THE ETHICAL AND PROFESSIONAL PRACTICE OF COUNSELING AND PSYCHOTHERAPY

LEN SPERRY
Florida Atlantic University

Boston New York San Francisco
Mexico City Montreal Toronto London Madrid Munich Paris
Hong Kong Singapore Tokyo Cape Town Sydney

Executive Editor: Virginia Lanigan
Editorial Assistant: Scott Blaszak
Marketing Manager: Kris Ellis-Levy
Production Editor: Gregory Erb
Editorial Production Service: Walsh & Associates, Inc.
Composition Buyer: Linda Cox
Manufacturing Buyer: Megan Cochran
Electronic Composition: Publishers' Design & Production Services, Inc.
Cover Designer: Joel Gendron

For related titles and support materials, visit our online catalog at www.ablongman.com.

Library of Congress Cataloging-in-Publication Data

Sperry, Len.
The ethical and professional practice of counseling and psychotherapy / Len Sperry.
p. cm.
Includes bibliographical references and index.
ISBN 0-205-43525-4
1. Counseling—Moral and ethics aspects. 2. Psychotherapy—Moral and ethical aspects.
3. Counselors—Professional ethics. 4. Psychotherapists—Professional ethics. I. Title.

BF637.C6S7 2006
174'.91583—dc22

2005056609

Printed in the United States of America

CONTENTS

Preface xi

PART I ETHICAL, PROFESSIONAL, AND CONTEXTUAL CONSIDERATIONS 1

CHAPTER ONE
The Ethical and Professional Practice of Counseling and Psychotherapy 3

MAKING COUNSELING PRACTICE DECISIONS IN THE PAST 5
MAKING COUNSELING PRACTICE DECISIONS TODAY 6
Professional Domain Considerations 7 / Ethical Domain Considerations 8
THE KEY ROLE OF ETHICAL CONSIDERATIONS IN MAKING COUNSELING PRACTICE DECISIONS 8
PREMISES AND PERSPECTIVES ON ETHICAL AND PROFESSIONAL PRACTICE 8
Basic Premises 8 / Three Perspectives on Ethical and Professional Practice 9
BASIC TERMINOLOGY 12
General Ethics 12 / Applied Ethics 12 / Ethical Dilemma 14 / Personal Ethics 14
THE DOMAINS AND DIMENSIONS OF ETHICAL THINKING AND DECISION MAKING 14
Professional Domain 15 / Ethical Domain 15 / Contextual Domain 15
A STRATEGY FOR DECISION MAKING IN COUNSELING AND PSYCHOTHERAPY PRACTICE 17

CHAPTER TWO
Personal and Developmental Ethics 20

THE PROFESSIONAL DEVELOPMENT OF COUNSELORS AND THERAPISTS 21
Levels of Counselor and Therapist Development 21 / Levels of Ethical Development 21
ETHICAL VALUES IN COUNSELING AND PSYCHOTHERAPY 25
Ethical Principles 25 / Ethical Values 25 / Ethical Values and Practices of Master Therapists 27
ETHICAL THEORIES IN COUNSELING AND PSYCHOTHERAPY 30
Six Ethical Theories 30 / Implications for Counseling and Psychotherapy Practice 30
ETHICAL CODES AND PRACTICE BEHAVIOR 31

FOSTERING ETHICAL DEVELOPMENT IN COUNSELING AND PSYCHOTHERAPY 32

Ethical Autobiography 32 / Ethical Decision-Making Style 33 / Ethical Acculturation 34

CHAPTER THREE
Multicultural, Relational, and Spiritual Issues in Ethics 37

THE RELATIONAL DIMENSION 38

The Relational Dimension in Counseling 38 / The Relational Dimension in Supervision 39 / The Relational Dimension in Ethical Decisions 40

THE MULTICULTURAL DIMENSION 40

Cultural Sensitivity and Competency 41 / Core Cultural Competencies 42 / The Primacy of Cultural Awareness 43 / Cultural Considerations and Ethical Decisions 44

THE RELIGIOUS AND SPIRITUAL DIMENSION 45

Spirituality 45 / Professional and Personal Stance Regarding Spirituality and Religion 46 / Levels of Professional Incorporation of the Spiritual Dimension in Counseling Practice 47 / Spiritual Assessment 49 / Spiritual and Religious Competencies for Counselors 49

CHAPTER FOUR
Organizational Ethics 53

ORGANIZATIONAL SYSTEMS AND DYNAMICS 54

Structural Subsystem 54 / Cultural Subsystem 54 / Administrative Subsystem 54 Staff Subsystem 55 / Strategy Subsystem 55 / Environmental Subsystem 55

DIFFERENTIATING PERSONAL, PROFESSIONAL, AND ORGANIZATIONAL ETHICS 55

THE CENTRALITY OF ORGANIZATIONAL ETHICS FOR ORGANIZATIONAL SUCCESS 57

The Central Role of Organizational Culture and Leadership 58 / Three Differing Perspectives 58

SYSTEMIC FACTORS IMPACTING ORGANIZATIONAL ETHICS 59

Conflict between Personal Ethics and Organizational Policy 59 / Impact of Organizational Dynamics on Ethical Dilemmas 61

ORGANIZATIONAL ETHICS AND PROFESSIONAL ETHICS 62

Confidentiality 62 / Informed Consent 62

COUNSELING PRACTICE AND ORGANIZATIONAL ETHICS 63

Financial Consideration 63 / Efficiency and Expediency 64 / Personal–Organizational Ethical Conflicts 65

ASSESSING AND EVALUATING ORGANIZATIONAL ETHICS IN A COUNSELING SETTING 66

Ethics Audits 66 / Organizational Ethics Inventory 67 / Ethics Compliance Audit 69

COMMUNITY VALUES 69

Impact of Community Values 70 / Recognizing Community Values 71

CHAPTER FIVE

Ethical and Professional Decision Making in Counseling and Psychotherapy 74

DECISION MAKING IN COUNSELING AND PSYCHOTHERAPY 75

Contextual Considerations 76 / Professional Considerations 76 / Ethical Considerations 76

APPROACHES TO ETHICAL DECISION MAKING 77

THE PROFESSIONAL AND ETHICAL PRACTICE DECISIONAL STRATEGY 78

The Eight Steps of the Decisional Strategy 78

CASE ILLUSTRATION OF THE ETHICAL AND PROFESSIONAL PRACTICE DECISIONAL STRATEGY 82

Applying the Ethical and Professional Practice Decision Strategy 85

PART II ETHICAL STANDARDS OF PROFESSIONAL PRACTICE 89

CHAPTER SIX

Confidentiality 91

THE CONTEXTUAL DOMAIN AND CONFIDENTIALITY 92

THE ETHICAL BASIS OF THE CONCEPT OF CONFIDENTIALITY 93

Beneficence and Confidentiality 94 / Nonmalificence and Confidentiality 94

Care and Confidentiality 94 / Respect for Privacy and Confidentiality 96

EMERGING BRAIN SCIENCE AND CONFIDENTIALITY 96

Attachment and Confidentiality 97

LEGAL ASPECTS OF CONFIDENTIALITY 98

Privileged Communication 98 / The Health Insurance Portability and Accountability Act (HIPAA) of 1996 99 / Personal-Developmental and Organizational Ethics in a Regulatory Context 100

EXCEPTIONS TO CONFIDENTIALITY 100

Abuse and Confidentiality 100 / Suicide and Confidentiality 101 / Threats to Others and Confidentiality 104

RIGHTS OF CHILDREN AND CONFIDENTIALITY 105

CHAPTER SEVEN
Informed Consent 109

THE CONTEXTUAL DOMAIN AND INFORMED CONSENT 110

THE LEGAL AND ETHICAL BASIS OF THE NEED FOR CONSENT FOR TREATMENT 112

KEY ELEMENTS OF AN INFORMED CONSENT DOCUMENT 113

SYSTEMIC AND MULTICULTURAL CONSIDERATIONS IN INFORMED CONSENT PROCEDURES 116

INFORMED CONSENT AND MINORS 118

Assent to Treatment 118 / Exceptions to the General Requirement of Parental Consent 119

INVOLUNTARY COMMITMENT AND INFORMED CONSENT 120

ONLINE COUNSELING AND INFORMED CONSENT 122

CHAPTER EIGHT
Conflict of Interest, Boundaries, and the Use of Power 126

THE CONTEXTUAL DOMAIN AND CONFLICT OF INTEREST, BOUNDARIES, AND THE USE OF POWER 128

Personal-Developmental 128 / Relational-Multicultural 129 / Organizational Ethics–Community Values 129

POWER IN COUNSELING AND PSYCHOTHERAPEUTIC RELATIONSHIPS 130

Abuse of Power as a Process and Not an Event 131

DUAL AND MUTUAL RELATIONSHIPS 132

BOUNDARY VIOLATIONS 134

Process versus Event 134 / Therapist Self-Care: A Way of Avoiding Boundary Violations 135 / Sexual and Nonsexual Boundary Violations 137

BOUNDARY CROSSINGS 139

A TEMPLATE FOR EVALUATING THE ETHICS OF NONSEXUAL DUAL RELATIONSHIPS 141

CHAPTER NINE
Competency and Professional Responsibility 145

COUNSELING AS A PROFESSION 147

Defining Profession and Professional 147 / The Counseling Profession 147

COMPETENCE AND WORK ORIENTATION 148

Three Work Orientations 148 / The Relationship between Work Orientation and Competence 149

ETHICAL AND LEGAL ASPECTS OF COMPETENCE 149

Ethical Aspects 149 / Legal Aspects 150

PROFESSIONAL COMPETENCE 150

Continuum of Competence 150 / Scope of Practice 152

ACHIEVING AND MAINTAINING COMPETENCE 153

Attaining Competence 153 / Maintaining Competence 154

INCOMPETENCE 155

Impairment versus Incompetence 155 / Three Types of Incompetence 155

DISTRESS, BURNOUT, AND IMPAIRMENT 156

Strategies for Preventing Burnout and Impairment 158

NEGLIGENCE AND MALPRACTICE 159

Negligence 159 / Malpractice 160

VIEWING COMPETENCE FROM THE THREE PERSPECTIVES 160

Perspective I 160 / Perspective II 161 / Perspective III 161

MASTER THERAPISTS AND COMPETENCE 162

COMPETENCE AND THE DEVELOPMENTAL, RELATIONAL, AND ORGANIZATIONAL DIMENSIONS 163

PART III ETHICAL AND PROFESSIONAL PRACTICE IN SPECIALTY AREAS 167

CHAPTER TEN

School Counseling 169

ROUTINE PRACTICE FOR SCHOOL COUNSELING 171

CONTEXTUAL ISSUES IN SCHOOL COUNSELING 172

Personal-Developmental 173 / Relational-Multicultural 173 / Organizational Ethics–Community Values 175

CORE ETHICAL ISSUES FOR SCHOOL COUNSELORS 179

Confidentiality 179 / Informed Consent 187 / Conflicts of Interest and Boundaries 192 / Competence 196

LEGAL ISSUES AFFECTING THE PRACTICE OF SCHOOL COUNSELING 201

Legal Rights of Parents and Confidentiality 202 / Mandatory Abuse Reporting 204 / Threat of Harm to Self or Others 207 / Case Law Related to the Practice of School Counseling 210 / Student Records 213 / Students with Special Needs 216 / Ethics and Sexual Behavior 218 / Spirituality and School Counseling 219

CASE ILLUSTRATION OF ETHICAL-PROFESSIONAL DECISION MAKING IN SCHOOL COUNSELING 221

CHAPTER ELEVEN
Mental Health Counseling 230

ROUTINE PRACTICE OF MENTAL HEALTH COUNSELING 231
CONTEXTUAL ISSUES IN MENTAL HEALTH COUNSELING 236
Personal-Developmental 236 / Relational-Multicultural 237 / Organizational Ethics–Community Values 238
CORE ETHICAL ISSUES AND CODES OF ETHICS FOR MENTAL HEALTH COUNSELORS 239
Confidentiality 240 / Informed Consent 244 / Conflicts of Interest 245 / Competency 257
REPORTS OF THE ACA ETHICS COMMITTEES 261
LEGAL ISSUES AND CASE LAW AFFECTING MENTAL HEALTH COUNSELORS 262
Duty to Warn/Duty to Protect 262 / Immunity from Suit for Breaking Confidentiality 265 / Client–Counselor Privileged Communication/Confidentiality 266
SPECIAL TOPICS IN MENTAL HEALTH COUNSELING 268
Managed Care 268 / Substance Abuse/Drug Addiction 270 / Group Counseling 271 / Spirituality and Mental Health Counseling 274
CASE ILLUSTRATION OF ETHICAL-PROFESSIONAL DECISION MAKING IN MENTAL HEALTH COUNSELING 275

CHAPTER TWELVE
Couples and Family Counseling and Therapy 285

ROUTINE PRACTICE OF COUPLES AND FAMILY THERAPY 286
HIPAA Considerations 287
CONTEXTUAL ISSUES IN COUPLES AND FAMILY THERAPY 291
Personal-Developmental 291 / Relational-Multicultural 293 / Organizational Ethics–Community Values 294
CORE ETHICAL ISSUES AND CODES OF ETHICS FOR COUPLES AND FAMILY THERAPISTS 297
Confidentiality 297 / Informed Consent 304 / Conflicts of Interest 309 / Competency 319
PREVALENCE OF ETHICAL BREACHES 323
LEGAL ISSUES AND CASE LAW AFFECTING COUPLES AND FAMILY THERAPISTS 325
Child Abuse 325 / Immunity for Reporting 327 / Threats to Others 330 / Communication Regarding a Third Party 331 / Threats to Self 332
SPECIAL ISSUES IN COUPLES AND FAMILY THERAPY 332
Training, Licensure and Certifications 332
CASE ILLUSTRATION OF ETHICAL-PROFESSIONAL DECISION MAKING IN COUPLES AND FAMILY COUNSELING 341

CHAPTER THIRTEEN
Rehabilitation Counseling and Career Counseling 352

INTRODUCTION TO CAREER AND REHABILITATION COUNSELING 353
Career Counseling 353 / Rehabilitation Counseling 354
ROUTINE PRACTICE OF CAREER COUNSELING 354
ROUTINE PRACTICE OF REHABILITATION COUNSELING 355
CONTEXTUAL ISSUES IN CAREER COUNSELING 357
Personal-Developmental 357 / Relational-Multicultural 358
Organizational Ethics–Community Values 359
CONTEXTUAL ISSUES IN REHABILITATION COUNSELING 360
Personal-Developmental 360 / Relational-Multicultural 363 / Organizational Ethics–Community Values 367
CORE ETHICAL ISSUES IN CAREER COUNSELING 373
Competency 373 / Informed Consent 374 / Confidentiality 374
CAREER-SPECIFIC ETHICAL ISSUES 375
Independent Practice 375 / Boundary Issues and the Use of Power 375 / Spiritual Issues 375
LEGAL ISSUES IN CAREER COUNSELING 375
CONCLUDING NOTE: PERSPECTIVE III AND RELATIONAL ISSUES 376
CORE ETHICAL ISSUES IN REHABILITATION COUNSELING 378
Competency 378 / Confidentiality 379 / Informed Consent 382 / Conflicts of Interest 383
SPECIFIC ETHICAL ISSUES IN REHABILITATION COUNSELING 385
Supervision 385 / The Use of Power: Giving It to Clients 386 / Spirituality 388
LEGAL ISSUES IN REHABILITATION COUNSELING 389
Privileged Communication 389 / Mandatory Reporting 391 / The Americans with Disabilities Act (ADA) and the Rehabilitation Act 391
CONCLUDING NOTE: PERSPECTIVE III 392
CASE ILLUSTRATION OF ETHICAL-PROFESSIONAL DECISION MAKING IN REHABILITATION COUNSELING 394

CHAPTER FOURTEEN
Ethical and Legal Issues in Supervision 403

THE ROUTINE PRACTICE OF SUPERVISION 405
The Supervisory Agreement 405 / The Development Issues Contract 407 / Written Documentation of Supervision 407
THE CONTEXTUAL DOMAIN OF SUPERVISION 407
Personal-Developmental 407 / Relational-Multicultural 411 /
Organizational Ethics–Community Values 417
CORE ETHICAL ISSUES IN SUPERVISION 419

Confidentiality 420 / Informed Consent 424 / Conflicts of Interest and Boundaries 428 / Competency 434

SPECIAL CONSIDERATIONS IN SUPERVISION 440

Fair Evaluation and Due Process in Supervision 440 / Multicultural Issues in Supervision 441 / Religious and Spiritual Issues in Supervision 442 / Clinical Supervision, Case Consultation, and Peer Consultation 443

LEGAL ISSUES AND CASE LAW AFFECTING SUPERVISION 445

Direct Liability and Vicarious Liability 445 / Proper Monitoring of Supervisees: Some Practical Considerations 446 / Key Legal Cases Involving Supervision 447

CASE ILLUSTRATION OF ETHICAL-PROFESSIONAL DECISION MAKING IN SUPERVISION 448

PART IV ETHICS AND EFFECTIVE COUNSELING AND PSYCHOTHERAPY 455

CHAPTER FIFTEEN

Striving for Personal and Professional Excellence: Ethics as a Way of Life 457

A WEEK IN THE LIFE OF BILL JAMES 457

Monday 458 / Tuesday 459 / Wednesday 459 / Thursday 460
Friday 460 / Commentary 461

A WEEK IN THE LIFE OF GERI JACKSON 461

Monday 462 / Tuesday 463 / Wednesday 464 / Thursday 466
Friday 470 / Commentary 471

CONCLUDING NOTE 471

Appendix A Ethical Theories 472

ETHICAL THEORY 472

TYPES OF ETHICAL THEORIES 473

Consequentialist Ethics 473 / Rights Ethics 475 / Duty Ethics 476 / Virtue Ethics 477 / Care Ethics 478 / Narrative Ethics 479

CASE ILLUSTRATION: THE ETHICAL THEORIES IN COUNSELING PRACTICE 480

Appendix B Dictionary of Key Ethical and Legal Terms 483

Author Index 490

Subject Index 492

PREFACE

Ethics, it seems to me and an increasing number of my colleagues, is more than a set of rules and strategies to avoid legal liability and professional censure. Rather, it is a way of *being* in relationship to clients, supervisees, students, and colleagues that both promotes development and prevents harm. *Being* in relationships promotes development *and* prevents harm. Some heady words to be sure, but words that reflect significant changes in professional practice today.

It would not be accurate to characterize this as a book about ethical issues in counseling and psychotherapy. It does not reflect the traditional or conventional perspective on ethics. More accurately, this is a book about the ethically sensitive, professional practice of counseling and psychotherapy. The title, *The Ethical and Professional Practice of Counseling and Psychotherapy,* was chosen intentionally to reflect this perspective.

At this time in the development of the helping profession, there really is no need for another book on ethics issues in counseling and psychotherapy. When ethics entered the curriculum of graduate programs in the 1970s and 1980s, there was a clear need for such a focus. Today's increasing focus on integrating ethics with cultural issues and spiritual and personal beliefs has reduced the appeal and immediacy of books, workshops, and courses with such a focus.

Unfortunately, this conventional perspective omits a number of considerations germane to the effective, ethical practice of counseling and psychotherapy. Mostly, these texts imply that ethical and legal issues are hazards that can result in professional censure and malpractice litigation. Accordingly, the purpose of a professional ethics course is to train professionals to reactively avoid such hazards by applying the principles or guidelines of their respective professional ethics code and a few relevant legal statutes. A more proactive stance is to view ethical, legal, and professional issues and challenges as opportunities for personal and professional development. The proposed book champions this proactive, developmental perspective. While covering the traditional core precepts of professional ethics in considerable detail—confidentiality, informed consent, conflict of interest and boundaries, and competence—it also advocates for counseling personnel to view ethical issues as challenges for personal and professional growth. And, it includes a number of critical topics that counselors and therapists face or will face in daily practice. These include organizational ethics, virtue ethics, the so-called "other" multicultural ethical areas—those involving of spiritual and religious issues—and the use of alternative interventions in counseling and psychotherapy. The basic assumption of this book is that, in addition to being knowledgeable about ethical codes and legal statutes, ethical counselors and therapists are also effective professionals who strive for personal and professional excellence.

This book is written in an accessible, concise, and easy-to-read style, and it endeavors to broaden the traditional focus of ethical study in mental health circles, just a bit, to include topics that students and practicing clinicians will find consistent with their own personal strivings and professional needs.

While other texts describe general principles of ethical practice, this book also *provides in-depth and extensive chapter-long coverage of* the application of these principles to the specialty areas of mental health counseling, marriage and family counseling, school counseling, career and rehabilitation counseling, and clinical supervision. This feature permits instructors to emphasize one or two of these areas in depth or to survey all the areas while providing students in different specialty areas detailed coverage and clinical illustrations, which precludes the need and expense for secondary texts and resources.

Learning-enhancers to facilitate reader learning and retention are another essential feature of the text. Each chapter includes learning objectives, extensive case examples, definitions of key concepts and terms, summary of key points, tables, and insets. There is also a dictionary (Appendix B) of all key terms. A separate chapter looks beyond professional codes of ethics, the traditional focus of other books, and emphasizes ways in which counselors and therapists can grow and achieve excellence in their personal and professional lives. This book covers organizational ethics, a topic no competing text addresses, because the organizational dynamics of a clinic, agency, or third-party payer significantly influences the ethical behavior of clinicians. Organizational ethics addresses questions such as, Why do otherwise good counselors and therapists in certain schools and clinics engage in ethically, legally, or morally questionable behavior? Since organizational dynamics can exert such powerful influence on ethical decision making, basic familiarity with it is essential. This text offers a special focus on ethical considerations involving spiritual and religious issues, as well as the use of alternative interventions in counseling and psychotherapy, including the common lawsuits brought against counselors and therapists using spiritual and alternative interventions—topics not covered in competing texts. A special section (Appendix A) describes the psychological and philosophical basis of ethical decision making for readers who want and need a more in-depth discussion, again not available in competing texts.

This book is intended to be a primary textbook for ethics courses in graduate counseling and counseling psychology programs as well as in undergraduate programs in human services and related areas. The largest section of the book, Part III, will be of particular interest to practicing counselors and therapists because of extended coverage of ethically sensitive, professional practice issues in mental health counseling, marriage and family counseling, school counseling, rehabilitation counseling, and clinical supervision.

This book approaches professional ethics a bit differently than other texts. It attempts to articulate various beliefs about ethics and professional practice that you may not yet have articulated for yourself. You may not agree with everything presented, but I trust you will find that the discussion and illustrated examples provoke critical reflection and perhaps even change the way you approach professional and ethical matters. Accordingly, it is my hope that this book will promote your own development as a professional counselor or therapist.

ACKNOWLEDGMENTS

Over the past thirty-five years I've published a number of texts and professional books. It has been my experience that developing a textbook is usually both challenging and gratifying, but always, it seems, more the former than the latter. However, having the opportunity to collaborate with cherished colleagues in the development of this book has been most gratifying and rewarding. My plan in developing Part III of the book was to collaborate with individuals with acknowledged expertise in the areas of mental health, couples and family, school, and rehabilitation counseling to draft these chapters. I found this expertise among departmental colleagues at Florida Atlantic University. For all practical purposes, Part III has become a departmental book of sorts, and I thank the following colleagues for their important contributions:

Michael Frain, Ph.D., Assistant Professor, Rehabilitation Counseling; Larry Kontosh, Ph.D., Assistant Professor, Rehabilitation Counseling; Alex O. Miranda, Ph.D., Associate Professor, Mental Health Counseling; Paul R. Peluso, Ph.D., Assistant Professor, Mental Health Counseling; Linda Webb, Ph.D., Assistant Professor, School Counseling.

I'm also most grateful for the expertise of two other cherished colleagues who have provided invaluable feedback as well as important chapters: James R. Bitter, Ed.D., Professor, Marital and Family Therapy, East Tennessee State University; and Maureen Duffy, Ph.D., Professor and Chair, Marital, Couple and Family Counseling/Therapy, Barry University.

Finally, I'd like to acknowledge the fine technical and professional support I've received from Virginia Lanigan, my editor at Allyn and Bacon, and her staff, particularly Scott Blaszak and Gregory Erb, and also Kathy Whittier of Walsh & Associates and the word processing support of Katherine Hendricks.

GETTING THE MOST OUT OF THIS BOOK

Learning about ethics doesn't have to be dry or boring. This text has been designed to capture your attention and help you make the most of this learning experience. Here are some activities that can focus your attention and personalize your learning.

■ **Understanding what professional ethics is really about.** Start off by turning to Chapter 15 before or while you read Chapter 1. Chapter 15 is very different from any other chapter in this text and very different from most other texts. Rather than containing theory, new concepts, or issues, Chapter 15 follows the lives of two experienced counselors over the course of a full week. You'll read about the professional issues they face with ethical sensitivity everyday. If you've had little or no professional experience, you'll get a glimpse of what professional counselors and therapists do and how they think about and respond to professional and ethical considerations.

■ **Boxing and keeping score as you read.** Each chapter contains several examples that illustrate and articulate key points in that chapter. These range from case examples to informed consent forms to supervisory contracts to key legal cases. They are indicated as "Box." As you read through a chapter, you'll regularly come across these boxes. Stop, read, ponder, and respond to questions that may be included.

■ **Coming to terms with new terminology, issues, and definitions.** Chapters begin with a list of key terms. These terms are defined in the chapter as well as in the Dictionary in Appendix B. When you come upon a new or unfamiliar term, look it up right away and make a note of it.

■ **Developing yourself professionally and personally.** A constant theme of this text is that counselors and therapists are on a developmental journey that begins in a training program and hopefully continues throughout their career. The developmental stages are first discussed in Chapter 2. Get in the habit in this course of monitoring the developmental trajectory or pattern in your professional and personal life and as you proceed through your career.

■ **Mastering course content.** In addition to your textbook, you have ready access to a Companion Website (www.ablongman.com/sperry1e), which can provide you with additional learning resources for self-review and self-assessment. Included on the Companion Website are multiple choice questions and short answer essay questions for all chapters. Your instructor will provide in-class activities and out-of-class assignments to increase your mastery.

■ **Mastering professional ethical codes.** Beginning counselors and therapists need a close familiarity with the general ethical codes (i.e., ACA, APA, etc.) and specialty codes (i.e., AMHCA, ASCA, IAMFC, AAMFT, etc.) To help you achieve a full understanding of these codes and their applicability to counseling practices various exercises, called Case Vignettes, are provided for Chapter 6–14 on the Companion Website. You'll be presented with a counseling situation in which a trainee or experienced counselor or therapist takes a course of action. You'll be asked to agree or disagree with the decision and then provide a reason or rationale—based on a professional ethical code and/or principles. Immersing yourself in these case vignettes will give experience in reading and applying the various ethical codes. You will have ready access to all of the professional codes of ethics listed above as a link for each of these chapters on the Companion Website.

■ **Doing in-depth analyses without tears:** Near the end of Chapters 5-14 are some detailed cases commonly seen in counseling practice in various settings. Since so much of counseling practice involves making professional decisions that have ethical implications, this text allows you to follow a counselor or therapist's decisional process. You can approach these cases in two ways. The first is to buzz through the background material and follow the considerations and decision-making process and get the overall sense of the case example. This is a relatively painless approach to learning. Unfortunately, it doesn't have much staying power or payoff. The other way is to read the background material and think about how you might approach the professional and ethical issues involved. Then, you can think through the seven steps of the decision-making process one step at a time. While this takes longer, the learning benefits are longer-term.

■ **Finding your unique ethical model and decisional-making style.** All of us view ethical and moral concerns through a specific lens or model. Chapter 1 summarizes six such models or theories. Identify the one or ones that make the most sense to you. Appendix A provides a more detailed description of each of these with a few exercises to help you further clarify yours. Everyone also has a unique style of approaching professional issues and concerns that has ethical implications. You'll be prompted to draft an ethical profile of yourself, which will include your ethical decision-making style, in Chapter 2. It's worth the time to complete this personal profile.

PART I

ETHICAL, PROFESSIONAL, AND CONTEXTUAL CONSIDERATIONS

Part I consists of five chapters that provide an introduction and overview of the text. Chapter 1 begins with a description of an emerging integrative understanding of ethical and professional practice. It distinguishes three perspectives of ethical and professional practice, and notes that Perspective III, which is characterized by a developmental, relational-multicultural, and contextual approach to the client, is the emergent trend. Chapter 2 explores the developmental dimension of the counseling process as it relates to understanding ethical issues and resolving ethical dilemmas. It chronicles the stages or levels of counselor and psychotherapist development from beginning student to master therapist level, noting how professional and ethical thinking and practice evolves through the levels. Chapter 3 focuses on the relational-multicultural dimension of the counseling process and emphasizes that ethical sensitivity is intimately related to cultural sensitivity and competence. Sensitivity to spiritual issues and their ethical implications are also discussed. Chapter 4 explores the organizational-community dimension of the counseling process and demonstrates how organizational dynamics of a school, clinic, or agency can and do impact the professional and ethical behavior of counselors and therapists. It makes the case that organizational ethics is a necessary complement to professional ethics. Chapter 5 basically integrates material from Chapters 1 through 4 and describes and illustrates an ethical decisional approach that is essentially a developmental, relational, and contextual strategy for making clinical-practice decisions in counseling and psychotherapy.

CHAPTER 1

THE ETHICAL AND PROFESSIONAL PRACTICE OF COUNSELING AND PSYCHOTHERAPY

It is Monday, 8:30 A.M., and Geri Jackson, who is licensed as a mental health counselor and a marriage and family therapist and is a professor at a local university, has a class that begins at 9:20: "I am arriving at my office for posted office hours, and Kathy has been waiting for me for about half an hour. This is the first day of the first week of courses for the fall semester, and Kathy finished the summer session with an F in a core course, but I do not know this yet. She has received nothing but As in the rest of the 18 credits she completed in our Counseling Program."

Geri: Have you been waiting long?

Kathy: Not really. I just need to talk with you.

Geri: Okay, let me get the door open. Come on in.

Kathy: I ran into some problems this summer: personal problems.

Geri: Do you want to tell me about them?

Kathy: Well, I had this one problem, and I decided that I couldn't complete the course on trauma and abuse. So I withdrew.

Geri: Okay.

Kathy: Then I had a bigger problem, and I didn't withdraw from my other course, and I got an F. I talked to the instructor, but he says that there's nothing he can do.

Geri: Can you tell me what the "bigger problem" is?

Kathy: Well . . . (a long, long pause) It's medical, I guess.

"It is clear to me that Kathy is hesitant to talk about whatever her 'problem' is. I don't want to push her on it, but I know she is in some minor academic difficulty that I might be able to help resolve if I have more details. My mind starts to wonder: Okay, it may be a medical problem. Maybe it's a medical problem that's life threatening or very embarrassing to discuss, especially early on a Monday morning. Maybe it's a medical problem that happened to someone else, perhaps her twin, and perhaps it totally galvanized her attention for the rest of the summer. I could respond to this as simply an academic problem, but she seems more distressed than that. If I open up the possibility of being concerned about her personal life, am I entering into a 'counseling' relationship? Is one session a relationship? Is the fact that I have a teacher–student relationship with her the determining factor about how personal I can get? Are these very thoughts already compromising my ability to respond to her as a human being with sympathy and compassion? And what is the line between sympathy for a student and empathy as a counselor; should there even be a line between the two? The professional requirement to avoid dual relationships and to not be both a counselor and a teacher for the same student is important, but not without impact at a lot of different levels" (Cf. ACA Code of Ethics, A.5.c and F.10.e [ACA, 2005]).

Geri: I can tell this is hard for you. I am willing to hear whatever you want to tell me, but if it would be easier for you to talk to someone else, we can arrange that.

Kathy: No. I don't want someone else. I just need to take care of this F.

Geri: Okay, let's start there. Changing the grade may be quite difficult. You have already talked to the instructor, and for whatever reason, he seems unwilling to work with you on this.

Kathy: Yes. That's right.

Geri: Your next level is to appeal the grade to the chair of the department, but she is unlikely to override the instructor or facilitate a change of grade without a very, very good reason—and something a little more specific than a medical problem. (pause) On the other hand, you have nothing but As in all of your other courses. That has to be taken into account. In fact, you have enough As so that you have not even dropped below a 3.0. You are not even on academic probation because of this F. You can, if you choose, simply retake the course. Both grades will remain on your transcript, and you may have to explain that to a potential employer someday, but if your grades are kept up and you pass comprehensive examinations, you graduate with your degree.

Kathy: (with some sadness in her voice) I have to think about this.

Geri: Okay. I'll be free tomorrow between 1 and 3 P.M. if I can help in any way.

So begins a new day in the life of a professional counselor and therapist. This snippet of case material is taken from a week in the professional life of a counselor, chronicled in Chapter 15. Your instructor may assign you to read that chapter at this time, or you might want to turn to it to follow Ms. Jackson through a typical week as she encounters situations that require her to make ethically informed professional decisions.

Counselors and therapists face increasing challenges such as competition among professional counselors and therapists, expanding local, state, and federal regulations, and mounting concerns about litigation and risk management surrounding professional practice. Nevertheless, counselors like Geri Jackson find this an exciting time to be practicing counseling and psychotherapy. Promising integrative approaches, innovative assessment and outcome measurement techniques, highly effective interventions, and clinically useful research findings from large meta-analyses and longitudinal and qualitative studies serve to make professional practice both challenging and satisfying. Amidst these various developments has been an emerging trend that is subtly but significantly reshaping our current understanding of the ethics of professional practice. This emerging integrative understanding of ethical and professional practice is vastly different from the current understanding. This chapter introduces this emerging trend. It also articulates the basic assumptions and premises of the book and defines basic terminology. Finally, it discusses the domains and dimensions of ethical thinking and decision making, as well as previews the next four chapters.

LEARNING OBJECTIVES

After reading this chapter you should be able to

1. State the five basic premises of the book.
2. Characterize the three perspectives on ethical and professional practice.
3. Define ethics, personal ethics, professional ethics, and organizational ethics.
4. Explain why contextual, professional, and ethical considerations underlie most decision making in counseling and psychotherapy.
5. List the eight steps of Ethical and Professional Practice Decisional Strategy.

KEY TERMS

applied ethics
ethical dilemma
ethics
organizational ethics
personal ethics
professional ethics

MAKING COUNSELING PRACTICE DECISIONS IN THE PAST

I well remember a graduate seminar with an admired professor who was asked about dealing with a client who mentions suicidal ideation in a counseling session. Almost reflexively the professor recounted how his mentor, a prominent advocate of the client-centered approach, dealt with a client who threatening to jump from a window in his office. Reportedly, the mentor followed the client's lead and empathically affirmed the client's decision but made no effort to dissuade or protect the client. The professor pointed out that is was simply another example of the time-honored clinical directive: Follow the client's lead. When another seminar participant asked if the mentor had no compunction about the client's successful suicide, the answer was no, because the client had assured the mentor that he had carefully considered the decision and was committed to it. Before any further discussion could ensue, another student asked a question that took the discussion in a completely different direction.

So for me, and probably most, if not all, of those in the seminar, the professor and his mentor had spoken and that was it. Presumably, this case example reflected an acceptable way to deal with suicidality in the late 1960s. As I recall, no one asked whether that professional decision was ethical. I certainly didn't ask, since I had uncritically accepted the clinical directive of following the client's lead. I had neither considered other sources of professional support for the decision, nor even thought that there might be ethical criteria to guide practice decisions. It was probably in the early 1980s that the legal ramifications of suicide appeared on the radar screen in the counseling profession. More recently, a number of states have enacted statutes that specify that clinicians have the duty to protect clients from harm, including suicide (Behnke, Winick, & Perez 2000). Accordingly, counselors working with clients contemplating suicide are expected to consider and decide upon several therapeutic options: hospitalize the individual, provide support in a protective environment such as a crisis center, attempt to establish a no-suicide contract with the client, give the number for a suicide hotline, be available to him or her by phone, and so on. These options are considered good professional practice and represent the expected standard of care in most communities.

Likewise, from an ethical perspective, several criteria for professional practice situations involving suicide began to appear. All of the therapeutic options mentioned above would be consistent with the basic ethical precept of counseling, that is, promoting the welfare of the client, which is Principle A.1.a of the ACA Code of Ethics (2005). Also, Principle B.1.c requires counselors to prevent clear and imminent danger to clients. It is noteworthy that these ethical principles about promoting client welfare and protecting clients from the harm of suicide provide a larger framework for evaluating various professional options and considerations to make important counseling-practice decisions.

Throughout that semester, that professor made it clear that there was only one criterion for making practice decisions: Follow the client's lead. Although that clinical directive has been very helpful to me and others, empirical research does not support the use of that clinical directive in all situations. There are specific situations in which research suggests the directive is contraindicated (Sperry, 1999).

MAKING COUNSELING PRACTICE DECISIONS TODAY

Until recently, there were essentially only three criteria, or sources of support, for making clinical practice decisions: (1) research, (2) clinical lore and opinions of supervisors and gurus in the field, and (3) personal clinical experience. About twenty years ago, a fourth criterion set emerged: legal statutes, ethical codes and standards, and ethical principles. Thereafter, other criteria were added, such as best practices, evidenced-based directives, and meta-analyses studies of clinical outcomes. Despite these various sources, many counselors and therapists remain comfortable basing their clinical practice decisions on only two of these criteria: the opinions of respected colleagues and personal experience. Less often do they base these decisions on research, best practices, or ethical principles.

Table 1.1 lists the various sources of support for making practice decisions.

The bottom line of this discussion is that, just as there are clinical situations in which reliance on only one form of professional support for practice decisions can be ill-advised, so can a single form of ethical support for a practice decision be ill-advised. Nevertheless, if the only ethical understanding the therapist had had been the ethical precept of promoting the client's welfare, in this case protecting the client from suicidal harm, quite likely this

TABLE 1.1 Criteria and Sources of Support for Clinical Practice Decisions

PROFESSIONAL	ETHICAL
Meta-analysis outcomes studies	Ethical sensitivity
Process and outcome studies	Ethical theory
Evidence-based directives	Ethical principles
Best practices	Ethical values, e.g., autonomy, beneficence
Theories and scholarly recommendations	Professional codes of ethics
One's own professional experience	Professional ethical standards
Professor, supervisor, or guru opinions	Standard of care
Clinical lore	Legal statutes and regulations

precept would have "trumped" the clinical directive of "following the client's lead," and the suicide may have been averted.

A basic tenet of this book is that providing effective, ethically sensitive counseling and psychotherapy requires more than considering either the professional or the ethical criteria; it requires considering *both* professional and ethical sources and criteria in clinical practice (see Box 1.1).

BOX 1.1

SHOULD A CLIENT'S TREATMENT EXPECTATIONS DIRECT THE COURSE OF COUNSELING?

Jeanine, complaining of "horrible dreams and nightmares," seeks professional counseling with you. Jeanine believes she is now "getting in touch with incest when I was young" and wants counseling specifically to help her process her early sexual trauma issues so she can "get on with life and feel better about myself." Should counseling directed at early trauma be offered that meets Jeanine's treatment expectation?

In this case, meeting the client's expressed treatment expectation may be totally reasonable and justified, or it may not be, depending on several considerations. Let's say that in the course of completing an initial evaluation of this client you find that in addition to her history of childhood sexual and emotional abuse, she comes from a chaotic and dysfunctional family, and discussing sexual abuse issues is a taboo subject in her culture. How might you proceed in deciding whether to accede to the client's treatment expectation? We suggest you begin by consideration of the professional domain and then the ethical domain.

Professional Domain Considerations

Based on the findings of this evaluation, it seems that several professional criteria, such as research findings, outcomes studies, and best practices, "override" the clinical lore directive to follow the client's lead, that is, accede to her request to focus therapy initially and exclusively on processing abuse issues. This case is discussed in considerable detail in Chapter 5, but briefly it can be said here that the client is too brittle and lacks the psychological resiliency to withstand a treatment approach focused initially and exclusively on abuse issues. Rather, it would seem both necessary and advisable to prepare her for the inevitably stressful processing of painful, traumatic material by increasing her resiliency before focusing on abuse issues.

Ethical Domain Considerations

Then, before finalizing your decision, we suggest that you consider the ethical dimension. While there is no ethical standard that directly addresses the particulars of this case, ethical sensitivity and ethical values would suggest that the client's welfare is best promoted by discussing the prospect of preparing the client, that is increasing her resiliency, for the inevitable regression that accompanies the processing of painful affects and memories. In this particular case, acceding, without reservation, to the client's treatment expectations would likely be unethical. Finally, we'd suggest you review the results of your professional and ethical considerations simultaneously. Such an evaluation leads to the conclusion that acceding to the client's request would be both professionally unsound as well as unethical.

THE KEY ROLE OF ETHICAL CONSIDERATIONS IN MAKING COUNSELING PRACTICE DECISIONS

You'll note that we did not approach this counseling practice decision as simply an ethical dilemma. In fact, in our estimation this case does not primarily or exclusively involve an ethical dilemma. Rather, such a counseling practice decision best begins first with a critical review of relevant professional considerations—including criteria or sources of support—and then with stepping back from those considerations to analyze relevant ethical considerations that bear on the case as well as professional considerations. In other words, ethical theory, principles, and values provide a larger perspective in which to critically evaluate professional considerations bearing on the case.

PREMISES AND PERSPECTIVES ON ETHICAL AND PROFESSIONAL PRACTICE

So what is this emerging trend in ethical and professional practice? Perhaps the place to begin is by listing the basic premises of this new trend. Next, three perspective on ethics in counseling and psychotherapy are described that offer a context in which to better understand how the professional practice is evolving.

Basic Premises

Ethical Practice and Professional Practice Are Integrally Linked. Sound professional practice is highly ethical, because ethical values "inform" professional practice. Ideally, ethical values are consistent with best practices, research, clinical lore, and professional experience, but when there is potential conflict ethical values "trump" clinical lore and clinical experience. This contrasts with the view that ethics is separate from professional practice and that it is merely an add-on or isolated consideration, rather than an integral consideration in professional practice decisions. Rather than being taught to think about how they might practice more ethically, it might be more useful for counselors and trainees to be taught how to practice more professionally. The disconnect between ethical considerations and professional practice considerations is difficult to justify as well as unhealthy for the individual and the profession. In addition to being knowledgeable about ethical codes and legal statutes, ethically sensitive, effective counselors and therapists will strive for personal and professional excellence.

Positive Ethics Is a Necessary Complement and Corrective to Negative, Defensive Ethics. Some clinicians, and many clinicians-in-training, view professional ethics as a necessary evil. In our current litigious society, ethics is taught in some professional workshops and seminars as a defensive or risk-management strategy. Positive ethics (Handlesman, Knapp & Gottlieb, 2002) counterbalances this view. It supplements negative ethics in acknowledging that risk management is a necessary consideration, but it is not a sufficient condition for ethical decisions. Positive ethics views ethical values rather than laws and codes as the starting point for ethical practice. It emphasizes ethical sensitivity as essential for professional practice and considers ethical reasoning and decision making to be contextual and not simply a linear process. In addition, positive ethics endorses ongoing self-care and personal and professional growth as essential to ethically sensitive, effective, professional practice.

Ethical Practice Is a Lived Relational Experience. Ethical and professional practice is not a solitary endeavor but involves relationships. Research on master therapists indicates that building and maintaining strong, healthy relationships with clients, colleagues, and family is key to both effective and ethically sensitive professional practice (Skovholt & Jennings, 2004).

Ethical Practice Is a Developmental Process. Research on stages of counselor and therapist development supports the view that a professional's ethical understanding and practice evolves, particularly in the context of supervision and peer and expert consultation, and promotes ethically sensitive professional practice (Stoltenberg, McNeill, & Delworth, 1998).

Ethical Practice Impacts and Is Impacted by Contextual Factors. Contextual factors such as culture and organizational dynamics can and do significantly influence an individual's ethical decisions and behavior. Organizational ethics encompasses individual and organizational dynamics, cognizant of cultural and spiritual considerations (Sperry, 2003).

Three Perspectives on Ethical and Professional Practice

A while back there was an episode of a sci-fi program, probably the *Twilight Zone,* that showed a mad engineer who was programming a humanoid to function as a customer services representative for a large department store that wanted to automate customer returns of merchandise. The scientist developed and tested out three different computer chips to estimate cost efficiency and elicit customer reactions. The first was a "letter of the law" chip by which the humanoid customer rep followed the return policy very strictly. The result was that cost effectiveness was best for this chip, but many customers felt put off by the seemingly "mindless" interpretation of store policy. For example, one customer who requested a return of an item purchased 15 days earlier and had a store receipt was rejected because of the 14-day return policy. The second was the "spirit of the law" chip by which the humanoid customer rep was very customer friendly and was quite liberal in following the return policy. Customer response was uniformly positive with this approach, and it was only slightly less cost-effective than the first. A third chip represented a mix: Sometimes the rep followed the letter of the policy strictly and sometimes it did not. The result was that some customers were frustrated and disappointed and some were not. Near the end of the program a disgruntled customer who had been rejected for a refund called the store with a bomb threat. The police team that responded unwittingly triggered a surge of electric power that "fried" the humanoid—with the "letter of the law" chip still inserted—which was being recharged at the time.

In many ways this story line is akin to the three differing perspectives on ethics. Though counselors and therapists are not humanoids, the perspectives they have on ethics do in a sense "program," or influence, their view of professional and ethical situations. And, these different perspectives can result in differing outcomes. Three perspectives characterize the current practice of counseling and psychotherapy (Sperry, 2005). The three are designated as Perspectives I, II, and III, and are best thought of as spanning a continuum wherein Perspectives I and III are near the end points and Perspective II is at the midway point (see Figure 1.1). Later, these perspectives are discussed in developmental terms in the careers of counselors and therapists.

Perspective I. In this perspective, ethics and professional practice are not usually considered linked or integrated. The focus of ethical thinking is limited to ethical codes, ethical standards, and legal statutes with an emphasis on enforceable rules and standards. Furthermore, risk management is the goal of ethical behavior. For the most part, personal and professional ethics are separated. This perspective is developmentally consistent with the needs of trainees, and beginning therapists and counselors look to codes and statutes for guidance in specific situations and circumstances. However, it also reflects the practice of some experienced counselors. In its most unadulterated form this perspective reflects a defensive, or negative, ethics.

Perspective II. Perspective II represents a midway position between Perspectives I and III. It tends to serve as the transition to Perspective III. It represents an effort to comply with ethical standards and rules, while at the same time being willing to consider self-reflection, contextual consideration, and self-care. The extent to which individuals holding this perspective experience cognitive and emotional dissonance is a function of how much allegiance they have to Perspective I: that is, the more allegiance, the less dissonance, and vice versa. Those who adopt Perspective II have some interest in integrating their personal and

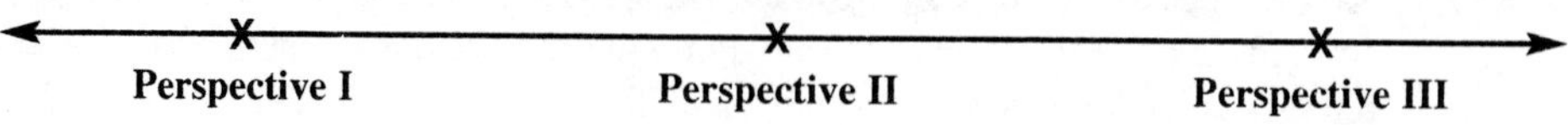

FIGURE 1.1 Continuum of Perspectives in Ethical Practice

professional values. Probably, the majority of counselors and therapists in practice today are somewhere between Perspectives II and III.

Perspective III. This perspective provides a comprehensive focus wherein it is possible to integrate professional codes, as well as other ethical traditions, with one's personal ethics. Here, virtues and values are considered as important as ethical codes, standards, and rules. The focus is on positive behavior and virtues, ethical ideals, character development, and integrating one's personal philosophy of life with one's professional goals and career aspirations. Self-care is valued and considered essential in this perspective, because it is believed that as professionals take care of themselves, they are better able to care for others. In this perspective, which values prevention, risk management is integrated with personal and professional development. Ethical decision making involves the professional, contextual, and ethical domains as well as the personal, relational, and organizational considerations. Ethical sensitivity is essential in this perspective, as is an integration of personal and professional ethical principles. Needless to say, this perspective reflects a positive ethics. It is also represents the actualization and realization of the emerging trend in the ethical and professional practice of counseling and psychotherapy. Table 1.2 summarizes some key distinctive features of Perspectives I and III.

The Transition from Perspective I to Perspective III. As professional ethics became part of the training of counselors and therapists in the late 1970s and early 1980s, it would be fair to say that Perspective I was the dominant mode in both teaching and in professional practice. While Perspective I remains common, particularly among trainees and beginning counselors and therapists, Perspective II probably reflects the sentiments of an increasing number of practitioners today. Perspective III seems to reflect other trends in the field involving consolidation and integration: for example, integrative therapies, incorporating the multicultural and spiritual dimension in treatment, and so on. Recent research suggests that master therapists and counselors live and model a growth-based, positive ethics that is characteristic of

TABLE 1.2 Characteristics of Two Perspectives on Ethical Practice

PERSPECTIVE I	PERSPECTIVE III
Ethics and professional practice is not usually considered linked or integrated	Ethics and professional practice are integrally connected
Attention is primarily on rule-based ethics, i.e., standards and statutes	Attention is primarily on virtue and relational or care ethics, while mindful of standards and statutes
Professional ethics is not usually viewed as integral to personal well-being	Professional ethics is usually considered integral to professional practice and personal well-being
Legal sensitivity and a proactive focus on risk management	Ethical sensitivity and mindfulness of the need to minimize risk
Professional ethics is usually considered separate from personal ethics	Professional ethics is usually integrated with with organizational and personal ethics
More characteristic of trainees and beginning therapists and counselors	More characteristic of master therapists and counselors

Perspective III (Skovholt & Jennings, 2004). As such, they provide a useful and necessary example of professional practice to other aspiring counselors and therapists.

A basic premise of this book is that the natural progression from beginning to advanced to master therapist and counselor involves movement from Perspective I or II to Perspective III. This book has been designed to describe and foster this developmental journey.

While these three perspectives appear to be discrete, it must be pointed out that ethical standards and legal statutes are not "confined" to Perspective I. All therapists and counselors, irrespective of the particular perspective they espouse, are expected to provide services reflecting a basic standard of care and mandatory ethical codes and standards.

BASIC TERMINOLOGY

It will be useful to have a common understanding of the terms used throughout this text. Since the emphasis in conventional texts, and in the traditional teaching of ethics involving counseling and psychotherapy, is on ethical standard, that is, professional ethics, there was little need to provide background information on the philosophical basis of ethics or describe ethical theories. This is consistent with Perspective I thinking. Furthermore, because there was no actual expectation that students would integrate their personal ethics with professional ethics, it was not even necessary to discuss personal ethics, much less professional ethics. However, because integrating personal and professional ethics, and recognition of contextual dimension of ethics, is characteristic of Perspective III, personal ethics and organizational ethics need to be defined and distinguished from professional ethics.

General Ethics

Ethics can be defined as the "philosophical study of moral behavior, of moral decision making, or how to lead a good life" (Brincat & Wike, 2000, p. 33). Ethics can be distinguished from morality. Morality is understood as the activity of making choices and deciding, judging, justifying, and defending those actions or behaviors, while ethics is the activity that studies how these choices were made or should be made. It is also useful to distinguish between good and bad and right and wrong. "Right and wrong apply only to actions, while good and bad describe not actions but motives, intentions, persons, means, ends, goals and so on" (p. 33).

The field of ethics is conceptualized as consisting of general ethics and applied ethics. General ethics aims to provide a moral framework for all individuals, not just those in corporations or professions. It is focused on more universal ethical issues and concerns. It starts from a conceptual framework that is seldom rooted in the concrete, but rather in the abstract. In other words, it usually begins with rules and theories and then applies them to cases. General ethics includes metaethics, prescriptive ethics, and descriptive ethics.

Applied Ethics

Applied ethics refers to the areas in which ethics comes out to meet the world, so to speak. In contrast with general ethics, applied ethics begins with cases or situations and uses them to understand or develop rules and theories. Applied ethics is typically subdivided into professional ethics, organizational ethics, environmental ethics, and social and political ethics.

More specifically, ethics that originates out of concern for the professions is called professional ethics, while the ethics that comes out of our concern for the environment is called environmental ethics, and so on (Brincat & Wike, 2000, pp. 56–60).

Professional Ethics. Professional ethics is the form of ethics that endeavors to help professionals decide what to do when they are confronted with a case or situation that raises an ethical question or moral problem; it considers the morality of one's professional choices and is informed by a code and standards of ethics specific to one's profession. Some cases and situations raise concerns that confront members of only select professions, such business executives or organizational consultants, while others deal with issues confronting all professionals. Professional ethics is subdivided into legal ethics, medical ethics, business ethics, and engineering ethics. In short, professional ethics considers the morality of one's professional choices. Typically, most professions have established codes of ethics to guide the ethical practice of members of that profession through professional organizations such as the American Counseling Association and the American Psychological Association.

Organizational Ethics. Organizational ethics is the form of ethics that recognizes the impact of organizational factors and involves the intentional use of values to guide decision making in organizational systems. Unlike business ethics and professional ethics, which characteristically view a given ethical concern from an individual perspective, organizational ethics views the same ethical concerns from a systems perspective (Sperry, 2002).

Unlike professional ethics, which focuses on a professional and his or her ethical concerns in practicing that profession, organizational ethics focuses as much on the organizational context as it does on the professional manager or executive who is considering an ethical matter. Organizational ethics emphasizes the impact of the organization and organizational dynamics, such as the mission of the organization; its responsibilities to clients and the large community; its relation to associated institutions and professional organizations; and the ways in which it provides leadership in order to meet these responsibilities. In short, organizational ethics involves the intentional use of values to guide decision making in organizational systems (Worthley, 1999, p. 9).

Akin to codes of professional ethics adopted by most professions or professional groups, one might expect there would be a corresponding code of organizational ethics. With the exception of the Joint Commission on the Accreditation of Hospitals and Health Care Organizations (JCAHO), which requires health care organizations to meet and maintain certain organizational ethical standards for JCAHO accreditation, there is no industry-wide code of organizational ethics. Nevertheless, some corporations, clinics, and school districts have established "codes of conduct" that provide guidelines for the ethical behavior of their employees.

Finally, it should be noted that while professional ethics can be differentiated from organizational ethics, it does not follow that ethical issues are automatically classifiable as either professional or organizational ethical issues. For instance, while confidentiality has been traditionally considered to be a professional ethical issue (Sperry, 1993), confidentiality also can and should be viewed from an organizational perspective (Worthley, 1999, p. 29). Similarly, while much has been written on the ethics of managed care (Sperry & Prosen, 1998; Worthley, 1999) little has addressed it from an organizational ethics perspective. This is most unfortunate because issues such as provider–patient relations, access of care, and conflict of interests are considerably broader than an analysis from a professional ethics perspective permits. In other words, it may be more appropriate and advantageous to consider and analyze ethical issues from both ethical perspectives: professional and organizational. Organizational ethics will be discussed in greater detail in Chapter 4.

Ethical Dilemma

Ethical dilemmas are situations involving an ethical consideration that confuses a professional, either because there are competing or conflicting ethical standards that apply or because there is a conflict between and ethical and moral standards. Ethical dilemmas may also arise when specific ethical standards seem unclear because of the complexity of the situation, or when other factors prevent a clear-cut application of the standard (Ahia, 2003).

Personal Ethics

Personal ethics is the form of ethics that reflects an individual's internal sense of how he or she should live and what he or she should strive for, and serves as the basis for moral decisions or judgments and guiding behavior. An individual's "moral compass," or conscience, reflects these ethical beliefs and values.

THE DOMAINS AND DIMENSIONS OF ETHICAL THINKING AND DECISION MAKING

This section offers a bird's-eye view of the rest of Part I. It sketches the integrative model of ethical decision making. The proposed model is a relational, developmental, and contextual process and strategy that is grounded in Perspective III and reflects the basic assumptions articulated earlier in this chapter. We refer to it as the Ethical and Professional Practice Decisional Strategy. Three interrelated domains are first briefly discussed, followed by a more detailed articulation of several dimensions of the contextual domain. Table 1.3 indicates the relationship of domains and dimension. Note that the contextual domain consists of three dimensions: personal-developmental, relational-multicultural, and organizational ethics–community values. These dimensions and domains form the basis of the Ethical and Professional Practice Decisional Strategy, which is described in the next section.

TABLE 1.3 Relationship of Domains and Dimensions of Ethical Thinking

Professional Domain

Ethical Domain

Contextual Domain
- Personal-Developmental Dimension
- Relational-Multicultural Dimension (includes Spirituality)
- Organizational Ethics–Community Values Dimension

Professional Domain

A basic assumption of this book is that, instead of being disconnected entities, ethical practice and professional practice are integrally linked. The implication of this is that to be an ethically sensitive therapist, one must also be competent and skilled in developing therapeutic relationships, formulating cases, planning and implementing interventions, and dealing with transference and countertransference. Furthermore, it requires the capacity to conceptualize technical and practice issues from a professional perspective, which includes input from several sources: the research literature, including evidence-based studies, best practices, counseling theories, scholarly debate, and clinical lore (i.e., clinical observations or methods that not empirically support but are revered and passed down from generation to generation) as well as supervision, consultation, and one's own professional experience.

Ethical Domain

In terms of the ethical considerations, the starting point is the therapist's own ethical sensitivity and self-knowledge. In addition, it is essential to have a working knowledge of ethical theory, principles, values, and professional codes and legal statutes. Furthermore, it is useful and sometimes necessary to have access to supervision and peer and expert consultation.

Contextual Domain

It was previously indicated that ethical sensitivity requires the capacity to recognize and deal with the ethical and moral aspects of professional and contextual domains in the counseling process. *Contextual* means any cultural, organizational, community, interpersonal, or personal dynamics that are operative. The contextual domain is emphasized in the approach to ethical thinking and decision making advocated in this book. The contextual domain involves three dimensions: the personal-developmental, the relational-multicultural, and the organizational ethics–community values dimensions.

The Personal-Developmental Dimension. This dimension primarily reflects a professional's ethical sensitivity and his or her capacity for dealing effectively with both professional and ethical considerations. It includes the individual's ethical values, ethical decision-making style, and level of counselor development. It also encompasses his or her unique personality style and needs, unfinished business, and blind spots in dealing with ethical issues, decision making, and resolving ethical dilemmas. We believe that self-knowledge about this dimension is essential to providing not only ethically sensitive but also effective counseling or psychotherapy. Chapter 2 develops this dimension more fully.

The Relational-Multicultural Dimension. Counseling theory, clinical lore, and research on psychotherapy processes and outcomes recognize the significant influence of the therapist–client relationship, positive and negative, on the client above all other factors in the counseling process. Because of its powerful influence, prohibitions against therapists' value imposition are found in the ethical codes of all counseling and mental health professions. We will primarily focus on a landmark study demonstrating the importance of the relational dimension in the lives of master therapists. Since master therapists reflect the epitome of the long and sometimes arduous journey of counselor development, it is useful and inspiring to understand their experiences, beliefs, and values.

Even though major studies have attested to the change potential of therapeutic relationships (Lambert, 1992; Wampold, 2001), empirical research recently reported on master therapists is noteworthy for clarifying its impact on the ethical domain. Master therapists report that establishing, maintaining, and honoring relationships were their core ethical values and that these relationships enhanced their ability to practice ethically. They believe that the healing potential of client–therapist relationships is the key to effecting positive changes in clients (Jennings, Sovereign, Bottoroff, & Mussell, 2004). Chapter 3 further develops this relational-multicultural dimension.

Multicultural Dimension. Basic to an effective therapeutic relationship is the therapist's sensitivity to the multicultural dimension, as well as the spiritual dimension, which is embedded within the multicultural dimension. The multicultural dimension is understood broadly to include race or ethnicity, gender and age, economic status, nationality, disability, sexual orientation, and religion and spirituality. A basic tenet of this book is that culturally competent counseling is ethically sensitive counseling. Of the many cultural competencies that counselors and therapists must develop, sensitivity to a client's ethical and spiritual worldview is critical.

Spiritual Dimension. Just as professional ethical standards require counselors and therapists to be sensitive to cultural issues, counselors and therapists are similarly required to be sensitive to religious and spiritual beliefs, values, and issues. This sensitivity is essential not only in engaging the client in the treatment process, but in effecting trust and therapeutic change. Since religious issues and client requests, such as that the counselor pray with him or her, can sometimes be discomforting and even engender negative countertransference, ethically sensitive therapists need to develop minimal competences such as being able to do a brief spiritual assessment and knowing when and how to refer the client to an appropriate minister or spiritual guide.

The Organizational Ethics–Community Values Dimension. The usual vantage point from which clinicians and clinic administrators deal with ethical dilemmas is personal ethics and professional ethics. Because of the powerful and pervasive influence of organizational dynamics in the clinical setting, it is helpful and, in many instances, necessary to consider the vantage point of organizational ethics. When the question arises, "Can otherwise good and ethical clinicians and administrators engage in morally questionable or even illegal professional practices?" neither the personal nor the professional ethics perspectives offers much of an explanation, because neither addresses the organization or its unique dynamics. An organization and its organizational dynamics can be thought of in systems terms; that is, the organization is a system with subsystems—structure, culture, strategy, administrators, and staff—that is embedded in the supra-system, the external environment of the organization, which includes community dynamics (Sperry, 1996, 2003). Each of these six subsystems can and does influence ethical decisions. Organizational ethics is the form of ethics that recognizes the impact of organizational factors and involves the intentional use of values to guide decision making in organizational systems. Unlike business ethics and professional ethics, which characteristically view a given ethical concern from an individual perspective, organizational ethics views the same ethical concerns from a systems perspective. Finally, it should be noted that community values and dynamics not only impact the organization, but also exert significance influence on individuals inside as well as outside the organization. Chapter 4 develops this dimension more fully.

A STRATEGY FOR DECISION MAKING IN COUNSELING AND PSYCHOTHERAPY PRACTICE

A basic assumption of this book is that good ethical practice is effective professional practice. One implication is that ethical practice and professional practice are interrelated and can be thought of as two sides of the same coin. Another implication are that the decision-making process in both is similar. Rather than seeing the decisional process involving ethical practice considerations as being distinctly different from the decisional process with professional practice considerations, we would contend that not only are these processes similar, but some aspects are essentially the same. It is our observation that counselors and therapists employ similar processes whether the issue is primarily a professional practice issue or an ethical practice issue. Because many have been socialized to think of ethical decision making as unique and separate from clinical or professional decision making, the similarities may not be intuitively obvious. We would contend that most, if not all, decision making in counseling and psychotherapy involves very similar processes, and that ethical decision making is not an arcane, isolated, and separate process.

The model of ethical decision making we propose is a relational, developmental, and contextual strategy as opposed to most of the other models, which are rational and linear strategies. The eight steps of the Ethical and Professional Practice Decisional Strategy are noted in Table 1.4. Chapter 5 offers a more detailed discussion of this decisional strategy, and illustrates its application in clinical practice. The reader will note that step "0" refers to an ongoing readiness to anticipate professional and ethical issues. Steps 1 through 7 are only operative when a problem or concern is present.

TABLE 1.4 Ethical and Professional Practice Decisional Strategy

0. Enhance ethical sensitivity and anticipate professional ethical considerations.
1. Identify the problem.
2. Identify the participants affected by the decision.
3. Identify potential courses of action and benefits and risks for the participants.
4. Evaluate benefits and risks re: professional, contextual, and ethical considerations.
5. Consult with peer and experts.
6. Decide on the most feasible option and document the decision-making process.
7. Implement, evaluate, and document the enacted decision.

KEY POINTS

1. In the past, professional practice decisions were made primarily based on experience, clinical lore, and research. In time, legal statutes and professional ethical codes of ethics emerged with specific standards for professional behavior. Unfortunately, professional ethics became increasingly separated from professional practice, a situation that seems to be changing now.
2. The basic premises of the book are that ethical practice and professional practice are integrally linked, that positive ethics is a necessary complement and corrective to negative ethics, and that ethical practice is a lived relational experience: It is a developmental process, and it impacts and is impacted by contextual factors.
3. Three perspectives characterize the current practice of counseling and psychotherapy: Perspectives I, II, and III. Perspective I represents a negative, or defensive, approach focused on codes and risk management, while Perspective III represents a more positive, integrative-contextual approach. Perspective II represents an intermediate position.
4. Decision making in the practice of counseling and psychotherapy is best accomplished by considering professional, ethical, and contextual considerations. The contextual domain—personal-developmental, the relational-multicultural, and organizational ethics–community values—is critical in decision making and is central to Perspective III thinking.
5. Ethics is the study of moral behavior, that is, moral decision making, or how to lead a good life. Professional ethics assists professionals in considering the morality of professional choices based on codes and standards of ethics specified by their professions. Organizational ethics recognizes the impact of organizational factors and involves the intentional use of values to guide decision making in organizational systems.
6. The steps of the Ethical and Professional Decisional Strategy are as follows: identify the problem; identify the participants affected by the decision; identify potential courses of action and benefits and risks for the participants; evaluate benefits and risks in light of professional, contextual, and ethical considerations; consult with peers and experts; decide on the most feasible option and document the decision-making process; implement, evaluate, and document the enacted decision.

CONCLUDING NOTE

Perspective III thinking reflects today's emerging integrative and contextual understanding of ethical and professional practice. Perspective III is integrative in its insistence that ethical and professional practice are deeply intertwined and contextual in recognizing that personal, relational, cultural, organizational, and community dynamics can and do impact professional and ethical thinking, decision making, and practice. While Perspective III differs from Perspective I, at the same time it affirms Perspective I's focus on knowing legal and ethical codes as well as anticipating and reducing liability. Furthermore, the chapter argued that decision making in the practice of counseling and psychotherapy is best accomplished by considering professional, ethical, and contextual considerations. It was noted that the contextual domain—personal-developmental, the relational-multicultural, and organizational ethics–community values—is critical in decision making, and is central to Perspective III thinking.

In short, this chapter has argued that contextual, professional, and ethical considerations underlie most decision making in counseling and psychotherapy and that good ethical practice is effective professional practice. Subsequent chapters in Part I develop these themes, with Chapter 2 discussing the personal-developmental dimension and its importance in the decision-making process.

REVIEW QUESTIONS

1. What sources of support for making ethical decisions would you be comfortable utilizing?
2. How would you describe your own "personal ethics"?
3. Do you think it is possible for you to reach Perspective III in your counseling career? What obstacles might interfere with your ability to reach Perspective III?
4. In your opinion, why is studying and understanding ethics important to the counseling profession?
5. In your opinion, how practical is the Ethical and Professional Practice Decisional Strategy? What, if any, part of this decision-making process might be difficult for you?

REFERENCES

Ahia, C. (2003). *Legal and ethical dictionary for mental health professionals.* Lanham, MD: University Press of America.

American Counseling Association. (2005). *Code of ethics* (Rev. ed.). Alexandria, VA: Author.

Behnke, S., Winick, B., & Perez, A. (2000). *The essentials of Florida mental health law: A straightforward guide for clinicians of all disciplines.* New York: Norton.

Brincat, C., & Wike, V. (2000). *Morality and the professional life: Values at work.* Upper Saddle River, NJ: Prentice-Hall.

Handlesman, M., Knapp, S., & Gottlieb, M. (2002). Positive ethics. In C. Snyder & S. Lopez (Eds.), *Handbook of positive psychology* (pp. 731–744). New York: Oxford.

Jennings, L., Sovereign, A., Bottoroff, N., & Mussell, M. (2004). Ethical values of master therapists. In T. Skovholt & L. Jennings (2004). *Master therapists: Exploring expertise in therapy and counseling* (pp. 107–124). Boston: Allyn and Bacon.

Skovholt, T., & Jennings, L. (2004). *Master therapists: Exploring expertise in therapy and counseling.* Boston: Allyn and Bacon.

Sperry, L., & Prosen, L. (1998). Contemporary ethical dilemmas in psychotherapy: Cosmetic psychopharmacology and managed care. *American Journal of Psychotherapy, 52*(1), 54–63.

Sperry, L. (1993). Chapter 11: Confidentiality and ethical issues. In *Psychiatric consultation in the workplace* (pp. 239–248). Washington, DC: American Psychiatric Press.

Sperry, L. (1996). *Corporate therapy and consulting.* New York: Brunner/Mazel.

Sperry, L. (1999). *Cognitive behavior therapy of the DSM-IV personality disorders.* New York: Brunner-Routledge.

Sperry, L. (2002). Organizational ethics in the corporation: Beyond personal, professional, and business ethics. In Kahn, J. & Langlieb, A. (Eds.), *Mental health and productivity in the workplace* (pp. 387–404). San Francisco: Jossey-Bass.

Sperry, L. (2003). *Effective leadership: Strategies for maximizing executive productivity and health.* New York: Brunner-Routledge.

Sperry, L. (2005). Health counseling with individual couples, and families: Three perspectives on ethical and professional practice. *The Family Journal: Counseling and Therapy for Couples and Families, 22,* 10.

Stoltenberg, C., McNeill, B., & Delworth, U. (1998). *IDM supervision: An integrated development model for supervising counselors and therapists.* San Francisco: Jossey-Bass.

Wampold, B. (2001). *The great psychotherapy debate: Models, methods, and findings.* Mahwah, NJ: Erlbaum.

Worthley, A. (1999). *Organizational ethics in the compliance context.* Chicago: Health Administration Press.

CHAPTER 2

PERSONAL AND DEVELOPMENTAL ETHICS

Ethical sensitivity requires the capacity to recognize and deal with ethical and moral aspects of the professional and contextual domains in the counseling process. This book emphasizes the importance of the contextual domain. We envision the contextual domain in terms of three dimensions: the personal-developmental, the relational-multicultural, and the organizational ethics–community values dimensions. This chapter focuses on the personal-developmental dimension of the counseling process, specifically as it relates to understanding ethical issues and resolving ethical dilemmas. It begins with a discussion of the developmental journey of counselors and psychotherapists and describes the process by which they develop personally and professionally in the course of learning and practicing the crafts of counseling and psychotherapy. This discussion includes a description of the process of ethical development. Then, the end point of professional and personal development, as manifest by master therapists and counselors, is described in terms of the core ethical values that underlie the highest level of professional expertise and ethical sensitivity. Finally, the chapter focuses on methods of fostering ethical development.

LEARNING OBJECTIVES

After reading this chapter you should be able to

1. Describe the four levels of professional development of counselors and therapists.
2. Describe the four levels of ethical development of counselors and therapists.
3. List and define the core ethical values of counseling and psychotherapy.
4. Describe how master therapists embody the core ethical values of counseling and psychotherapy.
5. List and briefly describe six ethical theories relevant to counseling and psychotherapy.
6. Discuss two methods of developing ethical sensitivity.

KEY TERMS

ethical principles
ethical theories
ethical values
ethical virtues
personal ethics

THE PROFESSIONAL DEVELOPMENT OF COUNSELORS AND THERAPISTS

Levels of Counselor and Therapist Development

Considerable interest in models of counselor development has been evident lately. Much of this interest is related to efforts to develop effective models and methods of clinical supervision. The Integrated Developmental Model originated by Stoltenberg, McNeill, and Delwarth (1998) is a widely utilized and respected model of supervision that specifies discrete levels of counselor development. Four levels of counselor and therapist development (adapted from Stoltenberg et al., 1998) are briefly described here. In the next section, the manner in which counselors and therapists at these various levels process and respond to ethical matters is described.

Level 1. Level 1 refers to beginning students who are completing course work and are involved in practicum training. These individuals tend to be highly motivated, extremely anxious, and dependent on supervisors for guidance and structure. Because of their lack of professional counseling experience, they tend to be highly self-focused and often exhibit limited self-awareness. Because this level represents the phase of professional infancy-moving-toward-toddlerhood, individuals at Level I are not expected to possess a sophisticated awareness of their strengths and weaknesses. Not unexpectedly, performance anxiety is high. Nevertheless, they strive to emulate experienced counselors and therapists as a means of developing the skills and confidence needed to move beyond their anxious, beginner's status (Stoltenberg et al., 1998).

Level 2. Level 2 refers to advanced students who are usually engaged in advanced counseling practica or internship training. Analogous to an adolescent who is struggling to establish a personal identity, individuals at Level 2 attempt to establish a professional identity while vacillating between functioning independently and regressing toward the dependency of Level 1. This can be a turbulent time. In contrast to the high motivation of those at Level 1, the motivation of the Level 2 counselor tends to fluctuate. This fluctuation is probably a function of having just enough experience to recognize the complexity of the counseling process. Even under optimal supervisory conditions, with shaken confidence, individuals at this level may experience transient feelings of despair and confusion. At this phase in the counselor's development, the autonomy–dependency conflict is likely to be heightened as the Level 2 counselor attempts to function independently. Nevertheless, the counselor's capacity for empathy is much more apparent at this level, as is the capacity to focus more intensively on client dynamics. As a result, individuals at Level 2 can be exquisitely susceptible to overt or covert client manipulations because of their tendency to overaccommodate to the client's perspective and needs. Accordingly, enmeshment is not uncommon at this level (Stoltenberg et al., 1998).

Level 3. Level 3 refers primarily to those who have completed training and are practicing counselors or therapists. As they transition from the potentially turbulent Level 2, trainees at Level 3 seem to be stable in their motivation and are no longer paralyzed by their doubts. As their professional identities take shape, Level 3 counselors are comfortable with their autonomy and have an accurate sense of their strengths and weaknesses. Whereas these counselors previously had only a limited awareness, they are now able to focus on the client, the process, and their own personal reactions simultaneously (Stoltenberg et al., 1998).

Level 4. Level 4 counselors, or what Stoltenberg and colleagues (1998) refer to as Level 3i, are characterized by a capacity to integrate the skills mastered in Level 3 as well as better integrate theory and practice. They exhibit a high level of self-awareness and concern for their impact on clients and colleagues. Individuals at this level are able to effectively monitor the impact of their professional life on their personal life and vice versa. When their professional accomplishments are recognized, they are typically humble about their efforts and successes. Not surprisingly, they are able to function interdependently with a wide range of clients, even the most chronic and difficult. They have achieved a solid professional identity and tend to be sought out by other colleagues for their advice and counsel. Notable is that they demonstrate stable and consistent motivation without concerns or doubts as to their self-efficacy. Finally, it is commonly observed that they demonstrate generativity and concern for younger colleagues and respect for peers. Table 2.1 summarizes these four levels.

Levels of Ethical Development

A predictable line or trajectory of professional development from the beginning trainee through the expert practitioner has been described in terms of four levels. It should not be too surprising that counselors and therapists at these various levels of professional development would process and respond to ethical matters in qualitatively different ways. In

TABLE 2.1 Levels of Counselor and Therapist Development

LEVEL	DESCRIPTION
1	Highly self-focused with limited self-awareness; anxious about making mistakes with clients and being evaluated by supervisors; dependent on supervisors; seek "correct" approach to client; need positive feedback and minimal confrontation; motivation and anxiety are high; they focus on skill acquisition
2	More able to focus on client and show empathy, but may have problems with client enmeshment or boundary issues; experience conflict between dependence and independence, which shows as resistance to supervisors; vacillate between feeling confident and confused
3	Becoming more self-aware, can remain focused on clients while reflecting on their personal reactions and use these in decisions about clients; show increased confidence in professional judgment; supervision becomes more collegial; motivation is consistent; have occasional doubts about their effectiveness
4	High level of self-awareness and concern for their impact on clients and colleagues; able to function effectively and interdependently with all types of clients; confident about their self-efficacy; demonstrate generativity and concern for younger colleagues and respect for peers

other words, just as there is a progression from professional infancy (Level 1) through professional adulthood (Levels 3 and 4), so too is there a progression in dealing with ethical dilemmas from a childlike, technical reliance and "letter of the law" interpretation of professional ethical standards (Level 1) to a more adultlike "spirit of the law" interpretation.

Level 1. Trainees at this level are generally eager to learn and use appropriate ethical and regulatory codes and statutes, although many view and "fear" codes and statutes as unquestioned precepts. Often, they demonstrate a "letter of the law" stance toward ethical issues and so will memorize codes. Some are overly preoccupied with risk management because of concerns of liability. Usually and fortunately, the ethical situations they encounter are typically clear and unequivocal. When complex cases arise, they are receptive to seeking extensive consultation, and such consultation is necessary and helpful in guiding and supporting them as they arduously traverse the decision-making process (Stoltenberg et al., 1998). Interestingly, some trainees adopt a laissez-faire stance and exhibit relative indifference to ethics issues, codes, and statutes and rarely seek consultation. Generally speaking, both types of trainees operate primarily from Perspective I.

Level 2. Trainees at this level tend to view codes and statutes as guidelines rather than as precepts. Typically, they quite aware of and committed to the ethical demand to respect and support their clients' welfare. Nevertheless, these trainees will occasionally avoid dealing with ethical and legal issues that conflict with their notion of what is in the client's best interest. Because of the trainees' developing need for autonomy, it is useful for teachers and supervisors to aid trainees in carefully considering options that pose conflicting interests. The challenge is to encourage the trainees' autonomy while continually monitoring their cases. Not surprisingly, ethical decision making becomes a central arena in which conflicts between trainees and supervisors get enacted (Stoltenberg et al., 1998). Some trainees may openly or covertly "defy" codes and statutes, or may selectively seek out consultants who agree with them. For the most part, trainees at this level operate primarily from Perspective I.

Level 3. At this level counselors and therapists are now capable of viewing standards and guidelines in a broader perspective, including both client rights and their professional responsibilities. Codes, standards, and statutes are more likely to be viewed as a starting point rather than an endpoint for ethical thinking. Consequently, they may review these codes and seek other input but then process alternatives and make decisions by balancing rights and responsibilities. In addition, they are disposed to developing a more personalized professional code of ethics. Their increasing personal and professional maturity provides an optimal environment for beginning to more fully integrate their professional identity and personal identity, including their gender, ethnicity, spirituality, and other individual differences and uniqueness (Stoltenberg et al., 1998). Furthermore, they seek personal–professional balance in their lives, particularly between personal and professional values, as they move beyond mandatory ethics to aspirational ethics. By and large, they operate primarily from Perspective II while moving into Perspective III.

Level 4. Counselors and therapists at this level find it relatively easy to balance mandatory and aspirational ethics. While they acknowledge code and statutory requirements, they exceed them; they move beyond competency to expertise and beyond nonmaleficence to self-knowledge. They continue to develop their character and virtues and act courageous in the face of ethical challenges. Typically, they consider the establishment and maintenance of strong, healthy relationships as a key to ethical sensitivity and competent practice. The integration of personal and professional identity begun in Level 3 continues. In the process of consolidating their own professional selves, they establish an integrated philosophy of professional practice that reflects high levels of both expert competence and ethical sensitivity. Furthermore, this philosophy of professional practice is comfortably integrated with their own personal philosophy of life and reflects their unique styles, beliefs, and values. Unquestionably, counselors and therapists at this level operate primarily from Perspective III. Table 2.2 summarizes four levels of ethical development in counselors and therapists.

To date, very little research on ethical values has focused on seasoned or expert therapists. However, the studies that have been reported are beginning to provide some understanding of the process of growth of professional judgment over the course of one's career (Conte, Plutchik, Picard, & Knauss, 1989; Hass, Malouf, & Meyerson, 1998; Jensen & Bergin, 1988). These studies suggest that when it comes to ethical considerations, seasoned therapists do differ from beginning therapists. For example, Pope and Bajt (1988) surveyed ethically knowledgeable and senior therapists and found that instead of using "textbook ethics" to guide their professional decision making, these experienced practitioners used "context-based ethics" developed over years of practice. What these authors refer to as "textbook ethics" we have called "technical ethics," and "letter of the law" ethics, and what they refer to as "context-based ethics" we have called "positive ethics" and "spirit of the law" ethics.

TABLE 2.2 Ethical Development in Counselors and Therapists

LEVEL	MANNER OF PROCESSING AND RESPONDING TO ETHICAL CONCERNS
1	Most have an uncritical and unquestioned view and "fear" of ethical codes and statutes; have a "letter of the law" stance toward ethical issues and so memorize codes and apply mechanistically; some take a laissez-faire stance and seem indifferent to ethics issues; both types operate primarily from Perspective I
2	Tend to view codes and statutes as guidelines rather than laws; may discount the clinical utility and value of codes and statutes, or may openly or covertly "defy" them; may selectively seek out consultants who agree with them; operate primarily from Perspective I
3	View codes and statutes as a starting point for ethical thinking and make decisions balancing rights and responsibilities; seek personal–professional balance in their lives as they move beyond mandatory ethics to aspirational ethics; operate primarily from Perspective II while moving into Perspective III
4	Balance mandatory and aspirational ethics; while acknowledging code requirements, they exceed these minimal standards; continue to develop their character and virtues and consolidate an integrated personal and professional view of life; operate primarily from Perspective III

ETHICAL VALUES IN COUNSELING AND PSYCHOTHERAPY

The terms *ethical principles* and *ethical values* have acquired various meanings in the professional ethics literature. It is our belief that precise denotations for key terms are important. The reader will note that our definition of an ethical value is what many professional ethics textbooks and articles refer to as an ethical principle. In philosophical ethics parlance, a value is "a single word or phrase that identifies something as being desirable for human beings" (Brincat & Wike, 2000, p. 141), whereas a principle is a normative statement about what ought or ought not to be done. In short, ethical principles are directives while ethical values are desirable and aspirational. Furthermore, principles typically link or combine two or more constructs or values. Whereas "beneficence" would be considered an ethical value, "the primary responsibility of counselors is to respect the dignity and promote the welfare of clients" (ACA, 2005, A.1.a) would be considered an ethical principle in that it combines three values and constructs: responsible counselors, respecting client dignity, and promoting client welfare.

To put it another way, principles build on and give direction to values. The direction principles give to values is presumably positive, but it can also be negative. For example, a gang of criminals can share the same values, such as autonomy, greed, control, and violence, but these shared values could violate some of society's basic ethical principles such as "the personal property of individuals should be safeguarded," "stealing and violence disrupt the common order," and related Bill of Rights and constitutional guarantees.

Ethical Principles

Again, an ethical principle is defined as a higher-level norm or directive within a society that is consistent with its moral principles and that constitutes higher standards of moral behavior or attitudes (Ahia, 2003). Ethical principles in the helping profession have been described as *prima facie* binding, meaning that they are binding in all situations when in conflict with equal or greater duties (Beauchamp & Childress, 1989). In our opinion, there are only a few basic ethical principles of counseling practice but several ethical values. Such basic ethical principles include "provide ethically sensitive, effective care," "respect and promote client welfare," and "act in the best interests of clients."

Ethical Values

Ethical values are beliefs, attitudes, or moral goods that are useful guides in everyday living (Corey, Corey, & Calanan, 2003). They are single words or phrases that identify something as being desirable for human beings (Brincat & Wike, 2000). Several ethical values have been specified for the counseling and psychotherapy profession, including beneficence, nonmalificence, autonomy, fidelity, integrity, and justice (Kitchener, 1984).

As professional associations shift from Perspective I to Perspective III thinking, they typically move from an exclusive focus on ethical standards to a focus on ethical principles and ethical values in addition to ethical standards. Recall that unlike ethical principles and ethical values, ethical standards are minimal expectations for practice. They represent obligations and form the basis for imposing sanctions when ethical standards are violated. In its recently promulgated revision of its code of ethics, now called the "Ethical Principles of Psychologists and Code of Conduct," the American Psychological Association (APA) prefaces its revised ethical standards with a set of five ethical principles. The purpose of specifying these five sets of general ethical principles, which we consider to be ethical values, is to guide and inspire psychologists toward the very highest ethical ideals of the profession. The five sets are beneficence and nonmaleficence, fidelity and responsibility, justice, integrity, and respect for persons (APA, 2002). This listing is very similar to the list of core ethical values proposed by Brincat and Wike (2000). Note that the first three sets in the APA listing incorporate the original five ethical values described by Kitchener (1984) and others, and add two others: integrity and respect for persons. The values chosen by APA are strikingly similar to those proposed by Brincat and Wike (2000). Following is a description of seven basic ethical values of counseling and psychotherapy, along with some of the key practice considerations associated with each ethical value.

Autonomy. Autonomy is a right to self-determination and self-direction. It includes freedom of choice. The ability to act on one's choices is, however, limited by the autonomy of others. Thus, an individual's choice is limited in situations such as kidnapping or murder, and it would be ethical to deny an individual's autonomy in such situations. Counselors and therapists can foster conditions of autonomy for their clients when they refrain from unnecessarily interfering in a client's decisions. Likewise they encourage and foster autonomy when they provide necessary information to clients in a forthright, honest, and understandable manner based on a given client's capacity to use this information in an autonomous manner. Counseling practice considerations related to this ethical value include competency, professional disclosure, informed consent, right to privacy, and the protection of confidentiality.

Benevolence. Benevolence is basically the obligation or responsibility to do good to others. It includes a duty to help current and potential clients, as well as people in general. It requires that counselors engage in professional activities in a spirit of helpfulness, work within the limits of their own competence, and provide for the public welfare. It also requires that counselors are able to provide the services that have been promised, and that the client has the right to expect. Counseling practice considerations related to this ethical value include competence to practice, informed consent, and dual relationships.

Nonmalificence. Nonmalificence is derived from Latin, and translated it means "doing no harm." Nonmalificence is often referred to as the most fundamental ethical value across all the helping professions. This ethical value includes avoiding, as well as preventing, harm to clients and others. It requires that counselors and therapists utilize only those interventions that are not likely to cause harm. Counseling practice considerations related to this ethical value include competence to practice, informed consent, dual relationships, and public statements.

Justice. Justice involves fairness and equity with regard to the treatment process as well as access to treatment itself and to necessary resources in treatment. In addition, counselors and therapists are obligated to assure that their treatment processes, as well as their agencies or institutions, do not discriminate in service provision. They must operate in a manner that reduces discrimination at the hands of others. Counseling practice considerations related to the ethical value of justice include due process considerations, access to grievance processes, and advocacy.

Fidelity. Fidelity involves honesty, loyalty, and promising to keep commitments. Because the bond of trust in the counseling relationship is considered to be vital to its effectiveness, this principle holds particular meaning for individuals in counseling and psychotherapy. Many theorists place particular importance on the healing characteristic engendered by the qualities nurtured by fidelity. Some interpretations of fidelity emphasize the nature of the promises made to clients and the social contract between the professional and client. However, reducing this concept to legalistic concerns, recognizing only specific, direct promises and overlooking those implied within the nature of the relationship, is limiting in regard to the counselor–client relationship. Counseling practice considerations related to this ethical value include professional disclosure, informed consent, maintenance of confidentiality, avoiding misrepresentation or withholding the truth, and avoidance of dual and multiple relationships.

Integrity. Integrity refers to promoting accuracy, honesty, and truthfulness in the practice of counseling and psychotherapy. It means not stealing, cheating, or engaging in fraud, subterfuge, or intentional misrepresentation. In addition, it means striving to keep one's promises and avoiding unwise or unclear commitments. Furthermore, in situations where deception might be ethically justifiable to maximize benefits and minimize harm, professionals have a serious obligation to consider the need for deception, the possible consequences, and their responsibility to correct any resulting mistrust or other harmful effects that might arise from the use of such methods. Counseling practice considerations related to this value include informed consent, maintenance of confidentiality, and avoidance of dual and multiple relationships.

Respect for Persons. Respect for persons means respecting the dignity and worth of all people, and the rights of individuals to privacy, confidentiality, and self-determination. It includes the recognition that special safeguards may be necessary to protect the rights and welfare of clients or others whose vulnerabilities impair autonomous decision making. It means awareness of and respect for cultural, individual, and role differences, including those based on age, gender, gender identity, race, ethnicity, culture, religion, sexual orientation, disability, language, and socioeconomic status. Furthermore, it means endeavoring to eliminate the effect of biases based on such factors, and of unknowingly participating in or condoning activities of others based upon such prejudices. Counseling practice considerations related to this value include informed consent, maintenance of confidentiality, multicultural sensitivity, and spiritual sensitivity. Table 2.3 provides a brief description of these ethical values.

Ethical Values and Practices of Master Therapists

Perhaps the most elegant research to date on ethical practice of experienced therapists is the master therapists study (Skovholt & Jennings, 2004). The study of ethical values was part of a larger investigation of the profile of and formative influences on master therapists. Five salient values that master therapists hold were identified. These include competence, relational connection, nonmaleficence, autonomy, and beneficence.

TABLE 2.3 Ethical Values in Counseling and Psychotherapy

ETHICAL VALUE	BRIEF DESCRIPTION
Autonomy	Taking responsibility for one's own behavior and self-directedness; freedom to choose without interfering with others' freedom
Nonmaleficence	Avoiding, minimizing, or preventing the infliction of harm on a client whether intentional or not
Beneficence	Promoting good for others and contributing to the welfare of clients and those with whom we work
Justice	Fostering fairness and equity and providing equal treatment to all individuals
Fidelity	Making honest promises and honoring commitments to clients and others, and maintaining genuine and consistent interactions
Integrity	Promoting accuracy, honesty, and truthfulness, while striving to keep one's promises and to avoid unwise or unclear commitments
Respect for Persons	Honoring the dignity, worth, individual differences, and rights of all people to privacy, confidentiality, and self-determination

Competence. The master therapists in the study clearly valued being exceptionally skilled in their clinical work. They were highly motivated to move beyond the minimum competency level required by ethical and practice standards and to become experts in the field. Despite years of training and experience, these therapists sought to continually upgrade their skills by seeking out formal and informal training in order to broaden their clinical abilities. This drive for competency combined with an awareness of their personal limitations inspired these therapists to become lifelong learners. In addition, through consultation and supervision as well as their own therapy, they availed themselves of opportunities to have others critically evaluate their work. Their commitment to professional growth bolstered their competence, which in turn increased their ethical sensitivity. Furthermore, as they became more confident in their skills and abilities, they reported becoming more tolerant of ambiguity as well as the complexity and uniqueness of each clinical situation in which they found themselves.

Relational Connection. The study's most significant overall finding was the importance that the master therapists placed on relational connectedness. Establishing, maintaining, and honoring relationships was another important ethical value for these master therapists. They highly valued their relational interaction and connection with clients, colleagues, family, and friends. Developing sound professional relationships with colleagues was considered a core value for them. They subscribed to the belief that, in order to maintain competence and build expertise, therapists must continually be in relationship with others in the field, for supervision, for consultation, and for collegial support and friendship. As would be expected, these therapists believed that the client–therapist relationship is key to effecting positive therapeutic changes in clients. It is clear that these therapists care deeply about their clients' well-being, and this caring attitude enhances the therapeutic relationship. It is interesting to note that the value these therapists placed on building strong therapeutic alliances is reflected in the emerging research on the link between the therapeutic relationship and treatment outcomes (Lambert, 1992; Wampold, 2001). The researchers point out that an ethics of care (Gilligan, 1982) is closely related to the ethical value of relational connection embodied by the master therapist. Additional results of this study are reported in Chapter 3.

Nonmaleficence. In addition to valuing helping others, master therapists are also aware of the tremendous potential of causing damage and harm in the context of the therapeutic relationship. They are mindful of the ways they may adversely affect clients and have developed measures to minimize this possibility. They believe in proactively managing their own personal and professional stressors, because left unchecked such stressors can lead to harmful behaviors. For them, humility offsets the potential for grandiosity and arrogance, which can result in harming clients.

These therapists are committed to self-awareness, with regard to both understanding and meeting their personal, emotional, and physical needs, as well as recognizing their own "unfinished business," personal conflicts, defenses, and vulnerabilities. Most important, they are aware of the potential for these issues to intrude upon their work with clients. They choose to fulfill their own needs with travel, exercise, spiritual practice, personal psychotherapy, and friendship. Finally, they are extraordinarily mindful of the need to recognize, monitor, and manage countertransference issues that potentially could be harmful to others.

Autonomy. The right of individuals to determine the courses of their own lives was another central value guiding the study's master therapists when making ethical practice decisions. These therapists appeared to be committed to encouraging clients' self-determination, while working to avoid imposing their own beliefs and values. Belief in the client's personal power may even foster a positive connection with the therapist. Because autonomy tends to be a central tenet of their own personal development, master therapists are committed to autonomy. Not surprisingly, these therapists believed that encouraging client autonomy is a central part of ethical practice. Finally, respectful attitudes toward clients' self-determination might also conceivably minimize the risk of harming clients.

Beneficence. Master therapists reported being committed to reducing human suffering and to working to improve the welfare of others. In their unique role as therapists, they have the opportunity to demonstrate caring by helping to transform painful experiences into sources of personal strength. They experience a great deal of satisfaction in helping others. Nevertheless, they acknowledge that rather than acting completely out of altruistic motives, they entered the field to meet personal needs to help others or to accrue other personal benefits from their professional work.

Summary and Implications. In short, master therapists in this study seemed to be operating on a higher order of virtue ethics. Virtue ethics emphasizes developing the virtue and character of the therapist, whereas rule-based ethics emphasizes meeting professional obligations. Rather than focusing on specific rules of conduct, such as confidentiality or bartering, these therapists seem to be operating from a more sophisticated and principled mindset when dealing with the intricacies of ethical practice.

Based on this study, students and practitioners are challenged not only to know their ethics codes, but to continue to develop their character as well as the ability to act courageously when dealing with ethically challenging situations. Because of the incompleteness and fluid nature of professional ethical codes, it is important to recognize the limitations of using only ethical standards to guide professional practice. This study reinforces the importance of several fundamental ethical principles: beneficence, nonmalificence, and autonomy. In addition, master therapists appeared to exceed ethical codes and requirements to be competent in their striving toward expertise. Finally, the study underscored the value that master therapists placed upon building and forming relationships, and how relationships enhanced their ability to practice ethically while increasing their understanding of the ethical demands of their professional role.

ETHICAL THEORIES IN COUNSELING AND PSYCHOTHERAPY

Ethical theory refers to the broad perspective that provides one an orientation to ethical situations. An ethical theory is "the way one chooses to live out and interpret one's values, or to put it on other terms, it is the way a professional puts into practice the choices made about what is valuable in his or her profession" (Brincat & Wike, 2000, p. 112). Major ethical theories include consequentialist ethics, rights ethics, duty ethics, virtue ethics, care ethics, and narrative ethics.

An ethical theory involves two tasks: The first is to provide an ethical orientation that includes assumptions about priorities, that is, what matters most: consequences, duties, character, relationships, and so on. The second is to resolve conflicts among values. Thus each moral theory provides a hierarchy of values and thus enables one to resolve ethical dilemmas and defend the solution reached (Brincat & Wike, 2000).

Six Ethical Theories

Of the several ethical theories, six are briefly described here and further elaborated in Appendix A. Table 2.4 offers a brief description of consequentialist ethics, rights ethics, duty ethics, virtue ethics, care ethics, and narrative ethics.

Implications for Counseling and Psychotherapy Practice

What possible utility or value, if any, do these theories have for counselors and therapists? There are actually several ways these theories are useful (Brincat & Wike, 2000). First, these theories provide insight into ethical thinking of ourselves and others. If you know that your supervisor or administrator is a consequentialist, you can expect that consequential reasons will be especially compelling to him or her. Theorists are distinguished not by their actions but rather by how they *decide* how they will act. Someone operating from a consequentialist perspective can be distinguished from someone with a care ethic by understanding why he or she made a certain decision. Second, these theories are useful in that they explain one's relationships to values. Knowing an individual's ethical theory is indicative of the values he or she deems important. For instance, beneficence and nonmaleficence are highly valued by consequentialists, whereas beneficence and compassion are

TABLE 2.4 Brief Descriptions of Ethical Theories

ETHICAL THEORY	BRIEF DESCRIPTION
Consequentialism	Theory that aims at realizing the best possible consequences. An act is considered good and right only if it tends to produce more good consequences than bad consequences for everyone involved.
Rights Ethics	Theory that assumes that individuals are the bearers of rights that are granted them. An act is considered morally good and right when it respects rights and wrong when it violates rights.
Duty Ethics	Theory that considers the intention of the person choosing, the means, and the nature of the act itself. An act is considered morally good and right if it is done for the sake of duty, has a good motive, its means are acceptable, and/or the nature of the act itself is good.
Virtue Ethics	Theory that defines virtues as that which makes one a morally good person. Ethics and morality are understood primarily in terms of internal dispositions and character rather than external behavior or actions.
Care Ethics	Theory that is rooted in persons and relationships, wherein ethical decisions are made by focusing on relationships rather than on actions, duties, or consequences. An act is considered morally good and right if it expresses care or is done to maintain a caring relationship.
Narrative Ethics	Theory that insists that narrative, or story, and its context are important in ethical decision making. An act is considered morally good and right if it reflects the ongoing story of an individual's life and the culture and tradition within which he or she lives.

more highly valued by those with care ethic orientation. Third, there are times when combining the insights from two or more theories can be helpful or even necessary. Certain value conflicts may be best dealt with by a duty orientation, while other ethical situations call for a virtue ethics perspective. Furthermore, some of the theories are particularly compatible with others. For example, a counselor with a preference for duty ethics may find it helpful to consider consequences along with duties. Similarly, a therapist with a narrative ethics perspective may find he or she needs a virtue theory or rights theory in order to establish a standard or goal for clients to strive toward in their life stories.

This has been a brief introduction and overview of ethical theories as they relate to the practice of counseling and psychotherapy. The interested reader is referred to Appendix A for a more detailed description and discussion of these six ethical theories.

ETHICAL CODES AND PRACTICE BEHAVIOR

In counseling and psychotherapy, ethical codes are intended to "set out expected and professional behavior and responsibility" (Eberlin, 1987, p. 384). However, studies involving ethical dilemmas often find the discrepancy between a counselor's or therapist's knowledge of what ought to be done and what he or she actually would do (Bernard, Murphy & Little, 1987). Why these inconsistencies? Researchers suggest that when the therapists thought the ethical infraction violated a clear professional code, they were more likely to act as they felt they should. This especially happened when the violation was bolstered by a legal precedent on given practices (Bernard et al., 1987). However, in situations that depend more on individual judgment, practitioners were less likely to "do the right thing." It appears that when written ethical guidelines are unclear, therapists rely on their own individual value systems and their understanding of ethical codes (Wilkins, McGuire, Abbot, & Blau, 1990). One possible explanation for the discrepancy between knowing and doing what is right is that some practitioners suffer from deficits in principles such as integrity and honesty (Smith et al., 1991). Rest (1984) theorized that a clinician who is reluctant to follow through with understood ethical behavior may lack the courage to act. To date, studies on therapist values have tended to focus on therapists' conceptualization what constitutes good mental health. Kitchener (1984) believes that parts of formal organizational ethics are too broad, whereas others are too narrow. In order to understand ethical decision making, it seems important to know the core values of the therapist that influence each unique situation.

FOSTERING ETHICAL DEVELOPMENT IN COUNSELING AND PSYCHOTHERAPY

Various educational and training methods have been utilized to foster ethical development in counselors and therapists. The most common method appears to be formal course work in professional ethics and legal issues as they impact the counseling process, the counselor, the therapist, and the profession. The second most common is ethics workshops. The emphases in both courses and workshops is on mastery of the content of ethical codes, standards, ethical principles and values, decision-making and resolution models, and legal issues and risk management. There is considerable debate about the effectiveness of such methods in increasing ethical sensitivity. Some have maintained that ethical sensitivity is fostered with methods that emphasize personal reflection, role modeling, and the ongoing experience of resolving actual ethical dilemmas in practice over memorization and the passing of paper-and-pencil tests (Gottlieb, Knapp, & Handlesman, 2002; Handlesman, Knapp, & Gottlieb, 2001). This section describes and illustrates two educational activities that foster ethical sensitivity. It also makes ethical sensitivity come naturally within a professional culture that is ethically sensitive.

Ethical Autobiography

In this exercise, individuals write about what it is in their backgrounds that helps them through things and identifies what is right and wrong, as well as what constitutes ethical professional behavior. The goal of this exercise is to increase one's ethical sensitivity. Individuals may capture their thoughts in two pages or fifteen pages. Length is not as important as the outcome, which is developing ethical sensitivity. This exercise has been shown to aid individuals in explicitly relating professional ethics to their personal morality. As a result, individuals "develop a good foundation for dealing with the inevitable conflicts that arise between their intuition and the professional code of ethics" (Kuther, 2003).

Ethical Decision-Making Style

Everyone studying counseling and psychotherapy has a unique history and unique needs, expectations, and dreams for his or her professional life, as well as a unique ethical decision-making style. This unique style reflects an individual's early and ongoing experiences with moral values and issues. Presumably, this style has been influenced and shaped by parents, relatives, peers, and valued adults such as teachers and coaches. This style remains implicit, meaning it is not consciously articulated, and it "informs" all or most of the student's ethical and moral decisions. A good clinical training program provides students the opportunity to become aware of and critically examine their implicit style. While this process may begin in an "Ethics and Professional Practice" course, it is usually during supervision that it is more likely to be accomplished.

Of the different ways of helping a student articulate his or her implicit style, the ethical genogram is a particularly useful method (Peluso, 2003). In this method an individual can understand his or her own style by drawing a family genogram chart and describing the various relationships and the ways in which key individuals, such as parents, dealt with moral issues and made moral decisions. The ethical genogram is the method utilized to articulate Jessie's ethical decision-making style in the case study in Box 2.1.

BOX 2.1
PERSONAL ETHICAL DECISION-MAKING STYLE

Jessie is a 28-year-old, recently divorced graduate student in a master's program in counseling. She has finished most of her course work and has started a half-time counseling internship. At the outset of the internship, her supervisor encouraged her to articulate her ethical decision-making style by completing an ethical genogram. Here is what she learned.

Prior to developing an interest in a career in mental health counseling, Jessie taught high school literature for five years after college and was married for two years to an alcohol-dependent sales manager. Although he was fun loving and carefree when they first met, he became progressively emotionally unavailable to her as his job required him to travel three weeks of the month. Their divorce was finalized three years ago.

Jessie is the eldest of three siblings. She describes her father as being substance-dependent on alcohol for most of his adult life and her mother as critical and emotionally distant. She admits to being angry at her mother for shaming and shunning her father when he was unable to maintain sobriety. As a child, Jessie viewed her mother's "tough love" attitude toward her father as unfair and cruel. As an adult, Jessie admits that her mother was frustrated and probably had no other alternative when faced with her father's repeated alcohol abuse episodes. Still, Jessie was very close to her father, finding him fun loving and caring, and she believed that somehow her father would not have drunk so much if her mother hadn't been so demanding and unreasonable. Not surprisingly, Jessie felt enmeshed in her parent's conflict, and she vowed she would make it on her "own terms" rather than by her mother's "strict rules and regulations." Nevertheless, she was also disappointed by her father's own "weakness" and difficulty making decisions and supporting the family, which resulted in her mother's "taking up the slack." Jessie found it incredulous that she was not particularly rebellious, nor did she engage in high-risk behaviors as an adolescent. The only time she came home intoxicated, the night of her senior prom,

(*continued*)

BOX 2.1 CONTINUED

she was perplexed that her mother said nothing and acted as if everything were normal despite Jessie's slurred speech and vomiting. While her mother held strongly to her religious beliefs and strict moral precepts, Jessie considered herself "more spiritual than religious."

Jessie's father's style of making tough decisions was to take the time to try to understand all ramifications, a process that became overwhelming, and as a result, he avoided making any decisions. On the other hand, her mother's style reflected her feeling of being forced to make the hard decisions her husband didn't or wouldn't make, and she vented her anger and vengeance accordingly. When it came to tough moral and ethical decisions, her mother tended to be strict and dogmatic, while her father reacted with hesitation and relinquishment. Jessie summed up her own implicit style by saying that she would consider all the facts and then act, "but never dogmatically." She was surprised to discover that her implicit style of making ethical and moral decisions was an uncomfortable blend of her parent's diametrically different styles.

Ethical Acculturation

Ethical acculturation refers to the process of becoming part of a professional culture that recognizes codes and rules but also prizes and models values, virtues, ethical sensitivity, self-care, moral traditions, and promoting positive behaviors rather than simply avoiding risky ones. In such an ethical culture, individuals are more than taught information and skills; information and skills are also modeled. Modeling involves being aware of one's ethical values, thinking explicitly about the ethics of practice, and then practicing in accord with those ethical values (Gottlieb et al., 2002).

KEY POINTS

1. There are four levels of professional development of counselors and therapists. They represent the developmental patterns of the perceptions, thinking, and behaviors of counselors and therapists from beginning trainee through master counselor and therapist.
2. The manner in which counselors and therapists at these various levels process and respond to ethical matters can be described in terms of progressive levels of ethical development. This progression ranges from a technical reliance and "letter of the law" interpretation of professional ethical standards to a more adultlike "spirit of the law" interpretation.
3. The seven core ethical values of counseling and psychotherapy are autonomy, nonmaleficence, beneficence, justice, fidelity, integrity, and respect for persons.
4. Ethical values can be distinguished from ethical principles: While an ethical value is a single word or phrase that identifies something as being desirable for human beings, an ethical principle is a normative statement about what ought or ought not to be done.
5. Among highly experienced or master counselors and therapists, five core ethical values are central to their personal and professional lives. These are competence, relational connection, nonmaleficence, autonomy, and beneficence.
6. Ethical theories are broad perspectives that provide an orientation to ethical situations. Six ethical theories relevant to counseling and psychotherapy are consequentialism, rights ethics, duty ethics, virtue ethics, care ethics, and narrative ethics.
7. Ethical sensitivity is essential to the effective and proficient practice of counseling and psychotherapy. Fostering the ethical development of counselors and therapists is presumably a goal of graduate programs, supervision, and continuing-education training.

CONCLUDING NOTE

Becoming an effective practitioner of counseling and psychotherapy involves a developmental journey or process in which counselors and psychotherapists grow personally and professionally in the course of learning and practicing their crafts. Developing ethical sensitivity—and, presumably, simultaneously developing professional expertise—lies at the heart of this developmental process. The end point of such professional and personal development is exemplified by master therapists and counselors. As the research suggests, these master therapists and counselors fully embody Perspective III ethical/professional thinking and decision making. We contend that the process of becoming a proficient and effective counselor or therapist involves increasingly embodying Perspective III thinking and decision making.

REVIEW QUESTIONS

1. At which level of ethical and professional development are you currently? What level do you aspire to reach?
2. Rank the seven core ethical values according to your opinion of their importance.
3. What are some of your ethical values? What are some of your ethical principles?
4. Do you think its necessary to utilize one of the six ethical theories outlined in this chapter in order to make a sound ethical decision?
5. How ethically sensitive are you? What can you do to increase your ethical sensitivity?

REFERENCES

Ahia, C. (2003). *Legal and ethical dictionary for mental health professionals.* Lanham, MD: University Press of America.

American Counseling Association. (2005). *Code of ethics. Revised edition.* Alexandria, VA: Author.

American Psychological Association. (2002). *The ethical principles of psychologists and code of conduct.* Washington, DC: Author.

Beauchamp, T., & Childress, J. (1989). *Principles of biomedical ethics* (2nd ed.). New York: Oxford University Press.

Bernard, J., Murphy, M., & Little, M. (1987). The failure of clinical psychologists to apply understood ethical principles. *Professional Psychology: Research and Practice, 18,* 489–491.

Brincat, C., & Wike, V. (2000). *Morality and the professional life: Values at work.* Upper Saddle River, NJ: Prentice-Hall.

Conte, H., Plutchik, R., Picard, S., & Knauss, T. (1989). Ethics in the practice of psychotherapy: A survey. *American Journal of Psychotherapy, 43,* 32–42.

Corey, G., Corey, M., & Calanan, P. (2003). *Issues and ethics in the helping professions.* Pacific Grove, CA: Brooks/Cole.

Eberlin, L. (1987). Introducing ethics to beginning psychologists: A problem-solving approach. *Professional Psychology: Research and Practice, 18,* 353–359.

Gilligan, C. (1982). *In a different voice: Psychological theory and women's development.* Cambridge, MA: Harvard University Press.

Gottlieb, M., Knapp, S., & Handlesman, M. (2002, August). Training ethical psychologists: An acculturation model. In S. Knapp (Chair), *New directions in ethics education.* Paper presented at the meeting of the American Psychological Association, Chicago.

Handlesmen, M., Knapp, S., & Gottlieb, M. (2002). Positive ethics. In C. Snyder & S. Lopez (Eds.), *Handbook of positive psychology* (pp. 731–744). New York: Oxford University Press.

Hass, L., Malouf, J., & Meyerson, N. (1998). Personal and professional characteristics as factors in psychologist's ethical decision making. *Professional Psychology: Research and Practice, 19,* 35–42.

Jensen, J., & Bergin, A. (1988). Mental health values of professional therapists: A national interdisciplinary survey. *Professional Psychology: Research and Practice, 19,* 290–297.

Kitchener, K. (1984). Intuition, critical evaluation, and ethical principles: The foundation for ethical decisions in counseling psychology. *Counseling Psychologist, 12,* 43–55.

Kuther, T. (2003). Promoting positive ethics: An interview with Mitchell M. Handelsman. *Teaching of Psychology, 30*(4), 339–343.

Lambert, M. J. (1992). Psychotherapy outcome: Implications for integrative and eclectic therapists. In J. Norcross & M. Goldfried (Eds.), *Handbook of psychotherapy integration.* New York: Basic Books.

Peluso, P. (2003). The ethical genogram: A tool for helping therapists understand their ethical decision making styles. *The Family Journal: Counseling and Therapy for Couples and Families, 14*(3), 286–291.

Pope, K., & Bajt, T. (1988). When laws and values conflict: A dilemma for psychologists. *American Psychologist, 43,* 828–829.

Rest, J. (1984). Research on moral development: Implications for training counseling psychologists. *Counseling Psychologist, 12,* 19–29.

Skovholt, T., & Jennings, L. (2004). *Master therapists: Exploring expertise in therapy and counseling.* Boston: Allyn and Bacon.

Smith, T, McGuire, J., Abbott, D., & Blau, B. (1991). Clinical ethical decision making: An investigation of the rationales used to justify doing less than one believes one should. *Professional Psychology: Research and Practice, 22,* 235–239.

Stoltenberg, C., McNeill, B., & Delworth, U. (1998). *IDM supervision: An integrated development model for supervising counselors and therapists.* San Francisco: Jossey-Bass.

Wampold, B. (2001). *The great psychotherapy debate: Models, methods, and findings.* Mahwah, NJ: Lawrence Erlbaum.

Wilkins, M., McGuire, J., Abbott, D., & Blau, B. (1990). Willingness to apply understood ethical principles. *Journal of Clinical Psychology, 46,* 539–547.

CHAPTER 3

MULTICULTURAL, RELATIONAL, AND SPIRITUAL ISSUES IN ETHICS

Ethical sensitivity involves the capacity to recognize and deal with ethical and moral aspects of professional and contextual domains in the counseling process. This book emphasizes the importance of the contextual domain. We envision the contextual domain in terms of three dimensions: the personal-developmental, the relational-multicultural, and the organizational ethics–community values dimensions. This chapter focuses on the relational-multicultural dimension of the counseling process, specifically as it relates to understanding ethical issues and resolving ethical dilemmas. The discussion begins with the relational dimension and proceeds to the multicultural dimension, with particular emphasis on ethical and professional considerations related to these dimensions. The multicultural is very broad and includes the spiritual and religious dimensions. Because clients are increasingly expecting counselors and therapists to deal with spiritual and religious issues, ethical aspects of the spiritual dimension are also addressed in this chapter.

LEARNING OBJECTIVES

After reading this chapter you should be able to

1. Explain this statement: Culturally competent counseling is ethically sensitive counseling.
2. Describe the components and processes of the relational or collaborative model of ethical decision making.
3. Describe a culturally sensitive strategy for resolving ethical issues and dilemmas.
4. Describe the relationship of the spiritual dimension and the multicultural dimension.
5. Describe spiritual sensitivity in terms of core cultural and spiritual competencies.

KEY TERMS

ethical sensitivity
multicultural dimension
relational dimension
religion
spiritual sensitivity
spirituality

THE RELATIONAL DIMENSION

This section emphasizes the role of the relational dimension in professional practice of counseling and psychotherapy and particularly the ethical implications of this dimension. After a brief description of the relational dimension and the relational view of ethics, we explore relational ethics in the counseling process, the supervisory process, and the process of ethical decision making.

The relational dimension refers to the therapeutic relationship and the context in which the process of therapy is experienced and enacted. While there are notable differences in the ways this relationship is described among the various psychotherapy approaches, most acknowledge the importance of this relationship. Across these various approaches, a correlation has been found between the therapeutic relationship and psychotherapy outcome. It is estimated that about 30 percent of the variance in psychotherapy outcome is due to "relationship factors," whereas 40 percent is attributed to "client resources" or "spontaneous remission" factors (Lambert, 1992). Based on his analysis of psychotherapy research, Strupp (1995) concludes that the therapeutic relationship is "the sine qua non in all forms of psychotherapy" (p. 70). Furthermore, the research of Orlinsky, Grawe, and Parks (1994) suggests that the quality of the client's participation in the therapeutic relationship is the essential determinant of outcome. In short, clients who are motivated, engaged, and collaborate in the work with the counselor benefit the most from the experience.

Important to the formation of the relational dimension is what Carl Rogers called the "core conditions" of effective counseling and psychotherapy: empathy, respect, and genuineness (Rogers, 1951). It appears that when clients feel understood, safe, and hopeful, they are more likely to take the risk of disclosing painful affects and intimate details of their lives, as well as risk thinking, feeling, and acting in more adaptive and healthier ways. However, these core conditions must actually be felt by the client, and these core conditions will be experienced differently by clients depending on their internal dynamics and cultural matrix. Duncan, Solovey, and Rusk (1992) contend that the most helpful alliances are likely to develop when the counselor establishes a therapeutic relationship that matches the client's definition of empathy, respect, and genuineness.

Professional ethics codes are sets of rules to which counselors and therapists are expected to conform; they reflect the justice or rights and duties orientation of our legal system, which situates obligations within the individual or personal dimension rather than within the relational dimension. Representing an individually focused understanding of ethics, the justice orientation is embodied in the stages of moral development (Kohlberg, 1981, 1984) and contrasts with the relational approach to ethics, which is rooted in an ethic of care (Gilligan, 1977, 1982). In such a relational approach to ethics, moral responsibility is directed toward the relationship rather than toward rights and duties, and ethical decision making is focused on how the relationship is affected by particular actions or inactions. Another view of relational ethics reflects a social constructionist perspective (McNamee & Gergen, 1999).

The Relational Dimension in Counseling

Both counseling theory and clinical lore have consistently elevated the relationship between client and counselor or therapist above all other factors in the counseling process. The experience of most practitioners seems to bear out the assumption that the quality of the client–counselor relationship is more important than theoretical orientation or intervention strategies and techniques. Research is continuing to empirically validate this assumption. We will briefly review some of this research, particularly research relating ethics to the relational dimension. We will primarily focus on a landmark study demonstrating the importance of the relational dimension in the lives of master therapists. Since master therapists reflect the epitome of the long and sometimes arduous journey of counselor development, it is useful and inspiring to understand their experiences, beliefs, and values.

Some of the results of the landmark study of master therapists were already reported in Chapter 2 (Skovholt & Jennings, 2004). Here we will describe in more detail the study findings regarding the relational dimension. One of the most important findings of this study was the emphasis these "master therapists placed upon building and forming relationships and how this enhances their ability to practice ethically" (Jennings, Sovereign, Bottoroff, & Mussell, 2004, p. 122).

Establishing, maintaining, and honoring relationships was found to be a core ethical value for these master therapists. They highly valued their relational interactions with clients as well as colleagues, friends, and the larger community. Furthermore, they upheld high ethical standards, particularly honesty and integrity in their relationships with others. Accordingly, they reported striving for congruence between their values and how they relate to others.

They also reported that in order to maintain their level of competence and expertise, they believed they must continually be in relation with others in the field.

Not surprisingly, they believed that client–therapist relationships are the key to effecting positive changes in clients. The healing potential of client–therapist relationships in terms of treatment outcomes is an increasingly common research finding. In an intensive and extensive review of the of the counseling and psychotherapy research literature, Wampold found that successful therapy outcomes depend more upon common factors, particularly the quality of client–therapist relationship, than any other factors. In fact, such relational factors accounted for over 70 percent of therapy outcomes (Wampold, 2001).

Finally, they believed that healthy relationships in their personal lives served as a safeguard against burnout and impairment. All told, the master therapists in this study demonstrated how their relationships bolstered their understanding of the ethical demands of their professional roles (Jennings et al., 2004).

The Relational Dimension in Supervision

In addition to the ethical significance of the client–counselor relationship, the ethical implications of the supervisee–supervisor relationship are immense. Many would agree that productive supervision cannot occur when the relationship between supervisor and supervisee is inadequate or problematic (Bernard & Goodyear, 2004; Bradley & Ladany, 2001; Holloway, 1995). Furthermore, because of the phenomenon of "parallel process," that is, the transfer of treatment from the supervisor, through the supervisee, to the client, it seems that how a supervisor relates to a supervisee will in some way affect the client, for better or for worse. In other words, if a supervisor is really concerned about client welfare, then he or she would do well to also be concerned about supervisee's welfare (Nelson, Gray, Friedlander, Ladany, & Walker, 2001).

Thus, a key task in early supervision is building a strong working alliance that will serve as a base from which future issues and dilemmas in supervision can be managed. Ongoing maintenance of the alliance should be the supervisor's responsibility throughout the course of the relationship. Furthermore, because supervision involves an evaluative component, it is essential that a strong supervisory alliance be based on mutually agreed upon expectations about the evaluative aspect of supervision. Incongruent expectations about the goals and tasks of supervision as well as about the process of evaluation can lead to misunderstandings, criticism, and harmful conflicts (Nelson, Gray, Friedlander, Ladany, & Walker, 2001). Chapter 14 further discusses the relational dimension in supervision.

The Relational Dimension in Ethical Decisions

For the most part, ethical decision-making models are rational and linear and assume an individual perspective, that is, a nonrelational perspective (Cottone, 2001; Davis, 1997). Davis has described a relational model of ethical decision making that is based on the values of cooperation and inclusion. He contends that effective ethical decision making is facilitated by a positive, collaborative relationship between counselor and client, and he implies that counselors and therapists who establish such relationships are less likely to face problematic ethical issues. Davis refers to the approach he advocates as a collaborative model for resolving ethical dilemmas.

Central to this model is a sequence of four steps:

- Step 1 identifies the participants involved in the dilemma.
- Step 2 articulates the viewpoints of each participant.
- Step 3 develops a solution, a resolution of the ethical dilemma, that is mutually satisfactory to all participants based on a group process focused on eliciting and discussing expectations and goals.
- Step 4 identifies and implements the individual contributions that are necessary to achieve the solution.

THE MULTICULTURAL DIMENSION

Diversity and the multicultural dimension are increasingly important today. This section describes the ethical implications of the multicultural dimension. We begin with a description of the multicultural dimension and then discuss cultural sensitivity and competence as a backdrop for our focus on cultural considerations in ethical decision making.

The multicultural dimension can be understood in a broad or narrow way. Narrowly, "multicultural" involves race or ethnicity. Broadly, it includes race or ethnicity, gender, age, economic status, nationality, disability, sexual orientation, and religion and spirituality. While counselors or therapists may be limited by their experiences (or lack thereof) in these various groups, they are nevertheless expected to recognize and respect diversity in their efforts to promote the welfare, respect, and dignity of their clients.

Today, professionals have become increasingly aware that when counselors and clients are from different cultural groups, differences may exist between them related to values, perception of situations, and even styles of communication. Furthermore, they are learning that even the counseling process may be uncomfortable and unacceptable to clients from some cultural backgrounds.

A basic premise of this book is that culturally competent counseling is ethically sensitive counseling. This section begins with a discussion of cultural sensitivity and cultural competency. It then proceeds to describe a strategy for infusing cultural sensitivity and competency into the resolution of ethical dilemmas. At this very practical level, culturally competent counseling is demonstrated to be ethically sensitive counseling.

Cultural Sensitivity and Competency

Effective counselors and therapists practice in a culturally sensitive manner. A key characteristic of culturally sensitive practice is being culturally competent. A major contribution to the counseling profession has been the development of multicultural competencies. Several authors (Arredondo et al., 1996; Pedersen, 2000; Sue, 1998; among others) have developed competencies as they apply to the counseling profession.

Sue and his colleagues (1998) have proposed that becoming a culturally competent practitioner requires three sets of competencies. The first set involves the practitioner's attitudes and beliefs about race, culture, ethnicity, gender, and sexual orientation. The practitioner would demonstrate capacity to monitor personal biases, develop a positive view toward multiculturalism, and understand how one's biases may interfere with effective provision of counseling services. The second set recognizes that cultural competency requires the practitioner to know and understand his or her own worldview. It also requires that the practitioner possess specific knowledge of the diverse groups with which he or she works and have a basic understanding of sociopolitical influences. The third set involves the capacity to effectively utilize assessment skills, intervention techniques, and strategies necessary in serving diverse clientele.

The Association of Multicultural Counseling and Development (AMCD) and the Association for Counselor Education and Supervision (ACES) teamed up to produce competency guidelines for counselors and other mental health educators, entitled *Multicultural Counseling Competencies and Standards* (Arredondo et al., 1996). These guidelines specify four major components of multicultural competency. The first guideline is awareness of the influence of one's own cultural heritage on one's experiences, attitudes, values, and behaviors. It also includes the way in which one's own culture limits or enhances effectiveness with diverse clients. The second guideline addresses one's comfort level with cultural differences and with clients from diverse cultures. It specifies the importance of developing an attitude that values and appreciates cultural differences, rather than one of disparagement or tolerance. The third guideline emphasizes the importance of honestly facing one's negative emotional reactions and preconceived notions about other cultures. It also specifies recognition of the harmful effects such reactions can have on clients and commitment to work on changing such attitudes. Finally, the fourth competency identifies respect and appreciation for culturally different beliefs, which is reflected in valuing bilingualism and honoring community support networks.

This important document also specifies the knowledge base necessary for practicing in a culturally sensitive, culturally competent manner. Finally, it describes several skills that counselors and therapists must develop and maintain to provide culturally competent counseling.

Core Cultural Competencies

Welfel (2002) provides a useful synthesis of these various competencies. She articulates five such competencies. In our opinion, counselors and therapists who manifest all five of these competencies can be considered to be culturally sensitive. These five competencies have been adapted and are briefly described here.

1. Demonstrate cultural awareness. The first competency specifies an attitude of openness toward other cultural values. Welfel contends that understanding the influence of one's cultural heritage on one's own development, values, beliefs, and social behavior is a prerequisite for this attitude of openness. The assumption is that if one understands the roots of one's behavior and culture, one is less likely to assume the universality or generalizability of it.

2. Understand the client's culture. The second competency requires knowledge of a specific culture or cultures. Unfortunately, ignorance of common cultural phenomena is reflected in misdiagnoses and mistreatment. Thus, knowledge of a particular culture is crucial for the counselor or therapist when clients are torn between following the path typical of their cultures and forging new directions.

3. Collaborate and consult with others. The third competency requires that the counselor have the capacity to involve and collaborate with other key individuals from the culture. Knowing when and how to engage such individuals can be crucial factor in resolving ethical dilemmas. Counselors and therapists also need to know how to seek out support for themselves as well as consult with peers and supervisors to become better informed about a client's culture.

4. Utilize culturally sensitive interventions. The fourth competency requires that the counselor can modify interventions or use interventions designed for cross-cultural counseling. Because conventional approaches to decision making and problem solving often do not sufficiently account for the cultural aspects of situations, counselors need to be skilled enough to adapt them or use alternative approaches designed for cross-cultural counseling (see Pedersen, 2000).

5. Demonstrate tolerance. Finally, the fifth competency requires that the counselor develop and demonstrate a tolerance for ambiguity and divergent views of right and wrong. This competency emerges from the principle of respect for autonomy. Welfel notes that if a client freely chooses a plan of action and has considered its alternatives, the counselor has a duty to respect the choice, provided it does not involve a serious risk to the client or others.

Box 3.1 summarizes these five competencies.

BOX 3.1
FIVE CORE CULTURAL COMPETENCIES

The counselor demonstrates the capacity to

1. Demonstrate an awareness of one's own culture and openness toward other cultural values.
2. Know and understand the client's culture.
3. Collaborate with key individuals from the culture to support the client, as well as seek support for oneself and consultation on cultural issues.
4. Utilize interventions that have been adapted to client need or interventions designed for cross-cultural counseling.
5. Develop and demonstrate a tolerance for ambiguity and divergent views of right and wrong.

Adapted from Welfel (2002).

The Primacy of Cultural Awareness

Of these five competencies, the first, the capacity to manifest or demonstrate awareness of one's own culture as well as openness toward other cultural value, may be the most difficult for many counselors and therapists. Why? The problem is "cultural encapsulation," a kind of cultural tunnel vision. Over forty years ago, Wrenn (1962) described the culturally encapsulated counselors as those who define reality according to their own set of cultural assumptions, are insensitive to the cultural values of others, and are, for all practical purposes, trapped in their own way of thinking that resists adaptation and rejects alternatives. Today, many students enter counseling training with such cultural tunnel vision. Because of limited cultural experiences, they may unwittingly impose their cultural values on other students and clients. The solution to the problem of cultural encapsulation is cultural sensitivity. For this reason it is imperative that counseling and psychotherapy training programs foster and expect cultural sensitivity from their faculty, staff, and students. In our view, the first step in becoming culturally sensitive is cultural awareness.

A counselor's own cultural identity, acculturation, religious and spiritual values, and gender role socialization—which can be thought of as the counselor's cultural worldview—can significantly affect his or her perception of a client's situation and circumstances. When it comes to ethical issues, the counselor's cultural worldview can frame a given situation as an ethical dilemma or not. Not surprisingly, the counselor's level of awareness of his or her own cultural worldview is an operative factor in ethical dilemmas. Box 3.2 illustrates this point.

BOX 3.2
CULTURAL FACTORS AND ETHICAL DILEMMAS

A Nigerian student with a newly diagnosed chronic, debilitating medical condition comes to the university counseling center seeking counseling to deal with distress about her health condition. The client, who had immigrated to this country a year ago, received the medical diagnosis two months ago. She is assigned a Hispanic counselor who values family connectedness. After some discussion, the counselor advises the client to return to her country of origin, where she could find family support. Since family support is also culturally valued by the student, the counselor's advice appears to pose no ethical dilemma. However, had the student been assigned another counselor who valued the client's freedom of choice, or autonomy, over family interdependence, the situation might pose a dilemma because of the potentially conflicting courses of action: stay or return home.

Cultural Considerations and Ethical Decisions

So far the discussion of cultural sensitivity and cultural competence has been decidedly theoretical and academic. What practical relevance, if any, do cultural considerations have in thinking about ethical matters? The answer is quite a bit. This will be immediately evident in the process of ethical decision making, or ethical resolution, particularly when an ethical dilemma is involved. The cultural critique of the counseling profession is that "despite the extensive advances in adding a cultural perspective to counseling theory, these conceptualizations have not necessarily been taken into account in the development of ethical decision-making models" (Garcia, Cartwright, Winston, & Borsuchowska, 2003, p. 275). However, these and other authors (Tarvydas, 1998) have suggested a necessary framework and a practical strategy for the resolution of ethical dilemmas.

The framework they propose includes five attitudes or virtues when approaching ethical dilemmas: reflection, attention to context, balance, collaboration, and tolerance (Tarvydas, 1998).

- *Reflection* involves the counselor's awareness of his or her own feelings, values, and skills as well as those of the other involved participants.
- *Attention to context* refers to being attentive to factors that are operative in the situation: for example, personal, relational, and cultural dynamics, organizational dynamics, and community sentiment.
- *Balance* involves the counselor's efforts to weigh each of the issues and perspectives presented by all the involved participants.
- *Collaboration* means that the counselor maintains an attitude of involving all participants in the decision to the extent that this is possible.

With regard to a practical and culturally sensitive strategy for analyzing and resolving ethical dilemmas, Box 3.3 offers some cultural considerations. Counselors and therapists would be well advised to consider these factors when they engage in ethical decision making.

BOX 3.3

SOME CULTURAL CONSIDERATIONS IN ETHICAL ANALYSIS AND RESOLUTION

- Collect relevant cultural information, such as immigration, family values, religious and spiritual values, and community relationships, as it impacts the problem.
- Determine the key participants involved based on the cultural values of the client.
- Determine whether the identification of the courses of action involved in the dilemma reflects your cultural worldview, the client's, or both.
- Evaluate the extent of cultural sensitivity of your professional ethical code; estimate the potential conflict between laws and ethical codes from a cultural perspective.
- Ensure that the courses of action selected reflect the culture worldviews of the participants involved.
- Use relational methods to reach agreement on potential courses of action.
- Identify culturally relevant resources and strategies for the implementation of the decision and plan.
- Anticipate cultural, personal, and organizational barriers to successful implementation of the plan.

Adapted from Garcia, Cartwright, Winston, & Borsuchowska (2003)

THE RELIGIOUS AND SPIRITUAL DIMENSION

Just as professional ethical standards require counselors and therapists to be sensitive to cultural issues, counselors and therapists are similarly required to be sensitive to religious and spiritual issues influencing their clients. This chapter will detail the ethical implication of a number of religious and spiritual issues in counseling practice. This section notes some of the more common spiritual and religious issues in counseling and psychotherapy.

It seems that increasing numbers of adults and older adults are searching for ways of incorporating spirituality into their daily lives. Survey research indicates that 94 percent of Americans believe in God, nine out of ten pray, 97 percent believe their prayers are answered, and two of five report having life-changing spiritual experiences (cited by Steere, 1997, pp. 43, 54). Thus, it should not be too surprising that clients expect counselors and therapists to incorporate the spiritual dimension in treatment.

The section begins by defining spirituality in a counseling context and then addresses a number of ethical issues involving this spiritual dimension. It also articulates the place of spirituality in the changing context of counseling.

Spirituality

The term *spirituality* conjures up various images and associations, ranging from the traditional, such as prayer and fasting, to the contemporary, such as crystals, meditation, and other forms of spiritual practices. In reality, spirituality is far more basic than any of its manifestations. Distinct from religion, which is the search for significance through the sacred in the context of a shared belief system involving, for example, doctrines and communal ritual practice (i.e., liturgy), spirituality is more about how individuals think, feel, act, and interact in their efforts to find, conserve, and transform the sacred in their lives. It has to do with one's deepest desire, a desire that all experience but cannot satisfy, since this desire is always and continually stronger than any satisfaction. Thus spirituality is primarily about what we do with that desire. Accordingly, spirituality is not something on the fringes of life, nor is it an option that only a few pursue or want to process in counseling or therapy. Rather, everyone has a spirituality that is reflected in everyday thoughts, feelings, and actions and is either life giving or destructive. Viewed from this perspective, spirituality and the spiritual dimension are not marginal to the treatment process nor primarily the domain of "spiritually sensitive" therapists. Rather, they are, or can be, considerations that are basic to any treatment process (Sperry & Shafranske, in press). Thus, recently trained counselors will have at least some formal training in religious and spiritual issues.

Professional and Personal Stance Regarding Spirituality and Religion

In terms of their professional lives, the main implication for that, counselors and therapists "usual and customary care" requires sensitivity to spiritual and religious factors in the clinical practice. In terms of their personal lives, it does not mean that, counselors and therapists are expected to change their basic beliefs or ideology about religion and the spiritual domain. More specifically, it means that counselors can maintain their status as agnostics, atheists, or as nominal or devout adherents to a specific faith or spiritual path. There are four possible stances regarding professional and personal sensitivity to religious and spiritual factors. Figure 3.1 depicts these stances. For instance, because the counseling professions support religious/spiritual sensitivity as usual and customary practice, a counselor or therapist must adopt stance 3 or 4, as stances 1 and 2 are out of compliance with the prevailing professional standard. Now, whether a counselor adheres to stance 1 or 2 is purely

Professional \ Personal	Low	High
Low	1	2
High	3	4

Key:

1 = disinterested or agnostic personal stance, and value-free or "scientific" professional stance

2 = personal spiritual journey, but value-free or "scientific" professional stance

3 = disinterested or agnostic personal stance, but sensitive to patients' spiritual/religious issues

4 = personal spiritual journey, and sensitive to patients' spiritual/religious issues

Stances 1 and 2 are inconsistent, while 3 and 4 would be consistent with ACA Code of Ethics (2005).

FIGURE 3.1 Spiritual Sensitivity and Professional and Personal Commitment

an individual matter. In short, counselors need only exhibit a modicum of sensitivity to religious/spiritual factors in their professional practice, irrespective of their own personal beliefs and behaviors. In the subsequent section, "Levels of Professional Incorporation of the Spiritual Dimension in Counseling Practice," it will be noted that while Level I (no spiritual assessment, no processing, nor referral regarding religious/spiritual issues) was acceptable in the past, today the professional practice of counseling must reflect Levels II through IV. Figure 3.1 graphically represents these types of commitment.

Levels of Professional Incorporation of the Spiritual Dimension in Counseling Practice

In a previous section, different stances or types of professional and personal commitment to religious/spiritual sensitivity were described. In this section, various ways in which psychiatrists can incorporate the spiritual dimension in their professional practice are discussed. Four levels of incorporation will be described and illustrated. These levels are differentiated based on the extent of incorporation of the following three therapeutic factors: (1) a spiritual history or assessment, (2) some degree of processing patients' religious and spiritual issues and/or utilizing spiritual practices with patients, and (3) the extent of referral and/or collaboration with religious/spiritual personnel such as chaplains, the patient's minister, priest, rabbi, or spiritual guide, and pastoral counselors. Box 3.4 summarizes these four levels.

This section briefly describes these four levels and illustrates Levels II, III, and IV. These leve's of incorporation are also related to stances or types of professional and personal commitment to religious/spiritual sensitivity. The reader will note that these illustrations portray both the psychiatrists' professional level of incorporation and their personal

BOX 3.4

LEVELS OF INCORPORATION OF SPIRITUAL DIMENSION IN COUNSELING PRACTICE

I. NONE	No spiritual assessment No processing of spiritual issues No spiritual advisor, even if indicated
II. LIMITED	Spiritual assessment No, or very brief, single processing of spiritual issues Referral to spiritual advisor if indicated
III. MODERATE	Spiritual assessment Some processing of spiritual issues Collaboration with a spiritual advisor if indicated
IV. MAXIMUM	Spiritual assessment Full processing of spiritual issues Collaboration with a spiritual advisor if indicated

commitment to religious/spiritual sensitivity, which is reflected in their unique religious beliefs, spiritual practices, and specific religious affiliations—or lack thereof. Please keep in mind that illustrations describing a particular psychiatrist's *personal commitment* are incidental and not necessarily characteristic of the specific levels of *professional incorporation* being described.

Level I: No Incorporation. At this level, geriatric psychiatry practice does not incorporate any of the three therapeutic factors. No spiritual assessment, not even a brief spiritual history, is undertaken; no processing of religious/spiritual factors or issues is undertaken by the counselor; nor does a referral or collaboration with religious/spiritual personnel occur. As noted in a previous section, this level of incorporation is inconsistent with the stated position of organized psychiatry regarding "usual and customary care."

Level II: Limited Incorporation. At this level, counseling does include at least one, and sometimes two, of the three therapeutic factors. At a minimum, the counselor undertakes a spiritual assessment, typically a brief or screening spiritual history. The counselor may also, based on the spiritual assessment, make a referral to appropriate religious/spiritual personnel if it is indicated, or even attempt a brief, single psychospiritual or spiritual intervention.

At this level of incorporation, the counselor's commitment to understanding and respecting a patient would involve a brief inquiry about spiritual and religious matters in the same way one would ask about work history and sexual matters in the course of completing a comprehensive counseling evaluation.

Level III: Moderate Incorporation. At this level, counseling includes all three therapeutic factors. In addition to the spiritual assessment, which typically is more detailed than a brief or screening spiritual history, the counselor is able and willing to engage in some processing of relevant spiritual/religious factors that have emerged from the assessment. This typically means that the counselor not only incorporates spiritual/religious factors in the case formulation but also engages in some processing of these factors or in some way incorporates psychospiritual and/or spiritual interventions or spiritual practice in the treatment process. If indicated, collaboration occurs with appropriate religious/spiritual personnel. Unlike in Level II, in which referral may be made, in Level III the counselor remains more actively involved in coordinating treatment issues and process.

Level IV: Maximal Incorporation. At this level, counseling fully incorporates all three therapeutic factors. Typically, following a more detailed spiritual assessment, the counselor is able to formulate religious/spiritual dynamics along with relevant psychological and social dynamics as well as biological factors. If indicated, collaboration occurs with appropriate religious/spiritual personnel. Counselors functioning at this level have sufficient training and experience to process relevant spiritual/religious dynamics as well as incorporate psychospiritual and/or spiritual interventions or spiritual practice in the treatment process. At this time, there are relatively few therapists and counselors who have the training and experience to practice at this level of incorporation. Generally speaking, those that do are usually also highly committed to their own personal development on the spiritual journey.

Spiritual Assessment

The process of eliciting religious and spiritual concerns and developing an appropriate treatment plan presumes that one has completed a spiritual assessment. Eliciting a religious history, or a spiritual assessment, as it is currently being called, is now considered an essential component of an initial evaluation. While there is no standardized format or protocol for such an assessment, the following are four questions that are quite useful in eliciting key information:

1. Is religion or spirituality important to you?
2. Do your religious or spiritual beliefs influence the way you look at your problems and the way you think about your health?
3. Would you like me to address your religious or spiritual beliefs and practices with you?
4. Are you part of a religious or spiritual community? (Koenig & Pritchett, 1998).

As noted earlier, the spiritual assessment is common among all three levels of incorporation: Level II, Level III, and Level IV. A high level of professional commitment to spiritual/religious sensitivity is taken (stance 3). Furthermore, the treatment plan that is implemented reflects a moderately high level of incorporation of the religious/spiritual dimension (Level III).

Spiritual and Religious Competencies for Counselors

In an earlier chapter we noted that counseling and therapy are not value-free and that values influence every facet of counseling process: assessment, goals of treatment, interventions used, and evaluation of treatment outcomes. We distinguished value exposure from value imposition. Value exposure involves the disclosure of counselors' or therapists' values when appropriate and without an agenda, whereas value imposition involves disclosure with an agenda. Most commonly value imposition involves effort to proselytize or to criticize the client.

A Committee of the Association for Spiritual, Ethical, and Religious Values in Counseling (ASERVIC) proposed a list of spiritual and religious competencies for inclusion in CACREP standards (see Box 3.5) (Favier, Ingersoll, O'Brien & McNally, 2001, pp. 178–180). Among others, these include the capacity to assess a client's religious and spiritual concerns, the capacity to demonstrate empathy involving a client's spiritual and religious beliefs and practices, and the capacity to assess the relevance of a client's spiritual and religious issues with regard to therapeutic goals. Presumably, supervisors are aware of these specific competencies and the level of the supervisee's competencies and will discuss the influence and impact of such client values and beliefs on treatment process, when operative.

Issues of transference and countertransference are not uncommon in counseling and therapy. It should not be too surprising that countertransference issues often arise when clients are describing or dealing with spiritual or religious matters. Supervisors would do well to acquaint themselves with specific strategies for managing countertransference involving such religious and spiritual issues. A clinically useful reference in this regard is Spero (1981).

BOX 3.5
SPIRITUAL AND RELIGIOUS COMPETENCIES FOR COUNSELORS

COMPETENCIES INVOLVING THE COUNSELOR

- Explain relationship among the spiritual, religious, and transpersonal dimensions.
- Describe one's spiritual, religious, and transpersonal beliefs and practices.
- Identify key life events and how they contributed to one's spiritual/religious beliefs.

COMPETENCIES INVOLVING THE CLIENT

- Demonstrate empathy regarding the client's spiritual or religious beliefs and practices.
- Acquire knowledge to better understand client's spiritual worldview.
- Assess the relevance of spiritual or religious issues regarding therapeutic goals.
- Identify when counselor's understanding or tolerance of spiritual, religious, and transpersonal issues is inadequate to serve client.
- Seek consultation and/or further education when indicated.
- Refer client to minister, chaplain, rabbi, or other spiritual leader when indicated.

Adapted from Association for Spiritual, Ethical, and Religious Values in Counseling (Favier, Ingersoll, O'Brien, & McNally, 2001, pp. 178–180).

Besides ethical issues involved with assessment of religious and spiritual values, beliefs, and concerns, counselors should be comfortable and willing to discuss these concerns with clients, and assuming they have sufficient training, utilize spiritually oriented interventions and methods. There are situations in which such intervention appears to be warranted. There are also situations and circumstances in which there are absolute contraindications as well as relative contraindications for such interventions (Sperry, 2001). One of the most sensitive and complex ethical issues that counselors and therapists face is requests from clients to pray with them. The advisability of utilizing prayer as a treatment intervention is an important professional and ethical consideration, and fortunately, the matter of indications and contraindications has been addressed (Koenig & Pritchett, 1998). Even though counselors may be not fully conversant in these matters, it is expected that they have access to such information through references or consultation.

KEY POINTS

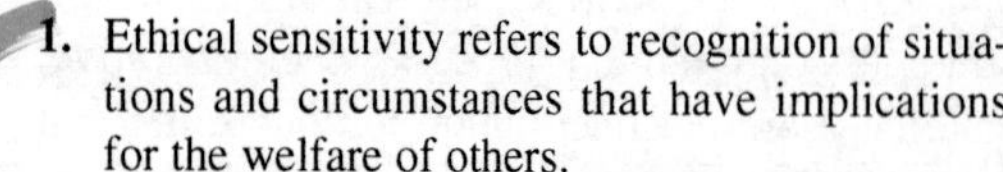

1. Ethical sensitivity refers to recognition of situations and circumstances that have implications for the welfare of others.

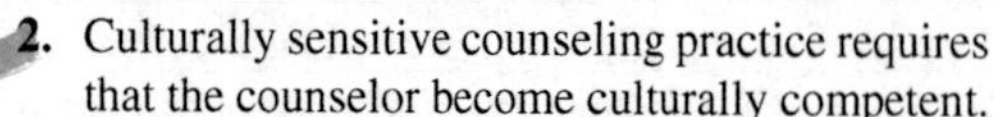

2. Culturally sensitive counseling practice requires that the counselor become culturally competent.
3. Becoming a culturally competent practitioner involves at least three sets of competencies. These include (a) the capacity to monitor personal biases, develop a positive view toward multiculturalism, and understand how one's biases may interfere with effective provision of counseling services; (b) the capacity to know and understand one's own worldview as well as the cultural worldview of the client; and (c) the capacity to effectively utilize assessment skills,

intervention techniques, and strategies necessary in serving diverse clientele.

4. When an ethical issue arises, the counselor's cultural worldview will frame a given situation as either an ethical dilemma or not.
5. The relational dimension involves the capacity for trust, mutuality, ethical sensitivity, and acceptance of uniqueness. It facilitates both the process and outcome of counseling.
6. Effective and productive supervision is unlikely to occur if the relationship between supervisor and supervisee is inadequate or problematic.
7. The multicultural dimension refers to factors such as ethnicity, nationality, economic status, gender, age, disability, sexual orientation, and religion and spirituality that impact the counseling process.
8. Since clients are increasingly expecting counselors and therapists to deal with spiritual and religious issues and concerns in counseling, counselors and therapists can expect to contend with the ethical aspects of these issues and concerns.
9. Spirituality is the unsatisfiable, deepest desire within everyone. It involves the ways individuals deal with that desire: how they think, feel, act, and interact in their quest to satisfy this insatiable desire.
10. Religion is the search for significance through the sacred within the context of a shared belief system. Examples of a shared belief system include shared doctrines and communal ritual practice such as liturgy or public worship.
11. Spiritual sensitivity refers to recognition of the importance and/or influence of religious or spiritual beliefs, values, and other factors on another's life.

CONCLUDING NOTE

This chapter has introduced the relational-multicultural dimension of professional practice of counseling and psychotherapy. The case has been made that cultural factors influence the counselor–client relationship and can and do impact ethical issues. Therefore relational and cultural factors need to be considered in decision making in ethical and professional practice. Effective counseling requires that counselors and therapists develop and enhance their capacity for cultural sensitivity and cultural competence. Such cultural competency further enhances ethical sensitivity. Thus, it can be concluded that culturally competent counseling is ethically sensitive counseling.

REVIEW QUESTIONS

1. How could you increase your own cultural competency?
2. What kinds of cultural factors do you think should be considered when making an ethical decision?
3. Do you think that spirituality and religion are appropriate topics for counseling? Explain your answer.
4. Do you think that nonreligious or nonspiritual counselors should be required to demonstrate spiritual sensitivity? Explain your answer.
5. What cultural factors might influence the counseling process? How can the counselor keep those factors from negatively interfering with the counseling process?

REFERENCES

American Counseling Association. (2005). *Code of ethics. Revised edition*. Alexandria, VA: Author.

American Psychiatric Association. (2000). *Diagnostic and statistical manual of mental disorders* (4th ed.; text revision). Washington, DC: American Psychiatric Association.

Arredondo, P., Toporel, R., Brown, D., Jones, J., Locke, D., Sanchez, J., & Stadler, H. (1996). Operationalization of the multicultural counseling competencies. *Journal of Multicultural Counseling and Development, 24,* 42–78.

Bernard, J. M., & Goodyear, R. K. (2004). *Fundamentals of clinical supervision* (3rd ed.). Boston: Allyn and Bacon.

Bradley, L., & Ladany, N. (2001). *Counselor supervision: Principles, process and practice* (3rd ed.). Philadelphia: Brunner/Routledge.

Cottone, R. (2001). A social constructivism model of ethical decision making in counseling. *Journal of Counseling and Development, 79,* 39–45.

Davis, A. (1997). The ethics of caring: A collaborative model for resolving ethical dilemmas. *Journal of Applied Rehabilitation Counseling, 28*(1), 36–41.

Duncan, B., Solovey, A., & Rusk, G. (1992). *Changing the rules: A client-directed approach to therapy.* New York: Guilford.

Favier, C., Ingersoll, R., O'Brien, E., & McNally, C. (2001). *Explorations in counseling and spirituality: Philosophical, practical, and personal reflections.* Pacific Groves, CA: Brooks/Cole.

Garcia, J., Cartwright, B., Winston, S., & Borsuchowska, B. (2003). A transcultural integration model for ethical decision making in counseling. *Journal of Counseling and Development, 81,* 268–277.

Gilligan, C. (1977). In a different voice: Women's conceptions of self and morality. *Harvard Educational Review, 47,* 481–517.

Gilligan, C. (1982). *In a different voice: Psychological theory and women's development.* Cambridge, MA: Harvard University Press.

Holloway, E. (1995). *Clinical supervision: A systems approach.* Thousand Oaks, CA: Sage.

Jennings, L., Sovereign, A., Bottoroff, N., & Mussell, M. (2004). Ethical values of master therapists. In T. Skovholt & L. Jennings (Eds.), *Master therapists: Exploring expertise in therapy and counseling.* (pp. 107–123): Boston: Allyn and Bacon.

Koenig, H., & Pritchett, J. (1998). Religion and psychotherapy. In H. Koenig (Ed.), *Handbook of religion and mental health* (pp. 323–336). San Diego: Academic Press.

Kohlberg, L. (1981). *Essays in moral development: Vol. 1. The philosophy of moral development.* New York: Harper & Row.

Kohlberg, L. (1984). *Essays in moral development: Vol. 1. The psychology of moral development: Moral stages and their nature and validity.* San Francisco: Harper & Row.

Lambert, M. J. (1992). Implications of outcome research for psychotherapy integration. In J. C. Norcross & M. R. Goldfried (Eds.), *Handbook of psychotherapy integration.* New York: Basic Books.

McNamee, S., & Gergen, K. J. (Eds.). (1999). *Relational responsibility: Resources for sustainable dialogue.* Thousand Oaks, CA: Sage.

Nelson, M., Gray, L., Friedlander, M., Ladany, N., & Walker, J. (2001). Toward relationship-centered supervision: Reply to Veach (2001) and Ellis (2001). *Journal of Counseling Psychology, 48*(4), 407–409

Orlinsky, D., Grawe, K., & Parks, B. (1994). Process and outcome in psychotherapy. In A. Bergin & S. Garfield (Eds.), *Handbook of psychotherapy and behavior change* (4th ed., pp. 270–376). New York: Wiley.

Pedersen, P. (2000). *A handbook for developing multicultural awareness* (3rd ed.). Alexandria, VA: American Counseling Association.

Rogers, C. (1951). *Client-centered therapy.* Boston: Houghton Mifflin.

Spero, M. (1981). Countertransference in religious therapists of religious patients. *American Journal of Psychotherapy, 35,* 565–575.

Sperry, L. (2001). *Spirituality in clinical practice: Incorporating the spiritual dimension in psychotherapy and counseling.* New York: Brunner/Routledge.

Sperry, L., & Shafranske, E. (Eds.). (in press). Introduction to spiritually-oriented psychotherapy. In L. Sperry & E. Shafranske (Eds.), *Spiritually-oriented psychotherapy: Contemporary approaches.* Washington, DC: APA Books.

Steere, D. (1997). *Spiritual presence in psychotherapy: A guide for caregivers.* New York: Brunner/Mazel.

Strupp, H. (1995). The psychotherapist's skills revisited. *Clinical Psychology, 2,* 70–74.

Sue, D. (1998). *Multicultural counseling competencies: Individual and organizational development.* Thousand Oaks, CA: Sage.

Tarvydas, V. (1998). Ethical decision-making processes. In R. Cottone & V. Tarvydas (Eds.), *Ethical and professional issues in counseling* (pp. 144–155). Columbus, OH: Merrill Prentice-Hall.

Wampold, B. (2001). *The great psychotherapy debate: Models, methods, and findings.* Mahwah, NJ: Lawrence Erlbaum.

Welfel, E. (2002). *Ethics in counseling and psychotherapy: Standards, research and emerging issues* (2nd ed). Pacific Grove, CA: Brooks/Cole.

Wrenn, C. (1962). The culturally encapsulated counselor. *Harvard Educational Review, 32,* 444–449.

CHAPTER 4

ORGANIZATIONAL ETHICS

Ethical sensitivity involves the capacity to recognize and deal with ethical and moral aspects of professional and contextual domains in the counseling process. This book emphasizes the importance of the contextual domain. We envision the contextual domain in terms of three dimensions: the personal-developmental, the relational-multicultural, and the organizational-community values dimensions. This chapter focuses on the organizational ethics–community values dimension of the counseling process. It begins by describing organizations and organizational dynamics as an introduction to organization ethics. Then it defines organizational ethics and distinguishes it from personal and professional ethics, as well as from business ethics. There is a discussion of how organizational dynamics influence various ethical practices and ethical dilemmas. Finally, the potential influence of community values on professional and ethical decision making is considered.

LEARNING OBJECTIVES

After reading this chapter you should be able to

1. Explain why otherwise good and ethical therapists and clinic administrators engage in morally questionable or illegal professional practices.
2. List the six subsystems of an organization that can influence ethical decisions.
3. Define organizational ethics and differentiate it from personal ethics, professional ethics, and business ethics.
4. Discuss how organizational dynamics influence the way therapists and counselors deal with confidentiality and informed consent issues.
5. Discuss how organizational ethics can either foster or hinder resolution of ethical dilemmas.
6. Explain how community values can influence professional and ethical decision making.

KEY TERMS

community values
ethical climate
ethics audit
organizational ethics
personal ethics
professional ethics

ORGANIZATIONAL SYSTEMS AND DYNAMICS

An organization and its dynamics can be imagined as a set of five overlapping, concentric circles representing the subsystems of structure, culture, strategy, leaders, and workers within a larger circle that represents the organization's external environment (Sperry, 1996, 2003). It should be noted that each of these six subsystems can influence ethical decisions.

Structural Subsystem

Structure refers to mechanisms that aid an organization in achieving its intended task and goals. The task is divided into smaller, person-sized jobs or roles and clustered into larger sets labeled *teams, departments,* or *divisions.* It specifies the reporting relationship of all roles, their span of control and scope of authority, and their location in a hierarchy of roles —called an organizational chart. An organization's structural system specifies the ways in which the person within a role performs. Roles are expectations that prescribe the boundaries of acceptable behavior for a particular job, that is, for the individual or individuals holding that job. Norms, on the other hand, define group behavior. Norms are shared group expectations about what constitutes appropriate behavior. They are not written expectations as are policies, but they are "known" by all nevertheless.

Cultural Subsystem

Culture refers to the constellation of shared experiences, beliefs, assumptions, stories, customs, and actions that characterizes an organization. The major determinants of culture are the values held by senior administrators, the history of the organization, and the administrators' vision of the organization. These translate into culture through the shared experiences, memories, stories, and actions of employees. The corporate culture provides a guide to action for new situations and for new employees. Culture is to the organization what personality and temperament are to the individual. Thus, culture defines an organization's identity to both those inside and outside the organization. The culture of a corporation may be difficult to describe in words, but everyone senses it. It gives an organization its unique "flavor," and essentially is "just the way we do things around here." It subtly controls the behavior of its members. Accordingly, management can influence its workers by effectively managing the organization's culture. Interestingly, mainstreaming and institutionalizing organizational ethics within the culture of an organization have been shown to be an essential component of ethical behavior in organizations (Sims, 1991). In fact, such an institutionalization of organizational ethics is necessary to "effectively counteract the increasingly frequent occurrences of blatantly unethical and often illegal behavior within large and often highly respected organizations" (Sims, 1991, p. 493).

Administrative Subsystem

The administrative subsystem involves both the leadership and management functions of an organization. Leadership refers to a process of influence, and its main functions include fostering high commitment and morale and empowering staff to provide high-quality services, to respect clients, and to collaborate and cooperate with each other. Management functions include planning, organizing, staffing, directing, and controlling. Thus, an effective leader creates a vision that tells members where the corporation is going and how it will get there. The leader then galvanizes members' commitment to the vision by being ethical, open, empowering, and inspiring.

Staff Subsystem

The worker subsystem involves the way employees relate to each other, their leaders, and the organization's mission and specific goals. Also called "followership" style, this subsystem is an important key to a leader's and the organization's success. Research shows that workers in a given organization have a preference for either the autocratic, democratic, or participative leadership style. Workers function best with leadership that corresponds with their followership style. For example, a subordinate with an affinity for the autocratic approach will respond favorably to the autocratic leadership style. The lack of match between leadership and followership styles probably accounts for conflict, stress, decreased worker productivity, and sustandard performance.

Strategy Subsystem

Strategy refers to the organization's overall plan or course of action for achieving its identified goals. Organizational strategy is based on the organization's vision and mission statements. The *vision statement* answers the question "What can the organization become, and why?" while the *mission statement* answers "What business are we in, and who is our customer?" Strategy answers the "How do we do it?" question. There are three levels of strategy: (1) the corporate strategy, which charts the course for the entire organization; (2) the business strategy, which is charted for each individual business or division within the corporation; and (3) the functional strategy, which deals with the basic functional areas—marketing, finance, personnel—within the organization.

Environmental Subsystem

These five subsystems interact and mutually influence one another. The configuration of these subsystems is also greatly affected by its suprasystem, the environment, especially during times of major changes such as economic recessions, war, or other natural disasters. The environmental suprasystem refers to those factors outside an organizational system that influence it and interact with it. The environment includes economic, legal, political, and sociocultural factors. It also includes technological factors such as a community's mental health needs, quality and availability of therapists, and standards of care.

DIFFERENTIATING PERSONAL, PROFESSIONAL, AND ORGANIZATIONAL ETHICS

This brief introduction to organizational dynamics has set the stage for discussing organizational ethics and the impact of the organization on ethical behavior. So what exactly is organizational ethics? Well, it is different from personal ethics and professional ethics, as well as business ethics. This section begins by briefly reviewing and differentiating personal, professional, and organizational ethics.

Personal ethics is concerned with an individual's internal sense of how he or she should live and what he or she should strive for, serves as the basis on which an individual makes moral decisions or judgments, and guides his or her behavior. They are the roots of one's "moral compass," or conscience (Shelton, 2000). Personal ethics reflect an individual's beliefs, values, and attitudes about the meaning and purpose of life, about right and wrong, good and bad, work and career, relationships, and others. They may be grounded in a religious tradition or reason.

Professional ethics endeavors to help professionals decide what to do when they are confronted with a case or situation that raises an ethical question or moral problem. Some cases and situations raise concerns that confront members of only select professions, such as business administrators or organizational consultants, while others deal with issues confronting all professionals. In short, professional ethics considers the morality of one's professional choices, and most professions have established codes of ethics to guide the ethical practice members of that profession; an example is the code of ethics for physicians articulated by the American Medical Association.

Business ethics has been defined as "the study of how personal moral norms apply to the activities and goals of a commercial enterprise. It is not a separate moral standard, but the study of how the business context poses its own unique problems for the moral person who acts as an agent of this system" (Nash, 1993, p. 5).

While business ethics and organizational ethics are often viewed as synonymous, they are actually quite different. "Business ethics focuses on the choices of the individual *in* an organization whereas organizational ethics focuses on the choices of the individual *and* the organization" (Boyle, DuBose, Ellingson, Guinn, & McCurdy, 2001, p. 16). Furthermore, organizational ethics studies both personal moral norms and organizational moral norms applicable to the activities and goals of an organization. Such norms are reflected in corporate strategy, structure, codes of conduct, contracts with employees and users of services, and corporate culture.

Organizational ethics is also distinct from professional ethics. Unlike professional ethics, which focuses on a professional and his or her ethical concerns in practicing that profession, organizational ethics focuses as much on the organizational context as it does on the administrators or clinicians who are considering an ethical matter. Organizational ethics emphasizes the impact of organizational and organizational dynamics such as the mission of the organization, its responsibilities to clients and the large community, its relation to associated institutions and professional organizations, and the ways in which it provides leadership in order to meet these responsibilities. In other words, organizational ethics is the study and practice of ethical behavior in organizations. It involves clarifying and evaluating the values embedded in an organization's policies and practices as well as seeking ways of establishing morally acceptable values-based practices and policies (Ells & MacDonald, 2002). In short, organizational ethics involves the intentional use of values to guide decision making in organizational systems (Worthley, 1999, p. 9).

Akin to codes of professional ethics adopted by most professions or professional groups, one might expect there would be a corresponding code of organizational ethics. Outside of health care organizations accredited by the Joint Commission on the Accreditation of Hospitals and Health Care Organizations, which requires organizational ethical

TABLE 4.1 Definitions

TERM	DEFINITION
personal ethics	The form of ethics that reflects an individual's internal sense of how he or she should live and what he or she should strive for and serves as the basis for moral decisions or judgments and guiding behavior. An individual's "moral compass," or conscience, reflects these ethical beliefs and values.
professional ethics	The form of ethics that endeavors to help professionals decide what to do when they are confronted with a case or situation that raises a ethical question or moral problem; it considers the morality of one's professional choices and is informed by a code and standards of ethics specified by one's profession.
organizational ethics	The form of ethics that recognizes the impact of organizational factors and involves the intentional use of values to guide decision making in organizational systems. Unlike business ethics and professional ethics, which characteristically view a given ethical concern from an individual perspective, organizational ethics views the same ethical concerns from a systems perspective.

standards to maintain accreditation, few clinics and agencies have adopted formal code of organizational ethics or even codes of conduct that provide guidelines for the ethical behavior of their staff.

Furthermore, it should be noted that, while professional ethics can be differentiated from organizational ethics, it does not follow that ethical issues and dilemmas are automatically classifiable as either professional or organizational ethical issues or dilemmas. For instance, while confidentiality has been traditionally considered to be a professional ethical issue (Sperry, 1993), confidentiality also can and should be viewed from an organizational perspective (Worthley, 1999, p. 29). Similarly, while much has been written on the ethics of managed care (Moffic, 1997; Sperry & Prosen, 1998), little has addressed it from an organizational ethics perspective. This is most unfortunate, because issues such as counselor–client relations, access of care, and conflict of interests are considerably broader than an analysis from a professional ethics perspective permits. In other words, it may be more appropriate and advantageous to consider and analyze ethical dilemmas from both ethical perspectives: professional ethics and organizational ethics. Table 4.1 summarizes these definitions.

THE CENTRALITY OF ORGANIZATIONAL ETHICS FOR ORGANIZATIONAL SUCCESS

For an organization to be successful, its ethical infrastructure must be aligned with its strategy and core values. Interestingly, ethical behavior has been shown to reflect such an alignment. When such alignment is not present "unethical behavior has been identified as a leading cause of operational inefficiency and poor quality" (Bottorff, 1997, p. 59). Accordingly, an organizational ethics strategy should "foster a virtuous organization whose ethical principles inspire appropriate decision making and moral behavior among its personnel" (Magill & Prybil, 2004, p. 227). While surprising to many, research findings are clear: Ethical organizations are more successful than unethical organizations (Verchsoor, 2003). Research evidence is mounting that the success of ethical organizations is reflected in several indices of performance. More specifically, ethical organizations have shown to have lower employee turnover rates, higher employee retention rates, higher quality of services, and higher levels of innovation. Furthermore, when the organization is a for-profit corporation, it also has higher profitability (Magill & Prybil, 2004).

The Central Role of Organizational Culture and Leadership

How does such an organizational ethics strategy develop in an organization? It must permeate all organizational dynamics ranging from strategy to structure to culture to leadership to followership to environment. Perhaps the two most important dynamics are culture and leadership. Recent research on the organizational factors that foster ethical decision making provides some clues. A preliminary study of an exemplary corporation and global leader in ethics found the following factors to be central to ethical decision making among employees: an organizational culture valuing ethics and rewarding ethical behavior, ethical analysis based on moral philosophy, consistency between individual values and organizational values, and ethics training (Bowen, 2004). Clearly, organizational culture valuing and rewarding ethical thinking and ethical behavior is a central factor.

Furthermore, because leadership directly drives all other organizational dynamics, an organization's ethical strategy must begin with the involvement of leadership. When organizational leaders convey moral integrity, encourage ethical sensitivity, and support and reinforce ethical behavior, an organization functions ethically.

What are the implications for counseling organizations? Such organizations, including mental health clinics, human services agencies, and schools, are well advised to consider ethics as important as counseling outcomes, quality services, student achievement, and legal and financial considerations. The administrators of such organizations must convey moral integrity, encourage ethical sensitivity, and support and reinforce ethical behavior. They support ethical behavior by upholding the organization's ethical values, requiring compliance with professional ethical standards, and by fostering a high degree of fit between personal values of staff and core values of the organization. Among other things it means hiring staff with ethical sensitivity and competence.

Three Differing Perspectives

While it is logical, the classification of ethics as personal, professional, or organizational ethics is not particularly useful in the real world. In the real world, a clinic administrator with certain values and ethical standards enters a profession with unique values and ethical code and takes a position with a corporation that has certain values and ethical standards. In other words, there are three points of view that are operative whenever that administrator confronts an ethical matter in the clinic setting: his or her own, the profession's, and the organization's. In the best of circumstances, all three sets of values and ethical standards are similar or compatible. In the worst of circumstances, all three are in conflict. For example, two clinic administrators face the same ethical dilemma. For one, the pressure to "ignore" an obvious conflict of interest is extremely distressing, while it seemingly nonproblematic for the other administrator. From the perspective of the first administrator, there appears to be an incompatibility or conflict between personal ethics and organizational ethics, which is presumably not the case for the second administrator. The first administrator might also feel the tug of his or her professional code of ethics, stemming from the professional perspective.

The point is that these three perspectives can and do exert influence on the many ethical considerations that administrators regularly encounter in the workplace, with one of these perspectives exerting more influence than the other two. For many individuals, because of the nature of organizational dynamics, there is significant pressure on clinicians and administrators to adopt the ethical perspective of their organizations.

SYSTEMIC FACTORS IMPACTING ORGANIZATIONAL ETHICS

By their very structure and culture, corporations can undermine the administrator's perspective, needed for functioning ethically in the workplace. "The inventive systems we create, the goals we set, the language we speak, the way in which information is gathered, and the channels through which it is communicated all contribute to any individual's ability to distinguish right from wrong" (Nash, 1993, p. 121). Specifically, Nash (1993) identifies four systemic factors, or organizational dynamics, that appear to be major contributing causes to unethical organizational behaviors: (1) the inarguable importance of the bottom line, (2) an overemphasis on short-term efficiency or expediency, (3) the seductive power of ego incentives, and (4) the difficulties of personally representing the organizational polity, of wearing two hats (p. 121). Each of these systemic factors will described and illustrated, along with strategies for dealing with ethical dilemmas arising from each factor, in subsequent sections.

Conflict between Personal Ethics and Organizational Policy

Every clinic administrator wears several hats in fulfilling his or her professional as well personal and family duties. Administrators routinely assume the roles of boss, coach, friend, advisor, loyal supporter, parent, and spouse. They also embody personal values that may or may not match actual—as contrasted with stated or written—organizational values. Problems arise when there is a conflict between the administrator's personal roles and values and organizational roles and values. Matters of personal ethics and conscience inevitably become involved. Administrators regularly face internal conflicts between what they would do as the head of any agency and what they as a private individuals or citizens might think is the right thing to do.

Needless to say, organizational influence on its staff, particularly administrators, is great indeed. Among other things, administrators are expected to protect and promote the organization's image. This obligation is germane to ethical dilemmas involving personal conscience versus organizational policy. Administrators noted that, while organizational loyalty may foster a "sweep it under the rug" climate, they also believed that "not airing dirty linen in public" is a sentiment widely shared by members of a corporation. Nevertheless, deference to the organizational viewpoint, while not bad per se, can and does influence ethical decision making. That is because the motivational power of a corporation's image is analogous to the influence of charismatic leadership. Just as employees tend to idealize charismatic leaders and defer to their directives, "the more charismatic the organizational image, the stronger is employee loyalty and commitment to the company's interest. . . . organizational charisma can prompt administrators to put on their 'organizational hats' and never take them off" (Nash, 1993, p. 217). As a result, they are unlikely to consider their own values and viewpoints, or judge issues from a broader perspective. In psychological terms, an administrator may then "confuse company loyalty, which is a reasonable duty, with *unquestioning* loyalty, which is not" (Nash, 1993, p. 217). See the case example in Box 4.1.

From an organizational ethics perspective, an administrator should consider more than the relationship between self and the friend. He or she should consider his or her relationship with other unit members, as well as with the corporation itself. There are implied obligations to each relationship, which can be boiled down to this organizational covenant: to provide value and receive a fair return in the process. According to Nash (1993), you, as the administrator, must provide value to the friend, to other employees, and to the corporation itself, and you have a right to expect a return from all three.

From this perspective, the problem would be framed differently. The initial issue would not be secrecy but rather the welfare of others. The interview or conversation would be viewed as an opportunity to provide value for all parties. Thus, without revealing the corporation's recent decision, the administrator would view this valued colleague's request as a source of information about his motivation, contributions to the team, and how well his needs are served by the corporation. By directing the discussion more broadly to the various reasons why he is job searching can offer both the corporation and you, the colleague, valuable insights. Rather than sidestepping the secrecy issue, the nature of secret and closely held information and their attendant responsibilities for all parties can be discussed. Just as the colleague is asking the you to keep his job search confidential, you can set the stage for the understanding that both of you have secrets that you are obligated and trusted

BOX 4.1

CASE EXAMPLE OF DIVIDED LOYALTIES

A friend and colleague comes to you for advice. Because of a recent promotion this individual now reports to you. He has been offered a position with a competitor and wants your advice on the matter. You have just learned that your unit has been given only one more quarter to improve performance or fold. No one else in your unit is aware of the organization's decision. Your colleague's input in the turnaround is critical, and you can't imagine getting through this without him. However, if you tell him that the unit may fold in three months, there is a good chance you will lose him immediately. Even if he passes up the other position and stays, word may leak out and demoralize the rest of the team. The ethical dilemma is this: Do you tell your friend about the top-management decision or not? If you tell him, he may respect your honesty and risk staying to work with you to valiantly bolster performance. Or, he may leave and divulge the information to the rest of the team, causing a major morale problem. However, if you conceal the information, you contribute to a culture of deception in employee relations that may be either destructive or beneficial in the short run, but will certainly catch up with you in the long run. What would you do?

to keep. You should tell him that you cannot tell him about job security but can expand the discussion as previously suggested.

This solution does not force the abandonment of the dual roles of friend and superior. It takes a long-term view of the problem at hand, rather than restricting the ethical analysis of the issue to a single decision. In this case, in developing relationships on the job and long before this issue arose, as the administrator you would have been careful to avoiding switching hats that is, being a special friend to the employee on some days to the exclusion of your organizational role as administrator.

To conclude this section, there are three strategies for dealing with these conflicts. The first strategy for resolving the conflicting voices of conscience is simplistic and straightforward: separate personal conscience from organizational roles and values and endorse the organizational view. The second strategy is to change roles and values as situations change. Well-intentioned administrators might be a friend one moment and spokesperson for the corporation the next moment. The third strategy is to strive for an *integrative* approach to personal ethics with organizational ethics rather than these *either/or* terms. Accordingly, instead of seeing staff productivity or billable hours as the first value and goal of an administrator, the administrator could focus instead on relationships and service to others, and view productivity as a byproduct of this focus.

Impact of Organizational Dynamics on Ethical Dilemmas

Counseling and psychotherapy practice today bears scant resemblance to clinical practice twenty years ago. Then clinicians, now called providers, practiced rather independently with little if any constraints on how they practiced. They made decisions about treatment length based primarily on client need, and their treatment outcomes were judged rather subjectively, usually by increases in referrals from satisfied clients and other referral sources. Today, clinical practice, particularly in mental health clinics and agencies, is characterized by an increasing emphasis on quality and accountability, particularly objective, quantifiable measures of accountability. Cost-effectiveness and treatment efficacy and efficiency have become the norm for the provision of behavioral health services. Clinical outcomes are key markers of quality and cost-effectiveness. The reactions of clinicians to the assessment of clinical outcomes range from wholehearted acceptance to anger and distrust. Those who are most negatively disposed view outcomes assessment as an intrusion into their clinical practice style or, worse, a breach of confidentiality. Few would doubt that the evolving emphasis on quality, cost-effectiveness, and accountability has impacted clinical practice style, particularly in delimiting clinician decision making. Yet, whether the assessment of outcomes actually constitutes a breach of confidentiality or other ethical principles is less obvious.

Since assessment of outcomes has been associated with cost control and quality improvement, such assessment is not only essential for certain types of accreditation; it is considered good business practice. As a result, many clinics have already begun to assess clinical outcomes.

The question "Can otherwise good and ethical clinicians and administrators engage in morally questionable or even illegal professional practices?" is not merely an academic question. While measuring clinical outcomes is a good business practice, several ethical dilemmas are associated with efforts to assess, monitor, and manage clinical outcomes. This section will describe organizational factors that foster both professional ethical dilemmas, such as confidentiality and informed consent, and more complex organizational ethical dilemmas, such as financial considerations, efficiency and expediency, and personal–organizational ethical conflicts, that both MBHO clinicians and administrators may face.

ORGANIZATIONAL ETHICS AND PROFESSIONAL ETHICS

Confidentiality and informed consent are two principles traditionally associated with professional ethics. This section discusses the influence that organizational dynamics can have on professional ethics.

Confidentiality

As with other aspects of the provider–client relationship, issues of confidentiality can accompany the use of outcomes assessment, monitoring, and management. Just as clients should be informed in writing of the extent to which confidentiality will be maintained in terms of provider communications and written records, they also should be informed as to how the data that they provide on clinical outcomes inventories will be held confidential. Clinics need to develop written policy and procedure language stating who has access to such information and how that information will be used. Since clinical outcomes data at the assessment level and the management level tend to be aggregate data, confidentiality issues are somewhat limited. On the other hand, at the monitoring level individual data and policies need to specifically indicate how providers and staff will safeguard such client data.

Earlier we indicated that confidentiality can also be considered an organizational ethics issue, which will be very briefly noted here. From an organizational ethics perspective, the structure and/or the culture of a clinic can effectively compromise confidentiality. All-too-common examples include inadequate structures—policies or enforcement of policies for limiting access to sensitive sections of client records—a clinic culture that "facilitates" detailed discussion of case material within earshot of nonclinical staff, and a staff's use of unflattering nicknames for problematic clients.

Informed Consent

Informed consent is a rather broad and complex legal and ethical issue. In managed care organizations, issues of informed consent often revolve around economic factors: For example, a managed care organization may pressure its staff not to inform clients about specialized or expensive treatments that it is not willing to pay for or reimburse. In short, they simply withhold information about specialized, expensive treatments, the antithesis of informed consent.

When it comes to the matter of clinical outcomes, the issue may have less to do with treatment options and more to do with *how* clinical outcomes information might be used. In this instance, informed consent issues might involve not only clients but also providers. This is particularly the case when it comes to client profiling and provider profiling. Let's look first at client profiling. Client profiling is a sophisticated process of combining a wide range of data on individual clients, beyond diagnoses, to predict the clients' likely responses to treatment and the overall costs of various treatment options. A managed behavioral health organizations (MBHO) administrator could make a treatment authorization based on cost predictions associated with client profiling, leaving little if any decision-making authority to the provider. For example, assume that profiling predicts that a client is likely to improve moderately with either psychopharmacotherapy alone or with focused psychotherapy alone, but would improve a bit more with psychotherapy combined with medication. The MBHO could decide to offer the client the least expensive treatment, psychopharmacotherapy, using a generic antidepressant already on their formulary. Or, if the profiling suggests that only a treatment option outside of the MBHO network is likely to be effective, MBHO management may forbid the provider from informing the client of that option. While it may be a good business practice to offer the client the least expensive treatments, it does so at the expense of informed consent.

Similarly, provider profiling can be the source of informed consent problems. Provider profiling is a sophisticated prediction method for identifying a provider's professional strengths and weaknesses. With provider profiling, MBHO management can profile an individual clinician's "success" in working with a variety of diagnostic presentations, by age, gender, and so on. It could use this profile to selectively refuse authorization for certain clients—those with which the provider has low success rates—or to systematically refer such clients to more "successful" providers. On the other hand, clinics could share profiling data with providers in order to establish supervision, coaching, or even specialized training such as specific CEU courses that could increase the provider's success rates in working with certain types of clients. Sharing such profiling information would constitute informed consent and show respect and concern for the provider.

COUNSELING PRACTICE AND ORGANIZATIONAL ETHICS

A basic premise of the organizational ethics perspective is that administrators, those individuals charged with making decisions for a given corporation, make decisions and engage in behaviors that reflect organizational values and, to a greater or lesser extent, their own values. By their very structure and culture, corporations can undermine the clinical perspective needed for functioning ethically in the workplace. "The inventive systems we create, the goals we set, the language we speak, the way in which information is gathered, and the channels through which it is communicated all contribute to any individual's ability to distinguish right from wrong" (Nash, 1993, p. 121). Specifically, Nash identifies some systemic factors, or organizational dynamics, that are major contributing causes to unethical organizational behaviors. In this article we will consider three: bottom-line, or financial, consideration, efficiency and expediency, and personal–organizational ethical conflicts. Each of these systemic factors will be described and illustrated, along with strategies for dealing with ethical dilemmas arising from each factor, in subsequent sections.

Financial Consideration

It is not unfair to say that corporations are preoccupied with the bottom line, since the bottom line is a quantitative indicator of organizational performance and success. But this indicator is limited and, in some instances, an inaccurate measure of qualitative factors such as client satisfaction, teamwork, and critical aspects of managerial functioning such as ethical behavior. In theory, the bottom line is morally neutral. Yet, in practice, high standards of conduct may be "linked to the bottom line for motivational and assessment purposes. . . . ethical conduct is motivated through the promise of a dollar reward" (Nash, 1993, p. 134).

Corporations who allow the bottom line to dominate their thinking become captive to a reductionistic approach to problem solving. "This can lead to a disregard, even disrespect, for others as empathic and relationship thinking is abandoned. As a long as the bottom line is in the driver's seat, other ethics norms will be either decorative or suppressed" (Nash, 1993, p. 158).

When a managed care organization (MCO) is preoccupied by bottom-line thinking, its moral muscle may give way to the scalpel of a cost-cutting agenda. Moral obligations such as effective treatment and quality care can be sacrificed at the altar of success, since bottom-line thinking tends to trap administrators into viewing ethical dilemmas as a choices between profitability and morality. Take the matter of clinical outcomes monitoring. While JCAHO and NCQA now require assessment of clinical outcomes, there is still some latitude in operationalizing this regulation. It is much less expensive to design and implement a system for before-after outcomes measurement than the more costly and time-consuming serial assessment of outcomes monitoring. Since outcomes monitoring, when compared to outcomes measurement, can significantly improve treatment efficacy as well as quality of care (Brill & Sperry, 1997), it is difficult to imagine how a clinic that represents itself as committed to effective, quality care can morally justify the use outcomes measurement only. More likely, their justification is financial, bottom-line thinking.

Efficiency and Expediency

Besides financial pitfalls, expediency is also a source of ethical problems. Short-term pressures can effectively silence moral reasoning because administrators have less time for considering the complex, time-consuming ramifications of ethical decision making. According to Nash (1993), short-term thinking is a twofold moral failure both of vision and of reckoning. First, it is a failure "to adopt a vision of business purpose that adequately encompasses the dynamics of value-creation and relationship-enabling activities" (p. 166). Second, it is a failure of reckoning, because by failing to look either far enough forward or far enough back, a administrator has "few tangible anchor-points for conscience to attach itself to decision making in an integrated, productive way" (p. 166). Nash (1993) reports that, in a survey of several hundred administrators, she found that "a short-term frame for performance was consistently cited as the single greatest stress factor on personal ethics" (p. 166). She notes that flooding the market with generic drugs as patents expire is an example of financial wrongdoing occurring when the time frame for decision-making was extremely constricted.

Subsequently, when legitimate pressures for efficiency and expediency dominate one's thinking and communications, there is an ever-present danger of becoming shortsighted. Values such as integrity, compassion, and honesty require an expanded time frame. Furthermore, effectiveness and efficacy can be incompatible with efficiency and expediency.

Short-term perspectives create both analytical and psychological barriers to such analyses. For the corporation, preoccupation with the short term precludes a consideration of long-term negative consequences and here-and-now process issues involving honesty and credibility, and unfittingly fosters an ethos of greed and underhanded organizational practices. For the individual, the short-term perspective suppresses awareness of cause and effect and fosters delusional thinking, which inevitably corrupts good leadership values.

In the short run, outcomes measurement systems are more efficient and expedient than outcomes monitoring systems and outcomes management systems. The successful implementation of a system that encompasses outcomes monitoring and outcomes management requires some basic changes in clinician practice patterns (i.e., independence and minimal practice constraints vs. standardization and practice guidelines) as well as in the overall culture of a behavioral health clinic or system (i.e., client need vs. cost as the criterian for treatment length) (Sperry, Grissom, Brill & Marion, 1996). Typically, these changes do not occur quickly or without resistance, and thus they do not lend themselves to expediency and short-term thinking. Nevertheless, such changes in practice patterns and clinical culture result in much improved treatment efficacy and quality of care.

Personal–Organizational Ethical Conflicts

Every individual wears several hats in fulfilling his or her organizational duties as well as personal and family responsibilities. Clinic administrators and clinicians routinely assume the roles of superior, coach, friend, parent, spouse, and behavioral health care advocate. These individuals also embody personal values that may or may not match actual—as contrasted with stated or written—organizational values. Business problems arise when there is a conflict between administrators' personal roles and values and organizational roles and values. Matters of personal conscience inevitably become involved. These people continually face internal conflicts between what they would do as loyal representatives of the corporation and what they as private individuals might think is the right thing to do. Such a conflict is known as the "two-hat" dilemma.

Needless to say, organizational influence on administrators is great—they are expected to protect and promote the corporation's image. Moral dilemmas often arise involving personal conscience versus organizational policy, that is, wearing two hats. In her research with organizational administrators, Nash (1993) found that "creating a good corporate image" was the most frequently cited organizational expectation after "making money" (p. 216). Interviewees viewed the morality of this goal with great ambiguity. These individuals noted that, while organizational loyalty may foster a "sweep it under the rug" climate, they also believed that "not airing dirty linen in public" is a sentiment widely shared by other members of a corporation. Not surprisingly, deference to the organizational viewpoint, while not bad per se, can and does influence ethical decision making. In psychological terms, it is relatively easy for individuals to confuse corporate loyalty, which is a reasonable duty, with unquestioning loyalty, which is not. As a result, they are unlikely to consider their own values and viewpoints, or judge issues from a broader perspective.

I've observed this "two-hat" dilemma among clinic administrators, particularly those who are associated with high-visibility clinics that are attempting to achieve or maintain their NCQA accreditation. It is not unusual for these administrators to feel pressured to "ensure" that a clinic or system comply with certain NCQA standards, standards that may be very difficult, if not impossible, to achieve given circumstances and resource allocation. The corporate pressure can be extremely high for these individuals to creatively document such "compliance." The fear of being viewed by top management and colleagues as disloyal and as non-team players can be paralyzing for administrators who feel ethically compromised. Needless to say, the real challenge for such clinics is to foster, instead, a culture that prizes ethical and moral excellence in addition to high productivity and quality care.

ASSESSING AND EVALUATING ORGANIZATIONAL ETHICS IN A COUNSELING SETTING

This section discusses the assessment and evaluation of organizational ethics as applicable to counseling settings. It describes ethics audits and an organizational ethics inventory. Chapters in Part III illustrate the use of this inventory in school counseling, mental health counseling, couple and family counseling, and career and rehabilitation counseling settings.

Ethics Audits

An ethics audit is an audit or investigation in which the implementation of ethical policies as well as ethical incidents in an organizational setting are reviewed and evaluated. In a counseling setting ethics audits can be helpful in evaluating the adequacy of current ethics-related practices in the organization, in modifying practices as needed, as well as in monitoring the implementation of these changes. Ethics audits first emerged in the 1980s in corporate settings as a response to various corporate scandals. In for-profit corporations, ethics audits are routinely completed by accounting firms. In short, an ethics audit is an investigation of how an organization's ethical policies are being implemented, as well as a review and evaluation of ethical incidents that occurred in the organization during a given time frame.

Recently, ethics audits have been introduced in health care organizations and human services agencies either because of accreditation requirements or because of the culture of accountability that managed care and the total-quality-assurance movement require. In the field of mental health, Reamer (2000) has advocated that ethics audits be required in social work training and practice.

How is an audit done? Formally, an audit is undertaken by an outside consultant—often a form of specialty accounting firm—who conducts interviews and surveys and reviews the organization's documents and documentation of ethics policy implementation and incidences. Typically, a standardized assessment device is utilized for identifying and reviewing pertinent ethical issues. Such a standard measure permits "benchmarking," or comparing results across organizations that have similar missions and structures. More informally, it can simply involve a brief review of the organization's core values, ethics policies, and ethical practices as they relate to professional ethical codes and standards, by means of short paper-and-pencil survey or inventory.

There are three types of ethics audits used in organizational settings, whether they are corporations, schools, agencies, or clinics: compliance audits, cultural audits, and systems audits.

Compliance Audit. The least comprehensive ethics audit is the compliance audit. This audit determines the degree to which the organization's ethics meets the minimum standards set forth in legal statutes, regulations, and policy, and the given profession's codes and standards. Reamer (2000) advocates this type of ethics audit in human services agencies. He contends that the audit should assess the extent to which "social workers and agencies have procedures in place to identify ethics-related risks and prevent ethics complaints and ethics-related litigation" (p. 356).

A detailed compliance audit for social work agencies has been developed and is utilized in a number of human services agencies (Reamer, 2001). It assesses the following ethical and legal factors: ethical risks, client rights, confidentiality and privacy, informed consent, service delivery, boundary issues and conflicts of interest, documentation, defamation of character, client records, supervision, staff development and training, consultation, client referral, fraud, termination of services and client abandonment, practitioner impairment, and the ethical decision-making process and method utilized by staff.

Cultural Audit. This type of audit assesses how employees or staff feel about the standards and behavior of the organization. Cultural audits assess perceived priorities and ethical effectiveness of individuals, groups, units, or the organization as a whole.

Systems Audit. This audit assesses compliance and culture as parts of a bigger whole, namely the degree to which the ethical principles, guidelines, and processes of the organization are integrated within the organizational system. Systems audits view the organization as a system and examine the ethics issues within that system and between that system and critical elements of the environment within which it operates. They examine the relationships within and between several components: environment, resources, core values, mission and strategic goals, and individual values as they relate to legal, regulatory, policy, and professional ethics.

Organizational Ethics Inventory

Why should a counseling trainee or professional counselor or therapist consider performing an organizational ethics evaluation of the counseling setting for which he or she will do an internship or be hired as a counselor? The main reason is that the organizational dynamics of a school, agency, or clinic can significantly impact the ethical and professional behaviors as well the job satisfaction of counseling interns and professional counselors and therapists. Organizations that have well-articulated ethical values, principles, and professional standards and that act on these values, principles, and standards tend to foster positive counseling outcomes in clients as well as personal and professional development and job satisfaction among staff better than organizations that do not. Staff commitment is likely to be higher, turnover is likely to be lower, and quality counseling outcomes are likely to result. This is particularly the case when a counseling intern's or school counselor's core ethical values and the school's actual ethical values are consistent. On the other hand, the less positive and healthy the ethical culture or climate of a counseling organization, the more likely counseling interns and school counselors will experience work-related stress. Accordingly, an evaluation of organizational ethics using an inventory—such as the one included below—can be a useful tool to assess the ethical climate of a particular school, agency, or clinic in which you might seek internship training or consider working as a professional counselor or therapist.

In terms of the three types of ethics audits described earlier, the Organizational Ethics Inventory provided in Box 4.2 is a systems audit, albeit a short and simplified one.

BOX 4.2
ORGANIZATIONAL ETHICS INVENTORY

Directions: Using the following 1–5 scale evaluate each of the following items based on your current experience with a particular counseling organization's ethical values, climate, and practices.

1 = disagree fully; 2 = disagree somewhat; 3 = neutral; 4 = agree somewhat; 5 = agree fully

_____ 1. There is a formal ethics policy that articulates the ethical values, principles, and professional standards to which this organization is committed.

_____ 2. The organization's actual core values and policies match its stated core values and policies.

_____ 3. The organization's commitment to its core values, ethical policies, and professional standards is championed by leadership and communicated routinely throughout the organization through staff orientation, training programs, and regular meetings.

_____ 4. Staff understands and agrees with the organization's core values and ethical expectations.

_____ 5. Staff are listened to when they identify ethical concerns about any aspect of their work.

_____ 6. Ethical behavior is recognized and rewarded while immoral and unethical behavior is sanctioned.

_____ 7. All staff and clients are treated with respect, fairness, and equality.

_____ 8. The organization's ethical commitment and elements of the ethics policy and professional standards are routinely discussed in staff and other meetings.

_____ 9. Confidentiality and client privacy is effectively safeguarded in this organization.

_____ 10. Increasing professional competency is highly valued and rewarded in this organization.

_____ 11. Establishing and maintaining appropriate boundaries and avoiding harmful conflict of interests is expected behavior.

_____ 12. Informed consent is provided to clients initially and on an ongoing basis.

_____ 13. There are formal processes in place for staff to report suspected unethical behavior and/or to ask questions to clarify understanding of the ethics policies and standards without fear of retaliation, retribution, or reprisal.

_____ 14. My ethical values and principles are consistent with the organization's values and principles.

_____ 15. The organization has a positive and healthy ethical culture, or climate.

_____ Total Score

ANALYSIS OF ORGANIZATIONAL ETHICS INVENTORY SCORES

Chapters 10 and 13 in Part III provide a scoring and analysis rubric for the use of this inventory in specific settings: school counseling, mental health counseling, couple and family counseling, and career and rehabilitation counseling.

Ethics Compliance Audit

How would a systems audit differ from a compliance audit in a counseling setting? The brief Ethics Compliance Audit in Box 4.3 is offered so readers can make their own comparison with the Organizational Ethics Inventory. The interested reader is referred to Reamer's inventory (Reamer, 2001), which is a full-scale compliance audit developed for a social work agency, but which seems applicable—or can be modified to be applicable—in any counseling organization.

BOX 4.3
ETHICS COMPLIANCE AUDIT

Directions: Using the following 0–3 scale evaluate each of the following items based on your current experience with a counseling organization's compliance with professional ethical standards and regulatory and legal statutes regarding the practice of counseling. More specifically, your rating should reflect the organization's level of risk for harm to clients or staff and/or malpractice involving the following dimensions.

0 = no risk; 1 = minimum risk; 2 = moderate risk; 3 = high risk

_____ 1. client rights
_____ 2. confidentiality and privacy
_____ 3. informed consent
_____ 4. delivery of professional services
_____ 5. boundary issues
_____ 6. conflicts of interest
_____ 7. documentation
_____ 8. client records
_____ 9. staff training
_____ 10. supervision

_____ Total Score

ANALYSIS OF COMPLIANCE ETHICS AUDIT SCORES
A total score of 10 or less—which represents minimal risk—could be considered acceptable. A total score above 10 or a rating of more than 2 on any individual item indicates that attention needs to be directed at reducing risk by increasing compliance with specific professional ethical standards, regulatory, and legal statutes.

COMMUNITY VALUES

Values are understood as what is considered good and desirable, and *ethos* refers to the fundamental character or the underlying sentiment that informs the ideals, beliefs, and norms of a community or society. As used in this book, the term *community values* refers to the ideals, beliefs, norms, and ethos that arouse an emotional response for or against them in a given community. The phrase "emotional response for or against" is key in this definition. In short, community values reflect the sentiments of what the majority of a community consider important, good, and desirable and influence their decisions and actions when their values are at stake.

Impact of Community Values

While some community values may be well articulated and openly discussed, and others are not necessarily articulated, communities will go to great lengths to safeguard what they hold as important and good. The perception that such community values are being compromised or threatened tends to provoke a defensive response in the community. Depending on the extent of that response, members and/or community leaders may take decisive action to "protect" the community from the actual or perceived threat.

Examples of community values and efforts to safeguard them abound. Voters in some towns and geographical areas may consistently vote down school referendums, while in other communities such referendums will be overwhelmingly approved because such expenditures are considered consistent with that community's valuing of children and educational advancement. Some communities are quite accepting and accommodating of homeless individuals, while other communities express their impatience and disdain for such individuals by expecting that loitering statutes will be enforced. Similarly, depending on its values, communities may or may not be receptive to the need for access to and provision of adequate treatment for the disabled and mentally ill and thus will predictably approve or disapprove initiatives for funding of services.

Needless to say, just as it is advisable for counselors and therapists to recognize and understand organizational ethics and dynamics, it is important for them to recognize and understand community values and dynamics. The case in Box 4.4 illustrates this point.

BOX 4.4
COMMUNITY VALUES IN ACTION

Jessie Rivera was considering applying for a newly advertised position as a rehabilitation counselor at a state-funded vocational rehabilitation agency in a metropolitan area about 200 miles north of where he was raised and attended college and graduate school. He was quite pleased the private agency in which he was completing his internship training and impressed with the way in which the larger community was receptive to the needs of the developmentally disabled. Unfortunately, that the agency could offer him only an entry-level position, while the upstate position was for an advanced-entry position at a higher salary. While Jessie was interviewing for the newly advertised position, he endeavored to assess organizational ethics and dynamics as well as community values with regard to receptivity to the needs of the disabled in that community. He was quite surprised to find that even though the agency was deeply committed to improving access and providing quality services, and even though the larger community vocalized its commitment to the disabled and to the new rehab agency, both the agency and the larger community were in reality quite insensitive to the needs of the disabled and agency's efforts to collaborate with local business in supporting sheltered workshops in that community. As a result of his investigation, Jessie decided to stay on at the private agency. Even though his salary was less, he believed it was more important that there was a good match among his core values, the core values of the agency in which he would work, and the values and ethos of the community in which he would work.

Recognizing Community Values

It is beyond the scope of this chapter to provide a detailed discussion of how counseling professionals can identify and/or change community values. Nevertheless, a few comments may be useful. A basic strategy for recognizing and understanding community values would involve the following: First, read local newspapers, particularly the so-called "op-ed" page or section, which includes letters to the editor and editorial opinions on local matters. It usually also contains one or more regular columns by national or local columnists. The opinions expressed in this page or section of the paper may closely reflect community values, or it may not at all. Determine this by asking a dozen different individuals in that community how they view their local newspaper. Second, try to ascertain the larger community's opinion about a particular agency or clinic or the local school system, or about particular leaders or news makers in that organization. Compare the community's comments about that organization or a leader's reputation to the "actions" the community takes about that organization or individual in terms of financial and/or emotional support.

KEY POINTS

1. Organizational dynamics can significantly impact the attitudes and behaviors of organizational members. As a result, otherwise good and ethical counselors and administrators can engage in morally questionable or illegal professional practices, reflecting a mismatch between the organization's core values and ethics and the individual's core values and ethics.
2. There are six subsystems of an organization that can influence ethical decisions: strategy, structure, culture, leadership, followership, and external environment. These subsystems reflect a school, clinic, or agency's organizational dynamics.
3. Personal ethics is an individual's internal sense of values and the basis for moral decisions. One's "moral compass," or conscience, reflects these ethical beliefs and values.
4. Professional ethics refers to ethical codes, standards, or guidelines of a profession that help professionals decide what to do when they are confronted with a case or situation that raises a ethical question or moral problem.
5. Organizational ethics reflects the impact of organizational factors and involves the intentional use of values to guide decision making in organizational systems.
6. While business ethics and professional ethics characteristically view a given ethical concern from an individual perspective, organizational ethics views the same ethical concerns from a systems perspective.
7. Ethical climate is one dimension of an organization's culture and reflects the shared perceptions that staff and colleagues hold concerning ethical procedures and practices occurring with the organization.
8. An ethics audit is an investigation of how an organization's ethical policies are implemented as well as a review and evaluation of ethical incidents occurring in an organization during a given time frame.
9. Community values are the ideals, beliefs, norms, and ethos that arouse an emotional response for or against them in a particular community.
10. Counselors and therapists would do well to recognize organizational ethics and community values and the degree to which they match or do not match their own core values. They also would to well to understand the impact and influence of organizational ethics and community values on their decisions involving professional and ethical matters.

CONCLUDING NOTE

Organizational ethics reflects the organizational dynamics that can powerfully impact the professional and ethical decision making of professionals within organizational contexts. While organizational ethics does not replace personal, professional, or business ethics, it significantly expands the ethical perspective to include organizational factors and dynamics. Similarly, community values also can impact professional and ethical decision making. Accordingly, effective and ethically sensitive therapists as well as school, clinic, or agency administrators would do well to become conversant in the organizational ethics and community values dimension. Recognizing and understanding these dynamics is essential to making specific, informed ethical decisions, as well as to evaluating the "fit" between an individual professional and the organization and community in which he or she is training or working or is considering training or working. An investigation of such organizational and community ethics and values can provide a plan for advocating and modifying organizational and/or community values. A simple strategy for increasing ethical sensitivity to organizational ethics and community values has been provided in this chapter. Hopefully, it will serve its purpose.

REVIEW QUESTIONS

1. What would you do if the organization that you work for holds different ethical values than you do?
2. Under what circumstances would it be appropriate to conduct an ethics audit?
3. What would you do if your personal ethics conflicted with your profession's ethics?
4. How can you determine an organization's ethical climate?
5. What are some of your community's values? How can you determine what your community's values are?

REFERENCES

Bottorff, D. (1997, February). How ethics can improve business success. *Quality Progress*, 57–60.

Bowen, S. (2004). Organizational factors encouraging ethical decision making: An exploration into the case of an exemplar. *Journal of Business Ethics, 52*(4), 311–322.

Boyle, P., DuBose, E., Ellingson, S., Guinn, D., & McCurdy, D. (2001). *Organizational ethics in health care: Principles, cases and practical solutions.* San Francisco: Jossey-Bass.

Ells, C., & MacDonald, C. (2002). Implications of organizational ethics to healthcare. *Healthcare Management Forum, 15*(23), 32–38.

Magill, G., & Prybil, L. (2004). Stewardship and integrity in health care: A role for organizational ethics. *Journal of Business Ethics, 50*(3), 225–238.

Moffic, S. (1997). *The ethical way: Challenges and solutions for managed behavioral healthcare.* San Francisco: Jossey-Bass.

Nash, L. (1993). *Good intentions aside: A manager's guide to resolving ethical problems.* Boston: Harvard Business School Press.

Reamer, F. (2000). The social work ethics audit: A risk-management strategy, *Social Work, 45*(4), 355–362.

Reamer, F. (2001). *Social work ethics audit: A risk-management strategy.* Washington, DC: NASW Press.

Shelton, C. (2000). *Achieving moral health.* New York: Crossroads.

Sims, R. (1991). The institutionalization of organizational ethics. *Journal of Business Ethics, 10*(7), 493–506.

Sperry, L., Grissom, G., Brill, P., & Marion, D. (1996). Changing clinicians' practice patterns and managed care culture with outcome systems. *Psychiatric Annals,* 27(2), 127–132.

Sperry, L., & Prosen, H. (1998). Contemporary ethical dilemmas in psychotherapy: Cosmetic psychopharmacology and managed care. *American Journal of Psychotherapy,* 52(1), 54–63.

Sperry, L. (1993). Chapter 10: Confidentiality and ethical issues. In *Psychiatric consultation in the workplace* (pp. 239–248). Washington, DC: American Psychiatric Press.

Sperry, L. (1996). *Corporate therapy and consulting.* New York: Brunner/Mazel.

Sperry, L. (2003). *Effective leadership: Strategies for maximizing executive productivity and health.* New York: Brunner/Routledge.

Verchsoor, C. (2003). Ethical corporations are still more profitable. *Strategic Finance* (June), 22–23.

Worthley, A. (1999). *Organizational ethics in the compliance context.* Chicago: Health Administration Press.

CHAPTER 5

ETHICAL AND PROFESSIONAL DECISION MAKING IN COUNSELING AND PSYCHOTHERAPY

In traditional or conventional texts on ethics in counseling and psychotherapy, this chapter would be entitled something like "ethical decision making in counseling and psychotherapy." In Chapter 1 a basic tenet of this book was noted: Good ethical practice is effective professional practice. What this means is that there is an intimate relationship between the two such that good ethical practice can and should reflect effective professional practice. Conversely, effective professional practice can and should reflect good ethical practice. In short, ethical practice decisions are not distinct from professional practice decisions, and the implications for counseling practice are significant. Since the process of decision making in both domains is similar, we have found it didactically useful to employ the shorthand "decision making in counseling and psychotherapy" in place of "ethical and professional practice decision making in counseling and psychotherapy." This chapter discusses this process of decision making and, in line with another basic tenet of the book, describes and illustrates the process in terms of ethical, professional, and contextual considerations.

LEARNING OBJECTIVES

After reading this chapter you should be able to

1. Explain this statement: Good ethical decision making is consistent with effective decision making in counseling and psychotherapy.
2. Identify the contextual, professional, and ethical considerations in decision making in counseling and psychotherapy.
3. Describe the seven-step ethical and professional decisional strategy.
4. Apply the seven-step decisional strategy to a counseling case.

KEY TERMS

professional and ethical decision making
professional and ethical practice decisional strategy

DECISION MAKING IN COUNSELING AND PSYCHOTHERAPY

A basic assumption of this book is that good ethical practice is effective professional practice. One implication is that ethical practice and professional practice are interrelated, and could be thought of as two sides of the same coin. Another implication is that the decision making process in both is similar. Rather than the decisional process with ethical practice considerations being distinctly different from the decisional process with professional practice considerations, we would contend that not only is the process similar, but some aspects of the process are essentially the same. It is our observation that counselors and therapists employ similar processes whether the issue is primarily a professional practice issue or an ethical practice issue. Because many have been socialized to think of ethical decision making as unique and separate from clinical or professional decision making, the similarities may not be intuitively obvious. We would contend that most, if not all, decision making in counseling and psychotherapy involves very similar processes, and that ethical decision making is not an arcane, isolated, and separate process. Consider the following case example in Box 5.1.

BOX 5.1
RESPONDING TO A CLIENT'S EXPECTATION FOR COUNSELING

A new client, Indira, comes to Domena, a licensed mental health counselor, for counseling. She says she has never had any counseling or therapy previously, but has been having some dreams and nightmares lately, and while watching the *Oprah* show she was surprised to learn that disturbing dreams like the kind she is having probably indicate early sexual abuse. She wants counseling to help her process what she believes are early childhood abuse issues. Domena, being a conscientious mental health counselor, listens to Indira's treatment expectations and then performs an initial evaluation that includes a family and developmental history. She will then make a decision about treatment goals and focus, mindful that the client's expectation may or may not be appropriate or realistic. Like Domena, practitioners engage in some form of decision making in which they weigh the benefits and risks of the client's request against relevant ethical, professional, and contextual considerations.

Whether the practitioner's decision-making process is instantaneous or takes a few minutes or more, every practitioner engages in some decision-making process. We would contend that whether the practitioner's decision making is intuitive and immediate, or is intentional and takes more time, a decision is reached after some kind of consideration of contextual, professional, and ethical factors. Let's look briefly at all three considerations as they relate to Indira's request and expectation for counseling.

Contextual Considerations

Context means any cultural, organizational, community, interpersonal, or personal dynamics that are operating. Indira's developmental history and personal level of coping and functioning were assessed. Her history is strongly suggestive of ongoing sexual abuse by an uncle from age 5 to 12, and she appears to have a limited capacity for dealing with the stressfulness of processing trauma and abuse issues. In fact, she meets criteria for borderline personality disorder, and her level of functioning is low-moderate, with a Global Assessment of Functioning (GAF) score of 55. Other key contextual considerations include the multicultural dimension. Indira is a Muslim, and discussion of sexual abuse history is a taboo subject within the family; talking about it to outsiders, such as physicians or therapists, is absolutely forbidden. In terms of the organizational ethics–community values dimension, it is noteworthy that the professional community in which Domena practices favorably supports the use of regressive therapies in working with trauma issues, including early sexual trauma.

Professional Considerations

Consideration of practice issues from a professional perspective includes input from several sources: the research literature, including evidence-based studies, best practices, and the like, as well as counseling theories, scholarly debate, and clinical lore (i.e., clinical observations or methods that are not empirically supported but are revered and passed down from generation to generation. Relevant best practices and research addressing treatment on abuse and trauma issues suggest that client readiness and psychological resiliency are important considerations. Even clients with relatively high readiness and resiliency, that is, reasonably high levels of psychological functioning, can find processing of traumatic memories and affects quite painful and distressing. It is not uncommon to deny or postpone such work with clients who do not possess sufficient psychological resiliency and have a high likelihood of regression during efforts to process extremely painful memories, particularly those involving early sexual abuse (Sperry, 1999). For example, for individuals with borderline personality disorder with low to moderate levels of functioning, some therapeutic approaches, such as Dialectical Behavior Therapy, discourage trauma work until later in the course of therapy.

Ethical Considerations

In terms of the ethical considerations, we begin with the basic ethical principle that acting in the best interest of client is the main criterion for determining the goodness and effectiveness of counseling. Ethical values involved in this case include autonomy, beneficence, and nonmaleficence. As is not uncommon, there is conflict among these three values. Autonomy involves respecting the client's wishes and right to self-determination. In this case it would mean acceding to Indira's expectation for counseling. Beneficence involves doing good, helping, and benefiting clients, while nonmaleficence involves the responsibility of a professional to do no harm to clients. Based on the professional consideration that there is a reasonable possibility that focusing therapy initially and primarily on abuse issues could be harmful to Indira, the conflict among the three values is reasonably resolved by recourse to the two essential ethical principles. Furthermore, focusing on abuse issues without first addressing the cultural issue, that is, the taboo against discussing abuse issues, is problematic. Unfortunately, there may be subtle or not-so-subtle pressure on Domena to proceed with what is likely to be a regressive therapeutic strategy with this client, since it appears to be the professional norm in that community.

In the case of Indira, providing ethically sensitive and effective care that is in her best interest might mean discussing the necessity and advisability of preparing her for the inevitably stressful processing of painful, traumatic material before beginning that process. Finally, it should be noted that, in this particular case, a basic tenet of standard clinical lore—"follow the client's lead," that is, accede without reservation to the client's treatment expectations—might be both unethical and professionally unsound. It is interesting to add that, in this instance, following this clinical directive does not allow for, or negates, informed consent.

It might be that the counselor or therapist only considers the professional and contextual dimensions. Still, based on these two factors, the decision would be the same: to delay on the client's request and to work initially on increasing the client's psychological resiliency. However, the value of including the ethical consideration is that the ethical provides a broader context for evaluating the professional and contextual considerations. In this case, the ethical principle of only acting in the client's best interest further confirms the decision to delay trauma work. In addition, the ethical principle of proving full informed consent reinforces the provider's responsibility of discussing and informing the client of the advisability—and rationale—for delay of the client's request.

APPROACHES TO ETHICAL DECISION MAKING

Several models of ethical reasoning exist in the literature. Kitchener (1984) describes a decision-making process that begins with information about a client's situation and is initially evaluated by the practitioner's immediate impression, his or her intuitive moral sense of the right thing to do. This intuitive sense is next evaluated at the "critical-evaluative" level—Kitchener's term for the formal process of evaluating the client situation in terms of general ethical principles, ethical theory, and professional codes, then weighing alternatives, considering possible outcomes, and evaluating the impact of one's decisions. Other decision-making approaches have been proposed. Most involve a linear, rational decision-making framework (Corey, Corey & Callanan, 2003; Remley & Herlihy, 2001; Welfel, 2002), while a few are more nonlinear (Cottone & Tarvydas, 2003; Davis, 1997).

The best of these approaches to ethical reasoning and resolution share an important attribute: They broaden the context of ethical thinking beyond immediate circumstances, simplistic calculations, and a single ethical standard or legal statute. The approach advocated in this book is based on very broad and comprehensive contextual analysis.

THE PROFESSIONAL AND ETHICAL PRACTICE DECISIONAL STRATEGY

Following is the formal decision-making strategy highlighted in this text. As previously noted, this formal strategy is basically an articulation of the informal model already used by many counselors and therapists in making professional practice decisions that have ethical implications. This decisional, or decision-making, strategy is a process that involves eight steps. Each will be briefly described here. Box 5.2 lists these steps, and Box 5.3 outlines several questions that guide the process employing this strategy.

BOX 5.2

PROFESSIONAL AND ETHICAL PRACTICE DECISIONAL STRATEGY

0. Enhance ethical sensitivity and anticipate professional-ethical considerations.
1. Identify the problem.
2. Identify the participants affected by the decision.
3. Identify potential courses of action and benefits and risks for the participants.
4. Evaluate benefits and risks re: contextual, professional, and ethical considerations.
5. Consult with peers and experts.
6. Decide on the most feasible option, and document the decision-making process.
7. Implement, evaluate, and document the enacted decision.

The Eight Steps of the Decisional Strategy

Step 0: Enhance ethical sensitivity and anticipate professional-ethical considerations. Ethical sensitivity is both a perspective on counseling practice and the capacity to interpret moral and ethical implications of situations irrespective of whether an ethical dilemma is present. Master counselors and therapists embody this perspective, which reflects their ongoing desire to foster the welfare and well-being of their clients. As ethical sensitivity increases and becomes second nature to counselors and therapists, they can more easily anticipate and respond proactively to various professional and ethical considerations, often before they emerge as challenges or dilemmas. For example, ethically sensitive therapists realize that protecting confidentiality and privacy, as well as keeping clients abreast of possible informed consent matters, is part of the ongoing process of counseling. Anticipating this ongoing responsibility, they respond proactively to these and other ethical-professional considerations. Not surprisingly, such a proactive stance seems to stave off the emergence of ethical issues and dilemmas. Accordingly, the challenge for beginning counselors and therapists is to enhance this sensitivity and proactive outlook. Since this book emphasizes the importance of the personal-developmental dimension, it is fitting that this the true starting-point of the decision-making strategy even though it is a general and ongoing process, rather than specific to a given ethical problem or dilemma.

Step 1: Identify the problem. Assuming that a problem exists, the process of decision making begins with information gathering and problem identification. It is essential to clarify whether the problem is primarily ethical, legal, professional, or some combination thereof. Oftentimes the problem is primarily professional and involves ethical or legal considerations. Sometimes the problem is first and foremost an ethical dilemma, with legal and professional considerations.

Step 2: Identify the participants affected by the decision. Because the relational dimension is critical to effective professional practice, identification of the key participants, those impacted by the problem or dilemma, is essential. The nature of your relationship with the client and other participants—the client's family, your supervisor, agency or school personnel, and others—is noted. Also noted is how the problem, and subsequent decision, is directly affecting or will directly affect you, your client, and other key participants.

Step 3: Identify potential courses of action and benefits and risks for the participants. While there many be many possible solutions to a problem, there are only a few realistic or probable solutions or courses of action. Brainstorming will help generate the possible solutions, while a realistic assessment of each will narrow these options down to probable courses of action. This step also includes a listing of risks and benefits of each of the short list of options for the key participants.

Step 4: Evaluate benefits and risks regarding contextual, professional, and ethical considerations. This step is the heart of the decisional process. As noted earlier, this step is involved in making many, if not most, practice decisions. Even though they might not be fully aware of their decisional process, many counselors and therapists routinely use such a process in their professional work. Typically, the process proceeds with an evaluation and consideration of the contextual, then the professional, followed by the ethical.

Step 5: Consult with peers and experts. This is a cross-check of the considerations in step 4. It involves a review of standard of care: what a reasonably trained counselor would do in similar circumstances. Besides consultation with peers and supervisors, consultation could include discussion with an ethics committee, lawyers, or other experts. Such consultation offers additional perspectives on the situation that one might miss either because of being too close to the case or because of one's own unrecognized blind spots. It also provides emotional support and encouragement in a difficult situation.

Step 6: Decide on the most feasible option and document the decision-making process. Involve the client, when appropriate. With additional information, it may be necessary to modify the courses of decision arrived at in step 3. Thereafter, arriving at the best or most workable decision involves careful consideration of available information from steps 4 and 5. It is a truism that the more obvious the problem or dilemma, the clearer the decision, while the more subtle the problem or dilemma, the more difficult the decision. Again, because of the centrality of the relational dimension in this process, involving the client, and possibly one or more key participants, should be considered. The extent of the client's involvement ranges from mutually reviewing the probable courses of action to limiting the discussion to the consequences of the decided course of action for the client. In any event, the decision, the decision-making process, and the rationale for the decision is then documented. Depending on your practice situation, you may be expected to inform a supervisor or an administrator about your decision.

Step 7: Implement, evaluate, and document the enacted decision. Implementing the decided course of action is the final step. The evaluation process includes the impact of the decision, in the short and long term, on the client. Since the decisional process has developmental ramifications for you, it can be quite useful to review the decision and the decisional process in terms of four common "ethical tests": publicity, universality, moral traces, and justice. The test of *publicity* raises the question, How comfortable would I be if my actions were reported by the media?, whereas the test of *universality* asks, Would I recommend my course of action to others who are faced with a similar predicament? The test of *moral traces* checks for those lingering feelings of doubt or discomfort that ethically conscientious professionals sometimes experience after they have made a decision. Next, the test of *justice* assesses the matter of fairness by querying, Would I respond the same way in a similar situation?

These "tests" can provide a sense of perspective and closure on what can be a confusing, anxiety-producing, and exasperating experience. Unfortunately, feeling satisfied or a sense of peace does not mean that the "right" decision was made. Sometimes, the best decision is not understood or well received by others. And, while this response may be unsettling to counselors and therapists whose personality style "needs" them to be liked and approved by others, making and implementing an ethically good but unpopular decision can be an opportunity for personal and professional growth. Finally, the formal decisional process concludes by documenting and evaluating how the decision was implemented.

BOX 5.3

PROFESSIONAL AND ETHICAL PRACTICE DECISIONAL STRATEGY: AN OUTLINE

1. Identify the problem
   - Is there an ethical dilemma here? If so, how do you define it?
   - What facts of the case lead you to define it this way?
2. Identify the participants affected by the decision
   - Which individuals are directly involved? Indirectly involved?
   - How does it affect you? Your client(s)? Others?
3. Identify potential courses of action and benefits and risks for the participants
   - What potential options or courses of action can you identify?
   - What are the risks and benefits of each course of action for each participant?
4. Evaluate benefits and risks re: contextual, professional, and ethical considerations

   A. Contextual

   (1) Personal-developmental

   (a) Ethical sensitivity and personal values
   - What's your ethical sense or intuition about the case?
   - How might your personal values be operative here?

   (b) Developmental level, ethical perspective, and ethical decision-making style
   - How is your developmental and perspective operative here? Your decision-making style?

(c) Blind spots re: ethical decision-making style
- How might your blind spots, unfinished business, or countertransference be operative here?

(2) Relational-Multicultural
(a) Nature of relationship with client and participants
- What is the level of trust and mutuality in the client? Other participants?

(b) Ethnic/gender/subculture
- What, if any, ethnic, gender, or cultural factors are operative?

(c) Spiritual-religious beliefs
- What are the spiritual and/or religious beliefs of the client and other participants and what is their influence? What is the influence of your beliefs?

(3) Organizational Ethics–Community Values
(a) Organizational ethics, values, and dynamics, i.e., school, agency, etc.
- What are the stated vs. actual core values? Dynamics? Impact of both?

(b) Community values, history, sentiment
- What is the community's attitude toward and impact on the dilemma?

B. Professional
(1) Standard of care
- What is the relevant standard of care in the community?

(2) Research, best practices, evidence-based, etc.
- If applicable, what does research, best practices, etc. have to say?

(3) Counseling theories and clinical lore/tradition
- What do scholars say about this issue? If there is disagreement, what arguments are most compelling?
- What does clinical lore, i.e., the counseling tradition, say about it?

C. Ethical/legal
(1) Ethical theories, values, and principles
- What theory(ies), value(s), and ethical principle(s) are applicable in this case?

(2) Ethical codes and standards
- Which professional codes are applicable? Standards?

(3) Legal statutes
- Are any legal statutes applicable? If so, which one(s)?

5. Consult with peers and experts
- What views do your supervisor(s), colleagues, lawyers, etc., offer in resolving the dilemma?
- If different from ethical standards and principles, how do they differ?

6. Decide on the most feasible option and document the decision-making process and rationale
- Are the original options still viable, or is revision necessary?
- What is the best option? What's your rationale for it?
- Should you inform your supervisor or an administrator of the decision?

7. Implement, evaluate, and document the enacted decision
- How should you implement the decision?
- What is the result of the various ethical tests: publicity, universality, moral traces, and justice?
- How will you document the decision, process, and rationale?

CASE ILLUSTRATION OF THE ETHICAL AND PROFESSIONAL PRACTICE DECISIONAL STRATEGY

Box 5.4 provides an example of a case presenting an ethical dilemma, followed by a discussion of the case.

BOX 5.4
A CASE OF THE AMBIVALENT FATHER

Tim D. is a 46-year-old Caucasian male who recently began psychotherapy for depression with Jeffrey, a licensed psychotherapist. Jeffrey has been licensed for about a year and has joined the clinic within the past three months. Although Tim has been prescribed an antidepressant by his family physician for the past four months, he has never had psychological treatment and believes that he needs it now. He reportedly made a suicide attempt two years ago but was not hospitalized and did not receive psychiatric treatment. He was married for ten years and has two children, currently ages 9 and 6, from that marriage. After the divorce one year ago, his former wife was granted custody of the children, and although he had weekend visitation twice a month, she refused to allow the children to visit Tim in his apartment. She also refused visitation to Tim's parents, who were actively involved with the children during the marriage. Approximately seven weeks ago she and Tim began to talk again, and she agreed that the children could visit him on alternate weekends. A week ago his younger daughter confided that her mother's boyfriend touched her indecently. Tim was upset and immediately called her and demanded that the boyfriend move out. She denied that anything had taken place, saying her male companion was not even there at the time of the alleged impropriety, and that if Tim did anything, the visitation would stop. Tim refuses to call Department of Child and Family Services or family court because of past experiences. When he contacted that agency on another matter, no action was taken. When his former wife learned of his complaint, she would not allow him to see the children for several months. Presently, he believes his only alternative is to maintain a close relationship with his children and hope that his ex-wife does not withhold access to the children by not doing anything to displease her, like getting her angry or filing a complaint. In the past he reportedly said that the children meant everything to him and without them he had little reason to live. He is a hardworking, conscientious, and drug-free individual who adamantly refuses to take any actions that may jeopardize access to his children. The psychotherapist acknowledges the probability of child abuse and that Tim continues to be depressed and has a history of attempted suicide. Jeffrey also believes that a potential ethical dilemma exists.

Step 1: Identify the problem. Jeffrey anonymously called the Department of Child and Family Services for an opinion and was told that reporting was not mandatory because the account of abuse was third-party information. He was told that since the situation did not appear to require mandatory reporting, the psychotherapist would not be legally bound to break confidentiality. Furthermore, Jeffrey was told that the Department of Child and Family Services's unwritten policy was to urge clients to call the state agency on their own. The problem was identified as an ethical dilemma involving client's autonomy and child welfare. Since Jeffrey had no basis for making a formal complaint himself, the matter of breaking confidentiality was not an issue.

Step 2: Identify the participants affected by the decision. There were at least seven participants involved and who were actually or potentially affected by the problem and its resolution. Tim stated he did not want to contact any authorities. Tim's younger daughter may be in danger, and possibly his older daughter; neither were likely aware of their options or how they could get help. The Department of Child and Family Services has responsibility for minors such as Tim's daughter and could be held liable for errors of its staff. Jeff could also be held liable for harm to Tim and his children. Tim's former wife could face an abuse investigation and be held liable. Finally, there were the grandparents, who could conceivably receive custody of the children.

Step 3: Identify potential courses of action and benefits and risks for the participants. Initially, there appear to be two potential courses of action. The first course of action is for Jeffrey to strongly urge Tim to contact the state Department of Child and Family Services, not to file a formal complaint, but, as per its unwritten policy, to do so anonymously. The second course of action is to refrain from urging Tim to contact the state agency. With the first option, the benefit is that the children would be removed from the potentially abusive environment, while the risk is that visitation may be withheld indefinitely. In the second option, the benefit is that Tim will presumably continue with visitation, while the risk is that child abuse may occur or continue.

Step 4: Evaluate benefits and risks re: professional, contextual, and ethical considerations.

Contextual Domain Considerations

The therapist was somewhere between Level 2 and Level 3 of counselor development and was aware of his pattern of independence and proactivity. As he pondered matters, he realized that Tim's passivity and fear of reprisal were problematic for him. He wanted Tim to be courageous and do the right thing, that is, formally report the abuse allegation. The therapist recognized that he would need to be especially vigilant in monitoring his countertransference toward his client, as well as carefully consider making decisions that were in his client's best interest rather than his own. Cultural, gender, and religious considerations did not seem operative in this case. Organizationally, the therapist's perception that the Department of Children and Family Services had a "policy" of convincing clients to self-report abuse was borne out. It also became clear that the clinic's "policy" on child abuse matters was conservative and reactive. His supervisor supported the state agency's policy and believed the therapist should adhere to both written and unwritten policies. Also, most of the professional staff at the clinic, including the clinic director, indicated that the state agency would not consider the matter reportable, since it involved third-party information. Thus, they urged him to monitor the situation only. He couldn't believe that he had taken a job in a place where there was little match between his values and the clinic's values, particularly in terms of client advocacy.

Professional Domain Considerations

In reviewing the research and scholarly literature, Jeffrey was impressed with how nondefinitive the literature was on situations akin to Tim's and his daughter's. While children's reports are often accurate, there were instances in which children or a parent in disputed custody situations made false allegations. Jeff was mindful that his information of the case of abuse was secondhand. In graduate school his professors and supervisors were strong advocates of clients' autonomy and the welfare and rights of minor children, particularly those who have experienced abuse. They were proactive in urging the reporting of any abuse.

Ethical Domain Considerations

Several APA and ACA codes and standards were applicable, most notably the following from the ACA Code of Ethics (2005): Section A.1.a on Primary Responsibility, the counselor's primary responsibility is to respect and promote the welfare of clients; Section B.1.d, Exceptions. The general requirement that counselors keep information confidential does not apply when disclosure is required to prevent clear and imminent danger to the client or to others or when legal requirements demand that confidential information be revealed; Section D.1.k, Negative Conditions. Counselors alert their employers to inappropriate employer policies or practices. They attempt to effect changes in such policies or procedures through constructive action within the organization; and Section D.1.j, Employer Policies. The acceptance of employment in an agency or institution implies that counselors are in agreement with its general policies and principles. Counselors strive to reach agreement with employers as to acceptable standards of conduct that allow for changes in institutional policy conducive to the growth and development of clients. The state's statute on mandatory reporting required reporting child abuse when the counselor reasonably believed a child had suffered abuse. However, the statute seemed equivocal about third-party reports of abuse, such as was the case with Tim's daughter. In terms of ethical values, there was clear conflict among nonmalificence, beneficence, autonomy, and fidelity.

Step 5: Consult with peers and experts. Since this was the first time Jeffrey had directly encountered the matter of child abuse, he believed he needed considerable consultation and help. He talked with several of his peers at his own and other clinics, as well as with his current supervisor. As noted earlier, most of the staff and his superiors at the clinic indicated that, because it involved third-party information, the state agency did not consider the matter reportable, and he was simply urged to monitor the situation and not pressure the client to file a complaint. The state licensure board's ethics committee was particularly concerned about confidentiality and the welfare of the children. There, recommendations seemed contradictory. In contacting a professor in his graduate program, Jeffrey was urged to pressure the client to report the allegation. Jeffrey also talked to an attorney who practiced family law that he knew through his health club. The attorney suggested petitioning the court to change the custody arrangement.

Step 6: Decide on the most feasible option and document decision-making process. Although initially somewhat confused, but mindful of Tim's position and reticence, his own personal needs, the organizational dynamics, the ethics codes, principles, and values, and input from consultations, Jeffrey chose the first option with a slight modification. He will strongly urge the client to call the state agency anonymously, but will not pressure him to make a formal report, thus respecting the client's autonomy.

Step 7: Implement, evaluate, and document the enacted decision. The implementation plan is as follows: First, talk frankly with Tim about the consequences of anonymous reporting as compared to not reporting. Second, strongly urge Tim to call anonymously for information about what would happen if the situation were reported. Third, if Tim will not call, stop trying to convince him. If Tim does call, provide him the necessary support. Fourth, inform the clinic administrator of the decision and document the decision, the process, and the rationale. After creating the plan, Jeffrey applied the ethical tests of publicity, universality, moral traces, and justice and was satisfied with the decision he made.

Tim agreed to call anonymously, and Jeffrey provided emotional support during this time. Three months later, DCFS reported that their investigation was inconclusive. As a result of the therapy, Tim's resolve to change the situation increased considerably, irrespective of his former wife's threats. With the psychologist's encouragement, Tim petitioned family court to change the custody agreement, and an extensive child custody evaluation completed by a noted expert proved sufficiently convincing. Custody was awarded to Tim's parents, and Tim and his two daughters made plans to move to his parents' farm.

Applying the Ethical and Professional Practice Decisional Strategy

Read the case in Box 5.5 and analyze the case, following the seven-step decisional strategy.

BOX 5.5
PRACTICE CASE

Sara H. is an elementary school counselor who has been referred Freddy B., a fourth grader, by his teacher, Justine C. This has been a difficult year for Sara professionally and personally, as she has felt overwhelmed by her increasing caseload and because of difficulty concentrating following of an acrimonious divorce that was finalized last August. Freddy has continued to do above-average work in class since his parents' divorce one year ago. However, his teacher has noted that Freddy tears up his worksheets and art projects as soon as they are graded and is not showing his typical enthusiasm for school activities. She has talked to him about the situation, but he denies that anything is wrong. In your first meeting with him, Freddy confides that his mother will no longer allow him to send letters and completed schoolwork to his dad, who lives upstate. He misses his dad and no longer thinks his schoolwork is important, so he tears it up. He asks you if you will send his letters and schoolwork to his dad occasionally, and Freddy gives you permission to discuss his concerns with his mother. She angrily forbids you to communicate with Freddy's father in any way. She tells you that she is the sole custodial parent and guardian, and that Mr. B. moved away rather than "be bothered with the responsibility of Freddy." She reluctantly allows you to continue counseling Freddy about his "behavior problems" in school, but tells you not to raise his hopes about seeing or communicating with his dad. While you continue to provide supportive counseling to Freddy, you consider the matter of contact with Mr. B. closed. By the end of the school year, you have not heard from Mr. or Mrs. B., and Freddy's problems have worsened. Was your decision not to contact Mr. B. correct?

KEY POINTS

1. Conventional decision making regarding ethical issues typically consists of linear process and involves specific steps: defining the issue or problem, specifying alternative courses of action, seeking input from relevant ethical codes and legal statutes, seeking consultation from peers and/or experts, deciding on a course of action, and implementing and evaluating the decision.
2. Good ethical practice can and should reflect effective professional practice, and effective professional practice can and should reflect good ethical practice.
3. Decision making in professional practice and ethical practice are remarkably similar in both strategy and process.
4. Decision making in professional practice and ethical practice can be interdependent in the sense that professional input and analysis (i.e., research, best practices, theory, or clinical lore) are first considered, and then ethical input (theory, values, principles, and codes) is considered in order to reinforce, refocus, or fine-tune the decision.
5. The Professional and Ethical Practice Decisional Strategy is a nonlinear, eight-step decisional strategy that emphasizes the integration of contextual, professional, and ethical considerations rather than simply ethical and legal considerations.

CONCLUDING NOTE

This chapter has described and illustrated a nonlinear approach to making professional practice decisions that have ethical implications. This approach is an alternative to the conventional ethical decision-making models, which are linear and noncontextual. The Professional and Ethical Practice Decisional Strategy is necessary, because it is assumed that professional practice and ethical practice are essentially interdependent processes, and that decision making in one domain should inform the other domain. They are interdependent in the sense that professional input and analysis are first considered, and then ethical input is considered in order to reinforce, refocus, or fine-tune the decision. This eight-step decisional strategy emphasizes the integration of contextual, professional, and ethical considerations rather than simply ethical and legal considerations.

While at first this strategy is sometime time intensive, the ultimate decision will reflect the specifics of the context as well as professional and ethical considerations that reflect the unique needs and demands of the context. Contextual factors considered are relational, cultural, organizational, and community factors. Also considered is the counselor or therapist's own personal and developmental issues, which means that the final course of action decided upon is made recognizing that counselors and therapists have their own needs and "unfinished business" that could otherwise unwittingly influence decision making.

REVIEW QUESTIONS

1. What sources of information or support would you use to assist you in making an ethical decision?
2. Under what circumstances might you have to make an ethical decision without using a specified decision-making procedure?
3. If you were faced with a difficult ethical decision, what cultural and professional factors would you consider?
4. If you were faced with a difficult ethical decision, what legal and ethical factors would you consider?
5. What would you do if you realized that you made a bad ethical decision?

REFERENCES

American Counseling Association. (2005). *Code of ethics. Revised edition.* Alexandria, VA: Author.

Corey, G., Corey, M., & Callanan, P. (2003). *Issues and ethics in the helping professions* (6th ed). Pacific Grove, CA: Brooks/Cole.

Cottone, R., & Tarvydas, V. (2003). *Ethical and professional issues in counseling* (2nd ed). Upper Saddle River, NJ: Merrill/Prentice-Hall.

Davis, A. (1997). The ethics of caring: A collaborative model for resolving ethical dilemmas. *Journal of Applied Rehabilitation Counseling, 28*(1), 36–41.

Kitchener, K. (1984). Intuition, critical evaluation, and ethical principles: The foundation for ethical decisions in counseling psychology. *Counseling Psychologist, 12,* 43–55.

Remley, T., & Herlihy, B. (2001). *Ethical, legal, and professional issues in counseling.* Upper Saddle River, NJ: Merrill/Prentice-Hall.

Sperry, L. (1999). *Cognitive behavior therapy of the DSM-IV personality disorders.* New York: Brunner/Routledge.

Welfel, E. (2002). *Ethics in counseling and psychotherapy: Standards, research and emerging issues.* Pacific Grove, CA: Brooks/Cole.

PART II

ETHICAL STANDARDS OF PROFESSIONAL PRACTICE

Part II consists of four chapters that describe the four most common ethical considerations in professional practice. It has been said that nearly all ethical and legal issues in professional practice can be subsumed under these four considerations. This chapter provides a broad overview of confidentiality, competency, informed consent, and conflict of interest, sometimes referred to as the "four horsemen" of professional ethics. Each of these considerations is defined and developed in general terms. Part III continues this discussion in more specific terms and illustrates the application of these four considerations in separate chapters devoted to the following specialty areas of professional practice: mental health counseling and psychotherapy, couple and family counseling/therapy, career and rehabilitation counseling, and clinical supervision.

Consistent with the basic premise of this book, the chapters in Part II describe these considerations both in terms of the basic, or minimal, ethical standards, that is, Perspective I, and in terms of a more positive view of ethics, Perspective III. Table II.1 provides a preview of the four chapters in Part II as it summarizes Perspectives I and III with regard to confidentiality, competency, informed consent, and conflict of interest.

TABLE II.1 Comparison of Key Ethical Issues in Terms of Two Ethical Perspectives

ETHICAL ISSUE	PERSPECTIVE I	PERSPECTIVE III
Boundaries and Dual Relationships, Conflicts of Interest	Boundaries viewed as rigid and inflexible; boundary crossings lead to boundary violations, which foster exploitive, harmful, and sexual dual relationships, all of which are unethical, below the standard of care, and/or illegal, and thus should be avoided. Conflicts of interest should also be avoided at all costs (this reflects both risk-management view *and* analytic therapy practice).	Boundaries viewed as more flexible; boundary crossings differ from harmful boundary violation and if appropriately employed, can increase therapeutic alliance and outcomes. Dual relationships are unavoidable in some locales and not unethical or below the standard of care unless harm/exploitation arises, i.e., conflict of interest. Sexual dual relationships are always avoided.
Competence	Viewed as achieving at least a minimum level of competence and maintaining it by completing minimum continuing education requirements. Impairment viewed as a legal liability. Goal is to avoid liability and censure.	Viewed as an ongoing, developmental process seeking to achieve expertise; lifelong learners continually monitor their level of competence and seek out needed supervision, consultation, and continuing education. Goal is to broaden and enhance clinical abilities.
Confidentiality	Viewed in the narrow, legal sense of the duties to warn or protect, mandatory reporting, HIPAA regulations, i.e., safeguarding records, and therapeutic privilege. Goal is to avoid legal liability and/or professional censure.	Viewed as the cornerstone of the counseling relationship, in which corrective secure attachments and positive therapeutic change can and likely will result. Arises from beneficence, nonmaleficence, respect for privacy, and an ethic of care.
Informed Consent	Viewed as primarily involving written documents signed by the client. Because the goal is to reduce risk and liability, the contents of the signed document are discussed with the client and that discussion is documented in the client's record. Full disclosure may be withheld.	Viewed in terms of written documentation as well as ongoing discussion with client about optimal treatment considerations that aims at full disclosure to the extent the client is competent. Goal is primarily to foster the therapeutic relationship, client well-being, and treatment outcomes.

CHAPTER 6

CONFIDENTIALITY

MAUREEN DUFFY

Most counseling and psychotherapy training programs have addressed education on confidentiality in clinical practice from a rule-based ethics perspective. Counselors learn about the ethical and legal codes they must adhere to in order to protect client confidentiality, and they learn about the legal and professional consequences of failure to do so. From a risk-management perspective, protecting client confidentiality is a primary value in order to reduce the risk of malpractice claims and other forms of civil lawsuits. This traditional form of ethics education emphasizes a Perspective I approach to thinking about confidentiality in clinical practice and ignores the contextual domain that provides a much fuller understanding of confidentiality as an ethic of care rooted in concern for the dignity and safety of the client.

It makes developmental sense for the beginning counselor to worry about not being sued and organizing clinical practice to reduce that risk. However, understanding the ethical ground from which confidentiality as a theory and a practice arises can help the beginning counselor to expand the process of self-reflection in challenging cases. Such self-reflection has the potential for helping the beginning counselor move more quickly from the Perspective I defensive mode to Perspective II, in which the professional and personal dimensions of one's work become more integrated, including how personal ethical values come to be reflected in one's work. This movement toward personal and professional growth and integration opens the door for counselor development at the master therapist level, which is marked by an ongoing reflexive awareness of the relational and multicultural aspects of one's clinical and personal development. The emergence of mastery is best described by Skovholt and Jennings (2004), who provide a picture of how and why master therapists live the personal- and professional-value-filled lives that they do.

This chapter will focus on understanding confidentiality from an integrative-contextual perspective by looking at the impact of disclosure (either deliberate or inadvertent) of private client information in the public domain. From this perspective, maintaining client confidentiality emanates from the ethical virtues of care for the other's dignity and privacy, respect for the autonomy of the other, and concern for the positive growth and development of the other. While situating confidentiality within a contextual framework, this chapter will also specifically consider the influence of recent federal privacy legislation (HIPAA) on counseling practice and the legal obligations of counselors in cases of abuse and neglect, suicide, threats to others, and protection of the rights of children. The ethical obligations of organizations and institutions to protect client confidentiality will also be explored from the contextual perspective of organizational ethics–community values. In addition, boundaries between the counselor and client, dual relationships, distinguishing counseling from friendship, and maintaining appropriate professional distance will be discussed as they relate to the role of confidentiality in counseling practice.

LEARNING OBJECTIVES

After reading this chapter you should be able to

1. Discuss confidentiality from the perspective of care for the privacy, safety, and autonomy of the other.
2. List the exceptions to confidentiality and describe these exceptions within the context of care for the other.
3. Discuss the implications of HIPAA on counseling practice and the impact of electronic communications and databases on protection of client confidentiality.
4. Explain the accountability that organizations have for maintaining client confidentiality.
5. Define professional boundaries in terms of ethical principles and obligations and describe counselors' responsibilities in evaluating and maintaining them.
6. Compare confidentiality from Perspectives I, II, and III.

KEY TERMS

autonomy
dual relationship
ethic of care
The Health Insurance Portability and Accountability Act of 1996 (HIPAA)
privacy
privileged communication
professional boundaries
rights of children
threats to others

THE CONTEXTUAL DOMAIN AND CONFIDENTIALITY

With reference to the practice of safeguarding client confidentiality, the contextual domain includes all relevant contexts that influence the client–therapist or counselor relationship. These contexts include the commonly understood obligations to uphold professional ethics and to adhere to state and federal laws regarding confidentiality. Examples of such laws and practices include privileged communication between client and psychotherapist, HIPAA federal laws to ensure the privacy of protected client health information, and adherence to the codes of ethics of the professional mental health associations of which one is a member. These contexts inform the understanding of ethics from a negative, defensive perspective in order to reduce risk of a lawsuit and professional sanction and to avoid liability.

A Perspective III understanding of the contextual domain, however, invites the therapist and counselor into an appreciation of confidentiality as a relational process in which the safety of the confidential client–therapist relationship provides an environment within which the client develops trust and explores the possibility of new behaviors. Confidentiality provides the basis for corrective secure attachments and the associated safe base for self-reflection and change.

At the personal-developmental level, maintaining client confidentiality becomes a practice of the psychotherapist that is linked to the therapist or counselor's values, self-discipline, and personal growth and development. The ethical therapist or counselor grows to appreciate the privilege and power involved in knowing intimate details of another person's life story and actively resists invitations to violate or breach that essential bond of confidentiality. At the organizational ethics–community values level, the policies and practices of the psychotherapy organization or agency and its level of awareness of the importance of confidentiality ultimately either enhance or constrain a therapist's or counselor's ability to understand and protect client confidentiality from a positive rather than a defensive ethics perspective. In the remainder of this chapter, we will highlight the understandings and practices necessary to safeguard client confidentiality from a positive integrative-contextual perspective.

THE ETHICAL BASIS OF THE CONCEPT OF CONFIDENTIALITY

The ethical basis of the concept of confidentiality can be found in an understanding of the principles of beneficence, nonmaleficence, care, and respect for the privacy of others. These principles converge when looking at the reasons why confidentiality is a cornerstone of effective counseling and mental health practice. By its nature, maintaining confidentiality is a relational process involving at least two people and, in contemporary counseling contexts, very likely involving organizations as well. Confidentiality provides the framework within which clients can disclose and explore aspects of themselves and their relationships that are problematic, personally painful, and that might cause embarrassment or harm if known outside of the counseling relationship.

Essentially, confidentiality ensures that the counseling process is safe for the client. If clients were not provided the professional and legal protection of confidentiality within the counseling relationship, it would be hard to imagine why anyone would go to counseling at all. Clients trust that the disclosures they make about their personal and emotional worlds will be safeguarded by their counselors and not revealed to anyone else. The very process of counseling depends on the development of this relationship of trust, which has confidentiality as a central part of its foundation. Confidentiality is a sacred trust between the healer or helper and the patient or client that has been recognized as a value going back to antiquity. The Hippocratic Oath from the fourth century B.C. states, "Whatsoever things I see or hear concerning the life of men, in my attendance on the sick or even apart therefrom, which ought not be noised abroad, I will keep silence thereon, counting such things to be as sacred secrets."

Beneficence and Confidentiality

The ethical principle of beneficence directs counselors to act on behalf of the welfare of their clients and to do everything they can to promote the growth and development of their clients. ("Client" should be understood as an individual, a couple, or a family group.) Beneficence is one of the roots of confidentiality because it provides a context of safety for the client. Providing a safe and respectful context for clinical counseling work is the basic step in promoting client welfare. Viewing confidentiality from the perspective of beneficence and the promotion of client welfare is very different from viewing confidentiality as a requirement that, if not met, is likely to result in professional and legal sanctions. It is helpful for counselors to think about the ethical principle of beneficence because it explains why most individuals who become counselors entered the profession in the first place—out of a desire to help others and to be of service.

Nonmalificence and Confidentiality

The ethical principle of nonmaleficence requires that counselors do their utmost to avoid doing harm to their clients. All harm done to patients or clients is not actively intended, or deliberate, harm. Harm can also be done unintentionally, and the principle of nonmaleficence requires that counselors be sufficiently knowledgeable and competent to examine their clinical and record-keeping practices in order to do everything they can to avoid inflicting unintended harm on their clients. In the medical world, medication errors and hospital-borne infections are a major source of unintended harm to patients (Bates, Shore, Gibson, & Bosk, 2003; Institute of Medicine, 2000; Leape, 1994). In the counseling world, asking questions or raising issues that the client may not have previously considered problematic could represent a source of unintended harm, as could leaving a client file open on a desk, visible to another client or staff member.

Care and Confidentiality

Counselors practicing from an ethic of care have an more expanded view of what is the best way to treat clients than if they were acting simply from an ethic of duty or justice. In her foundational work *In a Different Voice,* Gilligan (1982) points out differences between an ethic of duty or justice and an ethic of care and suggests that female moral decision making tends to be informed more by an ethic of care than by an ethic of duty. The distinction between these two ways of understanding ethical decision making centers on the classic difference between applying universal or general principles to the question of what constitutes a moral action versus making ethical choices primarily with regard to the particularities of an individual situation and its relational context. The ethic of duty or justice places primacy on the rules or general principles governing how to act, such as laws, professional codes of ethics for counselors, and even treatment principles. The ethic of care gives priority to the maintenance of the relationship and the needs of the other for acknowledgment, attention, and responsiveness to physical, emotional, and social needs. Gilligan and Attanucci (1988) summarize the distinction between an ethic of justice or duty and an ethic of care:

> A justice perspective draws attention to problems of inequality and oppression and holds up an ideal of reciprocity and equal respect. A care perspective draws attention to problems of

> detachment or abandonment and holds up an ideal of attention and response to need. Two moral injunctions—not to treat others unfairly and not to turn away from someone in need—capture these different concerns. (p. 73)

The process of counseling is filled with opportunities for the counselor to act from an ethic of care. Consider the example in Box 6.1.

BOX 6.1
ETHIC OF CARE IN COUNSELING

A client diagnosed as a borderline personality disorder with a self-cutting habit calls the therapist's office on Christmas day and leaves a desperate message suggesting that she is going to cut herself and that she feels intolerably lonely and abandoned. During the preceding week, the therapist had reinforced with the client her therapeutic intent to talk with the client only during scheduled appointments while also supporting the client's developing ability to manage her own feelings of abandonment and terror and reviewing previous strategies that the client had used to successfully self-regulate her emotions between sessions. The therapist received the message from her client during the afternoon of Christmas day as she was preparing Christmas dinner for her own family and several friends. She knew that should she decide to talk with the client, she would be violating the terms of the treatment plan agreement she had established with the client and that, additionally, she would be impinging on her own and her family's holiday celebrations. In this case, the counselor was not overly concerned about a suicide risk. Nonetheless, the therapist was concerned for the well-being of the client and was particularly concerned about the client's experience of emptiness and loneliness on Christmas day. In this instance, the therapist decided to break the terms of the treatment plan about not talking with the client between sessions and returned the client's call out of a sense of concern for the client's existential condition on Christmas day. The therapist asked the client whether she felt she needed to be a patient that evening or whether she believed she could tolerate the loneliness and anxiety she was experiencing. The call, happily, was shorter than the therapist had feared it would be, and the counselor felt comfortable that the client's need for additional care on Christmas day outweighed the solid treatment principles about no between-session contact incorporated into the treatment plan.

It is not always easy for beginning counselors to understand how an ethic of care can preempt a right or duty. This case example is included as a clear illustration of how the ethic of care can preempt and override an ethic of rights and duties. The counselor expressed flexibility, based on weighing both the needs of the client and the counselor's own personal needs on a holiday, in determining whether to make an exception to a fairly rigid treatment plan. Practicing the ethic of care in clinical situations requires that the therapist engage in a process of constant comparison between more narrowly understood ethical obligations like the duty to protect confidentiality and the duty to warn and make ethical decisions that include the more encompassing ethic of care. This case is primarily about ethics of care and secondarily about confidentiality. While this case is primarily an example of an ethic of care, confidentiality issues are also at play. If the therapist had chosen not to interact with her client on Christmas day and the client had ended up going to the emergency room, issues of confidentiality would have become so cumbersome due to difficulties in exchanging clinical information on a holiday that it could have led to an unnecessary hospitalization.

The ethic of care, rather than fear of litigation and professional sanction, should govern decisions about exceptions to confidentiality. These exceptions will be discussed later in the chapter.

An ethic of care encompasses the practice of confidentiality by directing counselors to safeguard the confidential nature of the psychotherapeutic relationship so that the client can develop an optimal level of trust with the counselor. This optimal level of trust allows for the creation of a safe context within which the client can begin the process of self-reflection and self-disclosure while decreasing self-censorship. This type of openness and trust is the cornerstone of a robust therapeutic alliance and is recognized as one of the major elements contributing to positive therapeutic change (Gaston, 1990; Hubble, Duncan, & Miller, 1999; Lambert & Bergin, 1994). With our current state of knowledge about what works in therapy, we know that the relationship between counselor and client accounts for a significant amount of client change and is most powerful when it reflects a context of safety, trust, and openness.

Respect for Privacy and Confidentiality

Respect for privacy and recognition of client autonomy go hand in hand. Ethical counselors recognize that it is the client, not the counselor, who has the right to control the dissemination of private mental health information. Private mental health information may contain diagnoses, personal disclosures, personal and family medical and psychosocial histories, and work or educational difficulties that, if known by others, could result in their disapproval or in outright discrimination against the client. While mental heath care is generally less stigmatized now than in the past, the specters of stigma and discrimination remain real possibilities from which ethical counselors must work to protect their clients. Without an assurance of privacy, clients could not be expected to reveal painful or embarrassing information to their counselors in the hopes of obtaining relief and help.

One of the paradoxes in a client's journey to change and healing is that private thoughts and feelings must ultimately be shared so that clients can separate themselves from those thoughts and feelings long enough to reflect upon them and assess their influence on their lives. Private thoughts and feelings that are troubling to a client can get field-tested within the counseling relationship without a risk of criticism or negative judgment. This safe space is the essence of the therapeutic relationship and is safeguarded by a respect for privacy and confidentiality. This supportive and trusting relationship between counselor and client is also one of the key ingredients in positive client change and successful therapeutic outcomes, irrespective of counseling model (Prochaska & Norcross, 2002).

EMERGING BRAIN SCIENCE AND CONFIDENTIALITY

Recent developments in brain science suggest that the therapeutic context generated by adherence to the principle of confidentiality potentially allows for a host of corrective emotional experiences to take place within the counseling relationship. Damasio (2003) makes a powerful case for understanding thinking and feeling as interconnected if not simultaneous processes that involve the mind, the body, thinking, feeling, and acting. This is so because, in the deep limbic structure, the amygdala is the first filter evaluating incoming stimuli, and it emotionally tags thoughts that are associated with particular experiences. Hence, Damasio takes the position that all thinking is emotionally tagged based on the context within which the thinking occurred and the degree of activation of the amygdala, which produces corresponding physiological responses. For example, a frightening experience is interpreted rapidly by the amygdala, which then initiates a cascade of biochemical body events associated with fear. Decision making or thinking that is done within this fear context will likewise be emotionally tagged with the biochemical sequellae (consequences) for fear. The decision to flee from a threatening situation is a good example of the interconnectedness of physiology, feeling, thought, and action. By contrast, a sense of safety experienced within a positive therapeutic relationship creates a context for comfort and security that allows for the exploration of thoughts and feelings, even difficult ones, without the initiation of the biochemical cascade associated with fear and threat.

Confidentiality is the foundation for the development of positive counseling alliances with clients because it builds safety and trust that then lead to client disclosures that are increasingly open and free of self-censorship. This safe and supportive context allows for looking or relooking at difficult personal and relational experiences within a context that the amygdala and other limbic structures interpret as secure and nonthreatening. The counseling work done within this safe and secure context becomes especially important because the limbic system has interpreted the counseling context and process as survival enhancing and therefore positive. Within this survival-enhancing relationship, corrective, secure attachments can be made between the counselor and client, further promoting the well-being of the client.

Attachment and Confidentiality

The consistency of the counseling framework, based on confidentiality, safety, and trust, promotes the development of consistent, secure attachments that have the potential to overwrite early insecure-attachment templates. In early insecure-attachment relationships with primary caregivers, clients learned that their needs would be inconsistently responded to or would be either minimized by emotionally dismissive caretakers or exaggerated by anxious caretakers. From attachment theory and the new brain science (Cozolino, 2002; Schore, 1994; Siegel, 1999) we know that early attachment relationships with primary caregivers foster particular kinds of neural network integration in the brain, predisposing individuals to react either securely or insecurely in the face of life's stressors and challenges.

Insecure attachment relationships have a tendency to transfer across relational contexts, because the brain has participated in this process by recruiting neural networks that leave a person vulnerable to either anxious fretting or overreacting or to inappropriate and insensitive dismissing of relational concerns. Even in the face of insecure primary childhood attachments, the counseling process can provide a context wherein the brain can begin to reorganize neural networks in ways that provide the client a greater repertoire of responses than their original reduced set based on insecure early attachments. The counseling context and process is the corrective environment, and this environment is built on confidentiality. Where confidentiality is respected and safety and trust are generated, the brain tags the work done in counseling in an emotionally positive way, and the client can begin to develop more detailed and enhanced self-narratives that are reflective of more

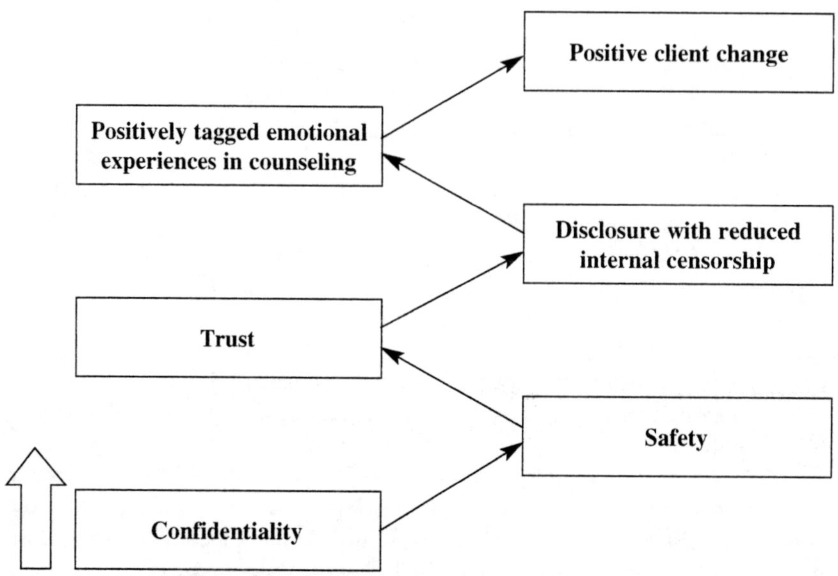

FIGURE 6.1 Relationship between Confidentiality and Client Change

enriched brain neural reorganization. Figure 6.1 illustrates the relationship among confidentiality, safety, trust, increased self-disclosure, the brain's recognition of secure counseling experiences as survival enhancing and therefore emotionally positive, and ultimately, client change and successful counseling outcomes. Parenthetically, these exciting developments in brain science are consistent with and provide additional support for the Perspective III ethical view advocated in this text.

LEGAL ASPECTS OF CONFIDENTIALITY

Privileged Communication

Privileged communication refers generally to the embodiment in statute of the right to privacy of communications between psychotherapist and client and freedom from forced disclosure, except as specified by law. In granting privilege to psychotherapeutic communications, society through the judicial system acknowledges the importance of privacy in psychotherapy for it to be effective and the chilling effect on the mental health professions that forced or unwanted disclosures would have. Affording privilege to psychotherapeutic communications also implicitly recognizes psychotherapy as a social good that improves the health and well-being of people. Individual states define and extend psychotherapeutic privilege as well as the exceptions to privilege differently. Common exceptions to privilege include the requirements to report abuse of minors, elders, or disabled adults; the duty to warn third parties of threats made against them in therapy; and situations during litigation in which psychotherapy clients bring into issue their own status as psychotherapy clients, such as citing temporary insanity as a defense for a crime.

In *Jaffee v. Redmond* (Lens, 2000) the U.S. Supreme Court established a federal right of privilege between psychotherapist and client by upholding the private interest of Redmond to receive counseling from a social worker and the larger public interest of promoting mental health through the provision of psychotherapy. Redmond, a police officer, sought counseling from a social worker after killing Ricky Allen when responding to a police call at his residence. Jaffee, the administrator of Allen's estate, sought access to the notes of Redmond's psychotherapy sessions. Both Redmond and her social worker refused to produce the notes, citing privileged communication, and so began the journey through the court system of *Jaffee v. Redmond* ending at the Supreme Court in 1996 with the establishment of a federal right of psychotherapeutic privilege.

The Health Insurance Portability and Accountability Act (HIPAA) of 1996

HIPAA, signed into federal law on August 21, 1996, brings the management and protection of private health information squarely into the domain of organizational and community ethics. The provisions of HIPAA require that organizations within which individual medical or psychotherapy practices are conducted be responsible and accountable for the procedures they use to protect clients' private health information. Individual mental-health-care providers must safeguard the privacy of psychotherapy assessments, treatment plans, and progress notes, but the umbrella agency or organization must also account for the standards it uses to safeguard these kinds of records. HIPAA was designed to provide a uniform and consistent set of procedures across the United States for protecting private health information. This standardization was thought to be necessary in order to inspire patient and client confidence in the handling of their private health information, especially in the era of electronic database storage and instantaneous transmission of data.

Some counselors may erroneously believe that the data they generate from counseling sessions does not come under HIPAA because they are not using email to transmit or receive client billing or mental health information. In fact, telephone and facsimile devices and the use of floppy disks, compact disks (CDs), or any other computer storage devices all fall under the purview of HIPAA. Therefore, every medical and mental health organization and individual mental-health-care provider must comply with HIPAA and establish safeguards for protecting clients' private health information in order to protect against existing or foreseeable threats to the privacy and security of such information.

HIPAA identifies necessary safeguards as including physical safeguards, administrative safeguards, and technical safeguards. Physical safeguards include evaluation of the security of the physical plant and actual storage cabinets and other physical procedures for protecting private health information. Administrative safeguards include the development of a set of written policies and procedures to be followed by personnel in the agency or organization in order to protect private health information. Examples would include an agency privacy statement distributed to all patients or clients, signed agreements to protect confidentiality completed by any and all personnel having access to areas where clients or their files might be found, and the establishment of procedures for discussing clients' private health information in secure areas where such discussions would not be overheard by others. Technical safeguards to protect private health information would include the use of secure firewalls on computers containing private health information, establishment of a system of secure passwords for those having access to such information, and procedures for monitoring and restricting access to clients' private health information.

HIPAA has become an integral part of modern law and ethics governing the security and confidentiality of client health information and of research using such information (Durham, 2002). The law was inspired out of a widespread awareness that, in the age of electronic transmission of data, private health information is more vulnerable than at any time in our history and that the nation has a duty to protect its citizens from the harm that could be caused by the misuse of health information.

Personal-Developmental and Organizational Ethics in a Regulatory Context

It is clear that HIPAA requires compliance with federal law about physically maintaining the safety and security of clients' private health information and the development of organizational policies to further protect their privacy. It is much more difficult to regulate organizational culture and the organizational attitudes related to the context and tone within which client's psychosocial histories, presenting problems, and counselor reactions are discussed.

Client histories can be discussed in demeaning, belittling ways or in respectful ways, and most counselors with even a little experience have been exposed to both kinds of practices. White and Epston (1990) raise the bar on the nature and context of counselor discussion of client histories by posing the question of whether the counselor would speak the same way about the client if the client were present in the room. How individuals and organizations respond to this question posed by White and Epston reflects entirely the ethical stances of both the individual practitioner and the organization. From the relational, constructivist view, we know that one cannot *not* influence, and any talk about a client is going to have ramifications for that client in terms of how he or she is viewed and responded to by others (Hoyt, 1998). Therefore, our talk about our clients when they are not present counts and makes a difference in how they ultimately will be perceived and treated. The Perspective III counselor has a heightened level of awareness about the power of any conversation, including offhand comments, to shape reality and incorporates this understanding into thoughtful and care-based self-restraint as a form of ethical practice.

EXCEPTIONS TO CONFIDENTIALITY

Abuse and Confidentiality

For the reasons discussed above, confidentiality is the gold standard in establishing a positive therapeutic alliance with a client. Clients can be expected to discuss painful or embarrassing material only within a context of safety and trust. Confidentiality, of course, is not absolute, and the reasons for the limitations of confidentiality can best be understood by turning once again to the ethical principle of beneficence. Beneficence requires us to work in the best interests of our clients and to do everything we can to promote their welfare. When clients are in serious distress, are vulnerable to exploitation by others, are in situations where their judgment and ability to reason are compromised, or where they are so constrained by others that their choices for effective action are significantly reduced, the principle of beneficence in counseling may require counselors to breach confidentiality in order to promote the welfare of the client.

While such actions could be construed as recentering expert knowledge in the hands of therapists by looking to the experts to make critical decisions for their clients, therapists who find themselves in such challenging situations have an obligation to reflexively examine their use of power and actively involve the client in critical decision making where possible. For example, in the clinical case described in Box 6.1, the therapist asked her client whether she needed to be a patient that day and what being a patient on Christmas day might mean for her. The client decided that she did not need to be a patient on Christmas day, and the therapist was satisfied that that was a safe and meaningful decision.

Physical and sexual abuse of minors, of disabled adults, and of the elderly are serious situations, and counselors in most jurisdictions are required by law to provide mandatory reports of such abuse. Most jurisdictions have a hotline or reporting agency where reports of abuse are directed. Generally, the reporting laws state that professionals have a mandatory obligation to report the abuse of a member of a vulnerable population (i.e., minors, the disabled, and the elderly). The reporting requirement usually describes the need to report in situations in which the professional either knows or suspects that abuse has occurred. In most jurisdictions, professionals who report abuse "in good faith" are protected from civil lawsuits for breach of confidentiality. Good faith reporting of abuse means that the professional has reason to suspect that abuse has been occurring and is filing the report in order both to promote the safety and welfare of the client and to comply with the law. Good faith reporting also means that the professional is acting on behalf of the client and not out of malice or intent to harm the client or alleged perpetrator. Abuse reporting does not usually require that the professional have proof of abuse, but rather that the professional have good reason, within the parameters of professional competence, to suspect that abuse is happening. Mandatory abuse reporting laws were established out of the recognition that vulnerable populations may be especially constrained from initiating effective action on their own behalf and require the protection of the eyes and ears of society, and especially of professionals, acting on their behalf.

While the ethical principle of beneficence and the intent of the abuse reporting laws may seem crystal clear to the average counselor, being confronted with an actual situation of suspected abuse can plunge a counselor into muddy waters indeed. The clinical case in Box 6.2 of Maria T. and Jorge illustrates a number of dilemmas and questions that counselors regularly face when dealing with suspected child abuse and mandatory abuse reporting requirements. How would an ethically competent counselor respond to the questions that Maria T. posed to herself during her period of critical self-reflection following the abuse report? The guidelines in Box 6.3 for counselors should be helpful in anticipating and managing mandatory abuse reporting requirements.

Suicide and Confidentiality

The primary problem with successful suicide is its irreversibility. Suicide represents a permanent solution to a usually temporary problem. In working with depressed clients and clients with other mood disorders, assessment of suicidality is always a significant clinical

BOX 6.2
CASE EXAMPLE OF MANDATORY ABUSE REPORTING

The therapist, Maria T., was an active member of her large church's parish council. The pastor and other members of her church regularly referred families to her who were having difficulties with their children. Maria T. accepted a referral from her church of a husband and wife and their 13-year-old son. The counselor did not know the family, but she was aware from her parish council involvement that the family was a sizable contributor to the church and that the father was a well-known accountant in town. The son, Jorge, who had been in the gifted program since elementary school, had begun to bring home slipping grades and was becoming increasingly detached from his friends at school. The parents had asked their pastor for a referral for counseling to someone who would share the values of their church. Both parents expressed genuine concern about Jorge and were very cooperative throughout the counseling process. During an individual session with Jorge, Maria T. noticed what she thought was a bruise peeking out from the leg of his pants and asked Jorge about it. Jorge proceeded to describe to Maria T. a series of regular beatings with a belt inflicted by his father for his low grades in school and for his refusal to socialize with schoolmates and parish friends.

Maria T. knew that she had no choice but to report the abuse to the Department of Children and Families, but she was wracked with anxiety about the impact of doing so both on the family and on her personally. Maria T. worried about whether Jorge would be removed from the home and whether that would be a worse outcome for him than suffering through the regular beatings. She wondered whether the mother would be charged with neglect for failure to protect her son from the abuse apparently inflicted by the father and what that would mean to the mother. Maria T. knew that a number of church members supported corporal punishment, and she worried that she would be blamed for the negative circumstances of the family arising from her abuse report. She worried whether she should have accepted any referrals at all from her church even though she was careful to accept only referrals of people whom she did not know or with whom she did not have any direct relationship. Maria T. wondered whether her relationship with this family constituted an indirect dual relationship. She also worried whether her own counseling practice would survive what was certain to become a notorious case in the community. Most important to Maria T., she worried whether the family, and especially Jorge, who needed the most help, would ever trust a therapist again after entrusting her with information that she was forced to disclose. In fact, Maria T. wondered whether the abuse reporting requirements did more harm than good in a case like this one.

concern. The more lethal a suicide plan appears to be, the more urgent is the requirement for therapeutic intervention. Suicide interventions can range from a no-suicide contract with the client to putting family members on a 24-hour suicide watch to hospitalizing clients involuntarily. Each of these interventions involves the autonomy of the client.

In the case of encouraging a client to enter a no-suicide contract for a specified period of time, the counselor encourages the client to resist the seduction of suicide, while planning for maximum psychological and social support for the client. In this case, the client's autonomy is not only respected but utilized. In the case of putting the family on 24-hour suicide watch, the autonomy of the client is respected insofar as the client is seen as capable of making a decision to act on a suicidal impulse, but the client's autonomy is mod-

BOX 6.3

GUIDELINES FOR MANAGING MANDATORY ABUSE REPORTING REQUIREMENTS

1. Work at developing and maintaining a high level of trust and communication with your client. This includes providing ongoing information to your client about the treatment process.
2. Ensure that your "Consent for Treatment" form contains a clear and detailed description of exceptions to confidentiality and the duty to report suspected child abuse, elder abuse, or abuse of disabled persons to the Department of Children and Families or its equivalent in your jurisdiction. Note that informed consent begins rather than ends with the signed consent form.
3. After the client has signed the "Consent for Treatment" form and before the formal counseling session begins, ask the client if he or she has any questions about any part of the "Consent for Treatment" form. Remember that ongoing informed consent enhances and strengthens the client–therapist relationship and confidentiality.
4. If you suspect abuse, remember that most jurisdictions distinguish between "proof of" and "suspicion of" abuse and that it is the professional counselor and psychotherapist's obligation to make a good faith report of *suspected* abuse. Proof of abuse is a higher standard that does not apply in most mandatory abuse reporting situations.
5. Remember that it is the Department of Children and Families's investigator that is the finder of fact in abuse cases, not the reporting counselor. The reporting counselor must only make a "good faith" report, which means that he or she is free of malice for all and is making a report based on professional counseling judgment.
6. If the suspected perpetrator is your client already when you make a good faith determination of suspected abuse, discuss with your client the need to report the abuse as required by law and indicated in your consent form, unless there is a risk that further abuse or harm might come to the abused minor or adult or the abused minor or adult does not wish you to notify the alleged perpetrator. In any case, communicate your ongoing commitment to your client's welfare and your willingness to continue counseling with your client, if appropriate, and/or to refer the client to a qualified counseling specialist for further care.
7. Consult with your supervisor and/or experienced clinical counseling colleagues for advice and support. Abuse reporting can be emotionally draining for counselors, and collegial support is very helpful.
8. When making abuse reports, include all information required by law, which usually includes the name and address of the person making the report, the name and address of the suspected victim, and the nature of the suspected abuse. In most jurisdictions, the identity of the person filing the report is kept confidential by the abuse investigator. However, if civil litigation is initiated, the identity of the person making the report may be disclosed.
9. Keep in mind the ethical principle of beneficence, and remember that it is not always easy or without personal cost to promote the welfare of clients who are members of vulnerable groups. Sometimes, counselors themselves who are tasked with helping members of vulnerable groups can have parallel experiences of fear and intimidation as they are responding to help the abuse victims take actions to become more safe.

erately overridden by the more compelling need to provide safety for the client by having family members provide round-the-clock surveillance. In the case of involuntary hospitalization of a suicidal client, the client's autonomy is severely restricted in order to promote the client's survival and therefore well-being and also to promote the opportunity for recovery from the depression and impaired reasoning usually associated with suicidality. It is too infrequently noted that, short of absolute deprivation of individual rights, such as keeping a person shackled, there is no fail-safe intervention for preventing suicide. Suicides happen in prisons with inmates on a 24-hour suicide watch, and they also happen in psychiatric hospitals with patients on a 24-hour suicide watch. Counselors who practice from a Perspective I defensive mode too easily overlook the fact that placing a suicidal client in a restrictive setting does not solve the problem of suicidality; it only solves the problem of custody.

The ethical codes of the American Counseling Association, the American Association for Marriage and Family Therapy, the National Association of Social Workers, and the American Psychological Association all obligate their clinical members to breach confidentiality and to act on behalf of saving their client's life in the event of clear and imminent danger of suicide. For counselors, suicide intervention juxtaposes the ethical principles of beneficence and autonomy. In order to save a client's life (beneficence) a client's freedom (autonomy) may need to be restricted temporarily.

The ethical counselor, practicing from Perspective III, will appreciate the importance of weighing the ethical values of beneficence and autonomy in making clinical decisions about what level of restriction to institute in order to intervene effectively with a suicidal client. Understanding the ethical principles that are in competition in the case of a suicidal client offers counselors an expanded opportunity for intervention, namely discussing with the client the issue of autonomy and its restrictions in order to protect life and soliciting the client's thoughts about what level of restriction of autonomy might be needed in the current situation. Involving the client in this kind of therapeutic conversation about the need for possible restriction of his or her autonomy paradoxically respects and utilizes the client's autonomy by encouraging self-reflection and the imagining of alternative scenarios. For the Perspective III counselor, even talk about restriction of autonomy can be collaborative and respectful.

Threats to Others and Confidentiality

All counselors in training are familiar with the *Tarasoff v. Regents of the University of California* (1974, 1976) case. In this case, a psychotherapy patient, Poddar, threatened to kill an unnamed woman who was apparently easily identifiable as Tatiana Tarasoff. Poddar told his therapist that he planned to kill her when she returned from Brazil. While the therapists involved in the case were concerned about Poddar's threats, nothing was done to further evaluate or restrict Poddar. Upon Tatiana's return, Poddar made good on his threat and stabbed Tatiana to death. In the *Tarasoff* case, the courts held that the right to privacy of psychotherapy patients is limited if they make threats to harm others. The case is used illustratively in counseling training programs to point out that confidentiality does not extend to threats to harm others made by clients in therapy and that, further, the psychotherapist has a duty to protect a third party if a threat against that third party is made by notifying him or her of the threat. Subsequent court rulings have clarified the *Tarasoff* decision, suggesting that violating client confidentiality is legitimate only when there is a specific intended victim and when the stated intent is to harm that specific victim (Barrett, 2000).

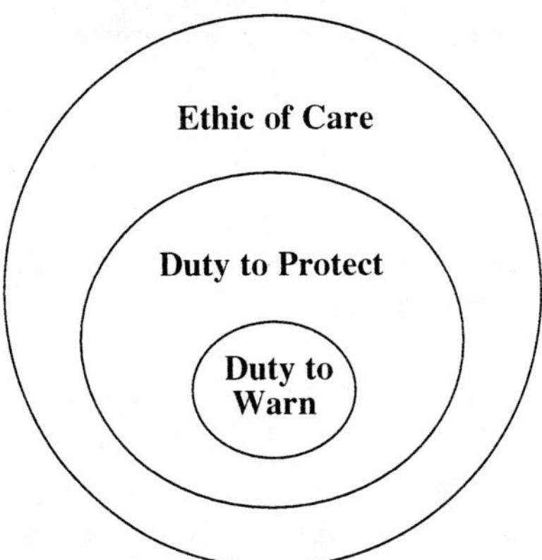

FIGURE 6.2 Relationship between the Ethic of Care and the Duties to Protect and Warn

The *Tarasoff* case generates a lot of conversational time in most graduate courses on legal and ethical issues in counseling, yet is not often cast within the framework of moral decision making that informs it. What *Tarasoff* directs counselors to do is to accept responsibility for making a moral choice to care for another if that other has been specifically named as an intended victim of harm, regardless of whether the therapist knows or has a professional relationship with the other. *Tarasoff* may indeed dictate a duty to warn in very specific circumstances, but it more generally dictates a duty to care and a duty to protect.

An ethic of care is at the heart of the principles informing ethical decision making for therapists. The ethic of care encompasses the principles of beneficence, nonmalificence, autonomy, and fidelity toward clients. It also invites therapists to know themselves, their competencies, and their limitations, and to actively pursue self-care and social and professional support. Within this encompassing ethic of care is the obligation to protect clients and, within very particular circumstances, the duty to warn. Protection of clients requires that therapists facilitate active client involvement in their own decision making and provide for adequate self-care. The duty to warn is a subset of the larger duty to protect arising out of the ethic of care and is applicable only under the circumstances described above.

RIGHTS OF CHILDREN AND CONFIDENTIALITY

The most salient dilemma in considering the rights of children to confidentiality is the potential tension between a child's right to privacy and a parent's right to know. Substance abuse, depression and suicidal thoughts, birth control and abortion, and aggression and violence are just some of the issues that may emerge in counseling settings with minors or initially in school settings where the child's behavior is brought to the attention of the school counselor. In such situations, what rights to privacy and confidentiality do minors have?

Remley (1993) held that parents probably have a legal right to know the content of counseling sessions with their children. On the other hand, Myers (1982) took the opposite position, stating that the therapist's duty to uphold confidentiality in therapy with minors extends to the minor client, not to the client's parent(s). Mitchell, Disque, and Robertson (2002) point out that, outside of the clearly defined exceptions to confidentiality—namely, child abuse, suicide, or imminent threats to others—both the law and the professional codes of ethics offer little guidance and much ambiguity about how counselors should handle the issue of client confidentiality with minors. To add to the confusion, in the highly charged post-Columbine period of tragic school violence, Isaacs and Stone (2001) conducted research about how and when counselors considered breaching the confidentiality of their minor clients. They found that younger age and greater perceived seriousness by the counselor of the disclosed activity increased the likelihood of breaching client confidentiality in the case of minors. In this study, counselors were more likely to respect the autonomy of older minors and to involve parents when they believed the issues at stake to be more serious.

An integrative-contextual view of the rights of children situates children within the context of both their families and their communities and includes an appreciation for how the parent–child relationship is constructed from a multicultural perspective. In this view, a reciprocal obligation exists on the part of families and communities to promote the welfare of their children and of children to act in accordance with their family and community standards. In such a view, the right to confidentiality for minors could be mitigated based on (1) immediate danger (suicide or threat of harm by another), (2) chronic danger (substance abuse or ongoing emotional distress), (3) patterns of disorganized or aggressive behavior, or (4) multicultural factors constructing the overarching right and responsibility of parents to know about and to intervene in situations in which their children's welfare is at issue.

In order to promote the welfare of children in these situations, the principle of beneficence would require involving others, especially parents, with the ability to provide more long-term resources and support. On the other hand, the rights of minors to confidentiality would be enhanced in situations in which their families or communities have demonstrated a failure to promote their welfare through (1) physical, sexual, or emotional abuse, or (2) neglect. Additionally, the rights of minors to confidentiality would be enhanced in the relational view in situations in which a young person is striving for developmentally appropriate autonomy and wishes to engage in counseling for the purposes of self-reflection and personal growth. While these relational guidelines are far from comprehensive and are themselves subject to changes in applicable laws, ethical codes, and cultural variations, they do provide some context for ethical decision making on the part of counselors and therapists about when to breach minor client confidentiality and when to uphold it.

Finally, we have presented confidentiality as a contextual consideration and have specified its relational connections. We add in closing that confidentiality is intimately related to the other three ethical considerations: informed consent, conflict of interests, and competence. While we have stated that confidentiality and informed consent go hand in hand, it is also implied that competence and conflict of interests are also closely tied to confidentiality.

KEY POINTS

1. Confidentiality is the cornerstone of the counseling process and arises from an ethic of care that values the privacy and autonomy of the other.
2. Confidentiality is a relational, multicultural, contextual activity designed to promote and enhance client welfare.
3. Confidentiality arises from the ethical principles of beneficence, respect for privacy, and nonmaleficence and is most richly understood as an ethic of care rather than as an ethic of rules and duties.

4. Confidentiality provides the foundation for a positive therapeutic relationship in which corrective secure attachments are likely to lead to positive therapeutic outcomes.
5. Privileged communication is a legal embodiment of respect for the privacy and confidentiality of communications between counselor and client.
6. The Health Insurance Portability and Accountability Act (HIPAA) of 1996 provides a federal mandate and standards for the protection of clients' private health information, including data from counseling and psychotherapy, for both individual practitioners and organizations.
7. Counselors need to reflect on their personal practices and the organizational culture related to how, when, and where discussions of client cases and counselor reactions to them are discussed.
8. Confidentiality is not absolute, and exceptions to it include abuse, suicide, and threats to others.
9. The ethic of care encompasses the duty to protect, which is outlined in the *Tarasoff* case. The duty to warn is a subset of the larger ethical obligation to protect.
10. Counselors can learn to manage mandatory reporting obligations in ways that enhance their personal-developmental and professional growth.
11. In general, children are not afforded a legal right to confidentiality, but the issue is debated in the professional literature. Cultural beliefs and values about the nature of the parent–child relationship and who should handle sensitive information are primary considerations for the ethical counselor.

CONCLUDING NOTE: PERSPECTIVE I VERSUS III

Confidentiality is the cornerstone of the counseling relationship and creates a context within which positive therapeutic change can happen. Far from being simply a defensive practice that a counselor must follow to avoid getting sued, confidentiality springs from the ethical principles of beneficence, nonmalificence, an ethic of care, and respect for privacy. Understanding the meaning of these ethical principles related to confidentiality helps counselors and therapists shift from a defensive, Perspective I view of ethics to a personally and professionally integrative, Perspective III posture. The Perspective III posture provides the professional with a much more expanded view of the nature of confidentiality and hence with greater flexibility and increased options for therapeutic interventions. The role of confidentiality in generating corrective, secure attachments within the counseling relationship and the influence of neural organization on thoughts, actions, and emotions, and vice versa, within a secure and trusting counseling relationship are vital elements for counselors to understand. Viewing confidentiality as ultimately helping to change brain activity is a radical departure from traditional understandings of the role of confidentiality in counseling. The legal aspects of confidentiality, including the duties to report and protect, can also be understood from an enhanced Perspective III standpoint revealing the ethical principles underlying these professional obligations. Counselors who understand confidentiality and its implications from a Perspective III vantage point are least likely to suffer burnout and are most likely to continue to develop personally and professionally and to experience greater degrees of professional freedom and creativity.

REVIEW QUESTIONS

1. Do you think that the fact that school guidance counselors cannot guarantee complete confidentiality compromises their potential effectiveness?
2. Currently, counselors do not have a duty to report spousal abuse. Would counseling an abusive spouse pose an ethical dilemma for you? Do you think the current duty-to-report laws are sufficient?
3. Under what circumstances would you hesitate to report suspected child abuse? What factors would you consider?
4. What would you do if your client who has a sexually transmitted disease told you that he often engages in unprotected sex with strangers? What factors would you consider?

5. Do you think electronic communication and the use of computers in counseling opens the door to breaches in confidentiality? What is your view on the use of electronic communication for confidential information?

REFERENCES

Barrett, R. L. (2000). Confidentiality and HIV/AIDS. In J. J. Gates & B. S. Arons (Eds.), *Privacy and confidentiality in mental health care* (pp. 157–172). Baltimore: Paul H. Brookes.

Bates, D. W., Shore, M. F., Gibson, R., & Bosk, C. (2003). Patient safety forum: Examining the evidence. *Psychiatric Services, 54,* 1599–1603.

Cozolino, L. J. (2002). *The neuroscience of psychotherapy: Building and rebuilding the human brain.* New York: Norton.

Damasio, A. (2003). *Looking for Spinoza: Joy, sorrow, and the feeling brain.* New York: Harcourt Trade.

Durham, M. L. (2002). How research will adapt to HIPAA: A view from within the healthcare delivery system. *American Journal of Law and Medicine, 28,* 491–502.

Gaston, L. (1990). The concept of the alliance and its role in psychotherapy: Theoretical and empirical considerations. *Psychotherapy, 27,* 143–153.

Gilligan, C. (1982). *In a different voice.* Cambridge, MA: Harvard University Press.

Gilligan, C., & Attanucci, J. (1988). Two moral orientations. In C. Gilligan, J. V. Ward & J. M. Taylor with B. Bardige (Eds.), *Mapping the moral domain: A contribution of women's thinking to psychology and education* (pp. 73–87). Cambridge, MA: Harvard University Graduate School of Education.

Hoyt, M. F. (Ed.). (1998). *The handbook of constructive therapies: Innovative approaches from leading practitioners.* San Francisco: Jossey-Bass.

Hubble, M. A., Duncan, B. L., & Miller, S. D. (1999). *The heart and soul of change: What works in therapy.* Washington, DC: American Psychological Association.

Institute of Medicine. (2000). *To err is human: Building a safer health system.* Washington, DC: National Academies Press.

Isaacs, M. L., & Stone, C. (2001). Confidentiality with minors: Mental health counselors' attitudes toward breaching or preserving confidentiality. *Journal of Mental Health Counseling, 23,* 342–357.

Lambert, M. J., & Bergin, A. E. (1994). The effectiveness of psychotherapy. In A. E. Bergin & S. L. Garfield (Eds.), *Handbook of psychotherapy and behavior change* (4th ed., pp. 143–189). New York: Wiley.

Leape, L. L. (1994). Error in medicine. *Journal of the American Medical Association, 272,* 1851–1857.

Lens, V. (2000). Protecting the confidentiality of the therapeutic relationship: *Jaffee v. Redmond. Social Work, 45,* 273–277.

Mitchell, C. W., Disque, J. G., & Robertson, P. (2002). When parents want to know: Responding to parental demands for confidential information. *Professional School Counseling, 6,* 156–162.

Myers, J. E. B. (1982). Legal issues surrounding psychotherapy with minor clients. *Clinical Social Work Journal, 10,* 303–314.

Prochaska, J., & Norcross, J. (2002). *Systems of psychotherapy: A transtheoretical analysis.* Belmont, CA: Wadsworth.

Remley, T. P. (1993, June). *Legal issues for professional counselors in schools.* Paper presented at the American School Counselor Association Annual Conference, McClean, VA.

Schore, A. N. (1994). *Affect regulation and the origin of the self: The neurobiology of emotional development.* Hillsdale, NJ: Erlbaum.

Skovholt, T. M., & Jennings, L. (Eds.). (2004). *Master therapists: Exploring expertise in therapy and counseling.* Boston: Allyn and Bacon.

Siegel, D. J. (1999). *Developing mind: Towards a neurobiology of interpersonal experience.* New York: Guilford.

Tarasoff v. Regents of the University of California (Cal. 1974). 529 P.2d 553.

Tarasoff v. Regents of the University of California (Cal. 1976). 551 P.2d 334, 331.

White, M., & Epston, D. (1990). *Narrative means to therapeutic ends.* New York: Norton.

CHAPTER 7

INFORMED CONSENT

MAUREEN DUFFY

Beginning counselors and therapists often view the informed consent process simply as a technical requirement to be completed before proceeding to the heart of the matter, which is the counseling or therapy process itself. In reality, informed consent is a relational process between counselor and client and not just a signed and witnessed work document to protect the counselor from liability. Informed consent typically unfolds in a four-part process. The first part of the process involves the client's reading an information sheet or booklet outlining the elements of the informed consent document. The second part of the process, assuming a well-trained counselor, involves the counselor's asking the client if he or she has any questions about any of the ideas covered in the informed consent document and includees the counselor summarizing the meaning of informed consent. The third part of the informed consent process involves the client's attesting to his or her understanding of informed consent by signing the informed consent document, which is usually witnessed by the counselor or, on occasion, by an intake worker. The fourth part of the process is the ongoing manner in which counselors and therapists inform their clients of developments or options as treatment progresses. This four-part process is key to effective professional conduct because it highlights the ongoing collaborative relationship between professional and client, particularly collaborative decision making. Howard (2002) insists that informed consent requires full client participation in the decision-making process.

LEARNING OBJECTIVES

After reading this chapter you should be able to

1. Describe the ethical and professional underpinnings of the informed process.
2. Indicate the ethical principles that are operative in informed consent.
3. List the key elements in an ethically and legally sound informed consent document.
4. Describe various systemic and multicultural factors impacting informed consent.
5. Discuss when minors can and cannot give informed consent.

6. Indicate how informed consent is operative in matters involving involuntary commitment.
7. Discuss how privacy and the absence of nonverbal cues can impact informed consent in online counseling.
8. Indicate why Perspective III views the primary purpose of informed consent as promoting client self-determination rather than protecting counselors from liability.

KEY TERMS

autonomy
collaborative decision making
informed consent
mandatorily referred clients
online counseling
self-determination

THE CONTEXTUAL DOMAIN AND INFORMED CONSENT

In the traditional view, informed consent is most often thought of as a document outlining the nature and conditions of the proposed treatment that is signed by the client and witnessed by the therapist or counselor. In the traditional, or Perspective I, view, informed consent is a static process beginning with the client's reading the informed consent document, asking any relevant questions, and then completing the process by signing the document. A contextual understanding of informed consent requires a radical departure from this view.

A contextual understanding of informed consent places the ongoing relationship between the therapist or counselor and client at the heart of the informed consent process. In this contextual, or Perspective III, view, informed consent is an ongoing relational process characterized by cooperative conversations with the client about the nature of treatment, its effectiveness, and future treatment plans and goals. Such a contextual understanding requires that the therapist or counselor and client take time during the therapeutic process to reflect on the treatment, consider the effect and/or meaning of the treatment for the client, and plan for future treatment in light of the outcome of periodic reflective conversations. These reflective conversations should include any new information, changed circumstances, or changes in the client's or therapist's point of view about how best to proceed in therapy. In this way, informed consent becomes a living, dynamic process that reflects the quality of the therapeutic relationship and the quality of the collaboration between therapist and client. In Perspective III, written documentation of informed consent is still obtained, but it is a product of the therapeutic relationship rather than an end in itself (see the case in Box 7.1).

The concern for Sally's past unsuccessful experiences of therapy that the new therapist demonstrated during the initial session had the effect of creating a very strong initial bond between Sally and her therapist. The therapist's acknowledgment of how disappointing Sally's unsuccessful therapy experiences must have been for her further strengthened the therapeutic alliance. Sally felt heard and cared about. By the therapist's proactively including collaborative reflection and evaluation about how therapy was going into the treatment plan, Sally left feeling relieved that there was a mechanism for review and changing course already built into the therapy process.

BOX 7.1
A RELUCTANT CLIENT ARRIVES FOR AN INITIAL APPOINTMENT

Sally had a long history of multiple failed therapy attempts. Her psychosocial history included childhood neglect and physical abuse; difficulties maintaining close, intimate relationships; and problems with chronic feelings of anger and dissatisfaction with her personal life. Her work history was in marked contrast to her personal history and was characterized by her outstanding success as a business owner and marketing consultant in the construction field. Sally wanted to feel less anger and also wanted to maintain her current relationship with a man with whom she thought she might even be able to have a long-term relationship.

Sally had tried therapy unsuccessfully so many times before that she felt pessimistic about its outcome. She was also exhausted and bored by the thought of having to tell her story all over again to yet another therapist. Her girlfriend was in therapy with someone whom she raved about and Sally thought she might call her girlfriend's therapist for an appointment and give therapy one last try. During her initial telephone contact with the therapist, Sally had briefly said she was going to try therapy one more time because her previous experiences had been unsuccessful.

The new therapist had pondered Sally's comments after the phone contact and knew that the initial appointment was going to be critical. When Sally arrived for her appointment, the new therapist ushered her into her office immediately and began the informed consent process, which included obtaining Sally's signature on a written informed consent document. During the process of obtaining informed consent from Sally, the new therapist emphasized how important it was going to be for her to frequently stop and reflect with Sally about how therapy was going and whether Sally felt it was meeting her expectations and whether they might need to adjust the therapy process and/or treatment plan. The therapist paid particular attention to acknowledging how tiresome it must be to tell your personal story over and over again and then, worst of all, to feel that little or nothing had been accomplished in the end. While she didn't want to set herself up for more disappointment, Sally left the new therapist's office feeling that something was different this time and also feeling the slightest bit hopeful. Sally liked that the therapist was proactively addressing the need to stop and reflect and review on how therapy was going and her openness to doing something different if it wasn't working.

These collaborative reflection and evaluation processes are excellent examples of informed consent as an ongoing relational process in which the nature of the treatment plan may change based on new ideas or information from either the therapist or the client or both. During these processes of review, the client is given the information necessary to make a continued informed consent decision about whether to proceed. By being open, disclosing, and by providing opportunities for review of the direction and effectiveness of therapy to date, the therapist is also strengthening the therapeutic alliance and demonstrating profound regard and care for the well-being of the client.

THE LEGAL AND ETHICAL BASIS OF THE NEED FOR CONSENT FOR TREATMENT

Consent for treatment is a critical condition of all counseling and psychotherapy. The importance of consent has its basis in the legal concept of a person's having the right to be free from unwanted touching and, indeed, the right to decline medical treatment (Rosoff, 1981). Consent for treatment in counseling and psychotherapy is akin to consent for treatment for medical procedures. It is a technical fact that providing counseling or psychotherapy without consent represents legal battery insofar as a person is being touched without his or her consent (Howard, 2002). In the case of counseling and psychotherapy, the touching that could theoretically constitute battery is understood as the "touching" of the emotional or psychological self and not necessarily the touching of the physical self.

What is most important in the understanding of informed consent; however, is the ethical and professional context within which it can best be appreciated. Driving informed consent is the ethic of care for the client and for the client's autonomy and right to self-determination. Irrespective of the belief of a professional counselor or psychotherapist about what would be best for a client, a client does, in fact, have the right to refuse or terminate counseling or psychotherapy, or consider and act on alternative treatment options. Refusing or terminating counseling in the face of a counselor's strong recommendation that a client begin or continue in counseling raises issue of power sharing between counselor and client, and in which party (counselor or client) power is most vested. The role of expert knowledge and who is deemed to possess such knowledge is at stake in such situations as well as the question of where power resides—in the counselor, in the client, or in the relationship between.

Traditional, individually based counseling models tend to share the medical model's paternalistic view of the client or patient as less powerful and less knowledgeable and, therefore, less capable of making informed decisions about whether it is in his or her own best interests to participate in counseling or psychotherapy. Relational models of counseling, including narrative and solution-focused models, reflecting-team models, and language-based systems models, demonstrate more explicit consciousness of the power-based foundations of the counseling relationship and, consequently, would be much less likely to appeal to expert knowledge to persuade a reluctant client to participate in counseling or psychotherapy. For example, in Anderson and Goolishian's (1988) language-based "Collaborative Language Systems Model," they encourage therapists to take a "not knowing" stance with all their clients.

It is important, therefore, for beginning therapists and counselors especially, to reflect upon the nature of the power relationships inherent in their preferred models of doing counseling and to think through how they might respond to a client who chooses to withhold or withdraw consent for treatment or to seek alternative treatments when they as counselors believe counseling is in their client's best interests. Irrespective of theoretical and clinical models of treatment, Walter and Handelsman (1996) found in their research study that clients rated mental health counselors as more trustworthy the more specific the information was that they shared with the clients in their informed consent procedures. They stated that ". . . clients may be more willing to trust therapists who are willing to share specific information and thereby share a portion of their power" (p. 259).

Informed consent is not primarily a device to protect the therapist from the threat of a civil lawsuit or, worse, a criminal charge of battery. It is designed primarily to enhance the personal agency and self-determination of clients by providing them with information necessary to make informed choices about optimal care and treatment for their relational, emotional, and psychological difficulties. Informed consent, understood as a relational process between counselor and client, can also promote and enhance the therapeutic relationship by providing a forum for discussion of the limitations of therapy and what would constitute realistic and reasonable expectations for change.

In terms of Perspectives I through III, Perspective I therapists and counselors view informed consent as primarily defensive practice, required to protect them from criminal charges of battery and civil charges of failure to safeguard client confidentiality. The Perspective I counselor is diligent about ensuring that the informed consent document has been provided to the client, explained to him or her, and appropriately signed and witnessed. The Perspective III counselor, practicing from an integrative-contextual stance, and having integrated the meaning of the ethical principles underlying professional practice into his or her own personal and professional development, views informed consent as a means of collaborative power sharing with clients and of promoting client autonomy and self-determination.

KEY ELEMENTS OF AN INFORMED CONSENT DOCUMENT

At least ten key elements should be included in an informed consent document. Box 7.2 lists these key elements, and this section describes each.

BOX 7.2

OUTLINE OF KEY ELEMENTS IN AN ETHICALLY AND LEGALLY SOUND INFORMED CONSENT DOCUMENT FOR COUNSELING AND PSYCHOTHERAPY

1. Nature of the treatment to be provided
2. Self-of-therapist information
3. Nature of the confidential relationship between counselor and client and a clear statement outlining exceptions to confidentiality
4. Potential risks and benefits of treatment
5. Alternatives to treatment
6. Competence and lack of coercion
7. Right to refuse or discontinue treatment without penalty
8. Office hours, contact information, and what to do in the event of an emergency
9. Fee structure and payment issues
10. Privacy of private health information

1. Nature of the treatment to be provided. The informed consent document should provide a clear description of the nature of the counseling services to be provided. The description should provide enough information about the proposed treatment that a reasonable person would be able to understand it. The nature of the treatment should be described in language that is comprehensible and understandable to an average person. Counselors are obligated to inform their clients of their theoretical framework and treatment approach

(McCurdy & Murray, 2003). In counseling, treatment approaches or modalities could include individual counseling, couples counseling, marital therapy, family therapy, group therapy, or some combination thereof. As a health care profession, there is probably no other discipline with as much diversity in approach to theory and treatment as psychotherapy. Depending on the theoretical model subscribed to by the counselor, clients could find themselves in vastly differing counseling situations ranging from a focus on past trauma (psychodynamic approaches) to a focus on identifying previously ignored versions of one's life and developing more satisfying personal and relational stories (narrative approaches). In order to provide clients with meaningful information with which to determine their mental health care, counselors must be willing and able to articulate their operating theoretical models. The process of counseling should also be explained in summative form. For example, clients should be informed that the counselor will utilize questions, reflections, discussion, history taking, a one-way mirror, reflecting teams, or audio- and/or videotaping, as is relevant for the particular counseling situation.

If appropriate, the client should be informed that the nature of the services to be provided could call for collateral contacts with physicians, teachers, extended family members, or social service system or judicial system representatives. As well as can be anticipated in advance, the doctrine of informed consent requires that the treatment provider lay out and describe what the anticipated course of treatment will include and who is likely to be involved. In order for the consent for treatment to be valid, the counselor must include sufficient information for the client to be able to make an informed decision about his or her mental health care.

2. Self-of-therapist information. This section would include a complete and accurate statement about the credentials of the therapist, licenses to practice, areas of special training and expertise, and type of services provided.

3. Nature of the confidential relationship between counselor and client and a clear statement outlining exceptions to confidentiality. Please see Chapter 6 for a discussion of the nature of the confidential relationship between counselor and client and the exceptions to confidentiality. It is imperative that counselors include a clear statement outlining the exceptions to confidentiality and the mandatory reporting requirements applicable under federal and state law and according to the professional ethical codes of the counselor's professional associations in their informed consent document. Failure to include this element in an informed consent document could open the counselor to a lawsuit for breach of confidentiality based on negligence or misrepresentation in not informing a client beforehand of the exceptions to confidentiality. Listing the limitations of confidentiality promotes the client's self-determination and autonomy, insofar as the client can then make an informed choice about whether to disclose certain categories of information to the counselor.

4. Potential risks and benefits of treatment. Any adequate informed consent document will also include a section outlining potential risks and benefits of treatment. This section may seem deceptively simple but it is not. Disclosure of risks and benefits is made by the counselor or therapist in the development of an informed consent document. The difficulty is that a client cannot be expected to know what risks and benefits may conceivably accrue outside of those presented by the counselor or therapist who is in the position of power and privilege, having expert knowledge over the process of psychotherapy. Therefore, in signing off on a risks and benefits disclosure as a part of an informed consent form, a lay client is relying on the representations of the counselor to provide a thorough and comprehensive summary of the risks and benefits in counseling and therapy.

Here again, reliance on basic ethical principles can help the counselor to navigate some unpredictable terrain. The ethical principle of fidelity—of being faithful to our professional knowledge base and to the promises we make to our clients—can best inform the task of drafting and disclosing a fair-minded risks and benefits statement about counseling and therapy. The informed consent document is not a sales tool or rhetorical device for accumulating clients; it is a mechanism for helping clients make informed decisions about their mental health care. Therefore, either exaggerating the benefits of therapy or minimizing the risks would be unethical because it would violate the ethical principles of fidelity and care. Our research and theoretical knowledge bases in counseling and psychotherapy provide us with ample evidence of the general effectiveness of therapy (Pinsoff & Wynne, 1995). On the other hand, Gottman's (1999) evidence-based marital therapy reminds us of the real possibility of providing ineffective therapy based on myth and unexamined assumptions rather than on empirical evidence. The benefits of therapy, understood as changing unsatisfying patterns of thoughts, feelings, or behaviors to more satisfying ones, can be accurately summarized, as can the smaller risk of counseling-induced emotional distress or interpersonal disruption, as in the case of the increased risk of divorce when one partner is in individual counseling and the other partner is uninvolved in the therapy process (citation). Our ethics and our knowledge base go hand in hand. Risks and benefits statements should be tied in fidelity to our professional knowledge base to what we know from the research evidence about how therapy influences peoples' lives.

5. Alternatives to treatment. Alternatives to treatment range from doing nothing to having an evaluation for medication, obtaining counseling from a counselor practicing from a different theoretical perspective, talking to trusted family members or friends, participating in self-help groups, utilizing body-based therapies like acupuncture, meditation, or massage, or utilizing some combination of available treatments.

6. Competence and lack of coercion. A person making an informed consent for mental health treatment must be competent and free from undue coercion. For example, a person actively under the influence of a mind-altering substance would hardly be in a position of competence required to make an informed consent for treatment. Likewise, a grandmother who reluctantly attends counseling because her adult daughter and son-in-law demand that she do so in order to continue seeing her grandchildren is not providing a freely given informed consent for treatment under such conditions of coercion.

7. Right to refuse or discontinue treatment without penalty. Informed consent documents must also clearly state that a person has the right to either refuse or discontinue treatment at any time without penalty.

8. Office hours, contact information, and what to do in the event of an emergency. In this section of the informed consent document, the counselor or counseling organization would include information about standard office hours, procedures for contacting the counselor after hours in the event of an emergency, and what to do in the event of a crisis, including emergency referral telephone numbers and addresses of crisis stabilization units, suicide hotlines, and domestic violence shelters.

9. Fee structure and payment issues. The fee structure of the counselor or clinic, payment expectations and arrangements, and issues relating to third-party insurance should all be clearly specified in this section of the informed consent document.

10. Privacy of private health information. How clients' private health information will be stored and utilized in conformity with HIPAA will also be clearly specified. For example, counselors and counseling organizations need to clearly state that clients' private health information will be used for purposes of providing treatment, for receiving clinical supervision, and where appropriate, for training, education, and research purposes. See Chapter 14 for an example of an informed consent for supervisor's document that addresses issues of privacy among many other key elements.

SYSTEMIC AND MULTICULTURAL CONSIDERATIONS IN INFORMED CONSENT PROCEDURES

Informed consent procedures are based on the western notion of the person as a self-contained, individual self. Western jurisprudence is based on this notion, as are the ethical principles of autonomy and self-determination. Emphasizing the right of the self to determine its own future protects against unwanted interference from governments, police power, religious institutions, and individual persons in positions of power and authority. The philosophical underpinnings of such a view assume that there are always clear boundaries between the self and others, and this is just not always the case when we consider the mutual influence of family, community, and culture on the individual. Kuczewski and McCruden (2001) remind us that "Although it is fine to speak about the rights of the individual, respecting patient autonomy usually requires a process of collaborative decision making. This process involves not only the patient and physician but those who are close to the patient. Patient autonomy becomes a reality when treatment decisions are made in the way that patients typically make their other significant decisions" (p. 34).

Kuczewski and McCruden (2001) situate the process of informed consent into a relational perspective and emphasize that the decisions about treatment that individual clients make will always reflect values and other elements of their culture as well as the values and priorities of their families. It is important, therefore, for the counselor at the informed consent stage to actively encourage clients to explore the meaning of counseling within the context of their culture and family. Sometimes it may be important for counselors to encourage the client to consult with family members about proceeding with treatment before making a decision to do so. With the client's permission, the counselor may also consider inviting significant family members of the client's choosing into the process of making informed consent for treatment decisions. There may be a practical advantage for the counselor in doing so when working with individual clients, insofar as family members who have been meaningfully involved in the informed consent to treatment stage will be more likely to support their family member through the counseling process.

The systemic implications of informed consent become quickly obvious when clients are involved with larger systems and find themselves in counseling in which the larger system also has a vested interest. For example, if a probation officer or the Department of Children and

Families is considering certain actions that are likely to affect the well-being of the client and impact the counseling relationship, what obligations does a counselor have, with the client's consent, to inform that larger system's representatives of the likely outcomes of their anticipated actions and to make recommendations on a client's behalf? The clinical case in Box 7.3 illustrates some of these issues in working with clients involved in multiple systems.

BOX 7.3

CASE EXAMPLE: HOW FAR DOES INFORMED CONSENT EXTEND AND TO WHOM IN MULTISYSTEM CASES?

A counselor was referred a case of a 12-year-old girl and her parents by the Department of Children and Families. The girl had been removed from her home after school personnel had made an allegation of sexual molestation by her father to the authorities. School personnel had been acting on information revealed to them by the girl herself. The case had wound its way through the juvenile justice system and was ultimately closed out as being "unfounded." After mandatory counseling, the child was placed back with her parents, although no one in the system was comfortable with the outcome. School personnel, who had been proactive in the case from the start, encouraged the family to continue family counseling privately. The Department of Children and Families was no longer involved in the case, and the father had engaged a private defense attorney after the initial allegation and was still in fairly regular consultation with his attorney.

One of the first things the counselor did was to stress the importance of establishing sacred and inviolate boundaries in the house for the girl that would not be breached by anyone. These boundaries included setting up the girl's bedroom and bathroom as a sacred and inviolate space that was hers alone to control and keep locked, as she wished. The boundary issue was more difficult for the mother to accept than for the father because the mother saw it as a violation of her idea of community and shared space within the family. The mother had vacillated between believing her husband, who denied the abuse allegation, and her daughter, who had made a convincing case for it.

After the question of spatial boundaries in the family had been agreed to, counseling quickly centered on the daughter's request for an admission from her father that he had abused her. Her father was fairly mute during counseling around this issue, neither admitting nor denying the abuse. The mother wanted to move on with her family life without having to explicitly address the issue of her husband's alleged abuse. The daughter, to her credit, was persistent in demanding acknowledgment of the abuse and said that she could get beyond it if her father admitted that he had done it.

With consent from the father to consult with his attorney, the counselor contacted the father's attorney and told him that the daughter's emotional and mental health and any possibility of reconciliation with her father depended on the father's acknowledging the abuse. The attorney's response to the counselor and to the father was to say that he could not advise his client to incriminate himself and that his client had the right to remain silent. Within a fairly short period of time, the mother said that she could not deal with the spatial walling off of her household and the competing demands for the father to acknowledge the abuse and face the reinitiation of criminal charges of sexual molestation or remain silent and hurt their daughter more. The mother filed for divorce, took her daughter, and left her husband.

Since the attorney was a key figure in this multisystem case, did the need for informed consent emphasizing the adverse consequences of certain courses of action in the therapy—namely, advising his client to remain silent—extend to him? This difficult case illustrates how full informed consent, in certain situations, sets constraints that can complicate rather than facilitate the therapeutic process. In this case, full informed consent stunted the therapy process because the father refused to participate meaningfully out of a fear of self-incrimination and ensuing legal consequences.

The counselor only spoke to the attorney on the phone, outlining the importance of the father's acknowledgment of the abuse for the daughter's recovery. Should the counselor have been a much stronger advocate for the daughter with the attorney by sending him excerpts from the professional literature emphasizing the importance of acknowledgment of abuse and by inscribing her phone advocacy in writing?

Reflecting most real-world clinical situations, this case involved not only informed consent but also confidentiality and boundaries/conflicts of interests. So, while the case highlighted the informed consent issue, the counselor also needed to account for the other two ethical-professional considerations—really three, because counselor competence was also implicitly involved.

INFORMED CONSENT AND MINORS

One of the more challenging areas of informed consent practice is the issue of the right of minors to be provided treatment and whether treatment requires the consent of parents or legal guardians. Ordinarily, minors cannot consent to their own treatment, and counselors must obtain consent from parents or legal guardians. For children who have been adjudicated dependent by a state court and are therefore in the custody of the state, the state's legal representative, usually an official from the state's Department of Children and Families or equivalent unit, is authorized to sign the consent for treatment. The rationale for requiring parental consent for the treatment of minors is the recognition of minors as a vulnerable group lacking full capacity to make informed decisions about their own care. If we consider age 18 to be the age of majority (however, the age of majority varies depending on the context; for example, one must be 21 to drink alcohol legally), there is clearly a difference between the decision-making capacity of a 7-year-old and that of a 15-year-old. These developmental differences complicate the issue of informed consent for minors and can be handled, if appropriate, by the use of an assent to treatment.

Assent to Treatment

An assent to treatment is a consent given by minors who have the capacity to have some meaningful understanding of the process of therapy that they are about to participate in. While not legally obligatory, an assent to treatment by a minor involves the minor in a respectful way in making decisions about his or her own mental health care. Most sensitive and skilled counselors already obtain assent for treatment from capable minors by discussing the process of counseling with them beforehand, answering any questions they may have, including those concerning what kind of disclosures might be made to their parents, and by clearly describing the exceptions to confidentiality. Some counselors develop a formal assent to treatment form for minors to parallel the consent to treatment form to be signed by their parents or legal guardians.

Exceptions to the General Requirement of Parental Consent

There are exceptions to the typical rule of requiring parental consent for the treatment of minors. Among them is the case of emancipated youth or youth in legal marriages. In both of these cases, most jurisdictions recognize the rights of minors to consent to their own treatment. Additionally, many state legislatures have specified certain exceptions to parental consent requirements, usually surrounding sexual and reproductive issues such as obtaining birth control or abortions or obtaining diagnostic testing and treatment for sexually transmitted diseases.

Many states also specify the right of minors over a certain age to seek evaluation for a mental health disorder and to seek crisis intervention for a period of time prior to obtaining parental consent. For example, for adolescents ages 13 and up, the state of Florida permits outpatient mental health diagnostic and evaluation services and outpatient crisis intervention, therapy, and counseling services not to exceed two visits in any one-week period prior to obtaining parental consent for treatment (2004 F.S. 394.4784).

The least problematic context for providing mental health treatment to minors is when the minor is brought to therapy by a parent or legal guardian who is authorized to provide consent on behalf of the minor. If individual counseling is to be the primary treatment modality for the minor, then the informed consent document should specify the nature and limits of confidentiality, what exceptions to confidentiality would be made, and to whom disclosure would be made, should the need arise (see the case in Box 7.4).

BOX 7.4

CASE EXAMPLE: A GRIEVING TEEN FROM A RELIGIOUS FAMILY CURSES GOD

A 16-year-old male adolescent was brought to therapy by his father and his father's fiancée. The teen's mother had been killed about eighteen months earlier in a motorcycle accident, and the teen, according to his father and his father's fiancée, had been demonstrating an angry and aggressive attitude in the house by talking back and generally disregarding directions. In addition, his grades were poor, and his father thought the teen should be doing better than he was eighteen months after his mother's death. The family members were evangelical Christians and relied on their religious beliefs and practices to help them through the mother's death and to help them understand that her death was part of a larger plan by God that they were not fully able to comprehend. The family agreed to individual counseling for the son because he was 16 and seemed to need professional help to deal with his grief. The counselor had a clear statement about the exceptions to confidentiality in his informed consent document and, further, had discussed with the father the developmental appropriateness of individual therapy for his adolescent son. The father agreed to the conditions of therapy for his son and agreed that individual counseling for him made sense.

(continued)

BOX 7.4 CONTINUED

The counselor and teen developed a strong therapeutic alliance fairly quickly, and it was obvious to the counselor that the teen had not really grieved his mother's death and that he was benefiting tremendously from the emotionally supportive context of counseling. The teen was beginning to express feelings of rage and anger at both his mother for dying on a motorbike and at his father for so quickly becoming involved with another woman and planning to get remarried. The teen freely expressed his rage and anger at God for letting all of this happen to his family and cursed God repeatedly. The teen was doing better at school and had substituted distance and aloofness for defiance in responding to his father. While the father was not happy with his son's aloofness, he saw it as better than aggressiveness and was pleased about his son's academic improvement. The counselor was pleased by the teen's increasing ability to identify and express his intense feelings of hurt, anger, and betrayal and felt that the teen was managing such strong feelings in an appropriate way and beginning to be less overpowered by those feelings.

Trouble emerged when the teen started cursing God to his father after they had gotten into an argument over how the teen had spoken to the father's fiancée. The father was furious and confronted the counselor about whether he permitted such behavior during the counseling sessions. The teen had told his father that the counselor let him curse God as much as he wanted and that the counselor didn't care whether he did it or not. The father demanded an accounting from the counselor of the subject matter of the counseling sessions with his son. The counselor attempted to defuse the situation and keep the teen in therapy by explaining to the father that anger at God was a fairly normal response to serious trauma. The father withdrew his consent for the teen to continue in therapy, and the case was lost to follow-up.

Was this case doomed to failure from the beginning, or should the counselor have provided more information to the teen's father prior to the beginning of therapy with the son? Should the counselor have anticipated areas of conflict with the father emerging during therapy and discussed them with him beforehand? Would providing a more thorough picture of possible behavior changes during therapy, including disimprovement, have increased the likelihood of the father's sustained commitment to his son's therapy?

INVOLUNTARY COMMITMENT AND INFORMED CONSENT

By its nature, involuntary commitment is the most far-reaching and powerful act a mental health care provider can take to care for and protect the well-being of a client. Involuntary commitment involves the loss of self-determination generally afforded to persons in free societies and therefore can never be undertaken lightly. It results in the deprivation of a person's civil rights in the same way that imprisonment results in the deprivation of one's civil rights, albeit that the initiating cause is different. It is a social control function and not a therapeutic function, and counselors need to keep these distinctions clear. Involuntary commitment relies on two powers of the state: the power of the state to act in the role of parent to a person deemed unable to care for him- or herself and the police power of the state to forcibly detain someone who has been determined to be a threat to him- or herself or to another (Behnke, Winick, & Perez, 2000).

The history of psychiatry in the United States and worldwide is replete with abuses of the power to involuntarily commit persons to psychiatric institutions. Abuse of this power has been undertaken for political purposes, for the domination of women, and for reasons of punishment and retribution. As a result of the checkered history of involuntary confinement to mental hospitals and because of the pervasive effects of such confinement on one's personal liberties, a mental health professional's decision to sign a certificate for confinement for involuntary examination must be based on the highest standard of care for the well-being of the client and on the highest standard of professional competence.

In general, the procedure for involuntary commitment in most states includes a referral for involuntary commitment during which the person may be held for a relatively short time against his or her will in order that a psychiatric evaluation may be conducted. After the evaluation is conducted and within the designated period of time, a legal hearing must be held if the results of the psychiatric evaluation indicate a recommendation for continued hospitalization that the patient disagrees with or refuses to comply with on a voluntary basis. During the hearing, the patient has a right to a private attorney or to a state-appointed one in order to represent his or her interests. The state attorney represents the interests of the receiving facility in continuing to hold the patient recommended for involuntary treatment. By definition, involuntary commitment eliminates the need for informed consent from the client or patient. On the other hand, involuntary commitment increases the need for informed awareness of the heavy legal and ethical responsibilities incumbent on the referring mental health provider to follow a demonstrable standard of clinical judgment and demonstrable adherence to the clinical ethic of care for one's client, including the duty to protect.

In Florida (Behnke et al., 2000), for example, the standards for referral for an involuntary psychiatric evaluation include the presence of a mental illness, the unwillingness or inability of the client to self-reflectively see the need for an examination and agree to one, and the fact that the person is at risk of harming him- or herself either through self-neglect or more proactively or is at risk of harming another. All of these conditions must be met in the state of Florida, for instance, before a mental health provider recognized by law to certify a person for an involuntary commitment can do so.

In the case of involuntary commitment, mental illness is defined by statute and tends to be more restrictive than the definition of mental illness found in the *Diagnostic and Statistical Manual of Mental Disorders, Fourth Edition, Text Revision* (DSM-IV TR) (American Psychiatric Association, 2000). It is therefore ethically incumbent on the counselors or therapists to be fully aware of the definitions and provisions of involuntary commitment statutes used in their jurisdictions. Because state laws use a good faith standard to evaluate the actions of mental health providers in referring persons for involuntary commitment, this standard tends to protect them against liability for their actions; however, the protection is not absolute. The good faith standard reduces liability while increasing the demands for ethical awareness and action on the part of the therapist. The use of power to deny someone his or her civil liberties should never be taken lightly, and should be done only if full accordance with the intent of the law—which is to care for and protect a mentally ill person who is a risk to him- or herself or to another and who is refusing, or incapable of seeing the need for, help through voluntary mental health care.

Many states also have involuntary commitment statutes for persons who are at risk to themselves or others because of impairment of judgment caused by substance abuse. Involuntary commitment for substance abuse statutes generally have been enacted in order to provide family members with a means of getting help for their loved ones who are denying or minimizing the risk of harm due to their impaired judgment caused by substance misuse. Counselors and therapists are often involved in the process of involuntary commitment of a patient for evaluation of a substance abuse risk to self or others either by providing information and assistance to family members or by bringing the at-risk substance abuser to the attention of the law enforcement authorities responsible for the implementation of the involuntary commitment procedures. In substance abuse involuntary commitment, there is also a two-step process involving an evaluation and then a legal hearing.

The ethical implications for counselors and therapists of involuntary commitment procedures center on awareness of the nature of the differential in the power relationship between the patient or client and the mental health professional. Even though legal safeguards in the form of hearings to review and protect the civil rights of the involuntarily committed person are in place and guaranteed by statute, there is no denying the significantly greater power of the mental health professional in the context of involuntary commitment. The mental health professional is recognized as the expert, and the mentally ill or substance-abusing person is by definition operating at significantly reduced capacity.

While the burden of proof is on the state to demonstrate impairment and risk to self or another, the power of privilege and discourse is vested in the hands of the counselor, therapist, or other mental health professional. The ethically competent therapist is mindful of this huge power differential, is continuously aware of the power of his or her recommendations to determine the freedom of the patient or client, ensures personal ethical behavior by ongoing reflection about clinical decisions, keeps updated about changes in civil commitment laws and procedures, takes seriously the ethics of ongoing professional development to maintain a high standard of professional competence, and consults regularly with colleagues about challenging clinical cases and decisions.

Participation in involuntary commitment procedures, which by definition bypass the need for informed consent, is no place for the Perspective I counselor who is practicing defensively and from the letter of the law. The Perspective III counselor who is reflexively aware of the influence of his or her presence and recommendations on the construction of reality about another and who has a history of personal and professional development and integration of ethical decision making is the only qualified practitioner skilled enough and ethically competent enough to participate in such serious proceedings in which the power differential and stakes are so high.

ONLINE COUNSELING AND INFORMED CONSENT

In October 1999, the Governing Council of the American Counseling Association approved their "Ethical Standards for Internet Online Counseling." These guidelines attempt to provide counselors offering online counseling services with some basic standards for addressing issues of confidentiality, privacy of communications, client access to the counselor, and backup plans for handling online client emergencies. Because of the unique nature of the online counseling relationship, the process of informed consent must include all of the standard key elements, but must also attend to online issues related to, for example, security of the websites and servers, expected turnaround time for counselor responses to client queries, determining the appropriateness of online counseling for a particular client, and providing backup professional help and referrals in the event of a client emergency. Additionally, the counselor must establish whether it is legal in his or her jurisdiction to provide online counseling to clients who may live in a state or states other than the one(s) in which the counselor is licensed.

The American Counseling Association's (1999) guidelines allow counselors to provide one-on-one counseling to clients only through secured websites or through email software using encryption technology. Counselors who do not have secure websites or encryption technology are allowed to provide only general mental health guidelines on particular topics, but may not provide personalized, individual counseling to online clients. Even so, these guidelines require the clients to sign waivers of confidentiality indicating that they are aware that, despite the best efforts to ensure the privacy and confidentiality of the online counseling process, the counselor cannot be held responsible for any breaches of that privacy that may occur. In other words, the client is required to assume the risk of a theoretical breach of confidentiality in order to obtain the benefit of the online service, and the counselor is required to use due diligence by providing an encryption package and/or a secure website.

Professional counselors are mandated by their ethical standards to assess the appropriateness of online counseling for their prospective clients through an intake procedure and to clearly inform clients of the limitations, risks, and benefits of online counseling as well as available face-to-face alternatives. The American Counseling Association also requires its members to provide online clients with the name and telephone number of at least one professional counselor located in their area as well as the standard information about how to access the online client in an emergency. These special requirements are in addition to the standard elements of informed consent discussed previously.

One of the areas not covered by the American Counseling Association's "Ethical Standards for Internet Online Counseling" (1999) but that is covered by the International Society for Mental Health Online's (2000) "Suggested Principles for the Online Provision of Mental Health Services" is the issue of language and context and the potential for confusion or misunderstanding because of the absence of nonverbal cues in the online counseling process. This issue seems important given that observation of the nonverbal presentation of affect is a significant source of client data for the treating counselor.

For the ethical counselor, the concerns about online counseling are real and require attention and reflection. On the other hand, there are benefits for clients of online counseling that are also real. A client can communicate through email at any time of the day or night and can communicate feelings when they are most intense. For some clients, these benefits may be significant.

KEY POINTS

1. Informed consent is a relational process between counselor and client and not just a signed and witnessed document.
2. Informed consent reflects the active participation in health care decision making of the client and involves a process of reading, talking, reflecting, negotiating, and writing.
3. The ethical principles of care, autonomy, and self-determination are at the heart of the informed consent process.
4. Lack of informed consent for treatment can technically be regarded as criminal battery.

5. Providing specific information about a client's proposed mental health care involves power sharing between counselor and client.
6. The informed consent document must be written in clear and easy-to-understand language.
7. The counselor must provide the client with information about the nature of the counseling process, the counselor's theoretical model and treatment approach, and who will be involved in the counseling process.
8. The counselor must also provide information about his or her credentials, licensures, and the nature of confidentiality in the counseling relationship and exceptions to it.
9. Risks and benefits of treatment, alternatives, and the right to refuse or discontinue counseling must also be discussed in the informed consent process, as well as information about payment and how to contact the counselor in an emergency.
10. The process of informed consent requires that a person be competent and free from coercion in agreeing to counseling or other mental health care treatment.
11. Cultural, familial, and systemic factors influence the informed consent process, and counselors need to be sensitive to how best to include these dimensions.
12. In general, minors may not consent to their own treatment, except as provided for by law, and require the consent of their parents or legal guardians. Counselors must respect the developmental status of minors and can include them in the informed consent process through collaborative discussion and/or the use of an assent to treatment form.
13. Involuntary commitment is a social control function designed to protect a client and/or others from harm. It involves a profound and serious use of power on the part of the mental health care provider and must only be used with a great deal of care, reflection, and professional consultation or supervision.
14. Online counseling presents unique issues in the management of informed consent, in particular issues dealing with privacy and the absence of nonverbal cues in the counseling process.
15. Informed consent is primarily means of promoting client choice and self-determination in mental health care and not primarily a tool for protecting the counselor from liability.

CONCLUDING NOTE: PERSPECTIVE I VERSUS III

Informed consent is a process that provides safeguards and benefits for both the client and counselor. However protective the process of informed consent may be for the counselor, it should be recognized primarily as a process for the promotion and enhancement of clients' well-being. At its best, the informed consent process is a relational one in which the counselor and client collaborate in a power-sharing agreement that enhances trust in the counseling relationship and process. Informed consent rests on an ethic of care for the client from within which the counselor meticulously lays out all the details needed by the client to make an informed decision whether the particular counseling service offered is best for him or her. The counselor defers to the authority of the client's rights to self-agency and self-determination by providing an accurate and comprehensive informed consent procedure.

The integrative, Perspective III counselor is not personally threatened or diminished by the detail and rigor of the informed consent process, but rather appreciates it as an ethical discipline and as a basic means of respect and care for the client. In the Perspective III approach, informed consent is a living, dynamic process in which the quality and strength of the therapeutic relationship creates a context for clinically appropriate, ongoing review of the direction and effectiveness of therapy that includes both the therapist and client in collaborative reflection and conversation. Through this process of collaborative review and reflection on the therapy process, the client gains more information about ongoing treatment plans and goals and is therefore able to make an ongoing informed consent decision about whether to continue in therapy or request changes. The Perspective III therapist or counselor welcomes the openness and collaboration with the client that is basic to the practice of informed consent as an ongoing relational process.

REVIEW QUESTIONS

1. Do you think that the informed consent process benefits the clients or the counselor more?
2. Do you think clients, during their initial counseling session, are capable of attending to and absorbing all of the information presented to them in an informed consent document?
3. Under what circumstances would you counsel someone without first obtaining informed consent?
4. Do you think it is ethical to counsel a child who does not consent to treatment?
5. What are your views on mandatorily referred clients? Do you think it is possible to obtain informed consent from these clients? Do you think effective counseling is possible for someone who did not choose to enter into counseling?

REFERENCES

American Counseling Association. (1999). *Ethical standards for internet online counseling.* [Online]. available: Http://www.counseling.org/Content/NavigationMenu/RESOURCES/ETHICS/

American Psychiatric Association. (2000). *Diagnostic and statistical manual of mental disorders* (4th ed., Text revision). Washington, DC: Author.

Anderson, H., & Goolishian, H. (1988). Human systems as linguistic systems: Preliminary and evolving ideas about the implications for clinical theory. *Family Process, 27,* 371–393.

Behnke, S. H., Winick, B. J., & Perez, A. M. (2000). *The essentials of Florida mental health law: A straightforward guide for clinicians of all disciplines.* New York: Norton.

Florida Statutes. (2004). 394.4784.

Gottman, J. M. (1999). *The marriage clinic: A scientifically based marital therapy.* New York: Norton.

Howard, M. L. (2002). Informed consent. *eMedicine,* 1–9. [Online]. Available: Http://www.emedicine.com/ent/topic181.htm

International Society for Mental Health Online (2000). *Suggested principles for online provision of mental health services.* [Online]. Available: Http://www.ismho.org/suggestions.html

Kuczewski, M., & McCruden, P. J. (2001). Informed consent: Does it take a village? The problem of culture and truth telling. *Cambridge Quarterly of Healthcare Ethics, 10,* 34–46.

McCurdy, K. G., & Murray, K. C. (2003). Confidentiality issues when minor children disclose family secrets in family counseling. *The Family Journal: Counseling and Therapy for Couples and Families, 11,* 393–398.

Pinsoff, W. M., & Wynne, L. C. (1995). The efficacy of marital and family therapy: An empirical overview, conclusions, and recommendations. *Journal of Marital and Family Therapy, 21,* 585–610.

Rosoff, A. J. (1981). *Informed consent: A guide for health care providers.* Rockville, MD: Aspen.

Walter, M. I., & Handelsman, M. M. (1996). Informed consent for mental health counseling: Effects of information specificity on clients' ratings of counselors. *Journal of Mental Health Counseling, 18,* 253–263.

CHAPTER 8

CONFLICT OF INTEREST, BOUNDARIES, AND THE USE OF POWER

MAUREEN DUFFY

Essentially, a boundary can be thought of as the frame and limits surrounding a therapeutic relationship that defines a set of roles and rules for relating for both client and therapist. Because of a power differential between clients and therapists, and because clients are in a vulnerable position, adequate boundaries serve to protect the client's welfare. The concept of boundary is central to understanding conflicts of interests and involves two polar positions: the categorical boundaries view and the dimensional boundary view, wherein boundary crossings and boundary violations are a major point of contention. In the categorical view, boundaries are seen as part of human interaction with the purpose of delineating role functions and of facilitating the therapeutic process (Fay, 2002). In this view, boundaries in professional relationships are considered immutable, not open to debate, and not to be crossed for any reason. Furthermore, such boundary crossings are viewed as a slippery slope that eventually results in serious boundary violations. In the dimensional view, even though professional relationships involve power differentials, relationships are not viewed as inherently abusive or exploitive (Fay, 2002). Even though boundaries are useful and necessary in professional relationships, they can be discussed openly by mental health professional and client, and boundary crossings, when appropriate, can facilitate the therapeutic relationship and treatment outcomes.

Boundary issues are important in counseling because of the inherently vulnerable position of a client in therapy. By exposing their emotional, cognitive, and interpersonal needs and difficulties during counseling, clients are in a position of reduced power and greater vulnerability in relationship to the therapist. The therapist has the ethical obligation to be conscious of this power imbalance and the vulnerability of the client and to act in accordance with ethical principles that promote the client's well-being and care.

This chapter is entitled "Conflict of Interest, Boundaries, and the Use of Power," so what do boundaries have to do with conflicts of interest? In counseling and psychotherapy a conflict of interest arises when a counselor or therapist has competing interests that would get in the way of faithfully exercising his or her professional judgment and skill in working with clients. An example would be a therapist who saw the wife of her husband's boss in therapy. The therapist's clinical judgment could be affected by a competing concern not to upset the client's husband because he had influence over the therapist's husband.

When the counselor's or therapist's needs and interests prevail—that is, come before the client's needs, interests, and overall welfare—abuse of power and boundary violations are classic indicators of such a conflict. The counseling and psychotherapy literature is filled with discussions of boundary violations such as harmful dual relationships, sexual exploitation of clients, and conflicts of interest (Corey & Herlihy, 1997; Doyle, 1997; Hill & Mamalakis, 2001; Lazarus & Zur, 2002; Reamer, 2001, 2003; St. Germaine, 1996; Stake & Oliver, 1991; Woody, 1998; Zur, 2004).

The literature on boundary violations and dual or multiple relationships in therapy is becoming more sophisticated and reflects increasing attention to the complexities of some dual relationships and the risk in applying a rigid and inflexible understanding of boundaries to ethical dilemmas. It should not be too surprising that conflicts of interest and boundary issues are among the most common ethical issues that are reviewed by licensure boards, certification boards, and professional ethics committees. This suggests the concern that practicing counselors and therapists experience about these issues.

A consensus exists that sexual relationships with clients and other dual relationships based on abuse of power, exploitation, and conflict of interest are uniformly unethical. However, there is growing recognition of the unavoidability of some dual relationships and even their desirability in certain situations (Lazarus & Zur, 2002; Reamer, 2003; Zur, 2004). Tomm (2002) contends that the ethical focus on dual relationships in psychotherapy misses the point and that the focus should be on exploitation and the profound harm caused by abuse of power in therapeutic relationships and not on dual relationships, many of which are unavoidable and desirable in the natural ecology of relationships.

From the theoretical point of view, a number of writers have provided a useful distinction between boundary violations and boundary crossings (Gutheil & Gabbard, 1993; Lazarus & Zur, 2002; Smith & Fitzpatrick, 1995; Zur, 2004). This distinction between boundary violation and boundary crossing is a useful tool for helping counselors to evaluate the ethics of proposed therapeutic relationships or strategies. Boundary violations occur as a result of exploitation of clients, abuse of power, coercion, deception, or misrepresentation. The classic example, of course, is that of the counselor who engages in a sexual relationship with a client. Boundary crossings, on the other hand, are described by Lazarus and Zur (2002) and Zur (2004) as any deviation from emotionally distant, psychoanalytically derived, office-based therapeutic practice and may be tremendously helpful for clients. Judicious therapist self-disclosure, going for a walk with a reluctant teenager, participating in worship services in a church where a client is also a member are all examples of boundary crossings that may actually promote client welfare and enhance therapeutic outcomes.

Perspective I ethics holds that boundaries are rigid and inflexible and applies a dichotomous right/wrong logic to resolving ethical dilemmas involving use of therapist power and boundary issues. Perspective III ethics holds that boundaries are more flexible and complex and that the distinction between boundary violation and boundary crossing is an ethically useful one because it calls attention to the more important question of whether exploitation and abuse of power are present in particular situations.

This chapter begins a general discussion of conflicts of interest and boundary issues that will be further detailed in the various chapters of Part III. The chapter begins by contextualizing and situating conflicts of interest, boundaries, and the use of power within the counseling relationship. It proceeds to describe and illustrate boundary crossings, boundary violations, and dual or multiple relationships and the various factors that foster appropriate boundaries.

LEARNING OBJECTIVES

After reading this chapter you should be able to

1. Develop a theoretical and working understanding of the concept of boundaries in the counseling relationship.
2. Define and understand the distinctions between dual relationships, boundary violations, and boundary crossings.
3. Develop a set of operating criteria with which to evaluate whether a boundary crossing or dual relationship is ethical.
4. Understand the origins of concern for respecting clinical boundaries as arising from the ethical principles of care, beneficence, and nonmaleficence.
5. Discuss the differences in understanding the issue of boundaries and use of power from Perspectives I, II, and III.

KEY TERMS

boundary
boundary crossings
boundary violations
categorical boundaries view
conflict of interest
dimensional boundaries view
dual (or multiple) relationship

THE CONTEXTUAL DOMAIN AND CONFLICT OF INTEREST, BOUNDARIES, AND THE USE OF POWER

All three contextual domains—namely, the personal-developmental, the relational-multicultural, and the organizational ethics–community values—have significant impact on the therapist or counselor with regard to the core ethical issues of conflict of interest, boundaries, and use of power.

Personal-Developmental

In the personal-developmental dimension, boundary violations such as romantic or sexual involvement with clients reflect therapist abandonment of relational responsibility (McNamee & Gergen, 1998) to their clients. Abandonment of relational responsibility represents therapist neglect of a primary clinical obligation to be aware of how one is viewing the client and the implications of that particular viewing of the client at that time. If the therapist assumes a superior, "I know what is best" attitude toward the client and neglects to reflexively examine that attitude, then the therapist is at greater risk of exploitative boundary violations of the client. Lack of attention to self-of-therapist issues, countertransference issues, and lack of appropriate consultation and supervision all leave the therapist more open to conflict of interest and boundary violations. Conversely, the therapist who appreciates the power imbalance inherent in the therapeutic relationship and who accepts the responsibilities of relationship with clients by seeking personal therapy when needed, participating in clinical consultation and supervision, and participating in active self-care is at reduced risk of conflict of interest and boundary violations.

Relational-Multicultural

At the relational-multicultural level, gender and multicultural factors are significantly involved in therapist decision making about particular practices in clinical situations. Touch is a good example. In Hispanic communities, for example, hugs or embraces are commonly exchanged between therapist and client at the beginning and end of a session. In this multicultural context, not to exchange a hug as a greeting or goodbye could represent a rejection or insult to the client. In another example, a male therapist who typically does not touch clients may pat the shoulder of a female client sobbing over the loss of her mother, as a gesture of support and caring. How surprised that male therapist might be if the female client reacted negatively and told the male therapist to stop patronizing her or if she asked him if he would make the same gesture of support to a male client in emotional distress. In this case, issues of gender would be at play. These examples underline the importance of therapists and counselors taking seriously the obligation to become multiculturally competent practitioners.

A therapist's past history of ruptures and disturbances in the therapeutic relationship may also be an indicator of future behavior and decision making about boundary violations and conflicts of interest. If the therapist or counselor had a history of accepting expensive gifts from affluent clients, it is not unreasonable to think that the therapist would continue to inappropriately accept such gifts. Likewise, if a therapist begins to violate boundaries and touch clients inappropriately, the likelihood is that such exploitative behavior would continue unless effective interventions could be introduced into the situation. Past experiences or ruptures in the therapeutic relationship are important areas of exploration in clinical supervision and in the exercise of personal-relational responsibility.

Organizational Ethics–Community Values

In the organizational ethics–community values dimension, the norms and practices of the organization and community also influence the degree to which a clear position is taken about maintaining boundaries between therapists and clients and avoiding conflicts of interest. Does the organization or clinic have clear policies about maintaining boundaries between therapists and clients and sanctions for violations of those boundaries? Are issues of power and exploitation raised and discussed in clinical supervision and professional development activities? Do the agency itself and its senior personnel model maintaining clear boundaries and avoiding conflicts of interest? In other words, to what degree would a novice therapist working in this organization recognize the organization's stance around boundary violations and conflicts of interest? To the extent that the organization has clear policies about conflicts of interest and boundary violations and makes space for dialogue about such issues, the likelihood increases that the therapists and counselors working there will be more aware of and less likely to commit boundary violations.

The therapist or counselor is also working within a particular community with its own norms and standards regarding tolerance for unethical and exploitive behavior. These community norms and standards also influence individual therapist and counselor behaviors. In communities where corruption at the highest levels of government and power are commonplace and brushed aside or laughed at, the community standard of what constitutes acceptable behavior for those in positions of power is lowered. Therapists and counselors are not immune to how high or low the bar for ethical behavior in their community is set for those in positions of authority. Therefore, ethical therapists or counselors would do well to examine the community standards for ethical behavior where they live and practice and consider initiating dialogue with other mental health professionals about the influence of those community standards on their own clinical ethics.

POWER IN COUNSELING AND PSYCHOTHERAPEUTIC RELATIONSHIPS

Counseling and psychotherapy involve a unique relationship. While counseling and psychotherapy involve the sharing of personal information and verbal, emotional intimacies, these intimacies are ordinarily unidirectional, that is, from the client to the counselor or therapist and not the reverse. The nature of the therapeutic relationship is set up to promote the psychological and emotional healing of the client, not of the therapist. While a therapist's personal growth may be enhanced as a result of a particular therapeutic relationship, that is not the primary goal of therapy: The primary goal of therapy is the enhancement of the client's experience and life. The ethical principles of beneficence and care require that the counselor keep in mind what is best for the client and develop treatment plans and interventions accordingly.

Because it is the counselor's task to keep in mind what is in the best interest of the client and because the counselor's decisions and actions should be tied to a professional body of knowledge, there is an inherent power imbalance in the relationship. The counselor is in the position of the privileged knower having expert knowledge about psychological, emotional, and relational life that the client may not have. The average client defers to such expert knowledge. This imbalance in power exists whether the counselor practices from an expert position or tries to practice more collaboratively from a "not knowing" position. In either case, the counselor as a professional has ethical responsibilities to maintain competence and to act in the best interest of the client at all times.

The psychotherapeutic relationship is a formalized one. It is regulated by state licensing boards, usually under the state's agency for health care administration, and sanctions exist for violating provisions of licensure laws. The psychotherapeutic relationship is also governed by the ethical codes of the various professional associations whose members practice any form of psychotherapy or counseling. This formal relationship emphasizes the needs of the client, not those of the therapist, and supports the predominantly unidirectional flow of personal and emotional disclosures.

As such, psychotherapy is not a mutually reciprocal relationship like friendship in which emotional disclosures and feelings are freely exchanged in a more uncensored way by both parties. While psychotherapy shares some elements of friendship, such as openness, trust, positive regard, and support (Berzoff, 1989), psychotherapy is not and was never intended to be friendship. It is intended to be a vehicle of positive change for the client. While the therapist may also be enriched as a result of the relationship, that is not the goal of therapy.

This being said, the therapeutic relationship can be a powerful one for both the counselor and client, and counselors who have their own unmet emotional or relational needs are at greater risk of using the therapeutic relationship more for themselves than for their clients. Abuse of power in the psychotherapeutic relationship and boundary violations are more likely when the therapist neglects his or her own emotional self-care and acts from unrecognized emotional or relational needs.

Abuse of Power as a Process and Not an Event

Exploitation of clients and therapist abuse of power are processes for which there are warning signs. It is the therapist's obligation to pay attention to these warning signs as a part of the larger ethical requirement of therapist self-care. A parallel example is the case of the recovering alcoholic who must understand relapse as a process of thinking and acting that precedes his relapse and not as the single event in which he picks up the glass of whiskey and starts to drink again. There are patterns of thought and behavior that might incline a therapist to abuse of power and there are circumstances of life that may make a therapist more vulnerable to boundary violations.

Abuse of power occurs across a continuum of therapist behaviors, ranging from predatory sexual exploitation of clients under the guise of therapist–client sex "being good for the client" to providing therapy to current students or supervisees to scheduling unnecessary appointments after treatment goals have been met in order to continue generating income. Not all of these behaviors would be considered predatory. Edelwich and Brodsky (1991) describe predatory professionals who exploit others to satisfy their own needs as severely character disordered. This category of professional usually does not self-refer for treatment or rehabilitation but must be identified by others in the profession when the unethical and illegal behavior becomes known.

Other sexual boundary violations include becoming sexually attracted to a client *and* acting on that attraction by becoming romantically involved with the client. The sexual attraction itself may not represent a boundary violation, but failing to appropriately address it by seeking supervisory consultation or by referring the client to another therapist is a boundary violation. In such a case, the therapist would have had an opportunity to become aware of the degree of sexual attraction to the client and think through what was in the best interest of the client and what would represent ethically important self-care. If the therapist did not take the opportunity to reflect on his or her own sexual feelings about the relationship and the clinical implications for the client, this would be an example of the process of thought and action or inaction preceding actual boundary violations. Ignoring warning signs indicating a need for either supervisory consultation and/or personal therapy leaves a therapist more vulnerable to abusing therapeutic power and violating therapeutic boundaries. Boundary violations appear as discrete events, but actually represent a more complex process of inattention to one's professional conduct and ethics and inattention to one's own emotional and psychological well-being.

DUAL AND MULTIPLE RELATIONSHIPS

In general terms, a dual relationship refers to engaging in more than one role with another individual. Some writers use the term *multiple relationships* for professional relationships that involve the professional engaging in two or more roles simultaneously (Catalano, 1997; Corey & Herlihy, 1997). In a counseling context, a dual relationship refers to having both a counseling and another kind of relationship, such as a social or business relationship, with a client simultaneously. Dual relationships can be described as either complimentary or conflicting. A complimentary relationship refers to one in which the client benefits as a result of being involved in both relationships. On the other hand, in a conflicting dual relationship there is a conflict between the professional and nonprofessional relationships that results in the loss of professional objectivity and some detriment to the client (Ahia, 2003). Complimentary relationships involve boundary crossings, while conflicting dual relationships involve boundary violations. In this book we espouse the position that dual relationships are potentially either ethical or unethical, depending upon whether harm, exploitation, or abuse of power is present in the dual relationship.

The meeting of one's own needs at the expense of the client's needs is an example of an abuse of clinical power that sets the stage for dual relationships that are exploitive in nature and therefore harmful to the client. Such exploitive dual relationships represent boundary violations, not boundary crossings. Tomm (2002) questions the focus of the ethical codes on duality rather than on exploitation and interpersonal power and influence. In the two clinical cases cited later, in Boxes 8.2 and 8.3, both Anita and Helen were subject to the interpersonal power and influence of their therapists who chose to use that influence by talking about their own experiences and feelings rather than by focusing on those of their clients. In both cases, the self-disclosures were an abuse of therapist power and influence. In an essay on dual relationships available online, Tomm (n.d.) states: "Therapists could become complacent about their power and influence if they believed that they could not exploit clients by virtue of not having dual relationships with them. A therapist who is inclined to exploit clients does not need a dual relationship to do so. Various forms of exploitation and abuse, including sexual abuse, can take place within the therapeutic relationship and in the therapy room itself" (para. 6).

Tomm (2002) does not let us forget that it is the power and potential for exploitation and harmful influence behind the duality and not the dual relationship itself that should be the focus of concern in evaluating a dual relationship. The issue of dual relationships is a sticky one for therapists, and Tomm and others (Lazarus & Zur, 2002; Reamer, 2003; Zur, 2004) also raise issues for serious consideration in suggesting that some dual relationships can actually be beneficial to clients and should be applauded and not condemned.

The key question then is how to evaluate dual relationships and distinguish exploitive ones from nonexploitive ones. Dual relationships involving sex with current clients are uniformly regarded as serious boundary violations that are exploitive and manipulative. In the mental health professions overall, Olarte (1997) cites data suggesting that between 8 percent and 12 percent of male therapists acknowledge having had sexual relationships with current or former clients. If these percentages referred to a disease, we would be talking in terms of an epidemic. Anecdotal information also suggests that most disciplinary actions by state mental health licensing boards involve charges of improper sexual relationships between therapists and clients. There is debate about whether and when sex with former clients is justified. The ethical codes and state statutes weigh in differently on the subject, ranging from a prohibition of sexual involvement with former clients for a number of years after termination of therapy to prohibition in perpetuity. Nonsexual dual relationships cover a much wider landscape of possibilities and range from dual relationships with students and supervisees to dual relationships with clients as business partners. If we take seriously the contributions of Lazarus and Zur (2002), Reamer (2003), Tomm (2002), and Zur (2004) in holding that nonsexual dual relationships can benefit clients, then their evaluation must be made on a more case-by-case basis and include an assessment of the degree of power and influence that the therapist has over the client in the dual relationship and whose needs are primarily being served. Box 8.1 summarizes possible dual relationships between counselors and clients and classifies them in terms of whether they represent sexual or nonsexual dual relationships. Ethical decision making will govern the conclusion that a counselor might come to in evaluating whether a particular potential nonsexual dual relationship might be helpful or hurtful to the client. The elements of a template for evaluating the ethics of nonsexual dual relationships will be discussed later in the chapter.

BOX 8.1
SEXUAL AND NONSEXUAL DUAL RELATIONSHIPS (MAY OR MAY NOT BE HURTFUL TO CLIENTS)

SEXUAL	NONSEXUAL
Predatory sexual behavior within the therapy session under the guise of its being therapeutic. This behavior is exploitive, manipulative, power-driven, unethical, and illegal.	Entering into business relationships or partnerships with clients during therapy.
Dating and/or becoming sexually involved with a client during therapy.	Becoming friends with clients and/or socializing with them during therapy or accepting existing friends as clients.
Dating and/or becoming sexually involved with a former client within a period of time after termination of therapy prohibited by either state law or professional association code of ethics.	Bartering therapy for goods or services from the client. This practice may or may not be acceptable, depending upon the context. Acceptable: In poor communities where bartering is accepted practice. Unacceptable: Client is massage therapist and therapist barters therapy for personal massages.
	Accepting a student, supervisee, or colleague as a client.

BOUNDARY VIOLATIONS

Boundary violations refer to exploitive or harmful practices in counseling and psychotherapy that occur when therapists cross standards of professional behavior for their own sexual, emotional, or financial gain. This section emphasizes the process of boundary violation and distinguishes sexual from nonsexual boundary violations.

Process versus Event

Similar to the earlier discussion on abuse of power as a process, boundary violations inevitably involve exploitation of the power differential between a therapist and a client as well as an erosion of appropriate boundaries. Increasingly, boundary violations are being understood as a process rather then isolated, discrete events that occur within the context of counseling. In this emerging understanding, boundary violations are viewed as the culminating instance in an ongoing process of ethical and boundary erosion that has taken place over a period of time (Peterson, 1992). By analogy, in substance abuse treatment, clients learn to conceptualize relapse not simply as a discrete event of satisfying an immediate craving but as a process of impaired thinking and action. In other words, relapse is not simply the event of taking a drink or drug again. Rather, it is a process of experiencing a craving, imagining and thinking about how good it will feel to use again, following by the conflicted deliberations over breaking one's resolve, the decision making, and the various behaviors of securing the substance that precedes the actual instance of taking or using the substance. This process is called abstinence violation.

Peterson (1992) provides compelling illustrations of how the boundary violation process typically plays itself out and occurs within the counseling relationship. This violation process is incremental, spans the course of several therapeutic sessions or encounters, and involves multiple boundary crossings. It seldom, if ever, involves a spontaneous action that the therapist or counselor acts out in response to an irresistible urge. Rather, it is a calculated, systematic series of actions for the purpose of meeting one's own needs. In the process, what initially appears as an innocent enough boundary crossing—the counselor sharing how he or she too has experienced loneliness and loss—is followed by other intensifying behaviors—giving or returning a hug, or extending the session a few extra moments. In a subsequent session the therapist might comment on the client's attractiveness, suggest they meet for dinner, or mention that he or she is recently separated or divorced or is otherwise available, and then escalate to more sexualized behaviors. This series of seemingly innocuous boundary crossings has one thing in common: They reflect a singular focus on the therapist's needs and interests more than those of the client's. In hindsight it is clear to an outside observer that such behaviors have little or no bearing on positive treatment outcomes. Inevitably, these violating behaviors harm the client.

Other sexual boundary violations include becoming sexually attracted to a client and acting on that attraction by becoming romantically involved with the client. The sexual attraction itself may not represent a boundary violation, but failing to appropriately address it by seeking supervisory consultation or by referring the client to another therapist is a boundary violation. In such a case, the therapist would have had an opportunity to become aware of the degree of sexual attraction to the client and think through what was in the best interest of the client and what would represent ethically important self-care. If the therapist did not take the opportunity to reflect on his or her own sexual feelings about the relationship and the clinical implications for the client, this would be an example of the process of thought and action or inaction preceding actual boundary violations. Ignoring warning signs indicating a need for either supervisory consultation and/or personal therapy leaves a therapist more vulnerable to abusing therapeutic power and violating therapeutic boundaries. Instances of abuse of power may appear to be discrete events, but actually represent a more complex process of inattention to one's professional conduct and ethics and inattention to one's own emotional and psychological well-being.

Therapist Self-Care: A Way of Avoiding Boundary Violations

Therapists themselves are human beings subject to the vicissitudes of life and to personal and family problems. It is more difficult perhaps for therapists to acknowledge a need for personal counseling than it is for others to do so because of a false but tacit belief that only incompetent therapists have problems. Loneliness, social isolation, relationship or marital problems, family problems, health problems, and financial problems leave therapists more vulnerable to boundary violations and to using clients to meet their own emotional or financial needs. Therapists with such personal problems should be strongly encouraged and supported by their profession and colleagues to seek counseling during these times of greater stress.

Abuse of power and committing boundary violations go hand in hand. By seeking personal counseling during stressful times in their lives, therapists are practicing an ethic of care for themselves and are thereby reducing their risk of practicing below the standard of care and committing boundary violations. Therapists are also obligated to maintain an ongoing awareness of power differentials in the therapeutic relationship and the effects of those differentials on the client. By being mindful of power differentials in therapy, therapists practice an ethic of care for themselves and their clients and thereby reduce the risk of boundary violations resulting from abuse of their power. The ethic of care applies to therapist self-care as well as to care of the client. Perspective II ethics includes a deliberate focus on personal and professional development. Times of personal life stress for therapists signal a need for increased attention to clinical decision making, increased use of supervisory and peer consultation, and perhaps personal counseling (see the case example in Box 8.2).

BOX 8.2

CASE EXAMPLE: HOW CAN BILL CARE FOR HIMSELF?

Bill was the supervising therapist at a community mental health center for years. He enjoyed a sterling reputation in the community and was the recipient of a number of community service and advocacy awards. His commitment to his clients was legendary, as were his teaching skills. In his weekly supervision groups, Bill started to joke about almost falling asleep with one of his

(continued)

BOX 8.2 CONTINUED

clients and having to make extra strong coffee before the client came in for therapy and sometimes even having to find a reason to get up out of his chair and walk around during the session. Bill couldn't figure out why he had such trouble staying awake with this one client. He let it go and didn't pay much attention to it. One of Bill's longer term clients told him with great trepidation that he was transferring to another therapist because he thought Bill had too much to do and looked tired all the time. One of Bill's new clients was having trouble with her young adult son, as was Bill, but for entirely different reasons. Bill's young adult son had fallen out of the middle class, rejected Bill's efforts to get him to attend school, and was employed randomly in day labor doing construction. He drank with the other construction workers after work, but apparently not to excess, and to Bill's great dismay seemed defiantly contented with his life.

Bill's new client, Anita, had a young adult son who ignored her constant efforts to connect with him and who went for months without letting her know how we was doing. He had an entry-level retail job, lived with a couple of other guys, and was financially responsible. Anita's reason for entering therapy was her great hurt and probable depression caused by her son's seeming indifference toward her. Anita was gentle in manner and childlike in her presentation of self. Bill had no trouble staying awake in his sessions with Anita and was activated by her stories of her son's indifference to her and wanted to protect her from more hurt. Over time, Bill disclosed to Anita his own story of disappointment with his young adult son and ultimately told her that if he had it to do over again he would never have any kids—that they sucked you dry and were ungrateful besides. Bill never knew the impact of his disclosure on Anita because she decided she didn't need therapy any longer and went home and wrote her son a stinging letter about his ungratefulness and cruelty to her and ended by telling him that she didn't give a damn whether he ever got in touch with her or not and that she was finished worrying about him and trying to have a relationship with him.

In this case, Bill's fatigue and careless attitude toward some clients contrasted with his hyperactivation and overinvolvement with a client whose life story paralleled his own in regard to her difficulties with her young adult son. Bill's self-disclosure was harmful to his client and arose from his own unresolved feelings about his relationship with his son. After hearing Bill's self-disclosure, his client took precipitous action by terminating therapy prematurely and writing a letter suggesting that a full-fledged emotional cutoff would be fine, when in fact that was exactly what she didn't want and what had given rise to her symptoms of depression. Bill's self-disclosure in this case was a serious boundary violation arising from his failure to act from an ethic of care for himself by seeking therapy for his own family problems.

In the case example in Box 8.3, the boundary violation has a mixed result in that the client felt her experience had been more normalized but she also felt abused insofar as she did not receive the attention and care she had paid for. Her clinician's actions during her session with him also raised concerns about his credibility and therefore called into question the treatment he had prescribed.

BOX 8.3

CASE EXAMPLE: WHOSE THERAPY IS IT ANYWAY?

Helen had sought therapy because of overwhelming life stress with her children. All of her three children had problems of one kind or another, but what brought her into therapy was the devastating news that her teenage son had been arrested for rape. She also had marriage problems that had been the focus of previous counseling. Her counselor was concerned about signs of severe depression and covert indications from Helen that she was potentially suicidal. Helen's counselor urged a psychiatric evaluation for medication, and Helen readily agreed. When Helen returned to the counselor for her next visit after her psychiatric consultation, Helen confirmed that the psychiatrist had prescribed antidepressants for her and that she had begun taking them. However, she complained that the psychiatrist spent almost the entire hour telling her about his hospitalization for organic brain syndrome and how his wife was trying to extort money from him during their divorce. Helen laughed and said that she left the session feeling not quite as bad about her own situation because she thought the psychiatrist was crazy but also feeling uncomfortable with him because of it. She also commented that he had pretty serious problems in his life, just as she had, and that made her feel not quite as ashamed. Helen stated that she got angry, though, when she had to write him his check for $250. She said that she felt *he* should have been paying *her,* or that at least it should have been a draw.

In this case, even though Helen received some benefit from her session with the psychiatrist through his sharing of his own personal ordeals and through her resulting feelings of being one of many in the world dealing with serious problems rather than feeling so alone, the psychiatrist clearly violated professional boundaries by not making Helen's concerns the primary focus of his clinical attention. He shared personal material that caused Helen to question his mental stability and potentially to lose confidence in him and in the treatment he prescribed, which she needed. This case is an example of a clear boundary violation that produced mixed results—some positive, some negative—for the client. Irrespective of the outcome, the boundary violation is clear and points to the psychiatrist's failure to maintain professional distance and take care of his own personal problems in supervision or in therapy. Even though the outcome was partially good for Helen, it is hard to see the operation of any of the primary ethical principles of good clinical practice (beneficence, nonmaleficence, respect for Helen's autonomy, and an ethic of care) at play in this case. What seems most clear is that the psychiatrist spent the hour with Helen meeting his own needs by verbalizing and processing his problems with her.

Sexual and Nonsexual Boundary Violations

The chart in Box 8.4 provides multiple examples of boundary violations that represent exploitation of clients and abuse of power by the therapist. Some of these examples of boundary violations may not represent true dual relationships as they are conventionally understood. The examples do, however, represent abuse of power by the therapist and attempts (either conscious or unconscious) to meet the therapist's own needs at the expense of the client's.

BOX 8.4

SEXUAL AND NONSEXUAL BOUNDARY VIOLATIONS (ALWAYS HURTFUL TO CLIENTS)

SEXUAL	NONSEXUAL
Therapist self-disclosure to client of personal, intimate sexual feelings, fantasies, or behaviors	Self-disclosure of details of personal life or thoughts and feelings unrelated to therapeutic need and for the primary benefit of the therapist
Therapist disclosure to client of specific sexual attraction, arousal, and feelings toward the client	Accepting gifts from clients that are of significant value and that do not represent a cultural symbol of appreciation or respect
Making sexual innuendos or telling racy jokes during counseling sessions	Meeting clients outside of the therapeutic setting for coffee or a meal for reasons unrelated to therapeutic goals
Holding, hugging, or comforting a client in a way that is intended to meet the therapist's sexual needs or to sexually arouse the client	Allowing sessions to become mutually enjoyable chats about politics, movies, books, or other topics of mutual interest to therapist and client that do not represent a focus on clinical goals
Making suggestive comments about the client's appearance or dress	Maintaining a client in therapy longer than is clinically necessary or scheduling appointments more frequently than is clinically necessary
Sexualized looking at or staring at the client's body and/or dress	Iatrogenically suggesting to a client that he or she has a problem that he or she had not identified as a concern and extending therapy as a result
Eliciting a detailed psychosexual history that is inappropriate and unnecessary given the client's presenting problem(s)	Giving personal, moral opinions or judgments to clients about their current or proposed behavior
Therapist sexually anticipating a particular client and dressing up for that client session	Not maintaining boundaries of clinical time during session; having sessions exceed the normal time for no therapeutic reason; telephoning client betweens sessions to meet therapist's need and not for clinical reasons
	Failure to respect client's privacy by sharing his or her personal stories with others not legitimately involved in the clinical case: telling the details of a client's story to one's spouse, significant other, or friend for its gossip value, even when protecting the identity of the client(s)

That the counselor or therapist has an unmet emotional, psychological, or relational needs is not the problem. The problem is the therapist's failure in self-care and in supervision, resulting in boundary violations and a standard of care below what is acceptable. Some of the boundary violations in the list below are more egregious than others. If recognized early, these thoughts or behaviors can signal to the therapist a need to deal with issues in his or her own personal life. In examining issues of power and abuse in therapy, it becomes clearer and clearer that therapist self-care should not be relegated to leftover time in the life of a therapist but, in fact, should occupy a central place in the therapist's own professional development. It also becomes clearer and clearer that the mental health profession and counselor education programs should take a much stronger stance in emphasizing the importance of therapist self-care and its relationship to issues of abuse of therapeutic power.

BOUNDARY CROSSINGS

Boundary crossings from the perspective of Lazarus and Zur (2002) and Zur (2004) represent relationships with clients that are well thought out and designed to enhance the therapeutic alliance and ultimately the therapeutic outcome. These authors make a signal contribution to the mental health field's discussion of boundary issues by pointing out that almost all therapy conducted within the framework of therapeutic models other than the psychoanalytic model and conducted anywhere other than in an office setting would be considered boundary violations under the field's current understanding of boundaries. Their point is well made, and the case for emphasizing the distinction between boundary violations, which are usually harmful to the client, and boundary crossing, which frequently can be beneficial to the client, is critically important now, since most counselors and therapists practice from models other than the psychoanalytic one.

Humanistic, behavioral, cognitive-behavioral, systemic, and multicultural models of therapy all require that the therapist take on a much more active role with the client and interact in ways that are engaging, as opposed to the distancing interactions required in the psychoanalytic tradition. It no longer makes sense to understand boundaries in the traditional psychoanalytic way, because most counselors and therapists are practicing from models that require active engagement with their clients. The chart in Box 8.5 provides examples of numerous boundary crossings (all nonsexual) that are either therapy-model specific or reflective of therapist behaviors designed to strengthen the therapeutic alliance.

BOX 8.5
EXAMPLES OF THERAPEUTIC BOUNDARY CROSSINGS

- Hugging a child during therapy to demonstrate support or in response to the child's reaching out for a hug
- Hugging an adult as a greeting or upon exiting as a culturally respectful and sensitive sign of acknowledgment

(continued)

BOX 8.5 CONTINUED

- Touching a client's hand, arm, or shoulder, or providing a nonsexual hug as a sign of support and acknowledgment

- Accompanying a client out in the community during behavioral exposure therapy or during *in vivo* desensitization therapy, e.g., accompanying the client on a steep escalator in the subway or to a reptile petting zoo
- Self-disclosure that is limited, judicious, and designed to promote client treatment goals
- Doing home-based family therapy and meeting with the family in the natural setting of their home, perhaps participating in shared meals with the family
- Intensive home-based parent education in which the therapist participates in everyday aspects of a family's life, such as helping to get the children ready for school and preparing a family meal, in order to provide psychoeducation and modeling
- Narrative therapy practices that include ongoing letter writing to the client and encouraging other members of the community to circulate alternative identities of the client through their own letter writing
- Doing therapy with adolescents in alternative settings, such as when going for a walk or sitting in a park
- Participating in milieu therapy in a residential treatment center by eating with the clients and talking to them during activity breaks
- Participating in religious ceremonies or rituals that are significant to the client and that not attending would represent a cultural insult
- Biofeedback and neurofeedback therapies that involve touching the client and hooking electrodes or other sensors to various parts of his or her body
- Guided imagery, visualization, and relaxation techniques that involve calling attention to body awareness and/or contracting and relaxing muscle groups
- Emerging body-centered psychotherapies that require touching a client's body or helping a client to focus on sensations within their bodies or body processes like breathing
- In substance abuse counseling, significant and detailed self-disclosure by a recovering therapist designed to promote client treatment goals and enhance the therapeutic alliance
- In small communities, exchanging greetings and friendly small talk when meeting clients in the normal course of living one's life and going to the store, place of worship, etc.
- Selecting a therapist for oneself or one's family based on knowing the therapist and having a high regard for the therapist's work rather than having to select a therapist whom one does not know in order to avoid the possibility of a previous relationship. This would be akin to physicians choosing the most capable physicians in their communities for their own or their families' needs.

Adapted from Zur (2004).

The above lists of dual relationships, boundary violations, and boundary crossings are designed to be comprehensive but not necessarily exhaustive.

A TEMPLATE FOR EVALUATING THE ETHICS OF NONSEXUAL DUAL RELATIONSHIPS

The challenge in understanding dual relationships and boundary issues from a more complex and flexible perspective is in coming up with meaningful guidelines for determining whether a particular relationship or action is going to be helpful or hurtful to the client and even to the therapist. Doyle (1997) points out that the professional associations' ethical guidelines alone do not give sufficient direction to counselors and therapists in handling difficult, complicated situations, as in the case of a recovering counselor and client. Ultimately, boundary issues will have to be examined within the context of the particular situations in which they arise. There are some general principles, however, that a counselor can apply to help in ethical decision making in what is now a much more complicated and less clear landscape where boundary issues are concerned.

Guideline 1: What does the code of ethics of the counselor's professional association say about the particular situation? What do state or federal laws say about the situation? Is there an explicit ethical standard or state or federal law governing the relationship or issue in question? If not, can a reasonable inference from the ethical codes or state or federal laws be made to cover the situation?

Guideline 2: What ethical principle(s) guiding clinical behavior would be helpful in deciding what the best course of action to take might be in the particular situation? How might the principles of beneficence, nonmaleficence, respect for the autonomy of my client, fidelity to the standards and values of my profession, and an overriding ethic of care for my client inform my decision about how to act in this particular situation?

Guideline 3: What theory of therapy or clinical model am I as the counselor or therapist operating from? Are the proposed actions or relationships congruent with the theory of my espoused clinical model? Are the proposed techniques congruent with this theory and accepted as a standard of care within the parameters of the particular clinical model?

Guideline 4: What particular issues or concerns emerge as a result of an examination of the imbalance of power between therapist and client in the situation under consideration? If the imbalance of power and the clinical implications of that imbalance were explicitly articulated and shared with my client, how would that openness inform my decision making in this particular situation? Additionally, what is my level of self-awareness about personal stressors in my life and their effects, my possible need for personal counseling or therapy, and my awareness of countertransference feelings about my client?

Guideline 5: What other influences are operating on my clinical and ethical decision making at this time? Do I have financial worries, family or relationship problems, or am I experiencing isolation or loneliness that might be influencing my judgment?

Guideline 6: Would it be helpful to seek supervision or consultation from trusted colleagues about this particular situation? How would the benefit of a second or third opinion impact my decision making? What do I imagine my supervisor would say if I were to consult about the particularities of this situation? Would I be able to support my decision and be confident of its ethical and clinical soundness? Is this a course of action that I would be comfortable letting my colleagues know about?

Guideline 7: What is my current program of professional and personal self-care? Am I taking care of my own emotional and relational needs? How am I doing that? Would it be helpful for me to seek personal therapy or to spend more time with my own family or relaxing? Do I have an adequate number of opportunities for social interaction, friendship, and emotional and sexual intimacy? In relationship to my clients, would I engage in this action with all clients in this same or similar situation, or do I see this client as special?

The above guidelines provide a richer template than simply examining the professional codes of ethics to provide guidance in the often murky waters of dealing with boundary issues and dual relationships. These guidelines include the professional codes and applicable state and federal laws but also point to the ethical importance of a more personal, reflexive examination of one's process of decision making about issues of boundaries and use of power in clinical relationships. They embody the stance of the Perspective III counselor, who acknowledges the need to pay attention to personal and professional development while also recognizing that the ultimate goal of therapy requires a strong relational view that attends to particularity and context.

KEY POINTS

1. Boundary issues are important in counseling because of the inherently less powerful, more vulnerable position of the client in relationship to the therapist.
2. The counselor has an ethical obligation to be conscious of the power imbalance in therapy and to consider its implications in particular clinical situations.
3. Dual or multiple relationships consist of having both a counseling and other kind of relationship with a client simultaneously or sequentially.
4. Boundary violations occur when a therapist participates in exploitive or harmful practices and crosses standards of professional behavior for his or her own sexual, emotional, or financial gain.
5. Boundary crossings differ from boundary violations in that they consist of therapeutic relational practices designed to strengthen the therapeutic alliance but do deviate from the detached, distant stance of the therapist in the analytic model.
6. The psychotherapeutic relationship is a formal professional one designed to promote the welfare of the client, not the therapist, and differs significantly from other kinds of relationships like friendship.
7. Dual relationships and boundary violations are of serious concern because of their exploitive, harmful nature and the abuse of therapist power inherent in them.
8. Exploitation of clients and therapist abuse of power are processes for which there are warning signs.
9. Abuse of power by therapists is a process of inattention to personal and professional development and is not a single event or set of events.

10. Therapists must proactively carry out a program of ethical self-care as a way of reducing the risk of committing boundary violations with clients.
11. Ethical decision making about dilemmas involving boundaries and dual relationships can be facilitated by attending to the seven guidelines in the section titled "A Template for Evaluating the Ethics of Nonsexual Dual Relationships."

CONCLUDING NOTE: PERSPECTIVE I VERSUS III

Boundary violations and abuse of power in the therapeutic relationship are continuing cause for concern among dedicated and ethical counseling professionals. These violations and abuses are significant because they represent therapist exploitation of clients, who by the nature of the therapeutic relationship are in positions of less power and greater vulnerability. Ethical counselors are conscious of the power imbalance in all of their interactions with clients and actively operate from the ethical principles of beneficence, nonmaleficence, respect for the autonomy of the client, and an overall ethic of care in protecting and promoting the client's welfare. Most importantly, ethical counselors recognize the relationship between their commitment to their own ongoing self-care and the resulting reduced risk of involvement in boundary violations. This recognition is a feature of counselors who understand that ethical practice always involves one's own personal and professional development (Perspective II) and leads to practice at the most sophisticated level and that is at the level of the relational or Perspective III practitioner.

The Perspective III practitioner will not shy away from embracing the complexities of understanding the differences between boundary violations and boundary crossings and examining the contextual elements that distinguish the two. Distinguishing between boundary violations, which by definition are harmful and exploitive, and boundary crossings, which may be helpful, requires that the counselor attend to the particularities of the context within which a specific clinical decision is made. This context includes awareness of the self-of-therapist issues discussed in this chapter, the multicultural and relational issues that influence individual clinical decisions in specific cases, and the organizational ethics–community values context whose norms and standards influence clinical thinking, practice, and ethical decision making. The Perspective III therapist or counselor has developed personally and professionally to a point of reasonable comfort with ambiguity and understanding the importance of clinical decision making in context rather than according to rigid, preset rules and standards that do not take into account the critical contextual factors discussed here. The Perspective III therapist or counselor is flexible, context-aware, and continuously self-reflective in relation to decision making about boundary issues and conflicts of interest.

REVIEW QUESTIONS

1. Under what circumstances would a social relationship with a current client be considered unethical? Under what ethical circumstances could you develop a personal or social relationship with a former client?
2. Ethics codes caution counselors and therapists against engaging in dual relationships. What are the reasons for this caution? What is your view on this subject?
3. Some believe that all boundary crossings are harmful, while others claim that some boundary crossings are essential to effective counseling. Briefly review both positions and then state your opinion.
4. What would you do if a client was attracted to you and said so? What would you say or do if you were attracted to a client?
5. What factors would you consider in responding to a client who offered you a gift? What would you say and do?

REFERENCES

Ahia, C. E. (2003). *Legal and ethical dictionary for mental health professionals.* Lanham, MD: University Press of America.

Berzoff, J. (1989). The therapeutic value of women's adult friendships. *Smith College Studies in Social Work, 59,* 267–278.

Catalano, S. (1997). The challenges of clinical practice in small or rural communities: Case studies in managing dual relationships in and outside of therapy. *Journal of Contemporary Psychotherapy, 27,* 23–35.

Corey, G., & Herlihy, B. (1997). Dual/multiple relationships: Towards a consensus of thinking. In B. Herlihy & G. Corey (Eds.), *The Hatherleigh guide series: Vol. 10. Ethics in therapy* (pp. 183–194). New York: Hatherleigh Press.

Doyle, K. (1997). Substance abuse counselors in recovery: Implications for the ethical issue of dual relationships. *Journal of Counseling and Development, 75,* 428–432.

Edelwich, J., & Brodsky, A. M. (1991). *Sexual dilemmas for the helping professional.* New York: Brunner/Mazel.

Fay, A. (2002). The case against boundaries in psychotherapy. In A. Lazarus & O. Zur (Eds.), *Dual relationships and psychotherapy* (pp. 98–114). New York: Springer.

Gutheil, T. G., & Gabbard, G. O. (1993). The concept of boundaries in clinical practice: Theoretical and risk-management dimensions. *American Journal of Psychiatry, 150,* 188–196.

Hill, M. R., & Mamalakis, P. M. (2001). Family therapists and religious communities: Negotiating dual relationships. *Family Relations, 50,* 199–208.

Lazarus, A., & Zur, O. (2002). *Dual relationships and psychotherapy.* New York: Springer.

McNamee, S., & Gergen, K. J. (1998). *Relational responsibility: Resources for sustainable dialogue.* Thousand Oaks, CA: Sage.

Olarte, S. W. (1997). Sexual boundary violations. In Hatherleigh Editorial Board (Ed.), *The Hatherleigh guide to ethics in therapy* (pp. 195–209). New York: Hatherleigh Press.

Peterson, M. (1992). *At personal risk: Boundary violation in professional–client relationships.* New York: Norton.

Reamer, F. G. (2001). *Tangled relationships: Managing boundary issues in the human services.* New York: Columbia University Press.

Reamer, F. G. (2003). Boundary issues in social work: Managing dual relationships. *Social Work, 48,* 121–134.

St. Germaine, J. (1996). Dual relationships and certified alcohol and drug counselors: A national study of ethical beliefs and behaviors. *Alcoholism Treatment Quarterly, 14,* 29–44.

Smith, D., & Fitzpatrick, M. (1995). Patient–therapist boundary issues: An integrative review of theory and research. *Professional Psychology: Research and Practice, 26,* 499–506.

Stake, J. E., & Oliver, J. (1991). Sexual contact and touching between therapist and client: A survey of psychologists' attitudes and behavior. *Professional Psychology: Research and Practice, 22,* 297–307.

Tomm, K. (n.d.). The ethics of dual relationships. [Online]. Available: http://www.familytherapy.org/documents/EthicsDual.PDF

Tomm, K. (2002). The ethics of dual relationships. In A. Lazarus & O. Zur (Eds.), *Dual relationships and psychotherapy* (pp. 32–43). New York: Springer.

Woody, R. H. (1998). Bartering for psychological services. *Professional psychology: Research and practice, 29,* 174–178.

Zur, O. (2004). To cross or not to cross: Do boundaries in therapy protect or harm? *Psychotherapy Bulletin, 39,* 27–32.

CHAPTER 9

COMPETENCY AND PROFESSIONAL RESPONSIBILITY

Clients expect that the counselors and therapists with whom they consult will be competent. But what exactly does competence mean in the counseling profession? Competency is about capability and performance, and neither is particularly easy to measure. Furthermore, professional competency is a process rather than an event. Much as they might desire, counselors and therapists do not achieve competence with the awarding of a credential, whether it is certification or licensure. Rather, competence is an ongoing, developmental process in which an initial level—usually a minimal level—of competence is achieved and maintained and then updated and enhanced as new developments and demands arise and the profession and the professional grows and changes. This chapter focuses on ethical and legal aspects of professional competence and the process of developing and maintaining competence. It conceptualizes competence on a continuum with differing levels and stages, examines the conditions of incompetence, distress, burnout, and impairment, and finally, relates competence to the three perspectives of ethical and professional practice.

LEARNING OBJECTIVES

After reading this chapter you should be able to

1. State at least three characteristic features of a profession.
2. Distinguish incompetence from impairment and describe the three types of incompetence.
3. Define scope of practice and indicate the counselor's responsibilities when expanding the scope of his or her practice.
4. Specify the four elements of negligence that must be met in a malpractice suit.
5. Profile competent practice from Perspectives I, II, and III.

KEY TERMS

impairment
incompetence
malpractice
negligence
profession
professional
professional competence
professional counseling
scope of practice
work orientation

Following are two cases, Boxes 9.1 and 9.2, that introduce the dimensions of professional competence. You will be asked to reflect on some questions now as well as later in the chapter when we return to these two cases.

BOX 9.1
ADAM: TWELVE YEARS OF COUNSELING EXPERIENCE

Adam completed his master's degree some twelve years ago and qualified for licensure as a licensed professional counselor a year later. Soon afterward he took a position as a staff counselor at a large community agency. He is married with two children, has become active in the Rotary Club, and is an assistant coach for the Little League team on which his son plays. He is quite comfortable with both his personal and professional life. Overall, Adam's annual performance reviews are positive but not exceptional. He is content to practice the way he was taught in graduate school and resists "new approaches." Eight years ago he was asked to provide supervision for interns, but he declined, saying he "needed more time to get up to speed first." A year later he was asked again and refused. The next time supervision assignments were made, the agency administrator assigned two interns to Adam. After about five weeks one intern complained that Adam seemed uninterested in supervising her, and the other intern asked for a reassignment, effectively ending Adam's short career as a supervisor. Completing continuing education requirements had become a challenge for Adam after the agency's policy on CEUs changed. Before, counselors could complete their hours on agency time if they scheduled their time wisely. Now, the majority of hours had to be met on the counselor's personal time or on weekends without agency reimbursement. Last month Adam received a letter from the state requesting he verify forty hours of CEUs over the past two years. He began to scramble, looking for workshops, since he could log only six hours of agency workshops. When one of Adam's younger colleagues asked another counselor how long Adam had been in practice, the tongue-in-cheek reply was "I believe it is twelve years. But I'm not sure if it is twelve years of progressive experience or one year of experience repeated twelve times."

BOX 9.2
JORGE: TWELVE YEARS OF COUNSELING EXPERIENCE, TOO

Jorge completed his graduate degree in the same year and the same class as Adam. During that time they became acquainted when they were assigned the same internship at a large state facility, but they didn't know each other particularly well. Jorge began to distinguish himself during the internship and was recruited to stay on as a staff therapist, and a year after he received his license, he was asked to become the assistant training director. This meant he would not only supervise interns but also schedule weekly seminars and case conferences. He is married, with two children. Over the years Jorge was heavily involved in his work at the state facility and took great satisfaction in helping clients as well as mentoring interns and younger staff. He read widely and wrote a column on new techniques for the agency's monthly newsletter. His colleagues regularly sought him out to consult on their difficult cases. He was an untiring advocate for wellness and self-care for counselors and therapists, and three years ago was appointed as a member of the state licensing board with the charge to create a task force on counselor self-care. Both Adam and Jorge completed the same internship and graduated from the same master's program, yet their professional lives seem to be evolving in very different ways. Their priorities, work orientations, and commitments seem to be quite different. What are some factors that may explain these differences? How would you describe their levels or degrees of professional competence?

COUNSELING AS A PROFESSION

Defining Profession and Professional

Because this is a book about professional ethics, it may be helpful to define terms such as *profession* and *professional.* Unfortunately, current usage of these terms is so broad as to render them nearly meaningless. Thus, let's provide definitions and a context for understanding these two terms. Technically speaking, the hallmark of being a profession is the *commitment* of a collective group of individuals to acquire *specialized knowledge and skills* in order to *serve the needs of others,* and to do so in a *competent and ethical manner.* Professionals are members of a profession who apply their specialized knowledge and skills based on standards of excellence for *meeting the client's needs rather than advancing their own personal interests.* Furthermore, they have an allegiance to a profession that has a comprehensive, self-governing organization that establishes *standards of competency, ethical codes,* and *practical guidelines* for providing specialized service to others (Brincat & Wike, 2000; Rich, 1984). The above italicized words and phrases—*commitment, specialized knowledge and skills, serve the needs of others, competent and ethical manner, client's needs over their own interests,* and *standards of competency*—well distinguish a profession and professionals from the efforts of nonprofessionals engaged in occupations that are not considered professions.

In terms of this extended definition, both counseling and psychotherapy would be considered professions. These professions have spawned a number of counseling and related mental health professional organizations that provide standards of competency, ethical codes, and practical guidelines for providing specialized counseling and therapeutic service. Professional training and certification or licensure attests to the acquisition of specialized skills and the attainment of minimal competencies in order to provide these specialized services. Presumably, the professions value and model commitment to meeting client's needs over the professional's own needs and interests.

The Counseling Profession

So what characterizes the counseling profession and professional counseling? In 1997 the American Counseling Association defined *professional counseling* as "the application of mental health, psychological and human development principles through cognitive, affective, behavioral and systemic intervention strategies, that address wellness, personal growth and career development, as well as pathology." They also note that within the counseling profession are several specialties such as mental health counseling, marriage and family counseling, school counseling, rehabilitation counseling, and others. Each specialty is based on specialized knowledge and therapeutic skills required by the clientele who seek out that specialty for assistance. Common to all these specialties are relationship, communication, and diagnostic, conceptualization, and intervention skills.

COMPETENCE AND WORK ORIENTATION

Work orientation is a research interest in both sociology (Bellah, Madsen, Sullivan, Swidler & Tipton, 1985) and psychology (Baumeister, 1991; Wrzesniewski, McCaukley, Rozin & Schwartz, 1997). Work orientation refers to a view and attitude toward work as determined by intrinsic values and aspirations and the experience of working. This orientation is reflected in thoughts, feelings, and behavior about work.

Three Work Orientations

Three work orientations have been observed among North American professionals, including professional counselors and therapists. Each reflects different intrinsic values and a sense of fulfillment. The three are job, career, and calling orientations.

Job. In the job orientation, individuals relate to their professional work as simply a job. Their main value in working is the material benefits of work to the relative exclusion of other kinds of meaning and fulfillment. In other words, for these individuals, work is simply a means to a financial end allowing them to enjoy their time away from work. Inevitably, the interest and ambitions of those with job orientations are expressed outside the domains of work (Wrzesniewski et al., 1997) and involve hobbies and other interests.

Career. In contrast, those with a career orientation value the rewards that come from work advancement within their school, clinic, or agency or through a professional organization. For those with this orientation, the increased pay, prestige, and status that come with promotion and advancement are the main focus of their work. Advancement brings higher self-esteem, increased power, and higher social standing (Bellah et al., 1985).

Calling. Finally, those with a calling orientation work neither for financial reward nor for advancement but value the sense of fulfillment that their work provides. In the past, calling denoted a "call" from God to engage in morally or social significant work (Weber, 1958), while today it means doing work that contributes to the well-being of others or making the world a better place (Davidson & Caddell, 1994). The determination of whether the work actually contributes to making a difference is largely determined by the professional. For example, a surgeon who views her work as a source of a comfortable six-figure income does not have a calling, whereas a street cleaner who sees his work as making the world a cleaner and healthier place probably has a calling.

A basic question underlying theory and research in this area involves the impact of work orientation on life satisfaction, fulfillment, and personal well-being. As hypothesized in sociological and psychological theory, research confirms that those with a calling orientation report higher job satisfaction and higher life satisfaction than those with either job or career orientations (Wrzesniewski et al., 1997). Interestingly, these professionals also derive more satisfaction from their work than from leisure, while those with job and career orientations rank satisfaction from leisure (i.e., hobbies and friends) higher than work satisfaction. What is increasingly clear is that, for professionals with a calling orientation, work is their passion, while for other professionals, their deeper satisfaction is found in leisure or in relationships outside of work.

The Relationship between Work Orientation and Competence

An individual can be a professional counselor or therapist and operate from a job, career, or calling orientation. The ideal implied in the ethics codes of both the American Counseling Association (2005) and the American Psychological Association (2002) is that counselors and psychologists would operate from the calling orientation. Presumably, the "fit" between profession and work orientation would be optimal. It should not be too surprising that master therapists would exemplify this optimal fit, since they appear to embody a calling orientation. In a subsequent section, it will be argued that this work orientation and attitude toward competence and expertise is compatible with Perspective III.

ETHICAL AND LEGAL ASPECTS OF COMPETENCE

Ethical Aspects

The ACA and APA codes of ethics and standards address competence (see Box 9.3). Both codes emphasize the importance of developing and maintaining professional competence. Beneficence and nonmaleficence are the ethical principles from which the standards on competence are derived. Both codes indicate the importance of scope of practice—practicing within the boundaries of knowledge and skills. Both also acknowledge that it is possible to extend one's scope of practice, but only after obtaining additional training and supervised experience. Finally, both specify continuing education or ongoing efforts to maintain competence.

BOX 9.3
ETHICAL CODES AND COMPETENCE

ACA CODE OF ETHICS, SECTION C: PROFESSIONAL RESPONSIBILITY (2005)

C.2.a. Counselors practice only within the boundaries of their competence, based on their education, training, supervised experience, state and national professional credentials, and appropriate professional experience.

C.2.b. Counselors practice in specialty areas new to them only after appropriate education, training, and supervised experience. While developing skills in new specialty areas, counselors take steps to ensure the competence of their work and to protect others from possible harm.

(*continued*)

BOX 9.3 CONTINUED

C.2.c. Counselors accept employment only for positions for which they are qualified by education, training, supervised experience, state and national professional credentials, and appropriate professional experience.

C.2.d. Counselors continually monitor their effectiveness as professionals and take steps to improve when necessary.

C.2.f. Counselors recognize the need for continuing education to maintain a reasonable level of awareness of current scientific and professional information in their fields of activity. They take steps to maintain competence in the skills they use, are open to new procedures, and keep current with the diverse and/or special populations with whom they work.

APA CODE OF ETHICS, SECTION 2: COMPETENCE (2002)

Boundaries of Competence

(a) Psychologists provide services, teach, and conduct research with populations and in areas only within the boundaries of their competence, based on their education, training, supervised experience, consultation, study, or professional experience.

(b) Where scientific or professional knowledge in the discipline of psychology establishes that an understanding of factors associated with age, gender, gender identity, race, ethnicity, culture, national origin, religion, sexual orientation, disability, language, or socioeconomic status is essential for effective implementation of their services or research, psychologists have or obtain the training, experience, consultation, or supervision necessary to ensure the competence of their services, or they make appropriate referrals.

(c) Psychologists planning to provide services, teach, or conduct research involving populations, areas, techniques, or technologies new to them undertake relevant education, training, supervised experience, consultation, or study.

2.03 Maintaining Competence

Psychologists undertake ongoing efforts to develop and maintain their competence.

Legal Aspects

In addition to the ethical aspect of competence are certain legal aspects. Because society expects professionals to be competent, professional associations and licensure boards hold professionals to a standard of competence. Two legal issues related to competence are credentialing and malpractice. Both are addressed in subsequent sections.

PROFESSIONAL COMPETENCE

Continuum of Competence

Current ethical codes and licensure laws and regulations give the impression that competence is an either-or phenomenon: A professional either possesses a "minimal level of competence" for licensure or certification or does not possess it. For example, competence is defined as "A counselor's capability to provide a minimum quality of services and within the counselor's (and his profession's) scope of practice. A counselor's competence is usually measured (for legal purposes) by what other reasonably prudent counselors will do under the same circumstances" (Ahia, 2003). In this definition, "minimum quality of service" refers to "minimal level of competence." We view competence in a broader sense, and so in this section we discuss a continuum of competence ranging from an absence of expertise to a full expression of expertise. This focus on expertise is intended to provide a perspective in which to better understand the concept of "minimum level of competence" in the context of professional practice.

Expertise means much more than simply possessing expert knowledge or skill. In distinguishing novices from experts, Skovholt and Jennings (2004) put it this way: "We know that experts and novices see the same words in a problem, chess pieces on a board, or notes on a musical score. The difference seems to be that experts see the words, pieces, or notes within a context of accumulated experience, knowledge, and wisdom. This allows the expert to see deeper, faster, further, and better than the novice" (p. 4). Becoming a competent professional counselor or therapist is a developmental process. This section describes five stages of the development of competence and expertise and the corresponding levels of professional practice. Figure 9.1 portrays a continuum of competence. Above the horizontal line are the designations "Deficient," "Minimal," "Moderate," and "Maximal," which represent competency associated with levels of professional practice. Below the line are the numbers 1 to 5, which refer to five stages of the development of expertise. These descriptions are adapted from Dreyfus and Dreyfus (1986), Skovholt and Ronnestad (1995), and Skovholt and Jennings (2004).

1. Beginning trainee. At this stage beginners or novices adhere to rules with little regard to others' subjective needs or the context in which they occur. For example, counseling students might cling to one counseling approach with little or no regard for the client's needs, circumstances, or expectations. In terms of licensure or certification requirements, these trainees would be considered not competent because of deficiencies in knowledge, skills, and experience.

2. Advanced trainee. Here trainees demonstrate a limited capacity for the subjective and contextual yet are still dependent on a counseling theory or approach to guide their thinking and practice. To some degree, they can integrate theory and practice with regard to client needs, circumstances, and expectations. While some trainees at this stage may demonstrate minimal levels of competency in applying some specific counseling skills and strategies, the purpose of ongoing education and supervision is to further develop and appropriately apply other skills and strategies.

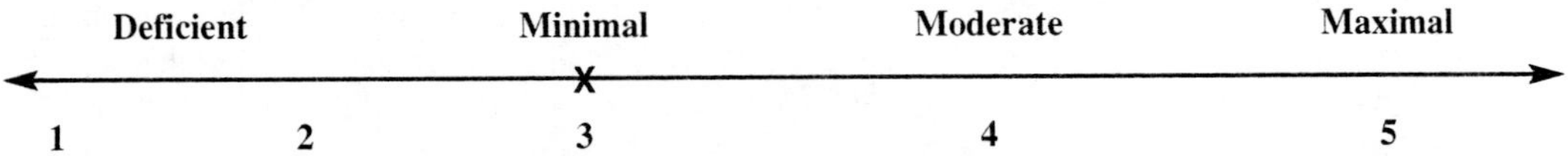

Deficient		Minimal	Moderate	Maximal
1	2	3	4	5

FIGURE 9.1 Continuum of Competence and Levels of Professional Practice

3. Entry-level professional. This stage represents the capacity to function with at least a minimal competence to practice counseling and therapy independently, which is the basic requirement for certification or licensure. At this stage of competence, new professionals can better integrate theory and experience and no longer make practice decisions that are contextless or based on textbook theory. Instead, they integrate theoretical knowledge with practice experience to determine which contextual factors are important to consider in the professional services they provide. Thinking about practice decisions tends to be slow, deliberate, and active. Nevertheless, once these individuals achieve licensure or certification, they are considered minimally competent to provide services and practice independent of the oversight of supervisors.

4. Proficient professional. Unlike in the preceding stage, practice decisions tend to be made rapidly and effortlessly. It is as if competence has become one's second nature. The reason for the proficiency is the capacity to incorporate intuition into one's professional practice. This evolving capacity to effortlessly recognize maladaptive patterns and employ interventions to modify and change such patterns is characteristic of this stage. Needless to say, job satisfaction as well as personal satisfaction tends to be high at this stage.

5. Expert professional. This level is characterized by the same seemingly effortless practice as the previous stages and is also marked by a level of reflection on several years of accumulated experience. Thus, their thinking, attitudes, and practice reflect "accumulated wisdom" (Skovholt & Ronnestad, 1995). They have relinquished reliance on textbook knowledge and operate instead from their own, internal, personalized theory of counseling or therapy based on the experience of years of intuitive and reflective professional practice. This level of expertise is reflected in the practice of so-called master counselors and therapists. It represents the epitome of subjectivity and contextuality.

What about incompetence and impairment? Incompetence and impairment would be located within the deficient range of competence. A detailed discussion of both incompetence and impairment is contained in a subsequent section of this chapter.

Scope of Practice

Scope of practice can be defined as the extent and limits of activities considered acceptable professional practice by an individual who is licensed or certified in a profession. More specifically, it refers to a recognized area of proficiency in professional practice involving specific competence, proficiency, or skills acquired through appropriate education and experience.

Scope of practice is a legal designation specified in licensure laws. For example, diagnosis and intervention are two key modalities that all states recognize as within the scope of practice of licensed psychiatrists and clinical psychologists and that many state licensure boards recognize as within the scope of practice of licensed mental health counselors. Scope of practice can vary widely in a profession from state to state. For instance, in the state of California, licensed Marriage, Family, and Child Counselors can extend their scope of practice to include psychological testing and hypnosis, provided they have had appropriate training and supervised experience. Until California licensure laws were modified, only psychologists and physicians could legally incorporate psychological testing and hypnosis in their practice. It appears that this broadened scope of practice is available only in

California. Currently, psychological associations in several states are pursuing legislation to increase their scope of practice to include prescription privileges.

ACHIEVING AND MAINTAINING COMPETENCE

Attaining Competence

Competence develops over time as a result of several educational experiences: didactic instruction, discussion, reading, supervised experience, and appropriate professional experience. For most counselors and therapists the process of becoming competent to engage in professional practice begins with graduate training. Accordingly, graduate faculty and supervisors bear the initial responsibility for producing competent professionals.

Selection. Graduate faculties have the responsibility for selecting individuals to their training programs who possess the requisite attributes necessary to become effective and compassionate counselors and therapists as well the requisite intellectual ability for developing the requisite skills and knowledge. Necessary attributes include the capacity for self-awareness and self-knowledge, curiosity about human nature, tolerance for ambiguity, self-esteem, and the capacity to explore one's own biases, values, blind spots, and personal issues. Both sets of requisites are essential. Possessing one or the other is not sufficient. Many faculty and site supervisors have observed that students with strong intellectual abilities who do not possess the requisite personal attributes are less likely to become effective and compassionate counselors and therapists than students who may be less intellectually gifted but possess the personal attributes.

Graduate Training. After being admitted into a graduate training program, the expectation is that formal coursework, experiential activities, supervised clinical experience, and academic and career advising will promote the development of at least a minimal level of competence. While the quality of instruction, faculty mentoring, and the quality of supervised experience are important factors in achieving the goals of graduate training, so is the student's motivation and the ability to learn. While coursework can provide a theoretical framework for conceptualizing professional practice, clinical experience is necessary to develop the specialized technical skills of the profession. The Continuum of Competence designates a shift from "not competent" to "minimally competent" as occurring in the transition from the second stage and the third stage. This shift occurs largely because of supervised clinical experience. Research indicates that appropriate and effective clinical supervision is essential in this development process (Stoltenburg, McNeill, & Delworth, 1998).

Credentialing. Typically, graduation from an accredited training program takes place somewhere in the transition between the second and third stage. To be able to practice independently, graduates must attain some form of credentialing. Usually this involves completing additional certification or licensure requirements in order to be formally acknowledged as having met the legal standard of competence, i.e., minimal competence. Credentialing provides a tangible marker of attaining this level of competence.

The terms *licensure, certification,* and *registration* can have various meanings and are sometimes used interchangeably, which unfortunately creates unnecessary confusion.

Technically, the term *licensure* refers to the most rigorous form of regulation. Licensure attests that only those who have been licensed (i.e., received a valid professional license) may practice that profession in a particular state or jurisdiction. *Certification* is a term used to signify that a particular title, such as "professional counselor" or "school counselor," can be used only by those who are certified. However, anyone can practice that profession without being certified as long as he or she does not use the title. Registration is the least regulated credential. Registration simply means that one has signed a government registry. The registration process does not involve a review of content of credentials.

The National Board of Certified Counselors offers national certification, which is a voluntary credential. All state departments of education in the United States require certification of school counselors employed in public school districts. In addition, some regional accrediting agencies, such as the Southern Association of Schools and Colleges (SAC), require counselors in private schools to be certified. Similarly, certification of rehabilitation counselors is available from the Council on Rehabilitation and Other Education Programs (CORE). In this remainder of this text, the term *licensure* is used to refer to state regulation of a profession, while the term *certification* is used to refer to national voluntary credentials and state department certification of school counselors.

Maintaining Competence

Once trainees have completed their formal training and are licensed or certified to practice, the responsibility for ensuring competence shifts away from educators and supervisors to the professionals themselves. Because credentialed counselors and therapists are now designated as independent professionals, they are expected to assume the burden for monitoring their own effectiveness and the scope of their practice. One indicator of a profession that distinguishes it from a nonprofession is that members of that profession can practice with autonomy—that is, independently—without the oversight of supervisors. The duty attached to this privilege of independence is that professionals must limit their practice to only those areas in which they are competent. For the most part, it is up to professionals to determine for themselves the limits of their competence and practice accordingly.

Continuing Education. There are several venues for increasing competence, for shifting from stage three to four. These include formal education, such as ongoing formal supervision, seminars, workshops, or other training that issues continuing education credits (CEUs), and informal education. Informal education includes reading, writing articles, book chapters, or papers, or reflection on one's own practice experiences. Due to the proliferation of new theories and knowledge, counseling approaches, and assessment and intervention strategies, it appears that it would impossible for a counselor or therapist to maintain more than a modicum of professional competence over the course of his or her professional career without additional education and training. Codes of ethics of both the ACA and the APA recognize the need for continuing education in order to maintain awareness of current advances in scientific and the professional realms. Likewise, most credentialing bodies have established continuing education requirements to maintain certification or licensure.

Until recently, credentialing bodies have specified only the number of hours of continuing education credit that must be accumulated within a given time frame. More recently, some licensure boards, particularly psychology boards, have begun specifying and mandating certain types of continuing education to meet perceived needs of the majority of practitioners in a particular state or jurisdiction. For example, some boards that recognized that their licensees had limited training in ethics or mandatory reporting laws regarding child abuse began requiring a specific number of hours of training in professional ethics and in the recognition and reporting of child abuse.

It is quite likely that this trend for mandatory training will continue and even increase. However, while mandatory continuing education in specified areas might meet the needs of many or most practitioners in a state, it is not sufficient to ensure continuing competence for individual practitioners. Thus, it remains up to each individual professional to recognize his or her own limitations and to seek to maintain skills by both formal and informal means (Keith-Spiegel & Koocher, 1985).

INCOMPETENCE

Incompetence is the incapacity to appropriately and competently perform the function of counseling role. Generally speaking, incompetence is the result of lack of adequate training or experience. While unwillingness or inflexibility can also result in incompetence, these are less common factors; however, either may confound training and experience deficits. Often, incompetence can be reversed with additional training, supervised experience, or personal therapy, assuming that the individual has sufficient readiness, willingness, and ability. Sometimes incompetence cannot easily be remediated, if at all.

Impairment versus Incompetence

There is currently little consensus on what constitutes impairment and what constitutes incompetence in supervisors. Some believe the two are essentially the same, as when Bernard and Goodyear (2004) defined impairment as gross incompetence. Others, like Lamb, Presser, Pfost, Baum, Jackson, and Jarvis (1987), contend that impairment is a reversal of previously adequate functioning and that incompetence is an inability to perform required functions.

While related, the two terms are sufficiently different to merit separate definitions. One of the reasons for distinguishing them is that ethical codes and legal statutes address incompetency and impairment separately. Another reason is that the interchangeable use of the terms can confound discussions and decisions. Thus, we believe it is necessary to precisely define and distinguish them.

Three Types of Incompetence

One way of clarifying the interrelationship among impairment and incompetence is to describe incompetence as comprising three components. The three components of incompetence are technical, cognitive, and emotional.

Technical Incompetence. Technical incompetence refers to the incapacity to appropriately and competently perform the counseling role and function because of a deficit in knowledge or specific skills, or the inability to apply knowledge or skills at the appropriate time or sequence. Usually, technical competence is remediable. Some skills, such as empathic responding, may be more difficult to develop proficiency in than others, such as cognitive restructuring. Commonly, involvement in a formal training, supervised experience, or focused, one-to-one coaching is sufficient to remediate the interventions of choice for lack of knowledge and experience. Usually, technical competence is remediable.

Cognitive Incompetence. Cognitive incompetence refers to the inability to accurately perceive, process, evaluate, and act upon information received. This form of incompetence can be transitory or permanent, and it may be mild or severe. Temporary cognitive incompetency can result from an infection or high fever, from drugs or substance use, or from a brief concussion or mild head injury that resolves in a short time. Permanent incompetence can result from irreversible brain damage resulting from an injury, drug or substance, poison or environmental toxin, or neurological condition such as Parkinson's disease, Alzheimer's disease, or another form of dementia. A mild cognitive deficit includes the influence of many substances, such as alcohol, or a substandard intellectual ability wherein an individual can function to some degree but below expectation, whereas in a severe form functioning is significantly disrupted. The applicant to a counseling or psychotherapy training program with a history of a head injury or brain tumor who evidences concrete thinking or perseveration might find it difficult to engage in counseling and therapy, which assumes a high capacity for symbolism, metaphor, and abstraction. Accordingly, this applicant might be adjudged cognitively incompetent and not offered admission. A practicing therapist who is beginning to demonstrate moderate signs of dementia would also be considered congitively incompetent.

When cognitive incompetence is not the individual's baseline functioning, but rather is a marked decline from an acceptable level of competence, as in evolving Alzheimer's disease, the cognitive incompetence can be considered "impairment." Thus, a continuum of cognitive incompetence can be conceptualized ranging from mild to severe, and wherein impairment represents a severe form of such incompetence in a previously competent individual.

Emotional Incompetence. Emotional incompetence refers to the inability to appropriately respond to others' emotional meaning and to appropriately modulate one's affects. Trainees or counselors who cannot appreciate another's frame of reference and respond empathically are probably demonstrating emotional incompetence. Similarly, those who are incapable of controlling overmodulated affects, such as rageful outburst, or demonstrate undermoduated or overly constricted affects, such as underreacting to another's distress, are probably also demonstrating emotional incompetence. Trainees or practitioners whose emotional life dominates or interferes with their professional work may be also be impaired. As in cognitive impairment, there is a continuum from mild to severe emotional incompetence. Where an otherwise competent trainee or practitioner is now demonstrating moderately severe to severe emotional incompetence, impairment probably exists.

DISTRESS, BURNOUT, AND IMPAIRMENT

Only recently has the problem of impairment been recognized in the counseling profession. Consensus on the definition of impairment has not been achieved. Largely this is because the terms *distress, burnout,* and *impairment* have been used interchangeably in the professional literature. One way of thinking about the relationship of these three conditions is on a continuum ranging from the least the most serious, in terms of their impact on a professional's performance. Thus, distress would be the least serious, impairment the most serious, and burnout at the midpoint between the two. As noted in the previous section, impairment can be understood as a type of incompetence.

The provision of counseling and psychotherapy can be stressful, and distress is not an uncommon complaint of counselors and therapists. Arguably, the counseling relationship itself can be a source of stress. In other interpersonal relationships such as marriage, there is considerable reciprocity and the mutual meeting of needs. Such mutual reciprocity does not exist in a counseling relationship, and counselors can feel needy and may even doubt the efficacy of their work. One study of stress in therapists found that the majority, 74 percent, viewed a lack of therapeutic success as the most stressful aspect of their professional work, while 55 percent felt depleted by the nonreciprocal attentiveness, giving, and responsibility that the therapeutic relationship demanded (Farber & Heifetz, 1982).

Stress can lead to distress, and many counselors and therapists experience distress at some point during their professional careers. One survey indicated that 82 percent of psychotherapists have experienced at least one episode of psychological distress (Prochaska & Norcross, 1983). Distressed counselors and therapists subjectively recognize that something is wrong with them and often experience anxiety and depression, feelings of helplessness, somatic symptoms, and reduced self-esteem. But, this does not necessarily represent impairment in their professional functioning, since the episodes of distress are transitory and can be easily reversed with a short vacation, a change of activity level, or even a day off.

On the other hand, continued, unalleviated distress can result in burnout. Burnout has been described as "physical, emotional, and mental exhaustion brought on by involvement over prolonged periods with emotionally demanding situations and people" (Pines & Aronson, 1988). Exhausted and depleted counselors and therapists tend to express negative attitudes toward self and their work and rarely have sufficient energy to attend to their clients. Burnout appears to be a process rather than a condition. Some writers have suggested that burnout is increasingly common and that few counselors will escape the experience of burnout during the courses of their careers, particularly after ten years in practice (Kottler, 1993). It appears that unalleviated burnout can lead to impairment.

Impairment can be described as the inability to provide competent client care. The professional skills and judgment of impaired counselors and therapists have diminished or deteriorated to such a point that they are unable to perform their responsibilities appropriately and effectively. Impaired judgment and actions can result in harm to clients. Impairment is often associated with alcohol and other drug abuse, and with the blurring of therapeutic boundaries that can lead to sexual exploitation of clients.

The ACA and APA codes of ethics provide clear guidelines regarding impairment (see Box 9.4). Both codes expect practitioners to refrain from professional activity when untoward effect will likely occur, whether it is less-than-competent service or harm to a client. Both codes also admonish that in such situations practitioners must limit, suspend, or terminate their professional duties or responsibilities.

BOX 9.4
ETHICAL CODES AND IMPAIRMENT

ACA CODE OF ETHICS, SECTION C.2.G: IMPAIRMENT (2005)

Counselors refrain from offering or providing professional services when their physical, mental, or emotional problems are likely to harm a client or others. They are alert to the signs of impairment, seek assistance for their problems, and if necessary, limit, suspend, or terminate their professional responsibilities.

APA CODE OF ETHICS, SECTION 2.06: PERSONAL PROBLEMS AND CONFLICTS (2002)

(a) Psychologists refrain from initiating an activity when they know or should know that there is a substantial likelihood that their personal problems will prevent them from performing their work-related activities in a competent manner.
(b) When psychologists become aware of personal problems that may interfere with their performing work-related duties adequately, they take appropriate measures, such as obtaining professional consultation or assistance, and determine whether they should limit, suspend, or terminate their work-related duties.

Impairment can be defined as the incapacity to perform professional functions of the counseling role due to a debilitating medical, substance-related, or psychological condition that results in diminished functioning from a previous higher level of functioning. Manifestations of impairment include clinical depression; substance abuse; sexual harassment, sexual misconduct, and other boundary violations; personality disorders; severe burnout; and medical conditions such as senile dementia or stroke. Psychotherapy or medical treatments are commonly forms of remediation for impairment, although sometimes limitation or loss of licensure or imprisonment is imposed, as in the case of sexual misconduct. Unlike the incompetent counselor, the impaired counselor is able to sustain some semblance of professional demeanor and functioning in the counselor role before exhibiting the recognizable incapacity characteristic of impairment.

Strategies for Preventing Burnout and Impairment

Burnout and impairment can be prevented. Preventing both requires a commitment to promoting self-care and wellness. Rather than being a luxury, self-care could be considered an ethical directive based on the premise that counselors and therapists cannot nurture and care for clients unless they can first nurture and care for themselves. An expert on self-care warns that "one-way caring" is an occupational hazard for helping professionals (Skovholt, 2001). He notes that those who spend most of their professional time caring for others need to acquire the art of caring for themselves.

Preventive self-care strategies are an important means of maintaining well-being. Brems (2000) has provided a detailed self-care plan for counselors and therapists to prevent burnout. Here is a brief overview of the two components of the plan:

Professional Self-Care Strategies

- *Continuing education:* Additional knowledge, skills, and experience can increase both confidence and competence.
- *Consultation and supervision:* Seeking expert input can provide considerable help in dealing with difficult and stressful cases.
- *Networking:* Keeping in regular contact with peers, former faculty members, and supervisors provides support as well as perspective on the rigors of professional practice.
- *Stress management strategies:* In addition to conventional de-stressing strategies, setting limits on the extent of help extended to others can be a necessary corrective for the tendency of helping professionals to give of themselves until they become depleted and exhausted.

Personal Self-Care Strategies

- *Healthy personal habits:* Maintaining a healthy pattern of nutrition, exercise, and sleep as well as moderation in substance use is not optional, it is a necessity.
- *Attention to close relationships:* Relationships with family and significant others provide emotional support and perspective on client and professional relationships.
- *Recreational activities:* Such activities, including hobbies, provide a welcome change of pace from the cognitive and emotional demands of professional practice.
- *Relaxation and centeredness:* Activities like meditation and controlled breathing provide a sense of connectedness and balance in life.
- *Self-exploration and awareness:* Recognition of one's vulnerability and seeking help and support when overwhelmed and consider counseling for personal problems are also necessary.

Chapter 15 continues and enlarges this discussion.

NEGLIGENCE AND MALPRACTICE

Counselors and therapists who perform incompetently can be subject to legal action as well as to sanctions by a licensure board or professional association. Since incompetent service is often negligent service, counselors and therapists can be sued for negligence in civil court.

Negligence

Negligence involves a failure on the professional's part to exercise foresight in performing a service. Negligence can also involve a lack of proper care or an omission or commission of an act that a reasonably prudent professional would or would not do under given circumstances. It is a form of carelessness that departs from the expected standard of care (Ahia, 2002). More succinctly, it has been defined as the dereliction of a duty (i.e., providing a reasonable standard of care) that directly causes damages (Behnke, Winick, & Perez, 2000).

Malpractice

Malpractice is a form of negligence. Malpractice is a violation of the professional duty or duties expected of a reasonably prudent professional, performing below the professional due-care standard. At its core, a malpractice suit involves four basic elements, the four Ds: **d**ereliction of **d**uty **d**irectly causing **d**amages (Behnke et al., 2000). Each of the four Ds is an essential element of a malpractice claim. If any one of the Ds is missing, the lawsuit cannot succeed. In a malpractice case, the plaintiff—the person who claims have been harmed and who brings the lawsuit—must demonstrate by a preponderance of evidence, i.e., at least 50 percent of needed evidence, that each of the four Ds is present. Box 9.5, which describes each of these four elements, is based on the work of Behnke and colleagues (2000).

In other words, in a malpractice suit it must be proved that a client–therapist relationship had been established, that the counselor's or therapist's conduct fell below an acceptable standard of care, that the conduct was the cause of an injury to the client, and that the client suffered harm as a result.

It is important to make a distinction between malpractice and the ordinary mistakes that are a part of professional life. For example, double-scheduling the same session time is unlikely to cause harm to a client and would be considered an ordinary mistake. However, using a regressive therapy such as rebirthing that results in a serious suicide attempt or suffocation death would be negligence and grounds for legal action.

BOX 9.5
THE ELEMENTS OF NEGLIGENCE AND MALPRACTICE: THE FOUR DS

Dereliction	The professional fails to provide care that is reasonable, i.e., within the standard of practice of an average member of the profession practicing within that specialty.
Duty	The professional has a legal responsibility to an individual that gives rise to a duty, i.e., an obligation.
Directly causing	The dereliction of duty must directly cause the damages.
Damages	The person bringing a negligence suit must have suffered harm.

VIEWING COMPETENCE FROM THE THREE PERSPECTIVES

Perspective I

The description of counselors and therapists who embody this perspective is limited to fully credentialed individuals rather than to students-in-training. In terms of professional practice, credentialed individuals with this perspective tend to view their professional work as a job and so are content to put in their time and be compensated to support their out-of-work life. Providing services that are minimally to adequately competent is their goal. Neither informal nor formal learning is a priority for them, and lifelong learning is simply a slogan that may apply to others. Thus, they will not ordinarily seek out supervision or consultation unless the situation demands it. It should not be surprising that they are likely to view formal continuing education requirements as impositions of their credentialing board or professional association, rather than as an invitation and encouragement to grow professionally and personally. The responsibility to monitor their level of competence seems to have little meaning for them, probably because they do not view ongoing education as necessary or important. Self-care is neither valued nor considered essential.

If attending in-house lectures or workshops is optional, they are unlikely to attend unless it relieves them of a work responsibility. If it is mandated, they may attend, but may do so with some reluctance. To log the necessary hours for licensure renewal, they may search for the least expensive or most accessible workshops or training programs, rather than base their choice on what knowledge or skill sets they need to enhance or develop. If the CEU event is industry sponsored with a free lunch or dinner, they may attend irrespective of the personal value of the content matter to their needs. In short, they set their sights no higher than somewhere between a minimal to adequate level of competence. For individuals in Perspective I it is not an issue of incompetence, but rather a matter of limited motivation to progressively increase their levels of competence.

Perspective II

Professional counselors and therapists operating from this perspective recognize that increasing competence is valuable either in terms of advancing their career or because the notion of being a lifelong learner has some appeal. Individuals here tend to view their professional work as a either a career or a calling. To the extent to which their goal is to advance their career they will become involved in informal and formal continuing education efforts. To the extent to which they recognize that their work involves making a difference in others' lives, they are also receptive to involvement in continuing education activities. Largely, their involvement in continuing education efforts is more intense and active compared to those embodying Perspective I, but not with the intensity or commitment of those in Perspective III. Self-care and wellness are more likely to be a reactive response to distress or burnout rather than a proactive initiative. Individuals embodying this perspective are more likely to function in adequate or proficient stages of competence.

Perspective III

Professional counselors and therapists operating from this perspective view competence as an ongoing, developmental process. For the most part, individuals here view their professional work as a calling. Accordingly, they are very invested in their work, and it provides them considerable job satisfaction as well as life satisfaction. Admittedly, they take the responsibility of monitoring their level of competence seriously and welcome opportunities to increase their expertise. Supervision, case consultation, and continuing education programs are important avenues for enhancing knowledge and skills. While some of these individuals are voracious readers and consumers of the professional and research literature in their field, most others manage to find a way to stay current with new developments. These counselors and therapists are often sought out by others for supervision and consultation, roles that they take seriously and in which they are likely to have attained a high level of proficiency. Self-care is valued and considered essential in this perspective, because it is believed that as professionals take care of themselves they are better able to care for others. Self-care and wellness are more likely to be a proactive rather than a reactive response. Not surprisingly, many of these individuals are considered by their peers to be master therapists.

MASTER THERAPISTS AND COMPETENCE

The landmark study of master therapists demonstrated the value they placed on being exceptionally skilled practitioners (Skovholt & Jennings, 2004). A basic conclusion of the study was that these therapists were not content to simply meet the minimum level of competence required by licensure law and ethical standards. Instead, they were highly motivated to become experts in their field. Even after years of experience and training, these therapists placed a high value on building and maintaining their professional knowledge base and skill set.

It was also found that even though they had achieved what others would consider an expert level of practice, these master therapists were continually seeking formal and informal training to further broaden and enhance their clinical abilities. This constant desire and ongoing effort to find opportunities for learning and growth in their profession was a defining characteristic of these master therapists. Their drive for competency combined with an awareness of their own limitations inspired these therapists to become lifelong learners.

These therapists spoke of the importance of finding professional growth experiences beyond traditional didactic venues such as professional conferences and workshops. They particularly looked to consultation and supervision, as well as their own personal therapy, as important avenues for change, challenge, and inspiration. It was important for them to have others critically evaluate their work. They also "spoke eloquently of bolstering the accumulation of clinical experience with sustaining professional relationships to grow professionally" (Jennings, Sovereign, Bottoroff, & Mussell, 2004, p. 111).

For master therapists, their commitment to professional development meant more than just amassing years of clinical experience. For them, experience combined with clinical consultation, ongoing traditional academic training, and professional reflection yielded a deeper level of professional growth. Their commitment to professional growth appears to have bolstered their competence, which in turn they believe is an important ingredient in conducting ethical work. It is interesting to note that the researchers in this study speculated that keeping current on new developments in the profession and exposing their work to others for feedback minimized the potential for unethical behavior among these master therapists.

Another finding of the study involved the relationship of competence and capacity for tolerance of ambiguity. These master therapists were less likely than other therapists to look for easy answers in their work with clients. Staying open to all experience was another hallmark of competent practice for them. They seemed to be searching constantly for the uniqueness and intricacies of a situation. This appreciation of complexities has ethical implications, helping prevent premature closure. Premature closure is the tendency to reduce anxiety by settling for the first solution that presents itself, or to use the same technique in virtually every situation. While premature closure is an effective anxiety reducer for the therapist, the premature solution or intervention chosen can be a poor fit for the client. Failure to be open to complexity and ambiguity leads to narrowing of case conceptualizations and treatment interventions, which can result in less-than-competent work.

Finally, there should be no doubt that these master therapists were functioning at stage 5 and at the maximal level of competence. Their values toward competency and expertise are also unmistakably reflective of Perspective III.

COMPETENCE AND THE DEVELOPMENTAL, RELATIONAL, AND ORGANIZATIONAL DIMENSIONS

In terms of the three contextual dimensions of ethically sensitive, professional practice, competent practice is sensitive to the developmental, relational, and organizational dimensions. By definition, Perspective III is a developmentally oriented perspective and in terms of competence, practitioners continually seek to develop their level of expertise. Relationally, as evidenced in the study of master therapists, these practitioners believed it was essential for them to have others review their work and understood the development of their expertise as related to growth in their professional relationships. While the master therapist study did not specifically address the organizational ethics–community values dimension, those who embody Perspective III attempt to integrate aspects of professional practice as well as personal well-being, mindful that professional ethics must be integrated with personal and organizational ethics. One implication of this sensitivity to the organizational dimension is that these practitioners positively impact the culture of their work setting by words and deeds such that increasing competency and expertise become a new norm.

Let's look again at the cases from the beginning of the chapter in light of these different aspects of competence (see Box 9.6).

BOX 9.6
ADAM AND JORGE: ADDITIONAL OBSERVATIONS

Admittedly, human behavior is complex and not easily explained. Nevertheless, the following observations can be derived from the case material. In terms of work orientations, it appears that Adam manifested a job orientation while Jorge manifested a calling orientation. In terms of levels of professional competence, Adam seemed to be functioning in the minimal to adequate range, while Jorge appeared to be functioning more in moderate to maximal range, and probably somewhere between the proficient stage and expert stage. Based on their attitudes, ideals, and professional behavior, Adam seems to embody Perspective I while more likely Jorge embodies Perspective III.

KEY POINTS

Some key points made in this chapter include the following:

1. A professional is a member of a profession who applies specialized knowledge and skills based on the profession's standards for meeting client's needs.
2. The law requires a minimum level of professional competence to engage in the practice of counseling and psychotherapy, whereas ethics encourages a maximal level of competence.
3. Counselors are required to practice within their boundaries of competence.
4. The development of professional competence begins with graduate training and education, and faculty and supervisors bear the initial responsibility for producing competent practitioners.
5. Training standards are established by accrediting bodies to ensure the graduates of accredited programs possess certain competencies. However, graduation from such programs does not guarantee competence.
6. Two forms of credentialing are licensure and certification. Licensure is a legal process that establishes minimum standards for counselors and therapists to practice in a given the state or jurisdiction.
7. While the purpose of licensure is to protect consumers and promote higher standards of practice, it is unclear whether licensure accomplishes these goals and ensures competence.
8. Certification is another form of credentialing that endeavors to ensure competence.
9. After counselors and therapists began to practice independently, they are responsible for determining their own level of competence.
10. Counselors and therapists are required to seek continuing education in order to maintain their competence.
11. When they experience distress, burnout, or impairment, counselors and therapists are required to protect their clients from harm and restore themselves to their previous levels of functioning.
12. When considering expanding their scope of practice to include client populations and interventions with which they possess little or no training or experience, counselors and therapists must seek additional training and supervision.
13. Malpractice lawsuits arise from claims of counselor or therapist incompetence. The four elements of malpractice must be proved for the suit to succeed.

CONCLUDING NOTE

In many ways all professional and ethical practice revolves around the concept of professional competency. It might be argued that, as a result of developing a high level of professional competence proficiency, master counselors and therapists less frequently encounter issues and dilemmas involving confidentiality, informed consent, conflict of interest, and boundary issues than do other counselors and therapists. How so? Well, it may be because that level of proficiency is reflected in their sensitivity to the professional, cultural, relational, and ethical dimensions of practice. Because ethical sensitivity is both a perspective on counseling practice and the capacity to interpret emerging moral and ethical implications of situation and respond proactively, it become second nature to master counselors to anticipate and respond proactively to various professional and ethical considerations, often before they emerge as challenges or dilemmas. The implication for training and development of counselors and therapists is obvious: Endeavor to increase ethical, cultural, and professional sensitivity and responsiveness.

REVIEW QUESTIONS

1. How would you react if a client accused you of being incompetent? Would your reaction be different if a colleague accused you of being incompetent?
2. Do you think that the requirements for extending your scope of practice are too strict? Too permissive?
3. Do you think that counselors are capable of monitoring their own level of competence?
4. What methods will you use to prevent burnout?
5. Do you think that continuing education requirements are sufficient means to maintaining competence?

REFERENCES

Ahia, C. (2002). *Legal and ethical dictionary for mental health professionals.* Lanham, MD: University Press of America.

American Counseling Association. (2005). *Code of ethics.* (Rev. ed.). Alexandria, VA: Author.

American Psychological Association. (2002). *The ethical principles of psychologists and code of conduct.* Washington, DC: Author.

Baumeister, R. (1991). *Meaning of life.* New York: Guilford.

Behnke, S., Winick, B., & Perez, A. (2000). *The essentials of Florida mental health law: A straightforward guide for clinicians of all disciplines.* New York: Norton.

Bellah, R., Madsen, R., Sullivan, W., Swidler, L., & Tipton, S. (1985). *Habits of the heart: Individualism and commitment in American life.* New York: Harper & Row.

Bernard, J. M., & Goodyear, R. K. (2004). *Fundamentals of clinical supervision* (3rd ed.). Boston: Allyn and Bacon.

Brems, C. (2000). The challenge of preventing burnout and assuring growth: Self-care. In C. Brems, *Dealing with challenges in psychotherapy and counseling* (pp. 262–296). Pacific Grove, CA: Brooks/Cole.

Brincat, C., & Wike, V. (2000). *Morality and the professional life: Values at work.* Upper Saddle River, NJ: Prentice-Hall.

Davidson, J., & Caddell, D. (1994). Religion and the meaning of work. *Journal for the Scientific Study of Religion, 33,* 135–147.

Dreyfus, H., & Dreyfus, S. (1986). *Mind over machine.* New York: Free Press.

Farber, B., & Heifetz, L. (1982). The process and dimensions of burnout in psychotherapists. *Professional Psychology: Resource and Practice, 13,* 293–301.

Jennings, L., Sovereign, A., Bottoroff, N., & Mussell, M. (2004). Ethical values of master therapists. In T. Skovholt & L. Jennings (Eds.), *Master therapists: Exploring expertise in therapy and counseling* (pp. 107–124). Boston: Allyn and Bacon.

Keith-Spiegel, P., & Koocher, G. (1985). *Ethics in psychology: Professional standards and cases.* New York: Random House.

Kottler, J. (1993). *On being a therapist.* San Francisco: Jossey-Bass.

Lamb, D., Presser, N., Pfost, K., Baum, M., Jackson, R., & Jarvis, P. (1987). Confronting professional impairment during the internship: Identification, due process, and remediation. *Professional Psychology: Resource and Practice, 18,* 597–603.

Pines, A., & Aronson, E. (1988). *Career burnout: Causes and cures.* New York: Free Press.

Prochaska, J., & Norcross, J. (1983). Psychotherapists' perspectives on treating themselves and their clients for psychic distress. *Professional Psychology: Resource and Practice, 14,* 642–655.

Rich, J. (1984). *Professional ethics in education.* Springfield, IL: Charles C. Thomas.

Skovholt, T. (2001). *The resilient practitioner: Burnout prevention and self-care strategies.* Boston: Allyn and Bacon.

Skovholt, T., & Ronnestad, M. (1995). *The evolving professional self: Stages and theories in therapist and counselor development.* New York: Wiley.

Skovholt, T., & Jennings, L. (2004). *Master therapists: Exploring expertise in therapy and counseling.* Boston: Allyn and Bacon.

Stoltenberg, C., McNeill, B., & Delworth, U. (1998). *IDM supervision: An integrated development model for supervising counselors and therapists.* San Francisco: Jossey-Bass.

Weber, M. (1958). *The Protestant ethics and the spirit of capitalism.* New York: Scribners.

Wrzesniewski, A., McCaukley, C. Rozin, P., & Schwartz, B. (1997). Jobs, careers, and callings: People's relations to their work. *Journal of Research in Personality, 31,* 21–33.

PART III

ETHICAL AND PROFESSIONAL PRACTICE IN SPECIALTY AREAS

Part III is the largest section of the book. It should be of particular interest to both trainees and practitioners because it provides in-depth, ethically sensitive coverage of most of the professional practice issues faced by counselors and therapists today. The five key areas of professional practice addressed in Part III are mental health counseling and psychotherapy, couple and family counseling/therapy, school counseling, career and rehabilitation counseling, and clinical supervision. Each chapter was designed to provide extensive coverage of the ethical and legal issues in each of these key areas of professional practice. These chapter further elaborate and illustrate the key considerations of confidentiality, informed consent, conflict of interest, and competency that were introduced in Part II. The following chapters are intended to serve as a ready reference source for students and practitioners alike. Presumably, these chapters are sufficiently inclusive that, as the need for information and clarification on ethical practice issues arise, readers can continually and confidently refer back to one or more chapters in Part III throughout their professional careers.

CHAPTER 10

SCHOOL COUNSELING

LINDA WEBB AND LEN SPERRY

Central to the discussion of the integration of professional and ethical practice in school counseling are the leadership and advocacy efforts school counselors make in the implementation of school counseling programs. The school counseling profession has been clear about the direction of school programs. In 1997, the American School Counselor Association (ASCA) established research-based standards reflecting what students should be able to do as a result of participation in school counseling programs in *Sharing the Vision: The National Standards for School Counseling Programs* (Campbell & Dahir, 1997). In 2003, ASCA furthered it efforts toward helping to more clearly define the role and mission of the school counselor and school counseling programs in *The ASCA National Model: A Framework for School Counseling Programs* (ASCA, 2003). This model is competency based and addresses the academic, career, and personal/social needs of students while providing direction regarding delivery, management, and accountability for a comprehensive developmental program. Most recently, ASCA has moved to help school counselors "operationalize" the national model through the development of *The ASCA National Model Workbook* (ASCA, 2004a). Each of these publications reflects professional efforts aimed at supporting counselors and educating all stakeholders in the school community about what counselors do and how they tie to the vision and mission of each school.

ASCA's *Ethical Standards for School Counselors* (ASCA, 2004b) also reflects a clear direction regarding counselor responsibilities to the profession. The preamble to ASCA's ethical code states:

> Professional school counselors are advocates, leaders, collaborators, and consultants who create opportunities for equity in access and success in educational opportunities by connection their programs to the mission of schools and subscribing to (the following) tenants of professional responsibility.

And among professional responsibilities:

> The professional school counselor adheres to ethical standards of the profession, other official policy statements, such as ASCA's position statements, role statement, and *the ASCA National Model,* and relevant statues established by federal, state, and local governments, and *when these are in conflict works responsibly for change.* (F.1.d)

However, it is not only following the call of the profession or adherence to ethical codes that motivates school counselors operating from Perspective III (as introduced in Chapter 1) to take leadership and advocacy roles regarding implementation of their school counseling programs but the integration of *professional practice, ethical codes,* and *personal ethics,* reflecting our internal sense of what is right and why we have chosen the counseling profession. With almost 54 million students in our K-12 schools being served by just over 100,000 school counselors (U.S. Department of Education, 2003), it becomes a strongly integrated personal, professional, and ethical obligation to follow the leadership of the profession that is providing direction in meeting the academic, career, and personal/social needs of all students through the implementation of comprehensive programs. Myrick (2003) describes our changing society in terms of school culture, educational expectations, high-risk behaviors, technology, lifestyles, family, poverty, crime, and violence and how these affect stress and anxiety among today's students. He notes the public demand for high academic performance from students coupled with the expectation these same students be responsible and socially productive citizens. Students need and deserve access to school counselors through school counseling programs aligned with the national model to support this development.

However, even with professional direction, ethical guidance, and knowledge of the far-reaching needs of our students in a changing society, many school counselors continue to struggle with implementation of comprehensive programs, citing being overwhelmed with non-counseling-related activities related to scheduling, discipline, administrative tasks, testing, and other assigned duties. It is the aim of this chapter of *The Ethical and Professional Practice of Counseling and Psychotherapy* to challenge school counselors to focus on one of the most important professional and ethical questions facing them today. It is one that each counselor must address prior to considering core ethical issues related to the practice of school counseling: *As a school counselor, am I tied to the vision and mission of my school and implementing the type of comprehensive program outlined by my profession to meet the academic, career, and personal/social needs of students?*

If the answer is no, what leadership and advocacy efforts are being made to work responsibly for change? If the answer is no, then the need for direction regarding ethics and professional decision making as related to individual and group counseling, classroom guidance, consultation, and the coordination of other services/activities related to implementation of a comprehensive program is secondary. The discussions in this chapter assume that the answer to this professionally and ethically fused question is yes; however, it is understood that for most counselors the answer may be somewhere in between. In the latter case (in between), the professional/ethical obligation is focused on being assertive in showing how you make a difference regarding improved outcomes for students and how you continue to take steps toward a more fully implemented school counseling program.

With the basic professional/ethical issue of program implementation at the forefront, this chapter will move ahead to frame core ethical and professional considerations inherent in school counseling practice and will present case examples using a Perspective III approach. The aim is to help the reader gain an understanding of this approach reflecting the infusion of professional and ethical practice as a guide for daily activities and decision making. The chapter begins with a description of the routine practice of school counseling followed by current professional contexts affecting decisions made by today's school counselors and the impact of organizational dynamics in schools and districts. Next, a discussion of key ethical issues including confidentiality, informed consent, conflicts of interest, and the duty to warn will be explored. Case examples and key legal cases with implications for school counselors will be highlighted. Finally, the seven-step ethical and professional decisional strategy introduced in Chapter 5 will be applied to the case of a high school counselor working with a student who has alleged abuse.

LEARNING OBJECTIVES

After reading this chapter you should be able to

1. Discuss professional and ethical obligations of school counselors regarding program implementation as related to the *ASCA National Model.*
2. Identify and discuss key elements of the American School Counselor Association's *Ethical Standards for School Counselors,* including standards and position statements.
3. Identify key policies and trends affecting the context of professional school counseling today.
4. Discuss the impact of organizational dynamics on the ethical decision-making process in schools and districts.
5. Discuss core ethical issues within the school counseling context including confidentiality, informed consent, boundaries, and competence.
6. Identify and discuss key federal legislation affecting the practice of school counseling.
7. Become familiar with the implications of key legal cases affecting the practice of school counseling.
8. Discuss ethical issues related to special topics including school records, students with special needs, sexual behavior, and spirituality.
9. Apply the ethical decision-making strategy to a case related to school counseling.
10. Compare the application of core ethical standards for school counselors from Perspectives I, II, and III.

KEY TERMS

academic development
accountability
ASCA
CACREP
career development
classroom guidance curriculum
National Model for School Counseling Programs
National Standards for School Counseling Programs
No Child Left Behind Act (NCLB) of 2001
personal/social development

ROUTINE PRACTICES FOR SCHOOL COUNSELORS

Routine practice for today's school counselors involves a wide range of services and activities as part of a comprehensive, developmental guidance and counseling program aimed at the academic, personal/social, and career needs of students. Consider the following examples typically within the routine practice of a school counselor that have clear implications for ethical and professional practice:

- Working with a small group of students whose families are going through a divorce
- Counseling a student who has made a written threat to harm herself in an English essay
- Providing information to a large group of students regarding coursework and credits needed for graduation and postsecondary endeavors
- Consulting with an administrator regarding the potential for violence by a student toward a teacher
- Counseling an upset student who has started the day with an argument with her mother
- Consulting with parents of a student you work with in group about ways to help their child manage anger
- Counseling a student when abuse is suspected but denied by the student

In each of these scenarios, the school counselor is in a position to facilitate change and provide support through the school counseling program. The cases are also examples that reflect both the professional and ethical practice challenges of the school counselor. Issues of informed consent, competence, limits of confidentiality, rights of parents, mandatory reporting, and the duty to warn are all embedded. Herman (2002) studied the prevalence of legal issues facing 273 school counselors and found frequent encounters with cases involving mandatory reporting, confidentiality, and the duty to warn. It is important for today's professional school counselors to be familiar with legal and ethical codes affecting routine practice, while reflecting a basic standard of care within the context of their school communities.

School counselors operating from Perspective I would likely focus on ethical codes and statues with a proactive focus on risk management. They might only consider ethical dilemmas when they present themselves as problems. School counselors moving toward Perspective III would approach these examples of routine practice with ethical sensitivity and with a developmental and contextual focus, yet remain aware of the need to minimize risk for counselors, students, and the educational community.

Ethics from Perspective III is integrated as part of routine practice and not seen as limited to specific ethical dilemmas. From Perspective III the routine practice of school counseling would include advocacy for the implementation of a developmental comprehensive program, as outlined by the profession's national model, aimed at meeting the needs of all students. It would involve assertive efforts to be involved in school improvement with programs linked to the school's vision and mission. It would involve taking every opportunity to share with key stakeholders how you have made a difference with students who have participated in your program. These have not typically been viewed as ethical issues. However, from Perspective III, professional and ethical issues become fundamentally fused. In this book and chapter, the authors emphasize the developmental progression toward a Perspective III approach to ethical-professional practice in counseling.

CONTEXTUAL ISSUES IN SCHOOL COUNSELING

The practice of school counseling at any individual school is uniquely shaped by a counselor's personal and professional development, relational skills, including influences and perspectives on spiritual and multicultural issues, and organizational and community dynamics. Professional counseling organizations, educational groups or boards, and local community values also contribute to the context and resulting decisions regarding school counseling practice.

Personal-Developmental

Four levels of counselor development and corresponding ethical development were discussed in Chapter 2. Development ranged from counselors dependent on others for structure, who tended to take a legalistic stance toward ethical standards, to counselors who had established a personal/professional identity with integrated skills, theory, and practice, who approached ethics from a balanced perspective. The importance of recognizing one's own personal development lies in the implications for counseling practice.

Consider the following example of a school counselor who was trained in a CACREP program and implemented a comprehensive school counseling program. Groups, classroom guidance, consultation, and individual counseling sessions were scheduled, based on the needs of the students, to reflect the mission of the school. While this scenario appears to be what school counselors strive to provide, there were personal issues that got in the way of providing effective services for students. One morning, a 6-year-old student came with a friend to the guidance office shortly after the bell had rung. Her dog had been hit by a car earlier that morning, and the child's mother brought her to school and explained to the teacher what had happened. The teacher agreed that it would be best for the child to stay at school, as the mother needed to go home to take care of the dog. Ten minutes into the school day, the student became weepy, and the teacher allowed her to walk with a friend to the counselor's office. When she arrived, the counselor was in her office, but it was not a time she normally saw students. The counselor refused to see the student, asked that the guidance aide schedule the student for a more appropriate time slot, and sent her back to class without being seen or even acknowledged. This type of personal ethic was not unusual and had a lasting impact on students and teachers in this school; it created a dynamic that discouraged self-referred interaction with the school counselor.

Relational-Multicultural

The relational-multicultural dimensions are broad subsets of the contextual domain affecting ethical decision making. The relational dimension reflects one's capacity for trust, sensitivity, and acceptance. The multicultural dimension refers to factors, such as ethnicity, age, disability, gender, sexual orientation, and spirituality, that impact the counseling process. Chapter 3 offers a complete discussion of the relational-multicultural dimension of ethical decision making with several sets of competency guidelines. Two factors have been chosen for discussion in this section. First, we will explore how the school counselor's view of the multicultural dimension is shaped by counselor education programs, and next, we will look more specifically at an increasingly talked-about topic—spirituality affecting the practice of school counseling.

Counselor Education Programs and the Multicultural Dimension. The degree to which school counseling students and practicing counselors embrace diversity as an important component of their program will reflect the school counselor's own experiences as well as the training program providing their preparation. Counselor education programs are posed to effect multicultural perspectives of school counselors through teaching, practice, and modeling. Accrediting bodies require universities to attend to diversity. For example, the National Counsel for the Accreditation of Teacher Education (NCATE) emphasizes standards aimed at helping colleges of education the host of many school counselor education programs, gaug their effectiveness in the area of diversity with regard to curriculum, faculty, and student experiences in the field. NCATE categorizes unacceptable, acceptable, and target outcomes. For example, the target curriculum standard for diversity emphasizes developing students who will learn to contextualize plans and challenges students toward cognitive complexity. The Council for the Accreditation of Counseling and Related Educational Programs (CACREP) also addresses multicultural perspectives and sets standards to acceptable and target practices. However, what counselor education programs "gear up for" during an accreditation cycle and what is infused as part of their program reflects the difference in stated and actual values. From Perspective III, a counselor educator or counselor education department would be driven by an ethic that promotes multicultural sensitivity that is reflected in its curriculum, clinical experiences, and recruitment and retention of students and faculty. The department would not be driven solely by the need to follow policy and accreditation guidelines. When stated and actual values regarding the multicultural dimension are in line, experiences of students are likely to be reflected in their personal and professional development.

Spiritual Dimension. Another dimension of the contextual domain with ethical implications for school counselors involves *spirituality.* In Chapter 3, the reader will remember, spirituality is described as how individuals think, feel, act, and interact in attempts to make meaningful the important things in their lives. Spirituality can, but does not necessarily have to, overlap religion.

The school counseling profession has recently provided a forum for discussion of spirituality in the 2004 special issue of *Professional School Counseling* (PSC), "Spirituality and the School Counselor." Here, spirituality is a defined as

> Human expressions of and attempts at "meaning-making" that are uniquely personal as well as communal or socio-cultural. It is a notion that reflects a person's attempts to make sense of his or her world. (Sink & Richmond, 2004, p. 291)

Sink (2004) recognizes spirituality as "fundamental to human functioning and assisting persons with their physical and mental health." He makes a case for the spiritual domain as part of a developmental perspective and outlines how "developmental competencies, guidance lessons and spirituality be sensitively infused" in an effort to become more holistic in meeting students needs. Sink (2004) also discusses the implications of spirituality for school counseling programs in addressing standards as outlined in the ASCA National Model (ASCA, 2003a). From individual or group counseling activities exploring questions regarding death and grief to large group developmental guidance activities that support wellness and student growth as a whole person, spirituality can be among the resources students draw upon and develop.

Ingersoll and Bauer (2004) suggest that spirituality is less controversial in today's schools when it is considered innate to human beings and developmental in nature, and they also advocate for integration of spiritual wellness into school counseling settings. They contend that many dimensions of spiritual wellness can be explored as part of a developmental program without overtly using the word *spirituality,* including issues of hope, forgiveness, compassion, meaning, and purpose. These issues would not be uncommon when helping students deal with grief and loss, helping develop compassion and an understanding of differences, or facilitating future goals and plans.

It is also important for counselors to be sensitive to the religious and spiritual climates of their school communities. Lonborg and Bowen (2004) propose that school counselors have an underlying knowledge of the religious and spiritual values of students as part of the larger school community and identify community resources that can help them optimize the multicultural dimension of their counseling programs. While it is important for counselors to be able to value the perspective of students and the community, it is just as important for them to have a full understanding and appreciation for their own cultural worldview (Sue & Sue, 2002).

These developmental views of spirituality seem to fit with a Perspective III approach to meeting the needs of students in school settings. Each involves understanding spirituality as part of human nature, not to be ignored as part of an individual perspective or as a resource from which to draw. Through this broader understanding, counselors have found ways to operationalize spirituality in their counseling programs.

Organizational Ethics–Community Values

The work of school counselors has been shaped by recent efforts within professional organizations as well as by national and state education departments and initiatives aimed at improved student achievement. School counselors are part of the educational community working toward helping students become more successful. It is important that they are knowledgeable and supportive of the school's mission and tie their program to this mission (ASCA, 2004b). Within the educational community, there has been a call for increased accountability with an emphasis on student achievement outcomes. Efforts within the school counseling profession have also reflected this call for increased accountability. This trend began to gain significant momentum with the development of the *National Standards for School Counseling Programs* in 1997 (Campbell & Dahir, 1997). These standards connect school counseling to education initiatives and the educational mission of schools and districts and focus on the academic, personal/social, and career needs of all students. It is no longer enough to show that school counselors are providing appropriate services; counselors are now being asked to show *how students are different* as a result of services provided through school counseling programs. To help answer this question, the American School Counselor Association has developed the *ASCA National Model: A Framework for School Counseling Programs* (ASCA, 2003a). In addition to helping counselors find ways to evaluate their programs based on student outcomes, the model was designed to assist counselors in the design, implementation, and evaluation of the success of their programs and to clarify the counselor's role.

Legislative policy, including the federal No Child Left Behind Act (NCLB) of 2001 (U. S. Department of Education, 2001), standards-based reform measures, and school improvement initiatives call for the enhancement of educational opportunities for all students. NCLB affects educational decision making in districts across the nation and places an increased emphasis on accountability for improved student outcomes for all students. Implications for school counseling professionals are evident. Robert Myrick (2003), a leader in the field of school counseling, has reemphasized the need for school counselors to show how they are part of the educational process and how they contribute to helping students learn more effectively. House and Hayes (2002) concur, while suggesting that it will take the involvement of all key players in the school setting, including the school counselor, to effect systematic change in student outcomes. The Education Trust National Initiative for Transforming School Counseling (2001) also supports this trend and promotes counselor use of interventions that are linked to improved student academic achievement. This type of focus increasingly calls for the use of interventions, strategies, and methods that have been shown to improve student outcomes as part of the school counseling program. Developmental programs are aimed at teaching the skills and strategies students need to be successful and to address social barriers affecting learning.

Professional ethics codes for school counselors also reflect the trends in education. The following statements are indicative of the professional and ethical climate in ASCA's *Ethical Standards for School Counselors* (ASCA, 2004b). Not only do they address professional and ethical practice, but they are also reflective of national standards, models, and the inclusion of the school counselor as part of an educational team tying into the school's stated mission.

The professional school counselor

- Has a primary obligation to the student, who is to be treated with respect as a unique individual. (A.1.a)
- Is concerned with the educational, academic, career, personal, and social needs and encourages the maximum development of every student. (A.1.b)
- Is knowledgeable and supportive of the school's mission and connects his or her program to the school's mission. (D.1.c)
- Conducts her- or himself in such a manner as to advance individual ethical practice and the profession. (F.1.b)
- Adheres to ethical standards of the profession, other official policy statements, such as ASCA's position statements, role statement, and the ASCA National Model, and relevant statues established by federal, state, and local governments, and when these are in conflict works responsibly for change. (F.1.d)

As pointed out in Chapter 4, organizational dynamics can significantly impact the ethical and professional behaviors of counselors in school settings as well as affect their job satisfaction. In that same chapter, organizational ethics was described as the study and practice of ethical behavior in organizations. It involves clarifying and evaluating the values embedded in an organization's policies and practices as well as seeking ways of establishing morally acceptable values-based practices and policies (Ells & MacDonald, 2002). Organizational ethics is as germane to a school district and individual schools as it is to a human services agency or a for-profit corporation. A school's organizational dynamics, most notably its culture and structure, reflect a particular school's or its district's actual core ethical values. Even though it may state that its core ethical value is to foster each student's highest educational development by providing qualified and committed teachers, its culture and structure, particularly its system of rewarding and sanctioning certain behaviors—its actual core ethical value—can be quite different. The example in Box 10.1 illustrates this point.

BOX 10.1
A SCHOOL'S STATED VS. ACTUAL CORE ETHICAL VALUES

There can be a distinct difference in a school's stated and actual core values as evidenced by the following examples.

School 1 is striving to improve the academic outcomes of its students as charged by local, state, and federal initiatives. The school counselor attended a counselor preparation program focusing on the implementation of a comprehensive model and has attended district meetings that reinforce its importance. Even though the school administration supports the concept of implementation of a comprehensive program (stated value) targeting academic student outcomes, the counselor does not fully implement such a model due to the demand focus on non-counseling duties related to tutoring and test administration. She is expected to cover classes as teachers plan, give supplemental practice tests to students who have not previously performed well on standardized tests, and organize test schedules and materials. In this case, the school's stated value is not evidenced by school counseling program implementation.

School 2 is striving to improve the academic outcomes of its students as charged by local, state, and federal initiatives. The school counselor attended a counselor preparation program focusing on the implementation of a comprehensive model and has attended district meetings that reinforce its importance. The administration supports the concept of the implementation of a comprehensive school counseling program tied to student achievement outcomes. The counselor in this school also has responsibilities tied to test administration. It is part of her annual plan and the school improvement plan. She is part of a team of teachers, administrators, and volunteers who support the organization of the testing process. The counselor is involved with test preparation, including helping students and teachers develop skills and strategies to help reduce the anxiety and stress associated with test taking, through collaborative work with teachers in classrooms and group counseling. The counselor also works in classrooms and groups throughout the year helping students link their social, emotional, and physical well-being to achievement outcomes (and test results). In addition, she will facilitate a brief workshop for teachers regarding test score interpretation. In this case, the stated value regarding implementation of a comprehensive program was evidenced by the focus on appropriate activities for the counselor related to testing.

The "stated value" of *supporting implementation of a comprehensive school counseling program* was similar in both schools. However, the counselor in the first school found herself with duties unrelated to implementation of her program. While one might consider the counselor in the second school "lucky" to find a school staff and administrator who supported implementation of her comprehensive program and whose actual values were in line with their stated values, we cannot underestimate the role of the counselor in facilitating that match. The counselor in the second school has taken clear steps—making sure she has explained to stakeholders how she can contribute to improved student outcomes through involvement in school improvement—to connect her program to the school's mission. The counselor in the second school is not simply "lucky" but a skilled proactive professional school counselor who understands her ethical obligation to work toward the implementation of a comprehensive school counseling program.

Assessing Organizational Ethics in School Settings. It is advisable for any professional working in a school setting to ascertain its organizational ethics. Ethical audits and organization assessment inventories and surveys, which were introduced in Chapter 4, are our way of assessing and evaluating a school's organizational ethics. Why should a counseling trainee or school counselor consider performing an ethical audit in the school or school system for which he or she will do an internship or be hired as a counselor? In other words, what is the value of such an assessment?

The main reason is that the organizational dynamics of school or school district can significantly impact the ethical and professional behaviors as well the job satisfaction of counseling interns and school counselors. Schools and districts that have well-articulated ethical values, principles, and professional standards and that act on these values, principles, and standards tend to foster both student educational and emotional development and the personal and professional development of teaching and counseling staff better than schools and districts that do not. Staff and student commitment is likely to be higher, staff and student turnover is likely to be lower, and quality educational programming is likely to result. This is particularly the case when a counseling intern's or school counselor's core ethical values and the school's actual ethical values are consistent. On the other hand, the less positive and healthy the ethical culture or climate of a school, the more likely counseling interns and school counselors may experience work-related stress. An ethical audit is one tool to assess the ethical climate of a particular school or district (see Box 10.2).

BOX 10.2

ASSESSING ORGANIZATIONAL ETHICS IN SCHOOL SETTINGS

Directions: Using the following 1–5 scale, rate evaluate each of the following items based on your current experience with a particular school's ethical values, climate, and practices.

1 = disagree fully; 2 = disagree somewhat; 3 = neutral; 4 = agree somewhat; 5 = agree fully

___ 1. There is a formal ethics policy that articulates the ethical values, principles, and professional standards to which this school is committed.

___ 2. The school's actual core values and policies match its stated core values and policies.

___ 3. The school's commitment to its core values, ethical policies, and professional standards is championed by leadership and communicated routinely throughout it in staff orientation, training programs, and regular meetings.

___ 4. Staff understands and agrees with the school's core values and ethical expectations.

___ 5. Staff are listened to when they identify ethical concerns about any aspect of their work.

___ 6. Ethical behavior is recognized and rewarded, while immoral and unethical behavior is censured.

___ 7. All staff and students are treated with respect, fairness, and equality.

___ 8. The school's ethical commitment and elements of its ethics policy and professional standards are routinely discussed in staff and other meetings.

___ 9. Confidentiality and client privacy is effectively safeguarded in this school.

___ 10. Increasing professional competency is highly valued and rewarded in this organization.

___ 11. Establishing and maintaining appropriate boundaries and avoiding harmful conflict of interests is expected and achieved in this school.

___ 12. Informed consent is provided initially and on an ongoing basis to students and their families.

___ 13. There are formal processes in place for staff to report suspected unethical behavior and/or to ask questions to clarify understanding of the ethics policies and standards without fear of retaliation, retribution, or reprisal.

___ 14. My ethical values and principles are consistent with the school's values and principles.

___ 15. This school has a positive and healthy ethical culture or climate.

Taking an integrated perspective, the school counselor will infuse his or her own personal ethics with ethical obligations to the profession, as outlined in relevant ethical codes, while being mindful of the organizational and community values that may also shape his or her practice.

CORE ETHICAL ISSUES FOR SCHOOL COUNSELORS

In professional ethics confidentiality, informed consent, boundaries, conflict of interest, and competency are viewed as the core ethical issues facing therapists and counselors, including those working in school settings. This section describes how these four considerations are typically experienced in school settings.

Confidentiality

Confidentiality is a particularly complex issue for counselors in schools. School counseling interns and practicum students are often surprised when they learn that issues of confidentiality and privacy constitute some of the most complex ethical considerations faced by counselors in educational settings. School counselors are challenged to balance ethical obligations to students who are minors, the rights of parents to be informed and involved in decisions regarding their children, and the need for teachers to better understand the issues affecting the learning of their students. The following discussion of confidentiality will include (a) a brief look at the codes, statements, and types of policies effecting decisions regarding confidentiality, (b) three approaches regarding confidentiality between students and school counselors, (c) a Perspective III approach to confidentiality when working with students in the schools, and (d) a look at cases with implications for ethical issues in other school counselor contexts.

Ethical Codes, Statements, and Policies. Both ASCA's *Ethical Standards for School Counselors* (ASCA, 2004b) and the American Counseling Association's *Code of Ethics and Standards of Practice* (ACA, 2005) provide guidelines to help school counselors understand and apply the principles of confidentiality when working in the school setting. Both of these codes are based upon a series of moral principles (Remley, Hermann & Huey, 2003) discussed in previous chapters, including veracity, justice, nonmalfeasance, beneficence, autonomy, and fidelity. ASCA's *Ethical Standards for School Counselors* (ASCA, 2004) outlines the following among the important tenants of confidentiality for the professional school counselor working with students.

- Making sure students are informed about the counseling process and procedure and understand the limits of confidentiality (A.2.a)
- Keeping information confidential unless disclosure is required due to safety or legal requirements (A.2.b)
- Informing third parties who are at high risk for contracting a communicable and fatal disease while providing conditions for disclosure (A.2.c)
- Requesting court disclosure not be required if it will bring harm to the student or counseling relationship (A.2.d)
- Protecting the confidentiality of students' records (A.2.e)
- Protecting the confidentiality of information received in the counseling relationship and informed consent for disclosure (A.2.f)
- Recognizing primary obligation for confidentiality to the student but balancing that obligation with the rights of parents to be informed (A.2.g)
- Respecting the rights and responsibilities of parents for their children and working collaboratively with parents when appropriate (B.1.a)

ASCA has also issued a position statement regarding confidentiality:

> A student has the right to privacy and confidentiality. ASCA recognizes that a counseling relationship requires an atmosphere of trust and confidence between the student and the counselor. Confidentiality ensures that disclosures will not be divulged to others except when authorized by the student or when there is a clear and present danger to the student or others. (ASCA, 2002)

In addition, school counselors must take into consideration the policies of individual states and school districts regarding the sharing of information with parents, teachers, or other school personnel. It is important to note that states and districts vary in their requirements for disclosure of information on issues such as those involving sexual activity, pregnancy, or drug use. Variations of disclosure policies also exist regarding the age or grade level of students. The requirement for sharing information on topics such as drug use with elementary and middle school parents may be different when working with high school students in that same district. Another district may have a policy regarding disclosure for all students regardless of age, while a third district may not require such disclosure at any level. This is only an example. School counselors must be aware of local and state policies affecting their practice in the schools.

While the guidelines appear fairly concrete about when a counselor should break confidentiality, the decisions counselors reach are varied. A survey of practicing school counselors by Davis and Mickelson (1994) found that, related to ethical dilemmas involving confidentiality and parent rights, the agreement rate was less than 50 percent regarding the preferred ethical or legal decision. Just as varied are the approaches to handling confidentiality with students in schools. The following is a look at three different approaches, as described by Littrell and Zinck (2005), to the challenges faced by school counselors regarding confidentiality when counseling students in an individual setting.

Confidentiality in the Individual Counseling Context: Three Approaches. The first approach involves keeping strict confidence except in exceptional circumstances or when mandatory reporting is necessary (Littrell & Zinck, 2005). The counselor only shares information with parents or teachers with the consent of the student. Collins and Knowles (1995) surveyed 13- to 18-year-old students regarding the importance of confidentiality. Overall, 99 percent indicated that confidentiality was either essential (53%) or important (46%), reflecting the significance of the issue to older students. Counselors adhering to this approach feel that students may not seek them out for help or trust them to share concerns if what they say is not going to be kept confidential. Other professionals agree with the importance of maintaining strict confidences (Ford, Millstein, Halpern-Felsher, & Irwin, 1997; Zingaro, 1983). Maintaining confidences is one way counselors develop trust, an essential element in developing an effective working relationship with students. This approach is inherent in both the ACA and ASCA ethical codes.

The second approach involves being very open with parents (Littrell & Zinck, 2005). Counselors using this approach may see confidentiality as keeping what the student discloses among the student, counselor, and parent. The counselor would share information with parents when deemed to be in the best interest of the student. While not necessarily disclosing specific content or dialogue of the sessions, counselors would provide information helpful to parents in deciding how they might best help their child. This would go beyond issues outlined in legal and ethical codes or district or school policy regarding required disclosure of specific types of information.

While Littrell and Zinck (2005) describe this more open approach with parents, some counselors may find it helpful for teachers also to have information that creates a heightened sensitivity to the needs of their students and allows for changes that will have positive outcomes for students. As previously reported in Chapter 6, Issacs and Stone (1999) surveyed school counselors about the circumstances in which they would share confidential information and found that elementary and middle school counselors would share confidential information more frequently than secondary school counselors. Counselors felt the age of the student and seriousness of the circumstance were important variables affecting the limits of confidentiality. As Remley (1985) notes, "the child's expectation of privacy is sometimes outweighed by the need to inform parents, guardians, or other adults" (p. 184). Significant adults, particularly parents and teachers, are important change factors in the lives of younger students.

Counselors using this approach would need to be certain students of any age are clearly informed about the counseling process and limits of confidentiality before counseling begins, with care being taken to remind students throughout the duration of counseling that information may be shared. This approach attempts to reflect the primary obligation for confidentiality to the student while balancing that obligation with an understanding of the rights of parents to be the guiding voice in their children's lives (ASCA, 2004b, A.2.g). That can be difficult indeed.

The third approach includes students' sharing information from counseling sessions with their parents to keep them informed and involved (Littrell & Zinck, 2005). Students can trust the counselor to keep information confidential but are encouraged, never forced, to share all or parts of the counseling session with parents following each session. With student permission, the counselor may also share information that would assist parents in guiding, supporting, or making decisions regarding their children. The counselor using this approach satisfies ethical requirements of confidentiality, supports the rights of parents to be involved and informed, and can build connections between students and their parents. If students are comfortable sharing, this might help initiate and build important parent–child connections, producing improved outcomes for the student. On the other hand, this could also create a difficult situation for students who are reluctant yet pressured by parents to share the contents of counseling sessions, creating further stress on the relationships.

Each of these three approaches may be appropriate given particular circumstances when working with individual students. However, individual counseling is but one of the direct services school counselors are prepared to provide targeting improved student outcomes. The tenets of confidentiality and disclosure of information have implications for other specific contexts of a comprehensive developmental guidance and counseling program. Counseling students in small groups, consulting with parents and teachers, and facilitating classroom guidance each have unique issues related to confidentiality.

Small-Group Counseling. Group counseling in schools generally involves students who have been referred based on a particular need affecting academic and/or social outcomes. These may include working on anger, academic skills, social skills, anxiety, dealing with loss, or changes in families. In each of these cases students are encouraged to share behaviors, experiences, and feelings that are causing concern or anxiety and to work on solutions in an environment of trust, encouragement, and support. It is important for the school counselor to explain the nature of confidentiality to students during the screening process and work with students to reach agreement about the need to maintain confidentiality in the group to build this trusting environment. The counselor should be sensitive to the types of disclosures students choose to make during sessions and continue to stress the importance of confidentiality. The ASCA has recognized that some topics may not be appropriate for group work in school settings (ASCA, 2004b A.6.c). Personally sensitive issues or those involving harm or abuse should be acknowledged, with an opportunity extended to the student to see the counselor at another time.

Groups facilitated in schools may be viewed differently by parents than groups facilitated in private mental health settings. Referrals to the school counselor may come from the students themselves, their teachers, or their parents. While parents may agree to the need for students to participate, they may be reluctant at the thought of "personal family issues" being shared at school. It is important to keep parents informed regarding the nature of group participation and the limits of confidentiality within groups. School counselors should be acutely aware of the sensitive nature of personal disclosures from a student, family, and community perspective while utilizing opportunities to maximize positive outcomes for students through involvement of teachers or parents.

The school counselor may use the age of the students, group focus, and school policy to make decisions regarding parent permission or parent notification of group participation. It is recommended when working with younger students and more sensitive topics regarding family privacy that counselors secure parent permission. As students become older or topics are less personally sensitive, such as academic skills, it continues to be important that parents are at least notified of the nature of the group and that their child has an opportunity to participate. The counselor should include contact information to answer any questions. In all cases, school and district policies should be followed.

Large-Group Guidance. Myrick (2003) suggests that once a group of students exceeds ten, it is no longer a small group, as the function and focus of the group changes due to the dynamics of multiple relationships and interactions. Large-group guidance in schools usually involves developmental or informational topics, with the counselor taking a teaching/coaching role while facilitating discussion, interaction, and practice among participating students. A broad range of topics may be covered in large-group guidance, each aimed at academic, personal/social, and career outcomes for students. The large-group format does not assume confidentiality—a concept that should be shared with participating students. However, the school counselor can take some steps to create a climate of support and caring in which students are taught to listen with empathy and support to others ideas in the classroom. Brigman and Webb (2004) outline classroom activities designed to build skills that foster trusting relationships within the classroom in their *Student Success Skills: A Classroom Manual.* Sears (2005) suggests ground rules to help create an atmosphere within the large group that encourage expression of ideas and feelings by students and to serve as a reasonable precaution to protect students against other students that include showing respect for different ideas and opinions and the need to respect the privacy of students who make personal comments. Counselors who are acting from an ethic of care will be sensitive to the personal needs of students as they arise in the large group by acknowledging the sensitive nature of personal disclosures and providing an opportunity for further exploration in a setting in which privacy can be maintained.

Consultation with Parents, Teachers, Administrators, and Community. Consultation with teachers, parents, and administrators provides an opportunity for the school counselor to work with significant adults in the lives of students while providing a holistic approach to understanding their academic and personal social needs. Consultation provides the vehicle for school counselors to interact with community and referral sources that are involved with the education and well-being of children and adolescents. It is recognized as an effective use of counselor time aimed at reaching the most students (Gysbers & Henderson, 2000; Myrick, 2003; Wittmer, 2000). The *National Standards* of the American School Counselor Association (Campbell & Dahir, 1997) include consultation as one of four services critical to the successful implementation of a comprehensive developmental school guidance and counseling program.

While ASCA's *Ethical Standards for School Counselors* (2004b) does not specifically address consultation, it does provide clear guidelines regarding confidentiality of the counseling relationship and ethical standards for sharing information with other persons or professionals. ACA's *Code of Ethics and Standards of Practice* (2005) specifically addresses the issues of confidentiality, sharing information with other professionals, and the need to involve the consultee by providing a clear understanding of the process aimed at positive growth and development (D.2.a–d).

Several ethical issues frequently arise as related to the school counselor's consultative role, including confidentiality and the nature of the relationship. Consider the example in Box 10.3 of the school counselor as a consultant.

BOX 10.3
SCHOOL COUNSELOR AS CONSULTANT

Ms. Morris is an elementary school principal who is well liked and respected by teachers, students, parents, and peers. She uses a leadership style that includes shared decision making and frequently consults other school staff regarding day-to-day concerns as well as continuous school improvement. The school counselor, Ms. Menendez, was recently asked to schedule a time to talk with the principal. During the meeting, the principal asked about her observations and experiences with a kindergarten teacher in her second year at the school who was having difficulty managing the behavior of several students in her class. This resulted from parent concern that was being communicated to the teacher and principal that the learning of all students was being affected. At the meeting, the principal also asked the counselor if she would consult with the kindergarten teacher, with the goal being to get at issues affecting classroom dynamics and the development of strategies aimed at reducing the incidents of misbehavior of targeted students while increasing academic time on task for the entire class. The principal asked to be kept updated as to how things were going with the teacher and her class. The principal made the request in the spirit of helping the teacher and knew the counselor had been effective in helping others with problem students in the past. What ethical considerations exist for the counselor with regard to the meeting with the principal and the suggested consultation with the kindergarten teacher?

School counselors, whose role includes being a behavior and relationship expert in their schools (Myrick, 2003), frequently consult with teachers about students with problem behaviors. In this case, the school counselor has the training and skills making her competent for the task at hand—helping the kindergarten teacher explore the problem behaviors in her classroom and working with her to develop a plan for intervention. However, in this case, attention must be given to several ethical issues if the counselor is to remain effective as a consultative resource for teachers and parents. First, it should be acknowledged that consultation, especially with teachers, is a peer relationship that does not involve evaluating or supervising teacher performance for administrative purposes. This type of dual relationship makes it virtually impossible for the counselor to establish a supportive, growth-oriented relationship during consultation in which the teacher feels free to share what is and is not going well in her classroom. The counselor cannot be perceived as someone who will routinely report concerns about teachers to administrators.

A second ethical concern for consideration involves the nature of the consultative relationship. In this case the principal is suggesting the counselor and teacher engage in a consultative process as a strategy aimed at helping the kindergarten teacher. It is important that this be a voluntary process and that a level of trust be present.

Issues of confidentiality also arise in this case. Who will approach the teacher regarding the possibility of consultation, and what will she be told about the meeting between the principal and counselor? How can the counselor reduce this new teacher's anxiety resulting from counselor-principal discussion of behavior concerns in her classroom? If the teacher does see consultation with the school counselor as a strategy that might help her with her class, how will the counselor handle requests from the principal to keep her informed?

The developmental level of the counselor, as previously discussed in Chapter 2, may likely impact the outcome of such a case. Counselors with a well-developed professional identity, who are comfortable with their autonomy and who have an accurate sense of their abilities, are most likely to be able to work with all stakeholders in a manner that demonstrates awareness and concern. Counselors who are less developed may be concerned about not "cooperating" with requests of administrators.

The counselor in this case suggested that the teacher be aware of several things prior to the consultation: (a) that the principal has talked with the counselor about students experiencing ongoing behavior problems in her class; (b) the counselor has been of help to other teachers with similar problems; (c) the counselor is available for consultation and/or collaboration; and (d) the counselor will maintain confidentiality with the teacher and will not be "reporting" back to the principal. The consultative relationship with the teacher would need to be built on the premise of trust and working together, with the teacher being informed of the confidential nature of the relationship. This option provides the counselor an opportunity to maintain effective, supportive relationships with this and other teachers in the school while being responsive to administrative requests.

Confidentiality and Perspective III. Confidentiality is indeed a complex issue for school counselors. It requires a careful case-by-case examination of the context—whether individual group counseling, classroom guidance or consultation. Confidentiality take into account the personal circumstances of the individual student such as age, family circumstances, ethnic and cultural factors, community mores—the organizational ethics of the school, and the immediacy of the situation. Counselors moving toward Perspective III would do well to recall that confidentiality is the cornerstone of the counseling relationship and that students tend to respond to the prospect of a conversation being held in confidence by the counselor with a sense of openness and trust. As noted in a previous chapter, counselors and therapists who practice in a genuine and respectful manner and value confidentiality tend to foster connection through emotional experiences as well as positive changes in their clients. Thus, safeguarding confidentiality is critically important. Obviously, there are circumstances when breaching confidentiality is necessary. In such circumstances, counselors practicing from Perspective III have already prepared their clients—that is, they have provided informed consent and addressed the limits of confidentiality—and view the process of discussing the sharing of confidential communication as a professional practice issue, not merely a legal or ethical one. They endeavor to engage the client in whatever way possible to be involved in providing information to a third party.

Recently, an ethically sensitive school counselor mentioned that, in her experience, confidentiality and informed consent go hand in hand. By this she meant that she informs students who want to talk with her about confidentially and its value and limits right from the outset. When certain concerns or issues are raised by the student, she again provides informed consent about confidentiality. For her, confidentiality is a professional counseling practice consideration as well as an ethical practice consideration. Needless to say, this school counselor operates from Perspective III. The example in Box 10.4 illustrates a case involving informed consent.

BOX 10.4
CONFIDENTIALITY AND INFORMED CONSENT

Jason, a ninth-grade student, asked to see the counselor. When he entered the office he appeared somewhat anxious. He had worked with the school counselor, Mr. Mathias, in large-group guidance but had never met with him individually. Mr. Mathias welcomed Jason, acknowledged his request to see a counselor, and briefly explained the counseling process. Mr. Mathias was mindful to include informing Jason of the confidential nature of disclosure in the session and that information would only be shared if Jason agreed that it would be helpful. Mr. Mathias added that there were a few exceptions to confidentiality he wanted Jason to understand and took the time to explain them, including the threat of harm to self or others. Mr. Mathias explained that he must always be sure students and others at school are safe. He asked Jason if he had any questions about the process and the nature of the confidentiality and if he thought this process might be helpful. Jason stated that he understood and wanted to proceed with the session. The counselor then asked Jason how he could be of help.

Jason's dilemma involved making a decision to provide information and the names of two students who were selling drugs on the school campus. These were students Jason knew; he wanted them to stop but did not want to get them in trouble. There was guilt and anxiety associated with either decision he made. Mr. Mathias focused on the guilt and anxiety and helped Jason to examine the risks and benefits of either decision. The counselor provided support throughout the decision-making process. At the end of the session, Jason said he wanted to disclose the information. Mr. Mathias reminded Jason that while he would not disclose Jason's name, he would likely disclose the names of the students selling the drugs, as their behavior posed a risk to the entire school community. He also said he could not guarantee how their identification might affect their status at school. Jason disclosed the names, and the counselor gave those names to the assistant principal.

This case demonstrates the nature of the relationship between confidentiality and our next core ethical consideration, informed consent. Mr. Mathias took care to consider the complex decisions and feelings facing Jason. He was careful from the start to make sure Jason was informed about the process and considered the need to re-address confidentiality as it became clear that it was at the center of the decision.

Informed Consent

Informed consent was discussed and defined in Chapter 7 as referring to the practice of obtaining consent for treatment that includes adequate information for the client to make an informed choice about participating. Several unique aspects arise regarding informed consent as it is applicable to school counselors. These include ethical considerations for large-group guidance and individual and group counseling as part of a comprehensive program. This discussion of the ethics of informed consent will include the role of the school counselor, with implications for individual and group counseling and large group guidance. A case example with questions regarding informed consent, along with a Perspective III discussion, will follow.

School counselors aim to implement comprehensive developmental school counseling programs that meet the needs of all students in their schools. They are part of the instructional staff that interacts with students on a day-to-day basis to help students achieve academic and social competence. However, the school counselor's role in helping students to achieve these outcomes may not be as obvious to parents as that of the teacher or a curriculum specialist. The ASCA takes the position that it is the responsibility of the school counselor to inform the school community, including parents, of the role of the counselor and services that will be provided.

> The professional school counselor makes counselees and their parents knowledgeable of the services available through the school counselor. School counselors provide written information regarding school counseling programs to the school publics; an explanation of legal and ethical limits to confidentiality may be included. Parental consent for services is obtained if state or local law or policy requires it. (ASCA, 2004c)

Variations in laws and policies from state to state, district to district, and even school to school require school counselors to be knowledgeable about the need to obtain written permission for services. Some districts provide policies regarding when parental permission is needed prior to a student receiving counseling services. This may include the right for minor students to consent to their own counseling services once they have reached the age at which the state's law allows them to consent for their own mental health services. Linde (2003) provides a list by state of the ages at which minors can consent to their own heath care (including mental health care). Other districts do not require parental permission, because the school counselor is part of the regular school staff providing services to students. However, if we consider informed consent beyond the required technical aspects of laws and policies, and look at it from an ethic of care perspective reflecting a relational power-sharing process, we may get our best direction in making decisions regarding informed consent.

Individual Counseling. School counselors work with individual students to provide counseling, support, and information. Individual counseling is one of several direct services provided by school counselors. According to Myrick (2003), the school counselor's work will consist primarily of brief counseling, as it is consistent with the time available and types of issues school counselors encounter as they work with individual students. A counselor may see the student once or plan to work with the student over several sessions.

Students may be referred by parents or teachers or may initiate contact with the counselor themselves. This creates a unique situation. When children and adolescents receive counseling outside of school, the parent or guardian is likely to be involved with the referral, give informed consent for the counseling services, and be in direct contact with the counselor providing demographic and/or background information. When children and adolescents are in school and go to see the school counselor as the result of a teacher- or self-referral, the parent may not be aware. Some districts have policies that require counselors to obtain parental permission for individual counseling if it exceeds one session. It would create an almost impossible situation for school counselors if they were required to turn away individual students when they were upset or needed support. Related to the issue of informed consent is confidentiality. While a school may require that a parent be informed or give permission for their child to enter counseling, it is important that the counselor inform the parents of the primary obligation of confidentiality to the student. The counselor would protect confidentiality and reveal information to others only with the informed consent of the student. Contexts and circumstances in which the counselor would encourage the student to share information with parents or teachers and exceptions to confidentiality have been previously discussed.

Small-Group Counseling. Students who have been identified as potentially benefiting from additional academic or social support may be referred for group counseling. Topics may include working on anger, academic skills, social skills, anxiety, dealing with loss, or changes in families. In each of these cases, it is important for the student and parent to understand the purpose, benefits, goals, techniques, expected behaviors, and limitations involved in group participation. Pregroup screening of prospective group members by the school counselor can provide the opportunity to share this information with students so they might better understand the nature of the group and decide if they would like to participate. It is also important for the counselor to stress the confidential nature of information shared during participation from the beginning of the group process. Students commonly share family and relationship issues as well as other private information and should expect disclosures to remain with in the group. However, it is recognized that, while the counselor can stress the importance of confidentiality, it cannot be guaranteed. The professional school counselor establishes clear expectations in the group setting and clearly states that confidentiality in group counseling cannot be guaranteed. Given the developmental and chronological ages of minors in schools, the counselor recognizes the tenuous nature of confidentiality for minors and renders some topics inappropriate for group work in a school setting (ASCA, 2004b, A.6)

The nature of confidentiality in the group process should be communicated as part of informed consent. The Association for Specialists in Group Work (ASGW) has developed *Best Practice Guidelines* (ASGW, 1998), which includes guidelines for screening prospective group members, issues of confidentiality, and informed consent. In addition to providing students with information about the group during the screening process, counselors can also assess whether each student will be a good fit for the group. Once this information is shared, students have an opportunity to "assent" to voluntary participation. Some question the ability of students, especially young students, to give informed consent arguing their lack of understanding and experience. However, giving information to students using developmentally appropriate language allows them to be involved in the decision-making process and promotes autonomy.

School policies vary regarding the requirement to inform parents of a student's group participation, and counselors should know the prevailing policy. The ASCA code (2004b) states:

> The professional school counselor notifies parents/guardians and staff of group participation if the counselor deems it appropriate and if consistent with school board policy or practice. (A.6.b)

The counselor seeking informed consent from parents will share the same types of information that were shared with students in the assent process. This can be done through a parent information letter that includes contact information and an invitation to call the counselor if they have any questions or information that might better help the counselor work with their child. Parents would then have an opportunity to give informed consent for their child's participation.

With older students, some counselors may send this type of letter but not require it to be returned as a condition of group participation. When parents are not informed by the counselor of a student's participation in a counseling group, they may feel they have missed an opportunity to collaborate with school personnel on issues affecting their child or become upset that they have not been kept informed. If confidentiality is breached by group members and sensitive information is shared outside of the group affecting a student or a student's family, parents may feel particularly distressed that they were not informed.

Large-Group Guidance. Another direct service school counselors provide is large-group guidance targeting skills and information that all students can use to help them develop socially and become better students. While large-group guidance topics are generally considered developmental in nature and part of the regular school curriculum, it is advised that parents be informed regarding topics and schedules. This can be done through school handbooks, guidance brochures, school or grade-level newsletters, or school websites. If there are questions, parents will have an opportunity to ask. Making parents aware of topics being discussed at school during classroom guidance can also act as a springboard to their own conversations on important topics. Consider the case presented in Box 10.5.

BOX 10.5
LARGE-GROUP GUIDANCE AND INFORMED CONSENT

Kathy is a school counselor who uses a developmental approach to guidance and counseling based on the ASCA model and her district's K-12 plan. The district plan includes a 6- to 8-session unit with students in grade five to target developmental tasks generally facing students as they transition to middle school and adolescence. During the unit, students are provided

(continued)

BOX 10.5 CONTINUED

information and a safe environment to discuss issues and gain understanding of the physical and emotional changes associated with these transitions. This includes information about reproduction and sexually transmitted diseases. Kathy refers to this unit as "Human Growth and Development" and has listed it on the annual calendar that goes home to all parents in September, along with the topics for other classroom guidance units planned throughout the year. Consent is not required for classroom guidance because it is generally seen as part of the regular school curriculum. Kathy has talked with other school counselors and is wondering if additional steps to inform parents regarding the curriculum would be best. What contextual issues might be relevant? If Kathy decided to get consent from parents, what steps might be taken to ensure "informed" consent? What are the benefits and risks involved in making participation contingent on parent consent?

Individuals with Disabilities Education Act. Students experiencing difficulty in school who do not improve with planned intervention or whose needs are not being met in the regular classroom may be considered for some type of formal evaluation to determine eligibility for special education services. While school counselors generally do not perform these types of evaluations, they are often part of the team of professionals gathering information and data that may be used as part of the evaluation. Attaining informed consent for these types of evaluations can have both legal and ethical components.

The current federal Individuals with Disabilities Education Act (IDEA), evolving from the original 1975 Education for All Handicapped Children Act (EAHCA), addresses the rights of parents with implications for informed consent. Amendments to IDEA in 1997 included expanding role of parents in several ways including participation in all meetings regarding evaluation, placement, and education of their child; examining all records relating to their child; and being notified of procedural rights as well as information they need to participate in educational decisions regarding their child (Alexander & Alexander, 2005). Each state is required to put procedures in place that will meet the requirements of IDEA in order to receive federal funds to support programs. Parents of students who are identified as eligible for evaluation for special education services must be provided information to be in a position to give an informed consent for evaluation. They must also be provided information that will allow them to make informed consent decisions regarding the placement and education of their children. While informed consent in this context is a legal issue, the level of care and consideration afforded parents making these difficult decisions becomes an ethical one as well. Consider the following two cases, one in which the counselor is careful to follow legal protocol, and one in which the counselor adds an ethic of care for the parents and their child to support the decision at hand (Box 10.6).

BOX 10.6

ETHICAL DECISION MAKING TO ENHANCE LEGAL DECISIONS

CASE 1

A counselor and teacher meet with parents regarding the placement of their child in exceptional education. The counselor is familiar with all of the policies and requirements of informed consent and follows important protocol related to parents' rights and informed consent. At the meeting, all information is reviewed, but the parents are somewhat hesitant to sign for permission for a special education placement. The counselor provides examples of how other students have been helped, and the classroom teacher, anxious for the student to begin receiving services, also encourages the placement. The parents voluntarily sign for the placement to begin.

CASE 2

In this case, the counselor is also familiar with requirements and protocol and is aware that the parents are somewhat hesitant. While the teacher is anxious for the student to begin receiving services outside of the regular classroom, the counselor asks the parents if they would like to schedule a visit to the classroom where their child would be served or further review the proposed placement. The counselor suggests they jot down questions they have for the ESE teacher, counselor, or others who would be involved in serving their child, because this is an important decision that could affect educational decisions for years to come.

What are your thoughts about the ethical perspectives of each of the counselors?

Informed Consent and Perspective III. In the case above it is evident that the second counselor is closer to Perspective III, as demonstrated by her ethical sensitivity and knowledge regarding procedures related to the evaluation and informed consent. It is her professional practice to fuse this type of sensitivity and offer opportunities for true informed consent that goes beyond what the law requires.

Informed consent in counseling should involve discussion with the client about the nature of counseling and its limits, including those involving confidentiality, possible risks, and so on. It may involve documentation and even having the student or guardian sign an agreement or waiver. This documentation would be the central concern from Perspective I. However, Perspective III recognizes the value of such disclosure and written documentation, but advocates ongoing discussion with the client—and family or teachers when appropriate and necessary—about interventions and counseling approaches with full disclosure to the extent that the client is capable of understanding and that is appropriate given age, level of maturity, and emotional disposition. The goal of informed consent in Perspective III is primarily to foster the therapeutic relationship, client well-being, and treatment outcomes, and secondarily to reduce liability for the counselor.

Conflicts of Interest and Boundaries

Conflict of interest refers to a conflict of professional experiences between loyalties or duties to a client or to multiple roles or relationships with a client. The assumption is that professionals will place the needs and interests of clients above their own needs and interests. When they do not, a conflict of interest exists. Needless to say, dual relationships complicate the boundaries between professionals and clients. Dual relationships in counseling have been previously defined as having a professional role or relationship as well as a nonprofessional role or relationship (i.e., social, business or personal) with a client simultaneously.

Boundaries are defined as the contextual framework, including constraints and limitations, within which the therapeutic relationship unfolds. As discussed in Chapter 8, counseling relationships that are characterized by harm, exploitation, or the abuse of power involve a breach of boundaries, reflect a conflict of interest, and are unethical. The discussion of boundaries in this section will examine relevant ethical codes and focus on the difference between boundary violations and boundary crossings. Several case examples will be offered for consideration followed by a Perspective III discussion.

The ASCA's *Ethical Standards for School Counselors* (2004b) specifically addresses dual relationships:

> The professional school counselor avoids dual relationships that might impair his/her objectivity and increase the risk of harm to the student (*e.g.*, counseling one's family members, close friends, or associates). If a dual relationship is unavoidable, the counselor is responsible for taking action to eliminate or reduce the potential for harm. Such safeguards might include informed consent, consultation, supervision, and documentation. (A.4.a)

The professional school counselor avoids dual relationship with school personnel that might infringe on the integrity of the counselor/student relationship. (A.4.b)

The ASCA standards point to the potential for harm and the infringement on integrity as guidelines. In cases involving incidences such as sexual relationships or exploitation, the potential for harm is clear. Social or emotional relationships with students serving the counselors needs are also clearly unethical. However, others require the school counselor to give careful thought to the professional, ethical, and contextual factors surrounding the relationship to ensure decisions are in the best interest of the student and provide optimal environments for well-being.

Dual relationships for school counselors typically involve multiple relationships with the student or the student's family and teachers as well as multiple contexts in which additional interpersonal relationships occur. The careful examination of each circumstance with regard to ethical codes, principles, and contexts is important to ensure the end result is in the best interest of the student.

Clarifying Boundaries for School Counselors. Let us consider several scenarios involving school counselors (see Box 10.7). Which might you consider boundary crossings? Boundary violations?

BOX 10.7

CLARIFYING BOUNDARY CROSSINGS FOR SCHOOL COUNSELORS

- Counselors' serving in their neighborhood or community schools encountering close friends or neighbors in professional settings, and students and coworkers in personal settings
- A counselor's asking an upset or excited student if he or she needs a hug and being available to provide a hug
- A counselor's disclosing personal information to a student or parent
- A counselor's taking gifts from students during holidays or the end of the school year
- A counselor's attending a student's performance or participating in an activity not affiliated with the school
- A school counselor's having lunch with a student at the picnic tables outside of the cafeteria or meeting with a student outside of the office

These types of scenarios are not uncommon. We will examine each issue to clarify the individual and contextual components that make the difference between a boundary crossing and a boundary violation.

■ **Counselors' serving in their neighborhood or community schools encountering close friends or neighbors in professional settings** and students and coworkers in personal setting School counselors, like many teachers, work in schools in their own communities and sometimes their own neighborhoods. This would likely result in working with teachers or administrators who are also friends or neighbors outside of the school setting or who have students in the school they are serving. It could also create a scenario in which the counselor's own children are in his or her school. Counselors would need to be particularly aware of other relationships that have already been established and mindful of the impact of those relationships on the counseling or consultative relationship with students, parents, or teachers. Individual case decisions would need to be made and steps taken to be ensure objectivity.

■ **A counselor's asking an upset or excited student if he or she needs a hug and being available to provide a hug.** School counselors have the opportunity to share many types of emotional experiences with students. A student who has recently experienced the loss of a family member may become upset in class, triggered by conversation she was not prepared to deal with, and referred to the counselor school. A student in counseling who has finally gained the courage to disclose the emotional abuse he has been suffering for years may be feeling relieved, scared, and uncertain about what will happen next. A high school student who has just been told about receiving a scholarship to the school she has always dreamed of attending may be ecstatic. Being available for students reaching out for a hug in these types of cases could be considered therapeutic boundary crossings that strengthen the therapeutic alliance. However, we cannot assume that hugs are always appropriate. For example, if the hug for the student with the loss is the result of unresolved emotions related to the counselor's personal circumstances triggered by the student, the hug could be considered a boundary violation versus a boundary crossing. In what contexts might a hug for the student who is disclosing abuse or the excited high school student be a boundary violation? What other types of touching may constitute a boundary crossing or a boundary violation for the school counselor?

■ **A counselor's disclosing personal information to a student or parent.** Counselor self-disclosure is another circumstance that may constitute a boundary crossing or a boundary violation depending on the context. Investigations have shown that the counselor–client relationship can be enhanced through counselor self-disclosure (Sermat & Smyth, 1973; Simonson & Bahr, 1974). However, it is important for counselors to consider what and how they disclose personal information to avoid burdening students or parents with counselor issues and avoid sounding like other adults who want to let students know "how it was when I was younger." Myrick (2003) suggests that counselor self-disclosure should involve more of the feelings associated with the event rather than the details of the event. The emphasis on the feelings associated with the event is likely to build a bond that cuts across differences. This could be particularly important in developing the therapeutic alliance. Myrick (2003) offers the following examples, the first reflecting an emphasis on the disclosure of feelings, and the second reflecting an emphasis on the event:

> Counselor disclosure with an emphasis on feelings:
>
> *I was unsure about what college I wanted to attend, too, when I was your age. There was a lot of pressure on me to make a decision. Those were confusing times.*
>
> Counselor disclosure with an emphasis on the event:
>
> *I remember when I was trying to decide between two colleges. I finally decided on the one closest to home because that is where my friends were going and I could get home easier when I needed to. Today I would look more at what courses were offered; but, I guess your first college major doesn't make any difference. Most people change. I know I changed my major three times.* (pp. 142)

The first disclosure would be an example of a boundary crossing, the second an example of a boundary violation, as it seems to serve as an outlet for the counselor to reflect on his or her own decision-making process.

■ **A counselor's taking gifts from students during holidays or the end of the school year.** Counselors' accepting gifts from clients is generally discouraged. However, in the school setting, it is customary for students to give gifts to teachers and other school personnel as a token of appreciation for the work and care they provide students throughout the year. Usually the gifts are small and may include items such as candy, small gift cards, and student-made gifts, candles, or baked goods. The counselors' accepting these types of gifts, and following up with a personal note of thanks, can provide the students with the gratification resulting from "giving" as well as strengthen the individual connections with the counselor, having received a personalized thank-you. Declining small gifts from students could in some cases result in hurt feelings or disappointment and actually harm the counselor–student relationship, particularly if the student is young and not able to fully understand why accepting gifts might not be appropriate. Accepting what the student offers would be considered a boundary crossing. However, accepting gifts from students can also clearly be a boundary violation. Consider the case of a school counselor in a private school where gifts were likely to include items such as expensive gift baskets, personal items, and large gift cards. The counselor accepted the gifts and then felt obligated to make sure the students received prompt attention with college placement decisions at the exclusion of other students' needs. This would plainly constitute a boundary violation. In addition to the size of gifts or the resulting treatment of students, school policy may also help clarify the difference between a crossing and a violation. If policy prohibits the accepting of gifts, it would clearly be a boundary violation to accept them.

■ **A counselor's attending a student's performance or participating in an activity not affiliated with the school.** In extending an ethic of care aimed building a therapeutic alliance with students that are difficult to reach, school counselors may consider actions that extend beyond the walls of the school. Consider this case of a school counselor who picked up a student for an event unaffiliated with the school. The counselor had been working with a student being raised by a grandmother in a subsidized housing project. The school counselor and student seemed to have little in common. However, the counselor noted that this student was chosen by the physical education teacher to represent the school at an upcoming track and field event. The counselor, who enjoyed running, took the opportunity to ask the student if he had ever run in the annual local homecoming run, which the counselor had participated in for years. The student replied that he usually attended the parade that followed the run (with his grandmother) but had never participated in the run. He expressed enthusiasm at the possibility of participating but said he would not have a way to get there. The counselor called the student's grandmother and asked if it would be all right for her to come by and pick up the student for the run and bring him to the grandmother on the parade route at the conclusion of the run. The conversation focused on the student's strengths, and the gesture implied counselor interest beyond the school setting. The relationship between the counselor and grandmother as well as the relationship between the counselor and student were greatly enhanced, and the student began to respond more positively in group counseling and in school in general. While this boundary crossing had positive outcomes, the school counselor would need to consider each situation carefully and consider any school or district policy that might prohibit such interactions.

Another important consideration for counselors who choose to cross this type of boundary is the need to balance personal and professional commitments. While the previous example demonstrated an ethic of care toward the student, the counselor would also need to consider his or her own personal and family needs. Take the example of the school counselor who made commitment to students' out-of-school activities—to be able to connect with these "hard to reach" students—a priority over the needs of her own family. Her boys suffered, as evidenced by drug use and other delinquent behaviors that may have resulted from lack of supervision or parental involvement in their activities. This would not indicate a program of responsible personal self-care. Balance in maintaining the emotional and relational needs of the counselor are crucial in determining appropriate boundary crossing.

▪ **A school counselor's having lunch with a student at the picnic tables outside of the cafeteria or meeting with a student outside of the office.** Counselors generally meet with students in spaces that will ensure privacy and the room to meet with groups of clients. As a result, most counselor–client encounters take place within these settings. In Chapter 8 it is suggested that there may be particular circumstances that counselors might choose to leave the office setting in support of therapeutic goals. For school counselors this may not always be a choice. Ideally, school counselors have private office space, space to work with groups of students, and conference facilities for meeting with groups of teachers and parents. In many instances, school counselors share office space and need to be creative about where they will meet with groups of students in crowded school environments. Not having a space that will support privacy is ethically unacceptable. However, counselors' meeting with students outside of a private office space, even if it is readily available, may be another example of a boundary crossing that may support the building of a relationship and an alliance with the student. A counselor's choosing to have a private lunch on campus with a student he or she is working with, to divert from therapeutic issues and focus instead on topics of mutual interest, would likely build trust and an assurance of sincere interest in the student's well-being. A counselor's choosing to meet with an anxiety-ridden student at home to help ease the home-to-school transition would likely increase the chances of successful reentry. School counselors who consider the benefits of boundary crossings in the context of balancing personal and professional needs are likely to reap the professional benefits related to improved outcomes for students.

Boundaries, Conflicts of Interest, and Perspective III. From Perspective I, boundaries between students, parents, teachers, and the school counselor are viewed as rigid and inflexible. The belief is that if school counselors engage in boundary crossings, they are in danger, since such crossings represent a slippery slope. The presumption is that such crossings in time lead to boundary violations that foster exploitive, harmful, or even sexual relationships. Perspective I advocates point to several highly publicized cases wherein both male and female teachers became sexually involved with their young adolescent students. On the other hand, Perspective III views boundaries more flexibly and emphasizes that appropriately employed boundary crossing can actually increase therapeutic alliance and outcomes. This, of course, assumes that the school counselor always places the student's needs, interests, and well-being above those of the counselor. Nevertheless, from any perspective—I, II, or III—harmful, exploitive, and sexual relationships are always unethical and to be avoided by school counselors.

Competence

Competence, as discussed in Chapter 9, is described as a developmental process reflecting the ongoing needs and demands of the student population as well as attending to the ongoing needs of the counselor. In this section we will review relevant ethical codes and discuss counselor work orientation as related to competence. We will also examine the ethical responsibility to attain, maintain, and enhance competence. This will be followed by a case example and Perspective III summary.

Ethical Codes Addressing Competence. The ACA's and ASCA's ethical codes both emphasize competence. The ACA code (reviewed in Chapter 9) specifically calls for counselors to practice within their boundaries and recognizes the importance of only accepting positions for which the counselor is qualified while seeking ongoing monitoring and education. The ASCA code also addresses these issues and specifically notes the need for ongoing personal as well as professional growth, and attendance to the hire of competent professionals.

The professional school counselor

- Functions within the boundaries of individual professional competence and accepts responsibility for the consequences of his/her actions. (E.1.a)
- Monitors personal well-being and effectiveness and does not participate in any activity that may lead to inadequate professional services or harm to a student. (E.1.b)
- Strives through personal initiative to maintain professional competence including technological literacy and to keep abreast of professional information. Professional and personal growth are ongoing throughout the counselor's career. (E.1.c)
- Accepts employment only for positions for which he/she is qualified by education, training, supervised experience, state and national professional credentials, and appropriate professional experience. (D.1.e)
- Advocates that administrators hire only qualified and competent individuals for professional counseling positions. (D.1.f)

Factors Affecting School Counselor Competence. Competence among school counselors is the result of many factors including: (a) the counselors' work orientation; (b) the graduate training program they attended; (c) the responsibility they take for enhancing competence after graduation; and (d) their commitment to professional and personal self care. This discussion of competence will address each of these factors.

Work orientation. School counselors enter the profession for a number of reasons. Some reasons align with the school counselor experiencing their work as a job, some a career, and some a calling. Box 10.8 illustrates examples of each.

BOX 10.8
SCHOOL COUNSELOR WORK ORIENTATION

A Job: Scenario 1. This school counselor has obtained a degree in education and taught in the schools. He chose the teaching profession based on the nine- to ten-month contract, convenient holidays, and the contracted work day ending at three to four o'clock. The stresses and pressures of working with students and parents on a daily basis have not been a good match, and moving to school guidance and counseling seems like a way to maintain a school schedule without leaving education.

(continued)

BOX 10.8 CONTINUED

A Job: Scenario 2. This school counselor has been in some other helping profession and already has a graduate degree in mental health counseling. She feels the demands and pressures of working with troubled adolescents and envisions working as a counselor in the schools as an easier job.

A Career: Scenario 3. This school counselor embraces his work as a career and values the opportunity to be more involved in school and professional organizations. He seeks opportunities to enhance professional development. He is motivated by the increased prestige or status that comes with his graduate degree and more selective status within the school community.

A Calling: Scenario 4. Previously a clinical social worker, this counselor returned to graduate school to become a school counselor as a way to reach and contribute to the well-being of increased numbers of students. She is committed to helping them reach their academic, career, and social potentials and derives personal and professional satisfaction from her work. This school counselor is passionate about making a difference through her comprehensive school counseling program. She is likely to have a *calling* for the profession.

In the cases of the *job* and *career* orientations, the performance of the counselors ends up being highly dependent on other elements of professional and personal development. If they attend a quality graduate training program and embrace the significance of their new roles, they are in a position to make a difference for the students they encounter, particularly if they continue to seek opportunities for professional development, as one with a career orientation would be likely to do. If not, they may not be prepared to advert administrative-type duties, nor will they have the skills to avoid getting bogged down with clerical tasks that get in the way of delivering the type of comprehensive program designed to meet the academic, personal/social, and career needs of all students. In this case, competence is greatly compromised.

Graduate training and certification. There are two key prerequisites for individuals who want to enter graduate training programs to work toward becoming competent professional school counselors. The first includes personal attributes necessary to become a helping professional and the intellectual capacity to develop the knowledge and skills for implementing a comprehensive school counseling program. In addition to the personal attributes of counselors described in Chapter 9, school counselors must also possess qualities that will allow them to work as part of an educational community, such as flexibility and a temperament that will allow them to work successfully as part of a team.

Students have the responsibility of choosing a graduate training program that will provide an opportunity for development of knowledge and skills that will prepare them for work in today's schools reflecting implementation of comprehensive developmental school counseling programs built on research-based National Standards for School Counseling Programs (Campbell & Dahir, 1997). These standards connect school counseling to education initiatives and the educational mission of schools and districts, and focus on the academic, personal/social, and career needs of all students. ASCA (2003) has provided frameworks to support implementation of these standards.

In most states, school counselors must also have certification from the State Department of Education. A counselor can also apply for certification as a Nationally Certified Counselor. These credentials attest to the minimal level of competence that school counselors must attain to enter the school counseling profession. ASCA has taken a strong stand on the issue of credentialing to support competence:

> ASCA strongly supports passage of a professional school counselor credentialing law in each state providing legal definition of the counseling profession and of qualified practitioners and establishing standards for entry and role definition in school settings, including a privileged communication clause. ASCA strongly endorses and supports the school counselor standards developed by the Council for Accreditation of Counseling and Related Educational Programs (CACREP) and encourages all state education certification and/or licensure agencies to adopt these professional standards for school counselor credentialing. Further, ASCA supports the credentialing and employment of those who hold a master's degree in counseling-related fields with training in all areas specified by the CACREP standards. Any school internship shall be under the supervision of a credentialed and/or licensed school counselor and a university supervisor. (ASCA, 2003c)

Maintaining and enhancing competence. Becoming a school counseling professional includes the ethical responsibility to continue to pursue the knowledge and skills reflective of the changing needs of students. This can include coursework, school and district in-service, workshops, conferences, and reading professional literature such as *Professional School Counseling* or the *Journal of Counseling and Development.* It can include networking with other school counselors regarding best practices. It can also involve ongoing counselor supervision, providing an opportunity for professional growth and development while serving to ensure competency.

While there are some requirements for maintaining professional certification, it is generally up to the school counselor to choose the type of continuing education and professional development efforts. Counselors who see their work as a "job" will probably choose the quickest and easiest routes to recertification regardless of topic. Those with a "career" orientation will probably be more conscientious about topics that will help to improve services to students and be members of professional organizations that provide literature and conferences as options. Counselors who have a "calling" for the profession engage in ongoing efforts to learn and explore topics and areas related to their own personal and professional development and greatly exceed any minimal requirements for maintaining their professional status.

Professional development seems to be accepted as necessary or essential, depending on your view. However, the idea of school counselors receiving supervision once they are in the field has not been as well received. In a recent article, Herlihy, Gray, and McCollum (2002) review the current status of school counselor supervision and its recent historical context and provide recommendations to help school counselors respond to ethical and legal issues associated with supervision, while seeing clinical supervision as an important tool in fostering the professional development of school counselors.

Chapter 14 of this text details ethical and legal issues related to supervision in counseling within relational, developmental, and organization contexts. An emphasis is placed on the importance of the supervisory relationship in establishing mutual accountability for client outcomes. It may be this perspective of shared responsibility that will make it easier for school counselors to embrace the idea of some type of ongoing supervision as part of the professional growth process.

Ethical issues related to supervision are twofold. First is the current lack of any clinical supervision once school counselors are in the field. Evaluations are generally completed by administrators based on their perception of what school counselors should be doing. While this type of evaluation can be used to indicate whether the counselor is completing agreed-upon tasks, it is not a good check for professional counseling competence. Generally, school counselors have not advocated for a change in this practice of no clinical supervision and have even resisted initiatives to include clinical supervision of their work with students (Henderson & Lampe, 1992). A national survey by Page, Pietrzak, and Sutton (2001) found that fewer than 10 percent of school counselors were receiving any type of clinical supervision, with one-third of the counselors feeling no need for supervision. Even when there is no formal mechanism for supervision, counselors working from Perspective III create and embrace opportunities for feedback aimed at professional growth. One alternative may include initiating opportunities for peer group supervision, coaching, and feedback on a regular basis. Another may be "self-supervision" as described in Chapter 14. Herlihy and colleagues (2002) explore training opportunities including credit-based coursework, peer supervision, collaborating with counselor educators, and working through school administrators to develop policy building in time for supervisory activities. Regardless of the mechanism, it is up to the school counselor to take stock of his or her needs and explore opportunities to maintain and enhance competence.

A second ethical issue involves school counselors being competent to provide supervision for practicum and internship students in their schools. ASCA's *Ethical Standards for School Counselors* outlines school counselors' responsibilities to the school and profession and states that counselors not accept responsibilities for which they not been trained. This would include supervising practicum and internship students. School counselors who provide supervision without specific training may not be able to provide practicum or internship students the support they need to make the most of the field placement in developing their skills (Dye & Borders, 1990). Training may be part of a student's graduate program or provided and required by school districts as a prerequisite for student supervision. A counselor operating from Perspective III would be compelled to seek training if needed to help students make the most of their internship experiences and for the future of the profession.

Professional and personal care. School counselors are not immune to the stress and burnout that affects helping professionals. The ratio of students to counselors varies, but it is not unusual, especially in large schools, for the ratio to be 500 or 600 (or more) to one. In comprehensive programs, counselors are involved in working with large numbers of students on developmental issues reflecting academic, personal/social, and career development needs. They work with small groups of students who themselves are experiencing stressful events such as loss or family difficulties. They work with a wide range of individual students who need support ranging from making tough decisions to handling extreme anger and are looked to for direction and support when crisis strikes. In addition, counselors face stress as they advocate, sometimes with resistance, for programs that will help students grow while dealing with requests for them to take on duties unrelated to students or their program.

While professional care involves activities aimed at enhancing competence, it also involves networking and support systems to help manage stress related to the work that counselors do. Counselors can talk about their successes as well as their needs and exchange ideas and support. It is also important to recognize the need to debrief after particularly stressful events or a crisis. Talking about the experience and its impact on the professionals involved is just as important as reviewing what happened and how it was handled. Consider the example of a school counselor who was involved with a grade level of students and team of teachers who witnessed a traumatic event on the playground after lunch. The counselor provided consultative and direct services to administrators, teachers, and students during an emotionally charged afternoon. While it was of the utmost importance that the counselor have the knowledge and skills to provide services, it was also important for the counselor to spend time at the end of the afternoon with other professionals processing the experience and emotions in preparation for the next steps. Taking the time to process along the way becomes a critical part of personal and professional care.

School counselors work with students to help them develop the personal and social skills they need to reduce stress and to maintain the mood and energy levels they need to perform. It is essential that they too, pay attention to these types of personal self-care strategies to maintain competence and avoid burnout.

Competence and Perspective III. It is not surprising that there are differing views of what constitutes competence in school counseling. Achieving school counseling certification and maintaining one's level of technical proficiency by completing minimum continuing education requirements is considered sufficient from Perspective I for meeting the ethical requirement of professional competence. On the other hand, from Perspective III, competence as a school counselor involves an ongoing, developmental process in which the counselor seeks to achieve a high level of technical expertise as well as personal, emotional, physical, intellectual, and spiritual development and well-being. From this perspective, counselors become lifelong learners who continually monitor their level of competence and seek out needed supervision or consultation and appropriate continuing education. They tend to view school counseling more as a calling than a career or job. The goal is to broaden and enhance their clinical abilities, relational skills, work satisfaction, and life meaning.

LEGAL ISSUES AFFECTING THE PRACTICE OF SCHOOL COUNSELING

Along with ethical dilemmas, school counselors are faced with issues that have legal implications. These include the legal rights of parents, the mandatory reporting of abuse, and the reporting of the intent to harm self or others, including suicide. These exceptions to confidentiality have been discussed in Chapter 6 along with guidelines for managing legal and ethical decisions. Case illustrations and guidelines based on those will be presented in this chapter.

Legal Rights of Parents and Confidentiality

The legal rights of parents to be involved with decisions regarding their children and ethical obligations to maintain confidentiality with students have been discussed. The severity of the ramifications of what students share, their age, the ability of parents to be of help in making changes, and what actions will positively affect outcomes for their children are all to be considered. Opposing views have been presented about the parent's right to know and the minor student's right to privacy, with no clear direction, aside from clearly exceptional circumstances as mandated by law. Consider the case of the school counselor working with a student who is reported to exhibit a pattern of substance of abuse at school and whose grades are falling (see Box 10.9).

BOX 10.9
LEGAL RIGHTS OF PARENTS AND CONFIDENTIALITY

Two ninth-grade students scheduled a time to see Dr. Macia, the school counselor. Upon meeting, Dr. Macia asked about the nature of their visit and let the students know if they chose to disclose information that suggested harm to any person in the school, she would need to make decisions about disclosure of such information. The students acknowledged, and shared their concern about a friend, Jennie, who had been drinking at school. They disclosed that she put vodka in her water bottle and drank throughout the day and that they are worried about her. This had been going on all semester. The students were concerned that this was not healthy and that, if Jennie were caught, she could be expelled. Dr. Macia asked the two students what they would like to see happen. They explained they wanted help for Jennie but did not want to be identified as having "told." Dr. Macia took some time with the two students to explore their feelings and provided encouragement for their decision to come to the counselor to explore "friendship" as related to their desire to seek help.

Dr. Macia had worked with Jennie the previous year providing support for several difficult academic placement decisions and felt some rapport had been established with Jennie and her mother. She had not met with Jennie's father but did know he was a prominent figure in the community. Dr. Macia checked on current progress with all teachers and arranged a time to talk with Jennie. She acknowledged the previous difficult placement decisions and inquired about her current progress. Jennie reported that everything was fine, even though six of seven teachers reported being concerned about school performance. Dr. Macia told Jennie what she had heard regarding the drinking at school and expressed concern for the stress and pressure Jennie must be feeling. However, Jennie was not ready to talk about it and did not confirm that she was drinking, nor did she acknowledge any of the difficulties reported by teachers. Jennie also quickly pointed out that she had never been caught drinking at school.

At this point, Dr. Macia had as evidence only the accounts of two other students that Jennie was actually drinking at school and thought carefully about what her next steps should be. Should she continue to see Jennie in an attempt to build a more trusting relationship, hoping that Jennie would disclose the concerns that were leading to her drinking at school, at which point she could encourage Jennie to talk with her parents about her need for help? Should she let the parents know what she had heard in an effort to enlist their support in getting help for their child? She also thought about the ramifications for this family if Jennie were caught with alcohol at school and expelled before she and Jennie had time to develop the type of relationship necessary for this type of disclosure.

The counselor in this case began by considering the problem—a ninth-grade student who was most likely drinking at school, indicated by impaired functioning as a student and person, who, if caught at school, would be expelled. Dr. Macia had no reason to discount the report of the two students who came to her. In their initial meeting, Dr. Macia was forthright with Jennie about why she had asked to see her and expressed concern.

Dr. Macia decided to invite Jennie to participate in several additional counseling sessions to explore stressors that were making it difficult to succeed as a student this semester. However, she decided she would consider the need to involve Jennie's parents if she were unable to reach an agreeable plan of action with Jennie. Dr. Macia was clear with Jennie about the limits of confidentiality prior to these sessions. After several sessions and continued resistance, Dr. Macia told Jennie of her need to let her parents know of the current concern regarding possible drinking at school and the concerns about performance from teachers. She invited Jennie's participation but she refused. The decision was made to arrange for a conference with Jennie's mother to let her know of the teacher's concerns and what was reported about her child's behavior. It was made clear that, while Jennie had not been caught, there was concern for what would happen to Jennie, her family, and the school if the situation persisted until either Jennie disclosed her substance abuse or was caught.

It was clear for Dr. Macia that her preferred option was to have Jennie disclose her drinking behavior and to encourage her to share the need for help with her parents; however, her defensive behavior could not be overcome in the short term. Dr. Macia was concerned about the right for her parents to know about the likely chronic drinking behavior of their child and the right to intervene at a point prior to irreparable damage—in this case Jennie's health, potential expulsion, and the resulting implications for the family. Dr. Macia also wanted the parents to have the opportunity to intervene in the identification and intervention of a behavior that could possibly affect academic and social outcomes for Jennie. Dr. Macia had a conference with Jennie's mother (the father was in court and could not attend) and explained what she had "heard." She explained that she did not have "proof" but had reason to believe, based on what she had heard and school performance this semester, that the drinking was likely to be true. Dr. Macia suggested the parent explore the situation and provided options for counseling and drug testing as an alternative to not knowing if the student was abusing alcohol with the potential for expulsion. The parent was initially caught off guard by the information but began to put together her own observations that might also indicate a problem. The mother was grateful the counselor had considered her right as a parent to make decisions about what actions to take regarding her child's reported behavior. Perspective III requires consideration of all personal and contextual factors in reaching decisions that are personally and ethically in the best interest of students. Given all factors, parent involvement seemed best in this case.

It should be noted that in this case the student did not initially come to the counselor for help. The counselor asked to see the student. As demonstrated here, that difference can greatly influence the dynamic of the relationship. If Jennie had come for help as a self-referral, Dr. Macia's explanation of the counseling process including limits of confidentiality would have likely led to a more trusting relationship, allowing them to work together in resolving issues and making decisions involving outside help.

Mandatory Abuse Reporting

State and district policy require teachers to be trained in identifying signs of abuse as well as the requirements and process of mandatory reporting of suspected abuse by educators. The school counselor may asked to provide this type of in-service to faculty, as they are often seen as playing a key role in the early identification of abuse among school-age children. To do this, counselors must be competent regarding the topic and process and be sure they have accurate information. Legal information will likely be provided by the state or district. Information about signs and indicators of abuse may also be provided by the state or district but should also be part of the school counselor's graduate training program. Counselors should seek ongoing professional development and identify other competent colleagues with whom to consult to ensure competence in this important area.

It is important for those providing in-service to teachers to help them understand that it is the responsibility of the person who has reason to suspect abuse to report the abuse to the proper authorities. A teacher seeing physical evidence of abuse on a student who displays troubling behavior over time, and who discloses the circumstances of the abuse to the teacher when asked about the physical marks, would be the mandatory reporter. It is not uncommon for teachers to consult with the school counselor and ask him or her to make the report even without solid reason to suspect abuse. However, the teacher should be directed to report, with counselor support for the process. The counselor may do this by offering to review the procedure and/or allowing the teacher to make the call from the counselor's office. The counselor may also provide encouragement that steps taken are in the best interest of making sure the student will be safe.

In other cases, a teacher will identify a behavior or physical mark that may be a sign of abuse and refer the student to the school counselor for the counselor to talk with the student to determine if there is reason to suspect abuse. In that case, the school counselor would be the first to have reason to suspect that the physical marks or behaviors are the result of an abusive situation and would be the mandatory reporter. The American School Counselor Association acknowledges the school counselor's responsibility to report suspected cases of child abuse/neglect to the proper authorities and goes on to define abuse as

> The infliction of physical harm upon the body of a child by other than accidental means, continual psychological damage or denial of emotional needs (e.g., extensive bruises/patterns; burns/patterns; lacerations, welts or abrasions; injuries inconsistent with information offered; sexual abuse involving molestation or exploitation, including but not limited to rape, carnal knowledge, sodomy or unnatural sexual practices; emotional disturbance caused by continuous friction in the home, marital discord or mentally ill parents; cruel treatment). (ASCA, 2003b)

While mandatory reporting laws are clear, reporting is not always emotionally easy for the school counselor, as he or she considers the potential behaviors and feelings of all involved, with the focus on the well-being of the student. Cases can become complex and may require advice or support from more experienced colleagues. The case in Box 10.10 highlights potential complexities. Chapter 6 (Box 6.3) provides an overview of guidelines for managing mandatory reporting requirements that may be helpful to school counselors.

BOX 10.10
MANDATORY ABUSE REPORTING

Julie, a gifted second-grade student, was referred for group counseling by her teacher and mother, both of whom had noticed some changes in behavior since the parents' divorce at the beginning of the school year. Julie had not seemed as happy, rarely smiled, and had less interaction with peers than in the past. Julie's mother was also a teacher at the school and was able to frequently consult with Julie's teacher and the school counselor. During the group, students were given an opportunity to express feelings about experiences related to joint custody. Julie began to talk about "not liking to be at Dad's" as a result of "some of the things that happened when I was there." Julie seemed very uncomfortable and did not want to say more. The counselor acknowledged her feelings and suggested they have more time after the group session to talk more. Julie said she would like that. At the end of the session, the counselor again reminded group members about the group agreement that had been established prior to the first session and the trust that had been developed within the group that allowed students to share difficult or personal situations. The agreement included not sharing information outside of the group.

At the beginning of the individual follow-up session, the counselor reminded Julie that while what she shared was private, if it became apparent that she was being hurt or in danger, the counselor would need to tell others who would be able to help sort out what was going on to make sure she (Julie) was OK. The counselor clarified she would tell Julie any steps she planned to take including if she would be involving anyone else. As the session proceeded, Julie remained somewhat hesitant to talk about her visits to her dad. The counselor asked if she would like to draw a couple of pictures instead and suggested she draw one doing something with her mother and one doing something with her father. Julie talked about her pictures. One picture was of Julie and her mom doing homework; the second was of Julie taking a bath with her dad sitting beside the tub. As Julie talked about the second picture she became somewhat withdrawn but appeared anxious to talk. Based on Julie's account, it appeared that her dad continued to be involved in her bathing and personal hygiene, including applying lotion to Julie before she was dressed, which made Julie very uncomfortable, as it usually involved his touching her "private areas." The counselor made sure she knew what "private areas" Julie was referring to. Julie said she had told her dad may times she could do all of this herself, but her dad "didn't listen" and even got mad so she didn't say anything any more. Julie said she did not tell her mom because her mom "doesn't like to talk about Dad." Julie also slept with her dad when she was with him, as he now had a one-bedroom apartment since the divorce. He told Julie did not want her to have to sleep on the couch. While she said that he did not touch her in the same way he did when he gave her a bath, she was still uncomfortable. The counselor asked Julie what she would want to have happen. Julie said she did not want her dad to continue to touch her this way and did not want to have to go there this weekend. Although this was not the determining factor in deciding whether to report suspected abuse, the counselor felt it was important to explore.

Julie's change in behavior, the nature and explanation of the picture as representative of true incidents, her emotions, the confrontation of her father met by anger, the divorce, and Julie's hesitance to talk with her mom all led the counselor to become very concerned about the potential of sexual abuse. The counselor let Julie know she was going to contact a person whose job it was to make sure that kids were not being hurt or abused, and that this person would come to talk with her. The counselor offered to answer any questions Julie posed. The counselor also acknowledged how difficult it was for children to share things like this and that she (the counselor) would see her in the morning.

The counselor has met the legal requirement of reporting suspected abuse. For a beginning counselor or counselor in training determining if there is evidence to suspect abuse may seem like the only decision that has to be made. However, there are professional, personal, and contextual factors that come into play that create other ethical dilemmas. You will remember that Julie's mother is a teacher in the school. The mother already has a professional relationship with the school counselor that will likely be affected in some manner by the report of suspected sexual abuse by the father. In addition, the school counselor wondered if she should tell the mother before the end of the school day that she has made the referral and to expect a visit from child protection or law enforcement authorities. In this case, the mother was not suspected of being involved in the allegations of abuse and would not pose a risk of harm to Julie. In addition, teachers in the school were often provided "professional courtesy" or given a "heads up" concerning personal situations. The counselor gave careful thought to the benefits and risks involved in doing so and consulted with a more experienced counselor. The mother/teacher might be more trusting of the counselor in professional contexts if she let her know what was happening ahead of time. However, informing the mother of the upcoming visit from child protection or law enforcement could create a difficult situation for Julie and influence the investigation. Even if the school counselor explained to the mother the need to let the professionals talk with Julie before becoming emotionally involved regarding the allegations, there would be no guarantee the mother could refrain.

While the report to authorities would remain confidential, the counselor knew the mother/teacher was likely to figure out the source of the referral. The counselor was prepared to communicate ongoing commitment to working with Julie and her mother regardless of the outcome of the investigation and to help the mother understand the importance of her (the counselor's) decisions in keeping Julie's welfare as the central focus. The counselor was also prepared to include both Julie and her mother in decisions regarding strategies for support for both of them at school during this difficult time, including who else should be aware of the current stressors. In this case, after several weeks and some initial anxiety, the mother/teacher shared that she felt the personal and professional relationship with the school counselor had actually been strengthened as a result of the concern and care that had been taken to make sure that decisions were based on what was best for Julie and not what might have been more comfortable for the adults. In this case example, a child's mother was also a teacher; however, similar dilemmas may arise in schools when the suspected abuse involves children with parents who are in important positions in the community or whose parents have other relationships with professionals at the school. While the decision to report suspected abuse is mandatory and not part of the dilemma, school counselors who stay focused on the best interest of the student, to include knowing how all participants may be affected, and who weigh the risks and benefits of each potential course of action are likely to be seen as personally interested, professionally competent, and ethically sound. The interested reader is referred to Sciarra (2004), who offers a particularly helpful review of incidents, factors, effects, and assessment of child maltreatment issues and examines abuse prevention.

There are several issues related to school counseling that have legal and ethical considerations aimed at the confidentiality, privacy, and informed consent related to student records, harm to self and others, and students with special needs.

Threat of Harm to Self or Others

When it comes to helping today's youth, the reality is that school counselors are on the school site and in contact with students, parents, and teachers on a daily basis. Other mental health professionals do not necessarily have this opportunity. As a result, school counselors are in a position to recognize cues and signals that a student may be in distress or depressed. The counselor may be cued by what a teacher or parent shares about a student, what the student discloses, or what he or she observes. Competency, confidentiality, and the duty to warn are among the ethical and legal issues school counselors must be mindful of as they proceed with decisions involving students who are in distress or may potentially cause harm to themselves or others. Suicide and the potential for school violence are among the opportunities for school counselor to make a difference.

Suicide. School counselors must be competent to make some assessment of situations involving potential suicides. It is not enough for a counselor to simply call a parent if he or she hears about a student talking of suicide. School counselors should be prepared to assess student risk of suicide. Below are some general principals for school counselors related to students with suicidal ideation (Capuzzi, 2003; McWhirter, McWhirter, McWhirter, & McWhirter 2004; Remley & Sparkman, 1993):

- Be knowledgeable about school board policy for dealing with suicidal youth.
- Consult with other professional counselors if possible. Especially consult if initial assessment indicates no need to notify parent.
- Do not be afraid to ask directly if the student has thought about hurting or killing him- or herself.
- Check for frequency and duration of suicidal thoughts. Ask if the student ever has attempted suicide.
- Check to see if the student has a plan. If there is a plan, check to see if student has access to means to carry out the plan.
- Check for overall and academic functioning, social support, sleep, nutrition, exercise, fun.
- Check for recent stressors, such as loss of a goal or relationship, serious family problems such as divorce, alcohol or drug abuse, physical abuse, or psychiatric treatment.
- Check for symptoms of depression and hopelessness.
- Ensure that student receives professional evaluation if threat appears real.

In cases where parent refuses to have the student evaluated when clear and imminent danger appears, refer to Child and Protective Services or police to ensure the student gets appropriate evaluation.

- Provide follow-up with the student, parent(s), and agency/therapist to ensure necessary support for student.
- Do not allow the student to leave school or to be unsupervised until the parent or guardian can pick him or her up and have the student evaluated. Stress to parent(s) the need for close monitoring of the student for the next 72 hours.

The situation in Box 10.11 presents an opportunity to think about how these principles come into play.

BOX 10.11

HARM TO SELF: A THREAT OF SUICIDE

Situation: Juan is a 12-year-old seventh grader who is referred to the counselor because a peer heard him say he was going to kill himself. The peer told her teacher, who referred Juan to the counselor.

Counselor response: The counselor told Juan the reason for seeing him was concern for his safety and that a student had told the teacher of hearing his statement. Juan admitted saying he was thinking of killing himself but denied he really meant it. The counselor explored how things were going with Juan and discovered he recently found out he did not pass the state mandated achievement test needed to be promoted. He also reported that he had no close friends at school or in his neighborhood. Although Juan said he did not have a plan for killing himself, he said he had thought of it several times during the last few weeks. Juan also said he had not talked to his parents about how bad he was feeling and had not seen a counselor. The counselor explained to Juan that his first goal was to make sure Juan was safe. While he believed Juan when he said he was not going to kill himself, the counselor talked with Juan about communicating his unhappy and hopeless feelings with his parents to make them aware that he may need some added support to make sure he got through this tough time. The counselor talked with Juan about the best way to do this. Juan mentioned he was scared of his parents' reaction to the failing achievement test score.

Juan and the counselor decided they would talk to the parents together and that the counselor would arrange for a conference before the day's end. To Juan's surprise, his parents were more concerned about his reaction to the test score than they were the test score. The counselor provided referral information to the parents, who required support in making a decision about taking Juan to have a psychological evaluation. The counselor gave the parents several appropriate referrals including a public mental health center where evaluations were free. The parents could sense the care and personal concern of the counselor and suggested the counselor and evaluator talk. The counselor had the parents sign a release to allow communication with the therapist conducting the evaluation. This would provide the school counselor the opportunity to share background information with the therapist and coordinate appropriate support for Juan at school. The counselor also discussed how the parents could provide support for Juan and ensure his continued safety. The counselor shared possible support services at the school including group counseling for social skills and tutoring based upon consultation with the therapist. A follow-up contact was agreed upon to check progress. At the end of the meeting with Juan and his parents the counselor told Juan he was available to check with him tomorrow to see how things went and that he would be thinking of possible things that could be done at school to help make things better.

What actions taken by the counselor most closely reflected Perspective III?

Remley and Sparkman (1993) highlight several key points in discussing the legal liability school counselors face when working with students who may be suicidal. These include (a) the difficulty in predicting who will attempt suicide, (b) overreactions due to being uninformed, and (c) involving adults. Predicting human behavior is limited. School counselors do have a duty to be informed about warning signs of suicide and to advocate for students who need protective care during suicidal periods. School counselors are expected to exercise professional judgment when trying to assess the potential for suicide. Judgment must be shown to be clearly substandard before negligence can be proven and malpractice established. Therefore, consulting with other professional counselors and following standard practices is essential to establishing that the counselor acted appropriately. Overreactions to the slightest suspicions of suicide include hysterical calls to parents, attempts to physically restrain students, and calls to emergency squads. These are detrimental to students and to the credibility of the school counselor. To automatically take the most extreme steps without first assessing that this level of action is warranted is both unprofessional and unethical. This type of overreaction can cause serious psychological injury to student and family. Counselors are right to be very diligent when faced with the possibility of a student being suicidal. To err on the side of caution is prudent with life and death at stake. However, appropriate investigation and judgment is needed to determine the level of reaction that is indicated.

Involving adults, usually school administrators and parents, can present problems when they are reluctant to take the situation seriously. According to Remley and Sparkman, (1993), legal liability for the school counselor ends when school authorities or parents have been notified that a student is at risk of suicide and preventive measures have been recommended. However, if these adults choose to ignore the warning and do not take recommended steps to protect the student, the counselor can take additional steps to meet the needs of the students. Three possible steps are (a) refer the matter to protective services for investigation and, if needed, a court order to have the student evaluated and treated; (b) report to a local agency responsible for involuntary evaluation, such as the police, that can take the student to an appropriate mental health facility for evaluation; and (c) provide counseling support at school. In the case of school administrators' not taking the situation seriously and recommending no further action, the counselor needs to make the case that this is not overreaction and is needed to comply with legal and ethical guidelines. The counselors can provide the administrator with the standard-of-practice guidelines and, if needed, request a ruling from the school board attorney. This frequently awakens another level of awareness of professional and legal thinking in the administrator and results in appropriate action. When the parent refuses to take the matter seriously, the counselor can explain the steps the parent will force the counselor to take. For example, the counselor will have to report the case to protective services, which will lead to an investigation and may involve a court order to do precisely what the counselor is asking the parent to do now. Many courts view parent refusal to have their child evaluated for risk of suicide as medical negligence. The analogy used is of a parent who refuses to take his or her child with a compound fracture to the doctor for medical treatment. In some cases, the counselor may believe a call to the police to take the student to be evaluated (Baker Act) is called for if the parent is not willing to take the student. Usually the parents will see that delaying action will not be in their or their child's best interest.

School Violence. School counselors have ethical and legal obligations to make efforts to prevent school violence. While even the courts recognize the difficulty in predicting school violence, school counselors remain in a crucial position to address issues related to school violence. Hermann and Finn (2002) make recommendations for school counselors addressing issues of school violence that include the following:

- Keeping up to date regarding violence prevention and intervention
- Creating violence prevention policies and programs
- Creating systems reflecting the seriousness of violence threats and referral systems to handle those threats
- Consulting with other professionals and identifying appropriate referral resources
- Keeping current on current legal issues and consulting legal counsel as needed
- Documenting action and maintaining liability insurance

Reddy, Borum, Berglund, Vossekuil, Fein, and Modzeles (2001) evaluate the relevance, risks, and effectiveness of current approaches to assessing the threat of school violence and offer a *threat assessment approach.* This threat assessment approach emphasizes the context of the situation and does not consider any single type of person as prone to violence, nor does it view targeted violence as a random act. Daniels (2003) reviewed the threat assessment approach and has provided implications for school counselors that include

- Remaining flexible and open to new approaches given there is little data on targeted school violence.
- Utilizing the threat assessment approach to help assess the level of risk based on individual and contextual factors.
- Looking for warning signs in troubled students. Daniels (2003) suggests using a list of 20 characteristics of youth who have killed at school developed by the National School Safety Center (1998) to help identify warning signs.
- Building a trusting, caring relationship with troubled students, creating opportunity for intervention including problem solving and anger management.
- Involving parents, teachers, and community resources in the intervention process.

School counselors play an important role in the prevention, assessment, and intervention aimed at preventing school violence.

Case Law Related to the Practice of School Counseling

Next, we will next take a look at some of the key legal cases that have had implications for school counselors (see Box 10.12).

BOX 10.12
SELECTED LEGAL CASES WITH IMPLICATIONS FOR SCHOOL COUNSELORS

NEGLIGENCE IN ACADEMIC ADVISEMENT

Sain v. Cedar Rapids Community School District (2001), 626 N.W. 2d 115, Iowa

Student was given erroneous advice by a school counselor resulting in the loss of an athletic scholarship. The loss was based on academic ineligibility as determined by the NCAA Clearinghouse. The Iowa Supreme Court found that school counselors must use care when advising students who need and rely on specific information such as courses and credits needed to pursue postsecondary endeavors. Stone (2002) presents this case and suggests the 2001 decision is a departure from the history of holding school counselors harmless and presents as a caution for practice. Stone (2002) also provides recommendations for school counselors in their role as academic advisors and advocates for them to continue to embrace the role while exercising a good faith effort to give accurate advice.

MANDATORY REPORTING

McDonald v. State (1985), 71 Or. App. 751, 694 P. 2d 569, Oregon

A teacher noted scratches on the neck of one of her students. The student told two versions of their origin: one of a kitten scratching her neck and another of her mother choking her as the student also reported had happened on several occasions. The teacher consulted with the principal and child development specialist, and a report was made to child welfare workers. The child was removed from the home. The allegations were unfounded, and the parents brought suit against the teacher, principal, and others. The courts decided the teacher and others involved acted in good faith and with reasonable cause to suspect child abuse and were granted immunity from the suit. Forty-nine states currently have mandatory reporting laws, many with clauses regarding immunity based on good faith and reasonable cause reporting.

HARASSMENT

Davis v. Monroe County Board of Education (1999), 562 U.S. 629, 119 S. Ct. 1661

A fifth-grade girl reported being tormented by a boy in her class. School officials were aware of the offensive nature and severity of the harassment but did not take any steps to remedy the ongoing problem. The U.S. Supreme Court determined that schools may be liable for peer-peer sexual harassment based on Title IX, but only when acting with "deliberate indifference."

Wagner v. Fayetteville Public Schools (1998), Administrative Proceedings of the U.S. Department of Education

These administrative proceedings involving the Office of Civil Rights of the U.S. Department of Education resulted when a school district failed to take meaningful action to prevent harassment based on sexual orientation and culminated in an agreement with the Fayetteville School District requiring the district to recognize harassment directed at gay and lesbian students, provide training for students and staff, and submit written reports monitoring progress. These proceedings are presented and discussed by McFarland and Dupuis (2001).

(continued)

BOX 10.12 CONTINUED

Gerber v. Lago Vista Independent School District (1998), 524 U.S. 274, 118 S. Ct.

This U.S. Supreme Court ruling found that schools (districts) can be held liable when teachers sexually harass students if an official of the school knows of the harassment and fails to take action.

DUTY TO WARN/PROTECT

Tarasoff v. Regents of the University of California (1976), 17 Cal. 3d 425, 551 P. 2d 334

This case involves the duty to warn and protect third parties of the potential dangers that may result from client behavior. Even though this is a California case with local jurisdiction, school counselors are not removed from the resulting implications. Issacs (1997) discusses implications of the *Tarasoff* case for school counselors in the context of their involvement in increasingly complex and sensitive issues making them more vulnerable to legal action. It is also discussed in further detail in Chapter 6 of this text.

Eisel v. Board of Education (1991), 597 A.2. 2d 447, Maryland

A student told the school counselor that her friend intended to commit suicide. When the counselor spoke with the student who made the suicide statement, the student denied ever making the comment. The counselor did not share the information with parents regarding the student's threat. Courts ruled that school personnel can be found liable if they fail to exercise "reasonable care" to prevent a student suicide, as was determined in this case. In later proceedings "reasonable care" was defined by the courts as taking each suicide threat seriously and taking precautions to protect the student, including notifying the parents of the threat or risk of suicide.

Gathright v. Lincoln Insurance Co. (1985), 286 Ark. 16, 688 S.W. 2d 931, Arkansas Supreme Court

A third-grade boy hung himself by a nylon cord in the school bathroom. The court decided the school had taken adequate safety measures and that students cannot be sheltered from every possible danger, whether self-inflicted or otherwise. The school was not held liable.

ABORTION COUNSELING

Arnold v. Board of Education of Escambia County (1989), 880 F. 2d 305, Alabama

Two students and their parents filed suit against the school district stating the school counselor had coerced and assisted the female student in getting an abortion, paid someone to drive the student to have the abortion, and provided paid tasks to the two students to earn money for the abortion. The courts found that the students were not deprived of their own free will, had chosen not to tell their parents, and were not coerced. During the trial it was discovered that the school counselor had repeatedly encouraged the students to consult with their parents and presented various alternatives that were rejected by the students, who admitted that the decision to obtain the abortion was theirs alone. Stone (2002) presents this case along with recommendations for school counselors.

SCHOOL CURRICULUM

Leebaert V. Harrington (2003), 332 F3d 134, U.S. Court of Appeals

A father argued his right to direct the education of his son by requesting that his son be excused from health education classes in his public school that included discussions of drugs, sexual harassment, family life, and AIDS. While the court acknowledged the importance of parents in the upbringing and education of their children, it ruled they cannot dictate or control the flow of information with regard to the curriculum of a public school they choose to send their child to.

ADHD

W.B. v. Matula et al. (1995), 67 F.3.d 484 (3rd Cir.)

The parent of a child with ADHD filed suit claiming school officials failed to properly evaluate, classify, and provide necessary educational services for the student. The case was initially dismissed, then sent to the U.S. Court of Appeals, where the court ruled there were violations of Section 504, IDEA, and constitutional rights based on the unwillingness of school personnel to recognize and accommodate the student's disability. Erk (1999) presents and discusses this and other cases with implications for the practice of school counseling.

EDUCATIONAL PLACEMENT

Florence County School District v. Carter (1993), 510 U.S. 7, 114 S. Ct. 361, U.S. Supreme Court.

The court decided that school authorities can be held responsible for reimbursing parents for expenditures on private education if the court finds that the student's educational placement is inappropriate and the parents' placement of their child in private school is appropriate. Congress has delineated what parents must do if they are to be reimbursed after withdrawing a child.

Note: Case summaries were based on explanations in Alexander and Alexander's (2005) sixth edition of *American Public School Law* except where otherwise noted. *American Public School Law* offers a thorough collection and discussion of cases affecting educators, including school counselors. In addition, ASCA has published *School Counseling Principles: Ethics and Law* (Stone, 2005). This resource provides a case approach to understanding statues and case law effecting school counselor practice.

Student Records

School counselors are involved on a regular basis with student records. While the maintenance of all records would not be a good use of counselor time or in alignment with ASCA's national model, school counselors are often involved in making sure student records are maintained according to state and federal regulations and help teachers and parents interpret their contents. One law having a direct impact on the maintenance and confidentiality of student records is *The Family Educational Rights and Privacy Act* (FERPA; 1974). Also known as the Buckley Amendment, this act establishes standards for schools to follow in handling student records. The act includes the right for parents and students (who have reached the age of 18 or entered a postsecondary school) to inspect school records and challenge their accuracy. In their sixth edition of *American Public School Law,* Alexander and Alexander (2005) provide a brief history of the events leading up to the establishment of the Act and outline its basic provisions.

Legal issues regarding student records can become complex, especially when there are custody issues involving minor children. School counselors are frequently involved with students who are experiencing academic, social, and emotional concerns associated with a parental divorce. This includes contact with parents who are resolving issues involving rights and custody. Under FERPA, an educational agency must give full access to records to either parent unless the school has been provided evidence of a court decision involving divorce or custody that specifically revokes the rights of one parent to make educational decisions regarding the student. The decision in the case of *Taylor v. Vermont Department of Education* in 2002 denied the mother access and the right to challenge school records after the father had been given custody and the right to make educational decisions for the daughter during the school year. Stenger (1986) suggests that school personnel be liberal in making a child's records available to parents while being strict about allowing access to nonparents.

Of particular interest to the school counselor is that FERPA also addresses personal records such as those that would be kept by a school counselor. Alexander and Alexander (2005) explain:

> Treatment records "made or maintained by a physician, psychologist, or other recognized professional . . . acting in his or her professional capacity" and used in the treatment of an eligible student may be excluded from the definition of "education records" in federal law and are not automatically accessible to the student. Further, "personal notes" that are defined as not education records are exempt from parental access. Personal notes are notes by an individual, such as a guidance counselor, to "jog the memory" when the child is counseled at a later date. (pp. 622–623)

According to Glosoff and Pate (2002), school counselors are often confused about the difference between protection from disclosing "personal notes" to parents and the rights of the court to subpoena such notes. Currently, school counselors are not protected by any right to privilege that would give them a legal basis to refuse to produce records or personal notes or to testify. However, school counselors can request that the court consider the confidential nature of their communication with their clients and the importance of maintaining that confidence as necessary for the counseling relationship. These conditions were supported in the 1966 Supreme Court Case of *Jaffee v. Redmond* (Remley, Herlihy, & Herlihy, 1997), also weighing harm to the counseling relationship as a result of disclosure of confidential information. This aligns with ASCA's ethical code (A.2.d) stating, "the professional school counselor requests that disclosure not be required when the release of confidential information may potentially harm a student or the counseling relationship."

Occasionally, the school counselor may provide counseling for a student over a period of time that extends beyond the routine practice and limits of brief counseling. In those cases it may be helpful to maintain notes that can help in planning and record keeping. SOAP (Subjective, Objective, Assessment, Plan) notes, developed by Weed (1971) and discussed in this text in Chapter 12, may provide a framework for organizing and keeping a record of services from planning to evaluation. However, as Remley, Hermann, and Huey (2003) note, while SOAP notes may provide some helpful guidelines for school counselors, they may not be feasible given the school counselor's large caseload.

Students with Special Needs

It is important for school counselors to be familiar with federal and state legislation designed to protect the rights and welfare of students, parents, and teachers. In Box 10.13 we give descriptions of terms that permeate the language of meeting needs of students with

BOX 10.13

KEY TERMS AND LEGISLATION RELATED TO WORKING WITH STUDENTS WITH SPECIAL NEEDS

The Americans with Disabilities Act of 1990 (ADA). This act prohibits discrimination against individuals at work, in school, and in public accommodations. Schools must make reasonable accommodations for people with disabilities. This act is not limited to organizations receiving federal funds.

Education for All Handicapped Children Act of 1975 (EAHCA, also known as Public Law 94-142). This legislation ensured the right of all students with disabilities to receive a free, appropriate public education, special education and related services, an individualized education program, due process procedures, and the least restrictive environment in which to learn.

Family Education Rights and Privacy Act of 1974 (FERPA). Also known as the Buckley Amendment, this law applies to all schools and districts that receive federal funds from the U.S. Department of Education. It has provisions for parental review of student records, determining who may access records, determining what information can be disclosed from a student record without consent, and guidelines for counselors' "personal notes."

Free and appropriate public education (FAPE). Under IDEA all handicapped children have the right to a free and appropriate public education (FAPE). FAPE has been defined as special education and related services that are provided at public expense, under public supervision, while meeting state standards, and in conformity with the required IEP.

Individualized educational plan (IEP). An individual plan written for students reflecting their educational needs, instructional goals and objectives, and evaluation procedures that will help monitor student progress towards goals and objectives.

Individuals with Disabilities Education Act (IDEA). In 1990, EAHCA (PL 94-142) was renamed the Individuals with Disabilities Education Act (IDEA, PL 101-476). Amendments to IDEA in 1997 affected several aspects of the statute (with implications for school counselors) including eligibility, evaluation, programming, discipline, and procedural safeguards. IDEA provides very specific procedures for providing a free and appropriate public education and applies only to education agencies that receive funds under IDEA.

Least restrictive environment (LRE). To the maximum extent possible students with disabilities are educated with students who are not disabled. Students with disabilities are removed from the regular classroom only when the severity of their disability is such that the use of supplementary aids and services in the regular classroom will not allow them to achieve satisfactorily.

Rehabilitation Act of 1973. This act states that no handicapped person in the United States shall be excluded from participation, denied benefits, or subject to discrimination based solely on his or her handicap. It pertains to any program or activity receiving federal financial assistance.

Section 504 of the Rehabilitation Act of 1973. Section 504 deals particularly with students with disabilities seeking equal educational opportunities and applies to all public educational institutions. Section 504 students must have record of a physical or mental impairment that substantially limits one of their major life functions (such as seeing, walking, hearing, or attending school) and be regarded as having such impairment.

(continued)

BOX 10.13 CONTINUED

Section 504 Plan. An accommodation plan written for students who meet requirements under Section 504. While the plan is often similar to an Individualized Education Plan (IEP), Section 504 is not as specific as IDEA regarding what shall be included in the plan.

Adapted from Alexander & Alexander (2005).

special needs, discuss key legislation with implications for school counselors working students with special needs, and introduce several key legal cases counselors will want to keep in perspective as they evaluate choices regarding personal, ethical, and professional obligations to students in the context of the school community.

School counselors have a responsibility to take an active role in providing guidance and counseling services to all students, including those with special needs. ASCA takes the following position:

> Professional school counselors encourage and support the academic, social/emotional, and career development of all students through counseling programs within the school. They are committed to helping all students realize their full potential despite cognitive, emotional, medical, behavioral, physical, or social disabilities. (ASCA, 2004d)

While providing counseling services to students with special needs and their parents may be the only contact some counselors have with the exceptional student education program, others may have a role in many of the activities that support the identification, placement, and ongoing educational programs for students with special needs. Some school counselors find themselves overinvolved with such activities, and their ability to meet the needs of other students is adversely affected. Counselors have a responsibility to their students, schools, and communities to advocate for the implementation of a comprehensive school counseling program taking into consideration the needs of all students. Consider the following ASCA (2004b) ethical standard:

> The professional school counselor delineates and promotes the counselor's role and function in meeting the needs of those served. The counselor will notify appropriate officials of conditions which may limit or curtail her or his effectiveness in providing programs and services. (D.1.d)

In addition, ASCA is clear in stating that it believes the school counselor should not have sole responsibility for providing information or administrative coordination and implementation regarding IDEA, IEPs or 504 plan development. However, school counselors are likely to have some role in these types of activities for students who experience learning and behavioral difficulties at school (Remley, Hermann & Huey, 2003). This involvement may or may not lead to referral for evaluation for a special education program. It should also be noted that, while the school counselor is not the professional who conducts the formal psychological evaluation for exceptional student education (ESE), the counselor is likely to be one of the school professionals directly involved in the process. Involvement for the school counselor varies from state to state and school to school but may include one or more of the following: (a) facilitating planning team meetings to discuss a student's learning or behavioral concerns and plan appropriate intervention, (b) providing individual or group counseling intervention based on identified student need, (c) meeting with parents to explain the evaluation process and the rights of parents and students, (d) explaining the results of evaluations and helping parents understand their child's disability, (e) being involved in the development of plans and accommodations that will help students improve their performance in the classroom, and (f) providing other support to students with special needs and their parents as indicated. As a result of the counselor's role in this process, it is important to be familiar with statues, laws, and policies that guide educational programs and protect the rights of students and parents involved in the process. Legislation and statutes having implications for the school counselor and all school personnel involved in serving students with special needs are included in Box 10.13.

Tarver-Behring, Spagna, and Sullivan (1998) suggest several types of activities for school counselors that would be appropriate when addressing the special needs of a student with a disability, working to develop empathy among nondisabled students, or collaborating with special education and regular education teachers. Among the suggestions is a concentration on social adjustment and peer acceptance that allows the school counselor to focus on the needs of all students, as well as information and resources that will facilitate successful inclusion in the classroom.

Increasing numbers of students are being diagnosed with Attention Deficit Hyperactivity Disorder (ADHD) (American Psychiatric Association, 2000). ADHD is not listed as a disability under IDEA, but students may be covered under IDEA as being *other health impaired* (OHI) or having a *specific learning disability* (SLD) or an *emotional handicap* (EH). ADHD students who do not qualify for special services under IDEA may be eligible for accommodation plans under Section 504 if the impairment can be shown to substantially limit the student's functioning in a major life activity, learning. As previously noted, ASCA clearly discourages school counselors from being solely responsible for the development and implementation of 504 plans. However, the school counselor can play an important role in supporting students with 504 plans (Sink, 2005). ADA would also require reasonable accommodations for students with disabilities that may include support by the school counselor. Advocacy can become particularly important for students with ADHD. While other disabilities are more clearly diagnosed and accepted, teachers generally have more difficulty accepting and accommodating students with ADHD. This may be due to the number of students who are inappropriately diagnosed or the inconsistency in behavior patterns of students with ADHD. ASCA provides a position statement regarding support for the rights of students with ADHD and a commitment on the part of the professional school counselor to promote the continuing development of each student. In addition to the position statement, ASCA acknowledges that the attitudes of counselors, parents, teachers, peers, and other professionals towards students with ADHD may have more to do with their educational success than any other factor. (Note: Erk [1999] provides information on the background, acts, statutes, and legal issues related to ADHD in *Attention Deficit Disorder: Counselors, Law, and Implications for Practice.*)

Ethics and Sexual Behavior

School counselors, as part of the educational community, are obligated to ensure that students attend schools in a safe and secure environment. This includes being free from harassment and sexual exploitation. Consider the following:

- Sexual harassment among students
- Sexual harassment between students and faculty
- Harassment of gay, lesbian, or bisexual students
- Sexual impropriety involving students and staff

Each of these examples present opportunities for the school counselor to impact outcomes related to the well-being of the students. School counselors can empower students with knowledge and skills to face incidences of harassment (Stone, 2000) through the developmental guidance curriculum at all levels. Beginning with kindergarten, school counselors can facilitate activities that help students learn about personal space and use stories and puppets to begin to develop empathy and talk about what it is like to be harassed. Developmentally appropriate language can be modeled for dealing with these difficult and sensitive situations. Counselors can plan activities at all levels of the developmental school counseling curriculum aimed at helping students appreciate and connect with one another while providing a safe environment in which to discuss issues related to harassment.

Counselors will be increasingly called upon to make sure gay and lesbian students are not harassed and are not discriminated against on the basis of sexual orientation. McFarland and Dupuis (2001) offer a discussion of legal and ethical issues related to the duty to protect gay and lesbian students from harassment in our schools. They provide reference to several resources with strategies that can be helpful to counselors as they become part of the leadership team aimed at providing safe schools, including *Making Schools Safe for Gay and Lesbian Youth: Breaking the Silence in Schools and in Families* (Massachusetts Governor's Commission on Gay and Lesbian Youth, 1993), *Homophobia 101: Anti-Homophobia Training for School Staff and Students* (Gay, Lesbian, Straight Education Network, 1998), and *Gay/Straight Alliances: A Student Guide* (Blumenfeld & Lindop, 1995). Advocacy for all students is central to the role of the school counselor. ASCA takes the following position:

> Professional school counselors are committed to facilitating and promoting the fullest possible development of each individual by reducing the barriers of misinformation, myth, ignorance, hatred, and discrimination based on sexual orientation. Professional school counselors are in a field committed to human development and must be sensitive to the use of inclusive language and positive modeling. ASCA is committed to equal opportunity and respect for all individuals regardless of sexual orientation. (ASCA, 2000)

Counselors are also in a position to provide training and information to students and faculty to protect them against exploitation from other students or faculty. This is particularly important given the increase in high-profile cases involving the exploitation of minor students by faculty.

Spirituality and School Counseling

Earlier in the chapter, we introduced the topic of spirituality from a developmental perspective and its role in the context of school counseling. However, there are some who are resistant to this developmental view of spirituality (Blake, 1996). Counselors operating from Perspective I are likely focus on this resistance and concerns primarily related to liability. From Perspective III, counselors consider the spiritual dimension as one that can affect emotional well-being, not to be avoided but to be explored as part of the holistic approach to working with students in schools. As stated throughout this text, Perspective III assumes the counselor will also weigh professional, ethical, and organizational variables in making decisions. Decisions regarding the practical applications of spirituality are no exception.

While our discussion of spirituality thus far has been general, we shift now to a few specific topics commonly challenged on legal and/or ethical grounds, including prayer, meditation, and imagery. We will also examine the Equal Access Act of 1984 and take a look at some guidelines for balancing personal and professional spiritual issues.

Prayer, Meditation, and Imagery. Consider the following scenarios, in which the school counselor

- Silently supports a high school student who prays in the counselor's presence about an important decision.
- Teaches students how to use relaxation and breathing techniques to refocus their energies.
- Facilitates a guided imagery exercise to explore alternatives to a problem situation.
- Teaches students how to use mental practice to see themselves as reaching their goals and being successful.
- Tells a story involving a spirit who gives a mythical animal character a second chance to make better decisions.

In each of these scenarios, the school counselor is using or introducing techniques and strategies aimed at facilitating the academic, social, and emotional well-being of students. While counselors operating from Perspective III would recognize the need to be aware of those who might consider any exercise by the school counselor that evokes an image, directs a thought, involves mythical characters, or involves a discussion of prayer or religion as inappropriate, they would not be wary of such activities simply to avoid an ethical or legal challenge. However, Perspective III would encourage counselors to seek an understanding of the core values and religious and spiritual contexts of their schools and communities and make decisions regarding the school counseling program with the views and beliefs of the larger culture in mind. Ethical and legal challenges are frequently avoided when counselors are multiculturally sensitive, are clear about the purpose of activities within the school counseling program, and use language that reflects that stated purpose. Let us look again at each of the scenarios.

A counselor may be asked by a student to pray with him or her regarding a decision or need for spiritual support. There would be many considerations in this case, including an understanding of the importance of prayer in this student's life, community values, and policies of the school or district, as well as a clear personal understanding of the counselor's own religious/spiritual beliefs. A school counselor in a private Catholic high school where students attend mass and pray in classes daily and who is also Catholic would likely pray with this student without hesitation. A counselor in a public high school with a clear policy regarding prayer, in a large city with a wide range of spiritual beliefs, would likely make a different decision. However, the counselor in the public high school operating from Perspective III would also recognize the need to have an understanding of the importance of prayer for this particular student and might acknowledge that importance with silent/emotional support for the student while he or she prays.

School counselors may teach students how to use relaxation and breathing techniques to refocus their energies, reduce anxiety, or manage their anger. Some may consider this a form of meditation. Counselors can be clear in their description of these activities and focus on these as strategies to put the student back in control of themselves, as the issue of "who is in control" is often at the root of the objection, particularly when relaxation and breathing techniques are paired with imagery. Language can be used to help clarify the intent of the exercise. Instead of *imagery* or *guided imagery,* which have different connotations to different people, the counselor might emphasize playing out alternatives to problem situations, using mental practice to increase successful social competence and academic achievement, and picturing successful outcomes. The specific language makes the intent of the exercise more clear.

In the case of using a story involving a spirit who gives a mythical animal character a second chance to make better decisions, the counselor would need to be sensitive in allowing students to decide what meaning to give the *spirit.* The idea of having a chance to start life over and make different decisions along the way is powerful. The use of animal characters allows for focus on the message, which is certainly spiritual in nature and not on any particular ethnic or religious group. However, in several school districts across the country it has been suggested that school counselors avoid certain programs that involve magical or mystical characters and ideas, as a result of community concern. As mentioned previously, operationalizing opportunities for students to explore developmental concepts involving spirituality requires one's own understanding of self, and sensitivity to the beliefs of the school community and local policy.

Equal Access Act and School Counselors. The *Equal Access Act* of 1984 was designed to guarantee groups with religious, political, or philosophical forums an equal right to meet on school campuses by withholding federal financial assistance to public secondary schools who deny students such an opportunity. Bullis (2001) sees the law and subsequent court decisions as having significant implications for school counselors, resulting from the insights they provide regarding how counselors approach religious and spiritual issues with students. He contends that counselors should take more than a superficial look at religious groups within the school community and those who ask to form groups who will meet in the school campus. Questions reflecting the role and purpose of the group as well as the membership are important and help position counselors to advocate for students and consult with administrators regarding such decisions. Counselors may respond to student need by facilitating the engagement of students and administration in discussions regarding religious and spiritual issues that may arise.

Guidelines for Balancing Personal and Professional Spiritual Issues. Lonborg and Bowen (2004) provide some guidelines to help counselors balance their personal and professional lives in relation to religious and spiritual issues: (a) anticipate ethical challenges associated with highly visible lives, (b) be prepared to answer questions regarding multicultural issues, (c) be familiar with norms and values important to the community; (d) be aware of one's own worldview including spirituality and the views of the community in which one works, and (e) advocate for multicultural competence throughout the educational community. Their final challenge to counselor educators was to more explicitly prepare students for the multicultural diverse, including spiritually diverse, communities they will serve. (Note: Readers are encouraged to consult the June 2004 *PSC* special issue, "Spirituality" for further discussion of the application and integration of spiritual development into school counseling programs.)

CASE ILLUSTRATION OF ETHICAL-PROFESSIONAL DECISION MAKING IN SCHOOL COUNSELING

Box 10.14 provides an example of a dilemma in school counseling, followed by a discussion of the case.

BOX 10.14
A CASE OF SEXUAL ABUSE THAT WASN'T

Jasmine Summers has been a counselor at Olympia Gardens High for two years. Earlier today, she met with Francisco, a 17-year-old junior whom she had seen one week ago for an individual counseling session. About two weeks ago, Francisco had told his track coach about an alleged sexual abuse, and the coach quickly reported it to child protective authorities and referred Francisco to Ms. Summers for counseling. Near the end of their second session, Francisco recanted his story that his mother's boyfriend, Cesar, had sexually abused him. With some trepidation he admitted that he fabricated the story, hoping that his mother would end her relationship with Cesar, because Cesar was verbally abusive to her when he was drinking. What professional, ethical, and legal issues does Ms. Summers face as a professional school counselor? What should she do? Following is an analysis of this case utilizing the ethical and professional practice decisional strategy.

Step 1: Identify the problem. Ms. Summers faces an ethical problem of determining how much confidentiality she owes Francisco, a minor, knowing that the welfare of Cesar, his mother's boyfriend, may be at stake as a result of the report of sexual abuse to authorities.

Step 2: Identify the participants affected by the decision. Francisco, his mother, Cesar, the school counselor, and the school.

Step 3: Identify courses of action/benefits and risks.

Option 1. Ms. Summers would tell no one about Francisco's recanting the sexual abuse and maintain confidentiality, letting Francisco decide what to do next.

Benefit: Client autonomy and trust will be maintained. Ms. Summers can have more discussion with Francisco to get a better sense of his motivation for retracting his prior claim of abuse, and Ms. Summers can be clearer about the actual facts.

Risk: Ms. Summers may be defying school policy and risk losing her job. Cesar may face a possible criminal conviction for something he did not do. Francisco's mother may end her relationship with Cesar for unsubstantiated reasons.

Option 2. Ms. Summers would tell Francisco that she needs to break confidentiality to inform those who needed to know that he has retracted the claim of sexual abuse, even if Francisco is uncomfortable with this option.

Benefit: If Francisco is now telling the truth, Cesar can be cleared from his charges of sexual abuse. The family can begin to deal with their issues together.

Risk: Francisco may abandon counseling or refuse to reveal any other personal information, due to loss of autonomy and trust. Francisco may change his statement again and say his first statement was the truth. Francisco may face punishment by his mother and/or Cesar. Although Ms. Summers's number one priority is Francisco, if the other students somehow learn that she disclosed Francisco's statements, perhaps they may refrain from using her counseling services when they may benefit from them. Ms. Summers may not have enough discussion time with Francisco to be sure of what the real truth is.

Option 3. Ms. Summers would call the investigator from children's services in the case and tell him or her about Francisco's retraction, even if Francisco is uncomfortable with this action.

Benefit: If Francisco is now telling the truth, Cesar can be cleared from his charge of sexual abuse. His mother will not leave Cesar, for this reason.

Risk: Francisco may abandon counseling or refuse to reveal any other personal information, due to loss of autonomy and trust. Francisco may change his statement again and say his first statement was the truth. Ms. Summers may not have enough discussion time with Francisco to be sure of what the real truth is and risk giving the investigator false information.

Option 4. Ms. Summers would encourage Francisco to make the needed disclosure(s) himself, but would not make a disclosure without Francisco's consent.

Benefit: Client autonomy and trust will be maintained. Francisco can take responsibility for his own actions. Ms. Summers can have more discussion with Francisco to get a better sense of his motivation for retracting his prior claim of abuse, and she can be as sure as possible about what is the real truth. If Francisco discusses the real problem with his mother and Cesar, they may be able to deal with their issues together. Then Cesar may be cleared from his false charges of sexual abuse.

Risk: Francisco may abandon counseling due to the repercussions of telling others. His mother and/or Cesar may punish him in some way.

Step 4: Evaluate benefits for each course of action based on domains/dimensions.

Contextual Domain Considerations

Personal-Developmental Dimension. Ms. Summers appears to be at Level 3 of counselor development and appears to function somewhere between Perspectives II and III. She is aware of her own values regarding confidentiality, abuse, and the rights of minors. There is no conclusive evidence of abuse or that Francisco is in clear and imminent danger. Also, Francisco is still his mother's responsibility, and so Ms. Summers cannot disregard her rights and responsibilities as a parent. Options 2 and 3 are unlikely, because they would not promote client autonomy and growth or enhance the trusting counselor–client relationship.

Relational-Multicultural Dimension. Although they have met only twice, sufficient trust in their relationship has developed so that Francisco was comfortable in talking with her about the fabrication rather than with his coach. His level of comfort probably reflects his belief that she is trustworthy and can help him with his dilemma. Francisco is from a third-generation blue-collar Cuban American family, while Ms. Summers is a second-generation Jamaican American. Thus, counselor and client are from different races, cultures, and genders. Nevertheless, Ms. Summers is aware of how persons in Francisco's culture tend to resolve issues and their views on confidentiality. She can be sensitive and objective in listening to Francisco and attending to his feelings. Accordingly, options 2 and 3 would not promote the sensitivity and objectivity.

Organizational Dimension. At Olympia Gardens High School Ms. Summers has a large support system in which she has a positive and open relationship with her colleagues. The district policy states that the welfare of students is of primary concern, and Olympia Gardens seems to rather consistently implement that policy, particularly in the Guidance Department, where counselors pride themselves on knowing and abiding by ACSA's *Ethical Standards for School Counselors.* Given these considerations, option 1 or 4 may be the best possible course of action.

Professional Domain Considerations

In reviewing the professional literature, Ms. Summers learned that the degree of confidentiality that a school counselor should maintain can be related to the child or adolescent's maturity and best interests. From this, she concludes that Francisco's age is relevant. His right to decide whether to disclose information or keep it private from his mother is greater than if he were several years younger. If she immediately discloses his information to others, she would probably fail to acknowledge his age and maturity. The professional literature also states that the counselor's primary responsibility is to the client and not his parents. However, the literature also notes that the counselor cannot completely disregard his parents' rights and welfare. With that in mind, choosing options 2 or 3 again seem problematic. Ms. Summers concludes that she must have further discussion with Francisco, respect his age and maturity, and be more certain of the truth of the situation before making any decision to breach confidentiality and disclose such sensitive material.

Ethical Domain Considerations

Ethical values are first considered. Ms. Summers concludes that respect for autonomy is crucial, since the professional literature suggests that an adolescent at 17 probably is mature enough to act autonomously. With this in mind, Francisco's right to make his own choice about what information is disclosed would be valued in option 1. Regarding the principle of fidelity, the counselor would remain loyal to the client and to the promises made to him. The principle of nonmaleficence suggests that the counselor has the duty to be as sure as possible about what the real truth is. With all of this in mind, options 2 and 3 seem untenable at this time. On the other hand, the principle of beneficence suggests that Ms. Summers ought to think about what course of action really helps the whole family the most. In this case, disclosure may be the best course of action. If Francisco discloses the information himself, the counselor would not be breaking any promises to him or to his family. The ASCA's *Ethical Standards for School Counselors,* A.1.a states that a counselor's primary obligation is to the student, who is to be treated with respect, while A.2.b states that counselors should keep information confidential except when disclosure is required to prevent danger to the student or others. The standard also indicates that, when in doubt, counselors should consult with other professionals. Disclosure of information may prevent the boyfriend being convicted for child abuse. The counselor should protect information received in the counseling relationship as specified by federal and state laws, written policies, and ethical standards. Information should be revealed only with informed consent from the student (A.2.f). This course of action makes option 4 more desirable.

The counselor acknowledges that primary obligation for confidentiality is to the student, but understands the legal and inherent rights of parents (A.2.g). ASCA standards (A.2 and B.1) address specific conditions for and limitations of disclosure of confidential information of a minor, informed consent, and parental rights and responsibilities. Ms. Summers had already explained the meaning of informed consent and limited confidentiality at the onset of the first counseling session with Francisco. This presumably set the stage for their working together. She also considered his parents' interests the legal liabilities to the school, and her ethical responsibility to protect all parties. These considerations support both options 1 and 4.

Step 5: Consult with peers and experts. Ms. Summer's professional and ethical responsibility is to consult with colleagues. ASCA advises that school counselors inform school administrators such as the principal about matters that may become a legal liability to the school. She talked first with the principal, who agreed with her assessment of the situation. He indicated there was no need for her to consult with the district's legal counsel at this time. In addition to talking to her principal, she consulted with two other counselors at Olympia Garden.

Step 6: Decide on best option and document the DM process. She now felt reasonably confident in her decision after reflection; reviewing the case, relevant literature, and policies; and consulting with a colleague. Considering Francisco's developmental maturity in discussing and understanding the concepts of abuse and lying, the risks and benefits of recanting, and his involvement in making an informed decision about confidentiality and the limitations of confidentiality, Ms. Summers felt she had a legal and ethical duty to encourage disclosure because of the harm to Cesar. The ACA and the ASCA codes state that the counselor should report abuse, but has not specified who should report the recanting of abuse. Francisco has not expressed unwillingness to tell his parents and social worker that he lied about the abuse. It is the counselor's recommendation that Francisco disclose this in her office. If Francisco makes the disclosure himself, he will learn the value of autonomy, self-responsibility, and self-determination, important outcomes of counseling. His confidence in the counselor will not be violated, and the counseling relationship will be preserved. The counselor reviewed state laws and ASCA, ACA, and school board policies, as well as consulted with a colleague. Ms. Summers thought about how all parties involved would be affected by her decision. After exploring contextual, professional, and ethical domains, and input from consultations, she chose option 4, with option 1 a close second. Fortunately, further discussion with Francisco reveals that what he really wanted was the support of the counselor to reveal the truth to his mother and Cesar. Obviously, this conversation confirmed Ms. Summer's professional and ethical analysis.

Step 7: Implement, evaluate, and document the enacted decision. Preparing Francisco for the disclosure is crucial. In order to maintain counselor–client integrity and prevent negative consequences for Francisco or compromising the counseling relationship, Ms. Summers discussed the process of disclosure with Francisco, made sure that he understood, and elicited his agreement. Further processing made it easier for him to follow through with his decision to make the disclosures. It was mutually agreed that Francisco would talk with the child protective services social worker by phone while in the counselor's presence. Then Ms. Summers would schedule a session with Francisco, his mother, and Cesar for the next day to facilitate the disclosure face to face. Francisco rehearsed what he would tell the social worker and his mother and Cesar. Ms. Summers and Francisco discussed likely reactions and possible outcomes of his recantation, their commitment to work through the process in counseling, and possible referral of the family for family counseling. Ms. Summers had Francisco promise not to disclose the information to his parents until they meet the next day. She documented the process in her case notes.

KEY POINTS

1. ASCA has developed *Ethical Standards for School Counselors* along with a series of position statements to address professional ethics and practice for school counselors.
2. The context of ethics in professional school counseling is shaped in part by the development of the *National Standards for School Counseling Programs* and the *ASCA National Model: A Framework for School Counseling Programs.*
3. One of the most fundamental ethical considerations facing today's school counselors is actively advocating and taking steps to implement a comprehen-

sive developmental school counseling program based on national standards and models.

4. Recent trends in the educational community focused on improved academic outcomes for students has resulted in an emphasis on counselor intervention and school guidance programs tied to the school's mission with similar outcomes.
5. A school or district's core ethical values are part of the organizational context that can impact the ethical and professional behavior of school counselors.
6. Ethical audits can help to ascertain a school or district's organizational ethics.
7. Confidentiality is a particularly complex issue for school counselors as they balance ethical obligations to minor students, legal rights of parents, and the need for teachers to better understand issues affecting the learning of their students.
8. Issues of confidentiality have implications for all direct services provided by school counselors, including individual and group counseling, consultation, and large-group guidance.
9. The Family Education Rights and Privacy Act (FERPA), also known as the Buckley Amendment, establishes standards for schools to follow in handling students' records and contains specific language used to describe records such as those kept by a school counselor.
10. School counselors working from Perspective II to III value the nature of informed consent to go beyond the documentation needed to avoid liability, and embrace it as vital in building a therapeutic relationship and optimizing client well-being and treatment outcomes.
11. While boundary violations are clearly unethical and may have legal implications, boundary crossings, if employed from an ethic of care for the student, parent, or teacher, can actually increase the therapeutic alliance and treatment outcomes.
12. Competence involves several aspects: (1) quality graduate training and appropriate certification, (2) maintaining and enhancing competence once a counselor is in the field, and (3) taking steps towards professional and personal care to help manage stress related to the work of school counselors.
13. There are many key legal cases related to mandatory reporting, the duty to warn, curriculum, the rights of parents, confidentiality, and the work counselors do with special needs students in schools.
14. The ethical decisions made by school counselors working from Perspective II or Perspective III will reflect the context of the profession, organization, and individual case with an emphasis on an ethic of care for what is best for all involved, while being mindful of ethical and legal codes.
15. The seven-step ethical decision-making process can help school counselors in their routine practice of school counseling.

CONCLUDING NOTE

From Perspective I, the ethical practice of school counseling seems straightforward, as it is directly tied to professional ethics and legal directives with implications related to state and federal funding, avoiding law suits, and pleasing superiors. However, the key objective of this chapter is to move school counselors toward Perspective III regarding ethical decision making in core areas using selected topics and cases. From Perspective III, counselors tie into the essential importance of understanding the implications of personal and professional development and the importance of considering all contextual domains in making ethical decisions regarding programs and students in our schools. Ethical decisions do not stand alone, nor should they. From Perspective III, ethical decisions are inherent in our professional practice, reflect ethical and legal standards of our profession, and are part of our person. From Perspective III, advocacy and efforts toward implementation of a comprehensive school counseling program aligning with ASCA's National Model are fundamental ethical obligations.

REVIEW QUESTIONS

1. Under what circumstances would a boundary crossing be considered useful or beneficial in a school counseling setting?
2. What would you do if a troubled student threatened to stop coming to counseling if you were to tell her parents about the things she said in session?
3. What is your opinion on the "assent to treatment" protocol used in counseling minors?
4. What type of information would you consider worthy of breaking a student's confidentiality to inform his or her parents about?
5. What do you think is necessary to maintain school counselor competence? Do you think that having an understanding of current youth culture should be part of the competency requirements?

REFERENCES

Alexander, K., & Alexander, M.D. (2005). *American public school law.* Belmont, CA: Thompson Learning.

American Counseling Association. (2005). *Code of ethics and standards of practice.* Alexandria, VA: Author.

American Psychiatric Association (2000). *Diagnostic and statistical manual of mental disorders.* (4th ed., Text revision). Washington DC.: Author.

American School Counselor Association. (2004a). *The ASCA national model workbook.* Alexandria, VA: Author.

American School Counselor Association. (2004b). *Ethical standards for school counselors.* Alexandria, VA: Author.

American School Counselor Association. (2004c). *Position statement: The professional school counselor and parent consent for services.* Alexandria, VA: Author.

American School Counselor Association. (2004d). *Position statement: The professional school counselor and the special needs student.* Alexandria, VA: Author.

American School Counselor Association. (2003a). *The American school counselor association national model: A framework for school counseling programs.* Alexandria, VA: Author.

American School Counselor Association. (2003b). *Position statement: The professional school counselor and child abuse and neglect prevention.* Alexandria, VA: Author.

American School Counselor Association. (2003c). *Position statement: The professional school counselor and credentialing and licensure.* Alexandria, VA: Author.

American School Counselor Association. (2002). *Position statement: The professional school counselor and confidentiality.* Alexandria, VA: Author.

American School Counselor Association. (2000). *Position statement: The professional school counselor and the sexual orientation of youth.* Alexandria, VA: Author.

Association for Specialists in Group Work. (1998). *Best practice guidelines.* Alexandria, VA: Author.

Blake, N. (1996). Against spiritual education. *Oxford Review of Education, 22,* 443–456.

Blumenfeld, W. J., & Lindop, L. (1995) *Gay/straight alliances: A student guide.* Malden, MA: Massachusetts Department of Education.

Brigman, G. A., & Webb, L. D. (2004). *Student success skills: A classroom manual.* Boca Raton, FL: Atlantic Education Consultants.

Bullis, R. (2001). *Sacred calling, secular accountability: Law and ethics in complementary and spiritual counseling.* Philadelphia: Brunner/Routledge.

Campbell, C. A., & Dahir, C. (1997). *Sharing the vision: The national standards for school counseling programs.* Alexandria, VA: American School Counseling Association.

Capuzzi, D. (2003). Legal and ethical challenges in counseling suicidal students. In T.P. Remley, Jr., M.A. Herman, & W.C. Huey (Eds.), *Ethical and legal issues in school counseling* (2nd ed., pp. 64–81). Alexandria, VA: American School Counselor Association.

Collins, N., & Knowles, A. (1995). Adolescents' attitudes towards confidentiality between the school counsellor and the adolescent client. *Australian Psychologist, 30*(3), 179–182.

Daniels, J. A. (2003). Assessing threats of school violence: Implications for school counselors. In T. P. Remley, Jr., M. A. Herman, & W.C. Huey (Eds.), *Ethical and legal issues in school counseling* (2nd ed., pp. 152–160). Alexandria, VA: American School Counselor Association.

Davis, J. L., & Mickelson, D. J. (1994). School counselors: Are you aware of legal and ethical aspects of counseling. *The School Counselor, 42,* 5–13.

Dye, H. A., & Borders, L. D. (1990). Counseling supervisors: Standards for preparation and practice. *Journal of Counseling and Development, 69,* 27–29.

Ells, C., & MacDonald, C. (2002). Implications of organizational ethics to healthcare. *Healthcare Management Forum, 15*(23), 32–38.

Education Trust National Initiative for Transforming School Counseling. (2001). *Achievement in America: 2001.* Washington, DC, Author.

Erk, R. (1999). Attention deficit disorder: Counselors, laws, and implications for practice. *Professional School Counseling, 2,* 318–326.

Ford, C. Millstein, S. Halpern-Felsher, B., & Irwin. C. (1997). Influence of physician confidentiality assurances on adolescents' willingness to disclose information and seek future health care: A randomized control trial. *The Journal of the American Medical Association, 278,* 1029–1034.

Gay, Lesbian, Straight Education Network. (1998). *Homophobia 101: Anti-homophobia training for school staff and students.* New York: Author.

Glosoff, H. L., & Pate, R. H. (2002). Privacy and confidentiality in school counseling. *Professional School Counseling, 6,* 20–27.

Gysbers, N. C., & Henderson, P. (2000). Comprehensive guidance and counseling programs: A rich history and a bright future. *Professional School Counseling, 4,* 246–256.

Henderson, P., & Lampe, R. (1992). Clinical supervision of school counselors. *The School Counselor, 39,* 151–157.

Herlihy, B., Gray, N., & McCollum, V. (2002). Legal and ethical issues in school counselor supervision. *Professional School Counseling, 6,* 55–60.

Herman, M. A. (2002). A study of legal issues encountered by school counselors and their perceptions of their preparedness to respond to legal challenges. *Professional School Counseling, 6,* 12–19.

Herman, M. A., & Finn, A. (2002). An ethical and legal perspective on the role of school counselors in preventing violence in schools. *Professional School Counseling, 6,* 46–54.

House, R. M., & Hayes, R. L. (2002). School counselors: Becoming key players in school reform. *Professional School Counseling, 5,* 249–256.

Ingersoll, R. E., & Bauer, A. L. (2004). An integral approach to spiritual wellness in school counseling settings. *Professional School Counseling, 7,* 301–308.

Issacs, M. L. (1997). The duty to warn and protect: Tarasoff and the elementary school counselor. *Elementary School Guidance and Counseling, 31,* 326–342.

Issacs, M. L., & Stone, C. (1999). School counselors and confidentiality: Factors affecting professional choices. In T. P. Remley, Jr., M. A. Herman, & W. C. Huey (Eds.), *Ethical and legal issues in school counseling* (2nd ed., pp. 48–60). Alexandria, VA: American School Counselor Association.

Linde, L. (2003). Ethical, legal, and professional issues in school counseling. In B.T. Erford (Ed.), *Transforming the school counseling profession* (pp. 39–62). Upper Saddle River, NJ: Merrill/Prentice-Hall.

Littrell, J., & Zinck, K. (2005). Individual counseling from good to great. In C. A. Sink (Ed.), *Contemporary school counseling: Theory, research and practice* (pp. 45–81). Boston: Houghton Mifflin.

Lonborg, S., & Bowen, N. (2004). Counselors, communities and spirituality: Ethical and multicultural considerations. *Professional School Counseling, 7*(5), 318–323.

Massachusetts Governor's Commission on Gay and Lesbian Youth. (1993). *Making school safe for gay and lesbian youth: Breaking the silence in schools and in families.* Boston: Author.

McFarland, W., & Dupuis, M. (2001). The legal duty to protect gay and lesbian students from school violence. In T. P. Remley, Jr., M. A. Herman, & W. C. Huey (Eds.), *Ethical and legal issues in school counseling* (2nd ed., pp. 341–457).

McWhirter, J. J., McWhirter, B. T., McWhirter, E. H., & McWhirter, R. J. (2004). *At risk youth: A comprehensive response* (3rd ed.). Belmont, CA: Brooks/Cole-Thomson Learning.

Myrick, R. D. (2003). *Developmental guidance and counseling: A practical approach* (4th ed.) Minneapolis, MN: Educational Media Corporation.

National School Safety Center. (1998). Checklist of characteristics of youth who have caused school-associated violent deaths. In *School associated violent deaths report.* Westlake Village, CA: Author.

Page, B., Pietrzak, D., & Sutton, J. (2001). National survey of school counselor supervision. *Counselor Education and Supervision, 41,* 142–150.

Reddy, M., Borum, R., Berglund, J., Vossekuil, B., Fein, R., & Modzeles, W. (2001). Evaluating risk for targeted violence in schools: Comparing risk assessments, threat assessment and other approaches. *Psychology in the Schools, 38,* 157–172.

Remley, T. P. (1985). The law and ethical practices in elementary and middle schools. *Elementary School Guidance and Counseling, 19,* 181–189.

Remley, T., Herlihy, B., & Herlihy, S. (1997). The U.S. Supreme Court Decision in *Jaffee v. Redmond:* Implications for school counselors. *Journal of Counseling and Development, 75,* 213–218.

Remley, T. P, Jr., Herman, M. A., & Huey, W. C. (Eds.). (2003). *Ethical and legal issues in school counseling* (2nd ed.). Alexandria, VA: American School Counselor Association.

Remley, T., & Sparkman, L. (1993). Student suicides: The counselor's limited legal liability. *The School Counselor, 40,* 164–169.

Sears, S. J. (2005). Large group guidance: Curriculum development and instruction. In C. A. Sink (Ed.), *Contemporary school counseling: Theory, research and practice* (pp. 152–189). Boston: Houghton Mifflin.

Sciarra, D. T. (2004). *School counseling: Foundations and contemporary issues.* Belmont, CA: Brook/Cole-Thomson Learning.

Sermat, V., & Smyth, M. (1973). Content analysis of verbal communication in the development of a relationship: Conditions influencing self-disclosure. *Journal of Personality and Social Psychology, 26,* 332–346.

Simonson, N., & Bahr, S. (1974). Self-disclosure by the professional and paraprofessional therapist. *Journal of Counseling and Clinical Psychology, 42,* 359–363.

Sink, C. (2004). Spirituality and comprehensive school counseling programs. *Professional School Counseling, 7*(5), 309–317.

Sink, C. (2005). *Contemporary school counseling: Theory, research and practice.* Boston: Houghton Mifflin.

Sink, C., & Richmond, L. (2004). Introducing spirituality to Professional School Counseling. *Professional School Counseling, 7,* 291–292.

Stenger, R. L. (1986). The school counselor and the law: New developments. *Journal of Law and Education, 15,* 105–116.

Stone, C. (2000). Advocacy for sexual harassment victims: Legal support and ethical aspects. *Professional School Counseling, 4,* 23–30.

Stone, C. (2002). Negligence in academic advising and abortion counseling: Court rulings and implications. *Professional School Counseling, 6,* 28–35.

Stone, C. (2005). *School counseling principles: Ethics and law.* Alexandria, VA: American School Counselor Assoc.

Sue, D. W., & Sue, D. W. (2002). *Counseling the culturally diverse: Theory and practice* (4th ed.). Hoboken, NJ: Wiley.

Tarver-Behring, S., Spagna, M.E., & Sullivan, J. (1998). School counselors and full inclusion for children with special needs. *Professional School Counseling, 1*(3), 51–55.

U.S. Department of Education. (2001). *No child left behind act of 2001.* Washington, DC: Author.

U.S. Department of Education, National Center for Education Statistics. (2003). *Digest of education statistics—2002.* Washington, DC: Author.

Weed, L. L. (1971). Quality control and the medical record. *Archive of Internal Medicine 127,* 101–105.

Wittmer, J. (2000). *Managing your school counseling program: K-12 developmental strategies.* Minneapolis, MN: Educational Media Corporation.

Zingaro, R. (1983). Confidentiality: To tell or not to tell. *Elementary School Guidance & Counseling, 17,* 261–267.

CHAPTER 11

MENTAL HEALTH COUNSELING

PAUL R. PELUSO AND ALEXIS O. MIRANDA

"The world is changing." This was the first line of narration in Peter Jackson's epic film adaptation of J. R. R. Tolkien's *Lord of the Rings,* describing the uncertainty of the times depicted in the story. However, it is not unlike the world that we face today, and especially the ethical practice of mental health counseling. Increased litigiousness, decreasing fees, managed care overregulation, intergroup squabbles over "turf," and lack of professional recognition by major governing bodies (e.g., Medicare, Medicaid) have eroded some of the goodwill that many counselors have for the profession. Ever since it evolved from the educational and guidance movement in the 1900s, mental health counseling has always responded to the needs and challenges of the times. Often these were client needs and challenges; however, the great challenges of the last twenty to twenty-five years have been professional in nature and included the rise of managed care, the consumer movement, and the specialization of the field (including licensure issues). The question that all counselors face in light of these challenges is how to respond in a way that embraces growth without losing the core identity of the profession. For example, the consumer movement was important because it helped professionals to think in terms of not what the counselor did *to* or *for* the client, but what the counselor did *with* the client. It forced counselors to consider their practice from a personal, organizational, relational, and multicultural perspective. Effective counseling by "master therapists" (referred to in the earlier chapters of this book) found a way to bridge the dichotomies that paralyze many professionals and then transcend them to the benefit of both counselor and consumer. It is the same with managed care and specialization. Both struggles have forced counselors to reevaluate how they practice, and how they are unique in doing it. Ethics are not isolated from these seismic shifts in the field. In fact, the impact of ethics on practice and practice on ethics is a dynamic process, subject to change. As Walden, Herlihy, and Ashton (2003), in discussing the evolution of counseling ethics, put it:

> We as counselor educators and supervisors are reminded of the need to be responsive to the world around us and to be sensitive to differing cultures and changing practices. As *the world in which we practice changes,* so do the standards that guide us (p. 109; italics added).

Indeed, no hobbit could have said it better! In this chapter, the integrative-contextual approach to mental health counseling will address the changes and challenges faced by counselors in the world today.

LEARNING OBJECTIVES

After reading this chapter you should be able to

1. Define ethically sound mental health counseling from an integrative-contextual approach that values good practice and ensures client welfare.
2. Relate the contextual dimensions—from the relational to the developmental to the organizational, including the multicultural—to the practice of mental health counseling.
3. Describe eight common ethical issues in mental health counseling and the specific ethical codes and standards relevant to them.
4. Understand the impact of managed care organizations on the ethical practice of mental health counseling.
5. Explain two common legal issues in the practice of mental health counseling.
6. Apply the ethical decision-making model to a mental health counseling issue, aware of the relational, multicultural, and other organizational and personal dimensions.

KEY TERMS

AMHCA
categorical boundaries
dimensional boundaries
HIPAA
MCO
PHI
power
SOAP notation

ROUTINE PRACTICE OF MENTAL HEALTH COUNSELING

It would seem that the day-to-day tasks of conducting the business of the practice of mental health therapy would not seem like major ethical concerns. However, there are several specific ethical codes and legal statutes that govern such day-to-day operations as advertising and assessment. Specifically, in the AMHCA code, Principle 7 is dedicated to competence, which addresses the fact that mental health therapists must not practice in areas outside of their training and competence (addressed below). Principle 4 deals with assessment and testing, and expressly states that any materials that are used must be within the therapist's scope of knowledge. Specifically, this means that the therapist must understand issues related to measurement and instrument validity and accurately provide interpretation of results in a fashion that clients can understand. Principle 12 is dedicated to private practice and reinforces the codes contained in the above sections, as well as also provides guidance about the payment of services, prohibition of payment for referrals, and other elements of practice (see Box 11.1). While the ACA code has similar codes interspersed throughout the ethics code, the AMHCA ethical code is noteworthy for expressly placing these within the context of private practice.

BOX 11.1
AMCHA ETHICS CODE PRINCIPLE 12: PRIVATE PRACTICE

A) A mental health counselor should assist, where permitted by legislation or judicial decision, the profession in fulfilling its duty to make counseling services available in private settings.

B) In advertising services as a private practitioner, mental health counselors should advertise the services in such a manner so as to accurately inform the public as to services, expertise, profession, and techniques of counseling in a professional manner. Mental health counselors who assume an executive leadership role in the organization shall not permit their name to be used in professional notices during periods when not actively engaged in the private practice of counseling. Mental health counselors advertise the following: highest relevant degree, type and level of certification or license, and type and/or description of services or other relevant information. Such information should not contain false, inaccurate, misleading, and partial, out of context descriptive material or statements.

C) Mental health counselors may join in partnership/corporation with other mental health counselors and/or other professionals provided that each mental health counselor of the partnership or corporation makes clear his/her separate specialties, buying name in compliance with the regulations of the locality.

D) Mental health counselors have an obligation to withdraw from an employment relationship or a counseling relationship if it is believed that employment will result in violation of the Code of Ethics, if their mental capacity or physical condition renders it difficult to carry out an effective professional relationship, or if the mental health counselor is discharged by the client because the counseling relationship is no longer productive for the client.

E) Mental health counselors should adhere and support the regulations for private practice in the locality where the services are offered.

F) Mental health counselors refrain from attempts to utilize one's institutional affiliation to recruit clients for one's private practice. Mental health counselors are to refrain from offering their services in the private sector when they are employed by an institution in which this is prohibited by stated policy that reflects conditions of employment.

From: AMHCA (2000).

From the ethical practice issues of mental health counseling, we turn our attention to the legal aspects of practice as it relates to the Health Insurance Portability and Accountability Act (HIPAA) of 1996. This federal law was fully implemented in April 2005, and has created several obligations that most mental health counselors must be aware of regarding confidentiality, informed consent, and the handling of client's health information. In particular, any provider who deals with protected health information (PHI) and transmits it electronically (including by fax machine) to a third party for payment (e.g., to an insurance company) must abide by the statutes. Some counselors who only see private, self-pay clients *and* conduct all their transactions by paper and through the mail may not be considered to be "covered entities" under HIPAA. However, it is best to err on the side of caution, since even sending emails containing basic client information could be considered electronic transmission, which requires the professional to be HIPAA compliant (Barstow,

2003; Wedding, 2004). Beyond the legal obligations of HIPAA, there is a basic principle of humanity that is important to focus on: namely, the right of people to keep information about their own persons (body, mind, and spirit) private. It is a right that all the helping professions (be they medical or mental health) have always striven to uphold, for at its heart are the issues of the fundamental dignity of the individual and a recognition of the "sacred" trust that the individual places in professional caretakers. When professionals lose their reverence for this trust, then abuse or carelessness occurs, which hurts the people we are entrusted to care for.

According to Barstow (2003), the privacy regulations for HIPAA have several requirements for counselors covered under the statute. Most of these responsibilities are congruent with sound ethical practices. These responsibilities include

- Providing clients with a notice of their health information use practices, and of their clients' rights with respect to health information.
- Appointing privacy officers (which can be themselves).
- Accounting for disclosures of health information to third parties.
- Establishing reasonable health information use practices to safeguard information.

Barstow (2003) notes that the requirements of these privacy regulations can be adapted to fit the setting in which the counselor practices. Therefore, a counselor working in a hospital setting would comply with the HIPAA regulations differently than a counselor in a solo private practice or an agency setting.

One of the requirements from HIPAA affecting a mental health counselor's daily practice is the status of psychotherapy notes versus other elements of the client's record. Psychotherapy notes are treated with even stricter requirements than other health care information under HIPAA and generally are to be excluded from individuals' regular medical records. Psychotherapy notes are defined by the regulations as follows:

> *Psychotherapy notes* means notes recorded (in any medium) by a health care provider who is a mental health professional documenting or analyzing the contents of conversation during a private counseling session or a group, joint, or family counseling session and that are separated from the rest of the individual's medical record. *Psychotherapy notes* excludes medication prescription and monitoring, counseling session start and stop times, the modalities and frequencies of treatment furnished, results of clinical tests, and any summary of the following items: diagnosis, functional status, the treatment plan, symptoms, prognosis, and progress to date. (U.S. Department of Health and Human Services, as cited in Barstow, 2003)[1]

In general, HIPAA underscored the right for clients to inspect, obtain a copy of, and request amendments to their protected health information if there are factual errors. However, now the practice of having to transmit psychotherapy notes to insurance companies for the purpose of payment is now ended. Although this is an improvement in confidentiality for clients, it means that counselors will have to separate their psychotherapy notes from the more basic treatment information they maintain in order to comply with the regulation.

[1]Commonly these types of notes are called progress or process notes.

Therapists may share their psychotherapy notes with their clients, but are not compelled to do so by the privacy regulation. In fact, counselors may deny clients access to their psychotherapy notes if there are concerns about clients' welfare if they were to read over the notes (Barstow, 2003; Wedding, 2004). However, clinicians who are both subtly precise and sensitive to the individual client (i.e., who operate from an integrative-contextual approach) tend to write their notes in a careful way that the client, in consultation with the counselor, should be able to accept (see Box 11.2).

BOX 11.2
NOTATION FOR MENTAL HEALTH COUNSELORS

While the regulations imposed by HIPAA have created many obligations for counselors, one regulation has granted permission for counselors to keep psychotherapy notes private from other elements of a client's record and not required to be transmitted to any outside source (for the purpose of payment). The result of this is that it creates an extra level of security or secrecy of the actual content of the psychotherapy session (i.e., what is said in the therapy session). However, there is no explicit ethical obligation for the counselor to keep an accurate record of what happens in the session.[2] Curiously, however, while the accepted "standards of care" (and some state laws) clearly indicate that there should be a record of what happens from session to session, there is no clear determination of *how* this should be done. While there are a number of different formats (described by their various acronyms: DAP, BIRP, etc.), they all essentially convey the same information. One of the more widely used formats is the SOAP note format. Developed by Weed (1971), SOAP stands for

Subjective. This is the section that contains the information given to the counselor by the client during the session. This includes the client's statements of fact, feelings, and a general sense of the session from the client's perspective.

Objective. This section contains factual information that the counselor observes directly. It should be written precisely, in quantifiable behavioral terms. Observations about mood, affect, appearance, and mental status should be recorded here.

Assessment. This is the counselor's clinical impression of the client based on the assessment and treatment plan, as well as the subjective and objective sections of the note. It is generally written in the multiaxial format of the most recent version of the *Diagnostic and Statistical Manual of Mental Disorders* (i.e., DSM IV-TR).

Plan. This is the section that contains the plan for treatment as well as the counselor's prognosis for the client. This often includes interventions used in session, specific recommendations for follow-up in the next session (i.e., "homework"), referrals for adjunctive intervention (e.g., psychiatric evaluation, group therapy, etc.), and the date of the next appointment.

Consider the following example:

Subjective. Client reported that wife has left him over his continued drinking. He fears that she will not return as she has in the past and that he will have to attempt recovery

[2]There are references in the AMHCA ethics code to the client's "record," but there is no specific information or guidance about what the record should reflect or contain.

alone. Reflected on family of origin, especially his parent's divorce, his estranged relationship with his father, and what this may mean for his own children.

***O*bjective.** Client was generally cooperative, though visibly upset throughout most of the session. Appeared disheveled, unkempt, and smelled like he had been drinking recently. Evidenced depressed mood and congruent tearful affect (i.e., crying spells). Was oriented to time/place/person/situation.

***A*ssessment.**

Axis I: Substance Abuse (If Initial Session)
Axis II: Deferred (Rule out Dependent Personality Disorder)
Axis III: Hypertension, Diabetes
Axis IV: Partner Relational Problem
Axis V: GAF = 50 (55 highest past year)

(If Ongoing) Continues to drink and experience depressed mood and denies suicidal ideation.

GARF = 55

***P*lan.** Scheduled individual therapy session this Friday (4/25/05). Continue to discuss destructive behavior patterns. Referred to AA meetings at least 1x/day. Prognosis guarded. This allows for coordination of services with other professionals, as well as a clear documentation of the course of therapy.

According to Cameron and turtle-song (2002) "using the SOAP format, the counselor is able to clearly document and support, through the subjective and objective sections, his or her decision to modify existing treatment goals, or to fine-tune the client's treatment plan" (p. 287).

Under HIPAA, mental health counselors must provide patients with a written privacy notice that describes how their PHI may be used or disclosed, as well as how clients can get access to it. The regulation requires the notice to explain the purpose of the consent form that the patient will initially be asked to sign and to clearly spell out that, if the patient refuses to consent to the disclosures, the therapist may refuse to treat the client. The client must be informed in the written notice of his or her right to request restrictions on certain uses and disclosures of PHI, if he or she should wish. The privacy notice must inform the client of the therapist's legal duties and the counselor's (or practice's) privacy practices with respect to PHI. Last, the privacy notice must inform the client of his or her right to complain to the secretary of the U.S. Department of Health and Human Services or other governing entities about believed privacy violations (Barstow, 2003; Wedding, 2004).

The HHS Office for Civil Rights (OCR), which is responsible for enforcement of compliance with HIPAA regulations, also has useful information for providers on its website, which is found at http://www.hhs.gov/ocr/hipaa. In addition, examples of forms created specifically for HIPAA covered providers (e.g., consent, privacy notice, authorizations, and policies and procedures) can also be found on the HHS web page, which can be downloaded and modified to each practitioner's specific needs.

In the next section, we switch from the surface issues related to mental health counseling and discuss some of the core elements of the integrative-contextual approach outlined in this text as they relate to mental health counseling.

CONTEXTUAL ISSUES IN MENTAL HEALTH COUNSELING

Personal-Developmental

Chapter 2 presents an excellent discussion of this topic for mental health counselors. It would be counterproductive to try to recapitulate the information again here. We will briefly discuss some of the unique (and not-so-unique) elements of mental health counselors' development personally as professionals in the field.

With the exception of marriage and family therapy (which has a rigorous process for becoming an Approved Supervisor from the American Association for Marriage and Family Therapy), mental health counselors pay particular attention to the process of supervision. Specifically, the Association for Counselor Education and Supervision (ACES) devotes considerable time and energy to the understanding of the process of supervision, particularly the development of new counselors. As a result, Stoltenberg, McNeill, and Delworth's (1998) four-tiered model of professional development (presented in Chapter 2) is considered a valuable starting point for evaluating the progress of counselors through the professional lifespan.[3]

The personal-developmental dimension of integrative-contextual ethics provides insights into not only a counselor's developmental skill level, but deeper levels of emotional maturity and good judgment. It is from this deeply held set of beliefs that the emotional "gut"-level response to often ambiguous clinical stimuli results (Peluso, 2003). It is not simply a matter of whether counselors have done their own personal "work" that indicates the level of maturity, but rather the level of insight into how these recurring issues, feelings, experiences can be used in an organic way to benefit the client. Rather than undergo "psycho-surgery" (i.e., intensive psychotherapy) whereby the counselor "finishes" all of his or her business so that it will never emerge, counselors who operate within an integrative-contextual approach that may have indeed undergone some personal experiences of trauma and recovery, utilize the knowledge, wisdom, or insight of their own struggle for the *client's* benefit. They recognize the client's right to have his or her own therapy without the burden of the counselor's "baggage" and balance it with their personal stories of honesty and integrity. They are aware of their (positive) influence and use it without either becoming manipulative out of a need for self-gratification or refusing to use their influence out of a fear of "imposing their values" on the client (which are the hallmarks of a Perspective I approach). This includes ethical decisions as well, related to conflicts of interest, power, multiple relationships, confidentiality, and boundary crossings.

Another area where the personal-developmental dimension plays a key role is in the emergence or prevention of burnout in counselors. Those counselors who do not subscribe to an integrative-contextual approach to ethics also tend not to examine either the personal-developmental or professional aspects of a situation. Rather, they look for expedience and a course of action characterized by a lack of entanglement. Paradoxically for these counselors, entanglements are inevitable when the personal-developmental dimension is ignored, which leads frustration, disillusionment, and finally overall therapeutic disengagement (commonly referred to as burnout). An alternate scenario is the case of the counselor who attempts to

[3]Note that issues relevant to supervision will be discussed in detail in Chapter 14; we merely focus on it from the point of view of the supervisee here.

compensate for the lack of personal fulfillment by overextending him- or herself, and "working harder, not smarter." This ultimately leads to exhaustion, "compassion fatigue," or burnout. Skovholt and Jennings (2004) reports that this is precisely the opposite of the "master therapist," who is continually seeking out personal growth and at the same time "taking care" of him- or herself by pursuing outside interests, learning and applying new skills, and/or being involved in his or her own therapy. In any case, the master therapist is continually aware of the particular impact of the personal-developmental dimension on overall professional demeanor.

Relational-Multicultural

Multicultural issues became the focus of professional counselors and writers approximately thirty years ago (Ibrahim & Arrendondo, 1986; Sue, Arrendondo & McDavis, 1992; Sue & Sue, 1999). Likewise, in response to this movement, professional organizations began to reflect in their ethics codes a respect for diversity, avoiding discrimination, and demonstrating cultural competency as a matter of the routine practice of mental health counseling. In fact, the AMHCA ethics code (Principle 1E.1) specifically and inclusively details the ethical obligation that mental health counselors have to their clients with regard to cultural sensitivity (see Box 11.3). As a result of the power of this movement, multicultural counseling became a meta-approach to counseling that would influence all of the established counseling approaches regarding the notions of monoculturalism. In addition, specific models of acculturation were developed, and targeted skill sets were taught to increase mental health counselors awareness, sensitivity, and, ultimately, facility in working with clients from cultural backgrounds different from the dominant culture (traditional Western culture). However, according to Garcia, Cartwright, Winston, and Burzuchowska (2003), "we found minimal reference to culture or how to integrate culture into ethical decision making processes systematically" (p. 269).

BOX 11.3
SELECTIONS OF AMHCA (2000) ETHICS CODE ON DIVERSITY

PRINCIPLE 1 WELFARE OF THE CONSUMER

E) Diversity

1. Mental health counselors do not condone or engage in any discrimination based on age, color, culture, disability, ethnic group, gender, race, religion, sexual orientation, marital status, or socioeconomic status.
2. Mental health counselors will actively attempt to understand the diverse cultural backgrounds of the clients with whom they work. This includes learning how the counselor's own cultural/ethical/racial/religious identity impacts his or her own values and beliefs about the counseling process. When there is a conflict between the client's goals, identity, and/or values and those of the mental health counselor, a referral to an appropriate colleague must be arranged.

From AMHCA (2000)

There have been several attempts at broaching the relational and, specifically, the multicultural dimension of ethical decision making. Cottone (2001) proposed a model of ethical decision making based on social construction that embraces the relational aspects and has informed additional ethical decision-making models such as the Transcultural Integrative Model (Garcia et al., 2003), and the integrative-contextual model that is articulated in this text. The integrative-contextual approach takes the elements of both Garcia and colleagues' model and Cottone's models (among others) and expands on them to include the personal as well as the organizational dimensions.

Another way that the integrative-contextual approach has expounded upon other ethical decision-making models is in the inclusion of spirituality in the model. Spirituality (and to some degree, religion) has always been a central pillar of U.S. society. From the founding of the colonies that would eventually become the United States, to the nation's reaction following the terrorist attacks on September 11, 2001, religion, spirituality, or the belief in a supreme being have played key, if not always visible, roles in the courses of Americans' lives. Popular surveys of adults routinely show an overwhelming majority of respondents acknowledged having a belief in a God or higher power, and a majority of those individuals report that they participate in some form of organized religious community (synagogue, church, mosque, etc.) regularly (Wolf & Stevens, 2001). However, if this is such a part of everyday life, why has there been such historical antagonism toward religion and spirituality by the therapeutic community? According to Wolf and Stevens (2001), psychotherapists historically excluded religion and spirituality because "from its outset, psychology has attempted to establish itself as a scientific domain" (p. 68). Religion and spirituality traditionally haven't fit nicely into a scientific conceptualization for investigation. However, this has begun to change, as well, as physicians, anthropologists, and psychologists have begun to study the impact of spirituality on a number of human phenomena (Genia, 2000). In mental health counseling, scientific rigor has not been emphasized as much as the personal experience of the client–counselor relationship, wider acceptance of a client's spiritual experiences.

Another obstacle to therapists' embracing a religious or spiritual perspective is the perception that religion is punitive, or limiting to one's freedom. This is in opposition to the nature of therapy, which is ideally supposed to help the client find new ways of self-expression that are neither limiting nor punishing. This can set the goals of therapy against the goals of the religion, which often has a creed and code of conduct that communicants must adhere to in order to maintain membership. However, on issues like homosexuality, marriage, and divorce, therapeutic ideals may conflict with a client's religious or spiritual ones, placing both the client and the counselor in a difficult position (Sperry & Giblin, 1996).

Mental health counselors who are unable or uncomfortable responding to clients within a spiritual frame of reference run the risk of shutting off a critical source of insight into the family's context, as well as denying a valuable resource for healing (Sperry & Giblin, 1996). Indeed, if this is the context in which a counselor views religion, then he or she may not be able to work with the client without inappropriately allowing his or her own countertransference into the therapeutic relationship, and is (at best) likely operating from a Perspective II approach.

Organizational Ethics–Community Values

As mentioned in Chapter 4, often a person's personal ethics, professional ethics, and an organization's ethics come into conflict. To review briefly, *personal ethics* is a unique set of beliefs and values by which one lives one's life. A counselor's *professional ethics* is the individual counselor's method for determining how to operate in an ethically sound, professional manner. This is based, in part, on personal ethics and on the ethical obligations of the profession. *Organizational ethics* refers to the institutional norms and organizational characteristics that go into making systemwide decisions. The organization's main focus is to ensure that individual staff behaviors and decisions execute the functions that the organization publicly proclaims that it will do. While it may be important for staff to feel a sense of connectedness that their needs are taken care of, there are times when that is a secondary consideration. This means that there may be situations where the staff must act in a way that they do not agree with in order to fulfill the mission of the agency or organization. Counselors who practice from an integrative-contextual approach must clarify the conditions of employment before they accept work at an organization. Daniels (2001) suggested that, when a counselor accepts employment at a given agency, she or he accepts tacitly the organization's policies and procedures.

At the same time, this does not excuse the organization from operating within the bounds of ethics. If an agency purposefully or unintentionally violates laws and/or rights, the counselor who practices from an integrative-contextual approach informs the agency administrators of such violation and works toward changing the policies and/or practices. The self-evaluation tool presented in Chapter 4 is a good starting point for assessing whether, in the counselor's opinion, the organization that he or she is working in is operating in an ethically consistent fashion and how much the personal, professional, and organizational ethics may be coming into conflict.

If the agency is not sensitive to ethical and professional considerations, there may be some times when the individual counselor's ethical concerns place him or her in jeopardy of breeching ethical obligations if the organization requires the counselor to act. Interestingly, the AMHCA ethics code (12.D) specifies that, if therapists find themselves in an employment situation where they feel there are questionable practices, they are obliged to withdraw from the employment rather than violate the ethics code. As a result, mental health counselors operating from an integrative-contextual approach must always be sensitive to the environmental factors, and the influence of the organizational structures and culture that surround them, as they practice.

CORE ETHICAL ISSUES AND CODES OF ETHICS FOR MENTAL HEALTH COUNSELORS

As mentioned above, the two primary professional associations for mental health counselors are the American Counseling Association (ACA) and American Mental Health Counselors Association (AMHCA). Ethical codes are changing instruments, just as the laws of a society change with the passage of time and with alterations in the social and cultural orders, and these have been updated recently. Since the ACA code is dealt with in other areas of this book, in the next section, we will refer solely to elements of the AMHCA ethics code. At a glance, there is considerable overlap between these two codes. The ACA code has eight major subsections, whereas the AMHCA ethics code has fifteen. In fact, the AMHCA code has agreement or overlap in the titles of six out of the eight ACA codes (see Box 11.4). A deeper analysis reveals more overlap in the additional sections. In general, however, the ACA code places more emphasis on research and teaching, while the AMHCA code places more emphasis on practice issues and consultation and even includes a section on Internet counseling. Specifically, the ethical codes related to the core ethical issues of confidentiality, informed consent, conflict of interest, and competency will be discussed.

BOX 11.4

SIDE-BY-SIDE COMPARISON OF THE MAJOR SECTIONS/PRINCIPLES OF THE ACA AND AMHCA ETHICS CODES

AMHCA Ethics Code "Principles"	ACA Ethics Code "Sections"
The Counseling Relationship	Welfare of the Consumer
Confidentiality, Privileged Communication, and Privacy	Clients' Rights
Professional Responsibility	Confidentiality
Relationships with Other Professionals	Utilization of Assessment Techniques
Evaluation, Assessment, and Interpretation	Pursuit of Research Activities
Teaching, Training, and Supervision	Consulting
Research and Publication	Competence
Resolving Ethical Issues	Professional Relationships
	Supervisee, Student, and Employee Relationships
	Moral and Legal Standards
	Professional Responsibility
	Private Practice
	Public Statements
	Internet Online Counseling
	Resolution of Ethical Problems

From ACA (2005) and AMHCA (2000).

Confidentiality

Confidentiality has long been regarded as the cornerstone of the helping professions and the counseling relationship (Keith-Spiegel & Koocher, 1985). Mental health professionals agree that confidentiality is a universally held value within the helping professions and other professions that rely upon information shared within the boundaries of a professional relationship. It is a prerequisite of the therapeutic process, as it protects the legal right to privacy of consumers of mental health counselors. Specific to the counseling field, Issacs and Stone (2001) defined confidentiality as "a variously accorded legal right of clients and a primary responsibility of mental health counselors who are charged with making professional judgments that protect clients" (p. 342). Siegel (1979) defined privacy as "freedom of individuals to choose for themselves the time and the circumstances under which and the extent to which their beliefs, behaviors, and opinions are to be shared or withheld from others" (p. 251). Privacy is a right guaranteed by the Fourth Amendment of the U.S. Constitution. Its basic premise is that all persons have rights to freedom and self-determination. However, the issue is not as simple as merely maintaining privacy, for though confidentiality is a relatively straightforward concept, the tricky element of confidentiality lies in the instance when it cannot be maintained.

The guidelines surrounding this have evolved in reaction to changing societal mores and the complexity inherent in the performance of professional duties, especially the information that is managed by counselors—conducting assessments, diagnosing and treating, consulting, researching, teaching, or submitting information to third parties for compensation. The two forces that have formed the framework whereby most counselors determine the limits of confidentiality are HIPAA regulations (see above) and case law (see below). However, the principle underlying confidentiality, according to Freeman (2000), is the issue of privacy and the obligation that counselors bear as a result of being employed by the client. Furthermore, he cited what Shah (1970) noted nearly four decades ago to be a conflict of what may best be construed as agency—a counselor acting on behalf of an institution and not a client when handling matters of privacy. Shah noted, additionally, that often counselors are faced with conflicts between obligations toward their institution, such in the case of an employer, and their clients. Shah maintained that, in such instances, a counselor must clarify these matters with a prospective client before establishing a professional relationship. We assume and expect, therefore, that a counselor practicing from an integrative-contextual approach assures informed consent before the establishment of a professional relationship. Informed consent, from the point of view of a counselor practicing from Perspective III, must address matters of agency.

In regards to confidentiality, the current AMHCA *Code of Ethics and Professional Practice* (2000) devotes an entire section to it. Box 11.5 lists some selected portions of the code, but most important are the underlying principles that are reflected in it. First, the obligation for counselors is to safeguard the client's information, and second is the idea that "confidentiality belongs to the clients" (AMHCA, 2000, 3C). This clearly reflects a focus on the client's right to privacy and places strong obligation on mental health counselors not to treat it lightly.

In addition, the right to privacy is inextricably linked with privilege. The legal concept of privilege refers to the right of a person not to have information shared with others in legal proceedings unless the person consents. Like confidentiality, privilege rests solely with the client. Siegel (1979) defined privilege as "a legal term involving the right not to reveal confidential information in a legal procedure. Privilege is granted by statute, protects the client from having his/her communications revealed in a judicial setting without explicit permission, and is vested in the client by legislative authority" (p. 251). In the AMHCA ethics code, this is reflected in Principle 3C and 3H, which direct the manner in which mental health counselors operate under court order or subpoena, a well as safeguard the protected information contained in client records.

No federal statute directly addresses privilege. However, recent case law (*Jaffee v. Redmond*) has supported the broad concept of counselor–client privilege. As a result, selected states extend privilege to therapist–client relationships. However, states' laws about privilege vary widely, and it is incumbent upon the counselors to investigate the specifics of the states

BOX 11.5
SELECTIONS FROM AMHCA CODE RELATED TO CONFIDENTIALITY

PRINCIPLE 3 CONFIDENTIALITY

Mental health counselors have a primary obligation to safeguard information about individuals obtained in the course of practice, teaching, or research. Personal information is communicated to others only with the person's written consent or in those circumstances where there is clear and imminent danger to the client, to others, or to society. Disclosure of counseling information is restricted to what is necessary, relevant, and verifiable.

A) At the outset of any counseling relationship, mental health counselors make their clients aware of their rights in regard to the confidential nature of the counseling relationship. They fully disclose the limits of, or exceptions to, confidentiality, and/or the existence of privileged communication, if any.

C) Confidentiality belongs to the clients. They may direct the mental health counselor, in writing, to release information to others. The release of information without the consent of the client may only take place under the most extreme circumstances. The protection of life, as in the case of suicidal or homicidal clients, exceeds the requirements of confidentiality. The protection of a child, an elderly person, or a person not competent to care for themselves from physical or sexual abuse or neglect requires that a report be made to a legally constituted authority. The mental health counselor complies with all state and federal statutes concerning mandated reporting of suicidality, homicidality, child abuse, incompetent person abuse, and elder abuse. The protection of the public or another individual from a contagious condition known to be fatal also requires action that may include reporting the willful infection of another with the condition. The mental health counselor (or staff member) does not release information by request unless accompanied by a specific release of information or a valid court order. Mental health counselors will comply with the order of a court to release information but they will inform the client of the receipt of such an order. A subpoena is insufficient to release information. In such a case, the counselor must inform his client of the situation and, if the client refuses release, coordinate between the client's attorney and the requesting attorney so as to protect client confidentiality and one's own legal welfare. In the case of all of the above exceptions to confidentiality, the mental health counselor will release only such information as is necessary to accomplish the action required by the exception.

H) Counseling reports and records are maintained under conditions of security, and provisions are made for their destruction when they have outlived their usefulness. Mental health counselors ensure that all persons in his or her employ, volunteers, and community aides maintain privacy and confidentiality.

*From AMHCA, 2000

they practice in. What is common about privilege is its express requirement for a professional to be licensed, certified, or registered as a professional. However, in selected states, privilege is extended to selected people who carry out the duties of mental health professionals. An example of a case involving privilege is illustrated in Box 11.6.

BOX 11.6
CASE OF CONFIDENTIALITY

Janice is a 24-year-old mother of two preschool-age children who recently left her abusive partner of several years. She is coming to counseling to address her depression and to get treatment for her explosive temper. During the course of therapy, she has improved her interactions with her children, which were seriously lacking in the beginning of therapy. In addition, she has demonstrated great strides in controlling her anger and in shaving genuine love for her children. However, in the assessment phase of her therapy, she disclosed to her therapist that she had physically disciplined her children with a belt, which left bruises on their bodies. In addition, she admitted to illicit drug usage, though she reported that this ended at the same time as the relationship. The parents of her partner (and the children's father) are seeking custody of the children, claiming that Janice is an unfit mother, and have subpoenaed the therapist's records. The therapist is aware of the potentially damaging effects of the information in the file that could be used against his client, despite her progress in treatment and the therapist's belief that Janice is a fit mother for her children. What would you do?

Regardless of what "Perspective" a counselor operates from, when a court order is issued from a judge, the therapist must comply. Yet, this is not generally the case when the subpoena is issued by an opposing lawyer. However, counselors operating from an integrative-contextual perspective, as a part of ongoing informed consent, would attempt to apprehend the likelihood of litigation and remind the client of the limits of confidentiality in the event of a court order. In this case, counselors from an integrative-contextual perspective need to consider how to act in accordance with their own best judgment, as well as in the best interest of the client. Steps that a counselor could take include contacting the client and discussing the specific elements of the record. The counselor would be well advised to work closely with the client's legal counsel to determine whether to assert privilege (which may or may not be recognized—see below for details) or have the subpoena quashed by the judge. If the client wishes the counselor to testify on her behalf, the counselor must also evaluate whether this would be helpful or hurtful to the client and act accordingly.

Confidentiality and Perspective III. At the core of all issues related to confidentiality, and the breaching of it, for counselors who adhere to an integrative-contextual approach, is the welfare of the client. In practice, these counselors not only know the limitations of confidentiality, but, as with the case above, inform prospective clients about these limitations and respect the privacy of all who procure counseling services. More important, counselors who practice from an integrative-contextual approach are proactive and act upon the premise that confidential communication supports positive counseling outcomes. Additionally, counselors provide information to third parties to the extent that it complies with legal mandates, court orders, and the protection of clients' dignity. They know that confidentiality protects the dignity of those who seek counseling and that proper respect for the issue upholds the integrity of the counseling process.

Informed Consent

Giving and maintaining informed consent is one of the methods whereby mental health counselors both respect clients' dignity and uphold the integrity of the counseling process. Informed consent is at the heart of ethical conduct (exemplified in Perspective III), as it places the client firmly in the position of making the choices about counseling based on full disclosure of counseling dynamics and counselor characteristics. It is a process of clarification and communication that sets the stage for the rest of the counseling. Does the therapist have a sufficient grasp of why the client is seeking help? Does the counselor know what the client's expectations or hopes or fears about counseling are? Does the client understand that he or she can question the therapist about the therapist's particular approach? Does the client understand how the counselor will likely operate? Does the client know the likely outcome of using such an approach to his or her problem (Pope & Vasquez, 1998)? Practically, informed consent necessitates description of enough information so that clients may anticipate the nature of the counseling process ("therapeutic regimes and schedules"), counseling material ("tests"), involvement of third parties ("reports, billing"), and the competence of the counselor who may provide the services ("statement of professional disclosure"). However, informed consent in not an event that occurs in counseling (as some professionals believe), but rather a process that unfolds as counseling progresses and as decisions need to be made.

Additionally, informed consent must deal with the "business" aspects of the therapeutic contract. Financial arrangements, missed appointments, length of session, and third-party payments should be discussed and clarified. In addition, the clients should be empowered to be involved in their treatment planning, goal setting, and/or questions about their progress. As discussed previously, clients should also be informed about how they can access their records, as well as about their rights regarding diagnosis and case notes (Ford, 2001). According to HIPAA regulations, clients have the right to petition to have their records amended, particularly if they choose to dispute what a professional has entered (e.g., inaccurate information, misquotes, diagnoses, etc.).

The ethics codes are clear about the need for providing informed consent, not only of the counselor's particular practice of counseling, but of their routine use of testing materials and billing practices. Box 11.7 presents some of the relevant codes. In addition, informed consent is also linked with confidentiality. In the AMHCA code, Principle 3A states that "mental health counselors make their clients aware of their rights in regard to the confidential nature of the counseling relationship. They fully disclose the limits of, or exceptions to, confidentiality, and/or the existence of privileged communication, if any" (AMHCA, 2000). In fact, mental health counselors must gain their client's consent (and be assured that they are fully informed) for testing, supervision, and research.

One of the major issues surrounding informed consent that mental health counselors face is what to do with individuals who cannot give consent. It is incumbent on the counselor to protect the rights of minors and clients who do not possess the capacity to make free choices regarding their participation in counseling. A portion of the relevant ethical guideline provides a general statement that does not remove the responsibility of informed consent when the client is disabled or a minor. However, consent is also a prerequisite for cooperation. As a result, even for minors and adults who cannot give consent, counselors working from and integrative-contextual approach must inform them of what therapy con-

BOX 11.7

SELECTED PORTIONS OF AMHCA CODE ON INFORMED CONSENT

PRINCIPLE 1 WELFARE OF THE CONSUMER

J) Informed Consent

Mental health counselors are responsible for making their services readily accessible to clients in a manner that facilitates the clients' abilities to make an informed choice when selecting a provider. This responsibility includes a clear description of what the client can expect in the way of tests, reports, billing, therapeutic regime and schedules, and the use of the mental health counselor's statement of professional disclosure. In the event that a client is a minor or possesses disabilities that would prohibit informed consent, the mental health counselor acts in the client's best interest.

sists of and give the opportunity to resolve any questions that they might have. Even if the client is a fully functioning adult, there are sensitive negotiations that often must take place as a part of building therapeutic rapport. In this instance, the process of giving informed consent can be transformed into "grist for the mill" or can leave a client feeling that he or she is being given the "cold shoulder." In the example in Box 11.8, we present a case where informed consent fosters the therapeutic process.

Informed Consent and Perspective III. Clearly, in this example the client was merely in an ideation phase with regard to suicidality. However, the counselor, operating from an integrative-contextual approach, conceived that informed consent is a two-way street that is essential to the success of counseling. Just as the counselor needs to inform the client of the practices of counseling, the limitations of confidentiality, and the treatment plan for the client, so too does the client need to keep the counselor informed of the relevant issues, feelings, thoughts, or events in his or her life. As a result, informed consent, from a Perspective III approach, is an ongoing, integral, and collaborative process of mental health counseling. This is in contrast to counselors operating from a Perspective I approach, who view informed consent as something that is done solely in the first session and that ends with a signature on a consent form.

Conflicts of Interest

The practice of mental health counseling is typically a solitary endeavor, from a professional standpoint. By and large, counselors operate alone in their offices (save, of course, for the client), unlike most other professionals. As a result, this can create the condition of isolation and insulation from others, whereby counselors don't have contact with other professionals (coworkers, etc.) and must rely solely on their own judgment, without feeling that they have to consult with anyone. This combination cannot only lead to burnout (as discussed earlier), but can also create problems recognizing conflict of interest, especially as it relates to power and boundaries. Counselors working from an integrative-contextual approach, while they

BOX 11.8
CASE OF INFORMED CONSENT

Harold was a 47-year-old man who was recently divorced after a twenty-three-year marriage. His presenting concern was mild depression following the dissolution of his marriage. He was very reluctant to come to counseling, but was urged to do so by his 21-year-old daughter. He was pale and thin in appearance and seemed to have recently lost weight. In addition, by his demeanor, it was obvious that he was leery about the counseling process. His only other experience with counseling was a session with his ex-wife that he thought was designed to help them work on their marriage. However, when he got there, it was revealed that his wife had been having an affair and that the purpose of the session was to inform him that she was leaving him. Harold began the initial individual counseling session questioning the counselor about whether "this stuff will do any good." The counselor, understanding Harold's hesitancy given his prior experience, discussed with him that Harold had control over the session and its content and that he would not "surprise" Harold. At the same time, the counselor sensed that Harold liked "straight talk" and told him that he would not "pull any punches" with him—that if he felt that there was something that was concerning him, he would say it. He explained to Harold the concept of informed consent, which would allow him to direct the course of therapy. At the same time, the counselor informed him that if there were issues that he thought were serious enough, he may have to make some tough decisions, but that he would consult Harold to the best of his ability.

The counselor, at this point, decided to take a chance with Harold and reflected to him that it would not be unheard of for a person in his position to have, at some point, considered that things would be better without him. Harold gave a recognition reflex response (a smile and nodding of his head) and admitted that he had thought that recently, but had told nobody about it. The counselor took the opportunity to talk to Harold about the options that he had if he continued to feel that way. He explained to him that there were differences between feeling that way, planning to do something about it, and actually preparing to do something harmful. He outlined for Harold the obligations that he had at each stage, but that they would work through it together. Harold thought that this was a logical explanation of the issue and began to feel more at ease with the counselor.

may find themselves in isolating situations, do not fall into the trap of (and do recognize the dangers of) *choosing* isolation and insulation. These will be discussed below.

Boundaries and Dual Relationships. "Power tends to corrupt, and absolute power corrupts absolutely."

Lord Acton

Lord Acton was a keen observer of the relationship between power and boundaries. Power over someone or something is corruptive in nature, and abuses will occur if it is not held in check by some delimiter or boundary. In the counseling domain, there is an inherent power differential embedded in the relationship between the client and the counselor, which has been the root cause of abuses in the past when there was nothing to hold back unscrupulous or even well-meaning therapists from acting in ways that today would clearly be inappropriate. Thus, boundaries have been set in order to protect clients from abuse and defend them against predatory counselors. Boundaries imply safety, security, and tidiness, which makes things run smoother (Sommers-Flanagan, Elliott, & Sommers-Flanagan, 1998). In therapy, clearly defined boundaries designed to protect clients are considered to be the *sine qua non* (Fay, 2002; Lazarus & Zur, 2002; Sommers-Flanagan et al., 1998). On this point, most counselors will agree. However, on many other points related to boundaries (e.g., the rigidity of the boundaries, and the extent to which they preserve therapeutic effectiveness) there is considerable variability across individual counselors and entire schools of therapy. As Williams (2002) points out:

> Two distinct and contradictory positions exist regarding boundaries in psychotherapy. On the one hand, authors argue that ethics concerns dictate a need for careful maintenance of boundaries as well as a need to sanction practitioners who violate. On the other hand, the tradition and practices of some forms of psychotherapy dictate that certain boundaries be routinely crossed. These two positions do not coexist well (p. 65).

Fay (2002) refers to these two positions as the "categorical" versus. "dimensional" views of boundaries, which will be discussed further below.

Categorical View of Boundaries. The categorical approach to boundaries takes the simple view that boundaries are a part of human interactions, and in place to delineate role functions and facilitate the therapeutic process (Clarkson, 2000; Fay, 2002). These are set *a priori,* and are, by and large, immutable and not open for debate (e.g., sexual contact with a client is never permissible; one must always provide informed consent to the client). Counselors who practice on this side of the argument are frequently criticized for maintaining a patriarchal hierarchy and not embracing a more egalitarian model of therapeutic interaction (Dineen, 2002; Zur, 2002). These clinicians are quick to point out, however, that there is often confusion between the ideas of the egalitarian nature of the therapeutic relationship and the power differential between counselor and client. One does not necessarily imply the other, nor does one exclude the other. Power differentials, as defined earlier, exist when one person has more influence, knowledge, or ability than the other person. Egalitarian relationships occur when both parties have relatively equal standing with one another and can mutually influence, share knowledge, and have the same ability level as the other. In viewing the therapeutic relationship, Pope and Vasquez (1998) note, "although certain approaches to therapy have emphasized egalitarian ideals in which therapist and clients are 'equal,' such goals are viewed only within a narrowly limited context of the relationship" (p. 46). In fact, the therapeutic relationship, by its very nature, cannot be egalitarian. It has a professional dimension to it that other egalitarian relationships do not have (e.g., collecting fees, billing, diagnosing), and it has a specific purpose that is its sole *raison d'être* (professionally helping one person who needs help) (Pope & Vasquez, 1998; Vasquez, 2003).

As Sommers-Flanagan and colleagues (1998) argue, by helping to define this relationship, the ethical codes also protect counselor and client:

> Professional ethics codes formally articulate professional relationship boundaries. As such, boundaries guide a host of potential interactions, some of which are more central to defining professional relationships, whereas other interactions are less specific, less impermeable, or less damaging to change. In professional relationships in which there is a clear power differential, there are boundaries of such clarity and precision that to violate them essentially redefines the relationship (i.e., sexual contact). (p. 38)

Hence, to some counselors, "any deviation from these boundaries [is seen] as a threat to the therapeutic process" and therapists must "regard such transgressions as potential of not inevitable precursors to harm, exploitation, and sexual relationships" (Zur & Lazarus, 2002, p. 5). However, counselors who embrace a categorical view of boundaries also cite legitimate, therapeutic reasons for maintaining boundaries (in addition to protecting clients from potential harm and structuring the relationship). For proponents of this point of view, one of the most significant curative aspects of psychotherapy may be that the client experiences, perhaps for the first time, an interpersonal relationship in which boundaries are adequately maintained. As a result of this, the client learns that the therapist is a separate person and is not dependent on the client to meet his or her emotional needs (as may not have been the case in past relationships). Clients learn through the experience of a relationship with clear boundaries that it is possible to have mature, adult relationships that are not exploitive in nature. In addition, clients learn how they can have healthy relationships that are conducted without manipulation, coercion, hidden agendas, or abuse (Williams, 2002). This can only be achieved if there are strong therapeutic boundaries and if these boundaries are strictly maintained.

Dimensional View of Boundaries. Some clinicians believe that the slavish devotion to boundaries is motivated either out of a need for counselors to enhance their own status and power (Zur, 2002) or out of fear, from which they have created these rigid, impermeable boundaries to provide a false sense of security in the vain hope that they will protect them from any harm. However, both of these positions comes at a therapeutic cost to the client, either by setting the conditions for exploitation or by creating distance in the relationship, which can have a negative impact on the treatment and are, themselves, unethical (Lazarus, 2002). In contrast to the categorical view of boundaries, they take a dimensional view of boundaries, in which relationships that have power differentials are not inherently abusive or exploitive (Lazarus & Zur, 2002). Boundaries are not eliminated, but rather discussed openly and co-created by client and counselor. "Contained within a definition of relationship boundary is the distinction between the expectations and interactions that would be considered appropriate within the relationship and those that would be considered inappropriate within the relationship. The boundary becomes woven into the relationship definition" (Sommers-Flanagan et al., 1998, p. 38). From this definition, then, decisions ranging from the course of treatment to whether the client and counselor can meet for a cup of coffee in a public restaurant become open to discussion, depending on the particular needs of the client at any given time.

This level of flexibility in boundaries feels at home to many practitioners of the humanist approaches, who seek to tear down the boundary between client and therapist (Williams, 2002) in order for the patient to feel equal to (rather than inferior to) the therapist. There is a tradition of sharing openly whatever impulses or thoughts come to mind in order to use raw honesty to bring about change, as well as to model for clients how to be more honest with themselves. Likewise, according to Williams (2002), behavior therapists use self-disclosure to model honesty and to talk about the particular efficacy of a treatment approach that has worked with them (e.g., reduction of phobic responses).

In addition to providing counselors with a comfort level and freedom to practice, practitioners who adopt a dimensional stance on boundaries believe that they are utilizing best practices with their clients. For many of these adherents, rigidity, distance, and coldness are incompatible with healing (Lazarus & Zur, 2002): "A boundary represents a limit, a set of conditions, a barrier between people, and rigid boundaries often conflict with acting in a manner that is clinically helpful to clients" (Fay, 2002, p. 150). Anonymity and neutrality inhibit the patient's growth and the therapist's effectiveness (Fay, 2002). Lambert (Lambert, 1992; Lambert & Barley, 2002) has demonstrated importance of warmth and rapport for an effective therapeutic relationship to develop (which can account for up to 30 percent of the treatment efficacy). According to Fay (2002) "while there are no unconditional adult relationships, an orientation that starts from a position of intimacy and openness to any approach that could help patients is apt to be more facilitative than an orientation that starts with 'anonymity,' contracts, and boundaries" (p. 150). Thus, the emphasis is on connection and collaboration, which requires a certain flexibility of boundaries in order to be effective.

It should be noted, however, that the dimensional approach is not synonymous with an absence of boundaries. Although he argues for more permeable boundaries, Lazarus (2002) concedes that there is a time and place for common sense with regard to boundaries for some clients: "It is usually inadvisable to disregard strict boundary limits in the presence of severe psychopathology; involving passive-aggressive, histrionic, or manipulative behaviors; borderline personality features, or manifestations of suspicious and undue hostility" (p. 27).

Williams's (2002) observation that the "dimensional" and "categorical" approaches do not coexist well is appropriate; however, are they completely incompatible? In terms of maintaining an intact therapeutic relationship, practitioners from both dimensional and categorical approaches (as well as most schools of psychotherapy) see the issues of boundaries as crucial. As Sommers-Flanagan and colleagues (1998) state, "when the concept of boundary in professional helping relationships is considered in the light of applied ethics, it is clear that the two are very much intertwined" (p. 38). The question remains: Which is more appropriate? Is there a way to determine this? An investigation into when boundaries break down and an analysis of boundaries from an integrative-contextual approach may shed some light on this.

When Is a Boundary Not a Boundary? Extensions, Crossings and Violations, and Perspective III. Most authors agree that there is an important distinction between boundary crossings and boundary violations (Dineen, 2002; Fay, 2002; Pope & Vasquez, 1998; Sommers-Flanagan et al., 1998). Zur and Lazarus (2002) differentiate them thusly:

> *Boundary violations* refer to actions on the part of the therapist that are harmful, exploitative, and in direct conflict with the preservation of clients' dignity and the integrity of the therapeutic process. Examples of boundary violations are sexual of financial exploitation of clients. A *boundary crossing* is a benign and often beneficial departure from traditional therapeutic settings or constraints. Examples of boundary crossings are making home visits to a bedridden sick client; taking a plane ride with a client who has a fear of flying; attending a client's wedding, bar mitzvah, or other function; or conducting therapy while walking on a trail with a person who requests it and seems to benefit from it. (p. 6; italics added)

Yet, for some, even these examples of boundary crossing translate into gross violations of sound ethical practice (Bernstein & Hartsell, 2000). According to Pope and his colleagues

(Pope & Bajt, 1988; Pope & Vasquez, 1998), most major breaks are usually preceded by minor breaks. Even Dineen (2002), who advocates passionately for a dimensional approach to boundaries, acknowledges the risks involved:

> "Breaking the rules" more often than not has nothing whatever to do with abusing, coercing, or manipulating patients and everything to do with acknowledging them as fellow human beings. It also has to do with risk taking because, in reality, it involves shifting power in the direction of the patient, who can at any time and for any reason lodge a complaint, claim to be a victim, or cast the psychologist in an evil light. (p. 134)

So, the question remains, are boundary crossings permissible, and when are they so? Just because a therapist *thinks* a boundary crossing is therapeutically justified or poses no harm to the client does not necessarily make it so. Both boundary crossings and violations must be examined according to the relevant ethical codes, especially in light of the prohibition on sexual relationships with current clients, as well as whether there is a danger of exploitation to the client. However, this does not imply that all boundary crossings are equally sticky. The questions of degree and proportionality are central to determining the potential effect of the boundary crossing. Since the aim of counseling is to empower clients to better deal with life experience, then the type of question that counselors working from an integrative-contextual approach must ask themselves is whether this particular boundary extension can be anticipated to further empower the client and not exploit the client. Furthermore, Sommers-Flanagan and colleagues (1998) suggest three additional questions for an ethically informed, mature counselor to reflect on in order to determine whether a boundary violation or crossing may be "bad." They are (1) Does the boundary violation "objectify" the client? (2) Is the therapist acting on impulse or out of a well-reasoned thought process? and (3) Is the boundary crossing or violation serving the needs of the therapist over the needs of the client?

Legally, some authors believe that boundary crossings are justified only if an impartial professional observer could answer these types of questions affirmatively. Hence, it would seem that the ultimate answer is to allow each counselor to set that standard for him- or herself, and if the counseler, the client, and an impartial colleague all agree, there is no need for absolute prohibitions (outside of violations of the law and the sexual prohibition). However, it is not that simple. There are boundary crossings that might seem harmless on the surface, but nonetheless represent subtle, unfolding, unforeseen ethical violations (Bernstein & Hartsell, 2000). Any alteration, extension, or crossing of the relationship boundary may either temporarily or permanently change the nature of the therapeutic relationship positively or negatively. This can occur even if the violation or crossing is inadvertent. Even if the therapist's intentions are good, he or she cannot know how the client will react to a particular crossing, which will necessarily cause a shift in the therapist's perception of the client. This may affect the amount and type of information that is shared in therapy, and even how the client feels about the therapeutic process itself. Of course, this does not mean these changes cannot be incorporated into the relationship, nor does it mean the boundary violation or crossing is automatically damaging to the therapeutic relationship (Sommers-Flanagan et al., 1998). In some cases, boundary crossings may increase familiarity, understanding, and connection and increase the likelihood of success of the counseling (Lazarus & Zur, 2002). However, it is incumbent on the counselor to evaluate, rather than ignore or underestimate, the impact of every boundary crossing or extension. According to Sommers-Flanagan and colleagues (1998), "The challenge to the professional and, we argue, the moral obligation of the more powerful person in any relationship is to be conscious of all boundaries and willing to extend or hold firm, depending on circumstances" (p. 39).

Looking at this issue from an integrative-contextual approach, boundary crossings have the potential to strengthen the therapeutic alliance and increase effectiveness. By definition, then, these crossings can be neither exploitive nor harmful. If the boundary crossing is harmful or exploitive, it is wrong, and does not proceed from an integrative-contextual approach but out of some selfish need or motive on the part of the therapist. As a result, it seems overly severe that some professional organizations feel they must prohibit all such crossings because some are harmful! This is equivalent to banning automobiles because some of them get into accidents. What often happens is that the car (or more precisely the car part, tire, etc.) that is faulty is removed. However, when operated properly and safely, cars are safe, and drivers arrive at their destinations more quickly than if they had to walk! It is the same with the occasional, ethically sound boundary crossing. The counselors who abuse this should rightly be sanctioned, but not all counselors should bear the burden.

Dual Relationships. Closely associated to the issues of boundaries and power for the ethical counselor is the role of dual or multiple relationships with clients. According to Lazarus and Zur (2002), a dual relationship refers to "any association outside the 'boundaries' of the standard client–therapist relationship—for example, lunching, socializing, bartering, errand-running, or mutual business transactions (other than the fee-for-service)" (p. xxvii). This is true if it occurs prior to, during, or following the termination of therapy (Ford, 2001). It is probably closer to reality to say that these relationships are not as much "dual" or "multiple" as they are "multifaceted," and that this other facet is usually in a social, professional, or financial domain (Pope & Vasquez, 1998). With other professionals (such as an accountant, physician, or lawyer), it is possible to have a multifaceted relationship in which business can be transacted between professional and client, and social interactions can take place outside of the professional milieu. This traditionally is not the case with counseling and psychotherapy. According to Vasquez (2003), these multifaceted relationships "tend to erode and distort the professional nature of the therapeutic relationship." However, other authors have argued that not all multiple relationships are necessarily harmful (Rubin, 2002; Zur & Lazarus, 2002). Zur (2002) and others maintain that the prohibition on contact with clients outside of therapy is an artifact of psychoanalysis (which maintained that any extra-therapeutic contact limited the analyst's ability to perform transference analysis) and, in fact, may result in decreased treatment effectiveness or more egregious unethical behavior (Coale, 1998; Lazarus, 2002; Scheflin, 2002). The tension between these two conflicting viewpoints can be confusing to the ethical practitioner. We will look at both sides of the argument, as well as the ethics code itself. We will conclude with a brief case example (Box 11.12) to illustrate our point.

Arguments For and Against the Prohibition on Multiple Relationships. Like many of the ethical codes, this code has evolved in response to several abuses by practitioners. Chief among these abuses have been the instances of sexual relationships between counselors and their clients. Given the emotionally intense and often intimate nature of the therapeutic relationship, as well as the potential for "transference" and "countertransference" of emotions to be aroused, the occurrence of therapist–client romantic and sexual relationships has endured, despite prohibitions and the possibility of severe sanction (Ford, 2001). One of the three most important determinants for the risk of harm to clients from engaging in dual relationships is the power differential within the therapeutic relationship, which was discussed earlier (Kitchener, 1988). As a result, all professionals are considered to be tainted, or "guilty by association." Furthermore, counselors in private practice, working alone, seem to be most vulnerable due to their isolation from others. Bernstein and Hartsell (2000) suggest as a guide a list of potential clients who should be referred by a therapist in order to avoid engaging in multiple relationships (Box 11.9).

BOX 11.9

A SUGGESTED LIST OF POTENTIAL CLIENTS TO REFER IN ORDER TO AVOID ENGAGING IN MULTIPLE RELATIONSHIPS

1. Personal friends
2. Financial associates
3. Social or organizational acquaintances
4. Students
5. Supervisees
6. Research participants
7. Individuals with whom you customarily barter
8. Anyone whom you have the responsibility to evaluate
9. Employees
10. Former and current sexual partners
11. Family members

Adapted from Bernstein & Hartsell (2000).

Pope and Vasquez (1998) list seven inherent problems in multiple relationships that make them detrimental to the therapeutic process. First, multiple relationships have the potential to distort the professional nature of the relationship between therapist and client. Second, multiple relationships can create conflicts of interest for the therapist, and thus compromise a therapist's objectivity and sound professional judgment. Third, multiple relationships can negatively impact a client's cognitive processes necessary for the maintenance of therapeutic gains following termination. Fourth, multiple relationships can affect the power differential in the relationship in a potentially exploitive way (e.g., misuse of therapeutic material for personal gain). Fifth, multiple relationships may encourage counselors to screen clients with potential future gain (social, financial, etc.), rather than sound clinical principles, in mind. Sixth, multiple relationships can create problems for therapists required to testify for or against clients with whom they have other relationships. Finally, seventh, counselors who choose to engage in sexual relationships with former clients, even though they adhere to the ethical standard, may still open themselves up to professional sanction by licensing boards if their former clients should file a claim. For these reasons, and many others, Pope and Vasquez (1998) advocate that "it is crucial to clarify our relationship to each patient and to avid sexual and nonsexual dual relationships which prevent that clarity and place the patient at great risk for harm" (p. 206).

According to Hoffman (1995), better training in preventing sexual relationships from occurring, not an all-out prohibition on all multiple relationships, is the only way to reduce the instances of inappropriate sexual relationships. Rubin (2002) concurs with this, adding that the problem is not the existence of the multiple relationship, per se, but that the danger of multiple relationships is "rooted in the failure to perceive and properly balance the complex motivations, feelings, and behaviors that characterize human interactions, professional or otherwise" (Rubin, 2002, p. 109). Clarkson (2000) also makes the case for better training, noting that

> it is impossible for most psychotherapists to completely avoid all situations where conflicting interests or multiple roles may occur. Furthermore, I believe that a profession that is built on the naïve and utopian ideal that such dual or multiple relationships can indeed be avoided does not equip trainee or experienced professionals with the awareness, attitudes or skills which make it possible for them to deal with these situations if and when they do arise—as I believe that they almost inevitably will. (p. 78)

However, even Zur (2002), who advocates strongly against the limitation of multiple relationships, concedes that

> [i]ssues of exploitation in general, and sexual or business exploitation in particular, are appropriately at the forefront of consumer advocates agendas. The valid concern is that helping professionals, especially psychotherapists, can easily exploit their clients by using their positions of power for personal gain. Hence, the effort to curtail exploitation and to protect consumers from harm is indeed essential. (p. 46)

Hence, most recent revision to the ethics codes provides some guidance for the practicing counselor. We present the relevant sections of the AMHCA ethical codes as a basis for making decisions about multiple relationships in Box 11.10.

Looking at the issue from a metalevel, Clarkson (1990, 2000) argues that the even present form of client–counselor relationships that exist (which are assumed to be "mono-" relationships) are already inherently multifaceted. In a review of research on the therapeutic relationship, she found evidence of five levels, or modalities (facets), of the psychotherapeutic relationship (across all the major schools of thought) that exemplify this multifacetedness (see Box 11.11). They are the working alliance, the transferential/countertransferential relationship, the reparative, developmentally needed relationship, the person-to-person relationship, and the transpersonal relationship. She asserts that, if therapists are already having to contend with multiple, and sometimes conflicting, roles in session, without a decrement to effectiveness, then the argument that this cannot be done outside of

BOX 11.10

AMHCA (2000) CODE, PRINCIPLE 1: WELFARE OF THE CLIENT

F) Dual Relationships

Mental health counselors are aware of their influential position with respect to their clients and avoid exploiting the trust and fostering dependency of the client.

1. Mental health counselors make every effort to avoid dual relationships with clients that could impair professional judgment or increase the risk of harm. Examples of such relationships may include, but are not limited to: familial, social, financial, business, or close personal relationships with the clients.
2. Mental health counselors do not accept as clients individuals with whom they are involved in an administrative, supervisory, and evaluative nature. When acting as supervisors, trainers, or employers, mental health counselors accord recipients informed choice, confidentiality, and protection from physical and mental harm.
3. When a dual relationship cannot be avoided, counselors take appropriate professional precautions such as informed consent, consultation, supervision, and documentation to ensure that judgment is not impaired and no exploitation has occurred.

L) Fees and Bartering

3. Mental health counselors ordinarily refrain from accepting goods or services from clients in return for counseling service because such arrangements create inherent potential for conflicts, exploitation, and distortion of the professional relationship. Participation in bartering is only used when there is no exploitation, if the client requests it, if a clear written contract is established, and if such an arrangement is an accepted practice among professionals in the community.

therapy is not tenable (as is the banning or discouraging of nonsexual, nonexploitive multiple relationships).

Perspective III and Multiple Relationships. So, if multiple relationships are already a part of current treatment, proponents of multiple relationships ask, "What is the reason for the prohibition?" Considering the integrative-contextual approach, we wonder the same thing! Zur (2002) contends that fear of being accused of abuse drives the prohibition of multiple relationships. He states that, since the terms of "dual" or "multiple" relationships have become synonymous with "sexual abuse" and other damage, counselors use the prohibition as "a magical amulet guarding against any and all possible harm to patients involved in therapeutic treatment (Zur, 2002, pp. 46–47). Another reason for the prohibition against multiple relationships is the need for therapists to be "hidden," "mysterious," or "anonymous" in order to be effective. Although this has its roots in the psychoanalytic stance of the therapist as a "blank screen," today's therapists use the prohibition to shield

BOX 11.11

A LIST OF MULTIPLE RELATIONSHIPS/FUNCTIONS INHERENT IN THE THERAPEUTIC RELATIONSHIP

1. *The working alliance*—the aspect of the client–psychotherapist relationship that enables the client and therapist to work together even when the patient experiences strong desires to the contrary.
2. *The transferential/countertransferential relationship*—the experience of unconscious wishes and fears transferred onto or into the therapeutic partnership.
3. *The reparative, developmentally needed relationship*—the intentional provision by the psychotherapist of a corrective, reparative, or replenishing relationship or action where the original parenting (or previous experience) was deficient, abusive, or overprotective.
4. *The person-to-person relationship*—the real core relationship, the subject relationship as opposed to object relationship.
5. *The transpersonal relationship*—the timeless facet of the psychotherapeutic relationship, which is impossible to describe, but refers to the inexplicable or spiritual dimensions of the healing relationship.

From Clarkson (2000, pp. 25–26).

themselves from being too familiar with their clients in the fear that clients will see their shortcomings or find them weak or inept and become contemptuous rather than awestruck (Lazarus & Zur, 2002). Clarkson (2000) and others contend that this is a potentially damaging and unethical position, which places the counselor's need for supremacy over the client's need for genuineness and an authentic therapeutic relationship, an inherently Perspective I viewpoint.

There are differences of opinion in the discussion of multiple relationships, which are compatible with the Perspective III approach, according to different theories of psychotherapy as different cultures. For example, seeing a couple in joint and individual therapy simultaneously is frequently an accepted part of systems-based therapy, but constitutes a multiple relationship to the psychoanalytic therapist (Zur, 2002). Or, in some cultures, extended kin networks are crucial for an individual's functioning, and refusing to consult with them formally or informally, under the aegis of avoiding multiple relationships, could place the client at odds with his or her cultural heritage. However, Pope and Vasquez (1998) contend that these are but two of several "rationalizations" that counselors engage in in order to continue their behaviors.

In thinking of the risks to the client and the "loss of the good" that can be done (the principles of beneficence and nonmaleficence), it might be helpful to think of multiple relationships in terms of a substance that has a therapeutic purpose, like Xanax. This is a drug that is intended for short-term use to decrease anxiety. When it is used according to the recommended dosage and purpose, it is very effective. However, it also can be used recreationally (not according to its recommended use), which can have intoxicating (and addictive) effects. When it is abused this way by a person, it seldom retains a therapeutic effect. Likewise, alcohol (another potentially addictive substance) is not intended for medicinal purposes. It is meant for recreational purposes. However, when it is abused for medicinal purposes (self-medicating for physical or psychological pain), it cannot usually be used again for recreational purposes. It appears that once that threshold is crossed, it cannot be reversed to serve its intended purpose. Likewise, multifaceted relationships with the counselor operating from an integrative-contextual approach do run the risk of decreasing the intended therapeutic effort and should be viewed very carefully (Ford, 2001) (see Box 11.12). However, just as there is no need for *everyone* to avoid Xanax or alcohol if needed or desired, there is no need for these counselors to completely rule out the benefit of a multiple relationship.

BOX 11.12
CASE STUDY

A grieving mother whose son was murdered has been working with a therapist for over a year. She feels close to the therapist because she has shared much of her grief and anguish over the loss of her son. She frequently ends sessions with a hug and tells the therapist how much she has been helped, saying, "I don't know what I would have done without you." She asked the therapist to come to her church and speak at a victims' memorial service in the hopes of helping others by talking about the grieving process, which the therapist did, with her permission. Now the client comes to the therapist with the idea of collaborating on a book together, sharing the story of her son and of her recovery process in therapy. The client enthusiastically states how it will be beneficial to others for her to share her story of loss and for the therapist to contribute about the process of healing from such a loss.

From an integrative-contextual approach, the counselor would have to consider several factors. First, how would the collaboration be helpful or hurtful for the client? The second consideration might be how the motivation of some fame or monetary gain may affect the therapeutic relationship as a business relationship emerges. Last, the issue of ownership of the story of the child would need to be discussed. Suppose that the counselor should think that issues related to the family would be important to discuss, and the client should agree though she has some misgivings. All of these decisions would need to be weighed against the issue of the impact on the relationship. One alternative to suggest may be have the client write it and read it aloud in session, with the decision of whether to publish it left until the end of the writing process. In addition, the counselor might agree to be an "editor" of sorts and provide feedback, or even agree to write a foreword or epilogue if the project is completed. In this way, whatever creative impetus that is sparking the client's interest is not thwarted by the counselor, as it might be if a Perspective I approach is adopted, whereby the issue would be dismissed immediately under the guise of "boundary violation."

Competency

When clients come for counseling they put their trust not only in the individual therapist, but in the institution of counseling as well. They are given assurances by licensing boards designed to protect the welfare of the public, and from degree-conferring academic programs designed to protect the integrity of the field, that when they enter into a therapeutic relationship that the counselor is properly trained and competent to practice. This is not to confuse an assurance of safety and skills with a guarantee of satisfaction, but rather to suggest that these individuals conform to the highest ethical standards and are capable to exercise good clinical practice without exploitation of any kind. This includes counselors' recusing themselves if there is any impairment in functioning or referring clients if they are not sufficiently competent to treat them (Pope & Vasquez, 1998). According to Ford (2001) therapists' strengths (i.e., areas of professional competence) enable them to help clients with problems that fall within their area(s) of expertise, while their acknowledging their limitations prevents them from "potentially harming clients by attempting to work with populations or problems outside the range of . . . professional training and experience" (p. 123). As a result, competency can be considered a logical and practical extension of the issues surrounding conflicts of interest.

Competence involves "a professional's understanding of her strengths and limitations, both of which are important to the practice of psychotherapy" (Ford, 2001, p. 123). The minimum standards for which an individual's level of competence as a counselor is based on his or her academic training and supervised experience. The ultimate culmination of this is to result in professional licensure or specialized certification. However, neither licensure nor education level is sufficient for any counselor to practice globally in every area of mental health treatment. Counselors are required to restrict their practice to serve only those clients and conditions that they are qualified to treat (Ford, 2001). In fact, most state licensure laws specifically state that counselors must practice "within their area of training, experience, and competence as well as to provide services that meet the *accepted standard of care*" (Stevens, 2000, p. 279).

According to Bernstein and Hartsell (2000), most counselors who get into trouble do so, not because of greed or ignorance, but out of a genuine motivation to help others. This clouds their judgment and leads them to stretch themselves too far into areas that they are not sufficiently trained or experienced in to meet the accepted standard of care, which usually leads to ethical breaches, violations of licensure statutes, and lawsuits with a "tragic result for a therapist" (Bernstein & Hartsell, 2000, p. 87). The major areas where counselors commonly find themselves practicing outside of the competency include: diverse client populations, new treatment models and interventions, and maintaining competence (Ford, 2001). The majority opinion for safeguarding oneself from this is to know and understand the relevant codes (Bernstein & Hartsell, 2000; Ford, 2001; Pope & Vasquez, 1998). Practicing within one's area of professional competence is addressed in the ethical codes of both the American Counseling Association and American Mental Health Counselors Association. Box 11.13 presents the relevant excerpts from the AMHCA code.

BOX 11.13

AMHCA (2000) ETHICS CODE PRINCIPLE 7: COMPETENCE

The maintenance of high standards of professional competence is a responsibility shared by all mental health counselors in the best interests of the public and the profession. Mental health counselors recognize the boundaries of their particular competencies and the limitations of their expertise. Mental health counselors provide only those services and use only those techniques for which they are qualified by education, techniques, or experience. Mental health counselors maintain knowledge of relevant scientific and professional information related to the services they render, and they recognize the need for on-going education.

A) Mental health counselors accurately represent their competence, education, training, and experience.

B) As teaching professionals, mental health counselors perform their duties based on careful preparation in order that their instruction is accurate, up to date, and educational.

C) Mental health counselors recognize the need for continued education and training in the area of cultural diversity and competency. Mental health counselors are open to new procedures and sensitive to the diversity of varying populations and changes in expectations and values over time.

D) Mental health counselors and practitioners recognize that their effectiveness depends in part upon their ability to maintain sound and healthy interpersonal relationships. They are aware that any unhealthy activity would compromise sound professional judgment and competency. In the event that personal problems arise and are affecting professional services, they will seek competent professional assistance to determine whether they should limit, suspend, or terminate services to their clients.

E) Mental health counselors have a responsibility both to the individual who is served and to the institution within which the service is performed to maintain high standards of professional conduct. Mental health counselors strive to maintain the highest level of professional services offered to the agency, organization, or institution in providing the highest caliber of professional services. The acceptance of employment in an institution implies that the mental health counselor is in substantial agreement with the general policies and principles of the institution. If, despite concerted efforts, the member cannot reach an agreement with the employer as to acceptable standards of conduct that allows for changes in institutional policy conducive to the positive growth and development of counselors, then terminating the affiliation should be seriously considered.

G) Ethical behavior among professional associates, mental health counselors, and non–mental health counselors is expected at all times. When information is possessed that raises serious doubts as to the ethical behavior of professional colleagues, whether association members or not, the mental health counselor is obligated to take action to attempt to rectify such a condition. Such action shall utilize the institution's channels first and then utilize procedures established by the state licensure board.

H) Mental health counselors are aware of the intimacy of the counseling relationship, maintain a healthy respect for the integrity of the client, and avoid engaging in activities that seek to meet the mental health counselor's personal needs at the expense of the client. Through awareness of the negative impact of both racial and sexual stereotyping and discrimination, the member strives to ensure the individual rights and personal dignity of the client in the counseling relationship.

These sections of the code clearly lay out the expectations of the field on practitioners, and represent the essence of sound, ethical behavior that each individual counselor must adhere to. What is remarkable is the reliance on the professional to police him- or herself. It is primarily within the purview of the individual practitioner to determine whether he or she has the requisite skills and experience to work with certain clients or to utilize certain techniques. It calls on the counselor to adhere strongly to the ethical principles and truly place the needs of the client over their own needs. But *how* exactly is this done from an integrative-contextual approach to counseling? We will discuss this further below.

Competence and Perspective III. No issue is more central to the idea and ideals of sound, principled, ethical practice than the competence of the counselor. It is a very simple standard to apply to behavior: Either the counselor is or is not competent to practice, practice with the population that he is working with, or practice using the particular skill set that is being utilized. It also reflects the values embedded in all five ethical principles. When it comes to ensuring that treatment is good or beneficial for clients, and that these clients are safeguarded from harm, competent professionals working from an integrative-contextual approach must yield any sense of pride and ego to the higher principles of beneficence and nonmalificence (Ford, 2001). According to Stevens (2000), competence is essential to the principle of autonomy, as clients have the right to decide whether they want to receive treatment from a counselor who either is unqualified to practice in a certain area or with a certain technique or is still in training. The status of the counselor's skills should be fully disclosed as a matter of informed consent (see above), and the client must be free to attain a referral to a more qualified practitioner if he or she requests it. This also reflects a level of advocacy for the client and fairness to the client that is part of the principle of justice. Last, the principle of fidelity is addressed by competence. Counselors who operate from an integrative-contextual approach must be fully open not only about their abilities and experiences, so too must they be open about their areas of weakness.

Looking further at competence from an integrative-contextual approach, competence for mental health counselors has two tenets: (1) You never achieve competence, you approach competence; and 2) competence is defined molecularly, not morally. Being that Perspective III counselors engage in lifelong learning throughout their career, the competence as a goal can never be achieved, as there is always something to learn. This brings up a dilemma: How can you practice if you search for the attainment of all knowledge? The answer is that you approach competence and embrace the gaps in knowledge (as well as disclose them to the client as part of informed consent). This is also where the second portion comes in, specifically that no one therapist is competent with every client and in every session (see the case example in Box 11.14). Instead, there are some sessions and some clients where the counselor is more effective, and others where he or she is not. The point is that *when* (not if) as a counselor one is "not up to par," one is aware of it, admits it quickly, and processes it *in vivo,* in the moment with the client. For the counselor operating from an integrative-contextual approach, *the inability or gap* becomes the issue to discuss, and both counselor and client, in a relational way probe the causes to see if there are active blockages to progress or serious unattended rifts in the relationship that have been unprocessed. In other words, the counselor uses his or her "weakness" as "strength" with the client in the hopes of promoting growth for both the counselor and the client. Again, this is closely associated with the personal-developmental dimension on the *molecular* (i.e., session by session) level. In contrast, at the risk of employing a cliché, the counselor employing the Perspective I approach sees competence as a "destination" rather than a "journey." It is something attained, rather than something aspired to, and it is something that, for these counselors, is defined *solely* by certification, degree, or licensure, and not as part of a more organic process.[4]

BOX 11.14

CASE EXAMPLE OF THE TRAINEE WHO WOULD BE A HYPNOTIST

Suppose that you work in an agency with other new professionals. One of the new, unlicensed counselors talks about just having come from a workshop on hypnotherapy and expresses interest in practicing it with some clients who have been treatment resistant. In fact, she says that she is working with several intransigent substance abuse clients who have not made progress and have frustrated her. You review her materials from the workshop, which explicitly state that advanced training is needed before utilizing this technique. You know that there are certified hypnotherapists who are practicing in the area who have much more experience than your colleague, but your colleague has always exercised good judgment in the past. What would you do?

From a Perspective I, defensive stance, the answer is clear and difficult at the same time. In order to "protect" the client, "protect" the profession, and (mostly) "protect" himself, the counselor must discourage the other counselor from engaging in hypnotherapy until she has the proper training and/or is under supervision. If she were to persist in her use of hypnotherapy, then you would have to attempt to resolve it with her or consult with her supervisor. If this does not resolve the dilemma, and you feel that she is continuing to engage in this practice without the necessary training and supervision, then action on the level of a formal complaint would result. From an integrative-contextual approach (Perspective III), however, the solution (on the outside) may look the same, but the process involved would be different. Obviously, the counselor must talk to the colleague, but first, he or she may need to consider a few things. First, it would be important as a counselor to look at him- or herself first and figure out what is most bothersome about this. Are there personal roadblocks to embracing hypnotherapy as a legitimate technique? Next, it may be helpful for the counselor to look at his or her own level of development. Is the counselor also feeling "stuck" with some clients and confused about what to do with them? Is the counselor afraid of being "left behind" in terms of skills acquisition? It is necessary to understand the potential influence of personal feelings in any "objection" to what the colleague is planning. Finally, before inviting the colleague to talk, it may be helpful for the counselor to review his or her own efforts at "lifelong learning" and approach the colleague as a potential source of information and learning. At this point, the counselor should have a conversation

[4]This is not to say that mental health counselors operating from a Perspective III approach *do not* value or obtain certifications, degrees, or licensure, but that they encompass these and see potential opportunities for growth and knowledge in *every* interaction (molecular), rather than in just the "official" training mechanisms (molar).

with the colleague (as in Perspective I ethics), but it will most likely be less contentious and confrontational. The counselor may share his or her frustrations with some clients, a desire to become more proficient, and an interest in learning new techniques. Any concerns that are raised will be viewed in the light of mutual curiosity and respect for the other as a professional, rather than questioning the colleague's ability to decide how to manage his or her own development. Instead, the counselor may congratulate the colleague for seeking out alternative ways of caring for these troubled clients.

REPORTS OF THE ACA ETHICS COMMITTEES

There are three methods for "policing" the behavior of mental health counselors in practice: state regulatory boards, lawsuits, and professional association ethics committees. Many times two or more are involved simultaneously, as when an infraction is such a blatant violation as to warrant civil action, sanctioning on the state level, and ultimately the judgment of the profession itself. The penalties for being found guilty can range from monetary damages, probationary status, further education, and additional supervision to, ultimately, the loss of a license to practice. The most serious sanction is to be suspended from a professional organization, as it signals behavior or individuals that are so unprofessional as to be beyond remediation. One of the chief duties of the Ethics Committee of the American Counseling Association is to "uphold and enforce the standards of the profession" (Walden et al., 2003, p. 106), and thus protect both the consumer and the ethically practicing individual as well.

Yet despite the awe-inspiring seriousness of these issues, very few counselors ever get to the point of requiring an investigation. In fact, Brown and Espina (2000) reported that, in the years between 1988 and 1998, there were only sixty-two active ACA members who were found guilty of violating state ethics standards. In 1998–1999, four members were found guilty nationwide; in 1999–2000, four cases were presented to the board; in 2000–2001, one case was adjudicated; in 2001–2002, three cases were adjudicated; and finally, in 2002–2003, twelve cases were brought against members (Brown, 2001; Hubert & Freeman, 2004; Sanders & Freeman, 2003; Williams & Freeman, 2002). It should be noted that often cases are brought to the Ethics Committee but are never adjudicated, either for lack of evidence or jurisdiction. However, this represents only a small fraction of the total membership of the organization who annually receives any sanction.

However, one of the more interesting facts that our investigation turned up was the number of informal ethics questions that were fielded by the Ethics Committee. From 1998 to 2000, over 600 inquiries were made annually regarding ethical issues. In the 2000–2001 year and 2002–2003 year, the number of inquiries doubled to 1,359 and 1,236, respectively.[5] Counselors who inquired overwhelmingly (approximately half the time) inquired about confidentiality issues, with questions regarding the therapeutic relationship (dual/multiple relationships) being the next classification of inquiries. The final group of significant questions related to relationships with other professionals, which frequently had to do with counselors having to lodge ethical complaints about another counselor (Brown, 2001; Brown & Espina,

[5]In 2001–2002, there were 798 inquiries.

2000; Hubert & Freeman, 2004; Sanders & Freeman, 2003; Williams & Freeman, 2002)! This reveals a trend by mental health counselors toward seeking out professional guidance about ethical issues in order to resolve ethical dilemmas. Furthermore, it seems that two of the major issues that counselors wrestle with are reflected in the core issues of confidentiality and conflicts of interest. This, coupled with the sheer number of inquiries, indicates that mental health counselors are aware and concerned about their professional obligations. However, it also attests to the need for counselors to learn a comprehensive method for evaluating the professional issues that are a part of everyday practice that is broad in scope and inclusive (hence, the integrative-contextual approach articulated in this text).

LEGAL ISSUES AND CASE LAW AFFECTING MENTAL HEALTH COUNSELORS

As mentioned earlier, there are inherent power differentials in the practice of mental health counseling. With these differentials comes the danger of abuse. The law, much like the ethical codes, acts as a counterweight to this power. There are an untold number of laws and standards that govern the behavior of therapists and their practice in every state, and keeping up with them can be daunting. However, the guideline with regard to the law is that ignorance of the law is no excuse for violating it. As a result, we cannot present an exhaustive list of the myriad statutes and court decisions affecting the practice of mental health counseling. We will, however, present a selected overview of the relevant case law related to critical issues that mental health counselors face every day, including duty to warn and duty to protect, immunity from lawsuit following a breach of confidentiality, and psychotherapist–patient privilege. However, we strongly urge all practitioners to become familiar with the statutes governing their practice by joining one of the national or state counseling associations.

Duty to Warn/Duty to Protect

The famous 1976 *Tarasoff v. Regents of the University of California* decision by the California Supreme Court created a new duty for California therapists. The details of this case have been laid out elsewhere in the text, and we will not deliberate on them here. However, as a result of *Tarasoff,* other states, as well as the various professional associations, have followed suit and created a duty-to-warn obligation. Specifically, when counselors receive information that their client poses "a serious danger of violence to another," the therapist must take steps "to protect the intended victim against such danger" (cf. *Tarasoff*). This was the crux of the "breakdown" that led to Tatiana Tarasoff's death. The counselor did not take the steps necessary to protect her, instead leaving it up to the authorities to handle the situation. He simply didn't "go the extra mile," which had devastating consequences. The ruling of the court found that protection is a higher obligation than merely warning. How, exactly, this is accomplished, is left up to the individual state regulations (if any). Although most states that have a *Tarasoff* statute, it is vitally important for therapists to check with their own state laws to understand the *extent* to which they are obligated to exercise their duty. In general, mental health counselors must be prepared make the effort to contact both the intended victim *and* local law enforcement in order to fully fulfill the duty to protect (see the case example in Box 11.15).

BOX 11.15
CASE OF A DANGEROUS CLIENT

Gerald is a 38-year-old man coming to therapy to discuss his mood swings, which have been getting progressively more pronounced. He is married, with three children, and reports having suspicions about his wife's fidelity recently. Over the first three sessions, you notice that twice he has come in preoccupied about his wife's having an affair and was unable to be redirected away from that topic. The other time, he acted as if he didn't care, stating that "I probably just exaggerated in my mind, she's really not the type of person who would cheat." You begin to suspect that this is related to the cyclical nature of his mood swings and have given him a provisional diagnosis of Bipolar Disorder. In addition, you have set an appointment up with a psychiatrist, but the first available appointment is not for another six weeks. Then, in the next session, Gerald comes in agitated and claiming that he knows who his wife's lover is and that it is a coworker she works with closely. He reports that they often stay late into the night at the office for some projects, but now states, "I have proof." He is vague about his proof, and becomes unfocused, making statements like "She'll never get away with it" and "I'll make her pay, make them both pay for making a fool out of me!" When you attempt to ascertain how serious he is, Gerald becomes evasive and suspicious, asking, "What are *you* going to do about it? Call the cops? Call my wife?"

In addition to the *Tarasoff* ruling, there are several others that have clarified or expanded these laws. Some states have not, as yet, adopted a *Tarasoff* law, but courts have maintained that therapists continue to have an obligation to warn or protect. Table 11.1 lists some of the more recent and important rulings regarding this subject. Several court rulings addressed an unintended consequence of the *Tarasoff* law, by which mental health therapists may refrain from doing a proper assessment and evaluation in order to avoid the pitfalls inherent in a breech of confidentiality. However, in the *Hedlund v. Superior Court of Orange County,* the court found that, if a therapist fails to properly diagnose a client's dangerousness, that could be a basis for liability. Likewise, in *Wilson v. Valley Mental Health,* the judge admitted similar concerns that the *Tarasoff* statute "may inadvertently operate to create an incentive on the part of therapists to avoid diagnostically appropriate examinations that could reveal specific threats and result in consequent duty to take preventative measures" (969 P. 2d 416 Sup. Ct., Utah, 1998). Further recognizing the potential burden to therapists, *Thompson v. County of Alameda* clarified the question of *general* threats made to a group of potential victims (e.g., "I'm going to kill a cop"). The court ruled that general, nonspecific threats do not constitute an imminent threat, particularly when there is no readily identifiable foreseeable victim, hence there is no duty to warn.

Clearly in this case, the client is a danger due to the fact that he is highly labile. In terms of the case law, and the duty to protect, it is clear from the *Hedlund* decision that the client has a diagnosis (though provisional), which makes it difficult (if not impossible) to ignore the threats that Gerald has made. In this case, the counselor cannot afford to guess whether he will actually carry out his plan, since there is enough in his descriptions to warrant concerns. As a result, the counselor must make some intervention to protect Gerald's wife, the coworker, and even Gerald himself. However, there are actually two concerns: One is what the counselor will do in light of the direct questions and Gerald's suspicions,

TABLE 11.1 Case Law Relevant to Duty to Warn/Duty to Protect

CASE NAME	CASE #/ JURISDICTION	RELEVANT FINDING
Tarasoff v. Regents of the University of California	California Supreme Court: 17 Cal. 3d 425 131 Cal Rptr. 14, 551 P.2d 334 (1976)	When therapists receive information that their client poses "a serious danger of violence to another," the therapist must take steps "to protect the intended victim against such danger."
Hedlund v. Superior Court of Orange County	Superior Court of Orange County, California: 34 Cal. 3d 695, 669 P.2d 41, 45 (1983)	It is the therapist's duty to warn family members potentially at risk from a client's violent acts. Extended the *Tarasoff* ruling by stating that merely failing to properly diagnose that a client was dangerous is a basis for liability.
Thompson v. County of Alameda	27 Cal. #d 741, 167 Cal. Rptr. 70, 614 P.2d 728 (1980)	In the absence of a readily identifiable foreseeable victim, there was no duty to warn. Therefore a threat to a general *group* of potential victims does not create enough danger to warrant a duty to warn.
Ewing v. Goldstein	2nd Dist., 2004 WL 1588240 (Cal. App. 2 Dist.) California (2004)	"Equally important information in the form of an actual threat that a parent shares with his or her son's therapist about the risk of grave bodily injury the patient poses to another also should be considered a 'patient communication' in determining whether the therapist's duty to warn is triggered."
Wilson v. Valley Mental Health	969 P.2d 416 Sup. Ct., Utah, (1998)	Court supported *Tarasoff* rule, but admitted concern that the statute "may inadvertently operate to create an incentive on the part of therapists to avoid diagnostically appropriate examinations that could reveal specific threats and result in consequent duty to take preventative measures."

and the other is how to handle the duty to protect. In dealing with the direct questions, the counselor must win Gerald's cooperation in de-escalating his mood and choosing not to act out while in his "manic" state. In dealing with the second issue of how to discharge the duty to protect, the counselor must get more details about who specifically is in need of care or protection. Speaking to Gerald on a general topic of safety (e.g., "My job is to make sure, to the best of my ability, that anyone in my care that I am responsible for is safe"), and being skilled enough to have built a solid working alliance with him are key tools for integrative-contextual counselors. Gerald will need to be gently convinced that his plan will be harmful to him (as well as others) and that he will feel differently about it in a little while. The counselor may have to go so far as to say that he cannot let Gerald go unless he goes for an immediate, emergency psychiatric stabilization, if he either remains agitated or is seemingly placating the counselor without abandoning his plan (i.e., "faking good"). In either event, the situation may seem unpleasant, but it is one that cannot be downplayed from an ethical, professional, or legal perspectives.

A related, but more indirect situation is when the therapist gets information about a client's threats of violence from a nonclient source. Does the therapist have an obligation to break confidentiality if he or she did not get information from the client directly? A recent decision, *Ewing v. Goldstein* ([2004]. Cal App. 2 Dist. WL 1588240), shed some additional light on this issue. The court found that a communication from a patient's family member to the therapist made for the purpose of advancing the patient's therapy is a patient communication within the meaning of the statute:

> Despite its privileged nature . . . the therapist's duty to protect that information must yield once the therapist comes to believe the information must be revealed to prevent danger to his or her patient or another . . . We discern no principled reason why equally important information in the form of an actual threat that a parent shares with his or her son's therapist about the risk of grave bodily injury the patient poses to another also should not be considered a 'patient communication' in determining whether the therapist's duty to warn is triggered . . . the information a patient's family member shared with the therapist in determining the existence of a material factual dispute as to whether the patient had communicated to the therapist a serious threat of physical violence to another, simply because the information did not flow directly from the patient to the therapist." (*Ewing v. Goldstein* [2004]. Cal App. 2 Dist. WL 1588240)

In other words, when the information comes from a source that has the closeness and credibility of a close family member, the therapist must consider it *as if* it came from the client him- or herself. The question arises when the family dynamics are so poor as to make the therapist question the sincerity or credibility of the family member who gives the information. These are questions that have not, as yet, been answered by case law.

Immunity from Suit for Breaking Confidentiality

The idea that a mental health therapist can be sued if he or she breeches confidentiality to either report abuse or execute a duty-to-warn obligation that may not be substantiated can have a chilling effect on whether a therapist reports. States have generally adopted some level of immunity from prosecution for mandated reporters. The *type* of immunity, however, varies from state to state and can be classified into one of two types: (1) absolute, such as in California, and (2) qualified, such as in Vermont. The importance of the type of immunity lies in the fact that any breach may inherently slanderous, distressing, and hurtful if untrue. An absolute immunity statute holds that therapists are immune from being sued for slander even if they make a report that they know is false, or act in bad faith to deliberately harm the person that is being accused. However, despite this possibility, states have decided that it is better to provide immunity and thus encourage therapists to report, than to subject therapists to suits, which might frighten them from making appropriate reports. However, it does not mean that therapists do not have to go through the due process of court proceedings. In fact, California courts have held that mandated reporters can still get sued, despite the absolute immunity, until a court can throw the case out (*Krikorian v. Barry*, 1987, 196 Cal. App. 3d 1211). In addition, the decision of *Stecks v. Young* (1995, 38 Cal. App. 4th 365) decided that immunity is not necessary where the report is true, it is only necessary where the report is false (Leslie, 2003).

By contrast, qualified immunity is a type of immunity that granted when certain conditions have been met (Leslie, 2003; Wedding, 2004). Generally, the condition is that the report must have been made without malice or intent to do harm for the immunity to apply. This creates the obvious problem that, any time a report is made, the alleged abuser can merely state that the reporter is not entitled to immunity because the statements were made with malice. However, there are times when a professional can abuse the system and make false claims in an attempt to hurt a client, or control his or her behavior. In one case, *Wilkinson v. Balsaam* (885 F. Supp. 651 D.VT 1995), a psychiatrist made a report that a client was allegedly abusing (including the use of satanic abuse and other acts), in order to bring him harm and pain. The court dismissed the report and held the psychiatrist liable, stating that the qualified immunity available under Vermont law did not apply due to the demonstrable presence of malice. Again, all practitioners are urged to investigate the laws of their state in regards to the level of immunity.

The state laws regarding children and reporting is clear; however, there are special cases that have resulted in court decisions that are important to discuss here. One clarification that was made by the courts was regarding the reporting of abuse that occurred in another state. In a decision by the Ninth Circuit Court of Appeal decision called *Searcy v. Auerbach,* (1992) 980 F. 2d 609 (9th Cir. 1992), the court found that a therapist was wrong in contacting the child protective agency of another state to report an allegation of abuse from his client. The therapist thought that he had immunity from prosecution under child reporting laws, but since the agency in his state was not informed, he was not covered by *his* state's immunity clause. The court sends a clear message that it was up to the agency to contact its counterpart in another state, not the therapist's responsibility. Therapists are only considered mandated reporters in the state in which they are licensed, though the standards of reporting would (presumably) be the same from state to state (Caudill, 2002; Leslie, 2003). These cases relevant to immunity from suit are summarized in Table 11.2. More information on the topic of child abuse will be discussed in the next chapter.

Client–Counselor Privileged Communication/Confidentiality

The last legal area we will look into is the recent legal recognition of the need for privileged communication between therapists and clients. While this had always been assumed by counselors (and in some cases wrongly so), it was not formally recognized on the federal level until 1996, with the *Jaffee v. Redmond* decision. In *Jaffee,* the U.S. Supreme Court upheld a lower court ruling that, since all fifty states recognize some form of psychotherapist–patient privilege, the Federal Rules of Evidence also (indirectly) recognize the same privilege (see Table 11.3). In addition, although the therapist in the case was a social worker, the justices expanded their comments to *all* mental health workers. This has widely been seen as an important step in the legitimization of counselors in the field of mental health care (Wedding, 2004). However, the *Jaffee* ruling also left some doors open to interpretation, including whether there is an exemption to the federal psychotherapist–patient

TABLE 11.2 Immunity from Suit for Breaking Confidentiality/Reporting Abuse

CASE NAME	CASE #/JURISDICTION	RELEVANT FINDING
Wilkinson v. Balsaam	1995; 885 F. Supp. 651 D.VT (Vermont)	Qualified immunity available under Vermont law did not apply due to the demonstrable presence of malice.
Krikorian v. Barry	1987; 196 Cal. App. 3d 1211 (California)	Until a court throws the case out, mandated reporters still get sued, despite the absolute immunity.
Stecks v. Young	1995; 38 Cal. App. 4th 365 (California)	Immunity is not necessary where the report is true, it is only necessary where the report is false.
Searcy v. Auerbach	1992; 980 F. 2d 609 (9th Cir. Federal Court)	A therapist was wrong in contacting the child protective agency of another state to report an allegation of abuse from his client. The therapist thought that he had immunity from prosecution under child reporting laws, but since the agency in his state was not informed, he was not covered by *his* state's immunity clause. Therapists are only considered mandated reporters in the state in which they are licensed.

privilege when a client is dangerous. In *United States v. Chase,* the U.S. ninth Circuit Court of Appeals decided that there was no dangerous-person exemption to the federal psychotherapist–patient privilege, and that any breach of confidentiality due to a threat to others would be discharged by duty-to-warn statutes, but that such information would not

TABLE 11.3 Case Law Related to Client–Counselor Privileged Communication/Confidentiality

CASE NAME	CASE #/JURISDICTION	RELEVANT FINDING
Jaffee v. Redmond	U.S. Supreme Court, 518 U.S. 1 (1996)	U.S. Supreme Court upheld a lower court ruling that since all 50 states recognize some form of psychotherapist–patient privilege, that the Federal Rules of Evidence also (indirectly) recognize the same privilege.
United States v. Chase	340 F.3d 978 (9th Cir. 2003)	U.S. 9th Circuit Court of Appeals decided that there was no dangerous person exemption to the federal psychotherapist–patient privilege, and that any breach of confidentiality due to a threat to others would be discharged by duty to warn statutes, but that such information would not be admissible at trial.

be admissible at trial, since the client would, presumably, no longer be a threat at that time. In other words, a therapist may breach confidentiality to prevent harm from coming to a person, but cannot divulge the elements of therapy without the client waiving privilege (which is the client's right, not the therapist's).

SPECIAL TOPICS IN MENTAL HEALTH COUNSELING

Managed Care

One of the central issues related to the practice of mental health is the interaction of counselors with managed care organizations (MCOs). Overall, mental health professionals do not see the relationship with MCOs as auspicious. Most surveys of providers indicate that mental health professionals, including counselors, view MCOs as intrusive and as a negative influence to the counseling process and the mental health professions (see Daniels, Alva, & Olivares, 2002). Interestingly, most of the detriment attributed to MCOs' influence relates to ethical dilemmas inherent in counselors' relationship to third-party payers, generally MCOs. However, with the implementation of HIPAA, it is likely that this perception will be somewhat diminished in the future.

Corcoran and Vandiver (1996) defined managed care as "the administration or oversight of health and mental health services by someone other than the clinician and the client" (p. 1). In general, MCOs aim to achieve two goals: assurance of quality of care and cost control. The latter, according to many counselors, is the true aim of the third-party-payer system because in a managed care environment the motivation is an increase in corporate profits. This is accomplished by restricting the number of sessions that a counselor has to work with a given client and limiting both the range of treatments available to clients and the number of clinicians in a given area. In addition, MCOs have systematically lowered the accepted rate of reimbursement for counselors to a point where many counselors have elected not to participate in provider panels (thus requiring their clients to pay out of their own pockets and not utilize their coverage).

The interaction between the intrusion of a third party in the practice of counseling and the emphasis on corporate profits lessens practitioner autonomy and quality of care. Additionally, the aforementioned interaction creates a conflict of interest for the counselors represented by the need to balance the duties toward their clients and those of the MCOs (see Box 11.16). One issue is, Who are the counselors working for, the clients that they are treating or the companies who are paying them? What if a client requires treatment that the MCO will not cover? Matters become even more complicated when "gag rules," or restrictions on the range of options that can be presented to a client, are imposed. In this case, are counselors truly advocating for the best care for their client if they do not present all the reasonable alternatives (regardless of insurance rules and regulations)? For the counselor operating from an integrative-contextual approach, a helpful question to ask is, Would I work with this client the same way if there were no MCO involved? If the answer is yes, then there is no professional or ethical conflict in working with the practices of the MCO. If the answer is no, then there are some serious issues of ethical practice that need to be addressed and resolved.

BOX 11.16
COUNSELOR CONFLICTS WITH MANAGED CARE ORGANIZATIONS

Amy is a counselor with twenty-five years' experience in the field. She has always resisted the "intrusion" of MCOs in her practice; however, financial pressures have forced her to be placed on the provider list for a major MCO. As a result, her referrals have increased, but so have the demands to fill out paperwork, precertifications, treatment plans, and recertifications. In addition, she has had to spend more time calling insurance companies when her claims are regularly declined and justifying her treatment choices. By now, Amy has learned what diagnoses the company will more quickly pay for, the modality of treatment that gets the largest reimbursement, and the maximum number of sessions that she can get a client qualified for. For example, while she routinely uses hypnotherapy on her private-pay trauma clients, but because the MCO does not consider that to be an empirically validated approach, she cannot utilize it for her insurance clients (even though she has had clients that would respond positively to it). Most recently, she has started a trauma group for survivors. However, the MCO pays $25 less for group treatment than for individual therapy. As a result, she bills for individuals sessions when she is seeing her clients in a group. She justifies it in her mind, saying, "They routinely stick it to me, so why shouldn't I stick it to them?" Do you agree or not?

Managed Care and Perspective III. In dealing with MCOs, counselors practicing from an integrative-contextual approach face certain duties that ensure ethical practice. Although the practice of counseling is a means for the counselor to earn a living, counselors who practice from an integrative-contextual approach must carefully evaluate whether they want to derive income from participation in MCOs. When counselors who adopt this approach enter into a professional relationship with MCOs, they behave with integrity, honesty, and respect for the organization. In the case above, though, the counselor was attempting to operate in a way in which she could serve her client and get paid for the session. While counselors have a right to have their services compensated fairly, it does not justify providing false documentation.

In addition, counselors must also resist the pressure to misdiagnose clients for the purpose of securing unwarranted lengthier treatment and consequent higher remuneration. In addition, as a function of informed consent, these counselors must discuss with clients all aspects of diagnosis and treatment (including the ramifications of diagnosis, particularly on their permanent medical record). The duty to facilitate informed consent may involve discussions about clients' out-of-pocket payment (in the case of deductible fees that complement a third party's payment for services), potential limitations in the choice of treatment for the clients' conditions, nature of and extent to which clinical information may be shared with an MCO, and potential detrimental effects of treatment on a client's employment or future acquisition of insurance benefits.

In addition, counselors who practice from an integrative-contextual approach ensure that they are competent to provide counseling services according to the demands of an MCO's clients. In other words, if an MCO asks these counselors to provide a certain type of treatment (e.g., brief, solution-oriented counseling), they will refuse to do so unless or until they have been appropriately trained and/or under the proper supervision before they provide such services to the public. Again, it is the responsibility of counselors who practice from an integrative-contextual approach to know the limitations of their competence and to seek continuing education or specialized training in accordance to what services that they will provide to the public before accepting inclusion in an MCO's list of providers.

Last, counselors who practice from an integrative-contextual approach have what Corcoran and Vandiver (1996) termed "the duty of fidelity" (p. 214). This means that counselors have a duty to resolve conflicts of interest in favor of (and advocating for) the client whenever possible. This may include the duty to protect clients' privacy by maintaining confidentiality and demanding that the MCO do so as well (again, as stated above, HIPAA regulations may bolster the counselors' claims of this duty). For example, counselors who practice from an integrative-contextual approach may feel that it is necessary to withdraw from a provider panel if they feel that the MCO is requiring them to act in ways that violate their professional standards or ethics codes. This is merely an extension of the organizational dimension discussed earlier in this chapter, whereby counselors tacitly adopt the policies, procedures, and even ethics of the larger organizations (Daniels, 2001). This may even include MCOs, because counselors are subcontractors of the corporation.

Substance Abuse/Drug Addiction

The National Institute of Drug Abuse (2005) estimates that drug abuse and alcohol dependency cost society nearly $67 billion per year. This figure includes factors that range from crime fighting to the cost of federally funded treatment programs. Often, these substance abuse treatment programs include several forms of counseling services. Counseling is a routine and necessary component of effective drug addiction and substance abuse treatment. Not surprisingly, treatment regimens that include counseling are effective when the goal is lasting abstinence and addresses the immediate reduction of drug use by focusing on the patient's ability to function. However, this often places the counselor in diametric opposition to the client's desires, especially when the client's level of denial is high. Thus, for many counselors in substance abuse, maintaining the high standards of a working therapeutic alliance may go by the wayside as power struggles take place. As a result, proper training and specialized supervision in addictive processes and working with a substance abuse population are all hallmarks of competency (and in keeping with the values of an integrative-contextual approach to counseling). In addition, certification as an addiction specialist demonstrates the counselor's commitment to this client base and problem area.

Counselors who work with drug-addicted/alcohol-dependent people, either in inpatient or outpatient settings, must also attend to legal and ethical issues particular to addictions or the organizations that provide inpatient treatment. For example, federal statutes demand confidentiality of information for patients who receive assessment or treatment. The U.S. Department of Health and Human Services (HHS) updated its definition of program in 1995 to identify those governed by federal regulations that protect confidentiality. Brooks and Riley (1996) indicated that the new definition identifies a program as federally assisted when it:

1. Receives federal funds in any form, even if the funds do not directly pay for the alcohol or drug abuse services; or

2. Is assisted by the Internal Revenue Service through grant of tax-exempt status or allowance of tax deductions for contributions; or

3. Is authorized to conduct business by the federal government (e.g., licensed to provide methadone or chemotherapy; certified as a Medicare provider); or

4. Is conducted directly by the federal government (e.g., an employee assistance program in a federal agency) or by a state or local government that receives federal funds that could be (but are not necessarily) spent for alcohol or drug abuse programs.

The restrictions about communications posed by certain federal statutes are more stringent than the privilege afforded to the traditional client–patient relationship. This is true whether the counselor is in private practice or part of a substance dependency treatment program.

Brooks and Riley (1996) emphasized these restrictions for substance abuse counselors and listed eight circumstance whereby counselors could breach confidentiality: (1) the patient consents to a release of information, (2) the disclosure of information is made to other members of a treatment program, (3) information disclosed does not contain information that identifies the patient as a drug- or alcohol-dependent person who is in treatment, (4) the information is released for a medical emergency, (5) the information is relevant to the commission of a crime by the patient, (6) a court order requires the release of information, (7) the information is in aggregate form and may be used for a program audit or research project, or (8) the information is about child abuse. From our perspective, this is congruent with the values that counselors who practice form an integrative-contextual approach hold on confidentiality.

Although the aforementioned points may serve as guidelines to protect the confidentiality of patients diagnosed with alcohol or drug dependency, there are other conflict-of-interest issues that a counselor who practices from an integrative-contextual approach must attend. For example, often, counselors who work with alcohol/drug addicted clients deal with matters related to the criminal justice system. This is explained by the frequent connection between substance abuse treatment and unlawful activity. If the unlawful activity places others in danger (as in the case of driving under the influence of alcohol or drugs), the counselor must evaluate the dangerousness of the situation and the relevance of the duty to warn others about a threat. However, this is never an easy matter for counselors, since it necessarily disrupts the therapeutic alliance. Thus, it is imperative that the counselor who practices from an integrative-contextual approach consult with supervisors, colleagues, or an agency to resolve these conflicts or act in a way that will minimize the harm to the client while discharging the duties assigned to them.

Group Counseling

One area that has continued to be a staple of mental health practice is group counseling. Although some writers believe that it hit its "high water mark" in the 1970s, it still continues to be a dynamic method for providing services to large numbers of people in need in an efficient manner. As an indicator of its importance as a treatment modality, all counselor training programs are required to provide a minimum level of training (as well as for state licensure). The Association for Specialists in Group Work (ASGW) requires at least one course in group work "that addresses such as but not limited to scope of practice, types of group work, group development, group process and dynamics, group leadership, and standards of training and practice for group workers" (ASGW, 2000), as well as a minimum of ten clock hours (with twenty recommended) of participation as a group member or in observation as a group leader (visit www.asgw.org for the full ASGW "Professional Standards for the Training of Group Workers"). While these are minimum recommendations, there are additional training and experiential requirements in order to be competent as a group therapist. There are different levels of specialization that a counselor can strive to master in group work. Specifically, they are Task Group Facilitation, Group Psychoeducation, Group Counseling, and Group Psychotherapy. Box 11.17 details the additional course requirements for the various specializations, while Box 11.18 details the additional clinical requirements to be competent in each specialization.

In addition to competence, advanced training in group work allows a counselor operating from an integrative-contextual approach to also be able to deal with the unique issues of confidentiality in groups. Specifically, group leaders cannot extend the guarantee of confidentiality that they give to the client to the group members, as they are not bound to the same requirement. Thus, any personal information that is shared has the potential to be shared without the client's consent to individuals outside the group. Therefore, it is a part of ongoing informed consent to remind group members of this possibility, and it is incumbent on the group leader to be skilled in creating an atmosphere where the group will respect this important element of group process. Another unique element of group counseling that counselors practicing from an integrative-contextual approach must face are the boundary issues and the conflicts of interest that can result from the group process. Examples of

BOX 11.17
BASIC COURSE CONTENT FOR VARIOUS GROUP SPECIALIZATIONS

Task Group Facilitation: Coursework in such areas as organization development, consultation, management, and sociology so students gain a basic understanding of organizations and how task groups function within them.

Group Psychoeducation: Coursework in community psychology, consultation, health promotion, marketing, and curriculum design to prepare students to conduct structured consciousness raising and skill training groups in such areas as stress management, wellness, anger control and assertiveness training, and problem solving.

Group Counseling: Coursework in normal human development, family development and family counseling, assessment and identification of problems in living, individual counseling, and group counseling, including training experiences in personal growth or counseling group.

Group Psychotherapy: Coursework in abnormal human development, family pathology and family therapy, assessment and diagnosis of mental and emotional disorders, individual therapy, and group therapy, including training experiences in a therapy group.

From AGSW (2000).

BOX 11.18
ASGW CLINICAL INSTRUCTION REQUIREMENTS FOR SPECIALIZATION

For Task Group Facilitation and Group Psychoeducation, group specialization training recommends a minimum of 30 clock hours of supervised practice (45 clock hours of supervised practice is strongly suggested). Because of the additional difficulties presented by Group Counseling and Group Psychotherapy, a minimum of 45 clock hours of supervised practice is recommended (60 clock hours of supervised practice is strongly suggested). Consistent with CACREP standards for accreditation, supervised experience should provide an opportunity for the student to perform under supervision a variety of activities that a professional counselor would perform in conducting group work consistent with a given specialization (i.e., assessment of group members and the social systems in which they live and work, planning group interventions, implementing group interventions, leadership and co-leadership, and within-group, between-group, and end-of-group processing and evaluation).

In addition to courses offering content and experience related to a given specialization, supervised clinical experience should be obtained in practica and internship experiences. Following the model provided by CACREP for master's practica, we recommend that one-quarter of all required supervised clinical experience be devoted to group work:

- **Master's practicum.** At least 10 clock hours of the required 40 clock hours of direct service should be spent in supervised leadership or co-leadership experience in group work, typically in Task Group Facilitation, Group Psychoeducation, or Group Counseling (at the master's practicum level, experience in Group Psychotherapy would be unusual).
- **Master's internship.** At least 60 clock hours of the required 240 clock hours of direct services should be spent in supervised leadership or co-leadership in group work consistent with the program's specialization offering(s) (i.e., in Task Group Facilitation, Group Psychoeducation, Group Counseling, or Group Psychotherapy).
- **Doctoral internship.** At least 150 clock hours of the required 600 clock hours of direct service should be spent in supervised leadership or co-leadership in group work consistent with the program's specialization offering(s) (i.e., in Task Group Facilitation, Group Psychoeducation, Group Counseling, or Group Psychotherapy).

From ASGW (2000).

this include clients needing individual treatment simultaneously with group treatment, outside contact with a client outside of group, and decisions to share personal information in the group. Again, these are all issues that counselors operating within an integrative-contextual approach to counseling must deal with in order to be effective in an ethical and professional fashion.

Last, a thorough understanding of group process, the relational nature of groups, and the unique cultural dynamics contained in sound ethical practice of group counseling and psychotherapy are the hallmarks of an integrative-contextual approach to ethics. Yalom (2000) describes some of the crucial factors for success in any group, such as an instillation of hope, altruism, interpersonal learning, the corrective recapitalization of the primary family group, and the development of socializing techniques. In addition, he describes the influence that the group members have on one another, and on the group leader, in a way that is very reminiscent of an integrative-contextual approach. Arguably, he is considered to be an example of a "master therapist" (described elsewhere in this text). As such, his writings evidence the best of group psychotherapy, as well as an integrative-contextual approach (though he does not explicitly write in those terms).

Spirituality and Mental Health Counseling

In the last decade or so, there has been a rediscovery of the usefulness of including spirituality in the therapeutic domain as an adjunct to therapy, or as a strengths-based resource to be incorporated. Counselors and clients alike can find some way of defining their own personal spiritual "space" with common elements (meaning, morality, and community) from which to have a shared dialogue regardless of the individual spiritual choices that one makes. Another influencing factor for the inclusion of spirituality has been the appreciation of non-Western and native healing traditions. In particular, the practice of prayer, meditation, yoga, and other "centering" exercises have been routinely incorporated either into individual stress management or as methods for couples or families to connect to one another. As these gained an audience in the therapeutic community, more traditional religious and spiritual traditions began to also gain acceptance as legitimate sources of support. This is particularly salient when clients make religious practices central themes of their lives, as well as central to their conflicts.

A final factor that has influenced the inclusion of spirituality into the mainstream of couple and family therapy practice is substance abuse treatment. Many of these modalities include a spiritual dimension as a part of recovery (following from Alcoholics Anonymous and other twelve-step recovery programs). Mental health counselors also have begun to view spirituality as part of the client's particular worldview, shedding some light on his or her presenting concern. Thus, spirituality has now become a regular aspect of any assessment, diagnosis, and treatment plan for couples and families (Sperry, Carlson, & Kjos, 2003). This is why, from an integrative-contextual approach, counselors must understand the impact of their default positions on cultural and spiritual issues on clients (see the case example in Box 11.19). However, the obligation doesn't stop there (as it would for Perspective II); rather, the clinician must be able to go beyond understanding and open him- or herself to being transformed by the experience with others. These counselors actually learn from the client and then expand both their experience and the client's.

Clearly, in the scenario in Box 11.19, Kendall has many countertransference issues that are being neither addressed in the session (which in this case may not be appropriate) nor dealt with in personal counseling or supervision. Instead, Kendall's outright rejection of her client's worldview does not move the relationship forward into an effective working alliance, but allows it to regress to the point that it eventually shifts into tacitly addressing Kendall's need to still be angry with God over her mother's death (at best, a Perspective II method of dealing with the issue). From the Perspective III approach, Kendall would recognize her potential personal weakness and either discuss it the first time it arose (e.g., "We

BOX 11.19
SPIRITUALITY AND THE COUNSELOR "ESTRANGED FROM GOD"

Kendall was a licensed mental health counselor who had been in private practice for fourteen years. She came from a Baptist family, but was not really devout in her faith. Six months ago, her mother died suddenly from a heart attack, and although she took six weeks off from her practice, she was still grieving the loss of her mother. Specifically, she had "a lot of anger toward God" over her mother's death, the suddenness of her mother's death, and her inability to say goodbye. As a result, she described herself as "estranged" from Him and expressions of religiosity. Recently, she took on a single female client who was from a nondenominational, evangelical Christian faith. In the first session, the client asked if Kendall would pray with her. She bristled at the suggestion and said coolly, "I don't do that, but I won't stop you from doing so." At the second session, the client again repeated the request, with the same response from Kendall. When they were walking out of the session, the client said, "I know that you don't believe in this, but I am going to pray for you," which Kendall ignored. Then in the next session, the client came in and said, "The Lord spoke to me about you, and He wants you to know that He loves you and wants you to open your heart to Him." Kendall burst into tears and left the room. When she regained her composure, she told the client that she was no longer able to work with her and offered a referral to another colleague in the building.

will not always share the same views on things, but it does not mean that we cannot find ways to learn and understand from each other. In this case, I will sit quietly and reflect while you prepare for the beginning of the session by praying."). In addition, she would be attuned to her strong emotional reactions and seek out the resources (i.e., grief counseling, supervision) to effectively deal with them.

CASE ILLUSTRATION OF ETHICAL-PROFESSIONAL DECISION MAKING IN MENTAL HEALTH COUNSELING

Box 11.20 provides an example of a dilemma in school counseling, followed by a discussion of the case.

Step 1: Identify the problem. In some respects, the issue of whether there is a dilemma begins with Patricia's initial "gut" feeling of unease at Dr. Jarrod's plan for dealing with the overload of cyber-clients. If she would explore it further, she would determine that there are several possible dilemmas in this particular case. First, there is the issue of counseling across state lines without fully understanding the legal aspects of it. Next, there are the elements of her lack of training in cyber-therapy, which made her feel uncomfortable. Dr. Jarrod's choice to expand his practice in this domain came after over twenty-five years in the field and specific training. Patricia was still unlicensed and beginning her career. However, if Patricia ignored her gut feeling (as was presented in the case), then the problem begins

BOX 11.20
A CASE OF WEB COUNSELING

Jarrod was a doctoral-level licensed mental health counselor with over twenty-five years' experience in private practice. He was well known in his community and well respected by his peers for his work with adolescents. In the last few years, however, he had experienced a substantial decrease in his income as managed-care insurance companies paid less for his services, and his number of full-fee private-pay clients began to shrink. Looking for new ways to generate income, Jarrod attended a daylong training on "tele-therapy" and cyber-counseling. He learned about several new ways of providing long-distance therapy to clients out of state. He began to offer services via a website referral service and soon was beginning to turn a healthy profit "seeing" long-distance clients over the Internet during his "off peak" hours of the day. Soon, he found that he had more clients than he had time. He also had several post-master's students to whom he was providing supervision in preparation for licensure. He made an arrangement to refer some of his "cyber-clients" to the unlicensed therapists, split the fee with them, and continue to provide supervision (also for a fee).

One of these interns was Patricia. She was a 27-year-old woman who graduated approximately one year ago from a CACREP-accredited mental health counseling master's program. She needed a little over one year of supervised practice before she would be eligible for licensure. She had worked with "Dr. Jarrod" for almost two years: one year as an intern in her master's program and one year as a post-master's supervisee. She felt very comfortable working with him and has been grateful for the guidance he has given her. So when he approached her with his scheme for seeing his "cyber-clients," she felt privileged, despite having some misgivings about counseling online. However, Dr. Jarrod said that he would take care of all the details (billing, etc.) and that all that she would have to do is maintain contact with the clients.

Patricia had been doing the Internet counseling for about three months when she began to work with Ron. Ron was a 46-year-old man who lived several states away. He was seeking counseling for work-related stress and feelings of depression over a recent separation from his wife of eighteen years and their children. Patricia's impressions of him convinced her that he was someone who used sarcasm to mask a vast reservoir of pain. As she worked with him, she found that he was prone to impulsivity and outbursts of temper. This precipitated his separation from his family and also led to his initially being referred for counseling. Throughout this time, Patricia consulted with Dr. Jarrod, who expressed concerns over his instability. The final straw came when Ron had a "bad day" at work and, in his words, "lost it." Ron had been out drinking the night before with some coworkers, although it was not something that he regularly did. The next day, he arrived at work late. His boss expressed dissatisfaction with this, which made Ron feel insecure and irritated. Later in the day, the entire department was in a meeting, and Ron was asked to give a status report on his project. He was missing some crucial information, and he had to state that he could not give a full report. At this point, his boss made a snide comment stating that, if Ron was not able to do his job, perhaps someone else should. Ron stormed out of the meeting without saying a word, but it was clear that he was upset. In processing the situation with Patricia, Ron seemed to become more agitated, saying that he could have "choked the life out of him right there" and that he would "really love to see him suffer." Ron expressed several destructive fantasies from slashing his boss's tires and putting sugar in his gas tank (to disable his engine) to "putting a bullet through his chest." This, Patricia knew, was not an idle threat, since he was trained in the military as a sniper and owned guns as a collector and a hunter. "In fact," Ron quipped, "I could do it like those guys in Maryland did, only I wouldn't get caught."

What follows is an analysis of the case from Patricia's perspective using the ethical and professional practice decision model.[6]

[6]Issues related to the ethics of supervision (and, hence, the issues of Dr. Jarrod) will be touched upon in Chapter 14. The reader is invited to read that chapter and then apply the specific considerations to Dr. Jarrod.

with the disclosure by Ron that he wants to kill his boss. The seriousness of this is compounded by the fact that he has the ability to do it and a specific plan to carry it out. Patricia must decide if she has a duty to protect Ron's boss and, if she does, how to do it.

Step 2: Identify the participants affected by the decision. Specifically, the individuals involved are Patricia, Dr. Jarrod, Ron, and Ron's boss. More generally, there are all of the other cyber-clients, which can be thought of secondarily to this dilemma (and its subsequent decision). In addition, there are the other trainees that Dr. Jarrod works with that may be affected by the decision as well.

Step 3: Identify potential courses of action, along with possible benefits and risks for the participants.

Option 0.[7] Patricia could have simply refused to "see" Ron, claiming that she is not comfortable in her skills to be able to deal with the responsibility of counseling online. She may also decide that she simply needs to attend some training on the subject before making an informed decision. She may also decide to confront Dr. Jarrod on the subtle pressure that she felt from him, as well as her fear of disappointing him and/or losing her position with his practice.

Option 1. Patricia could decide not to report Ron and to get more information. (**1a**) She could be surreptitious about this and not tell him of her concerns. (**1b**) She could express her concerns and establish a dialogue around his feelings. In addition, Patricia could ask for permission to contact his wife or other family in the immediate area.

Option 2. She could direct Ron to go and speak confidentially to the ombudsperson at his work and have a conversation about the issues with the boss and how he felt provoked. She could then ask Ron to sign a release to talk to the ombudsperson about his behavior as well as her concerns.

Option 3. Another option would have been to refer Ron to someone local to him, as these issues may be better dealt with if he had face-to-face contact with someone who could better gauge his demeanor.

[7]We refer to this as "Option 0" as a way to illustrate how, if Patricia had been attentive to her initial responses to seeing clients online, she would not be in the situation that she faces now. The point is that all professional decisions have consequences, whether we know it at the time or not.

Option 4. Because of Ron's hostile expressions and his history of impulsivity, Patricia could contact Ron's boss and inform him of the possible danger. In addition, she could contact the local law enforcement in the county where Ron and his boss live and work (which is the standard practice in Patricia and Dr. Jarrod's home state), under the *Tarasoff* "duty to protect" statute.

Step 4: Evaluate the benefits and risks for each course of action based on contextual considerations.

Contextual Domain Considerations

In terms of her personal-developmental stage, Patricia is moving between level 1 and level 2. However, it is not yet clear whether that distinction has been translated into her supervisory relationship with Dr. Jarrod, who may still see Patricia as a student and not as a new professional. It would also seem that Patricia has some issues around needing to please that may cloud her judgment when it comes to Dr. Jarrod, which may make her seem "less than" in his eyes. In addition, Patricia's unquestioning attitude toward (and deference to) Dr. Jarrod, while respectful to a male elder (a cultural value in her family of origin), may also blind both of them to the pitfalls of this course of action. She does not yet fully trust her own instinct and instead allows herself to "go with the flow," particularly if there is someone in authority directing her. This is an artifact of her family-of-origin dynamic, whereby she had many older siblings telling her what to do, without her having to make a decision on her own. In addition, her distance from Ron has put her at a disadvantage, as she has always felt that she could "get a read" on people when she worked with them face to face. However, she has not been able to determine the extent of Ron's therapeutic attachment, nor his seriousness about the threat that he has made. All of this has raised Patricia's anxiety level about the case.

Organizationally, there are several impediments to Patricia's acting freely according to her conscience. The fact that Dr. Jarrod is the owner/operator of the clinic makes for a tricky relationship (at best) and an exploitive relationship (at worst). In a very real sense, he has the power to make Patricia's decision very difficult, or at least the influence to persuade her to "sweep it under the rug" (an option that she has already ruled out). However, if this situation is handled properly (i.e., from an integrative-contextual approach), then the relationship between the two can evolve into something transformational for both of them. It will make a better supervisor of Dr. Jarrod and clearly will allow Patricia to become a professional in her own right (as well as see a potential role model for being a supervisor down the road).

Professional Domain Considerations

Patricia found that there was not much written about cyber-counseling and duty-to-warn issues. The National Board of Certified Counselors (NBCC) has published guidelines for web counseling, but complying with these is merely voluntary on the part of the counselor (Heinlen, Welfel, Richmond, & Rak, 2003; NBCC, 1997). In fact, according to their study, none of the 136 sites in their study was in full compliance with all 13 of the NBCC standards, especially Standard 9, which requires that "a counselor-on-call within the client's geographic region should be identified in the event of an emergency when the Web Counselor was unavailable" (Heinlen et al., 2003, p. 67). In fact, in their survey, most of the sites seemed to be negligent in the exposure to risk from dangerous clients, instead choosing to post "disclaimers" that suicidal or homicidal clients should not access web-based counseling. In the case of Patricia and Dr. Jarrod, this was not the case, and there was no local counselor on call in Ron's location.

Ethical/Legal Domain Considerations

As yet, however, there is no direct oversight of web-based counseling by ethics boards (Heinlen et al., 2003). However, according to the ACA and AMHCA codes, there are several relevant codes that relate to this case. According to Principle 14 of the AMHCA ethics code, "mental health counselors take responsible steps to ensure the competence of their work and protect patients, clients . . . and others from harm." The issue of practicing within one's competence is also reflected in section 14F.3. AMHCA Principle 3.C clearly states that "The release of information without the consent of the client may only take place under the most extreme circumstances. The protection of life, as in the case of suicidal or homicidal clients, exceeds the requirements of confidentiality." However, the key clause in this principle is in the introduction, where it states that "Disclosure of counseling information is restricted to what is necessary, relevant, and *verifiable*" (italics added). This is where the case of Ron's cyber-counseling makes things difficult. There is the impediment of distance, which makes verifying the information more difficult than if Ron was face to face with Patricia. At the very least, if Ron was co-located with Patricia, she could call in Dr. Jarrod for a consultation or videotape or audiotape the session for him (or someone else) to consult. Patricia conceivably could send Ron to a colleague that she knows professionally for a consult and get ready feedback. This is not as readily available to her at such a distance. The same section of the ethics code strictly prohibits the improper release of information.

In addition, Principle 14A clearly states that "mental health counselors shall become aware of the means of reporting homicidal clients in the client's jurisdiction." In terms of the legal aspects, Ron's state did *not* have a mandated reporter statute (a so-called "*Tarasoff* law"). In addition, Ron's state had only *qualified* immunity laws, meaning that Patricia and Dr. Jarrod were not immune from a civil suit for slander. Last, Ron's state did not have formal "reciprocity" with Patricia and Dr. Jarrod's home state for licensure purposes and viewed long-distance counseling as practicing without a license. As a result, both Patricia and Dr. Jarrod could be exposed to either a civil lawsuit that could cost a substantial amount or regulatory sanction and have their licenses revoked by their home state.

Step 5: Consult with peers and experts. While Dr. Jarrod was Patricia's primary supervisor, there was the potentially exploitive dual role. Dr. Jarrod had a financial stake in whether Patricia saw Ron, which could have compromised his ability to provide constructive feedback when Patricia raised her concerns. Patricia did reside in the same general area where her graduate program was. She could contact former professors or fellow students to provide another context for her decision making related to the concerns that she had about Ron's hurting his boss.

Fortunately, a former professor whom she, out of desperation, had confided in, helped her prioritize her options based on the facts at hand and not on the potential outcomes.

"Deal with the situation at hand and not the situation that might happen." When she looked at it from that angle, she realized that the only true fact was that Ron was genuinely in pain over this incident and that he was isolated. These were the conditions that, in the past, led to his acting out. However, Patricia did have a good working relationship with him. She had gotten an agreement from him not to act out for at least 24 hours, and she felt that she could at least use that "cooling off" time to come up with some viable alternatives. She resolved that this was an isomorphic issue, in which both she and Ron were isolated by these events and that *both* of them needed more resources than either of them could muster by themselves.

In addition, she contacted the legal help line provided through her professional organization to give her some information, particularly around the "dangerous client" issues, online counseling, and duty-to-warn issues across state lines/jurisdictions. After contacting the legal help line, Patricia learned that she could not just terminate with Ron (since that would be abandonment) and that, if she were to make a report, it would have to be done in her state, and it would be up to the state entity (in this case a sheriff's department) to decide whether to contact the local authorities in Ron's state. However, local law enforcement may not be up to date on the latest procedures and case law and may need some education around the issue. In addition, she would probably still be in a bind, since the duty-to-protect statute clearly mandated that she had an obligation to protect Ron's boss, if Ron did harm the boss.

Step 6: Decide on the most feasible option and document the decision-making process. First, Patricia decided that she needed to gather more information. She decided to express her concerns to Ron over his feelings along with a need to provide him with more support. In conjunction with this, she would seek to build a support system for Ron by getting permission to contact his wife for consultation, as well as the company's ombudsperson. She would further recommend that Ron see the ombudsperson or EAP personnel at work, reminding him that it was free and confidential. If he balked at these, or refused to comply outright, Patricia resolved that she would need to place a call to the local sheriff's office. She also noted that she may have to provide some relevant information about the legal procedures related to the duty to protect across state jurisdictions. Last, she made a decision to have a conversation with Dr. Jarrod about their relationship and what she needed from a supervisor at this point in her career and explore whether he would be able to provide that for her. She resolved to place her professional development ahead of her own immediate gain or her need to please a "superior." Ideally, after going through this process, Patricia would have a better understanding—as a result of considering her own contextual and professional issues (desire to please, to advance her own career, to not be seen as incompetent)—that she had bitten off more than she could chew. She may decide to no longer take cyber-clients until she has had more training. Regardless, she had determined that she was long overdue to have a conversation with Dr. Jarrod about the evolution of their supervisory relationship. For Patricia, this was the beginning of moving to the next level of maturity as mental health counselor operating with an integrative-contextual approach to ethics.

Step 7: Implement, evaluate, and document the enacted decision. Patricia did call Ron back the next day and expressed her concerns to him in a way that highlighted that she had some insight to the isolation that he was feeling. Ron confessed that he was embarrassed that he had spoken out the way that he had, and that, while the fantasy was "very realistic," his boss "wasn't worth it." While this still smacked of a lack of sympathy for his boss as a person, Ron was able to see that the consequences of his fantasy to lash out at his boss would only harm him in the long run. Patricia remarked that this was a mark of progress for him and honestly confided in him that she contemplated taking some action. "You mean you were going to tell on me?" Ron remarked defensively. Patricia replied, "I would have acted in a way that would protect everyone, and if that meant 'telling' on you, then yes, I would have. However, you just said so yourself that you would have only have hurt yourself if you had done something rashly. I was only going to try to protect you, but it seems like you beat me to it. So, let's talk about how it was that you protected yourself, and what to do about your boss when you have to face him later today . . ." With that the session went on as normal. Ultimately, Patricia did get Ron to contact the ombudsperson at work to discuss his boss and the treatment that he was getting from him.

This case illustrates some of the issues related to the most important duty that mental health counselors have, protecting our clients and the public at large. However, there is a multitude of ways that this obligation gets filled. Some ways seek to protect the counselor at the cost of the client; others protect the intended victim at the cost of the client. An integrative-contextual approach seeks to balance the needs all of the participants, and find a solution that serves these needs without sacrificing any of them.

KEY POINTS

1. Mental health counseling is, by virtue of its historical focus on privileging the client's perspective in treatment, inherently compatible to an integrative-contextual (Perspective III) approach.
2. Confidentiality is the cornerstone of all mental health counseling. Confidentiality protects the dignity of those who seek counseling, and ensures that proper respect for the client is upheld,
3. Counselors who practice from an integrative-contextual approach are proactive and act upon the premise that confidential communication supports positive counseling outcomes. Additionally, counselors provide information to third parties to the extent that it complies with legal mandates or court orders when all other avenues are exhausted.
4. The process of informed consent, from an integrative-contextual approach, is an continuing process of dialogue with the client, and a method of continually negotiating and maintaining the therapeutic relationship. It demonstrates a full partnership in the therapeutic process, and communicates genuine respect for clients' ability to make decisions about their care.
5. The idea that boundary permeability in the practice of mental health counseling can often lead to boundary crossings that, if they are not exploitative in nature, may facilitate the therapeutic relationship is in keeping with a Perspective III approach to ethical practice.
6. The multiple relationships and/or functions that are inherent in the therapeutic relationship are congruent with a positive, integrative-contextual approach. This calls into question the absolute prohibition on multiple relationships.
7. A lifelong desire to learn is the ultimate expression of competence and Perspective III ethics, while rigid reliance on board certifications as an expression of competence is indicative of a Perspective I approach to ethics.
8. While case laws may have shaped the Perspective I approach to ethics, mental health counselors can maintain a positive, integrative-contextual approach while upholding the law.

9. The integrative-contextual approach to ethics applies not just to the routine practice of mental health counseling, but also to subspecialties of mental health counseling (such as substance abuse counseling and group therapy). Mental health counselors who work in these areas generally evaluate their practice along similar dimensions as the positive, integrative-contextual approach.
10. Managed care organizations are a standard part of the practice of mental health counseling for many practitioners, though they are seen as having a negative impact on the field. Counselors who employ an integrative-contextual approach are mindful of the potential to operate in ways that are not beneficial to their clients (e.g., using misdiagnoses, etc.) and resist these pressures even if it means withdrawing from the panel.
11. Group counseling is an effective modality for delivering treatment to a large number of clients at the same time. However, there are particular issues and concerns that well-trained group counselors share in common with counselors operating from an integrative-contextual approach. These include confidentiality, informed consent, conflicts of interest, and competence.
12. Spirituality is a vital part of many clients' existence. In addition, it can be a powerful adjunct to positive treatment gains. While there has been some misunderstanding of this domain in the past, counselors operating from an integrative-contextual approach value the client's perspective and experience of the spiritual in a way that is accepting and respectful.
13. The application of the seven-step contextual ethical decision-making model allows mental health counselors to generate alternative solutions and evaluate them according to a positive, integrative-contextual model of practice, which assesses the impact that each has on the individual client.

REVIEW QUESTIONS

1. What would you do if the treatment your client required was not covered by his or her managed care organization, and the client could not afford to pay for the service out-of-pocket?
2. What would you do if a client threatened to physically harm you if you reported the abuse he disclosed in counseling?
3. Under what circumstances might you want to report a potentially dangerous situation learned about in counseling, even when you aren't mandated to report that type of danger?
4. What would you do if a client expressed a desire to speak his or her religion in counseling?
5. Would you begin counseling a client who is currently too symptomatic to concentrate on the informed consent process?

REFERENCES

American Mental Health Counselors Association. (2000). *Code of ethics of the American Mental Health Counselors Association.* Alexandria, VA: Author.

Association for Specialists in Group Work. (2000). *Professional standards for the training of group workers.* Alexandria VA: Author.

Barstow, S. (2003). *Public health programs and professional mental health counselors: Practice impact and advocacy needs.* Alexandria, VA: American Counseling Association.

Bernstein, B. E., & Hartsell, T. L. (2000). *The portable ethicist for mental health professionals: An A-Z guide to responsible practice.* New York: Wiley.

Brooks, D., & Riley, P. (1996). The impact of managed health care policy on student field training. *Smith College Studies in Social Work, 66*(3), 307–316.

Brown, S. P. (2001). Report of the ACA ethics committee: 1999–2000. *Journal of Counseling and Development, 79,* 237–241.

Brown, S., & Espina, M. R. (2000). Report of the ACA ethics committee: 1998–1999. *Journal of Counseling and Development, 78,* 237–241.

Cameron, S., & turtle-song, i. (2002). Learning to write case notes using the SOAP format. *Journal of Counseling and Development, 80*(3), 286–292.

Caudill Jr., O.B. (2002). Risk management for psychotherapists: Avoiding the pitfalls. *Innovations in Clinical Practice: A Source Book, 20,* 307–323.

Clarkson, P. (1990). A multiplicity of psychotherapeutic relationships. *British Journal of Psychotherapy, 7*(2), 148–163.

Clarkson, P. (2000). *Ethics: Working with ethical and moral dilemmas in psychotherapy.* London: Whurr.

Coale, H. W. (1998). *The vulnerable therapist: Practicing psychotherapy in and age of anxiety.* New York: Haworth Press.

Corcoran, K. J., & Vandiver, V. (1996). *Maneuvering the maze of managed care: Skills for mental health practitioners.* New York: Free Press.

Cottone, R. R. (2001). A social constructivism model of ethical decision making in counseling. *Journal of Counseling and Development, 79,* 39–45.

Daniels, J. A. (2001). Managed care, ethics and counseling. *Journal of Counseling and Development, 79*(1), 119–122.

Daniels, J. A., Alva, L. A., & Olivares, S. (2002). Graduate training for managed care: A national survey of psychology and social work programs. *Professional Psychology: Research and Practice, 33*(6), 587–590.

Dineen, T. (2002). The psychotherapist and the quest for power: How boundaries have become an obsession. In A. A. Lazarus & O. Zur (Eds.), *Dual relationships and psychotherapy* (pp. 115–139). New York: Springer.

Ewing v. Goldstein. (2004). Cal App. 2 Dist. WL 1588240.

Fay, A. (2002). The case against boundaries in psychotherapy. In A. A. Lazarus & O. Zur (Eds.), *Dual relationships and psychotherapy* (pp. 98–114). New York: Springer.

Ford, G. G. (2001). *Ethical reasoning in the mental health professions.* Boca Raton, FL: CRC Press.

Freeman, A. (2000). Treating high-arousal patients: Differentiating between patients in crisis and crisis-prone patients. In F. M. Dattilio & A. Freeman (Eds.), *Cognitive-behavioral strategies in crisis intervention* (2nd ed.; pp. 27–58). New York: Guilford Press.

Garcia, J. G., Cartwright, B., Winston, S. M., & Burzuchowska, B. (2003). A transcultural integrative model for ethical decision making in counseling. *Journal of Counseling and Development, 81,* 268–277.

Genia, V. (2000). Religious issues in secularly based psychotherapy. *Counseling and Values, 44*(3), 213–221.

Heinlen, K. T., Welfel, E. R., Richmond, E. N., & Rak, C. F. (2003). The scope of web counseling: A survey of services and compliance with the *NBCC Standards for the Ethical Practice of Web Counsleing. Journal of Counseling and Development, 81,* 61–69.

Hoffman, R. M. (1995). Sexual dual relationships in counseling: Confronting the issues. *Counseling and Values, 40*(1), 15–23.

Hubert, R. M., & Freeman, L. T. (2004). Report of the ACA Ethics Committee: 2002–2003. *Journal of Counseling and Development, 82*(3), 286–292.

Issacs, M. L., & Stone, C. (2001). Confidentiality with minors: Mental health counselors' attitudes toward breeching or preserving confidentiality. *Journal of Mental Health Counseling, 23*(4), 342–356.

Ibrahim, F. I., & Arrendondo, P. M. (1986). Ethical standards for cross-cultural counseling: Counselor preparation, practice, assessment, and research. *Journal of Counseling and Development, 64*(5), 349–351.

Keith-Spiegel, R. & Koocher, G. (1985). *Ethics in psychology: Professional standards and cases.* New York: Random House.

Kitchener, K. S. (1988) Dual role relationships: What makes them so problematic? *Journal of Counseling & Development, 67*(4), 217–221.

Lambert, M. J. (1992). Implications of outcome research for psychotherapy integration. In J. C. Norcross & M. R. Goldstein (Eds.), *Handbook of psychotherapy integration.* New York: Basic Books.

Lambert, M. J., & Barley, D. E. (2002). Research summary on the therapeutic and psychotherapy outcome. In J. C. Norcross (Ed.), *Psychotherapy relationships that work: Therapist contributions and responsiveness to patients* (pp. 17–32). New York: Oxford University Press.

Lazarus, A. A. (2002). How certain boundaries and ethics diminish therapeutic effectiveness. In A. A. Lazarus & O. Zur (Eds.), *Dual relationships and psychotherapy* (pp. 25–31). New York: Springer.

Lazarus, A. A., & Zur, O. (Eds.). (2002). *Dual relationships and psychotherapy.* New York: Springer.

Leslie, R. S. (2003). Ethical and legal matters: The dangerous patient and confidentiality. *Family Therapy Magazine, 2*(6), 43–45.

National Board for Certified Counseling. (1997). *Standards for the ethical practice of web counseling.* Greensboro, NC: Author.

National Institute of Drug Abuse. (2005). *NewsScan for January 10, 2005.* Retrieved June 9, 2005, from http://www.nida.nih.gov/newsroom/05/NS-01.html

Peluso, P. R. (2003). The ethical genogram: A tool for helping therapists understand their ethical decision making styles. *The Family Journal: Counseling and Therapy for Couples and Families, 14*(3), 286–291.

Pope, K.S., & Bajt, T.R. (1988). When laws and values conflict: A dilemma for psychologists. *American Psychologist, 43*(10), 828–829.

Pope, K. S., & Vasquez, M. A. (1998). *Ethics in psychotherapy and counseling: A practical guide* (2nd ed.). San Francisco: Jossey-Bass.

Rubin, S. (2002). The multiple roles and relationships of ethical psychotherapy: Revisiting the ideal, the real, and the unethical. In A. A. Lazarus & O. Zur (Eds.), *Dual relationships and psychotherapy* (pp. 98–114). New York: Springer.

Sanders, J. L., & Freeman, L. T. (2003). Report of the ACA ethics committee: 2001–2002. *Journal of Counseling and Development, 81,* 251–254.

Scheflin, A. W. (2002). Are dual relationships antitherapeutic? In A. A. Lazarus & O. Zur (Eds.), *Dual relationships and psychotherapy* (pp. 257–272). New York: Springer.

Shah, S. T. (1970). Privileged communications, confidentiality, and privacy: Confidentiality. *Professional Psychology: Research & Practice, 1*(2), 159–164.

Siegel, M. (1979). Privacy, ethics, and confidentiality. *Professional Psychology: Research & Practice, 10*(2), 249–258.

Skovholt, T. M., & Jennings, L. (2004). *Master therapists: Exploring expertise in therapy and counseling*. Boston: Allyn and Bacon.

Sommers-Flanagan, R., Elliott, D., & Sommers-Flanagan, J. (1998). Exploring the edges: Boundaries and breaks. *Ethics and Behavior, 8*(1), 37–48.

Sperry, L., Carlson, J., & Kjos, D. (2003) *Becoming an effective therapist.* Boston: Allyn and Bacon.

Sperry, L., & Giblin, P. (1996). Marital and family therapy with religious persons. In E. P. Shafranske (Ed.), *Religion and the clinical practice of psychology* (pp. 511–532). Washington DC: American Psychological Association.

Stevens, P. (2000). Practicing within our competence: New techniques create new dilemmas. *The Family Journal: Counseling and Therapy for Couples and Families, 8*(3), 278–280.

Stoltenberg, C. D., McNeill, B., & Delworth, U. (1998). *IDM supervision: An integrated developmental model for supervising counselors and therapists.* San Francisco: Jossey-Bass.

Sue, D. W., Arrendondo, P., & McDavis, R. J. (1992). Multicultural counseling competencies and standards: A call to the profession. *Journal of Counseling and Development, 70,* 477–487.

Sue, D. W., & Sue, D. (1999). *Counseling the culturally different: Theory and practice.* New York: Wiley.

Vasquez, M. (2003). Ethical responsibilities in therapy: A feminist perspective. In M. Kopala & M. A. Keitel (Eds.), *Handbook of counseling women* (pp. 557–573). Thousand Oaks, CA: Sage.

Walden, S. L., Herlihy, B., & Ashton, L. (2003). The evolution of ethics: Personal perspectives of ACA ethics committee chairs. *Journal of Counseling and Development, 81,* 106–110.

Wedding, D. (2004). Contemporary issues in psychotherapy. In R. Corsini & D. Wedding (Eds.), *Contemporary psychotherapies* (7th ed., pp. 475–492). New York: Wadsworth.

Weed, L. L. (1971). Quality control and the medical record. *Archive of Internal Medicine, 127,* 101–105.

Williams, M. H. (2002). Multiple relationships: A malpractice plaintiff's litigation strategy. In A. A. Lazarus & O. Zur (Eds.), *Dual relationships and psychotherapy* (pp. 224–248). New York: Springer.

Williams, C. B., & Freeman, L. T. (2002). Report of the ACA ethics committee: 2000–2001. *Journal of Counseling and Development, 80,* 251–254.

Wolf, C. T., & Stevens, P. (2001). Integrating religion and spirituality in marriage and family counseling. *Counseling and Values, 46*(1), 66–75.

Yalom, I. D. (2000). *Theory and practice of group psychotherapy* (5th ed.). New York: Basic Books.

Zur, O. (2002). In celebration of dual relationships: How prohibition of nonsexual dual relationships increases the chance of exploitation and harm. In A. A. Lazarus & O. Zur (Eds.), *Dual relationships and psychotherapy* (pp. 44–54). New York: Springer.

Zur, O., & Lazarus, A. A. (2002). Six arguments against dual relationships and their rebuttals. In A. A. Lazarus & O. Zur (Eds.), *Dual relationships and psychotherapy* (pp. 3–25). New York: Springer.

CHAPTER 12

COUPLES AND FAMILY COUNSELING AND THERAPY

PAUL R. PELUSO

The ethical practice of couples and family therapy, by virtue of its work with multiple clients in the same session, is a lived relational experience. This means that ethics do not, and cannot, reside in isolation, locked away in file cabinet, but must be expressed in the relationship with, to, and *among* one's clients. This very aspect of couples and family therapy is its greatest strength (i.e., working on multiple systemic levels at the same time) and one of its greatest challenges for its practitioners trying to employ a positive, integrative-contextual approach that is developmental-contextual in its scope. As with all aspects of practicing couples therapy (assessment, intervention, case conceptualization), ethical practice is not something that is learned once and never revisited. Instead, ethical practice is shaped by the therapist's growth and exposure to new ideas and concepts, developed in concert with client interaction, and reflective of broader organizational dynamics. In short, ethics from this perspective are a positive endeavor from a developmental, holistic perspective (rather than from a negative, reductionistic, fear-based one), which allows therapists to consciously incorporate and implement these principles in the practice of therapy. Therapists who view ethics from this perspective have the potential to grow and mature as clinicians with powerfully efficient tools for effecting change.

It is an indicator not only of a mature professional, but of a maturing field of service when there an emphasis on sound, ethically informed practice. In this chapter, we will explore the most recent revisions of the ethics codes of the two primary professional associations for couples and family therapists: the International Association of Marriage and Family Counselors (IAMFC) and the American Association for Marriage and Family Therapy (AAMFT). While we advocate for an integrative-contextual (Perspective III) approach in this chapter, it may seem odd that we will devote so much space to the various ethics codes (which are the sole focus of practitioners who employ a Perspective I approach to ethics). However, adopting an integrative-contextual ethics perspective *does not* mean that a therapist is somehow "above" the codes and can merely abandon or violate them at will because they follow the "principles," no more than someone who adopts a strict moral code can violate the law and justify it by his or her "superior" morality. Therapists who operate from Perspective III embrace the codes and the spirit (i.e., values) that they were written in, as well as the result on the individual clients and the broader system that the therapist is working with (i.e., the couple or the family). Hence, an integrative-contextual approach that is sensitive to the multiple domains of the personal-relational, professional, and legal/ethical is very much relevant to the day-to-day practice of couples and family therapy. First we will begin with a consideration of the ethical implications of the routine practices of couples and family counseling.

LEARNING OBJECTIVES

After reading this chapter you should be able to

1. Define ethically sound couples and family counseling from a relational perspective that values good practice and ensures client welfare.
2. Relate the contextual dimension—the personal-developmental, relational-multicultural, and organizational ethics–community values—to the practice of couples and family counseling.
3. Describe eight common ethical issues in couples and family counseling and the specific ethical codes and standards relevant to them.
4. Explain two common legal issues in the practice of couples and family counseling.
5. Apply the ethical decision-making model to a clinical issue, aware of the personal-developmental, relational-multicultural, and organizational-community dimensions.

KEY TERMS

ad hoc fallacy
boundaries
confidentiality
Family Systems Theory
long-arm statutes
play therapy
slippery slope
SOAP notation
spirituality

ROUTINE PRACTICE OF COUPLES AND FAMILY THERAPY

There are very few things that are "routine" about the practice of couples and family therapy in the modern era. The definitions of *relationship* and *family* are continually being challenged, and couples and family counselors must challenge themselves along with them. As a result, couples and family therapists are usually at the forefront of cultural and societal shifts long before the rest of the culture is cognizant of them. Whether it is single parenthood, unmarried couples living in long-term relationships, or homosexual unions, couples and family therapists have worked with the people who are living these existences well before they make the cover of a newspaper or magazine. Hence, there are a number of day-to-day tasks that take place in the practice of couples and family therapy that may not, on the surface, seem like major ethical concerns. In reality, however, there are certain ethical codes and legal statutes that govern such day-to-day operations as advertising and assessment. Specifically, in the IAMFC code, Section 3 is dedicated to Competence, which addresses the fact that couples and family therapists *do not* practice in areas outside of their training and competence (addressed below). Section 4 deals with assessment and testing, and expressly states that any materials that are used must be within the therapist's scope of knowledge. This means that the therapist must understand issues related to measurement and instrument validity and accurately provide interpretation of results in a fashion that clients can understand. Section 5 is dedicated to Private Practice and reinforces the codes contained in Sections 3 and 4, but also provides guidance about the payment of services, prohibition of payment for referrals, and other elements of practice (see Box 12.1). While the AAMFT code has similar codes interspersed throughout the ethics code, the IAMFC ethical codes are noteworthy for expressly placing these within the context of private practice.

BOX 12.1

SELECTED PORTIONS OF IAMFC SECTION V: PRIVATE PRACTICE

A. Members in private practice have a special obligation to adhere to ethical and legal standards, because of the independent nature of their work.
   1. Members keep informed of current ethical codes and ethical issues of the profession.
   2. Members maintain a working knowledge of legal standards in the geographical area and areas of specialty in which they work, abiding by these standards in their practice.
   3. Members continue professional growth and knowledge through consultation and supervision.

C. Members in private practice are responsible and respectful of client needs in their setting and collection of fees for service.
   1. Members provide a portion of their services at little or no cost as a service to the community.

From IAMFC (2002).

HIPAA Considerations

Perhaps no other piece of legislation or federal ruling in the last two decades has impacted the practice of couples and family therapy as much as the Health Insurance Portability and Accountability Act of 1996. While the act was passed in 1996, it was not *fully* implemented until April 2005. Sparked by several changes in the practice of health care delivery and the insurance related to it (managed care, etc.), HIPAA was designed to ensure uniform standards related to the protection of patient information in both the delivery of care and the transactions necessary for obtaining payment for services. As a result, any provider who deals with protected health information (PHI) and transmits it to a third party must abide by the statutes. As a result, couples and family therapists are covered regardless of the amount of contact they have with a given client. The HIPAA regulation accepts that different covered practitioners (by the nature of their discipline) may have different ways of complying with the law. There are, according to Leslie (2002a), several things that couples and family therapists must do the following in order to be compliant with the HIPAA requirements (see Box 12.2).

Under HIPAA, there is much that couples and family therapists must do; however, they are not incompatible with sound, ethical practice. Under HIPAA's "Privacy Rule," therapists must obtain written consent from a patient for the provider to use or disclose private health information, including records, for purposes of treatment, payment, or health care operations (see Box 12.3). This is different from obtaining written consent to treat, which must be separate. The consent form must contain specified information, but does not need to be obtained repeatedly, no matter how long the treatment or how many separate disclosures are made by the therapist. The consent form must advise the patient of his or her right to review the provider's privacy notice (Leslie, 2002a).

Under HIPAA, couples and family therapists must provide patients with a written privacy notice that describes how PHI may be used or disclosed, as well as how clients can get access to it. The regulation requires the notice to explain the purpose of the consent form that the patient will initially be asked to sign and to clearly spell out that, if the patient refuses to consent to the disclosures, the therapist may refuse to treat the client. Specific examples of each of the permitted disclosures must be given in the privacy notice so that the

BOX 12.2

PROCEDURES FOR COMPLYING WITH HIPAA

1. **Adopt written privacy policies and procedures.** These need to include *exactly* who has access to protected information, how it will be used within the entity, and under what circumstances the information may be disclosed. This includes nonclinical members of a staff (administrative, billing, and other clerical staff) and vendors who are not employees. A written agreement spelling out these requirements will need to be on file.
2. **Train employees.** Therapists or agencies must train employees on the policies and procedures with respect to protected health information (PHI, e.g., patient records).
3. **Designate a privacy officer.** Covered entities must designate an individual to be responsible for the development and implementation of the privacy policies and procedures. In small practices, the office manager will customarily be the privacy officer; in solo private practices, the therapist acts as the privacy officer.
4. **Designate a contact person.** A covered entity must designate a contact person who is responsible for receiving complaints concerning the policies and procedures or its compliance with such policies and procedures.
5. **Maintain documentation.** All forms dealing with consents, authorizations, notices of privacy practices, procedures and policies, training, and patient requests for records must be maintained on file and regularly updated.

Adapted from Leslie (2002a).

BOX 12.3
NOTATION FOR COUPLES AND FAMILY COUNSELORS

One of the new HIPAA regulations has granted permission for counselors to keep *psychotherapy notes,* which are not required to be transmitted to any outside source (for the purpose of payment), private from other elements of a client's record. This creates an extra level of security or secrecy for the actual content of the psychotherapy session (i.e., what is said in the therapy session). However, there is an additional issue with regards to couples and family therapy. Traditionally, couples and family therapists keep notes on the entire couple or family, not on each individual member. At the same time, clinicians must also keep track of each individual's contribution to the presenting issue, as well as the unique contribution of each person in the specific session or in progressing toward the therapeutic goals.

Curiously, however, while the accepted "standards of care" (and some state laws) clearly indicate that there should be a record of what happens from session to session, there is no clear determination of *how* this should be done.[1] While there are a number of different formats (described by their various acronyms: DAP, BIRP, etc.), they all essentially convey the same information. One of the more widely used formats is the SOAP note format. Developed by Weed (1971), SOAP stands for:

Subjective This is the section that contains the information given to the counselor by the client during the session. This includes the client's statements of fact and feelings, as well as a general sense of the session from the client's perspective.

Objective This section contains factual information that the counselor observes directly. It should be written precisely, in quantifiable behavioral terms. Observations about mood, affect, appearance, and mental status should be recorded here.

Assessment This is the counselor's clinical impression of the client based on the assessment and treatment plan, as well as the subjective and objective sections of the note. It is generally written in the multiaxial format of the most recent version of the *Diagnostic and Statistical Manual of Mental Disorders* (e.g., DSM-IV-TR). For couples and family therapy, on Axis V, a GARF score should be utilized as well as a GAF score.[2]

Plan This is the section that contains the plan for treatment as well as the counselor's prognosis for the client. This often includes interventions used in session, specific recommendations for follow-up in the next session (i.e., "homework"), referrals for adjunctive intervention (e.g., psychiatric evaluation, group therapy, etc.), and the date of the next appointment.

Consider the following example:

Subjective. Couple came to scheduled couples session. They report that sons are keeping agreements made in previous family therapy session. Today wife discussed husband's bipolar disorder and her frustration when he refuses to take his medicine, which is generally an

[1]There are references in the IAMFC and AAMFT ethics codes to the client's "record," but there is no explicit ethical obligation for the counselor to keep an accurate record of what happens in the session, nor is there specific information or guidance about what the record should reflect or contain.

[2]Space limitations do not allow for a full description of the GARF score. Please see GAP (2000) for a more thorough description of the GARF scale.

(*continued*)

BOX 12.3 CONTINUED

indication that he is beginning a prolonged manic phase. Husband expressed frustration that he cannot maintain treatment regimen and expressed fears that his wife may leave him. Reflected on family of origin dynamics, especially his parent's divorce and her mother's chronic mental illness during her childhood, and what this may mean for their relationship.

***O*bjective.** Clients were cooperative throughout the session. Appeared well-groomed and in good spirits. Mood and affect was congruent for topic of discussion for both participants. Both were oriented to time/place/person/situation.

***A*ssessment.**

(Initial)—Axis I: Bipolar Disorder, NOS
Axis II: Deferred
Axis III: Hypertension, Asthma
Axis IV: Partner Relational Problem, Parent-Child Relational Problem
Axis V: GAF = 50 (55 highest past year)

(Ongoing)—No suicidal ideation

GARF = 55

***P*lan.** Scheduled family therapy session this Friday (9/15/05). Continue to discuss family management patterns. Scheduled couples session for 9/30/05. Will begin to address wife's concerns over decreased libido in husband and lack of physical intimacy in relationship. Prognosis guarded.

client can understand the circumstances whereby his or her PHI will be utilized. The privacy notice should describe the uses or disclosures of personal health information that may be made without the client's consent. The client must be informed in the written notice of his or her right to request restrictions on certain uses and disclosures of PHI, if he or she should wish. In addition, the client must be informed of his or her right to inspect and copy PHI (e.g., therapy records), as well as amend PHI in the therapist's records that he or she believes is incorrect. The privacy notice must inform the client of the therapist's legal duties and the therapist's privacy practices with respect to PHI. Last, the privacy notice must inform the client of his or her right to complain to the secretary of the U.S. Department of Health and Human Services, or other governing entity, about believed privacy violations (Leslie, 2002a).

The HHS Office for Civil Rights (OCR), which is responsible for enforcement of compliance with HIPAA regulations, has useful information for providers on its website, which is found at www.hhs.gov/ocr/hipaa, as does Richard Leslie in his article "New Federal Privacy Regulations: What You Need to Know and Do" (2002a). In addition, examples of forms created specifically for couples and family therapists (like consent, privacy notice, authorizations, and policies and procedures) can be found on AAMFT's web page, www.aamft.org. These can be downloaded and modified to each practitioner's specific needs.

CONTEXTUAL ISSUES IN COUPLES AND FAMILY THERAPY

Personal-Developmental

When difficult situations arise, therapists are faced with difficult choices. The ethical codes are one method for providing professionals with guidance in these difficult matters. Often, however, these situations are complex and require some interpretation of the ethical codes, which can be ambiguous and inconsistent for providers wrestling with complex situations (Corey, Corey, & Callanan 1998; Haber, 1996; Kitchener, 1986). This struggle is often due to the emotional reaction and developmental level of the therapist, which often clouds his or her ability to understand the event and the issues surrounding it. Indeed, it has been noted that "ethical issues arise when existing guidelines do not provide direction. . . . when faced with ethical dilemmas or new issues, counselors must be able to critically evaluate and interpret the relevant codes, as well as evaluate their feelings as appropriate or inappropriate bases for ethical behavior" (Kitchener, 1986, p. 306). From the integrative-contextual ethics perspective, we feel that understanding, addressing, and incorporating the therapist's emotional and intellectual perspectives is the hallmark of Perspective III ethics.

According to Kitchener (1986), the intuitive level of ethical decision making consists of immediate feelings and reactions to the situation as well as personal ethical beliefs. This intuitive level is further described by Robson, Cook, Hunt, Alred, and Robson (2000) as a "pre-reflective response to an ethical dilemma, which is informed by the set of knowledge, beliefs, and assumptions that individuals carry with them" (p. 542). Thus, the intuitive level is the level at which therapists make a decision to proceed further in determining whether additional action is needed (Haber, 1996). However, many practitioners focus solely on the critical-evaluative level of ethical decision making, and not enough on the intuitive level:

> Decision making is based not only on the facts of the decision making but also on our feelings surrounding the facts and upon the values we hold that shape those feelings. All too often, our emotional, value-driven responses to decision making are undervalued and we "rationalise" [*sic*] our intuitive process—*post factum.* (Robson et al., 2000, p. 534)

Yet, to be unaware of or ignore the influence of these initial "gut" feelings or intuitions can lead to either underreaction or overreaction by therapists, which can lead ethical problems (Haber, 1996; Peluso, 2003; Robson et al., 2000).

Family therapists have claimed that these emotion-level responses are formed, in part, by the influences of the individual's family of origin (Aponte, 1994; Haber, 1996; Minuchin, 1974; Peluso, 2003). According to Aponte (1994), therapists—particularly those in training—should seek to understand their own families of origin as a matter of sound, ethical practice. It is clear that, at present, practitioners or educators have not paid enough attention to this level of ethical decision making. However, in order to better understand one's basic philosophical assumptions, and intuitive reactions to ethical dilemmas, an exploration of the family-of-origin dynamics that may have influenced them seems to make sense (Corey et al., 1998; Peluso, 2003).

As mentioned in Chapter 3, Peluso (2003) developed an extension of the genogram for understanding the influence of family of origin dynamics on present-day ethical decision-making styles. The "ethical genogram" is created in the same way as a regular genogram. Once the family of origin is drawn and the relationships between the supervisee and his or her family members are established, then additional questions related to overall ethical, or "tough," decision-making styles that were present in parents, siblings, and others can be discussed (see Box 12.4 for a sample list of questions).

In working through this process, a picture should begin to emerge that can indicate what types of ethical dilemmas might be difficult for the supervisee or therapist to recognize. Additionally, working through the ethical genogram can help determine whether a supervisee may have difficulty with "gray areas" versus "black-and-white" ethical decisions. When these underlying family-of-origin dynamics are uncovered, the therapist or supervisee has the opportunity to appreciate the context for, and the impact of, these forces on the initial appraisal of ethical decisions (see Box 12.5). As a result of the exercise, some therapists may discover the source of strengths or influences that they have never before realized. Others may come to an understanding of how a particularly negative pattern resulting from unresolved conflicts within the family of origin may impact ethical decision making. Therapists can process any particular insights that may arise or develop strategies to make better ethical decisions when certain potentially problematic conditions arise (Peluso, 2003). This is a powerful aspect to understanding the dynamics that get played out in therapists operating from a Perspective I or Perspective II approach, and the ethical genogram can be used as a tool for helping uncover these dynamics, and for assisting therapists in looking at the issues that can hamper their personal-professional development.

BOX 12.4

SAMPLING OF QUESTIONS FOR ETHICAL GENOGRAM

1. How did your father (or any parental figure in your youth) make tough decisions? Describe his style in two or three words.
2. How did your mother (or any parental figure in your youth) make tough decisions? Describe her style in two or three words.
3. Do you remember a particular instance in which a tough moral or ethical decision had to be made? What do you remember about it? Who made it, mother or father?
4. Was there conflict or disagreement between your mother and father when it came to making difficult or ethical decisions? Who usually prevailed? Why?
5. Is there anyone else who influenced your ethical decision making? Siblings, friends, teachers, or mentors? How did they influence you? Describe in two or three words their styles as they influenced you.
6. Were there additional influences on your ethical decision-making style (cultural, religious, philosophical, etc.)? How were you influenced by these, positively and/or negatively?
7. Did you ever break any rules or the law in your youth? Were you caught? How did your parents deal with it?

From: Peluso (2003).

BOX 12.5
SAMPLE FACILITATION AND SYNTHESIS QUESTIONS

1. What insights have you gained about your family of origin's influence on your ethical decision-making processes?
2. With this new information, what do you think might be some areas in which you would have difficulty making a decision about whether to take action?
3. What steps can you take right now to help you make better ethical decisions?

From: Peluso (2003).

Another unique element of couples and family therapy is the ability to work in a cotherapy situation with another therapist. This offers several possible (and interesting) dynamics to introduce in the session, but it also offers each therapist the ability to work closely with one another and provide a mirror for the other person to look into regarding his or her development. Many times the pairing includes a senior and a junior therapist, which allows for one to learn from the other. In this case, there is a power differential that must be addressed between the two so that the therapy is not affected. For example, the senior therapist may ask the junior therapist to attend to certain elements or to follow the senior therapist's "lead." Other times, there may be two therapists of intermediate (Level 2 or 3) development. This pairing requires a greater deal of maturity on the part of both counselors. The same level of development may place the cotherapists on an equal level, but they must also learn to negotiate each person's relative strengths and weaknesses, as well as utilize them for the client couple or family. Each person can choose to learn from the other and enhance his or her ability, or both can refuse, and inevitably create tension that will get translated into the therapy. The former is an example of Perspective III approach, and the latter an example of a Perspective I or II approach.

Relational-Multicultural

Family Systems Theory, the foundation on which most schools of couples and family therapy lies, has been cited as a catalyst for introducing a multiple modes of input and perspective in the therapeutic realm. Indeed, the idea that each person in the family could have a widely varied perception of the same series of events (i.e., daily family life) was a radical introduction into the psychotherapy of the 1950s and beyond. From this position, it was not a far leap to introduce the idea that broader cultural perspectives may mean that counselors and clients may have different perspectives based on their particular cultural backgrounds, or socioeconomic statuses. However, this shift did not happen overnight, and required decades of social change before being seriously considered in the therapeutic realm in the 1980s (Carter & McGoldrick, 2004). Today, we take for granted that therapists must be culturally sensitive and aware of their own biases and cultural encapsulation. We recognize the potential for harm that can be done by well-meaning therapists who do not consider how the imposition of their worldviews and values can impact a client or a family. For example, the structural family therapy technique of "unbalancing the system" is designed to force a type of crisis whereby the therapist can help the family restructure the family boundaries. However, this can often be a strategy that the therapist can use to impose his or her worldview (i.e., that parents must always be in control, that children should always have a voice) on a family that may not necessarily share it. When confronted with a situation in which the therapist is considering *any* technique, he or she must ask the question, Who is this best for, the client or me? In addition, couples and family therapists must consider whether there are any other approaches that would accomplish the same goal without creating a win/lose situation or being culturally insensitive. Likewise, a family therapist who does not take the time to understand both the macro- and microcultural aspects of family or couple's life risks missing out on information that could be just as crucial as other routinely collected family-of-origin dynamics (such as family history of addiction or divorce).

In fact, the IAMFC ethics code (Section I.B) explicitly states that couples and family therapists "strive to respect the diversity of personal attributes and do not stereotype or force families into prescribed attitudes, roles, or behaviors. Family counselors respect the client's definitions of families, and recognize diversity of families, including two-parent, single parent, extended, multigenerational, same gender, etc." Furthermore, the code goes on to indicate that a therapist's own cultural perspective can have a negative impact if not monitored. Hence, it is the clinicians' duty to be vigilant, specifically that they "do not impose personal values on families or family members. Members recognize the influence of worldview and cultural factors (race, ethnicity, gender, social class, spirituality, sexual orientation, educational status) on the presenting problem, family functioning, and problem-solving skills. Counselors are aware of indigenous healing practices and incorporate them into treatment when necessary or feasible" (IAMFC, 2002, Section I.F).

Organizational Ethics–Community Values

As mentioned in Chapter 4, often a person's personal ethics, professional ethics, and an organization's ethics come into conflict. To review briefly, *personal ethics* are an individual's "conscience," or the set of unique set of beliefs and values by which he or she lives his or her life. A counselor's *professional ethics* are the individual counselor's method for determining how to operate in an ethically sound, professional manner. This is based, in part, on the counselor's own personal ethics, and on the ethical obligations of the profession. *Organizational ethics* refers to the institutional norms and organizational characteristics that go into making systemwide decisions.

The organization's main focus is to ensure that individual staff behaviors and decisions execute the functions that the organization publicly proclaims that it will do. While it may be important for staff to feel a sense of connectedness that their needs are taken care of, there are times when that is a secondary consideration. This means that there may be situations where the staff must act in a way that they do not agree with in order to fulfill the mission of the agency or organization. At the same time, this does not excuse the organization from operating outside the bounds of ethics. The self-evaluation tool presented in Chapter 4 is a good place to assess whether, in the counselor's opinion, the organization that he or she is working in is operating in an ethically consistent fashion. If the agency is not sensitive to ethical and professional considerations, there may be some times when the individual counselor's ethical concerns place him or her in jeopardy of breaching ethical obligations if the organization requires the counselor to act. We present the case study in Box 12.6 to illustrate these points.

BOX 12.6
WHEN THE ORGANIZATION TAKES YOU BEYOND YOUR COMFORT LEVEL

Janet is a licensed couples and family therapist working in a nonprofit family counseling setting. A telephone intake came in—to provide counseling to a couple that had been charged with multiple domestic violence offenses—and was assigned to her. Janet's agency was one of the few centers in the area that offered these services. What made this case unique was that both partners were hearing impaired and required an interpreter from a translation service to come to the session and interpret (via sign language) between the couple and the therapist. Janet felt some misgivings about whether she was the appropriate counselor for the couple, since she did not have any training in working with couples with hearing impairment, nor did she know sign language. In addition, she was worried that she might not be effective working through an interpreter and that she would be "a step removed" from directly understanding (or being understood by) her clients. Furthermore, Janet was concerned about the confidentiality issues, since there was probably going to be a different interpreter at each session. Although she would normally accept challenging cases, she questioned her competence in working with these clients and felt that it might be better to find and refer the couple to a therapist in the area who knew sign language. Given the violent component of the relationship, she felt compelled ethically to not see the clients but make a referral right away.

- Do you agree or disagree with Janet's thinking about the case?
- What would you do?
- What ethical principles are involved in Janet's situation?

Janet reasoned that she was justified in deciding to refer the clients based on several ethical principles. First, she believed that, since she feels that she is not properly trained, she cannot be helpful to her clients (principle of beneficence), and with the violence in the relationship, her interventions may cause (or allow) an escalation of the violence (principle of nonmaleficence). In addition, Janet felt that presenting herself as a competent therapist to the couple would be false (principle of fidelity). However, when she presented her concerns and plan to refer the clients to her supervisor, he expressed some reservations about referring the clients. Specifically, he expressed a concern about exposing the agency to a lawsuit for discrimination. The supervisor consulted with the director of the agency, who concurred with the supervisor and stated that the couple could sue for unequal treatment under the Americans with Disabilities Act (ADA). Both Janet's supervisor and the director of the agency pressured her to see the clients, stating that one person's ethical concerns could not place the entire agency in jeopardy.

Janet countered by saying that, in the event that something were to go wrong in treatment, the agency would be at risk for a malpractice suit and that she could be held personally

(continued)

BOX 12.6 CONTINUED

responsible for not upholding her ethical duty of advocating for the best care for her clients. This, she feared, would result in disciplinary action from the state ethics board and possibly the loss of her license. However, neither her supervisor nor the director agreed with her assessment. In fact, Janet felt that (although it was not explicitly stated) if she refused to take the case and see the couple, she could lose her job for being insubordinate. She felt that she was in a bind between her job on the one hand and her license and principles on the other.

- What would you do?
- How would you resolve the dilemma?

In this scenario, Janet felt pressure to conform to the agency's needs. She knew in her heart that, if she were in a private practice, she would feel more comfortable in her decision that she was acting in the best interests of the clients. Although the agency does have the obligation to protect itself from therapists acting in an unprofessional manner for which it can be held legally accountable, and although a clinician's ethical considerations can never justify breaking the law, it is questionable whether the use of the ADA was accurate in this case. According to the Office of Disability Employment Policy, the U.S. governmental agency that administers the ADA, while professionals may be required to accommodate individual's disabilities by providing "auxiliary aids" (such as interpreters) in certain cases (i.e., lawyers, accountants, etc.), these aids are not required if they "result in an undue burden or in a fundamental alteration in the nature of the goods or services provided by a public accommodation" (see JAN, 2004). However, professionals who do not or cannot provide the auxiliary aid are not excused from finding a suitable alternative. Hence, in this case, Janet's concerns about taking the couple are justified, and her desire to refer the client would be warranted.

In addition to determinations of how one will practice, as demonstrated in the last case, the conflicts between one's professional ethics and the organizational ethics can revolve around differences with the *organizational culture.* Recall that an organization's culture is the shared beliefs, customs, and assumptions of the organization. These can be explicitly stated (as in a mission or vision statement) or, more likely, unwritten rules by which the organization and its staff govern themselves. Some organizations value competition and a "win at all costs" spirit, while others may value creativity and free expression, which then gets translated into elements like dress code, communications, or decision making. Sometimes individuals fit well with certain cultures while others do not. Many times it is not until a person is knee-deep into a situation that the realization hits that he or she is not a good fit. Again, as for Janet before, the answer is not as clear-cut as one would think. When issues of one's ability to make an income or support a family come into play, it becomes difficult to be a purist. Perhaps the best outcome is for a person to recognize that he or she is not in the best climate or organization for him or her and to take steps to find an alterative as soon as possible. In terms of a positive, integrative-contextual approach, this is the only way to preserve a practitioner's relationship with the most important person, him- or herself.

In the next section, we switch from the surface issues related to couples and family therapy and will discuss some of the core elements of practice, as well as their relevant ethical codes, from an integrative-contextual ethics perspective.

CORE ETHICAL ISSUES AND CODES OF ETHICS FOR COUPLES AND FAMILY THERAPISTS

As mentioned earlier, the two primary professional associations for couples and family therapists are the International Association of Marriage and Family Counselors (IAMFC)[3] and the American Association for Marriage and Family Therapy (AAMFT). Ethical codes are changing instruments, just as the laws of a society change with the passage of time and with alterations in the social and cultural orders, and these have been updated recently. In this next section, we will compare elements of both the IAMFC and the AAMFT ethics codes. At a glance, there is considerable overlap between these two codes. In fact, both codes have eight separate sections (or "principles"), with agreement or overlap in six out of eight (see Box 12.7). In general, the AAMFT code places more emphasis on research and teaching, while the IAMFC code places more emphasis on practice issues. We will discuss below the core issues of confidentiality, informed consent, conflicts of interest, and competency.

BOX 12.7
SIDE-BY-SIDE COMPARISON OF THE MAJOR PRINCIPLES/SECTIONS OF THE IAMFC AND AAMFT ETHICS CODES

IAMFC Ethics Code "Sections"	AAMFT Ethics Code "Principles"
Client Well-Being	Responsibility to clients
Confidentiality	Confidentiality
Competence	Professional competence and integrity
Assessment	Responsibility to students and supervisees
Private Practice	Responsibility to research participants
Research and Publications	Responsibility to the profession
Supervision	Financial arrangements
Advertising and Other Public Statements	Advertising

From AAMFT (2001) and IAMFC (2002).

Confidentiality

Confidentiality is a fundamental and essential element to effective psychotherapy and counseling. Clients must be confident that their therapists will keep information confidential if they are to feel comfortable revealing intimate information about their lives (Ford, 2001). As with any other type of therapy, couples and families are guaranteed a certain level of confidentiality. According to Bernstein and Hartsell (2000),

[3]It should be noted that IAMFC is a division of the American Counseling Association.

> The words *confidentiality* and *trust* are inextricably tied together in the lexicon of therapy. Few clients would consent to therapy if any of them thought that what they said in a therapy session would become part of the public domain or community gossip. Clients have a right to expect confidentiality. That is why under normal circumstances what is said in therapy is absolutely confidential and will *never ever* be repeated. (p. 34)

While this level of absolute secrecy cannot be guaranteed always (due to statutory limits on confidentiality, client's involvement in litigation, etc.), many clients proceed with the idea that this will be the case. This is the reason why it is crucial that confidentiality should be discussed at the beginning of therapy, as a part of informed consent and a thorough orientation to therapy. The limits of confidentiality related to any mandated reporter or duty to warn statutes should be covered (as discussed in earlier chapters). With couples and family counseling, however, the same level of confidentiality as individual therapy cannot be guaranteed. In individual therapy, the therapist is the only other person involved, and she or he has an ethical obligation to maintain confidentiality (if the client chooses to "break" confidentiality, that is his or her right, and not a violation!). So it is pretty much a safe bet. However, in couples or family counseling there is *at least* one other client present (and often more). Since the therapist cannot assume that any of the other family members in the therapy will keep confidential the information disclosed in session (i.e., talking to a friend or a family member), all that the therapist can guarantee is that he or she will not disclose any information about the clients (with all the aforementioned caveats). This lack of "security" regarding confidentiality needs to be brought to the forefront, and discussed openly with the clients, before going too far in therapy. Ford (2001) suggests that a couples or family therapist might "deal with the matter of confidentiality proactively by suggesting to the participants that is it undesirable for them to hide anything from each other because honesty and open communication is vital to improving their relationship" (pp. 113–114). In addition, discussing confidentiality as an issue of not respecting the rights of others can help to gain a consensus that each participant will keep information disclosed in therapy private.

Often, couples and family therapists will recommend individual meetings with parents, children, or individual spouses, but does the same type of confidentiality as would be extended if the client were in individual therapy exist? Or is everything that is shared open to disclosure to all of the members of the family/couple? The therapist should also disclose his or her position on the confidentiality of information gleaned through any individual meetings that may be an adjunct to the therapy, *prior to* any individual meetings. Some therapists extend confidentiality to the individuals and agree not to share any information in the individual meetings with the partner, while other therapists hold the position that *the couple* is the client and that to hold secrets in confidence would be counterproductive (Margolin, 1998; Pope & Vasquez, 1998; Woody, 2000).

There are pros and cons to couples and family therapists agreeing to keep secrets. The pros to having a policy of keeping secrets includes being able to get more reliable information from clients about what they may be thinking or feeling that they would be reluctant to offer if they knew it would be shared with their partners. For example, if a clinician is providing family therapy, would a daughter admit that she is pregnant, or a son admit that he is using and dealing drugs, or the father admit he has lost the family's savings on gambling and that he got fired recently, or the mother admit that she is engaging in an extramarital affair and plans to divorce her husband, if any of them knew that the therapist would not keep confidential from other family members information conveyed (Pope & Vasquez, 1998)? This avoids the case of the therapist's being blindsided by a hidden agenda from one of the family members that might sabotage treatment. The cons for this policy are that it requires the therapist to remember what information is accessible to the other members of the family and what information is to remain confidential. In addition, it places the therapist in the position of acting contrary to the goal of open communication between family members (Margolin, 1998). We will consider these in light of the ethical principles below. Regardless of the therapist's inclination, this information must be fully described at the outset of therapy as a part of sound, ethically based practice.

Confidentiality and Privilege in Couples and Family Therapy. Often therapists are confused about the differences among privacy, secrets, confidentiality, and privilege. Privacy involves information held by a person that the person would rather not share, but that does not affect his or her relationships with other people (Glick, Berman, Clarkin, & Rait, 2000). Examples of this might be how the person voted in the last election, the fact that she always dreamed about being a sports hero, her secret fantasy about having a billion dollars, or her first crush from kindergarten. These are personal fantasies, or aspects of the self that are not necessary to share in order to participate fully in a relationship. Secrecy, by contrast, is characterized by information or feelings that a person has that might have an affect on a relationship. These might be feelings of fear, ambivalence about the relationship, or shame about actions that the person has done (e.g., having an affair, using drugs). Therefore, the therapist's view of keeping secrets is intertwined with treatment issues of confidentiality, where privacy may not necessarily be. Confidentiality is a therapist's professional duty to keep secret the client's private information, which is based on an individuals' legal right to privacy. As mentioned above, confidentiality is both an ethical tenet and a traditional rule when offering therapy (Bernstein & Hartsell, 2000). Privilege is a client's legal right to prevent a professional from revealing confidential information in a legal proceeding (e.g., civil court case) as a witness. "Privilege resides in the client, and the professional has an obligation to protect this right, meaning that privileged communications can only be revealed when the client consents to 'waive' his right to privilege" (Ford, 2001, p. 112). Privilege prevents the therapist from disclosing private communications in court, while confidentiality prevents the therapist from disclosing private information to other members of the general public.

Legal privilege of communications between mental health professionals and their clients varies from state to state. Some states only recognize privilege in the context of certain legal actions (i.e., civil, criminal) but not all, while other states extend privilege to all actions (Ford, 2001). Even in states where privilege is granted for mental health information, many of the statutes governing them are so diluted by exceptions that they are of little use (Bernstein & Hartsell, 2000). Regardless, however, it is extremely important that couples and family therapists familiarize themselves with the relevant statutes and rules of evidence in the states in which they practice (especially the *Jaffee v. Redmond* ruling from the U.S. Supreme Court). Ironically, according to Ford (2001), couples and family therapy is generally excluded from privilege "because information revealed in a context in which more than two people are present is not considered confidential from a legal standpoint" (p. 112). So, for couples and family therapists who may seek to protect one client member of a family from another, this is frequently a nonissue.

Confidentiality and Litigation in Couples and Family Therapy. Since privilege is a right afforded by a court and given that the greatest threat to privilege and confidentiality is litigation, it is helpful to go over the aspects of confidentiality when a lawsuit is involved. In marital and family therapy, therapists must inform clients of the possibility that information discussed in the therapy sessions could be discoverable by or forced to be made known to the opposing attorney (such as in divorce or child custody proceedings). In litigation, the rules of evidence in that jurisdiction prevail, and the issue of confidentiality becomes one of privilege (Ford, 2001; Margolin, 1998). According to Bernstein and Hartsell (2000),

> In such cases, the rules of confidentiality state that what is said to the therapist in therapy is confidential and cannot be *voluntarily* repeated, but under the direction of a judge or other magistrate, or when directed under other rules of law, the therapist may be compelled to testify concerning the client, the client's records or the client's behavior as contained in the therapist's notes and intake data. (p. 34)

If a privilege is to be asserted by the client and the therapist, they (or their legal representative) must file a motion with the court. The privilege issues are decided by a judge, who determines what is or is not subject to being revealed in court. If the judge does not grant privilege, then the therapist is compelled to testify or risk being held in contempt for failure to testify and possibly be fined or incarcerated (Bernstein & Hartsell, 2000). When privilege is waived (by the client) or not granted by the court, then the professional is generally compelled to reveal the information (see IAMFC, 2002, Section II E), even if he or she does not think that it is in the client's best interest (Ford, 2001).

Even when under court order, the professional should always try to obtain the client's written consent before releasing confidential information (Pope & Vasquez, 1998). A client can waive confidentiality in writing (via a "Consent for Release of Information," or "Consent for Release of Confidential Information" form) and then the therapist can share case information about the client to the party named in the form. However, therapists must exercise caution when confidential information is released, as the "rule of unintended consequences" is generally in effect. This rule holds that "if the consequences prove to be terribly harmful to the client in an unintended, unpredictable, or unanticipated manner, the client could complain that the waiver was overreaching and that the release of information was not appropriately consented to by the client" (Bernstein & Hartsell, 2000, p. 35), which would leave the therapist vulnerable to legal or ethical sanction. Unwarranted violations of confidentiality represent the single greatest threat to the practice of couples and family therapy. Every aspect of the therapeutic relationship is based on the trust that a client places in his or her therapist. Therefore, it is the therapist's ethical duty to preserve clients' confidentiality and treat any deviations from that (agreed to or not) as sensitively as possible (Ford, 2001, p. 110).

Ethics Codes. We now present the portions of the ethics codes for IAMFC and AAMFT related to confidentiality in Boxes 12.8 and 12.9.

BOX 12.8
SELECTIONS FROM IAMFC CODE SECTION II: CONFIDENTIALITY

A. Nature of confidentiality

1. Members recognize that the proper functioning of the counseling relationship requires that clients must be free to discuss secrets with the counselor, and counselors must be free to obtain pertinent information beyond that which is volunteered by the client. Absent exceptions, this protection of confidentiality applies to all situations, including initial contacts by a potential client, the fact that a counseling relationship exists, and to all communications made as part of the relationship between a counselor and clients.
2. Members protect the confidences and secrets of their clients. Counselors do not reveal information received from clients. Counselors do not use information received from a client to the disadvantage of the client. Counselors do not use information received from a client for the advantage of the counselor or of any other person.
3. Unless alternate arrangements have been agreed upon by all participants, statements made by a family member to the counselor during and [sic] individual counseling or consulting contact are to be treated as confidential and not disclosed to other family members without the individual's permission.

B. Integration for legal and ethical limits on confidentiality

1. Members make reasonable efforts to be knowledgeable about the legal status of confidentiality in their practice location.
2. Members recognize that ethical standards are not intended to require counselors to violate clearly defined legal standards in their practice location.

C. Exceptions to confidentiality

1. Members may reveal a client's confidences with the consent of that client, but a counselor first makes reasonable efforts to make the client aware of the ramifications of the disclosure.
2. Members may disclose confidences when required by a specific law such as a child abuse reporting statute.

E. Practice management concerning confidentiality

1. Members assert the client's right to confidentiality when the counselor is asked to reveal client confidences.
2. Members notify the client when the counselor receives a subpoena which might lead to the counselor having to disclose the client's confidences.
3. When a member receives a subpoena to go to court, the counselor makes a reasonable effort to ask the court to recognize the value of the counseling relationship and the importance of confidentiality to that relationship, and consequently to excuse the counselor from disclosing confidential information.
4. When members are not excused from giving testimony, they exercise caution not to disclose information or relinquish records until directed to do so by the court.

BOX 12.9

SELECTIONS FROM AAMFT CODE PRINCIPLE II: CONFIDENTIALITY

Marriage and family therapists have unique confidentiality concerns because the client in a therapeutic relationship may be more than one person. Therapists respect and guard the confidences of each individual client.

2.1 Marriage and family therapists disclose to clients and other interested parties, as early as feasible in their professional contacts, the nature of confidentiality and possible limitations of the clients' right to confidentiality. Therapists review with clients the circumstances where confidential information may be requested and where disclosure of confidential information may be legally required. Circumstances may necessitate repeated disclosures.

2.2 Marriage and family therapists do not disclose client confidences except by written authorization or waiver, or where mandated or permitted by law. Verbal authorization will not be sufficient except in emergency situations, unless prohibited by law. When providing couple, family, or group treatment, the therapist does not disclose information outside the treatment context without a written authorization from each individual competent to execute a waiver. In the context of couple, family, or group treatment, the therapist may not reveal any individual's confidences to others in the client unit without the prior written permission of that individual.

As one can see, there is a lot of attention placed on this issue of confidentiality by therapists in general, but even more so for the practice of couples and family therapy. With multiple clients, there is a multiplication of responsibility on the part of the therapist to make sure that their information will be held confidentially. The IAMFC code seems more thorough than the AAMFT code when compared side by side. In particular, the IAMFC code takes great pains to instruct counselors about maintaining confidentiality within a practice, especially related to record keeping, computer terminals, and nonclinical staff (E 10–12). It should be noted that these are similar to the HIPAA standards adopted in 2003. In addition, the IAMFC code (A 3) states that unless otherwise arranged, any information gleaned from individual sessions should remain confidential. The AAMFT code echoes this position in code 2.2.

Confidentiality and Perspective III. Confidentiality, in light of the ethical principles and values, can be seen as an issue in which couples and family therapists must balance the needs of all clients involved. Therefore, the issue of beneficence is an issue of doing the good for *all* members of the couple or family. This is not always easy to do. Many times the principles of beneficence and nonmalfeasance are at odds, as what may be best for an individual or for most members of the family may not be "best" for one member. For example, if a person requires substance abuse treatment, it may be good for the family, but it may be bad or uncomfortable for the substance user. In addition, if the substance abuser is the sole provider for the family, a recommendation for substance abuse treatment may place an undue economic burden on the family. Likewise, beneficence and autonomy can be in conflict, as what is best for the family may infringe on the ability for one person to make decisions for him- or herself. At this point, a relational context is necessary to overcome these issues, as most straightforward methods of resolving ethical dilemmas begin to break down (i.e., a Perspective III approach is needed). Counselors working from a Perspective I approach are more likely to reactively frame the question as "the family is the client" and stop any further deliberation there. In contrast, counselors working from a Perspective III approach are more likely to say that "everybody is the client" and continue to work toward a solution that can be just. Opening a dialogue (or even better, continuing a dialogue that was started from the first session) about how it is difficult to achieve a balance and an outcome for all members, at all times, may be helpful. Discussing the need for cooperation from all family members to help the family surmount the particular challenge can be a good consensus builder. For the therapist, discussing the particular ethical principles openly with the family can help the family to see the therapist's struggle as not merely one of "taking sides" in a battle, but really striving to affect the best outcome for the family. Also, discussing the concept of privacy versus secrecy can help foster a more honest discussion in which the clients can process information openly. In this framework, issues of confidentiality (particularly where confidentiality cannot be kept) can be resolved. These issues are discussed in the case presented in Box 12.10.

From the Perspective III approach to ethics, there are several points of intervention with this couple. First, the issues of secrecy and contact outside of the therapeutic session must be discussed at the beginning. If it had been, then the dilemma in the case presented would be eased, but not completely alleviated (i.e., the therapist cannot just say "we talked about . . ." to the husband's question). Instead, the degree of danger that the wife felt that she was in and what she wants to do about her relationship would need to be weighed. In this case, it might be a good idea to suggest a one-on-one session with the husband to try to improve the relationship between the therapist and the husband and then gain some leverage. By improving the relationship, work can be done on the principal underlying issues. If the relationship between the husband, wife, and therapist is not improved to a point where the issue of abuse can be discussed in a context that values each person's needs, then the

BOX 12.10
CASE EXAMPLE OF CONFIDENTIALITY

You are seeing a couple who are coming to you for couples counseling around issues of poor communication, brought on by the wife's depression. Her husband is very reluctant to engage in therapy and showed up forty minutes late for the third appointment. During that time, the wife revealed that her husband is frequently emotionally and verbally abusive. She denies any physical abuse, but you are not sure that you can believe her, because she reported that they have been in therapy before (which the husband called "a waste of my time and money; that guy was a nut"). You suspect that the previous therapist must have found out about physical violence and attempted to address it before the couple was ready to, or that the therapist stopped the couple's therapy in favor of individual domestic violence treatment. At the next session, the husband again fails to show up, and the wife does confess to "occasional pushing and shoving" but then implores you to keep the information confidential. The husband returns to session the next week, and asks, "What did you two talk about while I was gone?" What do you do?

therapy will end up like the previous one. Another point about this case is the *professional* dimension of the case. From a Perspective III approach, the professional and the relational dimensions aren't separate, but are one and the same. Therefore, a discussion of the therapist's duty to protect is intertwined with the building a relationship with the husband, who may be the abuser. Indeed, it takes a mature and balanced individual to be able to walk this fine line and still keep all parties engaged in the therapeutic work.

Informed Consent

When couples or families decide to participate in psychotherapy or counseling, some or all of the participants generally have little knowledge of exactly what is involved. From the beginning of treatment, couples and family therapists are obliged to provide clients with information that will enable them to make an informed choice regarding about pursuing therapy. Since there is so much variability within the field (theoretical orientation, management of organizational or practice issues, managed care), therapists do not have a uniform method of obtaining consent, per se. However, there is agreement among couples and family therapists about the nature and purpose of consent and the basic topics that it should cover. According to Ford (2001),

> The fundamental point regarding informed consent is that the therapist does not ever want clients to be surprised during the course of treatment by some aspect of the therapeutic arrangement that had not been adequately explained in advance. Although the process of obtaining informed consent can be somewhat time consuming, each component of the treatment agreement must be explained so that the client can grasp it fully. (p. 103)

As a part of sound, professional practice, couples and families need to be fully oriented to therapy in an ethically responsible fashion. The process of providing information and gaining informed consent gives both the couple or family and therapist the opportunity to ensure that they adequately understand journey in which they are about to embark. It is a process of clarification and communication that sets the stage for the rest of the therapy: Does the therapist have a sufficient grasp of why the couple or family is seeking help? Does the therapist know what the clients' expectations, hopes, or fears are about therapy? Does the couple or family understand that they can question the therapist about his or her particular approach? Does the couple or family understand how the therapist will likely operate? Does the couple or family know the likely outcome of using such an approach to their problem? (Pope & Vasquez, 1998).

In the particular case of couples and family therapy, therapists must ensure that adequate informed consent and informed refusal (the couple or family's knowledge that they may decline part or all of the therapeutic endeavors) are provided for each person and that this consent addresses issues specific to therapy when more than one client is involved. For example, what are the limits of confidentiality and privilege for material disclosed by one of the clients? If one member of the family waives privilege, does the privilege still apply to the other members? What role will the therapist play? (Ford, 2001; Pope & Vasquez, 1998). Box 12.11 lists some of the fundamental questions that need to be addressed in order to ensure that the clients are fully informed about the processes of therapy before consent is given.

BOX 12.11

LIST OF THE ESSENTIAL ASPECTS OF FULLY INFORMED CONSENT FOR COUPLES AND FAMILIES

1. Do the clients understand who is providing the service and the counselor's qualifications (certifications and licensure)?
2. Do the clients understand the reason for, and the purpose of, the initial session?
3. Do the clients understand the nature, extent, and possible consequences of the clinical services that are being provided and what the possible alternatives are?
4. Do the clients understand the possible limitations of services (including therapist's status, managed-care-imposed limits, etc.)?
5. Do the clients understand the counselor's policies on fees and missed or cancelled appointments?
6. Do the clients understand the counselor's emergency contact procedures between sessions?
7. Do the clients understand the counselor's position on confidentiality for information received about other members of the couple or family in treatment?
8. Do the clients understand limits of confidentiality, privacy, and privilege?
9. Do the clients understand the counselor's supervision obligations to consult about the case?

Adapted from Pope & Vasquez (1998).

In addition to orienting the clients to therapy, it is the cornerstone of ethical practice to gain the clients' consent before treatment begins. This includes thoroughly going through the points mentioned above, as well as addressing any issues, fears, or questions that clients may have. Often, structural issues of how often the sessions will be or how much the therapy will cost will need to be dealt with, as well as subtle questions of clients' overall safety (psychological, confidentiality, and physical). It may seem that the requirement for a therapist to provide accurate, honest descriptions for informed consent can be overwhelming, if not impossible. It is important to keep in mind that (except in extreme situations); it is in the best interests of the client to be able make the determination for him- or herself. Indeed, informed consent should never be a "one-shot deal," but rather, should be an ongoing, recurrent process as the therapy evolves and as goals likely change (Ford, 2001; Glick et al., 2000; Margolin, 1998). For example, a family may consent to an initial psychological, neuropsychological, and medical assessment as well as to a course of family therapy based upon an initial, very provisional treatment plan to help with an acting-out child. Several months into treatment, the treatment plan may be significantly altered on the basis of the results of the assessments, additional information about family system, or the patient's changing needs. As the treatment plan undergoes significant evolution, the patient must adequately understand these changes and voluntarily agree to them (Pope & Vasquez, 1998).

Last, informed consent must deal with the "business" aspects of the therapeutic contract. Financial arrangements, missed appointments, length of session, and third-party payments should be discussed and clarified. In addition, the clients should be empowered to be involved in their treatment planning, goal setting, and/or questions about their progress. As discussed previously, clients should also be informed about how they can access their records, as well as about their rights regarding diagnosis and case notes (Ford, 2001). According to HIPAA regulations, clients have the right to petition to have their records amended, particularly if they choose to dispute what a professional has entered (i.e., inaccurate information, misquotes, diagnoses, etc.).

In the past, the fear was that giving clients too much information about therapy (the "warts and all" approach) would scare off clients or, at least, start the therapy off on the wrong foot. However, according to Pope and Vasquez (1998), the preponderance of evidence seems to point to the fact that clients who receive a frank discussion about the benefits and limits of therapy, at the outset, are more likely to follow through on treatment recommendations and be a full participants in the therapy (less symptomatic, less resistant, and more compliant). Therefore, not only on an ethical basis but as a part of good practice, proper rapport building, and relationship maintenance, therapists should utilize the informed consent process as a way to educate clients about the expectations of therapy as well as the process of therapy.

Consent and Diminished Capacity. Part of a sound, ethically informed therapeutic process demands that special attention and precautions are necessary when dealing with a person who either cannot give or has a diminished capacity to give proper consent for therapy. Consent is useless if it is not obtained from a person with the capacity to consent or the authority to consent for another individual. For example, a person who is under the influence of drugs or alcohol does not have the mental capacity to give informed consent to treatment. If a person presents him- or herself for therapy while under the influence of drugs or alcohol, informed consent would not be attempted until the person is clearly sober.

If informed consent is not possible because of a person's diminished mental capacity (as in the case of mental retardation, dementia, or a persistent psychotic episode), a therapist should find out if there is a legal guardian or a person with power of attorney who can provide informed consent. If there is no legal guardian, it is generally advisable for the therapist to decline to provide any treatment until one is appointed. Even if one is appointed, Bernstein and Hartsell (2000), recommend that the therapist request a copy of the court order appointing the guardian and review it to be sure there are no limitations to the guardian's authority (such as giving consent for mental health treatment). If there is any doubt, therapy should be postponed until the therapist has clarification of the guardian's legal authority to offer consent (by a lawyer or officer of the court). Even when clients have some diminished mental capacity, as a part of good, sound ethical practice, couples and family therapists should provide information to them as fully as possible given the client's ability to comprehend (Bernstein & Hartsell, 2000; Ford, 2001; Margolin, 1998).

Another group of clients with diminished capacity to give legal consent are minor children. Usually a minor child is defined as a child under 18 and unmarried. In some states, some minor children can be considered adults (for purposes of consenting to mental health treatment) when they have their status as a minor removed by either marrying or becoming emancipated from their parents (Bernstein & Hartsell, 2000). Even when minor children are participating in family therapy, and parental consent is legally required and given, the children must also be given similar information about the therapeutic process and agree to participate by giving their informed *assent,* or agreement. Central concepts of therapy should be presented to minor children in a manner that they can understand without excess jargon. Often the use of oral explanations, visual or pictorial aids, and having the clients orally demonstrate that they fully understand the information being presented are methods for ensuring that a thorough consent or assent process has been accomplished (Ford, 2001; Pope & Vasquez, 1998).

In today's society, where divorced parents often share joint custody of their children, it is increasingly difficult for family therapists to determine which parent has, or whether both parents have, the right to give consent for their children to be involved in family therapy. Just as with adult mentally incompetent clients, couples and family therapists should insist on obtaining a copy of the most recent custody order before therapy begins with children in divorced families. It is a good practice for therapist to keep a copy of any pertinent documents (such as a custody decree) in the child's file. Again, if there is uncertainty, couples and family therapists should consult their lawyers before providing services. After all, "consent in writing given by the wrong person or by a person without legal authority is no consent at all" (Bernstein & Hartsell, 2000, p. 64).

Ethics Codes. The ethics codes of both IAMFC and AAMFT have specific sections that give couples and family therapists some guidance about obtaining informed consent from clients. We present the relevant sections in Boxes 12.12 and 12.13.

BOX 12.12
SECTIONS OF THE IAMFC CODE REGARDING INFORMED CONSENT

1 N. Members inform clients (in writing if feasible) about the goals and purpose of counseling, qualifications of the counselor(s), scope and limits of confidentiality, potential risks and benefits of the counseling process and specific techniques and interventions, reasonable expectations for outcomes, duration of services, costs of services, and alternative approaches.

2 D. Informed consent about confidentiality

1. Members inform clients about the nature and limitations of confidentiality, including the separate but related status of legal and ethical standards regarding confidentiality.
2. Members use care not to explicitly or implicitly promise more protection of confidentiality than that which exists.
3. Members use care to get informed consent from each family member concerning limitations on confidentiality of communications made in the presence of a family or other group.
4. Members clearly define and communicate the boundaries of confidentiality agreed on by the counselor and family members prior to the beginning of a family counseling relationship. As changing conditions might necessitate a change in these boundaries, counselors get informed consent to the new conditions prior to proceeding with the counseling activities.
5. Members terminate the relationship and make an appropriate referral in cases where a client's refusal to give informed consent to the boundaries of confidentiality interferes with the agreed upon goals of counseling.

2 E 9. Members get informed consent from all clients prior to making an electronic recording of a counseling session.

BOX 12.13
SECTIONS OF THE AAMFT CODE REGARDING INFORMED CONSENT

1.2 Marriage and family therapists obtain appropriate informed consent to therapy or related procedures as early as feasible in the therapeutic relationship, and use language that is reasonably understandable to clients. The content of informed consent may vary depending upon the client and treatment plan; however, informed consent generally necessitates that the client: (a) has the capacity to consent; (b) has been adequately informed of significant information concerning treatment processes and procedures; (c) has been adequately informed of potential risks and benefits of treatments for which generally recognized standards do not yet exist; (d) has freely and without undue influence expressed consent; and (e) has provided consent that is appropriately documented. When persons, due to age or mental status, are legally incapable of giving informed consent, marriage and family therapists obtain informed permission from a legally authorized person, if such substitute consent is legally permissible.

1.12 Marriage and family therapists obtain written informed consent from clients before videotaping, audio recording, or permitting third-party observation.

2.6 Marriage and family therapists, when consulting with colleagues or referral sources, do not share confidential information that could reasonably lead to the identification of a client, research participant, supervisee, or other person with whom they have a confidential relationship unless they have obtained the prior written consent of the client, research participant, supervisee, or other person with whom they have a confidential relationship. Information may be shared only to the extent necessary to achieve the purposes of the consultation.

Both of the codes have areas of overlap, as well as some differences. The IAMFC code goes the extra step to caution therapists not to overpromise confidentiality to clients when obtaining consent, and then have to renege on the assurances.

Informed Consent and Perspective III. The issue of informed consent is, from a Perspective III approach, especially important for the ethical practice of couple and family therapy. With individual therapy, there is only one person's concern that must be taken into account in obtaining consent to treat. However, with couples or families, each person attending must give his or her consent, which means that all the clients must be fully informed. In addition, the therapist must decide whether all of the clients have fully grasped the issues before giving consent (see Box 12.14). From a positive, integrative-contextual approach, this means investing time in the initial session and taking steps to divest power and equalize the relationship, thus producing a more democratic atmosphere conducive to being fully informed of the therapeutic process. Last, the therapist must set the stage for the ongoing nature of consent throughout the counseling process, either to remind clients of the limits of counseling or to provide the opportunity for clients to reevaluate their involvement in counseling.

BOX 12.14
CASE EXAMPLE OF INFORMED CONSENT

Ramon and Sylvia came for couples counseling to discuss the conflicts in their eight-year marriage. Both clients immigrated from Colombia four years ago; however, while Sylvia has an advanced degree and is fluent in English, Ramon has a high school education and struggles with the English language, particularly reading and comprehending written English. The agency where they are receiving counseling has a lengthy consent form, designed to provide full details of the counseling process. The counselor suspected that Ramon was struggling to comprehend the written consent form. She started to go over it with the couple, but Sylvia become impatient with Ramon, and he stated that he understood everything and signed the consent form hurriedly.

Conflicts of Interest

Boundaries. In its simplest terms, a boundary is the marking point where one thing begins and another thing ends. The function of boundaries is to separate and to allow for categorization. We live with all sorts of boundaries every day. For example, the walls, doors, and windows of a house mark the boundary between inside and outside. Our genders, citizenship, and societal roles all entail some sort of boundary.

Boundaries have special meaning in Family Systems Theory (which is the theoretical seed-bed of almost all family and couples therapy). Utilized primarily by Bowen and Minuchin (and their subsequent followers), boundaries are those elements in a family that—if they are clearly defined—make the family work efficiently. For example, in a family, if the boundary between the parents and children is clearly defined, then the parents are able to effectively parent the children. If the boundary is poorly defined, as in the case of a parentified child who takes on many of the roles of a parent (e.g., cooking, cleaning, working outside of the home to provide income, and raising the children), then the parent's ability and credibility to act as a parent is diminished (since the child won't respect the parents and/or will feel some role confusion). Couples and family therapists will often look at the conation of the boundary in terms of its clarity or confusion, as well as its permeability (i.e., how well communication and functions can be exchanged) and its flexibility (i.e., how well the family or couple can adapt to change). Dysfunction results when boundaries are confused, too permeable, not permeable enough, too flexible, or not flexible enough.

Couples and family therapists must not only take into consideration the clinical aspects of boundaries in determining the relevant issues for treatment, but must also think about how they will influence, strengthen, or disrupt a couple or family's boundaries as a part of treatment. This intervention, in and of itself, is a boundary violation of a sort and must be thought of in light of the therapeutic impact on the couple or family, as well as the ethical values and principles. As a result, we will discuss the therapeutic and ethical aspects of boundaries in couples and family therapy by looking at the problem areas of boundary confusion, boundary permeability, and boundary rigidity in relation to the ethical principles of beneficence, nonmalfeasance, autonomy, justice, and fidelity.

Boundary Confusion. Boundary confusion between a therapist and clients can begin almost immediately. If the therapist is not clear with all members of a couple or family about the therapist's role and approach, then confusion will occur. It is the therapist's ethical responsibility to set a clear boundary in order to properly fulfill the obligation to "do no harm" (i.e., nonmalfeasance). According to Vasquez (2003),

> Many clients have had family or other relationships in which psychological or physical boundaries or both have not been clear, and they are therefore unable to set appropriate boundaries for themselves. The therapist is especially responsible for distinguishing the therapeutic relationship from those previous harmful relationships; doing so is vital to the success for the relationship. (p. 565)

Likewise, each client must be given the chance to hear and understand the expectations, likely outcomes, and procedures of the therapy. In addition, clients need to be able to express their needs, concerns, and expectations. All of these elements are critical to obtaining fully informed consent. This can only result if boundaries are clear and if all parties have relatively equal power (Sommers-Flanagan, Elliott, & Sommers-Flanagan, 1998).

Coale (1998) addresses an additional concern regarding boundary confusion. In what she calls an "implicit agenda" in boundary setting, therapist need is often served but seldom discussed. This secrecy can be harmful to a couple or a family if not discussed openly, as it introduces an element of confusion into the relationship. Since therapists are trained to place client's needs above their own needs the need to clarify the protective function of boundaries to the therapist is seldom discussed. Coale (1998) notes:

> For therapist as well as client, protection is a valid function of a boundary. After all, if we do not use boundaries for our own as well as our clients' needs, our usefulness to clients can be jeopardized. Both client *and* therapist have needs for protection and safety if they are to work together effectively. There are some kinds of clients, life situations, and personal issues faced by the therapist that require very firm boundaries. Others require very little boundary setting. A client who is in constant crisis and demands frequent responses from the therapist needs different boundaries than a client who rarely, if ever, reaches out for help. The therapist also needs different boundaries in the presence of varying situations in her own life. (p. 100)

Since there cannot be a "one size fits all" approach to boundaries, a therapist must have the capacity to discuss how the boundaries of a therapeutic approach will work, and will be adjusted and negotiated according to the clients' needs.

Like all aspects of boundary making, however, there is a "Catch-22" to this approach of boundary clarification. The danger on the one side is that, if client interest is the exclusive focus of the therapeutic boundary discussion, as may be a consequence of a too literal reading of the ethics codes, then the therapist's needs and self-protection agenda will be kept murky and secretive (only to emerge if the therapist perceives some danger in the client's behavior). This secret agenda gives clients the impression that all decisions made about boundaries are for their behalf. The danger of the other side is if therapists are too open with their clients about their own needs, then they are open to criticism from colleagues and professional organizations for inappropriately introducing their "needs" (viz.

countertransference) into the therapeutic milieu. Both of these creates boundary confusion, which, as in families, diminishes the effectiveness of the relationship, and is thus unethical (Coale, 1998; Pope & Vasquez, 1998). Perhaps Lazarus (2002) best captures the "middle ground" approach that is needed here by noting that, "in quality relationships, people honor one another's rights and sensibilities and are careful not to intrude into the other's psychological space" (p. 25).

Boundary Permeability. Boundary permeability describes the extent to which communication and functions are exchanged between the members of a family and, in the therapy setting, between clients and therapist. If the boundary is appropriate, then communication is clear between the parties; the functions to be carried out by the therapist are done so, and the functions that the clients are responsible for are likewise carried out. However, if boundaries are too permeable (that is, there is too much personal information shared between the therapist and the clients), then the therapist may be using the therapy for him- or herself. For example, a therapist may consider doing some family sessions at the client's home in order to gain a better perspective of the family's context and how they live. This is an example of good permeability of the boundary regarding the place of therapy (office vs. home), because it is done with the intention of better understanding the clients. However, if the therapist seeks outside contact (say, comes over for dinner) because he wishes to form a friendship with the family, this is a boundary violation. The boundary between personal and professional becomes too permeable and allows for too much crossover from one to the other. Peterson (1996) refers to this as a "role reversal" between therapist and client whereby the therapist relies on, or "leans" on, the client for personal support.

Like boundary confusion, overly permeable boundaries are a misuse of therapist power, intrusive into the client's lives, and secretive. As Coale (1998) notes,

> The key issue is not the boundary per se but what happens within the therapeutic relationship. The structure of the relationship and its boundaries do not determine its health or pathology; the way in which boundaries facilitate or impede the therapeutic process *on behalf of the client* is key. Is the client being objectified or exploited in any way? Is the therapist aware of the *client's* experience of the boundaries? Is the therapist open to discussing the boundaries and being honest about why she prefers certain kinds of boundaries over others with the client? Is she able to adjust herself in relation to the different kind of boundary needs with different kinds of clients? Is she getting enough of her own needs met outside of the office to prevent their intrusion into the therapy relationship? (p. 99)

As a result, the therapist must be cognizant, at all times, of the status of the boundaries in the therapy. In addition, the therapist must also be aware of his or her own tolerance level for "openness" or permeability, and be able to modify it in accordance with the clients' needs. For example, if the family is dealing with a member who has been sexually abused, family members may not feel comfortable initially in openly discussing their own sexual fantasies of power and control, even if the therapist has a good clinical reason to address the issue. In addition, the family may not be interested in hearing the therapist's own abuse history. It simply isn't appropriate for *that* family at *that* time, and forcing an issue or agenda becomes a boundary violation, as well as unethical. It is the ethical therapist, who is self-aware, understanding of the needs of the clients, and able to maintain a professional stance without infringing upon the client, that is able to maintain an appropriate boundary (Coale, 1998; Sommers-Flanagan et al., 1998; Vasquez, 2003).

Boundary Rigidity. The opposite of boundaries that are too permeable are boundaries that are too rigid. Rigid boundaries in a family maintain a status quo and do not allow for any growth, change, or flexibility. The dynamics underlying rigid boundaries are fear and power. In the face of change or growth, parents become fearful that they will not be able to control their children or that, by allowing their children more freedom, their children could get hurt. In order to control this, they rely on more restrictive or rigid boundaries and try to exert control. As a result, when circumstances do change (as when children begin to grow and take on more responsibility, or exercise their power), the family's inability to alter the relationships to accommodate this change creates confusion, hurt, and acting out. This can be explicit or implicit, but it is felt by all members.

In therapy, the same dynamics are at play with overly rigid boundaries. They are usually a therapist's response to fear or control, and clients are either implicitly or explicitly aware of it. However, according to some writers, it may be partially the ethics codes written to clarify boundaries that may be to blame (Coale, 1998; Lazarus, 2002). In particular, the explicit link between sexual misconduct (a true violation of a client, as well as a boundary) and any other boundary violations has created what Coale (1998) refers to as "some rather rigid and paranoid emphases of the maintenance of clear boundaries in therapy" (p. 95). In addition, the concerns over "risk management" preclude therapists from considering any techniques or procedures that may even run the risk of being seen as a violation of carefully delineated and regulated boundaries. Some techniques that have been at the heart of couples and family therapy (e.g., art therapy, play therapy, family sculpting, and role playing) become suspect in the cold light of litigation and licensing board action. Even such elements as therapist dress and using clients' first names are fair game for risk management (Coale, 1998). This has a chilling effect on therapists and can restrict their range of interventions to carefully prescribed verbal interactions. Where this rigidity can become ethically problematic is with clients who are not comfortable with verbal communication, who would respond better to a kinesthetic intervention (e.g., family sculpting), or who are unable to communicate verbally. When therapists cannot respond in a healing way to these needs, they are acting out of fear of reprisals and/or are attempting to control clients and make them conform to the therapist's dictates. The likely result will be some sort of acting out, whether covert (e.g., not returning to therapy), or overt (e.g., active resistance to the therapist).

Conclusion: What to Do? It is understandable if the reader is confused about what exactly constitutes a boundary violation. There seems to be no real guidance from the ethics codes or from "risk managers" except to say, Don't engage in any risky behaviors. However, according to some, that stance is questionable ethical behavior (Coale, 1998; Lazarus, 2002; Zur, 2002). Sommers-Flanagan and colleagues (1998) suggest the following three steps to determine whether a boundary violation may be "bad": (1) if the boundary violation "objectifies" the client, (2) if the therapist is acting on impulse or out of a well-reasoned thought process, and (3) if it is serving the needs of the therapist over the needs of the client. If any of these elements are involved (objectification, impulsive thinking, or serving therapist need), then—from a positive, integrative-contextual (Perspective III) approach—there is a violation of some sort. The therapist must consider if it is the result of some boundary confusion, permeability, or rigidity, and then seek out a solution (renegotiate the therapeutic contract with the clients, refer to another therapist, and/or seek out supervision or therapy for the therapist). Again, a therapist operating from an integrative-contextual approach will be attuned to these ruptures (big or small) and attend to them. Proper boundaries are at the heart of good therapy, and ethically minded therapists are encouraged to remember this:

> Therapy is about compassion, caring, empathy, empowerment, interconnectedness—the *being with* another's pain so that he feels heard, seen, understood, and accepted. Therapy is not about holding the client at a distance through the application of expert knowledge and risk management procedures. Therapy is, by definition, boundless in the sense that it connects the therapist and client in a mutual journey of healing, impacting both the client and therapist in the process, and breaking old boundaries of distrust, isolation, suspicion, and despair. (Coale, 1998, p. 97)

Dual Relationships. The therapeutic relationship is one that, by nature, engenders a great deal of trust in the clinician. At the same time, there is a heightened sense of vulnerability in the clients as they begin to do the serious work of therapy. When a therapist has more than one relationship with a client (i.e., business relationship, friendship, etc.), the ability to remain neutral or to act in the client's best interest is compromised (or at least can be called into question). Thus, the prohibition against therapists' having more than one relationship (that is, the professional, therapeutic relationship) is a boundary designed to protect both the clinician and the client(s) from manipulation, collusion, boundary confusion, and exploitation (Glick et al., 2000). However, there are some times when, professionally, therapists must have more than one professional relationship with a client, as they sometimes provide individual therapy to clients that they are seeing concurrently in couples or family therapy. Although these are both professional relationships (and not technically a "dual" role situation), seeing a client in two settings does introduce the potential for ethical complications about to whom the therapist has an allegiance (the family or the individual client) and sets the stage for accidental violations of confidentiality by discussing issues that may have been raised only in individual therapy (Ford, 2001).

The central element in this ethical prohibition on dual relationships, however, is the ban against having a sexual relationship with a client while he or she is under a therapist's care. This constitutes one of the greatest betrayals of the therapeutic relationship and is clearly unethical (Margolin, 1998; Woody, 2000). Yet, it is this very connection with sexual activity that has created some of the sharpest criticisms of the code dealing with the active discouragement of dual or multiple relationships.

As a result of the ban on sexual contact between a client and a therapist, *all* dual relationships are suspect. It is a "slippery slope" argument, which contends that any relationship that is outside of the professional realm has the potential to gradually (and inexorably) lead to sexual misconduct (Zur, 2002). This is not to say that this code has been put in place without reason. It is a sad commentary on our profession that several of our own colleagues have fallen prey to this or (even worse) have exploited a client at a vulnerable moment.

Regardless, however, any dual roles/relationship now "carries with it a connotation of sexual or other exploitative malfeasance" (Coale, 1998, p. 101). In fact, some experts even go so far as to suggest that practitioners who engaging in *any kind* of dual roles should have their licenses and professional association memberships suspended (Coale, 1998; Lazarus, 2002; Pope & Vasquez, 1998).

Unfortunately for those who wish to see all dual relationships banned, it is impossible for the therapist *not* to operate in two or more roles. Both interpersonally and intrapsychically, therapists must face dealing with clients on multiple levels. Interpersonally, therapists may have social settings in common with their clients (especially in small-town settings), such as church or religious communities, school or children's athletics leagues, or shopping areas where they may have to interact with their clients. In addition, they may have to occupy multiple professional roles as evaluator for court cases, or job-functioning, and mandated reporter in the case of abuse issues. Intrapsychically, the therapist must also contend not only with his or her role as professional when working with a client, but also with his or her role as a female/male, a parent, a spouse, a son/daughter, and so on. (Coale, 1998). All of these are dual roles that are not sexual in nature, which necessarily begs the question, Are there instances where a dual or multiple relationship is healthy or useful?

In the "real world" of most people's lives, there are individuals who have operated on more than one level at any given time. According to Coale (1998), these occasional dual roles can be "invigorating, healthy, and conductive to healing, as along as they are not secretive or skewed toward therapist interest at the expense of the client" (p. 103). For example, if a therapist is stranded due to car problems and a client drives by and offers to help (changes a tire, gives the therapist a ride), should the therapist refuse based on the fear of violating the dual role boundary? Probably not; in fact, the therapist would be silly to continue to be stranded. In fact, these occurrences can be empowering to the client, or humanize the therapist for the client. Again, the key is that the relationships must be neither secret nor exploitive.

There are dangers both in maintaining the strict boundary about dual relationships and in not paying attention to the potential for the exploitation of clients. "Relationships are messy and there are circumstances in which not participating in a dual role can me more destructive than doing so" (Coale, 1998, p. 105). There are also dangers in sending these relationships underground by making *any* dual relationship suspect in all situations. Yet, there is no way to avoid them. Karl Tomm (2002), a distinguished writer and practitioner in couples and family therapy, makes an important distinction between dual relationships and exploitation:

> Exploitation in relationships is always exploitation, regardless of whether it occurs in a dual relationship, a therapy relationship, a supervisory relationship, or a research relationship. A dual relationship is one in which there are two (or more) distinct kinds of relationships with the same person. For instance, a therapist who has a relationship with someone as a client and who also has another relationship with that person, such as an employer, an employee, a business associate, a friend, or a relative, is involved in a dual relationship. While dual relationships always introduce greater complexity, they are not inherently exploitative. Indeed, the additional human connectedness through a dual relationship is far more likely to be affirming, reassuring, and enhancing, than exploitative. To discourage all dual relationships in the field is to promote an artificial professional cleavage in the natural *patterns that connect* us as human beings. It is a stance that is far more impoverishing than it is provocative. (p. 33)

Ethics Codes. We now present from both IAMFC and AAMFT ethics codes related to dual relationships. It is noteworthy how extensive and wide-ranging the codes are regarding this issue—an indication of its relative importance to the profession. Of course, these are not without controversy and criticism, which will be addressed following the codes, presented in Box 12.15 and Box 12.16.

BOX 12.15

IAMFC CODE SECTIONS RELATED TO DUAL RELATIONSHIPS

SECTION I: CLIENT WELL-BEING

H. Members do not engage in dual relationships with clients. In cases where dual relationships are unavoidable, family counselors are obligated to discuss and provide informed consent of the ramifications of the counseling relationship.

I. Members do not harass, exploit, or coerce current or former clients. Members do not engage in sexual harassment. Members do not develop sexual relationships with current or former clients.

SECTION VII: SUPERVISION

B. Members who provide supervision respect the inherent imbalance of power in supervisory relationships. Thus, they actively monitor and appropriately manage multiple relationships. They refrain from engaging in relationships or activities that increase risk of exploitation, or that may impair the professional judgment of supervisees. Sexual intimacy with students or supervisees is prohibited.

BOX 12.16

AAMFT CODE SECTIONS RELATED TO DUAL RELATIONSHIPS

PRINCIPLE I: RESPONSIBILITY TO CLIENTS

Marriage and family therapists advance the welfare of families and individuals. They respect the rights of those persons seeking their assistance, and make reasonable efforts to ensure that their services are used appropriately.

1.3 Marriage and family therapists are aware of their influential positions with respect to clients, and they avoid exploiting the trust and dependency of such persons. Therapists, therefore, make every effort to avoid conditions and multiple relationships with clients that could impair professional judgment or increase the risk of exploitation. Such relationships include, but are not limited to, business or close personal relationships with a client or the client's immediate family. When the risk of impairment or exploitation exists due to conditions or multiple roles, therapists take appropriate precautions.

(*continued*)

BOX 12.16 CONTINUED

1.4 Sexual intimacy with clients is prohibited.

1.5 Sexual intimacy with former clients is likely to be harmful and is therefore prohibited for two years following the termination of therapy or last professional contact. In an effort to avoid exploiting the trust and dependency of clients, marriage and family therapists should not engage in sexual intimacy with former clients after the two years following termination or last professional contact. Should therapists engage in sexual intimacy with former clients following two years after termination or last professional contact, the burden shifts to the therapist to demonstrate that there has been no exploitation or injury to the former client or to the client's immediate family.

PRINCIPLE III: PROFESSIONAL COMPETENCE AND INTEGRITY

3.8 Marriage and family therapists do not engage in sexual or other forms of harassment of clients, students, trainees, supervisees, employees, colleagues, or research subjects.

3.9 Marriage and family therapists do not engage in the exploitation of clients, students, trainees, supervisees, employees, colleagues, or research subjects.

3.10 Marriage and family therapists do not give to or receive from clients (a) gifts of substantial value or (b) gifts that impair the integrity or efficacy of the therapeutic relationship.

PRINCIPLE IV: RESPONSIBILITY TO STUDENTS AND SUPERVISEES

Marriage and family therapists do not exploit the trust and dependency of students and supervisees.

4.1 Marriage and family therapists are aware of their influential positions with respect to students and supervisees, and they avoid exploiting the trust and dependency of such persons. Therapists, therefore, make every effort to avoid conditions and multiple relationships that could impair professional objectivity or increase the risk of exploitation. When the risk of impairment or exploitation exists due to conditions or multiple roles, therapists take appropriate precautions.

4.2 Marriage and family therapists do not provide therapy to current students or supervisees.

4.3 Marriage and family therapists do not engage in sexual intimacy with students or supervisees during the evaluative or training relationship between the therapist and student or supervisee. Should a supervisor engage in sexual activity with a former supervisee, the burden of proof shifts to the supervisor to demonstrate that there has been no exploitation or injury to the supervisee.

PRINCIPLE VII: FINANCIAL ARRANGEMENTS

Marriage and family therapists make financial arrangements with clients, third-party payers, and supervisees that are reasonably understandable and conform to accepted professional practices.

7.5 Marriage and family therapists ordinarily refrain from accepting goods and services from clients in return for services rendered. Bartering for professional services may be conducted only if: (a) the supervisee or client requests it, (b) the relationship is not exploitative, (c) the professional relationship is not distorted, and (d) a clear written contract is established.

Tomm (2002) is highly critical of the ethical codes related to dual relationships (focusing specifically AAMFT code), believing that the focus of the ethical codes must address issues of exploitation by bad therapists and not the avoidance of dual relationships. He continues:

> But the present AAMFT position against duality is more serious than a simple injunction against relationship complexities that have the potential to be constructive. Not only is the "baby" being thrown out; a pathologizing social process is being understood to take place. It is a process that gives priority to professionalism over personal connectedness. This priority is pathologizing because it fosters human alienation and promotes an increase in interpersonal hierarchy. In the name of professionalism, we, as marriage and family therapists, are being encouraged to avoid becoming involved in the personal lives of our clients, students, trainees, employees, or research participants. In effect, we are being told to maintain our "professional distance." The active maintenance of this impersonal distance draws attention to and emphasizes the power differential between the persons involved. This distancing promotes a process of objectification and disposes us toward more of a vertical hierarchy in human relations. When social systems are restructured in this way, it is the professional whose status is raised. Consequently, the status of those being "served" is lowered in a reciprocal manner. This is one of the more sinister aspects of professionalism. (p. 40)

In addition, Tomm (2002) notes that the ethics board takes the problem one step farther in the wrong direction. The remedy provided in the code is for the therapist (or supervisor) to obtain supervision (of his or her choosing) to keep the bounds of the dual relationship clear. Nowhere is there suggested the idea of allowing the client (or supervisee) to have a choice in the matter. The client (supervisee) is not given a "voice" to bring in a third party of the client's choosing to help maintain the boundaries (Coale, 1998). This would be a step toward balancing out the additional power differential that exists in the case of a potentially exploitive relationship, over and above the existing differential inherent in the therapeutic relationship (Tomm, 2002).

The absolute prohibition of dual relationships is, in its structure, an *ad hoc* fallacy of logic. *Ad hoc* is short for the Latin phrase *ad hoc ergo propter hoc,* which translates into "because one thing follows another once, one thing will always follow another." Popularly this is captured in the syllogism "All cats die; Socrates died; therefore, Socrates was a cat." In terms of the ethical prohibition on dual relationships, according to Tomm (2002) and others, the syllogism is "All exploitive relationships are bad. Exploitive relationships are dual in nature. Therefore, all dual relationships are bad." In addition, prohibiting all dual relationships provides an elegant solution from an evaluative perspective. One does not need to sort out the "good" dual relationships from the "bad" ones (a process that could be unbearably burdensome in a legal sense), but rather to examine whether duality exists. If so, it is bad and the practitioner is punishable. If not, there is no harm. Context and circumstance have no place here. However, it begs the question, Who is this process best for, the client, the therapist, or the evaluating bodies? If it is the first, then it can be seen as ethical and justified. If it is for the other two, then it does not meet the principle of beneficence, or justice, and instead borders on malfeasance (Coale, 1998).

In terms of the ethical principles, it should be noted that those dual relationships that are exploitive (including sexual relationships) are neither good, just, nor truthful. In addition, these relationships are always bad (for both client and practitioner), and they deny the client the ability to make a free choice. Hence, they are in violation of *all* of the ethical principles.

However, what about the nonexploitive dual relationships? Can they be beneficial, respect the client's autonomy, promote justice for the client, and allow for truth to be maintained? In other words, can a therapist have nonsexual dual roles/multiple relationships with clients *and* operate within the framework of the ethical principles? Again, it depends on the therapist's ability to clearly define and maintain boundaries, as well as to negotiate these with the client's best interests at heart, while openly admitting the ways that the therapist's own personal, emotional, and even financial needs are being met by the therapeutic relationship. Then, perhaps, the relationship can be seen as ethical. In our opinion, this is a much higher standard than any specific code can ever hope to attain. It is also the starting point of any good, ethical practice of psychotherapy or counseling. The issue is presented in the case study in Box 12.17.

BOX 12.17
CASE EXAMPLE OF DUAL RELATIONSHIPS

You are about to start a session with a new couple, who are in your waiting room. As you go out to meet them and invite them back into the office for the session, you recognize that they are members of your church/synagogue community, where they are actively involved. The couple also recognizes you, but never associated your name (which they got out of their insurance company's provider list) with your face. In keeping with all relevant ethical practices, you offer to refer them to another therapist and help them make the appointment. The couple reacts visibly, starting to become upset, and protests, saying, "We have been waiting and looking forward to this for two weeks, I'm not sure that we could wait another two or three more. We really need the help *now*." What would you do?

Conflict of Interest/Boundaries and Perspective III. By now, this may seem like a "no-brainer" (viz. an integrative-contextual approach); however, often the simple cases can trip up well-meaning therapists. In addition, the simple cases can provide the starkest relief of the issue for discussion. The above scenario is one in which the main issue *has* to be "what is in the best interest of the clients." The couple seems to be in acute distress and is specifically asking for help. A competent counselor who can balance the surface issues of multiple relationships should be able to see the couple, and, after some discussion about how to handle the inevitable meeting in public, provide treatment with no problem. In fact, to send them away, knowing that they would have to wait a considerable length of time for a new appointment, is *not* acting in the best interest of the clients. Thus the therapist working from a Perspective III approach, after some negotiation, would see the clients with no compunction whatsoever. In fact, the shared spiritual component could be utilized positively in therapy as a resource for healing and to create a quick rapport with the couple. A therapist who operates from a strictly Perspective I approach might do the opposite. The ethical code mandate to "avoid all dual relationships" would loom large in his or her thinking, and the therapist would probably stick to that rule hard and fast. Another possibility would be that the therapist in question (operating from a Perspective I approach) would be apt to exploit the situation for his or her own gain (power, prestige, money, etc.). As a result, the couple would either be sent on their way, with an apology and a referral, or be seen and exploited by a truly bad therapist. In either case, the couple would be poorly served by the profession.

Competency

The practice of couples and family therapy is very complicated. A therapist must work with more than one person's concerns, and a delicate balance must be struck among all of the members of the family. It is easy to alienate a member of the family, or naturally align with either partner in a couple, or with the children against the parents (or vice versa). Models of individual psychotherapy, while sufficient for operating on a basic level, are not applicable to the increasingly intricate elements of working effectively with a couple or a family. Hence, being competent to practice couples and family therapy involves more than just training to be a therapist. Even licensure in couples or family therapy may not always be enough to ensure that a practitioner is competent to practice family therapy. Many states will allow therapists trained and licensed as professional counselors or mental health counselors to sit for licensure without having additional coursework or certified training and supervision in the practice of couples or family therapy. As we have already noted, it is unethical for a therapist to practice in an area in which he or she is not properly trained.

So what's the big deal? you may ask. After all, counseling is counseling, right? Not exactly. Just as in Chapter 11 we presented the example of a licensed therapist who performed hypnotherapy without proper training, which was unethical, we maintain here that those therapists who arbitrarily see couples and families (with their myriad complexities and issues) without proper training and supervision are potentially putting themselves, and their clients, at risk. This is not to say that many therapists who are not trained exclusively as couples and family therapists cannot ethically and effectively function as couples or family therapists. Retraining, or additional training on top of an initial background in individual therapy, can be ideal for practitioners who want to be broad in their knowledge and abilities, as well as deep. It is this kind of love for the field and lifetime learning that Jennings and Skovholt (2004) noted was a crucial component of "master" therapists. Too often, however, therapists who receive a minimal amount of exposure to the theories of couples and family therapy (to say nothing of actually practicing couples and family counseling, or CFT) in their training are asked to provide these services without the proper instruction, experience, and supervision. They forgo the process of getting the additional information that would lead them to appreciate the dynamics and understand the turbulent emotions that can arise in couples and family therapy that can lead to treatment failures or greater harm. This is blatantly unethical, particularly if clients are not aware of the therapist's deficits and believe that they are receiving proper care.

Even properly trained couples and family therapists must be clear about their identity, consistent with their training. From a legal standpoint, this clarity is to protect the public from unscrupulous practitioners who might exploit the client's naïveté about competency in order to "make a buck." From a more integrative-contextual approach, being clear about one's identity and competency level helps the therapist keep a balance between appropriate expertise (in matters relating to couples and family therapy) and being imbued with proficiency in areas outside of his or her professional realm. O'Malley (2002) cautions that therapists are particularly at risk of being "elevated" in client's eyes, because there are usually trust and dependency issues at some level of the relationship. In certain situations where referrals are made or an opinion is asked for (usually pertaining to a diagnosis or other medical consideration), the therapist must make it clear that he or she is only making suggestions and help the client to come to his or her own informed decision.

It is also not enough to say that a person is trained and licensed as a couples and family therapist. This does not necessarily mean that the therapist is qualified to comfortable with or capable of working with all of the subpopulations and issues that the term implies. For example, some family therapists do not have sufficient training (or comfort) working with young children or adolescents. Other therapists may work well with family and parenting issues, but not with couples issues. Last, some therapists have the necessary specialized training to work with high-risk or highly emotionally charged issues like domestic violence, sexual abuse, incest, or substance abuse, while others may not. All of these areas of competence must be fully disclosed at the onset of therapy, and as the issues become salient in therapy as a part of sound ethical practice. If they are not, then the clients are at risk for making themselves vulnerable to someone who cannot adequately treat the problem or concern, which will then "turn them off" to therapy (even with a skilled clinician who can offer some relief) and thus cause them to continue to live in pain, fear, or terror.

Ethics Codes. Due in large part, then, to the unique issues that couples and family therapists are confronted with (relative to the other mental health professionals), as well as the potential for great harm and abuse, the ethics codes of the two major organizations place great emphasis on ensuring the competency of therapists. This is a statement to the public, as well as to the profession, that therapists will be well equipped to handle the issues that clients present, or be knowledgeable enough to know when they cannot provide treatment. Both IAMFC and AAMFT codes devote an entire section to the professional competency of couples and family therapists, especially the educational components of competence. In addition, both codes highlight the fact that training and competency is not a static event (based on one's degree or licensure status), but an ongoing process of maintaining competence that *all* therapists must go through.

Of special note in the latest revision of the AAMFT code (AAMFT, 2001b) is Section 3.14 (see Box 12.18), which gives couples and family therapists an ethical reason to refuse to testify and give their opinions when a client couple or family are involved in divorce proceedings, custody or visitation disputes. In the past, when therapists would work with a couple or family that resulted in divorce, or when a custodial parent would enter into therapy with his or her children, the therapist was in jeopardy of being compelled to testify in court if the other parent wanted to make some changes to a custody order. This generally put therapists in a bind, especially when the presenting concerns did not have anything to do with custodial issues, and/or when the therapist did not perform any kind evaluation for custodial fitness. The therapist who testified could have potentially opened him- or herself up to

BOX 12.18

AAMFT CODE 3.14

3.14 To avoid a conflict of interests, marriage and family therapists who treat minors or adults involved in custody or visitation actions may not also perform forensic evaluations for custody, residence, or visitation of the minor. The marriage and family therapist who treats the minor may provide the court or mental health professional performing the evaluation with information about the minor from the marriage and family therapist's perspective as a treating marriage and family therapist, so long as the marriage and family therapist does not violate confidentiality.

liability issues. Under the new standard, therapists may still have to testify, but "unless the therapist's only role with the family has been the performance of a forensic evaluation using the standard of care protocols commonly used in the community, a couples and family therapist should only reveal information gained in the role of a treating therapist and not as an evaluator" (O'Malley, 2002, p. 53). Now, the therapist can state that giving such an opinion would be a violation of the ethical code, which may carry more weight with a court. At the very least, a therapist can (and should) delineate these functions for couples and families when this may be potential issue. This provision is not in the latest revision to the IAMFC code presented in Box 12.19, but may be incorporated in the future.

BOX 12.19

SELECTED SECTIONS OF IAMFC CODE RELATED TO COMPETENCE

SECTION III: COMPETENCE

A. Members have the responsibility to develop and maintain basic skills in marriage and family counseling through graduate work, supervision, and peer review. An outline of these skills is provided by the Council for Accreditation of Counseling and Related Educational Programs (CACREP) Environmental and Specialty Standards for Marriage and Family Counseling/Therapy. The minimal level of training shall be considered a master's degree in a helping profession.

B. Members recognize the need for keeping current with new developments in the field of marriage and family counseling. They pursue continuing education in forms such as books, journals, classes, workshops, conferences, and conventions.

G. Members are committed to gaining cultural competency, including awareness, knowledge, and skills to work with a diverse clientele. Members are aware of their own biases, values, and assumptions about human behavior. They employ techniques/assessment strategies that are appropriate for dealing with diverse cultural groups.

H. Members take care of their physical, mental, and emotional health in order to reduce the risk of burnout, and to prevent impairment and harm to clients.

On first inspection of the ethical codes related to competence, there seems to be a lot of overlap between the two codes. However, the IAMFC code seems to emphasize specific educational aspects, whereas the AAMFT code discusses the application of competency (or lack thereof) in practice. Both codes make a special effort to point out that therapists must not be careless about the use of titles, certifications, expertise, and how they present (market) themselves to the public. This is to give the client the most accurate information about their therapist from which to make an informed decision before entering into a therapeutic relationship with a particular therapist.

Looking at competency from a principles perspective, it is easy to see that this issue touches all five ethical principles. Competency is a *prima facie* issue when it comes to the principle of fidelity. By definition, if you are practicing beyond your ability, then you are not honestly representing yourself to your clients. This is a blatantly unethical practice in terms of the code and the principle behind it. Couples and family therapists who act in an ethically informed way must be "up-front" with the client about their limitations. As noted above, not to do so violates the principle of autonomy, as it robs the client of a fully informed decision about treatment. Likewise, with the principle of nonmalfeasance, it would seem that doing no harm is next to impossible to avoid if you don't know what you are doing. In fact, doing "good" would be more a matter of luck or chance than skill! The only way that good can result from a therapist who is practicing in an area that he or she is not comfortable with is if the therapist is seeking supervision at the same time. This and referral are the only just solutions to a therapist's dilemmas related to competency. They are the mark of a truly competent, mature, and ethical family therapist, as illustrated in the following case study (see Box 12.20).

Competence and Perspective III. In this scenario, from an *integrative-contextual* perspective, treatment decisions are made collaboratively, where the client's autonomy is honored as well as the fidelity of the therapist. The therapist must be able to actively and truthfully advocate for the family by being completely honest about the lack of skill, and the potential of the family coming to harm (nonmalfeasance) is mediated by the therapist entering family therapy supervision. The main issue here is that the therapist is concerned with how her opinion will be heard by the family. She knows that she wields considerable influence with the family, although she has not encouraged it and has taken great pains to emphasize the clients' power. As a result, she knows that, while she has information to share, she is not doing it as a medical professional (something that she is not trained to do), but as a fellow human being with some similar experiences. It is clear that, if she feels that there may be biological cause behind her client's behavior, then a referral to a physician is in keeping with the standards of practice for the field. However, should she disclose her experiences? Should she make a recommendation to an endocrinologist immediately, or refer the clients to their primary care physician or a general practice psychiatrist? As with any personal disclosure, the question that must be asked is, For whose benefit is this disclosure? It may help the family make a decision to pursue the medical route to hear a "personal story," or it might be just as well to not disclose the therapist's personal knowledge of the story but discuss it in the "third person" ("I heard of a case once . . ."). The therapist may decide to make the referral for a "general checkup" related to the depression and get a release from the family to follow up with the physician and "coordinate care" (a practice that is routinely

BOX 12.20
CASE EXAMPLE OF COMPETENCE

You are a family therapist in practice, and you have been working with a single-parent family (mother and three children) for some time. The oldest daughter has been displaying symptoms that may call for a diagnosis of major depression (increased sleeping, dysphoria, change in mood, etc.). However, you observe that there have been no significant events or occurrences that would account for a depression to set in, and both she and her family concur that this has been the case. You have no reason to believe to the contrary, as you were thorough in your original assessment, as well as in subsequent interviews. In addition, you notice that she has been showing some signs that her condition may be have a biological etiology. You have some personal experience with a sister-in-law who had a thyroid condition that initially presented as depression. She saw an endocrinologist and had the condition medically treated with a positive outcome. You think it may be the same thing with this case. You also know that the family takes what you say very seriously and may be influenced by your story (to the exclusion of any other possibility). What should you do?

done in the field), at which point, the therapist can share her observations and knowledge. However, if the recommendation is too vague, the family may not pay much attention to it. Again, from an positive, integrative-contextual approach, it would be foolish not to consider the weight that her opinion will have, but it is also a greater risk to the integrity of the therapeutic relationship not to have a reasonable conversation with the family about all medical options (with all caveats included). Hence, in choosing this path, the counselor is operating from an integrative-contextual perspective and utilizing the ethical decision-making process, in collaboration with the client, as a method for ensuring the most beneficial outcome.

PREVALENCE OF ETHICAL BREACHES

In the previous sections, we discussed specific aspects of the ethics codes and presented case examples of the difficult situations that many couples and family therapists face. It may seem that, with so many different ways that the everyday practice of CFT could potentially get into trouble, it would seem that there are plenty of complaints before ethics boards. However, the number of practitioners who are charged, sanctioned, or even stripped of their licenses is not as many as one may think. In this section, we present data on the prevalence and consequences of breaches of the ethics codes. We do so because so often beginning clinicians and the denizens of Perspective I risk management use sanctions by governing boards and professional associations to justify a restrictive (and possibly unethical) approach to ethics, creating an unwarranted fear of prosecution and sanction. We hope this information is helpful in providing some much needed context to the debate.

There are three types of complaints: legal (malpractice), regulatory, and ethical (Woody, 2000). According to Woody (2000), it is impossible to obtain precise numbers of legal complaints, since many cases are settled out of court or are in protracted litigation and are not reported anywhere. However, Peterson (1996) asserts that malpractice suits are on the rise. Likewise, the occurrence of complaints about therapists' unethical behavior brought before state licensing boards is increasing.

The AAMFT, like many other professional associations, maintains a committee on ethics and professional practices. Operating under the AAMFT bylaws, the ethics committee interprets the code of ethical principles, considers allegations of violations of this code made against AAMFT members, and if the case is heard by judicial counsel, adjudicates the charges against the member (AAMFT, 2001b).

In a report of the AAMFT Ethics Committee of ethical violations, there have been a total of 1,120 ethics cases in the last fifty years (AAMFT, 2001a). The committee reported that it gets approximately fifty to sixty each year, referred by a state licensure board, a fellow member or practitioner, or a client. The most frequent part of the ethics code that was violated by members was the aspects of the code that related to dual/multiple relationships (Principles 1.3, 1.4, 1.5, 1.7, and 3.8 in Box 12.16). This accounted for 40 percent of the cases that were reported. In addition, of this group, 65 percent involved sexual attraction or sexually inappropriate behavior. The second largest group of violations (13%) was for issues related to competency and impairment of the therapist. Many of these issues dealt with operating outside of one's area of training or expertise, or where personal deficiencies weaken one's ability to practice ethically or professionally. Nine percent of cases were related to disciplinary actions by state regulation boards (a violation of AAMFT ethics), and violations of confidentiality, advertising, and termination (Principle 1) were responsible for 6 percent each. The remaining 20 percent of categories include being convicted of a felony or misdemeanor, noncompliance with the ethics committee (refusing to comply with an investigation), and financial impropriety. Each of these categories represented 5 percent or less of the overall cases reported. Clearly, however, therapists have the greatest problem dealing with the boundary between professional and personal relationships (sexual or otherwise). It would appear that this is an area where further training must be targeted.

Given the percentages above, a therapist might feel discouraged about the occurrence of ethics violations. However, once these issues were identified, what were the results of the investigation? Most of the cases that are identified to the Ethics Committee are not followed up with the necessary waivers of confidentiality (approximately 65%), and the case must be closed. Hence, only 49 percent of initiated complaints actually make it to the Ethics Committee. According to AAMFT (2001a), in the decade 1990–2001, only 281 cases were adjudicated, and of these, 17 percent resulted in termination from membership (the ultimate sanction under the AAMFT Ethics Committee). Over half of the cases (52%) resulted in no action because of the charge being dismissed, investigated and found to have been no violation, or being for a violation that was so minor as to not warrant disciplinary action. Twenty-seven percent of the cases are found to have ethics violations and require some rehabilitative action for the therapist. Often, this includes personal counseling, temporary suspension of practice, or practicing under continuing supervision.

These statistics reveal that, at least for one governing body, the prevalence of ethical complaints over the course of a decade is relative small, given the thousands of members.[4]

[4]An exact, unduplicated count of membership over the period of 1990–2001 could not be readily obtained. However, the number must be well into the thousands.

LEGAL ISSUES AND CASE LAW AFFECTING COUPLES AND FAMILY THERAPISTS

All couples and family therapists in practice must do so with multiple contexts in mind. They practice within the context of their discipline, their theoretical perspective, their particular ethical codes, and finally, the laws of the state where they are licensed. In practicing within these multiple contexts, therapists must balance each of these domains, especially the legal one. Indeed, therapists face peril by ignoring the law, as ignorance of the law is no excuse for violating the law. State laws, in part, provide for disciplinary action, including revocation of license, for violations of the duty to report. In addition, wrongful breaches of confidentiality also subject practitioners to liability in civil actions for damages (Leslie, 2003). Therefore, we present an overview of the legal issues and case law related to child abuse, threats to others, and the confidentiality issues in dealing with clients who are a threat to themselves.

Child Abuse

Couples and family therapists are usually more intimately involved in circumstances related to child abuse and the mandated reporting of it. Whether it is with custody battles, or families that are under extreme stress, issues related to child welfare usually play a role. However, this is often a confusing area, as the line of demarcation between mild and severe, what is reportable and what is not reportable, is often fuzzy. We will address some of the definitions related to the duty to report child abuse (see Box 12.21).

BOX 12.21
DEFINITIONS RELATED TO CHILD ABUSE REPORTING

Immunity Therapists are protected from being sued (in civil or criminal court) by clients or suspected parties if they are required to report child abuse. This varies widely from state to state, with some states requiring that, in order to be entitled to the immunity, the therapist must have acted "in good faith."

Child A person under the age of 18.

Emancipated minor A child who has been given the legal right to separate from his or her parents. Each state has its own law with respect to the emancipation of minors and the consequences of emancipation. With respect to the issue of reporting child abuse and neglect, some states require child abuse reporting even with respect to emancipated minors, while others may not.

Standard for reporting Like other elements of mandated reporting, each state is different. The basic question to be answered is whether you need a mere suspicion, a reasonable suspicion, or something closer to probable cause in order to be mandated to report child abuse. Many states use "reasonable cause to believe" as the standard while others use "reasonable suspicion" as the standard. Other statutes require the reporter to "know or suspect."

Physical abuse This is usually considered to be a physical injury inflicted by other-than-accidental means. It usually will involve bruises, contusions, abrasions, lacerations, swelling,

(continued)

BOX 12.21 CONTINUED

scalding, burning, or other injuries. Slapping, spanking, or other nonsevere forms of corporal punishment, which result in no physical injury, may not constitute child abuse depending upon the particular circumstances and applicable state law.

Sexual abuse Sexual abuse of a child usually includes sexual assault (e.g., rape, incest, sodomy, or oral copulation) and sexual exploitation (e.g., employment of a minor to perform obscene acts or assisting a child to engage in prostitution).

Neglect This refers to the maltreatment of indication of harm to, or threats to the health or welfare of a child by any adult responsible for the child's well-being. It typically includes both overt acts (e.g., deliberate starving) and omissions (e.g., not getting proper medical attention), and can range from nonsevere (e.g., failure to immunize) to severe (e.g., not feeding a child for a week as punishment). In most states, neglect must be reported, regardless of severity.

Emotional abuse The difficulty with emotional abuse is defining the cases of mild emotional abuse. Severe emotional abuse (e.g., barricading a child in a closet) generally will always have to be reported, but *mild* emotional abuse (e.g., scolding, teasing, punishment), while potentially harmful, may not be *reportable* under the law. As with the other instances, state laws vary.

From Leslie (2003).

According to a Department of Health and Human Services study (HHS, 2003), every state except Indiana, Missouri, and Vermont has mandated reporting statutes for mental health professionals. In Indiana, while there are no specific statutes for mental health counselors, everyone is considered a mandated reporter. In addition, most states provide mandated reporters with immunity from civil and criminal liability for making reports that are required or authorized. In general, however, the statutes granting immunity for making required reports is comprehensive, and at the same time the possible consequences of a failure to report are substantial (including criminal, administrative, and civil liability) (Leslie, 2003). Hence, this is not an issue for therapist to be ignorant of!

While it is clear that couples and family therapists have an obligation to protect the welfare of children, especially when they vulnerable to exploitation or being abused, it is not always clear about what is reportable and when it is so. Consider the case example in Box 12.22.

BOX 12.22

ABUSE IN THE PAST, DISCLOSED IN THE PRESENT

Phil, a licensed couples and family counselor, was seeing a couple in their mid-thirties who had been having sexual difficulties. The wife, in the course of therapy, admitted for the first time that she had been molested by a babysitter several times over the span of four years when she was a child. She said that she remembered who it was, but was not sure if he still lived in the area. The abuse happened over twenty years ago. What should you do?

This example begs the question of whether there is a *legal* statute of limitations on the reporting of child abuse. The general answer is that there is usually no statute of limitations on reporting abuse, although there may be a statute of limitations on *prosecuting* the accused child abuser. Another factor to consider is the time and manner of reporting the abuse. Generally, this varies from state to state, but a telephone report must be made as soon as possible. In some jurisdictions, a written report may also be required to be made within a short period of time. If the therapist fails to comply with the law in a timely manner, he or she may be held criminally liable. Reports are usually required to be made to a child protective services agency, the police, or the local sheriff's department (Leslie, 2003). The reporting duty is generally considered to be an individual duty, though there may be some vicarious liability on the part of the therapist's supervisor or employer (see Chapter 14 for more information on supervisors' responsibility).

The state laws regarding children and reporting is clear; however, there are special cases that have resulted in court decisions that are important to discuss here (see Table 12.1). One clarification that was made by the courts is regarding the reporting of abuse that occurred in another state. In a decision by the Ninth Circuit Court of Appeals' decision called *Searcy v. Auerbach* (980 F. 2d 609 [9th Cir. 1992]), the court found that a therapist was wrong in contacting the child protective agency of another state to report an allegation of abuse from his client. The therapist thought that he had immunity from prosecution under child reporting laws, but since the agency in his state was not informed, he was not covered by *his* state's immunity clause. The court sent a clear message that it is up to the agency to contact its counterpart in another state, not the therapist's responsibility. Therapists are considered mandated reporters only in the state in which they are licensed, though the standards of reporting would (presumably) be the same from state to state (Caudill, 2000; Leslie, 2003).

Immunity for Reporting

The idea that therapists can be sued if they report abuse that may not be substantiated can have a chilling effect on when a therapist reports. As mentioned above, states generally adopt some level of immunity from prosecution for mandated reporters. However, the level of immunity can be classified into one of two types: (1) absolute, such as in California, and (2) qualified, such as in Vermont. The importance of the type of immunity lies in the fact that a child abuse report is inherently slanderous, distressing, and hurtful if untrue. An absolute immunity statute holds that therapists are immune even if they make a report that they know is false or act in bad faith to deliberately harm the person that is being accused. However, these states have decided that it is better to provide immunity, and thus encourage therapists to report, than to subject therapists to suits that challenge the abuse allegation. Despite this, however, it does not mean that therapists do not have to go through the due process of court proceedings. In fact, California courts have held that mandated reporters still get sued, despite the absolute immunity, until a court can throw the case out (*Krikorian v. Barry,* 1987, 196 Cal. App. 3d 1211). In addition, the decision of *Stecks v. Young* (1995, 38 Cal. App. 4th 365) decided that immunity is not necessary where the report is true; it is only necessary where the report is false (Leslie, 2003).

TABLE 12.1 Case Law Affecting Couples and Family Therapists

CASE NAME	CASE #/JURISDICTION	TOPIC	RELEVANT FINDING
Wilkinson v. Balsaam (Vermont)	885 F. Supp. 651 (D.VT 1995)	Qualified Immunity from Suit for Breaking Confidentiality	Qualified immunity available under Vermont law did not apply due to the demonstrable presence of malice.
Krikorian v. Barry	1987; 196 Cal. App. 3d 1211 (California)	Immunity from Suit for Breaking Confidentiality	Until a court throws the case out, mandated reporters still get sued, despite the absolute immunity.
Stecks v. Young	1995; 38 Cal. App. 4th 365 (California)	Immunity from Suit for Breaking Confidentiality	Immunity is not necessary where the report is true; it is only necessary where the report is false.
Searcy v. Auerbach	980 F. 2d 609 (9th Cir. Federal Court 1992)	Immunity from Suit for Breaking Confidentiality/ Reporting Abuse	A therapist was wrong in contacting the child protective agency of another state to report an allegation of of abuse from his client. The therapist thought that he had immunity from prosecution under child reporting laws, but since the agency in his state was not informed, he was not covered by *his* state's immunity clause. Therapists are considered mandated reporters only in the state in which they are licensed.
Tarasoff v. Regents of the University of California	1976; California Supreme Court: 17 Cal. 3d 425 131 Cal. Rptr. 14, 551 P. 2d 334	Duty to Warn/Duty to Protect	When a therapist receives information that their client poses "a serious danger of violence to another," the therapist must take steps "to protect the intended victim against such danger."
Hedlund v. Superior Court of Orange County	1983; Superior Court of Orange County, California: 34 Cal 3d 695, 669 P. 2d 41, 45	Duty to Warn/Duty to Protect	It is the therapist's duty to warn family members potentially at risk from a client's violent acts. Extended the *Tarasoff* ruling by stating that merely failing to properly diagnose that a client is dangerous is a basis for liability.

CASE NAME	CASE #/JURISDICTION	TOPIC	RELEVANT FINDING
Thompson v. County of Alameda	1980; 27 Cal. #d 741, 167 Cal. Rptr. 70, 614 P. 2d 728 (California)	Duty to Warn/Duty to Protect	In the absence of a readily identifiable foreseeable victim, there was no duty to warn. Therefore, a threat to a general *group* of potential victims does not create enough danger to warrant a duty to warn.
Ewing v. Goldstein	2004; 2d Dist., 2004 WL 1588240 (Cal. App. 2 Dist.) (California)	Duty to Warn/Duty to Protect	"Equally important information in the form of an actual threat that a parent shares with his or her son's therapist about the risk of grave bodily injury the patient poses to another also should be considered a 'patient communication' in determining whether the therapist's duty to warn is triggered."
Wilson v. Valley Mental Health	1998; 969 P. 2d 416 Sup. Ct. (Utah)	Duty to Warn/Duty to Protect	Court supported *Tarasoff* rule, but admitted concern that the statute "may inadvertently operate to create an incentive on the part of therapists to avoid diagnostically appropriate examinations that could reveal specific threats and result in consequent duty to take preventative measures."
Jaffee v. Redmond	1996; U.S. Supreme Court, 518 U.S. 1	Client–Counselor Privileged Communication/ Confidentiality	U.S. Supreme Court upheld a lower court ruling that, since all 50 states recognize some form of psychotherapist–patient privilege, the Federal Rules of Evidence also (indirectly) recognize the same privilege.
United States v. Chase	2003; 340 F. 3d 978 (9th Cir.)	Client–Counselor Privileged Communication/ Confidentiality	U.S. 9th Circuit Court of Appeals decided that there was no dangerous person exemption to the federal psychotherapist–patient privilege, and that any breach of confidentiality due to a threat to others would be discharged by duty to warn statutes, but that such information would not be admissible at trial.

By contrast, qualified immunity is a type of immunity that granted when certain conditions have been met. Generally, the condition is that the report must have been made without malice or intent to do harm for the immunity to apply. This creates the obvious problem that, any time a report is made, the alleged abuser can merely state that the reporter is not entitled to immunity because the statements were made with malice. However, there are times when a professional can abuse the system and make false claims in an attempt to hurt a client or control his or her behavior. In one case, *Wilkinson v. Balsaam* (885 F. Supp. 651 [D.VT 1995]), a psychiatrist made a report about a client that the client was allegedly abusing (including the use of satanic abuse, and other acts), in order to bring harm and pain. The court dismissed the report and held the psychiatrist liable, stating that the qualified immunity available under Vermont law did not apply due to the demonstrable presence of malice (Leslie, 2003).

Threats to Others

The famous 1976 *Tarasoff v. Regents of the University of California* decision by the California Supreme Court created a new duty for California therapists, and subsequently for couples and family therapists across the country. The details of this case have been laid out elsewhere in the text, and we will not deliberate them here. However, as a result of *Tarasoff,* other states, as well as the various professional associations, have followed suit and created a duty-to-warn obligation. Specifically, when therapists receive information that their client poses "a serious danger of violence to another," the therapist must take steps "to protect the intended victim against such danger" (cf. *Tarasoff*). How, exactly, this is accomplished, is left up to the individual state regulations (if any). This is why it is vitally important for therapists to check with their own state laws to understand the extent to which they are obligated to exercise their duty. However, in most states that have a *Tarasoff* statute, therapists generally will make an effort to contact both the intended victim *and* local law enforcement (Leslie, 2003).

Tarasoff was particularly significant for couples and family counselors, particularly since the issue involved was a couples issue (Poddar was spurned as a lover). Indeed, the issues of power and control over another person are central to the issue of family or domestic violence that couples and family therapists face on a daily basis. The "duty to protect" obligation created by the *Tarasoff* rulings places an extra obligation on the couple or family counselor when they confront the issue, specifically since the perpetrator and the victim are *both* clients. In the past, most treatment guidelines for partner violence eschewed doing couples therapy out of a concern for the victim (Jacobson & Gottman, 1998). This was mostly an artifact of the conceptualization of the victim's having no power and being always in jeopardy at the hands of a mostly untreatable perpetrator. While a number of couples experiencing domestic violence fall into this category, recent research and treatment indications have begun to view partner violence as encompassing a wide array of types and dynamics. Some of these couples' dynamics seem to be amenable to treatment in couples therapy. However, there are two key provisos, things that the counselor working from a Perspective III approach *must* do before seeing a couple or family where there is violence: First, perform a thorough assessment to determine the extent and underling dynamics of the violence, and second, put in place appropriate safeguards to protect both partners and/or all family members (Sperry, Carlson, & Peluso, 2005).

Communication Regarding a Third Party

What happens when a client tells a therapist that he or she knows that someone is in danger of being hurt, or that the client is in danger him- or herself? Does the therapist have an obligation to intervene and break confidentiality? In general, unless there are specific statutes to the contrary, the therapist would probably have to keep the communication confidential. This is because immunity statutes do not protect breaches of confidentiality without reasonable, firsthand information. In the case in which the client gives information that cannot be substantiated, the therapist can be held accountable if he or she breaks confidentiality and there is no threat. However, *ethically,* the therapist would want to explore what would be in the client's best interests and help the client resolve what to do in order to help him- or herself or the intended victim (Caudill, 2000; Leslie, 2003).

A related, but more direct, situation is when the therapist gets information about a client's threats of violence from a nonclient source. Does the therapist have an obligation to break confidentiality if he or she did not get information from the client directly? A recent decision, *Ewing v. Goldstein* (2nd Dist., July 16, 2004 WL 1588240 [Cal. App. 2 Dist.]), shed some additional light on this issue. Specifically, the parents of a man who was killed by his girlfriend's former boyfriend filed suit against the killer's psychotherapist when they learned that the killer's father had informed the therapist that his son was planning to consider harm to his former girlfriend. The therapist felt that because this information was given to him secondhand, he did not have an obligation to warn. In addition, he felt that he could not, by law, break confidentiality, because the information neither was communicated from the client himself, nor did it include an indication of lethality. The therapist won, but was overturned on appeal, with the court holding that a communication from a patient's family member to the therapist made for the purpose of advancing the patient's therapy is a patient communication within the meaning of the statute:

> Despite its privileged nature . . . the therapist's duty to protect that information must yield once the therapist comes to believe the information must be revealed to prevent danger to his or her patient or another . . . We discern no principled reason why equally important information in the form of an actual threat that a parent shares with his or her son's therapist about the risk of grave bodily injury the patient poses to another also should not be considered a 'patient communication' in determining whether the therapist's duty to warn is triggered . . . the information a patient's family member shared with the therapist in determining the existence of a material factual dispute as to whether the patient had communicated to the therapist a serious threat of physical violence to another, simply because the information did not flow directly from the patient to the therapist." *Ewing v. Goldstein* (2nd Dist., July 16, 2004 WL 1588240 [Cal. App. 2 Dist.])

In other words, when the information comes from a source that has the closeness and credibility of a close family member, the therapist must consider it *as if* it came from the client him- or herself. The question arises when the family dynamics are so poor as to make the therapist question the sincerity or credibility of the family member who gives the information. These are questions that have not, as yet, been answered by case law.

Threats to Self

Most state laws provide for situations in which the patient specifically threatens suicide. According to Leslie (2003), in this case, therapists may not be under a *duty* (as defined by law) to make a disclosure, but they usually have the *right* to do so (as defined under the customary standards of care, and the ethical principles of beneficence and nonmalificence). The therapist's duty under such circumstances always involves the duty to provide competent care, and he or she should be knowledgeable about how to treat a suicidal patient. Consultation from another licensed health practitioner or a clinical supervisor, if available, is always advised, and should be documented in the client's record.

The usual treatment during an acute episode of suicidality is temporary hospitalization and stabilization. However, in many states, there is no provision for emergency, involuntary hospitalization for couples and family therapists. Close coordination with other medical professionals working with the client (e.g., psychiatrists, primary care physicians, etc.) can help the couples and family therapist provide the best treatment when a client is suicidal or a danger to him- or herself. Communications with other professionals for the purpose of coordinating care or diagnosis are not generally considered to be breaches of confidentiality, especially under emergency circumstances, but proper written consent should be routinely obtained to avoid any problems.

In some states, the local law enforcement entity (police, sheriff's department) must be contacted in order to properly safeguard the client and transport him or her to a facility. In addition, during episodes of suicidality, spouses, partners, and other family members are routinely contacted, and a plan of care is coordinated (hospitalization, etc.). Family and couples therapists are usually in a better position to make these contacts, as at least one of these individuals is also a part of the therapy. Again, state laws vary widely, so it is important for therapists to understand the specific laws in the state where they practice (Leslie, 2003).

SPECIAL ISSUES IN COUPLES AND FAMILY THERAPY

There are many unique elements to the ethical practice of couples and family therapy. We present a brief discussion of a few critical issues for consideration. These include training, licensure and certifications, ethical decision making, and cyber-therapy and the use of technology in couples therapy.

Training, Licensure and Certifications

Training is the process of becoming cognitively, behaviorally, emotionally, and personally ready to be a couples and family therapist (Fraenkel & Pinsof, 2001). In addition, we would add *ethically ready to be a couples and family therapist* to the list. The minimum level of training in order to practice as a couples and family therapist is a master's degree in one of the helping professions (professional counseling, social work, psychology, or couples and family therapy). Students in non-CFT programs (professional counseling, social work, and psychology) usually will need to seek out additional course work and specific internship experiences in a couples and family therapy setting in order to achieve a satisfactory level of competence. Meanwhile, students in a CFT program will not, because the focus of their practicum and internship training experiences is primarily on couples and family work. Training programs will usually be accredited by an accrediting body of their respective profession (i.e., COAMFTE for couples and family therapy programs), which is an indication of the desire of the program to adhere to a set of standards shared by the profession for proper training of students.

However, despite the standardization of content to be taught, there is still wide latitude as to how that knowledge is presented. The question that most training programs must face is how to provide students with maximum exposure to the various schools and techniques of therapy, give students the experience of practicing from these various theoretical orientations, and allow them sufficient time to make an informed choice and master the theory that they choose. Some programs offer training in certain theories, with the idea that students will get a depth of training over a breadth of knowledge. Other programs have begun to look at ways of training students from an integrative perspective to give students the essential building blocks of skill, technique, and theory upon which the student will be able to construct (or adopt) a particular theory of practice (Cornille, McWey, Nelson, & West, 2003; Fraenkel & Pinsof, 2001; Norcross & Beutler, 2000). Added to this is the question of *how* to teach ethics. Although it is a requirement, the perspective from which it is taught, and the level of integration with the *whole* of the student's training, varies as much as the other curricular elements. In some programs, ethics may be taught in a separate course with little or no integration with other elements of practice (Perspective I ethics), and in other programs it may be well integrated within all coursework (Perspective III ethics).

Licensure laws for couples and family therapists provide a mechanism for the public (and other parties) to identify qualified practitioners of couples and family therapy. Therapists who obtain a license (the most common titles used for this license are "Marital and Family Therapist" or "Marriage and Family Therapist") have met certain educational and clinical experience criteria. All states require a minimum of a master's or doctoral degree and at least two years of postgraduate supervised clinical experience before becoming eligible for licensure. In addition, applicants for licensure must take a licensure exam designed to test the therapist's knowledge of the practice of couples and family therapy, *including ethics.*

In 2003, forty-seven states (including the District of Columbia) had statutes regulating couples and family therapy in the United States. By comparison, in 1986, only eleven states regulated MFTs. This represents an era of tremendous growth in the recognition of the field as a separate discipline, as well as the premium that individuals are placing on becoming legitimized and regulated (AAMFT, 2004). This means that each of these states have a licensure board that polices its members for violations of ethics. While this is designed to protect the public, there are those who feel that licensure boards are overly punitive in handling ethics cases, and thus reinforce a Perspective I ethics (Tomm, 2002). Specific information about individual state requirements can be obtained by contacting the boards listed or through the Association of Marital and Family Therapy Regulatory Boards (www.AMFTRB.org) or the American Association of Marriage and Family Therapy (www.aamft.org).

In the best of all circumstances, only those therapists who have been trained in couples and family therapy would practice it. The skills necessary for being effective with couples or families require some mastery. Yet, too often, therapists practice couples and family therapy with only minimal training and supervision. While there are strong prohibitions in the various ethics codes about practicing within one's level of competence (IAMFC Section 3; AAMFT Principle 3), in most states, there is no real regulation or limitation placed on what therapists do, so long as they are licensed. Hence, many mental health counselors, social workers, and psychologists work with couples or families regardless of training and competence (there are exceptions, most notably in California, where there are stricter guidelines). This is not to say that there aren't many of these licensed professionals who do not get additional training and supervision in couples and family therapy, or even become dually licensed as a couples and family therapist (like the author of this chapter, for example). The *point* is that, with few exceptions, there is no way to stop licensed professionals *before the fact* from practicing couples or family therapy without proper training. It is only after a malpractice suit or an ethics charge is made that there are remedies for this practice (sanctions, etc.). While there are some efforts to tighten up the regulation of this, at the present time we must rely on each therapist to consider his or her own level of competence to practice couples and family therapy.

Just as we have been discussing the difficulty to proactively police the practice of couples and family therapy, the same holds true for some specialty areas that require advanced training and certification to achieve the proper mastery. It is up to the professionals to accurately portray themselves and practice within the scope of their training and competence (again, please see IAMFC Section 3 and AAMFT Principle 3). While there are numerous certifications in both theoretical schools (e.g., NLP) and in the use of certain techniques (EMDR, hypnotherapy) that require advanced training, we will focus our discussion on three types of certifications appropriate to couples and family therapists: sex therapy, play therapy, and divorce mediation.

Sex Therapy. The role of sex in a relationship is central. It provides a point of emotional and physical connection between partners, as well as a source of mutual comfort and pleasure. It is also a biological function of human beings that is subject to the limitations of the human condition. When sexual dysfunctions occur, it is a relationship issue. Hence, there are many overlaps between sex therapy and couples therapy. As a result, researchers have estimated that as many as 75 to 80 percent of all couples seeking therapy have sexual difficulties and that approximately 80 percent of the couples who are seen in sex therapy have significant relational problems (Heiman, LoPiccolo, & LoPiccolo, 1981; McCarthy, 2002; Schnarch, 1997). According to Glick and colleagues (2000), approximately 50 percent of all relationships will experience a sexual problem at some point. This rate is true for homosexual couples as well as heterosexual couples. Therefore, it is important for couples therapists to be well versed in the areas of sexual function, as well as the treatment of sexual dysfunction. As part of an integrative-contextual approach, the therapist's own experiences, issues, or biases regarding sex should be examined as a part of the personal-developmental domain.

While couples and family therapists frequently deal with sexual issues, and *should* be familiar and comfortable with issues related to sex, there is advanced certification for sex therapy. Some states (e.g., Florida) require certification prior to practicing and strictly regulates the advertising of such services, while others do not. The American Association of Sex Educators, Counselors, and Therapists has outlined the necessary training in order to become a certified sex therapist (see Box 12.23). It signifies that you have met the advanced training requirement in the physical, biological, psychological, emotional, and sexual aspects of a relationship as they relate to intimacy. The field of sex therapy has emerged out of the shadows of shame and misunderstanding to be recognized by the public as a legitimate treatment modality for couples who experience sexual dysfunction. Certification in sex therapy is the means for maintaining that level of integrity in the practice of it.

BOX 12.23

BASIC REQUIREMENTS FOR CERTIFICATION AS A SEX THERAPIST

1. Must be an AASECT member
2. Must have two years' post-master's clinical experience
3. Must be licensed to practice in the state you live
4. Must have 90 clock hours of education covering general knowledge in human sexuality
5. Must have a minimum of 60 clock hours of training in how to do therapy with patients/clients whose diagnoses include the Psychosexual Disorders
6. Must have completed a minimum of 250 hours of supervised clinical treatment of patients/clients who present with sexual concerns
7. Must have completed a minimum of 50 hours of supervision with an AASECT Certified Supervisor

Note: Please contact The American Association of Sex Educators, Counselors, and Therapists (*www.aasect.org*) for complete requirements.

Play Therapy. Like sex therapy, play therapy is another specialty area that family counselors have unique opportunities to practice. Children are regularly the "identified patient" of a more distressed family system, or they truly have mental or emotional illnesses to contend with. Verbal communication is not their primary or preferred mode of communication (at least at the level of adults), but rather symbolic representations are. As a result, the use of play becomes a powerful technique for observing and decoding a child's representational world. This world will generally give the therapist clues as to the children's perceptions of their environment, their experiences, and their relationships to others. Play therapy has proven to be a powerful tool for helping children who are traumatized or experiencing significant disruption in their lives due to illness, divorce, or death in the family, to name a few (Kottman, 2003).

There are unique professional and ethical considerations that play therapists must deal with. In particular, working with children requires specialized knowledge and training. The American Association for Play Therapy provides certification for registered play therapists and registered play therapy supervisors. The requirements for play therapists are summarized in Box 12.24. The American Association for Play Therapy also publishes a code of practice that provides guidelines about confidentiality issues, as well as other professional issues, many of which are compatible with the IAMFC and AAMFT ethics codes.

BOX 12.24
REQUIREMENTS FOR CERTIFICATION AS A REGISTERED PLAY THERAPIST

Academic. Applicants must have a master's degree in a medical or mental health profession and 150 clock hours of instruction in play therapy.

Clinical. Applicants must have two years (2,000 hours) of clinical experience (one year post-master's), must have provided a minimum of 500 hours of supervised play therapy experience, and must document supervision of both general and Play Therapy clinical experience.

Note: According to the Association for Play Therapy (*www.a4pt.org*).

Divorce Mediation. Divorce mediation is the process by which a couple meets together with a trained mental health professional or an attorney educated in mediation and the psychology of conflict resolution. Most mediators view divorce differently and really work toward a solution that is best for all parties; there are no winners or losers, and each person assumes responsibility for his or her actions. The differences in an issue for the couple are mediated in a task-oriented manner until a settlement is reached. The overall goal is to negotiate the best settlement possible that will maximally satisfy each partner's needs and interests now and in the future. At the very least, the process consists of systematically isolating points of agreement and disagreement, developing options, and considering accommodations. Even if all the elements of the dispute cannot be resolved, the conflict may be reduced to a much more manageable level (Taylor, 2002). An advisory attorney rewrites the mediated settlement in legal terms and relates impartially to the family as the client, "not to two parties in conflict." The settlement task for mediation includes division of marital property, possible spousal maintenance of rehabilitative alimony, required child support, shared parenting responsibilities, and custodial arrangements for the children (Folberg & Milne, 1988; Taylor, 2002).

In fact, many couples therapists offer mediation services as a part of their practice, since many of the skills necessary in conducting successful therapy significantly overlap with successful mediation (Taylor, 2002). The four areas that a mediator tries to influence in creating a cooperative settlement outcome are communication, attitudes, negotiating methods, and outcome goals (Erickson & McKnight-Erickson, 1988). The mediator works hard to teach people how to cooperate. A communication process is used to resolve practical and emotional issues of divorce in a mutually cooperative manner. Given the two parties' different values, different abilities, and limited resources to face the future, mediation provides a participatory process for them to achieve a successful termination of a partnership that has created children, shared income, and accumulated assets.

Requirements for certification as a divorce mediator vary by jurisdiction and are generally set in conjunction with the state bar association. The minimum requirements usually include some training in conflict resolution, with some jurisdictions mandating additional training for work when children are involved (e.g., Texas). Because this is an evolving, and potentially lucrative, area of practice, however, there is also great potential for abuses and unethical behavior. As yet, the professional organizations have not established guidelines about mediation.

Cyber-Therapy and the Use of Technology in Couples Therapy. The use of technology, and especially the Internet, in the practice of couples counseling is an evolving frontier of the field. Like many frontiers, there are more questions than answers for therapists who are considering the use of these technological advances to improve their services to clients. In particular, only the American Counseling Association (ACA) has specific addition to its Code of Ethics for Internet online counseling (Leslie, 2002b). Other associations have position papers and statements about online therapy, but with all of these, the prevailing message is *caveat emptor* (let the buyer beware). We will briefly outline some of the concerns below.

The first question about counseling online is, Is it legal? The answer is not so simple: yes and no. Actually, the legality of online counseling (i.e., telemedicine) varies from state to state. However, this brings up the first (and oft-cited) problem in the debate over online counseling: Where does the counseling take place? More specifically, what body of laws is enforced to protect either the practitioner or the client? Are they the laws in the state where the client resides, or where the counselor resides? According to Leslie (2002a), "the majority view is that the health service is performed in the state where the patient is at the time of treatment" (pp. 39–40). The same principle applies to licensure, as not all states recognize the licensees of other states.

Hence, online counselors may run the risk of being charged with the crime of practicing without a license in the state where the client is, regardless of their status in their state (Leslie, 2002a). In addition, since many of the professional associations have not made ethical determinations about the use of the Internet in couples counseling, the risk of running afoul of the ethical codes is increased. However, to complicate this situation even more, most states have what are called *long-arm statutes.* These statutes allow a state to assert its jurisdiction over an out-of-state resident for the purposes of litigation if he or she conducts commerce in that state. For example, you can be subject to laws of Texas, even if you practice and live in Florida, if you have engaged in acts that constitute doing business in Texas. The existence of long-arm statutes and the conflicting pattern of state licensing laws means that couples and family therapists who want to provide long-distance therapy (either by the Internet or by telephone) should seriously consider the fact that they could be called on to defend themselves in a lawsuit in a different state (Caudill, 2000).

Other ethical issues related to online counseling are informed consent (verbal vs. oral), handling e-mail communication from clients, and whether not physically being present with the clients, and observing nonverbal behavior, affects the quality of therapy. However, perhaps one of the most serious ethical issues has to do with assuring the confidentially and security of online counseling. The security of communication over the Internet, whether written, voice, or video, cannot be guaranteed unless encrypted or conducted on a secure network. Even then, the occurrence of hacking or the transmission of sensitive information over public telephone lines makes it impossible to absolutely guarantee complete confidentiality. The risks to clients of all of these issues must be disclosed as a part good clinical practice. However, there are some potential benefits to online counseling, such as increased access to quality services (especially in remote areas), reduction in travel costs and overall inconvenience, and the potential for greater continuity of care (Leslie, 2002a). Obviously, technology, in one form or another, will continue to play a part in the practice of counseling. The use of faxes, voice mail, and electronic reimbursement of claims has not ended, but has enhanced the practice of counseling. As with any new growth area, however, the expansion of technology has outpaced the ethical and legal regulation of it. What remains to be seen is how these questions will be addressed in the future, and how the answers to these questions will impact the profession as a whole. Caudill (2000) suggests the following for therapists to protect themselves from long-distance malpractice (see Box 12.25).

BOX 12.25

WAYS THAT COUPLES AND FAMILY THERAPISTS CAN PROTECT THEMSELVES FROM LONG-DISTANCE MALPRACTICE

1. Extensive and substantive notes of all long-distance therapy contacts with patients should be kept, in order to have an "official" record of the transaction.
2. Have a detailed informed consent form that complies with national standards on informed consent and that reflects within it that there are controversies about the use of long-distance therapy. In addition, the consent form should specify the state under whose laws the services will be provided, and the state in which he or she is licensed. Last, the consent form should state that, if warranted, the client may be referred to a local practitioner.
3. Therapists engaged in long-distance therapy should check with their malpractice carriers to see whether they have coverage, as well as to inform them that they will be engaged in long-distance therapy.
4. Only licensed practitioners should provide long-distance therapy. Do not have interns or students engage in this practice.
5. The consent form should reflect the therapist's state policy/laws regarding mandated reporting (e.g., child abuse reporting and the duty to warn).
6. Written consent and an intake form should be obtained by mail or email from the client. The form should include statements regarding client's age and ability to give consent as well as an assertion that the statements contained are true to the client's knowledge.

Adapted from Caudill (2000).

Spirituality and Couples and Family Therapy. Just as with the multicultural approach, couples and family therapists have also been able to more readily adopt an open stance about religion and spirituality as an important aspect of family living and as a powerful resource for the family. Indeed, in the last decade or so, there has been a rediscovery of the usefulness of including spirituality in the therapeutic domain as an adjunct to therapy, or as a strengths-based resource to be incorporated. In family therapy, no one has been more on the forefront of this movement to incorporate more spirituality with family therapy than Harry Aponte. According to him, spirituality can be broadly defined as "the transcendent aspect of life that gives to our lives meaning (philosophy and/or theology), morality (ethics and/or virtue and sin), and spiritual practice and community (social network and or faith community along with the spiritually transcendent)" (Aponte, 2002, p. 282). Hence, from this definition, everyone (therapist and client family alike) can find some way of defining his or her own personal spiritual "space," with common elements (meaning, morality, and community) from which to have a shared dialogue, regardless of the individual spiritual choices that one makes. Aponte (2003) suggests that use of the spiritual in the therapeutic milieu is on the same level as the biological, psychological, or family system in importance.

Interestingly, the most recent update to the AAMFT Code of Ethics does not specifically address the issues of client's religious or spiritual background (except to say that couple and family therapist do not discriminate based on religious beliefs). However, the IAMFC code *does* address these issues, from cautioning the therapist against imposing his or her values on the client to openly embracing spirituality and religion as legitimate aspects of the counseling process (see Box 12.26).

BOX 12.26
IAMFC CODE SECTION 1: CLIENT WELL-BEING

E. Members assist clients to develop a philosophy on the meaning, purpose, and direction of life. Counselors promote positive regard of self, family, and others.
F. Members do not impose personal values on families or family members. Members recognize the influence of worldview and cultural factors (race, ethnicity, gender, social class, spirituality, sexual orientation, educational status) on the presenting problem, family functioning, and problem-solving skills. Counselors are aware of indigenous healing practices and incorporate them into treatment when necessary or feasible. Members are encouraged to follow the guidelines provided in Multicultural Competencies (cf. Arredondo, P., Toporek, F., Brown, S., Jones, J., Locke, D. C., Sanchez, J., & Stadler, H. [1996]. *Operationalization of the multicultural counseling competencies.* Alexandria, VA: American Counseling Association).
G. Members do not discriminate on the basis of race, gender, social class, disability, spirituality, religion, age, sexual orientation, nationality, language, educational level, marital status, or political affiliation.

In addition, the IAMFC code specifically directs its members to utilize the spiritual or religious resources of their clients to benefit their treatment progress:

> Members should pursue the development of clients' cognitive, moral, social, emotional, spiritual, physical, educational, and career needs, as well as parenting, marriage, and family living skills, in order to prevent future problems.

Clearly, the IAMFC code emphasizes the organization's efforts to welcome the client's religious and spiritual life as a part of the client's whole being, as well as part of the family's or couple's life. From a contextual perspective, this allows the therapist to appreciate the clients' spiritual life and utilize it as a resource for treatment and for coping (Bevcar, 2003). At the same time, the IAMFC code is clear in its cautioning therapists against the imposition of their own personal values on to clients (1F) and the pitfalls that this can engender.

In terms of viewing the issues of spirituality from a Perspective III approach to ethics, determining what is good for the client (i.e., whether the client is involved in religious practices that are helpful or harmful) can be difficult. What is a "cult" for one person may be a "church" for another. Just as with case scenario to follow, when one person in the family decides to convert to another faith or denomination within a faith, or decides not to claim a faith at all (becomes agnostic or atheistic), that can frequently can cause the family some distress. What happens when a person embraces a non-Western, "New Age," or other faith unfamiliar to the rest of the family? What is the therapist's obligation and to whom? Is the therapist supposed to get the one family member to return to the family's faith, or help the family to accept their loved one's choice? It is here that the therapist may find him- or herself in some conflict with regards to the ethical principles. In the other example, if the counselor values client autonomy, but the religious and spiritual norms of the couple value conformity with certain religious precepts (i.e., gender roles, dress, etc.), what should the therapist do? In Box 12.27, these issues are explored with a case example.

BOX 12.27
CATCHING THE PRODIGAL DAUGHTER BEFORE IT'S TOO LATE

The Higgins family (parents John and Beth) and their 19-year-old daughter Sarah come for therapy to discuss some substance abuse issues that developed when Sarah went off for her first year of college. The Higginses attend a Southern Baptist church and do not use alcohol. They feel strongly that alcohol consumption is a sin and that their daughter is "backsliding" as a result. Sarah admitted to drinking to the point of getting drunk on several occasions, but that it was no big deal. Her parents revealed that her grades were so poor that she had to withdraw from school and that this was due in part to her drinking. In addition, she has stopped attending church (as opposed to being greatly involved in the church in high school), which is an issue of great concern to her parents. Sarah says that she is an adult and that she should make up her own mind about what she chooses to do.

Since there is an increased likelihood for the therapist to misguidedly impose his or her values on the client, it would seem that it would be important for the therapist to filter their interventions through the lens of a positive, integrative-contextual approach. According to Odell (2003), spiritual work must value all forms of client safety (physical, emotional, psychological, and relational), especially given the nature of the subject and the potential for abuse in each of the above realms. It is the therapist's obligation to ensure that the client's exposure to this kind of harm (nonmalfeasance) in therapy is minimized. In Sarah's case, then, the therapist must explore with the family how to have a dialogue about *everyone*'s differing perspectives of faith and the expression of faith without shutting anyone out. Close on the heels of nonmalfeasance, the issue of autonomy becomes important as well. It is an essential human quality for clients to have the freedom to choose what they believe to be true (viz. spirituality) and how they choose to express it. This is especially true in determining their particular belief system. Couples and family therapists are obliged not to impose their value system or indoctrinate clients in any way (and if they feel that they have to, they are obliged to refer the client out). This is because spiritual work in therapy may call for a deeper level of relationship with the client than other elements of therapy. Clients may feel a deeper obligation to live consistently with their beliefs. This personal commitment can assist the therapists in pointing out internal inconsistencies (e.g., confronting a client who is committed to her faith, which prohibits adultery, but who is having an affair). Again, in the case above, there may be personal inconsistencies in *all* of the family members. It would be helpful to ascertain what the family's spiritual tradition teaches about fallibility and forgiveness. This must be done respectfully within the process of working through issues and giving the client the choice of how to become more congruent between beliefs and actions (Odell, 2003). If the therapist attempts to impose his or her beliefs on the client, then the client's choices of what to believe and how to live according to those beliefs are robbed.

Aponte (2003) sees very little distinction between developing an appreciation of the spiritual in therapy and the ethical value of advocating for justice in the community. In fact, the opposite is true: To deny the spiritual is to act unjustly to the client. Odell (2003) asserts that clients who do not participate in the lives of others tend to be worse off and that couples and family therapists especially are trained to foster connection between family members as well as larger systems. He notes that "spiritual and religious work in therapy must be done emphasizing *responsibility* to the client's larger community, including the family, and both the faith community (if one identified) and the larger society" (p. 27) as a part of sound (and ethical) therapeutic practice.

CASE ILLUSTRATION OF ETHICAL-PROFESSIONAL DECISION MAKING IN COUPLES AND FAMILY COUNSELING

Box 12.28 illustrates an ethical-professional dilemma for a couples and family therapist.

BOX 12.28
CASE EXAMPLE

The Simmons family came to family therapy following a long, painful six months. The parents are Arthur and Andrea, both 38 years old, who have been married to each other for seventeen years. They have three children, a 16-year-old daughter, Savannah, a 12-year-old son, Jerry, and a 4-year-old daughter, Rose. Culturally, the Simmons are African American, and they report that they are "very active" in their faith community (a Pentecostal Christian congregation). For the last three years, Arthur and Andrea have been having ongoing conflicts with Savannah about the way she dresses, monitoring what she watches on TV, and generally disapproving of her taste in music. "It is all disgusting," her mother said, "killing, drugging, and sex." Both parents felt that they were doing "what responsible parents ought to do" and expressed a religious obligation to their parenting. Savannah replied that they "obsess" over her and that they are "unfair" and "too strict." She also stated that they "pick on me" and favor her brother over her.

(*continued*)

BOX 12.28 CONTINUED

Matters had come to a head approximately six months ago when Arthur and Andrea discovered that Savannah had been "dating" a 25-year-old man, who was her former music teacher from middle school. The school and police launched an investigation and arrested the teacher. During the course of the investigation, it was revealed that they had been sexually intimate, which was particularly devastating to Arthur and Andrea. They learned that the relationship had lasted over a year, and Savannah (who did not want to say anything about the relationship) did not want the relationship to end.

As a result of this, and the scandalous publicity that the story generated, they relocated approximately 200 miles away in a new town. Arthur was able to be transferred by his employer, while Andrea stayed with the children and home-schooled them. The family came to therapy in order to "help Savannah to deal with all of this." However, it was clear that the entire family, especially Arthur and Andrea, needed help. In the initial session, the family presented as appropriately concerned about their daughter's welfare, as well as stressed by the upheaval over the past few months (media attention, leaving their community, starting "fresh" in unfamiliar surroundings, etc.). Both Arthur and Andrea presented as mature, emotionally stable individuals with professional backgrounds (she had been an accountant; he was employed as an engineer). They were fearful about the choices that their daughter was making, and her defiance of their guidance and "authority." In session, Andrea began to tear up whenever discussing Savannah's relationship, and Arthur would either turn away or comfort her. Savannah, for her part, did not show any emotion at all when her mother became emotional. In fact, it was remarkable that Savannah seemed to be "distant" and "cold" emotionally toward her family, particularly her mother and brother. Her parents described her as being closer to her father, while Savannah failed to acknowledge whether she felt close to either of them. In regard to the relationship with her former music teacher, Savannah refused to discuss it in session. Jerry mostly listened and contributed one-word answers to the conversation, despite repeated attempts to engage him. He presented as typical 12-year-old boy who is interested in his Play Station and basketball. Rose was not present in the session.

The counselors worked as co-therapists in the family sessions. They were a Caucasian male (Alan) and a Caucasian female (Susan). In terms of their religious/spiritual backgrounds, Alan was of a Protestant denomination, and Susan was from an evangelical Christian denomination. Early in the intake process, Arthur and Andrea inquired about this, stating "it is important for us to have a Christian counselor." It was made clear that neither counselor was certified as a Christian counselor (a certification that requires specialized training), but that the spiritual dimension was seen as an important component of the therapeutic process. This seemed to make them feel more at ease when they came to session, as they disclosed that a previous therapist rejected their spiritual beliefs as "fundamentalist," and they felt too uncomfortable to return to therapy.

In the second family session, despite this conflict, there seemed to be more of a relationship between Savannah and her father, as she tried to comfort him when he became upset in session. There was even a "thawing out" of the relationship with Savannah and her mother as they discussed a recent impromptu "dance party" that Andrea and the children had one afternoon listening to "oldies" on the radio. Yet, the most animated discussion continued to be about the parent's dislike of Savannah's dress. In these exchanges, Savannah vigorously defended herself, stating that she had a "right" to dress the way that she wants. Her parents remained adamant about the lascivious way that she dressed and the negative influence that her music was having on the household. Attempts to refocus the conflict back to the client's stated purpose of helping Savannah (and the family) deal with the trauma of the relationship were to little avail. The counselors decided after the second family session that it might be a good idea to see Savannah individually for a session and see if some rapport might be built in order to move forward on the issue. Susan agreed that, given the issues involved, it would be better for Savannah to have a female therapist.

In the next, individual session with Savannah, Susan attempted to get her to discuss the relationship. She did indicate that she did not feel the relationship was wrong and that she should have been allowed to continue it. She was upset that "he got in trouble over it," and thought that it was "a big deal over nothing." Savannah stated that she had several other friends with boyfriends in their 20s and 30s, and that the only reason why she got caught was because he was a teacher. She felt that she was mature enough to make her own decisions and would try to keep in touch with him. When Susan began to ask more about her relationships with her family, Savannah stated that her mother and father paid Jerry to beat up on her and touch her sexually. She denied that they ever did anything to her, but that they also "paid" her to let her brother touch her bottom, her crotch, and her breasts. Susan asked her how long ago it happened, and she replied that it was several years ago but could not be specific. She asked Savannah if she had told this to anyone during the investigation, and she said that she had not. Susan was very surprised to hear this and did not know what to do. She told Alan about the content of her session, and they both realized that they had a difficult dilemma on their hands. What follows is an analysis of the case using the ethical and professional practice decision model.

Step 1: Identify the problem. Both Susan and Alan have some doubts as to the veracity of Savannah's story. Her behavior has not indicated that she was abused or traumatized. In addition, the actual claim that her parents paid her to accept abuse (physical and sexual) from her brother also seems bizarre. Typically, instances of abuse are direct, not indirect, particularly when dealing with incest, and it is unlikely that *both* parents would be involved. While it is not *impossible,* it is unlikely, in Alan and Susan's opinion. In addition, Susan and Alan agree that Andrea and Arthur seem to have a genuine care for Savannah's well-being. They don't *feel* that Andrea and Arthur actually did this. Although they readily admit that not all child abusers *appear* malevolent on the surface, neither of them has a "gut" feeling nor suspicion about this case (as in other cases dealing with allegations of incest or child abuse). However, there is the strong mandate for them to report any allegation of child abuse that is made by a child. This is where their dilemma lies. Do they report an allegation that they do not believe is credible, but that they cannot dismiss out of hand, or do they disregard the law and hope that there isn't any truth to the allegations?

Step 2: Identify the participants affected by the decision. Specifically, the individuals involved are Susan, Alan, Andrea, Arthur, Savannah, and Jerry. If the Department of Family and Children's Services becomes involved, Rose could be affected too. If there is legal action taken, Susan and Alan's organization, as well as their supervisors, could be impacted by their course of action.

Step 3: Identify potential courses of action, along with possible benefits and risks for the participants. Alan and Susan felt that they had three options, and none of the options were particularly palatable for them.

Option 1. Alan and Susan make a report to the child protective services department.

Benefit: Alan and Susan would be discharging their duty according to the letter of the law.

Risk: Although there would be few negative repercussions for them, if Alan and Susan did make a report of the allegation, as the law in their state required, it could launch an investigation, and the kids could (theoretically) be taken away either temporarily or permanently. However, it is more likely that it will cause more chaos for the family that may very well be needless. This course of action also runs the risk of ruining any therapeutic rapport, regardless of the outcome, and the family may refuse to continue therapy.

Option 2. Susan and Alan could delay making the report until they had more information, or not report at all.

Benefit: It would preserve the therapeutic relationship with the family.

Risk: They wondered, if they choose not to report the allegation, how it might affect Savannah. It could destroy any trust or rapport with her, as she may feel dismissed or disregarded. Would she feel that it is the adults versus her, and would that merely set up more power struggles and reinforce her mindset? In addition, they considered what the personal consequences would be if they did not make the report given the fact that it does violate the mandated reporter law of their state.

Option 3. Susan and Alan could let Andrea and Arthur make the report directly and follow up.

Benefit: This approach would give Andrea and Arthur the courtesy of first hearing the accusation in private and to process their reactions in a safe environment. Then the parents could decide how to best prepare themselves to both confront Savannah and inform the authorities. This would have the benefit of giving the family a neutral place to appropriately discuss the allegation and the issue surrounding it. The therapists should adopt a stance that would attempt to preserve as much of the therapeutic relationship as possible and communicate to the parents that, while the report was a necessary part of the therapy, Susan and Alan would do everything possible to make the process bearable.

Risk: The parents may distrust the therapists and refuse to make the report, forcing Alan and Susan to do it. In addition, the parents may accuse the therapists of taking their daughter's side when she was making up a lie to strike back at them. Ultimately, this may lead to a withdrawing from counseling (perhaps permanently).

Step 4: Evaluate the benefits and risks for each course of action based on contextual considerations.

Contextual Domain Considerations

In terms of their personal-developmental stage, Alan and Susan have very similar experiences, and both seem to be moving beyond Level 2 and toward Level 3. Both counselors are feeling more confident about their ability to appraise situations and make treatment decisions. In addition, they have worked as co-therapists for a while and have developed a good peer supervisory relationship. Each knows that, if the other had a strong objection or opinion, he or she would voice it. They each feel strongly that, while the law is clear about mandated reporting of abuse allegations by a minor, there can be some accommodation in the way their obligation is fulfilled that will not be callous or indifferent to their circumstances, thus protecting the therapeutic relationship. Moreover, in this particular instance, they are sensitive about the impact that their disclosure will have on Savannah's relationship with her parents, recognizing that it is vital for the family to begin the healing process from the trauma that they have experienced. Hence, Option 1 is less appealing.

In terms of the relational issues with the clients, Susan has acknowledged that she has some sympathy for the Simmons's plight, given the similarities in their spiritual backgrounds. Recently, Susan's mother died following a long illness, during which she had spent a lot of time caring for her mother. Therefore, she and Alan discussed the possible countertransference to Andrea and the sense of irritation she feels at Savannah for putting her mother through more pain. Alan, for his part, does shares neither the spiritual nor cultural backgrounds of the clients, but is open to exploring how their spiritual lives provide courage and strength, as well as possibly truncate their range of expression of their frustration (though not the feelings of frustration themselves). Alan's particular struggle is with the expression of strong emotions in family sessions, stemming from his family-of-origin issues related to an often unpredictable, alcoholic mother. In the past, this has led him to "overintellectualize" in session with clients when things become tense. As a result of his own therapy, as well as supervision, he has been able to identify when this happens. Likewise, he and Susan have worked out a method for signaling one another when Alan was beginning to prematurely shut down a family's emotional process. In addition, both acknowledge the fact that they are Caucasian and may not readily understand the Simmons's struggle, being an African American couple that is raising a teenage daughter in the present time. They believe that they can create a place in the therapy to discuss how this can cause high levels of anxiety and give them a chance to explore this issue in an open forum while simultaneously "educating" Susan and Alan. Last, both work in an organization that stresses supervision, especially for difficult situations, and provides plenty of opportunities for it. In addition, the organization takes a client-focused stance and advocates strongly for its staff to consider all the potential benefits and consequences of making a report before doing so.

Professional Domain Considerations

Professionally, the issues related to child abuse are clear. Couples and family therapists are in unique positions to be able to play an effective role in prevention and correction of abuse, and the law gives them the tools to do it (viz. mandated reporting laws). However, this means that there must be vigilance on the part of practitioners. Too often in the past, it has been easy to either say, "She or he doesn't fit the stereotype" or ignore the matter altogether. Sadly, this meant that children continued to experience abuse, even while in some form of professional "care" (from doctors, therapists, etc.). At the same time, there are also the treatment issues related to the whole family. For Susan and Alan, it means that, while they cannot simply ignore Savannah's statements, they must decide on how to act. The first thing is to obtain more information and corroborate the allegation while being sensitive to the family. Coale (1998) recommends that all allegations (child and adult) of abuse must be evaluated within the *context* in which the individual is living. She recommends that, unless there are overwhelming reasons (e.g., danger to the victim) to the contrary, the family *must* be included in the treatment discussions, including how to handle the report of abuse. The question for Alan and Susan, then, is how to deal with Savannah's allegations as quickly as possible, in a way that does not disregard the impact on the therapeutic process with either the parents or Savannah, but opens the family up to making further therapeutic progress (which makes Option 2 less realistic).

Ethical/Legal Domain Considerations

According to the IAMFC code, as well as state law, there are several relevant codes that relate to this case. Principle II, Section C.2 clearly states that "members may disclose confidences when required by a specific law such as a child abuse reporting statute." The AAMFT code has a similar section (2.1), but does not explicitly reference child abuse. However, this is assumed under state law, which is in place in Susan and Alan's state. The convergence of ethics code and state law is unequivocal and not open to much leeway. As a result, Option 2 must be ruled out, given their level of concern.

Step 5: Consult with peers and experts. Susan and Alan consulted with their supervisor, a licensed psychologist and marriage and family therapist with over twenty years' experience in the field. He agreed that there were some startling aspects to the allegation, which did not seem to fit. While he expressed sympathy for the parents and what they have gone through, he encouraged them to think about the larger picture of what Savannah's behavior might be trying to say on "metalevel" about her perceptions of the family or of the family's response to all of the trauma. He reminded them that she probably perceives her household as even stricter now than before, so that her power to make choices for herself is limited or that the choices that she makes are scrutinized. She may not be accepting the spiritual worldview that dominates her parent's lives and is struggling to come to her own determination of how she will live her life. Regardless of the truth of the allegation, he also suggested that Savannah may be struggling to find some deeper meaning for the experience that she had with the teacher and the feelings that it brings up. He reflected that she may not feel that she can say anything positive about the relationship, which limits her ability to cope with the aftermath of it (the publicity, the relocation, etc.). While he took the obligation to report seriously, he endorsed Option 3 as the best of the ones proposed.

In addition, Alan contacted a former professor who had some expertise on sexual abuse survivors to provide another context for their decision making about Savannah. The professor provided some guidance about how to approach the parents and concurred with the other professional about the veracity of the story. However, she did express to Alan the concern that Savannah may feel (or actually be) scapegoated and "blamed" at a time when she is reaching out for some help. The professor encouraged Alan to make sure that Savannah's needs were taken into account when implementing the final plan. A final resource for them would also be the agency's lawyer, to discuss the impact of such a disclosure on the agency, as well as the legal consultation help line provided through the professional organizations that Susan and Alan belonged to, in order to give some information about their own course of action. However, in this case, they did not use this option.

Step 6: Decide on the most feasible option and document the decision-making process. Following extensive consultation, the consensus about a course of action seemed to revolve around Option 3. This seemed to both relieve Alan and Susan of their legal responsibility (which was clear, despite their misgivings), but also hold out the hope of preserving as much of the therapeutic relationship as possible. Alan and Susan would have to be skilled in simultaneously managing Arthur and Andrea's anxiety and probably disappointment, while keeping them engaged in the long-term therapeutic goals. This may include couples counseling in addition to the family counseling that they were undergoing.

For Savannah, it was decided that it would be made clear that her concerns were being taken seriously because of the serious nature of her allegations. Susan and Alan knew that they had to check their suspicions of her story, so as to not participate in a "blaming of the victim." In her individual session, Susan told Savannah that she would have to make some form of report of this allegation, which did not elicit much of a response from Savannah. In addition, she was be reminded of the limits to confidentiality that she was informed of at the beginning of counseling. She would also be offered individual counseling as an adjunct to the family counseling. They decided that they would frame her context in the larger picture of feeling helpless and wanting to reassert her own control over something, after she had lost *everything*.

Step 7: Implement, evaluate, and document the enacted decision. Both Alan and Susan decided that the best course of action would be to invite the family back for the next regularly scheduled session and bring Arthur and Andrea in alone first to discuss the allegation. This would allow them to process it with the therapists and to hear the course of action that would be taken next. Next, they would bring in Savannah and discuss what had been talked about with her parents, then give her an opportunity to confront her parents, process her feelings with Susan, or to wait for an investigator from Child and Family Services. Next, the counselors would invite the parents to contact the local Department of Child and Family Services and report the allegation themselves; then Susan would speak to the investigator and report what she had heard. Savannah would be invited to participate as well, if she chose, and be given the option to talk in the session room (with her parents present) or in a separate room alone. Then the entire family would process the event and discuss the next course of action.

The parents came into the session and were shocked by the information. Andrea began to break down and cry, saying, "it's not true, it's not true." Arthur was visibly agitated and also denied the allegation. Susan and Alan validated their feelings and reflected how this might seem like one more unbearable stressor, but reframed it in the context of helping Savannah process part of the trauma that has happened to her. They were invited to view this sequence of events as a way to start healing not only her wounds, but the wounds inflicted on the family as well. Susan stated that all of the losses brought about a sense of victimhood that all three of them shared, and that they could each find ways to empower one another to not let this "rob them of their joy" (a reference to Scripture). Understandably, they struggled to accept this and chose to focus on the fear of having their children taken away from them. It was explained to them that, while the allegations were serious, there were other circumstances (e.g., the investigation surrounding the relationship with the teacher) that would also be taken into consideration. This seemed to reassure both of them.

When Savannah came into the session, she did not betray any emotion when Susan told her what was told to her parents. When she was asked how she felt, she replied, "fine." Her mother was surprised and asked, "When did we ever do this? When did we ever make you feel this way?" Savannah seemed to change her story when she replied that, when Jerry used to play rough with her, Arthur and Andrea would tell her to ignore him or to keep playing with him. When asked specifically about the sexual aspects, Savannah stated, "He would sometimes touch my butt." She never gave any explanation about other sexual acts and never directly accused her parents of participating in any activity. They then contacted the Department of Family and Children Services, who opened a preliminary investigation into the matter. When Savannah saw her father begin to silently weep, she finally showed some emotion and said, "I don't know, I guess I didn't know what else to say. I didn't mean to hurt you." Andrea expressed her anger, saying, "Well, you have a funny way of showing it! Now we are going to go through all of this!" Alan intervened to de-escalate the tension, and refocused attention on the family's experience at that moment and over the last six months.

Within two weeks, Savannah and Jerry had been interviewed at school, and both Arthur and Andrea were interviewed. Susan was also interviewed, and the case was ultimately closed. The Simmons family continued therapy for three months and focused on the need to process what had happened to them and find strengths in what they have endured. In addition, they worked on negotiating how to work with one another. They were able to use the sessions effectively, with Savannah attending several individual sessions. By discharge, everyone agreed that they were working more closely with one another.

KEY POINTS

1. By virtue of its work with multiple clients in the same session, couples and family therapy is a lived relational experience that is unique in its practice, as well in the application of Perspective III ethical considerations.
2. Family systems theory, as a result of its focus on multiple levels of interaction at the same time, makes it easy for couples and family therapists to adopt a positive, integrative-contextual approach to ethical practice.
3. The process of informed consent, from an integrative-contextual approach, is a continuing process of dialogue with the client, and communicates genuine respect for the clients' ability to make decisions about their care.
4. Confidentiality is the cornerstone of all couples and family therapy. Confidentiality protects the dignity of those who seek counseling. Proper respect for the confidentiality of clients upholds the integrity of the counseling process.
5. Couples and family therapists who practice from an integrative-contextual approach are proactive and act upon the premise that confidential communication supports positive counseling outcomes.
6. Boundary permeability in the practice of couples and family therapy can often lead to boundary crossings that, if they are not exploitive in nature, may facilitate the therapeutic relationship. This is in keeping with a Perspective III approach to ethical practice.
7. The multiple relationships and/or functions that are inherent in the therapeutic relationship are congruent with a positive, integrative-contextual approach. This calls into question the absolute prohibition on multiple relationships.
8. A lifelong desire to learn is the ultimate expression of competence and Perspective III ethics, while rigid reliance on board certifications as an expression of competence is indicative of a Perspective I approach to ethics.
9. While case laws may have shaped the Perspective I approach to ethics, couples and family therapists can maintain a positive, integrative-contextual approach while upholding the law. This is especially true in the areas of mandated reporting of abuse and of protecting the client or someone else from harm in a way that is proportional to the needs of the client as well as the demands of the situation.

10. The positive, integrative-contextual approach to ethics applies not just to the routine practice of couples and family therapy, but also to subspecialties of couples and family counseling (such as sex therapy, play therapy, and divorce mediation). Couples and family therapists who work in these areas generally evaluate their practice along similar dimensions as the positive, integrative-contextual approach.
11. Play therapy is an effective modality for delivering treatment to children in families. However, there are particular issues and concerns that well-trained play therapists share in common with counselors operating from an integrative-contextual approach. These include confidentiality, informed consent, conflicts of interest, and competence.
12. Divorce mediation is a method for couples and family therapists operating from an integrative-contextual approach to provide clients with a framework to contain the potential long-term damage to the individuals (particularly children) in the family by focusing on strategies for relationship maintenance.
13. Sex is a crucial dimension of couples' functioning. As such, clinicians operating from a Perspective III approach recognize the inherent value of exploring with clients the intricacies and impact of sexual functioning as an integral part of the relationship and of evaluating their own areas of discomfort with sexual issues.
14. Spirituality is a vital part of many couples' and families' existence. In addition, it can be a powerful adjunct to positive treatment gains. While there has been some misunderstanding of this domain in the past, couples and family therapists operating from an integrative-contextual approach value the couple or family's perspective and experience of the spiritual in a way that is accepting and respectful.
15. The application of the seven-step contextual ethical decision-making model allows couples and family therapists to generate alternative solutions and evaluate them according to a positive, integrative-contextual model of practice that assesses the impact that each has on the couple or family.

REVIEW QUESTIONS

1. What would you do if a client you were seeing both individually and in couples counseling asked you to not tell her husband that she is having an affair?
2. Do you think confidentiality can be guaranteed in family counseling? Why or why not?
3. Do you think the additional requirements for play therapy, divorce mediation, and sex therapy are warranted? Why or why not?
4. Under what circumstances would you recommend that a couple divorce?
5. Do you think that family counseling can be effective if one or more of the family members refuses to take part in the counseling process?

REFERENCES

American Association of Marriage and Family Therapy. (2001a, June/July). Do all ethics complaints end in termination of membership? *Family Therapy News*, 8–9.

American Association of Marriage and Family Therapy. (2001b). *AAMFT code of ethical principles for marriage and family therapists*. Washington, DC: Author.

American Association of Marriage and Family Therapy. (2004, March/April). What do MFTs get paid? *Family Therapy Magazine*, 32–33.

Aponte, H. J. (1994). How personal can training get? *Journal of Marital and Family Therapy*, 20(1), 3–15.

Aponte, H. J. (2002). Spirituality: The heart of therapy. *The Journal of Family Psychotherapy*, *13*(1/2), 13–27.

Aponte, H. (2003, September/October). The soul of the marriage and family therapist. *Family Therapy Magazine, 2*(5), 15–19.

Bernstein, B. E., & Hartsell, T. L. (2000). *The portable ethicist for mental health professionals: An A–Z guide to responsible practice.* New York: Wiley.

Bevcar, D. S. (2003). Utilizing spiritual resources as an adjunct to family therapy. *Family Therapy Magazine, 2*(5), 31–33.

Carter, B., & McGoldrick, M. (2004). *The expanded family life cycle: Individual, family, and social perspectives* (3rd ed.). Boston: Allyn and Bacon.

Caudill, O. B. (2000, February/March). Let your fingers do the walking to the courthouse: Long distance liability. *Family Therapy News.*

Coale, H. W. (1998). *The vulnerable therapist: Practicing psychotherapy in and age of anxiety.* New York: Haworth Press.

Corey, G., Corey, M. S., & Callanan, P. (1998). *Issues and ethics in the helping professions.* Monterey, CA: Brooks/Cole.

Cornille, T. A., McWey, L. M., Nelson, T. S., & West, S. H. (2003). How do master's level marriage and family therapists view their basic therapy skills? An examination of generic and theory specific clinical approaches to family therapy. *Contemporary Family Therapy, 25*(1), 41–61.

Erickson, S. K., & McKnight-Erickson, M. S. (1988). *Family mediation casebook: Theory and process.* Philadelphia, PA: Brunner/Mazel.

Folberg, J., & Milne, A. (1988). *Divorce mediation: Theory and practice.* New York: Guilford.

Ford, G. G. (2001). *Ethical reasoning in the mental health professions.* Boca Raton, FL: CRC Press.

Fraenkel, P., & Pinsof, W. M. (2001). Teaching family therapy-centered integration: Assimilation and beyond. *Journal of Psychotherapy Integration, 11*(1), 59–85.

Glick, I. D., Berman, E. M., Clarkin, J. F., & Rait, D. S. (2000). *Marital and family therapy* (4th ed.). Washington, DC: American Psychiatric Press.

Haber, R. (1996). *Dimensions of psychotherapy and supervision: Maps and means.* New York: Norton.

Heiman, J., LoPiccolo, L., & LoPiccolo, J. (1981). The treatment of sexual dysfunction. In A. Gurman & D. Kniskern (Eds.), *Handbook of family therapy.* New York: Brunner/Mazel.

International Association of Marriage and Family Counselors. (2002). *IAMFC ethical codes.* Available from http://www.iamfc.org/ethicalcodes.htm

Jacobson, N. S., & Gottman, J. M. (1998). *When men batter women.* New York: Simon and Schuster.

Job Accommodation Network (JAN). (2004). *ADA questions and answers.* [Online]. Retrieved October 2004 from www.jan.wvu.edu/links/ADAqta.html

Kitchener, K. S. (1986). Teaching applied ethics in counselor education: An integration of psychological processes and philosophical analysis. *Journal of Counseling and Development, 64*(1), 306–310.

Kottman, T. (2003). *Partners in play: An Adlerian approach to play therapy* (2nd ed.). Alexandria, VA: American Counseling Association.

Lazarus, A. A. (2002). How certain boundaries and ethics diminish therapeutic effectiveness. In A. A. Lazarus & O. Zur (Eds.), *Dual relationships and psychotherapy* (pp. 25–31). New York: Springer.

Leslie, R. S. (2002a, March/April). New federal privacy regulations: What you need to know and do. *Family Therapy Magazine, 1*(2), 41–43.

Leslie, R. S. (2002b, September/October). Practicing therapy via the Internet: The legal view. *Family Therapy Magazine, 1*(5), 39–41.

Leslie, R. S. (2003). Ethical and legal matters: The dangerous patient and confidentiality. *Family Therapy Magazine, 2*(6), 43–45.

Margolin, G. (1998). Ethical issues in marital therapy. In R. M. Anderson, T. L. Needles, et al. (Eds.), *Avoiding ethical misconduct in specialty areas* (pp. 78–94). Springfield, IL: Charles C. Thomas.

McCarthy, B. W. (2002). Sexuality, sexual dysfunction, and couple therapy. In A. S. Gurman & N. S. Jacobson (Eds.), *Clinical handbook of couple therapy* (3rd ed., pp. 629–652). New York: Guilford.

Minuchin, S. (1974). *Families and family therapy.* Cambridge, MA: Harvard University Press.

Norcross, J. C., & Beutler, L. E. (2000). A prescriptive eclectic approach to psychotherapy training. *Journal of Psychotherapy Integration, 10*(3), 247–261.

Odell, M. (2003). Intersecting worldviews: Including vs. imposing spirituality in therapy. *Family Therapy Magazine, 2*(5), 26–30.

O'Malley, P. (2002). Demystifying the AAMFT code of ethics principle three: Professional competence and integrity. *Family Therapy Magazine, 1*(4), 50–56.

Peluso, P. R. (2003). The ethical genogram: A tool for helping therapists understand their ethical decision-making styles. *The Family Journal: Counseling and Therapy for Couples and Families, 14*(3), 286–291.

Peterson, C. (1996). Common problem areas and their causes resulting in disciplinary actions. In L. J. Bass, S. T. DeMers, et al. (Eds.), *Professional conduct and discipline in psychology* (pp. 79–81). Washington, DC: American Psychological Association.

Pope, K. S., & Vasquez, M. A. (1998). *Ethics in psychotherapy and counseling: A practical guide* (2nd ed.). San Francisco: Jossey-Bass.

Robson, M., Cook, P., Hunt, K., Alred, G, & Robson, D. (2000). Toward ethical decision-making in counseling research. *British Journal of Guidance and Counseling, 28*(4), 532–547.

Schnarch, D. (1997). *Passionate marriage: Love, sex, and intimacy in emotional committed relationships.* New York: Henry Holt.

Skovholt, T. M., & Jennings, L. (2004). *Master therapists: Exploring expertise in therapy and counseling.* Boston: Allyn and Bacon.

Sommers-Flanagan, R., Elliott, D., & Sommers-Flanagan, J. (1998). Exploring the edges: Boundaries and breaks. *Ethics & Behavior, 8*(1), 37–48.

Sperry L., Carlson, J., & Peluso, P. R. (2005). *Couples therapy: Integrating theory, research, & practice* (2nd ed.). Denver, CO: Love.

Taylor, A. (2002). *The handbook of family dispute resolution.* San Francisco, CA: Jossey-Bass.

Tomm, K. (2002). The ethics of dual relationships. In A. A. Lazarus & O. Zur (Eds.), *Dual relationships and psychotherapy* (pp. 44–54). New York: Springer.

Vasquez, M. (2003). Ethical responsibilities in therapy: A feminist perspective. In M. Kopala & M. A. Keitel (Eds.), *Handbook of counseling women* (pp. 557–573). Thousand Oaks, CA: Sage.

Weed, L. L. (1971). Quality control and the medical record. *Archive of Internal Medicine, 127,* 101–105.

CHAPTER 13

REHABILITATION COUNSELING AND CAREER COUNSELING

MICHAEL FRAIN, LARRY KONTOSH, AND LEN SPERRY

Rehabilitation and career counseling have much in common, starting with the common roots from which each has grown. They began in this country with Parsons's (1909) seminal work. From this tradition comes the idea that job choice can and should be a purposeful and planned-for event. They deal with the interface of human behavior and the demands of occupations and labor markets. Each deals with models of career choice, assessment of work capacity, and the applications of workplace behavior to successfully chart a lifelong career or change one's direction. Both apply interventions to nonpathological, but potentially dysfunctional, behavior that may be causing individual angst or may block a person's occupational entry, reentry, or tenure. They also deal with lifestyle and self-actualization issues. As individuals grow and develop, their expectations of fulfillment change. Thus, both counseling specialties help address personal adjustment and satisfaction.

From this common ground, each of these specialties has developed unique branches that allow unique contributions to human development. This chapter further explores these specialties. Inherent in understanding the ethics of these counseling fields is the need to understand the relational (Perspective III) approach they both take in understanding clients.

LEARNING OBJECTIVES

After reading this chapter you should be able to

1. Describe legal issues germane to rehabilitation and career counseling.
2. Describe the fields of career and rehabilitation counseling, the types of clients practitioners work with, and the underlying goals of counseling.
3. Describe the unique relationship between clients and counselors in a rehabilitation setting, indicating the unique responsibilities each one has and the overall model used to achieve these goals.
4. Understand the ethical issues that face rehabilitation counselors and their clients, including the societal barriers that are present.

5. Describe how the core ethical components of confidentiality, informed choice, conflict of interest and dual relationships, and competency are handled in a rehabilitation and career counseling setting.
6. Apply the ethical decision-making moc l, multicultural, and other organizational
7. Identify the career counseling compete
8. Identify the professional association as

KEY TERMS

Americans with Disabilities Act
case closure
consumer
Client Assistance Program
creaming
essential functions
independent living

INTRODUCTION TO CAREER AND REHABILITATION COUNSELING

Career Counseling

Career counseling as a counseling specialty has its origins in the social reform movement of the late nineteenth and early twentieth century, beginning with early attempts to systematize job choice and placement at a critical time in U.S. history. As the country shifted from an agricultural economy to an industrial one, and as a huge wave of immigration brought thousands of workers here, the relationship between occupational need and worker skill set became the focus of theorizing for many researchers (e.g., Williamson, Jones, Roe, Holland), thus spawning a variety of worker assessments and job typologies.

The vocational guidance model originally focused on an adult's initial job choice and theorized that the best choice was a congruent match between job factors and worker traits. Gradually, this matching concept filtered into the school systems. Post–World War II, with the influx of veterans onto the nation's campuses, the model expanded to include the choice of college majors and postcollege employment. The growth in the desire by workers to planfully select their initial jobs caused models of career choice to be developed and become a focus of research efforts.

The economy has shifted its composition from an industrial to an information/service economy. The composition of one's work skill set thus has taken on new dimensions. The work skills needed by the labor market have begun to polarize. Skills tend to be either highly complex and advanced or low level. Additionally, high-level skills change quickly in response to the formation of new industries, new occupations, new work methods and data, and new advances in science and technology. Often, the demand for new skills exceeds the supply-side response. That is, individuals often are technologically or informationally disenfranchised because their expertise does not meet the advanced demands of the labor market. Employer-based training thus has become a significant source of technical education. Postmodern career-development theories have recognized contextualism and phenomenological impact in an effort to address to complexities of career choice, development, change, role conflict, and salience.

Career counseling is exceptional in the role it plays in human intervention and the methods its employs. It addresses the common sources of personal angst and human dysfunction.

Rehabilitation Counseling

Rehabilitation counseling as a profession blends three models of professional philosophy and practice: the Medical Model, the Vocational Guidance Model, and the Mental Health Model. From the Medical Model, the profession inherits the task of addressing the functional aspects of physical and mental impairment. This service includes the requirement of understanding medical diagnoses along with the functional and adaptional strengths and limitations they might present. The Vocational Guidance Model focuses the profession on understanding the vocational impact of a person's functional capacity and its potential impact on employability, competitiveness, and independence. This function requires advanced knowledge of the world of work and the functional demands of the labor force. The Mental Health Model focuses rehabilitation counselors on helping people address their psychosocial needs and their family and interpersonal relationships, abilities, and needs. This task demands therapeutic interventions aimed at increasing adjustment and fulfilling needs. Additionally, since this profession begins during the Social Reform movement in the early twentieth century in the United States, underlying each of the above models is the requirement for rehabilitation counselors to be advocates for the clients they serve and to facilitate the self-advocacy of persons with disabilities. Thus rehabilitation counseling is a composite profession that applies a varied and wide range of knowledge and skills to the individual situation. It is also a profession that takes seriously its role as advocate.

Rehabilitation counseling is based on several fundamental tenets that are in line with a relational (Perspective III) ethics viewpoint. The Adlerian concept of the holistic nature of people is basic to the profession. Rehabilitation counselors focus on the whole person in context. Thus, a counselor addresses the physical, emotional, and spiritual needs of the person as he or she impacts and is impacted by the environment, relationships (e.g., interpersonal, work), and societal organizations.

ROUTINE PRACTICE OF CAREER COUNSELING

Career counselors practice in a variety of settings: schools, colleges, counseling centers, and in independent practice. In these venues, counselors generally deal with career choice, career development, or career change. Career counselors focus on the relationship between clients' abilities (e.g., work skills, achievement levels, and aptitudes), their vocational assets and limitations, and the goals or life adjustments they seek. As part of the counseling relationship, aptitude, interest, or skill testing is often used to provide objective data about the client. Career exploration often includes the gathering of data about occupations, environments, and lifestyles. A synthesis of this information is done and processed so that plans for choices can be made. Once goals are set, a plan is developed to achieve them.

Often workplace dysfunction can be the client's presenting problem. In this regard, the counselor helps the client focus on work behaviors, the cognitions that produce them, and workplace expectations. The gap between expectations and performance becomes the focus of the counseling sessions. The counselor helps the client develop ways address behaviors that are causing problems at work or may prevent promotion.

Career change, whether it is voluntarily chosen or forced due to labor market issues beyond clients' control, is another area in which career counselors help clients. In this area, the counseling focus is on understanding the world of work and the options it may present for the client. Testing and other personal data provide a useful assessment of the client. But, knowledge of the labor market—local, national, and international—is critical to informed choice making.

Other counseling issues are routine to the practice of this specialty. They include dealing with indecisiveness, dysfunctional indecision, low levels of labor market access, family-versus-work role conflict, basic and advanced education and skill acquisition, promotional issues and upward mobility, acquisition of supervision skills, geographical relocation, and workplace discrimination (e.g., race or the glass ceiling), to name a few.

The typical practice of career counseling is as diverse as the clients its serves. It requires abilities that are unique to the specialty and advanced in skill. It deals often with the ordinary person under dysfunctional circumstances (vs. pathology) and addresses work and its importance in the broadest application. It is focused on client values, needs, and expectations for occupational and lifestyle fulfillment.

ROUTINE PRACTICE OF REHABILITATION COUNSELING

Little is "routine" concerning the practice of rehabilitation counseling. The profession developed out of a foreseen need by the federal government to have counselors work with individuals, initially those returning from war, who had become disabled. The initial plan set forth by the federal government acknowledged that veterans returning from serving their country who had suffered an injury during the war, and could no longer work at their previous occupation due to the injury, deserved to be helped by the government in acquiring new vocational skills and assistance in finding employment connected to these new skills. Such ideas by the government led to legislation such as the Smith-Sears Act of 1918, the Disabled Veterans Rehabilitation Act of 1943, and The Vietnam Era Veterans' Readjustment Assistance Act of 1974 (Szymanski & Parker, 2003). The practice of rehabilitation counselors doing career counseling with returning veterans was so successful that the logical next step of offering vocational services to all U.S. citizens with disabilities was apparent to all. Out of this initial emphasis on public vocational counseling, the role of rehabilitation counselors has grown tremendously. Currently, the rehabilitation counselor sets up shop in a variety of practice settings, which include the state and federal systems, but also private practice and not-for-profit agencies.

While, once, training involved only a vocational component, rehabilitation counselors now are trained as generalists who are skilled in both career and personal adjustment counseling (Cottone & Tarvydas, 2003). The scope of practice statement that has been endorsed by the three major governing bodies of rehabilitation (CRCC, ARCA, and NCDA) emphasizes the appropriateness of many differentiated models of practice for the rehabilitation counselor, to include assessment, diagnosis and treatment planning, career counseling, individual and group counseling, case management, program evaluation, research, interventions, consultation services and job analysis, development, and placement (CRCC, 2001b). Thus, while many see rehabilitation counseling as a practice with a more restricted or specialized range of clients, in reality, this is not the case, as rehabilitation counselors work with people who have physical, mental, developmental, cognitive, emotional, and addiction disabilities to help them achieve their personal, career, and independent-living goals in the most integrated setting possible (CRCC, 2001b).

While official statements of practice are essential in order for outsiders to understand a profession, in reality, the rehabilitation profession is growing at such a rate that further explanation is necessary. Much as ethical practice from a Perspective III standpoint is always an evolving aspect of the counseling world, the role of counseling also evolves as society changes and needs arise. This has been seen in the rehabilitation world, with the tremendous need for case-management services in the managed care industry. Rehabilitation counselors fit nicely into this role because of their excellent knowledge concerning medical aspects of disease and their vocational case management skills. With these skills, rehabilitation counselors are able to work with clients in a variety of managed care settings, such as employee assistance programs, employer-based disability management programs, disabled student service offices, and agencies that serve chronic illnesses such as HIV and AIDS (Leahy & Szymanski, 1995). The rehabilitation counselor in this position works with clients in developing a plan for vocational, psychosocial, and medical needs, by coordinating services and informing clients of rehabilitation options that are available to them.

More traditionally, rehabilitation counselors have worked in a state or federal rehabilitation system in which clients are directed to their services due to having a disability that limits one or more aspects of their major life activities. Counselors working in this role have the ultimate responsibility of working with clients to help them attain their maximum life potentials. The counselor does this through a variety of methods, which include individual counseling with the client and also helping clients adjust to their disability and find ways to achieve their maximum potential through accommodations, education, or training. Through these methods, persons with disabilities come to understand their capacities as opposed to their limitations.

The unique knowledge rehabilitation counselors have has made them well suited for a number of practice settings outside the traditional state rehabilitation agency. Rehabilitation has long been instrumental in working with psychiatric rehabilitation patients both in forensic and hospital settings (Cottone & Tarvydas, 2003). Similarly, drug and alcohol abuse programs are often staffed by rehabilitation counselors and benefit from the holistic approach to treatment, which can include medical, social, and vocational aspects for the client. Like many settings rehabilitation counselors inhabit, the substance abuse programs often take advantage of the team approach to rehabilitation, wherein the rehabilitation counselor works with the medical doctor, the recreational therapist, the occupational therapist, and others to develop a holistic plan with the client, so that all aspects of the client are included in the rehabilitation process. The team approach allows clients to work on skills and knowledges concurrently, such as can be seen in the client in a rehabilitation hospital soon after lower-limb-removal surgery, due to a drunk motor vehicle accident. The client can work on mobility skills with the physical therapist but make the mobility skill lesson vocationally useful as well by planning a trip to a potential employer, thereby working on both physical and vocational skills at the same. In this way, all the professionals who work with the client may integrate their planning with the client so the client benefits from a holistic approach that coordinates services in order that rehabilitation can occur in an integrated fashion as opposed to through separate, disjunctive service.

Importantly, while rehabilitation counseling has a very broad area of practice, there are clearly identified standards of practice for what constitutes appropriate professional practice (Cottone & Tarvydas, 2003).

The various practice settings in which rehabilitation counseling takes place have expanded greatly from the traditional ones. Rehabilitation counselors enjoy a wide variety of opportunities for specialty practice (Leahy, 1997). One traditional area of practice is in the public sector. The state-federal vocational rehabilitation (VR) system has for decades been the primary source of employment. In this venue, rehabilitation counselors determine eligibility for service, counsel with the consumer to determine a rehabilitation goal, contract and broker the agreed-upon services, case manage the process, and guide the successful conclusion of the plan. Another traditional practice setting for rehabilitation counselors is the private nonprofit sector. In this area, rehabilitation counselors are employed by rehabilitation centers (e.g., Goodwill) or community-based organizations that do advocacy and other types of services delivery. Rehabilitation counselors are the interface between the consumer and the service-providing organization. Thus, counseling, negotiation, and in-house case management are critical skills. Finally, there is the private for-profit sector. In this sector, the major employers are workers' compensation carriers and insurance companies, via long-term disability programs. Also in the for-profit sector, there is a large area devoted to private practice. Rehabilitation counselors in private practice are direct service providers of vocational rehabilitation services (e.g., vocational evaluation, job development, job placement), as well as providing expert testimony and life-care planning in various types of litigation (e.g., personal injury). The types of services rendered include transferable skills analysis and assessment of lost earning capacity and labor market access.

Nontraditional practice areas include employee assistance programs, employer-housed disability prevention and management programs, school-to-work transition programs, mental health centers, university-based offices for services for students with disabilities, and rehabilitation hospitals and medical clinics. The expansion of the venues of practice demonstrates the versatility of rehabilitation counseling and the wide usefulness of the unique skills that rehabilitation counselors possess.

CONTEXTUAL ISSUES IN CAREER COUNSELING

Personal-Developmental

Ethical sensitivity is very important. The degree to which a career counselor is ethically sensitive is the degree to which the counseling relationship will be relational and responsive to the unique happenings associated with it. Career counselors need to not only understand the letter of the Code of Ethics, but practice with attention toward virtue and relational care. This book attempts to make the point that ethics and professional practice are connected and should be integral. While risk management is important, ethical sensitivity demands a relational and developmental focus.

Ethical decision making is a fundamental skill that career counselors need to learn and apply. Following a decision-making model is one way to establish ethical sensitivity and to relationally apply the value tenants found in codes of ethics. The seven-step model suggested in Chapter 5 is one that is useful clinically. It allows for application of ethical principles as well as focuses on a care-giving approach to problem solving that considers risk management. Additionally, while career counselors generally focus on adults, there can be times when their client is a child. Following the advice found in the chapter on school counseling is fundamental.

A career counselor's professional development is an important factor in effective practice. Initial preparation imbues the counselor with the basic competencies necessary for ethical practice. As a career counselor has more professional experiences, it is necessary for the professional to reinforce those values that form the basis of excellent practice, as well as learn new ways to apply those values so that client differences can be honored and respected. Thus, while there are rules that assert one course of action (e.g., avoid dual relationships), the seasoned professional knows that not all situations rise to the level of violation or can be avoided. Thus, the issue is how the counselor applies the principles in the code and manages the situation to avoid harm and to remain care giving.

Further, the career counselor's personality, style, and core values need to be addressed and known by the counselor. Personal developmental issues, one's values, and unfinished business impact the quality of the counseling relationship. Thus, self-knowledge and dealing with these issues is fundamental to the professional development of good counselors. For counselors to be ethically sensitive and effective, they need to be self-aware. They also need to be aware of when their core values and beliefs might negatively impact the counseling relationship. The profession does not expect the career counselor to adopt the values and beliefs of the client, nor to affirm them, nor refute them. The profession only expects the counselor to be effective in the counseling relationship. One does not have to accept and adopt the values of Hannibal Lector in order to be an effective counselor to Hannibal Lector.

Privileged communication is a legal concept that prevents a counselor from being forced to disclose information the counselor obtained during the counseling relationship. It is the assertion on behalf of the client that the client's right to privacy be respected.

Privilege is determined on a case-by-case basis. It is a tenet supported by various counseling professional associations and has been accepted by the federal courts system (*Jaffee v. Redmond,* 1996). The concept is vital to the counseling relationship and to ethical practice.

Relational-Multicultural

The quality of the counseling relationship has been shown to be the best predictor of good outcomes. In career counseling, the issues addressed are more likely than not to be nonpathological in the DSM sense. However, sometimes persons do seek career counseling under very dysfunctional circumstances. The scope of the relationship and the issues involved can be broader and more varied than customary. Research and the reports of master therapists conclude that the quality of the counseling relationship is critical and will affect client fulfillment, decision-making ability, and goal attainment. Thus, a relational focus is critical to outcome success. Career counselors need to build effective relationships with their clients. They need to be ones in which the bond between client and counselor is resilient and strong.

One important part of a relational focus is the recognition of the culture of the client and the role it plays in the counseling relationship. For the practicing career counselor, culture includes more than race, nationality, and ethnicity. It is gender, age, socioeconomic status (SES), disability, sexual orientation, religion, and spirituality. Each of these personalogical issues affects the quality of the relationship between the client and the counselor. Career counselors need to be culturally competent. That includes understanding the client's worldview, rate and level of assimilation and acculturation, and culturally based values. Values determine behavior, problem solving, and counseling outcomes. Culture can determine the type of services to be provided, and the language(s) needed for effective communication.

Organizational Ethics–Community Values

Awareness of the community and its makeup is critical. The diversity of the client base often impacts the amount of access a client has to occupational information and to the Internet. The PhD program consists of a minimum of 60 credit hours including general required courses and a specialized coursework in one of three areas: Child and Adolescent Development in School and Community; Children, Adolescent, Couples, and Family Intervention; or Optimizing Human Development and Health. All of these resources are vital links to up-to-date employment and labor market information. Access requires not only provision of books and hardware (i.e., ports of entry), but also technological skills to use the data and "surf the net." Unfortunately, two problems present. Persons from minority groups often have limited or no access to computers or the Internet, nor the skills to use them effectively. Thus, their ability to obtain quality knowledge about employment and educational opportunities is equally limited. Additionally, local libraries may not catalogue recent occupational information in print form. Lacking either print or electronic access or operational skill to utilize these resources impacts the knowledge at hand with which to make decisions and establish goals for one's future.

Organizational ethics and the system dynamics associated with it are also important for the career counselor. The uniqueness for the career counselor lies in the large likelihood of being in independent practice without organizational auspice. For those who do practice in organizations, the systems approach discussed in Chapter 4 is useful for assessment of this dimension. An organization's goals, culture, and expectations clearly impact the individuals who work there. It is incumbent on professional career counselors to understand the relationships between organizational goals, objectives and operational dynamics, and the personal values and standards the counselor has. Where these two sets of values differ rests the potential for conflict.

For career counselors in independent practice, it is useful to view the environmental system as the organizational system. Within the environment there are business dynamics that impact the career counselor. Counselors must compete to stay in practice. They need to provide quality services in order to generate income. Counselors can be judged by the quality of the outcomes of their relationships with their clients. Methods of business solicitation, marketing, and advertising impact the public persona that career counselors present to the community. Supply and demand for career services, location of office space, and operational overhead can each affect whether the career counselor continues in practice.

The profession has also tasked career counselors with advocacy for its clients. Advocacy is usually done in the environmental system. Testimony before governmental committees and personal visitation to a principal on behalf of a student represent examples of advocacy.

As with any branch of counseling, it is important for the career counselor to ascertain the organizational ethics in which they are involved. Organizational ethics audits were introduced in Chapter 4 as one means of assessing and evaluating a career counselor's organizational ethics. Career counselors are encouraged to look at the assessment later in this chapter to evaluate the work of setting ethics of their own.

CONTEXTUAL ISSUES IN REHABILITATION COUNSELING

Personal-Developmental

Patterson (1998) and others have pointed out the purpose of a code of ethics: to provide standards for a profession, to give society some guarantees about a profession, and to give the counselor some guidance on how the profession ought to work (Shertzer & Stone, 1980). We must also realize that, despite the continual revision of ethical codes and the good that is contained in them, the code is not widely used as a guide in rehabilitation counseling (Brubaker, 1977; Cottone, 1982). While this is likely due to many reasons, one seems to be the disconnect many counselors and students feel between learning a code of ethics and following one in actual practice. For instance, students can often identify that informed choice is a part of the code, but don't always understand how having a client sign a blanket "consent to share information with other agencies" form at the initial meeting may go against the ethics of informed choice. We think the code of ethics for professional rehabilitation counselors is excellent and should be understood by all counselors; however, the way one practices ethics in a rehabilitation setting needs to be understood in practical terms as well. Ethical behavior is much more than rote following of a code of ethics (a Perspective I approach), but recognizing the code should be a part of the process (Patterson, 1998; Tarvydas, 1987). The next step in ethical behavior is understanding how the code fits in with the everyday practice of counseling individuals with disabilities.

Ethics for the rehabilitation counselor in part must come from an understanding of self, as well as being able to relate the relational (Perspective III) view spoken of in earlier chapters to life as a counselor. Every interaction in counseling has ethical linings to it, and thus, ethics should be recognized as a core concept of the rehabilitation process, *not a* mode of response that occurs when a counselor feels there is an ethical dilemma present; all of counseling is ethical. With this in mind we feel the mindset of rehabilitation is to promote positive relational ethics, understanding that the field is looking for the good in all including rehabilitation counselors.

In order for rehabilitation counselors to view relation ethics in client-oriented way, the knowledge of self becomes paramount. There is little doubt the vast majority of counselors know and truly attempt to do no harm (Gatens-Robinson & Rubin, 2001); however, counselors need to build empathy skills in order to understand quality-of-life perspectives from the client's point of view in order to adjust their beliefs about how life ought to be for individuals with disabilities (Gatens-Robinson & Rubin, 2001). Indeed, this should include ethical principles of helping, including beneficence to act in a manner that promotes the well-being of clients (Beauchamp & Childress, 1989), autonomy to show respect for clients' freedom of choice (Kitchener, 1984), and justice in treating all clients fairly (Welfel, 1987)—but it most go beyond this as well. Counselor education programs should help develop empathy and insight skills in counselors-to-be. The programs should strive to go beyond simple simulation exercises that do more harm than good (Wright, 1983), and move toward developing empathy by having students invest time and understanding into the world of disability through being a part of that world for extended time, by learning to listen to those who are disabled and being able to understand their worldview and how it may differ from that of the student. By developing those skills as other knowledge is being attained by the student, a more cohesive identity, one in which positive ethics is interwoven, for the student's identity of themselves as a rehabilitation professional is cultivated. This identity includes, at its core, a positive ethics approach as an enmeshed part of everything they do as rehabilitation counselors.

We believe the rehabilitation profession understood the Perspective III relational concept long before other professional areas and has been working toward a positive relational ethical identity for some time. Indeed, the most recently revised code of ethics in rehabilitation, which went into effect on January 1, 2002, identified the need for the rehabilitation professional to become more aware of the worlds of people from different cultures and worldviews. Similarly, the revised code acknowledges the shortcomings of past codes, which had inadequate coverage of the personal needs and values of clients (Tarvydas & Cottone, 2000). Rehabilitation has a proud history of trying to understand the world of clients and should be proud of the continuing emphasis the code places on understanding clients.

The recently revised code of ethics for professional rehabilitation counselors also reflects the 1999 task force in rehabilitation that thoughtfully developed supplemental standards to the code in order to consolidate the code and make it relate more directly to the general counseling code, as rehabilitation has become aware that the rehabilitation professional's role has changed over time and is involving more counseling attributes than before (Tarvydas & Cottone, 2000). With these changes, the rehabilitation field acknowledges that the code is a living document, one that must be encouraged to grow and change in response to the evolving role of rehabilitation (Pape, 1987).

The recent revision of the Rehabilitation Code of Ethics emphasized changes in important areas, one of the major revisions being an infusion of a major emphasis on multicultural considerations (Cottone & Tarvydas, 2003). Any document on ethics becomes somewhat obsolete the minute it is printed due to the continual evolution of needs and changes in society and the profession (Pape, 1987; Marshall, Leung, Johnson, & Busby, 2003). The new code of ethics contains eleven sections and 197 standards, making it a large document to maintain in short-term memory. Ethical codes by their nature must be reactive and address how to deal with failings that are brought to ethical committees; a code must be enforceable by a group of peers in the field (Tarvydas, 2003). Therefore, a code of ethics is often much different than the actual practice of ethics in the profession.

One way that actual practice can be more proactive should be in the way multicultural issues are dealt with by the field. Educators are always attempting to cultivate skills in their students, knowing that as professionals their students will need to be proficient in interacting with a wide range of people who may be very culturally different than the counselor. And, if the rehabilitation professional is not culturally aware, numerous problems can arise, such as unintentional racism, misinterpretation of culturally based behaviors, misdiagnosis, and misuse of assessment, to begin the list (Alston & Bell, 1996; Byington, Fischer, Walker, & Freedman 1997). While the hope would be that all professionals in the field are culturally aware, the rehabilitation counseling foundation is based on the core rehabilitation-philosophical assumptions of valuing human differences and of the basic dignity and worth of all persons (Tarvydas, 2003). However, this hope has not always been realized, as can be heard from past clients of this system.

The issue comes at an important time for career and vocational counselors, as the U.S. labor force will reflect cultural shifts to a more "Brown," "Black," and "Gray" workforce over the next twenty years (Fisher & Chambers, 2003). Thus, counselors must work with clients to develop "mutual respect and demonstrate positive regard for one another's culture in order to work competently together" (Marshall et al., 2003, p. 56). Some have proposed that, in order to do this, multicultural competencies and standards should be put in place in the field (Middleton, Rollins, Sanderson, Leung, Harley, Ebner, & Leal-Idrogo, 2000). Others have suggested that it is imperative that counselors learn to delve into the lived realities of those who are culturally different than the counselor; it is only through this method that the counselor can truly help with meaningful life decisions such as employment (Marshall et al., 2003).

Whatever the reason, it is evident that in order to be an ethically proficient counselor one must be able to understand cultural differences and show empathy for those who have had different histories. Some have suggested this can be done through integrating cultural issues into existing training and courses. Others suggest that the best approach is through a single-course design that stresses the systematic classroom teaching about issues of culture, race, and ethnicity (Marshall et al., 2003; Smart & Smart, 1992). The field must continue to treat clients first and foremost as individuals, but must never consider the individual out of his or her social context (Ivey & Ivey, 1999).

We acknowledge these issues are a part of this living document and also look to the educators to continue to see the development of students into rehabilitation professionals to be an ever-changing responsibility. As that responsibility looks toward the future, we see the great possibility of integrating a positive relational ethical aspect into the minds and hearts of counselors, so that all that they do reflects, and is an obvious sign to others, that the professional recognizes the ethical aspect in everyday living—interacting with all clients, service providers, and colleagues in a manner that exhibits the rehabilitation professional's call to see the positive in others and emphasize strengths of all.

With a focus on the continued move from Perspective I to positive relational ethics, there needs to be an understanding as to both how to develop ethical skills and also how these skills are influenced after being learned. While we encourage counselor education programs to begin the skill building of students, we obviously recognize the responsibility that is left with the counselor to continue to build empathy skills and understanding of client situations as their time from school becomes more distant. In addition to the individual variables concerning an ethical life, we acknowledge that often organizational variables can be very influential in the way intended positive ethics can play out in the world. Organizational variables, especially philosophy and expectations as well as individual supervisors, can have great effects on the well-intentioned rehabilitation counselor (Ferrell & Gresham, 1985). Later in this chapter, we will address organizational dynamics and the role it can play for a counselor attempting to use relational ethics as a guide.

Relational-Multicultural

One of the unique aspects rehabilitation counseling brings to the counseling field is the primary obligation of counselors to advocate for their clients and for the inclusion of all individuals with disabilities into the societal mainstream (Canon 2 of the Code of Ethics, 2001a). The concept is laudatory and has been updated in the new code of ethics to place an emphasis on advocating not just for one's own clients, but to empower all persons with disabilities by providing appropriate information and supporting their own efforts at self-advocacy (Tarvydas & Cottone, 2000). While acting in the interest of the client has always been central to the ethical concept of rehabilitation (Howie, Gatens-Robinson, & Rubin 1992), the new provision goes a step farther to recognize that what a counselor does affects many more individuals and society beyond any single client. This recognition underlies the important aspect of self-determination that the profession has recognized as central to ethical practice for individuals with disabilities (Cottone & Tarvydas, 2003). This tenet of rehabilitation is reason for pride and respect among those in the profession; indeed, other than social work, no other profession emphasizes this core obligation. However, a further explanation of ethical advocating is needed (Tarvydas & Cottone, 2000).

The provision of advocating for all people with disabilities requires rehabilitation counselors to "strive to eliminate attitudinal barriers, including stereotyping and discrimination and to increase their own awareness and sensitivity to such individuals" (CRCC, 2001a, p. 6). This indicates that rehabilitation counselors must advocate in society for what they believe are proper adaptations and changes to society in order that persons with disabilities are fully included. Environmental adaptations such as accessible transportation and buildings are an obvious place to start, but as Greenwood (1987) advocated, promotion must also be seen in society and services, with fields leveled to give equal access to jobs and schools to individuals with disabilities. The change in the code acknowledges that rehabilitation counselors must be the leadership in this challenge to make a society more equal for all. Rehabilitation counselors are required to lead all other professions in interpreting and supporting work-related values in collaboration with their clients (Tarvydas & Cottone, 2003). The rehabilitation profession is now in a unique position that allows rehabilitation professionals to have contact with various other medical and psychological professions through integrated work settings and the use of these professions for referral information. The rehabilitation professional is called on to take an active role in changing the way these professions view disability. The rehabilitation counselor needs to help educate medical professionals to look for strengths, instead of merely diagnosing weaknesses with patients who are disabled. Similarly, the profession needs to teach clients how to deal with service providers and vendors who are not promoting full access to the environment through attitudinal and corporate barriers such as pricing the worker who is disabled out of the market on key items that would allow for greater access to important aspects of society. In essence, this is a call to the rehabilitation field to bring a relational ethical way of being to all with whom they come into contact. This obligation makes this aspect of rehabilitation counseling a part of all activities with clients, and all of society the counselor comes in contact with, making it a proactive requirement, thus teaching that self-advocacy should be a part of all interactions, not just when requested by clients.

An important change is the acknowledgment that one of the best ways to help change society is through teaching, and assisting persons with disabilities with, self-advocacy skills (Vash, 1987). Counselors can do this in many ways, role modeling for clients how to advocate for things, allowing clients to deal directly with individuals who are suppressing their participation, and teaching what should be expected of an adapting society based on laws, moral principles, and the standards of the code of ethics. Rehabilitation believes in the human dignity of all individuals, the value of individual abilities, and the freedom of choice for individuals (Szymanski, 1987). An ethical counselor understands and promotes these ideals through demanding that all services to clients are provided in a nonpaternal, equal manner, with choices given to clients to assure that changes can be made if relationships are encroaching on the dignity and freedoms of the individual with a disability. Thus, from the beginning of all relationships with clients, counselors should work to help clients understand that the relationship is truly one of equality, allowing clients the freedom to choose many aspects of the relationship: how interactions will take place, the rules and obligations of the counselor to their place of employment, what information needs to be exchanged, and how disagreements will be handled.

It is understood that the relationship does not always start out equally: The rehabilitation counselor has power over the clients concerning eligibility for programs, and this imbalance should be institutionally changed, as discussed later in this chapter. The counselor also has knowledge of the field of rehabilitation from years of schooling and service to the field. This creates an imbalance of power that can and should be acknowledged and shared. Also to be acknowledged is the unique insight only clients have about themselves. The rehabilitation client shares the intimate details of his or her life with the counselor in order to provide the counselor with a picture of the client's needs and desires, strengths and weaknesses (Gatens-Robinson & Rubin, 2001). It is paramount in such situations that the counselor should share his or her knowledge of rehabilitation, counseling, work, and whatever else is appropriate to the particular client he or she is working with at the time.

From the initial contact, it is understood that the primary obligation of the counselor is to the client and all individuals with disabilities who are receiving services from rehabilitation counselors (CRCC, 2001a). A secondary responsibility is recognized to families and other parties, with the understanding that interdependence is a facet of everyone's life (Cottone & Tarvydas, 2003). The ethical rehabilitation counselor therefore recognizes that his or her primary obligation is to help the client attain the skills and knowledge necessary to become a self-advocate. These goals are over and above the desires of the federal or state system or other organization that may be concerned about the employment or health recovery of the client above the gains that are needed for clients to become self-advocates. It is also understood that very often rehabilitation counselors are meeting with clients after many life changes have taken place, and the rehabilitation client may not be fully aware, or fully capable of understanding, all the decisions and responsibilities the client now has. Therefore, the counselor must often act as an advocate for the client, to significant others and to other professionals, during the time the client is being taught self-advocacy and given the appropriate information that will be needed to make important life decisions down the road. It may also be appropriate, with the client's consent, to teach significant others how to advocate with, and on the behalf of, the client. This may especially be the case in instances in which the client is still a minor or the client is not his or her own guardian.

Rehabilitation counselors recognize that many laws have been put in place to attempt to achieve a level playing field for persons with disabilities. These laws, while perhaps laudatory, have not resulted in real change for whole population of persons with disabilities. This is in part due to societal values that place high regard to those with physical attractiveness, and the societal belief of "spread" that states that, when one attribute about a person is seen as below average, all other aspects are as well (Gatens-Robinson & Rubin, 2001; Wright, 1980). The Perspective III rehabilitation counselor understands that these societal beliefs affect all who are different from the mainstream, resulting in unemployment and underemployment as well as the lack of opportunity for many. All facets of society are affected by these misguided values; for instance, Kolata (1993) found that businessmen sacrifice $1,000 in salary for every pound they are overweight. In addition to employment areas, there is a greater recognition that a larger percentage of those with disabilities than those without disabilities do not go to movies, restaurants, cultural events, or grocery stores (Taylor, Kagay, & Leichenkor, 1986). It is for these reasons that rehabilitation counselors are called to advocate, not only for the clients they serve, but for human dignity of all individuals, for both individual and societal adaptation that will allow a more dignified lifestyle to be led by all.

Relational: Client's Context. The only way to truly advocate for clients is by understanding the place in this world that persons with disabilities occupy, in a professional, nonpaternal way, through heightened empathy on the part of the rehabilitation counselor. Rehabilitation counselors are aware of difficulties that politically opposed and socially stigmatized individuals face in having the opportunity to participate fully in their worlds (Cottone & Tarvydas, 2003). Indeed, the recent change to the code of ethics for rehabilitation counselors has placed explicit attention on multicultural issues, along with understanding that all people with disabilities have faced a pileup of demands that is more difficult to overcome because of their disabilities. Rehabilitation counselors have adopted an explicit general value system that honors all human diversity and are aware of the problems presented by social, vocational, economic, and political barriers to those who are not understood or those who are devalued (Cottone & Tarvydas, 2003). Indeed, the ethical rehabilitation counselor recognizes that attitudinal and other social and economic barriers and limited access are often the most severely limiting aspects of disability (Cottone & Tarvydas, 2003).

The enlightened rehabilitation counselor understands that significant similar experiences are not usually shared by the counselor and the client (Gatens-Robinson & Rubin,

2001). Persons without disabilities, as well as those from majority cultures, often have trouble understanding how day-to-day life affects individuals from a minority culture. The advantages given to those without a disability are rarely recognized until deep reflection is done by the counselor and awareness of how different it would be to walk in another's shoes becomes more apparent. Schools are therefore encouraged to teach students empathy through real-life experiences that go far beyond the simulation exercises in which students may participate in an activity or two in a wheelchair. What must be encouraged is a deeper understanding of what minority status means on a day-to-day basis, in order to understand the real value of specific services for clients (Gatens-Robinson & Rubin, 2001). Students should be encouraged to go outside their comfort zones to understand minority cultures. We recommend going beyond the simulation exercises, which promote sympathy more than empathy, by encouraging students to make a commitment to understanding disability thorough whole new eyes. Students in our classes in the past have attempted to develop more empathy through a number of activities including using public transportation as their only mode of transportation for a semester, going to another religion's services for a semester, and giving up a desired substance for a period of time. We find that students are very inventive in finding ways to help increase their own empathy toward others; by being allowed to choose activities for themselves, they often explore with more exuberance and find the change in understanding others to be quite dramatic. Professionals, too, should continue to find ways to increase their own empathy, especially as diseases such as HIV/AIDS become prominent among clients requesting services.

It is important that counselors understand the context of the society they are living in and be able comprehend how societal rules and perceptions affect members of that society. For instance, the United States places a high value on independence, so much so that any sort of dependency is viewed negatively (Gatens-Robinson & Rubin, 2001). The overriding belief is that dependency always ought to be minimized and self-sufficiency maximized; the strong pervasiveness of freedom, autonomy, and independence has deep roots in the U.S. political and social history (Fowler & Wadsworth, 1991). While these beliefs may have merit, they often are not as prevalent in reality as they are in the belief system. Few Americans grow their own food or build their own transportation, but Americans still view themselves as being able to survive independently, even if this perception does not coincide with the reality of their situations. However, this lack of dependence on others is often used as a discrimination device against persons with disabilities. The ethical rehabilitation counselor works hard to conceptualize societal attitudes and how they may affect individuals with disabilities both economically and psychologically. The counselor, through empathy, can then help clients understand how societal misconceptions may be affecting the clients and their own self-worth. Through this understanding, clients can choose more positive societal values and begin to look inside for self-worth.

In spite of the best efforts of rehabilitation professionals to conceptualize clients, by taking into account the historic contexts in which the clients find themselves, unexpected problems still arise. While many counselors now come from diversified backgrounds, and programs have been promoting inclusion of all in the education and practice of rehabilitation counseling, there is still much debate over the inclusiveness and fairness of the rehabilitation system. For instance, numerous authors (e.g., Atkins & Wright, 1980; Wheaton,

1995; Wilson, Harley, McCormick, Olivette, & Jackson, 2001) have suggested that acceptance rates for persons from minority groups are significantly below rates for dominant-culture clients. The significance to rehabilitation and career counselors is even greater due to the increasing rate of ethnic populations in the United States and to the higher rates of disabilities that are seen in many minority populations such as African Americans (Alston & Bell, 1996; Middleton et al., 2000).

Expectancies concerning the counseling process are heavily influenced by cultural values, and minorities often have different expectations than counselors (Byington et al., 1997). Numerous authors in rehabilitation suggested that the code of ethics in rehabilitation does not emphasize services to minorities enough.

While virtually everyone served in the rehabilitation field is a minority, there has been a struggle in the field to understand how the "pileup of demands" of being a minority in various aspects of one's life (e.g., a woman, a person of color, a person with a disability) affects clients and the services they receive. Thus, the ethics of the rehabilitation counselor should strive to understand the context of the many minority statuses a person may have, and how those situations affect the rehabilitation process for that individual.

Organizational Ethics–Community Values

Beginning with the Smith-Fess Act of 1920 (PL 236, or Civilian Vocational Rehabilitation Act), rehabilitation counseling is a profession begun out of grants started by the federal government rather than out of a business marketplace. As such a profession, there have been dynamics associated to it that are rarely seen in other professions. The profession has relied on grants, and still does to some extent, to continue to exist. This reliance has often resulted in the field struggling with the expectations of its lifeblood. The question of how to appease the funding source while still providing appropriate services to clients has long been a struggle for the profession.

While the majority of rehabilitation counselors no longer work in the federal/state system (Chan, 2004), it is likely that most rehabilitation counselors still must directly or indirectly depend on governmental support to exist. Counselor educators rely in part on long-term training grants; counselors in supported employment settings rely on referrals and payment from the state system; and even the nontraditional rehabilitation counseling positions that are appearing, such as employment in rehabilitation hospitals, often rely on patients on Medicaid or Medicare whose ability to pay for rehabilitation counseling services often depends upon payment rulings made by the federal system. In all, rarely do funds for rehabilitation services come from sources other than the state or federal government. It is obvious that rehabilitation counseling is a profession with many masters, but one with a lot of the power.

Perhaps because of the need to satisfy a state and federal system that is outside of the counseling field, rehabilitation organizations often put counselors in precarious ethical situations in which the counselor must choose which master to follow. The stated goal of rehabilitation is that individuals with disabilities reach their maximum potential; this creed is often superseded by state organizations that desire counselors to close as many cases as possible in a timely, cost-efficient way (see the case example in Box 13.1).

BOX 13.1
THORNY ORGANIZATIONAL ETHICS ISSUES

Organizational dynamics can present many difficult problems for rehabilitation counselors, as this example will illustrate. In the late 1990s, a state rehabilitation organization in a midwestern state was feeling the need to increase the amount of successful (status 26) closures. In past years, the agency had attempted to increase closures through staff training, hiring an on-staff job developer, and outreach to the disability community. Perhaps due to these efforts, the organization indeed substantially increased the number of clients it closed successfully, for a few years in a row. However, the desire to increase the number of clients closed successfully remained.

The leaders of the organization examined ways to increase closures and came up with an idea: They would have counselors contact clients who had been previously closed successfully and see if these clients needed further services. If the clients suggested they needed more services, the counselors would open their cases going through the same eligibility determinations and plan writing that accompany any new case. In each case, the counselor would then provide the service the client needed, and provided the client stayed employed, the case, after the appropriate time, would be closed, the client declared successfully rehabilitated (status 26).

As a rehabilitation counselor, what, if any, ethical concerns does this case raise for you? The agency, when questioned about the new, if unwritten, policy by a rehabilitation counselor, reacted by suggesting all clients the agency serves are severely disabled, thus clients who are working are just as in need of services as anyone else in the system. The agency also reacted to individual counselors who questioned the policy by listening to concerns and then doing unscheduled caseload evaluations of the counselor. The agency also responded to counselors who questioned the policy by asking, in passing remarks, if the counselor "was being ethical today," an obvious attempt to belittle the questioning of the organization.

The counselors who questioned the policy did so with the following points: The rehabilitation field has been asked to serve those who are most disabled; individuals who are working, while perhaps benefiting from services, rarely are the most disabled. Second, they noted that a stated goal of rehabilitation is to promote independence of clients. By asking if services are needed without clients' requesting services, the agency was acting paternalistic; independent clients ideally would be able to acquire needed services from their employers or would understand how to go about getting needed services without being checked up on. Finally, counselors argued that, with caseloads as large as they always seem to be for any state rehabilitation worker, spending time contacting and supplying services to those who had previously been deemed successfully rehabilitated was taking away time and services from the majority of clients and people with disabilities who had not been successfully rehabilitated.

There are other issues in the case that neither the counselors nor agency discussed. How a case should be reopened and what factors constitute a successful closure are factors perhaps important in agency settings.

- How would you handle this situation if you were a rehabilitation counselor at this agency? if you were an administrator? What if you were a client? If you were a client, would it make a difference if you were one of those already successfully rehabilitated?
- If in a situation in which you believed you were being asked to do something that did not fit your ethical view, how would you react, and who would you want to discuss your situation with? Are there some situations in which "the end justifies the means," such as the fact that, if your agency had more closures, you would receive more funds to work with those who are looking for employment?

- Do you think the agency or the counselors did anything wrong in this situation?
- What are your thoughts about the indirect consequences that often come along with discussing the ethics of your organization, such as having your caseload reviewed, or being passed over for promotions due to the organizational questions that you bring up? Is it better sometimes to go along quietly? Is it OK not to follow organizational policies you do not feel fit your view of ethics, but not to raise questions about the policy?
- Often, administrators or other people in the rehabilitation system are not rehabilitation counselors. They may feel the rehabilitation code of ethics does not apply to them. What are your thoughts on this?

For a long time it has been understood that the status 26 case closure is the primary measure of success for the rehabilitation counselor in the state system (Kuehn, 1991). Counselor's performance, agency's funding, and state's reputations are often linked to the number of status 26 case closures that happen. Generally, a status 26 closure occurs when a rehabilitation counselor helps a client with a disability attain employment and that client stays in that employment setting usually for at least ninety days.

Organizational dynamics can be tenuous for rehabilitation counselors anywhere they work. There is the constant question of whom the counselor is working for: Is it the client or the person paying the counselor's salary? Some counselors may decide that they follow the policy of the one who pays them, while others fight for everything they think their clients deserve. Ideally, the agency goals and the relational ethics of the counselor are compatible; however, in the current system, this often is not the case.

Creaming, eligibility determination, limited choice to clients, and serving clients with unqualified personnel are just a few of the ways that organizations can be at odds with the Perspective III ethical standards counselors are expected to uphold. Creaming, the process of selecting persons with the least severe disabilities and serving those clients at the expense of others, can lead to much quicker and cheaper positive rehabilitation outcomes for agencies. This however, smacks in the face of the Americans with Disability Act's (1990) call for agencies to serve those with the most severe disabilities first (see Box 13.2). Eligibility decisions

BOX 13.2

ORGANIZATIONAL DYNAMICS: WHO SHOULD GET SERVED FIRST?

The Americans with Disabilities Act mandated that those with the most severe disabilities should be served first. Should this be the case?

Let's suppose you work as a rehabilitation counselor at a state vocational rehabilitation agency. Your state is under an order of selection, meaning that you serve those with the most severe disabilities first. In practice, this means that many people who have a documented disability that prohibits them from fulfilling one or more life functions will never get services under an order of selection. One day, two clients come into your office looking for help:

(*continued*)

BOX 13.3 CONTINUED

The first client is Ron; he has recently been forced to leave his job as a ramp service worker for a major airline due to back problems that prohibit him from bending or lifting heavy objects. Ron indicates to you that he wishes to get back to some kind of work soon because he enjoys work and needs the financial rewards that come with being employed. He indicates that he worked for twenty-one years with the airline, generally getting good to excellent reviews by his supervisors and missing work only twice due to illness during that twenty-one-year span.

Ron hopes to get an injury settlement from the airline, but that may be unlikely or at least a lengthy process, due in part to the airline's recently filing for bankruptcy. Due to layoffs at the airline, working in another position did not pan out at this time; other airlines do not have openings that would fit Ron's employment needs. In checking Ron's history, you see he appears to be a very reliable and hard worker; however, his educational history shows that he has not yet completed high school. His transferable skills are good, but would seem to be limited by his lack of a high school diploma, which would be needed in most jobs that he appears most suitable for at this point in his life, such as a plant supervisor or shipping manager, positions very similar to the lead position he held with the airline. Ron indicates that one reason he did not finish high school was because of an undiagnosed learning disability. As a vocational counselor, you are aware that with some minor accommodations, mainly with computer equipment, you could work with Ron and through short-term training, he could attain his GED and be able to easily find work in the area at a salary in the lower range of what he was making before his injury. The total cost to your agency would be small, less than $1,500 for computer equipment and fees for training such as for books and classes in some job development skills that could help Ron, such as resume-writing skills. Your time as a counselor on this case would seem to be minimal, and you project Ron could be back working within six months to a year.

The second client, Chris, is a 29-year-old paraplegic who has not been employed at any time thus far in life. Chris went to school in a small town that did not provide any accommodations for the wheelchair that he uses or for the difficulty he has manipulating small objects. Chris was not able to write and often could not go to school due to the medical condition. He did graduate from high school, but admits that the "most of the teachers just let me pass without doing much of the work."

He comes into your office hoping you can help him get a job. He states that he does not know what he would like to do, but that he does like computers, and maybe computer programming would be interesting. His current skills in relation to computers are not very good; he can use voice commands to turn the computer on and off but can do little else.

Chris is a friendly guy, but his professional skills do not meet the standards you expect in an office environment: His hair is disheveled, he has not shaved for a few days, and he speaks a bit crudely for your tastes. His mobility skills with his wheelchair are at a similar level, as noted by the broken frame on the picture of your dog, which fell off the table after Chris ran into it today.

As a vocational counselor, you are aware that Chris has many needs before he could become employed. You are not sure that he could ever use a computer at a competitive rate, due some concerns about his speech. You surmise he would probably need a new wheelchair and at least four years of schooling in order for him to reach his potential. And, due to his medical history, you are concerned that any training would often be disrupted by long stays in the hospital.

After some time and assessment, you sit down with Chris to write a plan together. The two of you estimate it will take him six years to become employed, and the plan is estimated to cost a little over $200,000.

Examining this situation from a relational ethic viewpoint, if you could only choose one of these individuals to take on as a client, which client would you choose? What ethical concerns must you consider? If your agency director indicated that, because of the order of selection your state is under, you must serve only the individual with the most severe disability, what would be your course of action? How would you help these clients advocate for themselves? If your state was not under an order of selection and you could work with both of these clients, what percentage of your time would you spend with each of them? How do you think others would handle this situation? Would any of your thoughts be any different if you were working as a private rehabilitation counselor in your own agency? If you got paid only when one of your clients had been working for six months, would this affect your decision?

The community plays a key role as well in the determination of services for individuals with disabilities. Generally, services are provided through government programs that are supported by taxpayers. Therefore, the values of the community and the legislature are often a determinant for the amount and quality of services received by individuals for disabilities. Rehabilitation services grew out of the community desire to help returning soldiers who became disabled in World War I (Rubin & Roessler, 2001). The community continues to value certain disabling conditions over others. Individuals who become disabled through no fault of their own and those who have physical disabilities are believed to be more deserving of help than individuals who become disabled through their own negligence or who have mental disabilities in the minds of the majority of taxpayers (Rubin & Roessler, 2001). Rehabilitation counselors need, then, to understand that services and, ultimately, employment to individuals with disabilities rest with the views of the whole community. Programs that highlight the benefits of rehabilitation counseling and allow people with disabilities to be a part of the community allow individuals with disabilities to be seen by the community at large as normal human beings, deserving of opportunities similar to others in the community.

Organizational Ethical Audits in Rehabilitation Counseling Settings. It is advisable for any professional working in a rehabilitation counseling setting, usually an agency, to ascertain its organizational ethics. Organizational ethics audits were introduced in Chapter 4 as one means of assessing and evaluating a rehab setting's organizational ethics (see the example audit in Box 13.3). Why should a counseling trainee or rehabilitation counselor consider performing an organizational ethical audit of the agency for which he or she will do an internship or be hired as a counselor? In other words, what is the value of such an assessment?

The main reason for audits is that the organizational dynamics of an agency can significantly impact the ethical and professional behaviors as well the job satisfaction of counseling interns and rehabilitation counselors. Agencies that have well-articulated ethical values, principles, and professional standards and that act on these values, principles, and standards tend to foster both positive client outcomes and the personal and professional development of its staff better than agencies that do not. Staff commitment to their work and the agency is likely to be higher, staff turnover is likely to be lower, and quality of client services is likely to be positively impacted. This is particularly the case when a counseling intern's or a rehabilitation counselor's core ethical values and the agency's actual ethical

BOX 13.3

ASSESSMENT OF ORGANIZATIONAL ETHICS IN A REHABILITATION COUNSELING SETTING

Directions: Using the following 1–5 scale rate, evaluate each of the following items based on your current experience with a particular agency's ethical values, climate, and practices. Then add up your rating as a total score. An analysis of total score ranges is included below.

1 = disagree fully; 2 = disagree somewhat; 3 = neutral; 4 = agree somewhat; 5 = agree fully

_____ 1. There is a formal ethics policy that articulates the ethical values, principles, and professional standards to which this agency is committed.

_____ 2. The agency's actual core values and policies match its stated core values and policies.

_____ 3. The agency's commitment to its core values, ethical policies, and professional standards is championed by leadership and communicated routinely throughout it in staff orientation, training programs, and regular meetings.

_____ 4. Staff understands and agrees with the agency's core values and ethical expectations.

_____ 5. Staff is listened to when they identify ethical concerns about any aspect of their work.

_____ 6. Ethical behavior is recognized and rewarded, while immoral and unethical behavior is sanctioned.

_____ 7. All staff and clients are treated with respect, fairness, and equality.

_____ 8. The agency's ethical commitment and elements of the ethics policy and professional standards are routinely discussed in staff and other meetings.

_____ 9. Confidentiality and client privacy is effectively safeguarded in this agency.

_____ 10. Increasing professional competency is highly valued and rewarded in this agency.

_____ 11. Establishing and maintaining appropriate boundaries and avoiding harmful conflict of interests is expected and achieved in this agency.

_____ 12. Informed consent is provided initially and on an ongoing basis to clients.

_____ 13. There are formal processes in place for staff to report suspected unethical behavior and/or to ask questions to clarify understanding of the ethics policies and standards without fear of retaliation, retribution, or reprisal.

_____ 14. My ethical values and principles are consistent with the agency's values and principles.

_____ 15. The agency has a positive and healthy ethical culture, or climate.

_____ Total Score

ANALYSIS OF ORGANIZATIONAL ETHICS SCORING FOR A REHABILITATION COUNSELING SETTING

The following ranges provide a cross-sectional, here-and-now view of ethical and professional considerations within a particular rehabilitation counseling setting. In combination with other indicators of organizational structure and culture, it can provide a useful perspective in which to think about how the clinic/agency values and prioritizes ethical and professional considerations, allocates resources, and concerns itself with meeting client needs and quality services as well as staff needs and job satisfaction.

61–75 The agency appears to be highly sensitive to ethical and professional considerations and to staff/clients' well-being.

44–60 The agency appears to be reasonably sensitive to ethical and professional considerations and staff/clients' well-being.

31–43 The agency appears to be relatively insensitive to ethical and professional considerations and staff/clients' well-being.

0–30 The agency appears to be grossly insensitive to ethical and professional considerations to the point of fostering or sanctioning unethical and/or illegal behavior.

values are consistent. On the other hand, the less positive and healthy the ethical culture or climate of an agency, the more likely counseling interns and its counseling staff may experience work-related stress. In short, an organizational ethical audit is one tool to assess the ethical climate of a particular agency.

CORE ETHICAL ISSUES IN CAREER COUNSELING

There are several issues that are critical to career counseling that place significant responsibilities on counselors. How these issues are handled is fundamental to the success of the counseling relationship.

Competency

Counselor competency in career counseling is very important. The National Career Development Association (NCDA) identifies eleven potential competency areas. They are career development theory; individual and group counseling skills; individual and group assessment; information resources; program management and implementation; coaching, consultation, and performance improvement; diverse populations; supervision; ethical and legal issues; research and evaluation; and technology (NCDA, 1997).

But, given the diversity of practice venues, populations, and services expected, counselors often specialize within the field. Counselors focus on job placement, career change, or lifestyle counseling. Additionally, some specialize in an industry; some offer outplacement counseling or resume preparation. Some help with interviewing and job hunting. Some specialize by type of clients served (e.g., Hispanic). Counselors need to be sure that the services they offer are within the scope of their abilities and skills and that the labor market knowledge they possess is current and accurate. Further, multicultural concerns not only are found in practices that specialize in a particular population (e.g., Native Americans), but also apply to the general population as it becomes more diverse and pluralistic.

Testing is often used as an assessment tool. Counselors need to be sure they use tests that they have been trained in and can correctly and accurately administer, score, and interpret. They need to professionally and carefully help clients use the results to make choices in their best interests. The NCDA code of ethics states, "NCDA members neither claim nor imply professional qualifications which exceed those possessed, and are responsible for correcting any misrepresentations of these qualifications by others" (NDCA, 2003).

Informed Consent

Concomitant in importance with counselor competence is client informed consent. Counselors need to be clear, in the beginning of the counseling relationship, what services they can provide and what information and services will have to come from other sources. Clients can have unrealistic expectations of the results of the counseling session (e.g., guaranteed placement), so outcome expectations need to be dealt with early and clearly. Clients often seek help in times of crisis (e.g., job loss). Counselors need to clearly define the limits of their service and the time that is usually needed for delivery and results.

When tests are used in the assessment process, counselors need to be sure the need for measured, objective data arises out of the client's need for additional information in order to make an informed choice. The client should be told the need the test will address, and how the data could be useful for the client's purposes.

Client competency, or clients' ability to make informed choices in their best interests, is an assessment that is increasingly necessary in the counseling relationship. As more people seek career counseling, the ability of the counselor to access client competence has become critical. Impairments to competence include, but are not limited to, substance abuse, developmental disabilities, injury, medication usage, or emotional distress.

Age presents a unique informed consent situation. Our society sees persons below the age of majority as being **not** competent to make many of their own decisions (e.g., about access to medical care). Being not competent is different from being incompetent. Incompetence is the condition of being inadequate or unsuited for effective action. It implies the impact of an agent or condition (internally or externally) that is averse to clients' normal functioning. Because of the variety of services that are offered by career counselors, the client's ability to competently understand the counseling relationship and the nature of the services offered is critical, is the fundamental responsibly of the counselor, and is necessary to best practice.

Confidentiality

Confidentiality is fundamental to any counseling relationship. Because career counseling often deals with workplace dysfunction and adverse conditions that impact personal fulfillment, confidentiality as also critical in this specialty. Often, to aid in the assessment of the client's presenting situation, the counselor may request collateral information (e.g., employer recommendations, performance appraisals). Sometimes these documents may be used for eligibility reasons or to better understand the client's work capacity. These documents become part of the documentation of the case; in order for them to be used in the client's best interests, they need to be keep confidential.

Career counselors who do job development and placement need to be careful what they reveal to potential employment sources. Counselors may have access to test results, employer evaluations of the client's performance, or other third-party information about the client (in each case, both supportive and adverse). What is revealed needs the client's written approval and should be used to support the client's counseling goals.

CAREER-SPECIFIC ETHICAL ISSUES

Independent Practice

Career counseling is one specialty of counseling that is frequently practiced independently of organizational auspice. Counselors in solo or group practices often offer career counseling as part of a menu of varied services. Others specialize in career services exclusively. Career services are not often reimbursable by insurance carriers, though sometimes they can be part of services available though Employee Assistance Programs or some government-funded programs. Often, the client directly pays for the services. The NCDA code of ethics suggests, in part, that NCDA members "consider the financial status of clients and the respective locality" (NCDA, 2003, A.5).

Boundary Issues and the Use of Power

The counseling relationship is, in the traditional perspective, a relationship of unequal power: that is, the counselor by education and experience has more power in the relationship than the client. Counselors carefully check or apply their power in order to aid the client in goal achievement. In career counseling, a relationship of shared power is the best way to be effective and affords good outcomes. In such a relationship, mutual decision making regarding process, goals, and expected outcomes can be the most rewarding to clients. Further, test results, supplemental information obtained from third-party sources, and insights gained from experiential exercises are best utilized by and for the client.

Power abuse is most often seen in instances regarding dual relationships. Dual relationships can and do present themselves. They often are unavoidable. For example, a career counselor in private practice may find that a relative seeks job advice.

Spiritual Issues

Career counseling as per several theorists (e.g., Super, 1990; Rounds & Tracey, 1990) considers lifestyles and environmental issues in addition to occupation. Thus, often spirituality and religion impact goal setting, outcomes, and fulfillment. Religious vocations, spiritual transcendence in environment and activities, and religious values impacting decision making (e.g., abortion) are examples of the kinds of concerns clients can bring to the counseling relationship. Koenig and Pritchett's (1998) spiritual assessment is useful and should be done early in the relationship. Counselors' clear understanding of what level of incorporation of the spiritual dimension into their practices is appropriate is critical to being receptive to clients' needs.

LEGAL ISSUES IN CAREER COUNSELING

Several legal issues are unique in career counseling. One is privileged communication. Privilege, in law, is the recognized exclusion of confidential information revealed in session from being part of professional testimony in court. Like most ethical and legal standards, it is not absolute. The information needs to be imparted in session, and the request for privilege needs to be made to and granted by a judge. If allowed, the professional is excluded from having to reveal the information.

In any practice (e.g., sole, group, or agency or organizationally based), the integration of legal and ethical standards into to professional relationships remains the responsibility of the professional counselor. The difference between confidentiality and privilege needs to be explained during the informed consent process at the beginning of the relationship.

Another legal issue that needs close scrutiny is licensure. While career counseling is not licensed in most states, the use of the title counselor may be restricted under the title protection sections of the licensing law. Many career counselors find it practical to become licensed as mental health counselors (if the state in which they practice so licenses). Licensing affords a level of protection to both the client and the counselor. Careful, prudent practice usually dictates that practitioners obtain certification or a license from the state in which they practice, as appropriate. Career counselors need advanced skill, knowledge, and experience. As a result, licensure and certification have become very important in this field.

Two organizations currently offer national certifications. The NCDA offers several certifications that address the uniqueness of this specialty. They include Master Career Counselor (MCC) and Master Career Development Professional (MCDP). The Center for Credentialing and Education (CCE) is an affiliate of the National Board for Certified Counselors (NBCC). It offers certification as a Global Career Development Facilitator (GCDF), Approved Clinical Supervisor (ACS), and Distance Credentialed Counselor (DCC).

Licensure is less specific. Currently, no state licenses career counseling as a counseling specialty. Many who specialize in this area seek licensure as mental health or couples and family counselors. Because most states that license counselors also have title-protection sections in their licensing law, for career counselors to use the title of counselor they need to seek licensure in one of the specialties that are included in a state's licensing law. The absence of specific licensing of career counseling has given rise to the use of a variety of other titles by persons who are not license eligible but yet practice. Thus, career coaching, job coaching, placement advising, and the like are used by persons who practice in this area.

A counselor's duty to protect is fundamental to the counseling relationship. It is grounded in the core values of beneficence and nonmaleficence. These values underpin the NCDA code of ethics. Another application of this principle is the mandatory-reporting requirement found in many state licensing laws. The requirement to report certain behaviors (e.g., child abuse) is an obligation that accrues to those who are licensed. Thus, though codes of ethics are founded on similar principles, it is law that requires the extra step of mandatory reporting. To do so, states usually set up reporting agencies that are staffed to handle the calls.

CONCLUDING NOTE: PERSPECTIVE III AND RELATIONAL ISSUES

Key to understanding the ethical principles outlined in this chapter and book is the idea of adopting these practices not as a risk-management tools but as one's method of practice. One is confidential because it fosters the therapeutic relationship, but confidentiality is not absolute. Its limitations need to be explained in the beginning of the client relationship as part of informed consent. Informed consent exists not to protect the counselor, but because

it underpins good practice. Many dual relationships canno aged so that they cause no harm to the client and protect th ical to a relational practice.

As the U.S. labor market increases in its complexit new skill sets are demanded, the need for labor-market- Career counselors need advanced skills, education, and the present certifications that are available.

The critical ethical and legal issues discussed above underlie cur... specialty. Ethical concerns for client protection and the development of a strong relation ship between counselor and client protect good outcomes. See Box 13.4 for two case examples in which a counselor must determine the best career-counseling strategy.

BOX 13.4
TWO CASE EXAMPLES

COLLEGE CAREER CENTER

A career counselor is working for the campus career center. He is approached by a new female freshman who is having difficulty choosing her major. The student is 18 and comes from a small town. She has had limited work experience. After school, she worked as a clerk in an ice cream store. Once, when she was younger, she worked as a page in the public library. She has come to the state university to begin work on a college degree, but is unable to decide if she wants a career or if she wants to marry and raise children. Her mother is a professional seamstress, and her father is a truck driver. Each has urged her to pick a different job, because they do not want their children to follow in their footsteps.

The student is bright. Her college admissions scores were above average. Additionally, her high school grades were nearly all As. Her best grades were in English and history, and she has expressed interest in mathematics. However, she does not want to teach and is unable to express an occupation that would allow her to follow her math interest.

The university offers 192 majors in several academic departments, a bewildering assortment. The student is unfocused and unable to determine the steps she needs to take to make a choice of major. How does the career counselor aid the student in prioritizing, problem solving, and career choice?

INDEPENDENT PRACTICE

A young upwardly mobile professional in the software design industry approaches a career counselor to help her make the next career move in what promises to be a productive and rewarding career. The client, however, has recently been passed up for promotion and feels that a person with less skill got the job because he was male. The counselor interviews the client regarding her work history and job experiences and finds out that at two previous employment situations she was also passed up for promotion. The client admits to filing a complaint against the second employer with the EEOC for employment discrimination. The client is unable to explain any commonalities among these experiences. How does the career counselor help the client objectively look at these three situations to find the job behavior patterns that might need to be addressed? How should the counselor obtain objective information about the client's work performance?

ICAL ISSUES IN REHABILITATION COUNSELING

Competency

Since we know that ethical conduct in the sense of relational ethics goes beyond common sense, sound judgment, and work experience (Flowers & Parker, 1984), and we know that it is a skill that can be learned by practitioners (Handelsman, 1986), we outline a developmental model that can be used for educators and practitioners to develop a relational model of ethics for students and those in the field alike.

First, as Sue and colleagues (1992) have pointed out, achieving self-awareness can help rehabilitation professionals prevent their values, biases, and preconceived notions from inhibiting their optimal effectiveness with clients (Sue, Arredondo, & McDavis, 1992). However, the rehabilitation community has recognized that many individuals enter the profession with a greater ability to feel sympathy than empathy for clients (Wendell, 1989). It is understood that society as a whole has taken a paternalistic view of people with disabilities; thus, it is to be expected that, unless trained otherwise, those entering the profession will not have the empathy skills and therefore will underestimate what is needed for persons with disabilities and will place potential limits on what they consider as their scope of obligation to persons with disabilities (Gatens-Robinson & Rubin, 2001).

Second, as a profession, we recognize that surveys of rehabilitation counselors indicate that the majority of ethical violations are due to ignorance and poor judgment rather than outright willful disregard for the code of ethics (Van Hoose & Kottler, 1985). When combined with the finding that 45 percent of rehabilitation counselors are aware of ethical violations by colleagues (Patterson, 1998), ethical problems are seen as a system failure rather than an individual shortcoming. As a systemic shortcoming, rehabilitation needs to address how to deal with ethics as a profession as well as on an individual basis.

Therefore, a developmental model needs to address the core competencies that core are required of all rehabilitation-counselor-education programs, and the tenets that make up relational ethics need to be recognized. A core requirement that accredited programs have a specific class on rehabilitation ethics is a start. However, including ethics as a part of all required classes in an integrated fashion makes much more sense from the relational view of ethics. In order for students to understand and actually use their ethical knowledge in practice, they must see how it is a part of their rehabilitation counselor identity, and not something that should be pulled off the shelf for the occasional "ethical dilemma" that arises. For instance, while teaching a job development class, educators often emphasize how important it is to give choice to clients throughout the process and may even do exercises that help students understand how they have developed self-determinism and how frustrating it can be when that value is not addressed in the rehabilitation plan. This is excellent teaching on the part of the rehabilitation educator and helps students understand how the ethical principle of autonomy is incorporated into the daily interaction counselors have with clients. Emphasizing the relational aspect of the rehabilitation tenet of self-determination through autonomy only reinforces the identity of what a rehabilitation counselor is for the student. Incompetent behavior is the result of poor training, which can be seen in counselors who exhibit poor judgment, often through an inability to recognize their own limitations (Van Hoose & Kottler, 1985).

On an individual basis, using the relational ethics outlined earlier in this text will help students and practitioners mold their knowledge of ethics and rehabilitation tenets into one big mass of an integrated self.

Confidentiality

Perhaps due to the complex relationship rehabilitation counselors have with clients, families, and service providers, confidentiality issues are frequently misunderstood by both the counselors and clients. Accordingly, the Commission on Rehabilitation Counselor Certification (CRCC) tried to address these issues in the most recent code of ethics. To begin with, whether direct client contact occurs or whether indirect services are provided, rehabilitation counselors are obligated to adhere to the code (CRCC, 2001a). Furthermore, rehabilitation counselors are required to explain the limitations of confidentiality and any foreseeable situations that might limit confidentiality to the client (Cottone & Tarvydas, 2003).

While confidentiality issues are often cited as being the most difficult situations to handle for counselors, this can be particularly true for counselors in the rehabilitation profession, due to the many individuals who may be involved in the rehabilitation process and due to various legislative issues, which can vary significantly for rehabilitation counselors depending on jurisdiction.

The counselor will often be faced with situations in which others expect or desire him or her to break confidentiality guised in the belief that in doing so the client will benefit in the end. Families, schools, and other agencies that may truly desire the best for the client often also expect to be afforded unlimited access to information concerning the client. This often puts the counselor in the unenviable role of having to battle with individuals whom they hope will be supportive of plans that the counselor and client make together, thus creating adversaries of individuals they may later desire to have as teammates.

Persons with HIV/AIDS. Aside from these areas of rehabilitation that relate to confidentiality issues, there is an additional area that appears to be more unique to the rehabilitation setting that will be discussed here, the situation of clients with HIV/AIDS.

Rehabilitation counselors have recognized HIV/AIDS as a chronic illness that affects clients similarly to other chronic illness such as diabetes and arthritis, with additional stigma attached (Frain, Berven, & Chan, in press). Counselors have also struggled with duty-to-warn issues related to the *Tarasoff* case that often arise when clients with HIV/AIDS continue to participate in behaviors that may be putting others at risk for infection. This struggle continues in part due to state laws that are not consistent concerning duty to warn in the case of HIV/AIDS (Hopkins & Anderson, 1990). In addition, rehabilitation counselors do not report a general consensus in terms of their behavior and the profession's role in the duty to warn a partner or other concerning a client with HIV/AIDS (Stanard & Hazler, 1995).

Many attempts have been made to lay out guidelines to help counselors understand how to approach the duty-to-warn issue with clients. Woods, Marks, and Dilley (1990) suggested that counselors should have knowledge about the following facts before they have a duty to warn or a duty to protect another individual: (a) The client is HIV infected; (b) the client engages in unsafe behavior on a regular basis; (c) the behavior is actually unsafe; (d) the client intends to continue the behavior; and (e) HIV transmission is likely to occur.

These ideas are very similar to those in the *Tarasoff* case, which has been mentioned in earlier chapters, in which three conditions mandated a duty to warn: (a) There must be a genuine therapist–patient relationship; (b) the patient must have communicated a serious and imminent threat of physical violence toward another; and (c) the threat must be against a reasonably identifiable victim or victims (Dalton et al., 1986; Harding, Gray, & Neal, 1993; Woods et al., 1990).

Combining the *Tarasoff* case with duty-to-warn and confidentiality issues related to HIV and AIDS has proven to be tricky for the rehabilitation counselor and psychology in general. Communicable diseases have always been a part of our society, and physicians and rehabilitation professionals have attempted to work with clients with these diseases in a professional manner that respects both the client and the public welfare. The courts have offered guidance in some areas of disclosure. For instance, a state's duty to protect its residents was reason for rulings that physicians were correct to forgo confidentiality for the good of the state. Cases such as *Wojcik v. Aluminum Company of America* (1959) and *Simonsen v. Swenson* (1960) dealt with a physician's decision to warn people about the possibility of contagious disease in order to prevent the spread of the disease (Knapp & VandeCreek, 1990). In these cases, courts ruled that, if a physician is aware of a patient with a contagious disease and aware that the patient was not warning those who could become inflicted with the disease, the physician has the obligation to warn others about the possibility of becoming infected.

Rehabilitation counselors are not physicians, however, and one argument in opposition to the *Tarasoff* approach with HIV clients contends that breaching confidentiality based on the counselor's ideas of imminent danger of a partner is going beyond the scope of the field of expertise of the counselor (Harding et al., 1993). It forces counselors to render a medical opinion concerning how the disease is transported and the likelihood of infection from different sexual practices and needle-sharing situations.

Additional authors suggest that the *Tarasoff* ruling is not comparable to the situations involving HIV/AIDS clients for a number of reasons. First, the threat in *Tarasoff* is a direct, active threat, not the passive one seen with clients with HIV/AIDS (Kermani & Weiss, 1989). Second, the concept of clear and imminent danger is a hard one to decipher. The danger is relative to the type of sexual activity the client participates in, the manner of protection the client may use to shield a partner from infection, and, perhaps, how the client chooses to share needles as an IV drug user (Stanard & Hazler, 1995). Third, some have questioned how disclosing a client's status because of general concerns of infection fit into the *Tarasoff* concept of an identifiable victim. If the counselor is not aware of who is likely to contract the disease, it is difficult to warn those individuals.

These ideas have not led to a consensus in the rehabilitation community concerning client confidentiality and HIV status; numerous philosophical discussions continue on the subject (e.g., Knapp & VandeCreek, 1990; Patterson, 1998). Ethically, a rehabilitation counselor may feel a duty to warn a partner concerning the HIV status of a client, even if the legal obligation is not present. Additionally, mandatory reporting of AIDS cases to public health officials is present in all fifty states. However, it is a rare case in which this obligation falls from the physician to the counselor.

CRCC and APA have not indicated clear standards for counselors to follow concerning HIV-positive clients (Melchert & Patterson, 1999). The APA maintains the following position:

1. A legal duty to protect third parties from HIV infection should not be imposed.
2. If, however, specific legislation is considered, then it should permit disclosure only when: (a) the provider knows of an identifiable third party who the provider has compelling reason to believe is at significant risk for infection; (B) the provider has a reasonable belief that the third party has no reason to suspect that he or she is at risk; and (c) the client/patient has been urged to inform the third party and has either refused and/or is considered unreliable in his/her willingness to notify the third party.
3. If such legislation is adopted, it should include immunity from civil and criminal liability for providers who, in good faith, make decisions to disclose or not to disclose information about HIV infection to third parties. (APA, 1991, p. 1)

The CRCC Code of Ethics has not taken as protective a stance on client's confidentiality rights. The CRCC stance on contagious and fatal diseases is that, "where allowable by law," the rehabilitation counselor will disclose information concerning disease to a third party, "who by his or her relationship with the client is at high risk of contracting the disease" (CRCC, 2001a). This, according to CRCC, should only be done after the counselor is sure the third party has not been told by the client and the client has no intention of doing so in the near future. This policy appears controversial for an organization that purports to support all people equally and always work in the best interest of the client. It goes against other major governing bodies, the Centers for Disease Control in addition to APA, by missing the burden of service to the client. This canon asks rehabilitation counselors to make judgment calls that appear to be outside their area of expertise, with possibility of resulting grievous damages to clients—in a vocational atmosphere that has seen numerous corporations already show a bias toward this group of individuals due to beliefs about HIV/AIDS and homosexuality. Cracker Barrel restaurants, for one, had a long-time written policy (until 2002), stating that homosexuals did not fit in with the "family" nature of the restaurant and would not be employed by the restaurant (*People of the State of Illinois v. Hubert,* 1992; Verona, Layton, & Morrison, 1998). This canon appears to further the discriminate toward this group of individuals; however, others have argued that the protection of the third party is worth breach of confidentiality. We encourage all rehabilitation professionals to examine this issue for themselves and attempt to understand the situation from all parties involved in order to decide the best course of action in such cases.

A rehabilitation counselor should be aware of the various state and federal laws regarding duty to warn in the case of a client with HIV/AIDS. However, they should also keep in mind the relational positive ethics that are the foundation of the rehabilitation counselor–client relationship. The relationship should start with an understanding of how confidential and potentially embarrassing or career-damaging issues such as HIV will be handled before the client indicates HIV/AIDS status. The counselor is aware that many incorrect assumptions abound around HIV status and that it is still legal in some areas to be terminated from employment for one's sexual orientation, which is often questioned after HIV status is known. Thus, while the laws give guidance on what to do, a much deeper approach is needed with clients, with an understanding that releasing certain information can be extremely damaging to many areas of the client's life. While information about any disability brings with it certain negative stereotypes, this is compounded in the case of HIV/AIDS, where the public generally reacts with avoidance, indignation, and blame directed toward the lifestyle and beliefs of the individual with HIV/AIDS.

Informed Consent

With all clients, counselors should fully inform the client about any information that will be shared with other parties, how that information will be shared, and who will be able to potentially access such information. This should be fully understood by clients before any information is accessed in order that clients are able to refuse any services if they desire not to share specific information. In working with individuals with disabilities, it is sometimes the case that individuals do not have the capacity to make all decisions for themselves. This may be due to a disability such as severe mental retardation, or it may be due to the recent onset of a disability. In these instances in which another individual has the legal right to make confidentiality decisions on behalf of the individual with a disability, the individual should still be consulted and a part of the decision and have an awareness of how information will be shared with others.

In the rehabilitation field, however, things should go further than just informing clients and giving informed choice. The rehabilitation professional must recognize that clients with disabilities have been consistently faced with barriers to choice. These barriers have been seen environmentally, architecturally, and attitudinally (Patterson, Patrick, & Parker, 2000). While all of these barriers have seen change in recent years, and some architectural ones have begun to crumble through legislation, barriers represent a unique obstacle to choice for the client who is disabled.

Informed choice is not a new concept in the rehabilitation field. Levine (1959) and Patterson (1960), and countless others since, have emphasized that clients should be given choice in regard to their vocational desires. More recently, that concept of choice has spread to other concepts concerning clients, often heard in the disability community's mantra of "nothing about us, without us," but as strong an underlying concept as informed choice appears to be in theory, in practice it does not always seem to come through as clearly. Who among us in the rehabilitation field has not at some time come across a particular client and spoken of their unrealistic vocational goal and the need therefore to take a more parental approach to therapy with such clients? In my own work as a rehabilitation counselor, I remember a particular likable client, shy and always struggling in social situations, who indicated he wished to host a television talk show such as Oprah's when asked about his short-term employment goals. And in my own naïveté, that of a young rehabilitation counselor, I felt the compulsion to take a stronger role in his vocational goals.

However, Patterson and colleagues (2000) point out a much more relational ethical viewpoint on this common attitudinal barrier, as they discuss the often-heard unrealistic goal of clients with disabilities in terms of Super's Life-Span, Life-Space Theory (1990), which discusses the fantasy stage and its typicalness for clients who have a limited knowledge of the world of work. Thus, informed choice for career and rehabilitation counselors must acknowledge the barriers to exploration that have existed for many rehabilitation clients and take a proactive approach to making informed choice a real experience for clients. Salomone (1988, 1996) has presented a five-stage model that uses a relational view for helping clients who are in the infancy stage of understanding their world to move to a more appropriate view of the world around them. The model suggests counselors help clients (a) gain an understanding of self, (b) gain an understanding of the environment, (c) gain an understanding of the decision-making process, (d) implement educational and career decisions, and (e) adjust and adapt to the world of work (Salomone, 1988, 1996).

Informed choice, therefore, can be seen as both something that should be promoted by the counselor as a part of an ethical practice and also something that needs to be cultivated. Counselors can use Salomone's model to help clients in self-exploration through a number of methods: giving appropriate and honest feedback to clients, using family and significant others as a part of feedback, and allowing societal natural consequences. In the vocational aspect of this, counselors can urge clients to participate in many activities that are familiar to the rehabilitation counselor, including job shadowing, informational interviews, job simulations, job tryouts, situational assessments, and similar other techniques (Patterson et al., 2000).

Rehabilitation professionals find themselves often in medical settings and with health-related concerns. The idea of informed choice can be related to informed consent as it is understood in health care (Patterson et al., 2000). Much as informed consent can only be given by clients after they understand the procedures that will happen to them and after they fully understand the other options that are available to them, along with the risks and rewards of each method, informed choices can only come after clients have been "informed" about choices that are available to them. Counselors in this field must contently stay cognizant that they are often dealing with clients who have had to face barriers in their lives that have reduced their overall awareness of the world around them.

In all situations, the rehabilitation counselor should desire to protect the best interest of the client. One important way of doing this is through the use of minimal disclosure as a safeguard to client confidentiality (Cottone & Tarvydas, 2003). The counselor should reveal only the minimal amount of information necessary to other parties (Cottone & Tarvydas, 2003). This often means contacting the other parties and consulting with the client about the information that is necessary to share with these parties. This situation often comes up when a client has a file that includes information concerning medical, psychological, and personal information that has been collected by the counselor but is not a part of the service needs of another who is requesting the file. Often a job developer will get a release signed by the client to access the client's entire file without the client's realizing that personal information such as medical procedures and family situations are contained in the file that have no bearing on the services that will be provided by the job developer. In these instances, the counselor should be proactive in understanding, with the aid of the client, what information contained in the file would be a logical help in obtaining the best services from the individual requesting the information. Often, through this discussion with the client, the counselor can better understand what information should always be minimally shared. Concurrently, the client is able better recognize what information may be shared when he or she signs open-ended consent forms and can then put further limitations on how information is shared. This type of disclosure is also a part of the knowledge concerning HIPAA that counselors should have, which will be discussed later in this text.

Conflicts of Interest

The CRCC Code of Ethics clearly states, "The primary obligation of rehabilitation counselors is to their clients, defined in the Code as individuals with disabilities who are receiving services from rehabilitation counselors" (CRCC, 2001a). Thus, the well-being of the person with a disability can mitigate the relationships that the rehabilitation counselor has with other parties interested in the rehabilitation process. The protection of and determination of the application of the core values that underlie rehabilitation counseling are the basic responsibilities of the rehabilitation counselor. Simple as this philosophy sounds, there are real-world realities that often pit the counselor against other interests that may not always be in the best interest of a client.

Rehabilitation counselors who work in insurance or worker compensation settings as well as EAP programs often find that their own companies' interests lie at least in part with saving money. A counselor may get the message that an important part of his or her job is getting a client rehabilitated at the lowest cost possible, which often can conflict with the most appropriate rehabilitation choices for a client. Rehabilitation counselors recognize that clients are individuals who have strengths and are more than just their disabilities.

A central tenet of the rehabilitation philosophy is to understand and emphasize what people can do, as opposed to the limitations they have. Thus, the new emphasis in psychology on the medically based diagnostic paradigm has troubling implications for the long-valued, asset-focused, nonstigmatizing rehabilitation model that centered on functional assessment (Cottone & Tarvydas, 2003). Counselors are thus faced with the dilemma of either doing the bulk of their work and communication with other professionals in a way that shows they are contemporary in their knowledge in the use of the DSM-IV and related medical diagnoses, and therefore focusing on the limitations that clients have, or remaining true to the emphasis of the rehabilitation field on the self-worth and abilities of individuals over their diagnoses.

This dilemma reaches far beyond just rehabilitation counselors; all counselors and therapists in the United States have seen a gradual movement toward the medicalizing of the profession. In the rehabilitation community, there are many benefits to being associated more closely with the medical profession. Clients can be treated more holistically and receive coordinated services in many hospitals with doctors, nurses, rehabilitation professionals, occupational therapists, and the like, all working together for the common goal of the success of the client. While this mixing has numerous benefits, the medicalization of the profession also has some serious relational ethical drawbacks. A greater percentage of the insurance industry, government eligibility statutes, and other service providers are requiring a DSM-IV diagnosis in order to extend benefits or services to clients. These DSM-IV and medical diagnoses at the root emphasize deficits that clients have—ignoring the dignity of worth of all individuals, the ability of people with disabilities to become self-sufficient and contributing members of society (Bozarth, 1981)—by creating a cast of people who are, first and foremost, recognized by their disabling label.

Rehabilitation counselors have a long tradition that incorporates philosophy and the practical importance of addressing client's holistically, even when emphasizing vocational concerns (Cottone & Tarvydas, 2003). The move toward including rehabilitation counselors as a part of hospital treatment teams has allowed clients' goals to be seen more holistically from the outset after injury. Clients are able to begin to plan for vocational concerns, which may be addressed and made part of recovery while in the hospital. For instance, rehabilitation counselors are working with physical therapists in designing activities that will aid clients not only in their physical recovery, but also in their vocational recovery. Thus, an outing that once only emphasized exercise and an increase in stamina now includes using that exercise to learn a bus route to the client's place of employment. This holistic approach to the rehabilitation of clients has allowed the transition back to their lives at home to become smoother with a quicker return to normal activities.

One of the most important of those activities is work. Work is seen as a central value and one of the most meaningful human activities by both the counselor and client (Cottone & Tarvydas, 2003). A holistic approach to clients helps them to see the many positives they are bringing to their places of employment. Rehabilitation counselors should emphasize the positive impact clients make through their work, while at all times being aware of potential adaptations that can be made to the workplace to take full advantage of the knowledge and skills that people with disabilities take to the workplace. It is natural for clients and others to notice and emphasize the shortcomings that can accompany disability. For instance, a bank teller who is newly confined to a wheelchair may notice and hear from others about the difficulties created by his not being able to reach things in the vault and by the need for accommodations to be made to the work site, while ignoring the employee's continued high performance in both balancing his drawer and having high customer satisfaction. Thus, it is often left up to the rehabilitation counselor to be the one who notes the things that are going well and their relative importance as compared to things that may have changed since the disability occurred.

SPECIFIC ETHICAL ISSUES IN REHABILITATION COUNSELING

Supervision

Codes of ethics have generally dealt with the practice of rehabilitation and career counseling, with not much guidance concerning supervision (Tarvydas, 1995). Clinical supervisors in rehabilitation and career settings have a myriad of roles with those they supervise, often being a teacher, therapist, evaluator, and consultant to the supervisee (Burns & Holloway, 1989). The roles of supervisors seem to be increasing even as the need for knowledge is growing exponentially. Unfortunately, this increased role and knowledge expectation comes with little guidance from codes of ethics. Supervision ideally should focus on the professional development and skill enhancement of the one being supervised and assure that the client is receiving quality professional counseling services (Goodyear & Bernard, 1998).

Supervision can come in many settings; in rehabilitation it is usually done by university or agency personnel. Practice settings for rehabilitation supervisors include public rehabilitation programs, private not-for-profit community-based organizations, independent living centers, universities and colleges, mental health centers, private (proprietary) rehabilitation companies, K-12 school systems, insurance companies, business and industry, hospitals and medical centers, and correctional facilities (Saunders & Peck, 2001). It is a job that comes with little training but heavy responsibilities. These responsibilities are increasing in all settings as the professional worlds of psychology and rehabilitation have entered an era in which access to licensure and certification has become essential for practitioners in order to compete for third-party reimbursement and maintain professional credibility (Tarvydas, 1995). With students pushing for credentials, supervisors are often put to task on having specialized knowledge outside their areas of competence in order to help students with their goals of attaining certain licensures or certifications. This is the lament of many rehabilitation educators with the certified rehabilitation counselor (CRC) credential who are now supervising students pursuing licensure as professional counselors (e.g., Licensed Professional Counselors or Licensed Mental Health Counselors). Recent studies (e.g., Ferrin, Frain, Leech, & Holcomb, 2004) suggest that more than 25 percent of graduates with rehabilitation master's degrees are seeking professional licensure, with many others seeking certifications in diverse fields such as substance abuse counseling and vocational evaluation. With the move to more diverse roles by graduating students, at a time when there is, appropriately, increased knowledge on the part of consumers as to what counselors should know, supervisors are under stress to ethically serve students concerning issues about which they were never taught themselves.

Supervision in the rehabilitation and career counseling environments can come with many delicate ethical issues for the supervisor. First, the supervisor and supervisee are often in a position in which they are governed by a number of codes of ethics. It is not uncommon for a rehabilitation supervisor to be working under the CRCC code, the ACA code, and the state or federal code of the agency at which the supervisor are employed. This has caused confusion for some who see a difference in some aspects of the code (Saunders & Peck, 2001). Second, the majority of supervisors in the field hold master's degrees in rehabilitation or a related field that, often, has not allowed for any specialized training in the aspects of being a supervisor. Fortunately, CRCC and ACA have begun to rectify this situation by infusing the CRCC Code of Ethics into the ACA Code of Ethics in order to start to lessen the confusion that comes with multiple codes (Saunders & Peck, 2001). Finally, the CRCC Code of Ethics has recently added a section on supervision in order to help answer questions posed by this position. However, while this new input can be helpful, supervisors need to recognize the code as just a guideline, and they must stray abreast of the supervision literature in order to stay current in the field. This can be difficult in the nonacademic roles that most supervisors currently play (Patterson, 1998; Tarvydas, 1995).

The Use of Power: Giving It to Clients

With the Rehabilitation Act Amendments of 1998 demanding that "individuals must be active participants in their own rehabilitation program, including making meaningful and informed choices about the selection of their vocational goals, objectives and services" (Tarvydas & Cottone, 2000), the need to teach clients their equal roles in the process went from a moral responsibility to an ethical duty as well. It is imperative that clients be provided with the vital information they need concerning their rehabilitation processes in order that they are able to make informed choices concerning their own rehabilitation processes (Tarvydas & Cottone, 2000). Unfortunately, families and persons with disabilities often cite the counselor and other rehabilitation professionals as being stressful to deal with and not helpful in terms of resource acquisition (Kosciulek, 1994).

It becomes the ethical responsibility of the rehabilitation counselor to recognize the needs of and prepare persons with disabilities to be able participate fully in the collaborative process that is the rehabilitation process (Tarvydas & Cottone, 2000). This may be a process of helping clients develop self-determination in order that they understand and take ownership of their own knowledge, skills, and attitudes. With many clients who have had little chance in their life to make decisions for themselves due to limited experiences, this may be a slow process with skill teaching and role playing along the way in order that clients develop the competencies and capacities to exercise autonomy in their life. The rehabilitation professional has an obligation to facilitate this learning and the freedom of choice and action that comes along with such development (Gatens-Robinson & Rubin, 2001).

The rehabilitation process is a unique one among the counseling professions that requires rehabilitation counselors have a strong obligation of beneficence toward clients (Howie et al., 1992). Beneficence is often problematic for rehabilitation professionals due to the tendency to become overall parental or authoritarian with clients (Patterson, 1998). It can be a particularly difficult act to balance due to the special knowledge rehabilitation professionals have concerning the special needs and risk conditions of a certain groups of individuals, along with being in a unique position to be able to help assess the risks and benefits of courses of actions from these individuals (Howie et al., 1992). In addition to often being the sole access to needed information and resources, rehabilitation counselors, especially in the state and federal system, are in a position of power that allows them to dispense or withhold resources and information that could promote the welfare of clients (Gatens-Robinson & Rubin, 2001). While it may be that this role should change and counselors not be case managers and eligibility determinants, it is a role in which many counselors find themselves in the realities of practice today. It is thus the duty of counselors to work with clients so that there is less disparity between the roles of counselor and client. Counselors should work on educating clients and the community so that knowledge they hold becomes common knowledge among persons with disabilities in order that they may access resources and information without needing the counselor to play an intermediary role in the process.

The counselor must be proactive in pushing the client to adapt these skills. The rehabilitation client who comes for services at midlife often has the expectation that the rehabilitation counselor will follow a medical treatment model, in which the professional is the expert and the client unquestioningly follows the professional's advice. Rehabilitation services, as affirmed by the passage of the Rehabilitation Act of 1973, differentiates rehabilitation services from the medical model, emphasizing the importance of the consumer's role, and mandating involvement in the rehabilitation services planning process through the completion of the Individual Written Rehabilitation Plan (IWRP) (Rubin & Roessler, 1995). The IWRP, now called the Individual Plan for Employment, or IPE, is a plan for the services and the relationship between the counselor and client. It should be codeveloped by the counselor and client and reviewed periodically; it is the driving part of the ongoing process between the client and the counselor (Tarvydas & Cottone, 2000). In addition to the long-term goals and plans the IPE outlines, it should also contain information from the client regarding how he or she is involved in choosing alternative goals (Rubin & Roessler, 1995).

The Rehabilitation Act is in sharp contrast to the attitude that the professional knows what's best for the client, especially in cases where the client may seem to have an emotional or mental illness that leads to what are perceived to be bad choices (Guess, Benson & Siegel-Causey, 1985). Beauchamp and Childress (1989) note that any limitations on autonomy should be limited to areas of true incompetence of the individual. It is the underlying assumption with all clients that they have the ability to make competent and rationale decisions, and they have the legislative and moral right to make such decisions (Kitchener, 1984; Patterson, 1998). Even in cases in which legal guardians or others have the final say for clients, counselors should work with clients to get assent to any decision about the client.

Clients and rehabilitation counselors themselves are aware of the need for more autonomy in the current rehabilitation process. Counselors note that there are numerous reasons why clients do not show self-determination through autonomy: The consumers have unrealistic vocational goals; the clients request more services than are necessary to achieve suitable employment; the clients feel the need to have the most expensive services to meet their needs; and the expectations of clients are often not in balance with the realities of the world (Patterson, Patrick, & Parker, 2000). These barriers have been noted in the rehabilitation profession for some time and emphasize the need for counselors to educate clients to bring them into the reality the counselor works in. In addition, these points also should enlighten federal and state agencies to help put parameters on services and funds that are available in order that clients and counselors can understand the options that are available to them. It is human nature to desire the top-of-the-line service or equipment; we see this in all aspects of human life: People make choices about the quality in regard to expense and other real-world realities when the realities impact them. People who are invested in the cost of the products and services they use are more likely to investigate the best options in terms of what they need and in the realities of cost and practicality. Therefore, counselors need to work to bring those clients who are unfamiliar with the realities of the world up to date on how their decisions and desires actually affect their rehabilitation process, and counselors must advocate for a system that is individualistic yet with solid enough parameters that counselors and clients can understand the practicalities of the system.

An example may be beneficial here. In the late 1990s, the state system in which this author worked allowed clients $10,000 over the life of their case for equipment. Clients could ask for and be granted an additional $2,000 for equipment if the needs of the case warranted such an addition. By making clients aware of this financial constraint from the beginning and helping clients understand how equipment needs and cost would be a part of different aspects of their rehabilitation plan, clients were able to take ownership of cost-containment strategies early on in order to have available funds for equipment needs at the end of the plan, when they may begin work. It was a concept similar to "saving money for a rainy day" lessons everyone had learned as a child; thus, it made sense to clients, and they could now take a more active role in some aspects of their rehabilitation process. Counselors in this situation often have difficulty when the clients desire to spend funds in ways the counselors do not agree with, and all parents out there can attest to some difficulty during the learning stages of money management. However, it seems to be learning from these decisions that allows relationships to move from paternal to self-determining. We encourage counselors to help clients understand the business world of adaptive equipment, role-model their comparison-shopping skills, and allow clients to take over this aspect of the process as much as the agency allows. This ownership ideally will help clients, not only with a better understanding of the realities of equipment purchases, but also with the opportunity to become more realistic in all decisions and goals in the clients' lives. Fortunately, emerging concepts in rehabilitation education point along these same lines.

Spirituality

Informed choice, self-determination, and empowerment fit in well with a respect for the spirituality of a client. Rehabilitation counselors may face clients with very different beliefs and cultures from their own. Allowing clients to define the role spirituality, along with family and similar concepts, will have in the rehabilitation process allows clients to take charge of their rehabilitation plan. While the earlier beliefs that a disability was a punishment from God have moved away from the mainstream, the influence of religion and spirituality on illness and disability can still be very strong in some individuals and cultures. Counselors who take Perspective III attempt to recognize how many facets of the client's life will be involved in the rehabilitation process. By respecting and understanding how these facets can help the clients reach their goals, a counselor is respecting the rehabilitation process.

LEGAL ISSUES IN REHABILITATION COUNSELING

Privileged Communication

The concept of privileged communication is also one that is not easily understood by rehabilitation professionals. Rehabilitation counselors should not assume privileged communication extends to their practice (Cottone & Tarvydas, 2003). Indeed, wise counselors will investigate the legal protections that are granted to them in the area they practice. Generally speaking, privileged communication status is granted to only those who hold a license in that jurisdiction (Cottone & Tarvydas, 2003). Many rehabilitation counselors will therefore not be granted privileged communication status with their clients, due to their status as Certified Rehabilitation Counselors (CRCs) and not Licensed Professional Counselors (LPCs) or similar licensure. While this privilege is often being reviewed through court cases, and rehabilitation counselors should work with their legislatures to make changes to include rehabilitation professionals, it is important for counselors to understand and relate to clients their status in terms of privileged communication.

Privileged communication is a legal term describing specific types of relationships that enjoy protection from disclosure in legal proceedings. Privilege is granted by law and belongs to the client in the relationship. When privilege exists, the client is protected from having the covered communications revealed without explicit permission (Koocher & Keith-Spiegel, 1990).

Recently, the Supreme Court decision *Jaffee v. Redmond* (1996) held that communications between psychotherapists (including psychologists) are privileged in federal courts under certain circumstances. The court ruled that "the confidential communications between a licensed psychotherapist and the patient in the course of diagnosis or treatment are protected from compelled disclosure under Rule 501 of the Federal Rules for Evidence (*Jaffee v. Redmond,* 1996). Mary Lu Redmond was a police officer in a suburban Chicago neighborhood. In 1991, she shot and killed Ricky Allen while responding to a "fight in progress" call. After the shooting, Officer Redmond sought counseling from a licensed clinical social worker. Later, Jaffee, acting as administrator of Mr. Allen's estate, sued Redmond, citing U.S. civil rights statutes and Illinois tort law. Jaffee wanted access to the social worker's notes and sought to compel the therapist to give oral testimony about the therapy. Redmond and her therapist refused. The trial judge instructed the jury that refusing to provide such information could be held against Officer Redmond. The jury awarded damages based on both the federal civil rights and state laws.

On June 13, 1996, the Supreme Court overturned the lower court's decision, upholding the existence of privilege under federal Rules of Evidence to patients of licensed psychotherapists by a vote of 7 to 2. The two dissenting justices who did not warrant such a privilege in this case argued that psychotherapy should not be protected by judicially created privilege and that social workers were not clearly experts in psychotherapy. Thus, this case set a new national standard that affords privilege protections across jurisdictions (Ong, Lee, & Frain, 2002).

This Illinois case suggests that all those working with licensure in the helping profession in a counselor role have the right to privileged communication, even if they are not a psychologist or licensed in the jurisdiction. However, this case has yet to be applied to other areas; thus, counselors need to investigate on their own how their rehabilitation status affects their privileged communication status.

Often, there is confusion, and privileged communication is confused with confidentiality (Patterson, 1998). Privileged communication is the legal right of counselors not to testify in court regarding confidential information (Hummell, Talbutt, & Alexander, 1985). Conversely, confidentiality refers to an ethical decision not to reveal information concerning a client. Thus, a counselor is required to explain to clients the limits of confidentiality based on the jurisdiction he or she is practicing in, and therefore discuss the foreseeable situations that could arise that would limit confidentiality (Cottone & Tarvydas, 2003). There are two types of privileged communication that counselors should make clients aware of: absolute and conditional. Generally, rehabilitation counselors have conditional privileged communication, indicating that in some, but not all, situations the communication between the client and the counselor is privileged (Denkowski & Denkowski, 1982). Counselors should always be aware, though, that, unless professionals have been granted privileged communication by statute, none exists (Hummell et al., 1985).

And there are many limitations and exceptions concerning how privilege is distributed to individuals. For instance, students, such as unlicensed individuals working in counseling roles during their internships, may not be covered by privilege in accord to communication with a licensed supervisor, but state laws vary widely in this regard. Additionally, there are many instances in which circumstances mandate the practitioner by law to breach confidentiality and report certain information to authorities. For example, a rehabilitation counselor may be obligated to report cases such as child abuse to state authorities (Ong, Lee, & Frain, 2002). When law and ethics do diverge for a rehabilitation counselor, often the only recourse is for the counselor to choose civil disobedience, doing so usually on one's own, as the APA and CRCC ethical codes offer little guidance: "If psychologists' ethical responsibilities conflict with law, psychologists make known their commitment to the Ethics code and take steps to resolve the conflict in a responsible manner" (Koocher & Keith-Speigel, 1990).

Rehabilitation counselors also face many unique situations to the field concerning confidentiality. Because rehabilitation counselors may work in many settings including school, forensic, state, and federal, they must be aware of how confidentiality issues affect the different settings in which they work. We encourage those who work with minor students to examine Chapter 10 in this text, which discusses specific issues related to ethics, confidentiality, and the issues that concern students who are under 18 years of age. We are also aware that many rehabilitation counselors are practicing in federal addiction treatment facilities or addiction facilities that receive federal funding, both of which have very specific limits of confidentiality based on their setting status. (In particular, counselors in federally funded addiction treatment facilities are granted privileged communication regardless of their licensure status.). Additionally, it is recognized that rehabilitation counselors often find themselves in settings that lend themselves to doing much work in a group setting, including group therapy, but also group case management and group assessments. Cottone and Tarvydas (2003), among others, point out the awareness that counselors should relate to clients concerning limits of confidentiality that result from the group setting.

Mandatory Reporting

The *Tarasoff* case mentioned throughout this book also applies to rehabilitation counseling and psychology for counselors who have clients who make threats to others. Rehabilitation professionals may find themselves in a situation wherein a client makes a threat to another identifiable person, and the counselor believes this threat to be serious enough to warrant intervention. The counselor is responsible for taking action to warn the identified person of the threat of bodily harm from the client. This is an extreme measure and should be done with caution and after consultation with other rehabilitation professionals whenever possible.

Many rehabilitation professionals are also in positions in which mandatory reporting of certain actions is their responsibility. In most jurisdictions, this applies to cases of child abuse for individuals under the age of 18, cases of elder abuse for individuals over the age of 65, and individuals with some form of disability. In all of these cases, the rehabilitation counselor must report situations in which the above individuals were neglected or abused. Generally, this reporting should be to the police or the department of children services or similar government agency that oversees the affected individual. This mandatory reporting applies to almost anyone in a position of contact with clients or consumers; thus, case managers, rehabilitation counselors, and job coaches, among others, are all responsible to take action under mandatory reporting situations.

The Americans with Disabilities Act (ADA) and the Rehabilitation Act

Rehabilitation was formed and has been shaped by legislation. One of the most important pieces of legislation is the Americans with Disabilities Act of 1990 (ADA; PL 101-336). Considered the civil rights act for people with disabilities, this piece of legislation has many important legal aspects a counselor should be aware of. First, disability is defined in the act as it was in section 504 of the Rehabilitation Act of 1973: "(a) physical or mental impairment that substantially limits one or more of the major life activities of such individual: (b) a record of such an impairment, or (c) being regarded as having such an impairment" (Adams 1991, p. 28). This definition of disability explains who is covered by the five titles of ADA. The titles give people with disabilities equal rights to employment through reasonable accommodations, and nondiscrimation in terms of access to public and private services as well as telecommunication services. While a complete capsule of legislation as it applies to persons with disabilities is outside the scope of this book, it is assumed that a counselor working with individuals with disabilities would be aware of legislation and how it effects the individuals he or she works with; there are numerous excellent sources for obtaining this information (e.g., Chan & Leahy, 1999; Rubin & Roessler, 1995; Szymanski & Parker, 2003).

Box 13.5 summarizes the legal issues discussed in this section.

BOX 13.5
KEY LEGAL ISSUES IN REHABILITATION COUNSELING

Privileged communication: Rehabilitation counselors have the right of privileged communication with clients. Therefore, they do not have to disclose information they received from a client.

Mandatory reporting: Although information is privileged between a counselor and a client, counselors must report certain information, depending on the jurisdictions they are working in. Generally, cases of child abuse or neglect, elder abuse or neglect, and abuse to individuals with disabilities must be reported to the proper authorities by the counselor.

Rehabilitation Act of 1973: Mandated that counselors must use consumer involvement to help promote the rights of individuals with disabilities.

Americans with Disabilities Act of 1990: Expanded on the prior Rehabilitation Act and gave more rights to individuals with disabilities.

CONCLUDING NOTE: PERSPECTIVE III

During the 1970s and the 1980s, there was a focus on normalization and mainstreaming, which was used as the mantra for rehabilitation professionals in their professional activities (Wolfensberger, 1983). More recently, empowerment has been the "mantra" that permeates the rehabilitation process (Emner, 1991). Perspective III recognizes and advances the ideas of empowerment in an ethical manner by integrating professional codes and personal counselor development into the actual practice of rehabilitation counseling.

The term and associated philosophy of empowerment emerged out of research in community psychology and the practice of political activism in the 1980s (Flaherty & Parashar, 2002). With origins in the community development movement of the 1970s, empowerment refers generally to the capacity of disenfranchised persons to understand and to become active participants in matters that affect their lives. In practice, this represents a Perspective III ethical stance toward helping clients develop skills that allow self-determination. Self-determination allows clients to be the source of information without relying on professionals or helpful-minded family members. In order to have self-determination, clients must have knowledge and awareness about themselves in regard to their relative standing in the world. Therefore, they must be able to self-monitor and evaluate themselves in order to understand and self-manage their performance and make adjustments when they are performing at undesirable levels. With this awareness comes the self-efficacy and appreciation of oneself that allows for planning and decision making in regard to employment and other aspects on life. This decision-making process is aided greatly by the ability of clients for self-advocacy in asking for what they need from not only the rehabilitation professional but also those they will meet after being rehabilitated, such as employers. Self-determination is a key component to empowerment that has been recognized as lacking in many clients in the rehabilitation process due to the overprotection that clients have often become accustomed to because of well-meaning parental and teacher shielding and isolation.

In modern health promotion parlance, empowerment "has come to represent efforts to foster bottom-up social change through consciousness raising, self-help, capacity development and political action" (Simons-Morton & Crump, 1996, p. 291). Through a Perspective III approach and empowerment education, theoretically, individuals within groups can develop motivation and skills enabling them to advocate for social reforms to better the lot of the group or broader community.

Empowerment has been defined in many ways. Fawcett and colleagues (1994) defined empowerment as "the process of gaining some control over events, outcomes, and resources of importance to an individual or group" (Fawcett, White, Balcazar, Suarez-Balcazar, et al., 1994, p. 472). Along the line of relational ethics, Conger and Kanungo (1988) suggested that empowerment is primarily relational, or that empowerment concerns the extent to which one has control or influence over another or a group. Thus, it seems the empowerment process increases interpersonal or political power so individuals can take action to improve their life situations (Guiterrez, 1990). This is an essential skill that must be taught to clients in the rehabilitation field, since the field is fraught with professionals who attempt to help too much, and whose clients have come to have a dependency on service providers typically due to the clients' lack of awareness of real choices (Olney & Salomone, 1992).

Empowerment skills must be cultivated with clients due to the diseases of vulnerability and loss of social opportunity that are prevalent for many persons with disabilities. Proponents of the discrimination model acknowledge that biological agents may cause various psychiatric symptoms, and disease vulnerabilities may, in turn, lead to diminished skills and social support networks. However, social misconceptions about these symptoms, and the "illness" they entail, have a much more damaging effect on social functioning. A primary way to threat the "injustices" toward people with disabilities is to enable them to obtain power over their lives in their community (Flaherty & Parashar, 2002). That is the essence of what empowerment is about. Empowerment values provide a belief system that governs how professionals and clients work together. These values include attention toward health, adaptation, competence, and natural helping systems. An empowerment approach considers wellness versus illness, and competence versus deficiency (Flaherty & Parashar, 2002). This suggests that rehabilitation counselors should work with persons with disabilities toward their becoming as independent as possible, by helping them to develop skills for the changing conditions that pose barriers in their lives. Additionally, counselors need to work with others to overcome obstacles that limit the full integration of all individuals into their communities (Flaherty & Parashar, 2002).

The empowerment process involves work through which people, organizations, and communities gain mastery and control over issues that concern them, develop a critical awareness of their environment, and participate in decisions that affect their lives. It provides individuals with opportunities to develop and practice skills necessary to exert control over their sociopolitical environment, such as decision making and resource-mobilization skills and the ability to critically analyze their sociopolitical environment. Critical awareness refers to an individual's knowledge of how to acquire those resources and the skill to manage the resources once they are obtained (Kieffer, 1984).

Perspective III processes also consist of collective learning and opportunities to influence the sociopolitical environment. They are processes in which efforts to gain a critical understanding of the relevant social environment are central, to gain access to resources are paramount, and to work with others to achieve common goals are fundamental (Cornell Empowerment Group, 1989). Maton and Salem (1995) state that empowering interventions enhance group-based systems, provide opportunities to develop knowledge and skills, create a supportive resource pool, and include shared and inclusive leadership. Therefore, rehabilitation counselors should have as a goal with all clients, organizations, and in all positions to empower them to become more self-reliant and self-governing and less controlled by external forces.

The rehabilitation community is moving more toward a Perspective III approach, as can be seen in attempts to help foster the concept of empowerment and self-determination in persons with disabilities, and in counselors themselves. It has become part of the code of ethics, and numerous authors have presented models to aid counselors in understanding how to promote the empowerment concepts to individuals and the community at large. Kosciulek (1999) offered the Consumer-Directed Theory of Empowerment (CDTE) as a model for guiding the development of rehabilitation services that promote consumer empowerment. His model emphasizes the awareness that there must be a continual stress on increased consumer participation at all levels (Seelman & Sweeney, 1995). The belief is that, through this model of rehabilitation service delivery, there will be an increase of community integration and empowerment as well as increased quality of life for individuals with disabilities (Kosciulek, 1999). This will happen through the acquisition of values and attitudes that are incorporated into the individual's worldview (Bolton & Brookings, 1996). This internal and psychological factor includes a sense of control, competence, confidence, responsibility, and participation that comes from the relational relationship between the rehabilitation counselor and the client. In addition to this psychological factor, CDTE also promotes the situational and social factor that is concerned with the manner in which individuals with disabilities behaviors are influenced by their environment. Through the relational approach to clients, counselors can help individuals with disabilities to have control over important resources, and they are then best able to determine the courses of their lives, solve their problems in living, and develop adaptive social networks (Flaherty & Parashar, 2002).

While the empowerment approach is an essential part of the rehabilitation process, it needs to be understood that this is a Eurocentric approach. Many clients the rehabilitation counselor will work with need skills and education in order to make informed choices. Similarly, many rehabilitation counselors will need work to integrate their own personal beliefs into their counseling practice. Rehabilitation counselors must also recognize the necessity for releasing some power to their clients who are not of the predominant culture in order allow expanded choice after proper education and skills have been realized by the clients.

CASE ILLUSTRATION OF ETHICAL-PROFESSIONAL DECISION MAKING IN REHABILITATION COUNSELING

This section applies the ethical-professional decisional strategy to a rehabilitation counseling dilemma, introduced in Box 13.6.

BOX 13.6

CONFIDENTIALITY AND DUTY TO WARN WITH PERSONS WHO ARE HIV POSITIVE

In Julie Morrison's work as a rehabilitation counselor, she has a client with whom she has been working for three months. Karen, a 38-year-old client, confides one day to Julie during a meeting between the two that she has tested positive for the HIV virus. She has just gotten confirming results on this day from an HIV clinic at a nearby university; she is very distraught. She recently got remarried, after being divorced just over a year ago; she believes she contracted the virus during the time she was single from an individual she had intercourse with while on vacation.

The previous issue in the counseling relationship had been adjusting to her hearing loss and working on finding suitable employment for Karen. Karen is a Licensed Practical Nurse who had been working at a local hospital with oncology patients. She left her job voluntarily six months ago because her life had suddenly changed due to a car accident that left her with damaged hearing. She wishes now to go back to work as a nurse but is in the process of learning sign language and adjusting to her disability.

During the course of the meeting, Karen states that she is terrified at the thought of telling her husband about her HIV status, that she does not wish for him to know about her past sexual experience, and that she does not want to cause suspicion by not continuing to have normal sexual relations with her husband. She acknowledges, "I just need some time to figure out what to do about all this, and then everything will be fine." Being a nurse, she is aware of precautions in their sexual practice they can use, and she knows how to deal with any blood spills she may have.

In addition to concerns about her husband's contracting the virus, Julie is also aware from previous meetings that Karen enjoys "going out" some weekends when her husband travels, and Karen has confided in Julie that she sometimes finds herself spending the night with men she meets.

Karen indicates that she was tested seven months ago, before she left work, and did not have the virus, and was tested twelve months before that using the Western Blot method, which she believes detects the HIV virus even in its earliest stages.

Step 1: Identify the problem. There are many aspects of relational ethics taking place. As a counselor, Julie may recognize that many people with HIV are stigmatized and that many individuals make assumptions concerning a person due to his or her HIV status. In a case like this, a counselor may first be challenged with his or her own feelings concerning working with someone who carries a life-threatening virus. In addition, a counselor should be aware of how his or her own feelings concerning how the virus was contracted and, perhaps, the client's social activities affect the counseling process. Furthermore, some counselors might feel uncomfortable concerning the employment goal of oncology nurse for someone who has HIV. There may be questions in the counselor's mind concerning how advocating for this client may affect clients in the future, or if advocating to employers about this client should include full disclosure concerning her HIV status.

Step 2: Identify the participants asffected by the decision. In this case, it appears many people could be affected by Karen's HIV status. The counselor and Karen are obviously affected, as they may be the only two individuals who are fully aware of Karen's HIV status. Who else is affected? Well, it seems Karen's husband may be at risk for contracting HIV if precautions are not taken. As a counselor, how comfortable would you be concerning Karen's continuing normal sexual relations with her husband? Would you feel comfortable talking about the precautions they are taking? Would you feel obligated to contact the husband? What about the other relationships she may be in and her past husband: How should they be involved in this case? Future employers also seem to be affected by the problem. Should a nurse disclose HIV status to an employer, to patients, to the community at large? When and how should this be done if disclosure is an option? What ethical and moral codes are involved? How would the organization you work for respond to this situation?

Step 3: Identify probable courses of action and benefits and risks for the participants.

Option 1. For a relational counselor who looks for assets in individuals, this case may bring up various emotions; however, on top of the emotional and ethical implications there may also be an educational component that is important for the counselor to understand. There are many misperceptions concerning the spread of the HIV virus, and the counselor would want to be up to date in order to be able to separate reality from myth. The counselor then may want to talk with Karen concerning some of her reservations about telling others about her HIV status. By trying to understand why Karen may be afraid to tell her husband or future employers, the counselor may better understand some of Karen's decisions and help her make the best decision for herself. The counselor and Karen may get to the point where Karen wishes to disclose her status to some individuals who may be at minimal risk for contracting the virus, such as sexual partners, but does not wish to disclose to others whose risk is also minimal, such as patients or coworkers. Ideally, the client and counselor would understand the risks and benefits as best possible, understanding that many aspects of this decision, such as others' reactions, may be unpredictable.

Option 2. The other option would be for Julie to break confidentiality and tell those who could potentially be affected by Karen's HIV status. Julie might contact Karen's husband and explain the risks he is taking, as well as potential employers where Karen may potentially work and expose patients to risks of which they are unaware. Benefit: The individuals who could be at potential risk for contracting the virus would be aware of the risk and take proper precautions. Risk: Karen may be indelibly harmed in terms of her future employment and her relationship with her husband and others.

Option 3. Julie may choose to wait and see what Karen will do after the initial shock of the diagnosis has passed. Perhaps she will enter into an agreement with Karen that Karen will not participate in any activity that could potentially put anyone at risk, such as sexual activity, until the counselor and client meet again. They may then set up frequent appointments in order to discuss the issue further. Benefit: The counseling relationship remains open and potential decisions concerning disclosure can be thought through and investigated properly. Risk: Karen may agree to some stipulations in the office but not abide by the agreement once she leaves. She may then abandon the counseling relationship and not reveal this information to future counselors.

Step 4: Evaluate the benefits and risks for each course of action based on domains/dimensions.

Contextual Domain Considerations

In order for a counselor to make appropriate ethical actions using a Perspective III approach, the counselor must understand the context that the client is coming from. The counselor should move beyond the immediate thoughts of threats to others and also consider what disclosure will mean for the client. Will the client forever after be subject to minority status and scapegoating, along with diminished opportunities? The counselor must also look at his or her own thoughts and values about HIV, sexual behavior, and personal life choices. This examination may help the counselor understand the blind spots that may be affecting his or her thoughts on how to proceed with an individual with HIV. As a rehabilitation counselor, one is expected to advocate for all individuals with a disability: How would your actions concerning this one client affect the opportunities for other clients? Should that affect your actions?

Step 5: Consult with peers and experts. As with any ethical decision, as well as general practice in counseling, talking to others can be very helpful to a counselor for sorting out his or her own contextual values from the actual situation taking place. Experts in the field of HIV may be helpful for a counselor in understanding risk factors and other aspects of HIV that are not familiar to the counselor.

Step 6: Decide on the most feasible option and document the decision-making process. Involve the client, when appropriate. A relational view of ethics in the rehabilitation field would strongly support the idea that the client should be involved in the counselor's decision-making process. Therefore, the most feasible course of action would depend greatly on the desires of Karen, as well as the counselor's investigation concerning the possibility of harm toward identifiable others. Ideally, the counselor would help Karen advocate for herself in a manner that is appropriate and accurate and that allows her to reach her maximum potential. In a situation in which Karen chooses not to disclose, the rehabilitation code of ethics suggests the counselor is responsible for warning others. This viewpoint seems counter to the relational view of ethics, and the main author strongly encourages counselors to consider a relational view. The author also strongly encourages the rehabilitation professional to consider the ACA and other codes in regard to informing others in cases with HIV. Other codes do not require the counselor to inform others in the case of HIV/AIDS.

Step 7: Implement, evaluate, and document the enacted decision. Based on the decision that has resulted in the client–counselor relationship, there could be a number of ways to implement the decision. Ideally, Karen would feel comfortable enough to take an active role in implementing the decision and would be open to the counselor's evaluating and documenting the result of the decision.

As in any ethical dilemma, there are many things you may wish to consider. Here are some other aspects of this case you may wish to consider: What concerns do you have concerning Karen's confidentiality and the harm she could do to others? Why do you think Karen chose to confide in you? If Karen would have believed she got the virus another way, such as a blood transfusion after her accident, would that affect your thinking in this case? If, instead of Karen, this were a gay male under similar circumstances, how would your approach to this case differ?

KEY POINTS

1. Regulation of the practice of career counseling is largely voluntary via professional societies and national certifying agencies. Voluntary certification is critical to a foundation of best practice.
2. Cultural context provides a basis of communication and understanding that is vital to the counseling relationship and effective outcomes.
3. Ethnic/racial diversity, while increasing in U.S. society, impacts access to occupational information, computers, and the Internet. The ownership of a computer and an Internet service subscription is differential by income level. Access to information is a function of means and ability. While there may be some pubic websites available, one's clients may not possess the necessary skills to obtain the information needed to make occupational decisions in their best interests.
4. Understanding by counselors of their core values and the impact of core values on counseling effectiveness is fundamental to effective practice.
5. Rational practice and the adoption of core practice values as one's own professional values is best practice.
6. Rehabilitation and career counseling are specialties that work with unique populations on numerous issues with employment, and quality outcomes are the central tenets of both disciplines.
7. Rehabilitation counseling works with individuals with various types of disabilities in numerous settings in order to help them achieve their full potential in life, in employment, living situation, and access to their environment.
8. Rehabilitation counselors advocate for people with disabilities, but more important, the rehabilitation counselors work with people with disabilities in order that they can advocate for themselves.
9. Rehabilitation and career counseling are specialized areas with unique licensing and certifications, but also are directly related to many similar organizations such as ACA and APA.
10. The Code of Ethics for Rehabilitation Counselors has recently been revised in part to emphasize the areas of multiculturalism and supervision that were lacking in the previous document.

REVIEW QUESTIONS

1. What is your impression of career counseling and how do you think it compares to mental health counseling?
2. Do you think that the relationship that exists between a rehabilitation counselor and his or her client is different from the relationship that exists between a mental health or school counselor and his or her client? Explain your answer.
3. What societal barriers exist for rehabilitation or career counseling?
4. How do you think empowerment can be instilled into rehabilitation counseling clients?
5. How do you think rehabilitation counseling clients are different from general counseling clients? Do you think they should be treated differently? Explain your answer.

REFERENCES

Adams, J. E. (1991). Judicial and regulatory interpretation of employment rights of persons with disabilities. *Journal of Applied Rehabilitation Counseling, 22,* 28–46.

American Psychology Association. (1991). *Legal liability related to confidentiality and the prevention of HIV transmission.* Washington, DC: APA Council of Representatives.

Americans with Disabilities Act of 1990, 42 U.S.C. 12101.

Alston, R. J., & Bell, T. (1996). Multiculturalism in rehabilitation education: History, pedagogy, and future trends. *Rehabilitation Education, 10,* 2.

Atkins, B., & Wright, G. (1980). Three views of vocational rehabilitation of blacks: The statement. *Journal of Rehabilitation, 46,* 40–46.

Beauchamp, T., & Childress, J. (1989). *Principles of biomedical ethics* (3rd ed.). New York: Oxford University Press.

Bolton, B., & Brookings, J. (1996). Development of a multifaceted definition of empowerment. *Rehabilitation Counseling Bulletin, 39,* 256–264.

Bozarth, J. D. (1981). Philosophy and ethics in rehabilitation counseling. In R. M. Parker & C. E. Hansen (Eds.), *Rehabilitation counseling* (pp. 59–81). Boston: Allyn and Bacon.

Brubaker, D. R. (1977). Professionalization and rehabilitation counseling. *Journal of Applied Rehabilitation Counseling, 8,* 208–217.

Burns, C. I., & Holloway, F. L. (1989). Therapy in supervision: An unresolved issue. *The Clinical Supervisor, 7,* 47–57.

Byington, K., Fischer, J., Walker, L., & Freedman, E. (1997). Evaluating the effectiveness of multicultural counseling ethics and assessment training. *Journal of Applied Rehabilitation Counseling, 28,* 15–19.

Chan, F., & Leahy, M. (1999). *Health care and disability: Case management.* Lake Zurich, IL: Vocational Consultant Press.

Chan, T. (2004). *Qualified personnel recruitment and retention: Challenges and opportunities.* Paper presented at the National Conference on Rehabilitation Education, Washington, D.C.

Commission on Rehabilitation Counselor Certification. (2001a). *Code of professional ethics for rehabilitation counselors.* Rolling Meadows, IL: Author.

Commission on Rehabilitation Counselor Certification (2001b). *Scope of practice for rehabilitation counseling.* Rolling Meadows, IL: Author.

Conger, J. A., & Kanungo, R. N. (1988). The empowerment process: Integrating theory and practice. *Academy of Management Review, 13,* 471–482.

Cornell Empowerment Group. (1989). Empowerment through family support. *Networking Bulletin,* 1(1), 2.

Cottone, R. R. (1982). Ethical issues in private-for-profit rehabilitation. *Journal of Applied Rehabilitation Counseling, 13,* 14–17.

Cottone, R. R., & Tarvydas, V. M. (2003). Ethical and professional issues in counseling. Columbus, OH: Merrill Prentice-Hall.

Dalton, H. L., Burris, S., & Yale Law Project. (1986). *AIDS and the law: A guide for the public.* New Haven, CT: Yale University Press.

Denkowski, K., & Denkowski, G. (1982). Client–counselor confidentiality: An update of rationale, legal status and implication. *Personnel and Guidance Journal, 60,* 371–375.

Emner, W. G. (1991). An empowerment philosophy for rehabilitation in the 20th century. *Journal of Rehabilitation, 57,* 7–12.

Fawcett, S., White, G., Balcazar, F., Suarez-Balcazar, Y., et al. (1994). A contextual-behavioral model of empowerment: Case studies involving people with physical disabilities. *American Journal of Community Psychology, 22*(4), 471–496.

Ferrell, O. C., & Gresham, L. G. (1985). A contingency framework for understanding ethical decision making in marketing. *Journal of Marketing, 49,* 87–96.

Ferrin, J., Frain, M., Leech, L., & Holcomb, J. (2004, October). *Employment patterns of rehabilitation counselors: A national study using Multiple Regression Analysis.* Paper presented at the National Training Conference on Rehabilitation Education, Washington, DC.

Fisher, J., & Chambers, E. (2003). Multicultural counseling ethics and assessment competencies: Directions for counselor education programs. *Journal of Applied Rehabilitation Counseling, 34,* 17–21.

Flaherty, S., & Parashar, D. (2002). *Consumerism, empowerment and independent living.* Unpublished manuscript, University of Wisconsin at Madison.

Flowers, J. G., & Parker, R. (1984). Personal philosophy and vocational rehabilitation job performance. In W. G. Emner, A. Patrick & D. K. Hollingsworth (Eds.), *Critical issues in rehabilitation counseling* (pp. 45–64). Springfield, IL: Thomas.

Fowler, C., & Wadsworth, J. (1991). Individualism and equality: Critical values in North American culture and the impact of disability. *Journal of Applied Rehabilitation Counseling, 22,* 19–23.

Frain, M., Berven, N. L., & Chan, F. (in press). Family resiliency, uncertainty, optimism, and the quality of life of individuals with HIV/AIDS. *Rehabilitation Counseling Bulletin.*

Gatens-Robinson, E., & Rubin, S. E. (2001). Societal values and ethical commitments that influence rehabilitation services delivery behavior. In S. E. Rubin & R. T. Roessler (Eds.), *Foundations of the vocational rehabilitation process*. Austin, TX: Pro-Ed.

Goodyear, R. K., & Bernard, J. M. (1998). Clinical supervision: Lessons from the literature. *Counselor Education and Supervision,* 38(1), 6–22.

Greenwood, R. (1987). Expanding community participation by people with disabilities: Implications for counselors. *Journal of Counseling and Development,* 16, 2.

Guess, D., Benson, H. A., & Siegel-Causey, E. (1985). Concepts and issues related to choice-making and autonomy among persons with severe disabilities. *Journal of the Association for Persons with Severe Handicaps, 10,* 79–86.

Guiterrez, L. (1990). Working with women of color: An empowerment perspective. *Social Work,* 35, 149–153.

Handelsman, M. M. (1986). Problems with ethics training by "osmosis." *Professional Psychology: Research and Practice, 17,* 371–371.

Harding, A., Gray, L., & Neal, M. (1993). Confidentiality limits with clients who have HIV: A review of ethical and legal guidelines and professional policies. *Journal of Counseling and Development, 71,* 297–305.

Hopkins, B., & Anderson, B. (1990). *The counselor and the law.* Alexandria, VA: American Association for Counseling and Development.

Howie, J., Gatens-Robinson, E., & Rubin, S. E. (1992). Applying ethical principles in rehabilitation counseling. *Rehabilitation Education, 6,* 41–55.

Hummell, D. L., Talbutt, L. C., & Alexander, M. D. (1985). *Law and ethics in counseling.* New York: Van Nostrand Reinhold.

Ivey, A., & Ivey, M. (1999). Toward a developmental diagnostic and statistical manual: The vitality of a contextual framework. *Journal of Counseling and Development, 77,* 484–491.

Jaffee v. Redmond et al., 1996 WL 314841 (U.S. June 13, 1996).

Kermani, E., & Weiss, B. (1989). AIDS and confidentiality: Legal concept and its application in psychotherapy. *American Journal of Psychotherapy, 43*(1), 25–31.

Kieffer, C. (1984). Citizen empowerment: A developmental perspective. *Prevention in Human Services, 3*(2–3), 9–36.

Kitchener, K. (1984). Intuition, critical evaluation, and ethical principles: The foundation for ethical decisions in counseling psychology. *Counseling Psychologist, 12*(3), 43–55.

Knapp, S., & VandeCreek, L. (1990). *What every therapist should know about AIDS.* Sarasota: Professional Resource Exchange.

Kolata, G. (1993, January 4). A losing battle. *Chicago Tribune,* pp. T1, T3.

Koenig, H., & Pritchett, J. (1998). Religion and psychotherapy. In H. Koenig (Ed.), *Handbook of religion and mental health.* (pp. 323–336). San Diego: Academic Press.

Koocher, G., & Keith-Spiegel, P. (1990). *Children, ethics, and the law: Professional issues and cases.* Lincoln, NE: University of Nebraska Press.

Kosciulek, J. (1994). Dimensions of family coping with head injury. *Rehabilitation Counseling Bulletin, 37,* 244–257.

Kosciulek, J. F. (1999). The consumer-directed theory of empowerment. *Rehabilitation Counseling Bulletin, 42*(3), 196–213.

Kuehn, M. D. (1991). An agenda for professional practice in the 1990s. *Journal of Applied Rehabilitation Counseling, 22,* 6–15.

Leahy, M. J. (1997). Qualified providers of rehabilitation counseling services. In D. R. Maki & T. F. Rigger (Eds.), *Rehabilitation counseling: Profession and practice* (pp. 95–110). New York: Springer.

Leahy, M. J., & Szymanski, E. (1995). Rehabilitation counseling: Evolution and current status. *Journal of Counseling and Development, 74,* 163–166.

Levine, L. S. (1959). The impact of disability. *Journal of Rehabilitation, 25,* 10–12.

Marshall, C., Leung, P., Johnson, S., & Busby, H. (2003). Ethical practice and cultural factors in rehabilitation. *Rehabilitation Education, 17,* 55–65.

Maton, K. I., & Salem, D. (1995). Organizational characteristics of empowering community settings: A multiple case study approach. *American Journal of Community Psychology, 23*(5), 631–656.

Melchert, T. P., & Patterson, M. M. (1999). Duty to warn and intervention with HIV-positive clients. *Professional Psychology: Research and Practice, 30*(2),180–186.

National Career Development Association. (1997). *Career counseling competencies.* Retrieved May 26, 2005, from http://www.ncda.org

National Career Development Association. (2003). *Ethical standards.* Tulsa, OK: author.

Middleton, R., A., Rollins, C., Sanderson, P., Leung, P., Harley, D., Ebner, D., & Leal-Idrogo, A. (2000). Endorsement of professional multicultural rehabilitation competences and standards: A call to action. *Rehabilitation Counseling Bulletin, 43,* 219–240.

Olney, M. F., & Salomone, P. R. (1992). Empowerment and choice in supported employment: Helping people to help themselves. *Journal of Applied Rehabilitation Counseling, 23,* 41–44.

Ong, L., Lee, G., & Frain, M. (2002, March). *Ethical issues in rehabilitation.* Paper presented at the American Counseling Association Conference. New Orleans, Louisiana.

Pape, D. (1987). Teaching professional ethics: The heart of the matter. *Rehabilitation Education, 1,* 129–131.

Parson, F. (1909). *Choosing a vocation.* Boston: Houghton Mifflin.

Patterson, J. B., Patrick, A., & Parker, R. M. (2000). Choice: Ethical and legal rehabilitation challenges. *Rehabilitation Counseling Bulletin, 43,* 203–208.

Patterson, J. B. (1998). Ethics and ethical decision making in rehabilitation counseling. In R. M. Parker & E. Szymanski (Eds.), *Rehabilitation counseling: Basics and beyond* (3rd ed.). Austin, TX: Pro-Ed.

Patterson, C. H. (1960). The counselor's responsibility in rehabilitation. In C. H. Patterson (Ed.), *Readings in rehabilitation counseling* (pp. 113–116). Champaign, IL: Stipes.

People of the State of Illinois v. Hubert. 91CM-6948 (St. Clair County, IL, March 18, 1992).

Rehabilitation Act of 1973, 87 stat. 355, 29 U.S.C. 701.

Rounds, J. B., & Tracey, T. J. (1990). From trait-factor to person-environment fit counseling: Theory and process. In W. B. Walsh & S. H. Osipow (Eds.), *Career counseling: Contemporary topics in vocational psychology* (pp. 1–44). Hillsdale, NJ: Erlbaum.

Rubin, S., & Roessler, R. T. (1995). *Foundations of the vocational rehabilitation process* (2nd ed.). Austin, TX: Pro-Ed.

Rubin, S., & Roessler, R. T. (2001). *Foundations of the vocational rehabilitation process* (3rd ed.). Austin, TX: Pro-Ed.

Salomone, P. (1988). Career-counseling: Steps and stages beyond Parsons. *Career Development Quarterly, 36,* 218–221.

Salomone, P. (1996). Career counseling and job placement: Theory and practice. In E. Szymanski & R. Parker (Eds.), *Work and disability: Issues and strategies in career development and job placement* (pp. 365–420). Austin, TX: Pro-Ed.

Saunders, J. L., & Peck, S. L. (2001). The code of professional ethics for rehabilitation counselors: The administrator and supervisor perspective. *Journal of Applied Rehabilitation Counseling, 32,* 20–27.

Seelman, K., & Sweeney, S. (1995). The changing universe of disability. *American Rehabilitation, 3,* 2–13.

Shertzer, B., & Stone, S. (1980). *Fundamentals of counseling.* Boston: Houghton Mifflin.

Simons-Morton, B., & Crump, A. (1996). Empowerment: The process and the outcome. *Health Education Quarterly, 23*(3), 290–292.

Smart, J., & Smart, D. (1992). Curriculum changes in multicultural rehabilitation. *Rehabilitation Education, 6,* 105–122.

Smith-Fess Act (Vocational Rehabilitation of Persons Disabled in Industry Act of 1920), 41, Stat. 735.

Stanard, R., & Hazler, R. (1995). Legal and ethical implication of HIV and duty to warn for counselors: Does Tarasoff apply? *Journal of Counseling and Development, 73,* 397–400.

Sue, D. W., Arredondo, P., & McDavis, R. (1992). Multicultural counseling competencies and standards: A call to the profession. *Journal of Counseling and Development, 70,* 477–486.

Super, D. (1990). A life-span, life-space approach to career development. In D. Brown, L. Brooks & Associates (Eds.), *Career choice and development* (pp. 197–261). San Francisco: Jossey-Bass.

Szymanski, E. M. (1987, Fall). Rehabilitation counseling: A profession based on values. *Interaction,* p.1.

Szymanski, E. M., & Parker, R. (2003). *Work and disability: Issues and strategies in career development and job placement* (2nd ed.). Austin, TX: Pro-Ed.

Taylor, H., Kagay, M., & Leichenkor, S. (1986). *The ICD survey of disabled Americans: Bringing disabled Americans into the mainstream.* New York: Louis Harris and Associates.

Tarvydas, V. M. (1987). Decision-making models in ethics: Models for increased clarity and wisdom. *Journal of Applied Rehabilitation Counseling, 18,* 50–52.

Tarvydas, V. M. (1995). Ethics and the practice of rehabilitation counselor supervision. *Rehabilitation Counseling Bulletin, 38,* 294–305.

Tarvydas, V. M. (2003). The ethical imperative for culturally competent practice. *Rehabilitation Education, 17*(2), 117–123.

Tarvydas, V. M., & Cottone, R. R. (2000). The code of ethics for professional rehabilitation counselors: What we have what we need. *Rehabilitation Counseling Bulletin, 43,* 188–196.

Vash, C. L. (1987). Fighting another's battles: When is it helpful? Professional? Ethical? *Journal of Applied Rehabilitation Counseling, 18,* 15–16.

Van Hoose, W. H., & Kottler, J. A. (1985). *Ethical and legal issues in counseling and psychotherapy* (2nd ed.). San Francisco: Jossey-Bass.

Verona, T., Layton, K., & Morrison, M. (1998). Notable legal developments affecting lesbians and gay men. *Lawbriefs,* 1, 1–5.

Vietnam Era Veterans' Readjustment Assistance Act of 1974, 38 U.S.C. 4212.

Vocational Rehabilitation Act of 1918 (PL 65–178).

Welfel, E. (1987). A new code of ethics for rehabilitation. *Journal of Applied Rehabilitation Counseling, 22*(1), 30–33.

Wendell, S. (1989). Towards a feminist theory of disability. *Hypatia, 4*(2), 104–124.

Wheaton, J. (1995). Vocational rehabilitation rates for European Americans and African Americans: Another look. *Rehabilitation Counseling Bulletin, 38,* 224–231.

Williamson, E. G. (1964). *Vocational counseling.* New York: McGraw-Hill.

Wilson, K. B., Harley, D. A., McCormick, K., Jolivette, K., & Jackson, R. L. (2001). A literature review of vocational rehabilitation acceptance rates and explaining bias in the rehabilitation process. *Journal of Applied Rehabilitation Counseling, 32,* 24–35.

Wolfensberger, W. (1983). Social role valorization: A proposed new term for the principle of normalization. *Mental Retardation, 21,* 234–239.

Woods, G., Marks, R., & Dilley, J. (1990). *AIDS law for mental health professionals: A handbook for judicious practice.* San Francisco: The AIDS Health Project.

Wright, B. (1983). *Physical disability: A psychosocial approach.* New York: Harper & Row.

Wright, G. (1980). *Total rehabilitation.* Boston: Little, Brown.

CHAPTER 14

ETHICAL AND LEGAL ISSUES IN SUPERVISION

LEN SPERRY AND MAUREEN DUFFY

It has been reported that failure to supervise properly is the seventh most common cause of disciplinary action taken by regulatory boards against mental health professionals (Sacuzzo, 2002). Supervisors are liable not only for their own negligent actions as supervisors but also for the actions of their supervisees. For example, if a supervisee disclosed confidential information about a client to someone outside the clinical setting or engaged in inappropriate behavior with a client inside or outside the counseling setting, the supervisor could be held liable for the supervisee's actions. Why, then, would anyone in their right mind even entertain the thought of assuming supervisory responsibilities in the first place? The answer is that supervision is a necessary component of counseling and psychotherapy training and vital for the future of the profession. It involves multiple roles as well as multiple ethical and legal challenges for the supervisor. The challenge is for competent professionals who aspire to provide supervision to find ways to increase their ethical sensitivity and minimize their legal liability (Bernard & Goodyear, 2004). This chapter details and illustrates key ethical considerations as well as critical legal issues within a relational, developmental, and organizational context. This chapter is as important for students who will be or are receiving supervision as it is for those providing supervision. Students not only assume the role of supervisee but, because of the nature of professional training, most will later assume the role of supervisor.

LEARNING OBJECTIVES

After reading this chapter you should be able to

1. Define clinical supervision, compare it to relational supervision and self-supervision, and contrast it to case consultation and peer consultation.
2. Relate the contextual dimensions of the relational, the developmental, and the organizational—including the multicultural—to the process of supervision.

3. Describe eight common ethical issues in supervision and the specific ethical codes and standards relevant to them.
4. Explain two common legal issues in clinical supervision and risk-management strategies for their prevention.
5. Apply the ethical decision-making model to a supervisory issue, aware of the relational, multicultural, and other organizational and personal dimensions.

KEY TERMS

case consultation
clinical supervision
direct liability
fair evaluation and due process in supervision
liability
peer consultation
relational supervision
self-supervision
standard of care
supervisor impairment
supervisor incompetence
vicarious liability

This book frames ethical and professional issues in counseling within several contexts: the relational, the developmental, and the organizational. We begin with discussion of the developmental dimension, or context, of supervision. Four levels of supervisor development are described, including the impact of the supervisor's developmental level on supervisees. The dynamics and ethical implications of stunted or fixated development are addressed with regard to incompetence and impairment among supervisors. Also discussed are ways in which the supervisor can promote the ethical development of supervisees by articulating the supervisees' ethical decision-making styles, as well as their own ethical and professional development through self-supervision. Next, we describe the relational context of supervision and compare and contrast the relational view of supervision with the traditional view. Then, the roles, responsibilities, and accountabilities of both supervisor and supervisee are discussed and illustrated. Finally, the organizational dimension or context of supervision is presented in terms the impact of organizational dynamics on supervision, supervision agreements, and the developmental issues contract. As noted earlier, this chapter is designed to be clinically useful for supervisees as well as supervisors. Accordingly, a case illustrates a supervisee's use of the ethical decision-making model to deal with a difficult supervisory dilemma.

The next section explores and illustrates four core ethical considerations in supervision. These are confidentiality, informed consent, conflicts of interest and boundaries, and competency of both supervisor and supervisee. We then address other ethical considerations such as multicultural issues, spiritual and religious issues, due process issues, and expert and peer consultation in relation to supervision. Also explored are two legal issues: fair evaluation and due process in supervision and supervisor liability. Although much consideration in this chapter has been afforded to Perspective III, this chapter also is cognizant of the place of Perspective I in the supervisory process. According, specific recommendations for risk management are highlighted.

THE ROUTINE PRACTICE OF SUPERVISION

There are various styles and methods of clinical supervision, which are reflected in the various ways in which supervision is practiced: from a supervisor and supervisee reviewing process notes or videos to a group supervision utilizing one-way mirrors or reflecting groups. Nevertheless, amid this diversity of supervisory styles, there are a number of routine procedures and practices that are personally helpful to supervisees and supervisors as well as administratively useful. This section reviews three such practices.

The Supervisory Agreement

Written agreements can be particularly useful in formalizing the supervisor–supervisee relationship as well as for structuring the process of supervision. While not necessary for administrative supervision, since the relationship and tasks are specified by the job description of both the supervisor and supervisee, such a written agreement can be invaluable in clinical supervision, particularly for relationally oriented supervision. Because such written agreements articulate the expectations and boundaries of the supervisory relationship, they can reduce subsequent misunderstandings. They also serve to educate the supervisee regarding the nature of supervision, supply a model for approaching informed consent with clients, and provide a sense of safety for both parties by structuring the relationship (Remley & Herlihy, 2001). The key elements of such an agreement are noted in Box 14.1.

BOX 14.1
KEY ELEMENTS IN A RELATIONAL SUPERVISORY AGREEMENT

Elements in a Relational Supervisory Agreement

- Purpose of the supervision
- Professional background of the supervisor
- Specific expectations and responsibilities of supervisor and supervisee
- The structure of supervision and supervisory sessions
- Boundaries of the supervisory relationship
- Supervisor's philosophy of supervision
- Method of evaluation and developmental plan
- Provision for ethical and professional practice

An example of a supervisory agreement illustrating relational supervisions is in included in Box 14.2.

BOX 14.2
EXAMPLE OF A CLINICAL SUPERVISORY AGREEMENT

Jessica Swenson, MS, LMHC, staff counselor, and supervisor, agrees to provide clinical supervision to William A. Brahos, an intern, for the purpose of meeting the clinical education requirements for his master's degree in counseling as well as for professional licensure. Jessica is licensed by the State of Florida as a Mental Health Counselor since 1997, has complete state requirements to provide clinical supervision, and has supervised several practicum students and interns in the past four years. Her professional expertise includes counseling adults and couples.

William agrees that it is his responsibility to meet to meet all requirements necessary for his graduate degree, to provide counseling services to his assigned clients following the clinic's protocol for internship students, and to be prepared for every clinical supervision meeting with case progress notes, process notes, and videotapes. Jessica's responsibilities include facilitating supervision sessions, monitoring and evaluating William's clinical work with clients in his case loads, and completing the clinical supervisor's section of any forms necessary for evaluation of his performance and to verify hours for licensure. They also involve ensuring that William develops accurate diagnoses and clinically useful case conceptualizations and treatment plans, applies various theoretical models and interventions appropriately and effectively, and utilizes proper case report writing and documentation methods.

The supervisory sessions will be structured in a one-to-one format and will be scheduled for a minimum of one hour per week. This hour is set aside as an appointment, and the expectation is that both will treat it as such. In the event that either cannot make a scheduled supervision appointment, it is that person's responsibility to reschedule as soon as possible. William is also encouraged to participate in the weekly clinical supervision group with other practicum and internship students at this site. It is understood that the supervisor of that group will evaluate performance and verify hours for this professional activity separately. Because evaluation of professional performance is involved, we will not establish a personal relationship, offer gifts, or initiate social interactions during the course of this supervision.

Jessica's philosophy of supervision is that clinical supervision is an essential and necessary part of becoming an effective counselor or therapist. She believes that regular, scheduled supervision is essential to help interns deal with a wide range of professional and ethical issues, including transference and countertransference. Accordingly, her role as clinical supervisor is to model appropriate and ethically sensitive professional attitudes and practice, and to advise, monitor, and evaluate William's clinical efforts in the ethical and professional practice of counseling. Jessica has an open-door policy, and William is encouraged to stop by when needed as it is feasible.

Jessica will complete a written evaluation of William's progress and performance at the midpoint and then at one week before completion of this internship. Jessica will provide a copy of both evaluations for discussion and action prior to being submitted to the university supervisor. The midpoint evaluation will result in a developmental plan—or developmental contract—that will be reviewed by both prior to being sent to William's university supervisor. By signing below, both parties agree to provisions outlined including the expectation to adhere to all the standards of practice and ethical guidelines as well as the policies and procedures of this clinic site.

______________________________	______________________________
Jessica Swenson, MS, LMHC	William A. Brahos
Date: ______________________	Date: ______________________

The Developmental Issues Contract

The use of a developmental contract has been advocated as unique approach to counselor and therapist development within the context of supervision (Skovholt & Ronnestad, 1995). Specifying a formal contract that explicitly states the goal of developing awareness of a particular value—as it pertains to ethical decision making—can be a useful educational activity. For instance, when the matter of improving "relational connections" with clients arises in supervision, the supervisor might suggest a contract in which the supervisee attends to specific relational dynamics for a particular period of time or with a particular client population. Then, as ethical issues arise in supervision, both the supervisee and supervisor are charged with examining how attending to relationships might be part of finding an ethical solution to a particular concern or dilemma. The hope is that developmental contracts will increase both the supervisor's and the supervisee's comfort levels in dealing with developmental issues in supervision, since they make value training a more intentional and tangible, overt part of the supervisory process.

Written Documentation of Supervision

Supervisors in some agencies are required to document their work with supervisees, usually to promote accountability and reduce liability for the agency. For some supervisors, this requirement involves little more than logging—usually in a notebook or computer—all the client cases that are reviewed and discussed with a particular supervisee on a given date. Other supervisors add additional information to their entry for a specific supervisory session, such as "dangerous to self or others," potential dispositions, and other problems of specific clients and considerations such as privacy and confidentiality matters or boundary issues involving the supervisee, along with other risk-management considerations.

Even if it is not required, written documentation can be a valuable exercise for both supervisee and supervisor. In our experience, a written log or notes of the highlights of specific sessions can be reviewed when completing an evaluation of the supervisee. It is useful to keep track in writing of the supervisee's progress, and even lack of progress, along with discussions of supervisee countertransferences, assessment of supervisee's level of professional development, ethical decision-making style, and particular concerns, to can help focus the supervisory process. It can also useful for supervisors to reflect on the process of their supervision and examine their own countertransferences to supervisees, their level of development as supervisors, and so on.

THE CONTEXTUAL DOMAIN OF SUPERVISION

This section describes the three contextual domains impacting the professional and ethical practice of supervision. They are the personal-developmental, relational-multicultural, and organization ethics–community values dimensions.

Personal-Developmental

Chapter 2 detailed four levels of counselor and therapist development and the characteristic way in which individuals at each level conceptualized and responded to ethical issues and concerns. That chapter also described the arduous developmental trajectory from beginning student to expert or master therapist and counselor. Supervision plays a pivotal role in this developmental journey. In this section, we describe a similar developmental trajectory of supervisors from a beginning level to an expert level of supervision. Four progressively differentiated levels of supervisor development and the impact of the supervisor's level of development on supervisees is discussed, particularly with regard to ethical considerations. This section also addresses other developmental considerations such as personal ethical decision-making styles and self-supervision. It also describes what might be considered developmental delays or fixations among supervisors, with a detailed discussion of supervisory incompetence and impairment.

Levels of Supervisor Development and Ethical Issues. Four levels are briefly summarized in Table 14.1 and discussed in the following narrative.

Level 1 Supervision. Level 1 supervisors are typically new to supervision and may be highly anxious or somewhat naive in their role as supervisor. Because structure can reduce their anxiety, they tend to focus on doing the "right" thing, and commonly assume the "expert" role with supervisees. Providing feedback and doing evaluations tends to be uncomfortable for them and so they prefer structured evaluations, i.e., checklist, rather than written narratives. Not surprisingly, they may have difficulty with levels 2 and 3 supervisees, but do better with level 1 supervisees. Furthermore, they have a vested interest in encouraging supervisee to adopt their own favored theoretical orientation and treatment methods (Stoltenberg, et al, 1998).

Level 2 Supervision. Level 2 supervisors view supervision as more complex and multidimensional than Level 1 supervisors. Assuming that a supervisor is a Level 3 therapist, Level

TABLE 14.1 Four Levels of Supervision

LEVEL	DESCRIPTION
1	Limited technical and relational supervisory skills as well as experience; often anxious and focused on doing things "right," they can be overly structured in working with and evaluating supervisees; can work adequately with Level 1 supervisees
2	Often a short-lived period of transition to Level 3; failure to make the transition shows in tendency to lose objectivity, to emphasize supervisee's global deficits, a laissez-faire attitude, and even to do therapy instead of supervising supervisees; they need ongoing, expert supervision; difficulty with all but Level 1 supervisees
3	Capable of making accurate and appropriate appraisals of their supervisees and can be expected to provide a balanced assessment of the supervisees' strengths and limitations; work reasonably well with supervisees at any level
4	The so-called "master" supervisors; effortlessly capable of integrating theory and practice and modeling this integration; can accurately and effectively monitor and evaluate supervisee performance; work very well with supervisees at any level

2 supervision tends to be a short-lived period in his or her professional development. Many of these individuals transition to Level 3 supervision with minimal difficulty. However, for those who fail to make this transition, their supervisory behavior is often problematic. For example, they may overfocus on a supervisee and lose the objectivity necessary to provide both appropriate guidance and confrontation. When it comes to evaluation, they may emphasize the supervisee's global rather than specific deficits and may erroneously conclude that the supervisee is either unable or unwilling to implement supervisory feedback. Other risks are associated with not making the transition to Level 3 supervision. They adopt a laissez-faire attitude toward supervision, or out of frustration in their supervisory role, they may engage in counseling or therapy with supervisees. Needless to say, these supervisors tend to be a difficult match for all levels of supervisees; however, working with Level 1 supervisees is less problematic. Needless to say, seeking out expert, ongoing supervision is a necessity for such Level 2 supervisors (Stoltenberg, McNeill, & Delworth, 1998).

Level 3 Supervision. Because Level 3 supervisors have achieved the level of experience and expertise characteristic of Level 3 therapists, they are likely to view supervision as a highly valued professional activity. Thus, they can be expected to approach supervision in a responsible and caring manner. Supervisors at this level are reasonably adept at integrating theory and practice. Unlike Level 1 and 2 supervisors, these individuals have developed the capacity to make accurate and appropriate appraisals of their supervisees and can be expected to provide a balanced assessment of a supervisee's strengths and limitations (Stoltenberg et al., 1998).

Level 4 Supervision. Also referred to as Level 3i, Level 4 supervisors have been referred to as "master" supervisors (Stoltenberg et al., 1998). Over the years, they have developed considerable technical as well as relational supervisory skills. They are most likely to be highly proficient counselors and therapists and are likely to be considered "master therapists" by their peers. They tend to be quite adept at integrating theory and practice and can accurately and effectively monitor and evaluate supervisee performance. They can work equally well with supervisees at any level, being particularly adept with the more difficult of the supervisees, Level 2 supervisees.

Ideally, those providing formal clinical supervision will already be at, or evolve into, Level 3 and 4 supervisors. Realistically speaking, supervisees are too often assigned to Level 1 and 2 supervisors. What are the personal, professional, and organizational ethical and legal considerations for supervision?

In terms of personal ethics, it would seem that those providing clinical supervision would take the duties and responsibilities of mentoring supervisees seriously and endeavor to become effective supervisors in terms knowledge, skills, and experience in supervision. That means becoming effective, that is, Level 3 or 4, counselors or therapists themselves, as well as becoming effective, that is, Level 3 or 4, supervisors. This means engaging in training programs as well as continuing to be supervised by a masterful supervisor. It also means a commitment to one's own personal development in addition to this professional development.

In terms of professional ethical and legal considerations, Level 1 and 2 supervisors are more likely to be involved with ethical and legal issues than are Level 3 and 4 supervisors.

Issues of supervisory competence and supervisee's welfare are not uncommon with Level 1 and 2, and of course, doing counseling therapy with supervisees is clearly unethical. In terms of negligence and direct liability, failing to match supervisees with clients they are competent to work with and inadequately monitoring supervisees' work with clients seem to be particularly problematic with Level 2 supervisors.

In terms of organizational ethical considerations, clinical or program directors and other administrators have the responsibility to assign supervisees to only those supervisors who can effectively meet the requisite supervisory function. While not every supervisor can be expected to function at Level 3 or 4, ethically sensitive programs and administrators will foster a culture of effective supervision, provide supervisor training, and appropriately reward effective supervision. In tough economic times, that means allocating resources and personnel so that supervisees function as trainees and not as junior staff, assigning those with supervisory talent a reasonable number of supervisees, and ensuring that supervisors have sufficient time to occasionally meet with the supervisee's clients, review tapes and transcriptions, and adequately monitor and evaluate the supervisee's clinical work.

Personal Ethical Decision-Making Styles. Every supervisee comes to supervision with a unique history, needs, expectations, and dreams for his or her professional life, and a unique ethical decision-making style. This unique style reflects one's early and ongoing experiences with moral values and issues. It is has been influenced and shaped by parents, relatives, peers, and valued adults in one's life, such as teachers and coaches. This style remains implicit, meaning it is not consciously articulated, and it "informs" all or most of the supervisee's ethical and moral decisions. A good clinical training program provides students the opportunity to become aware of and critically examine their implicit styles. While this process may begin in an "Ethics and Professional Practice" course, it is usually during supervision that it is more likely to be accomplished. Of the different ways of helping supervisees articulate their implicit styles, the ethical genogram is a particularly useful method (Peluso, 2003). In this method, an individual can understand his or her own style by drawing a family genogram chart and describing his or her various relationships and the ways in which key individuals, such as parents, dealt with moral issues and made moral decisions. The ethical genogram was the method utilized to articulate Jessie's ethical decision-making style in the case of Jessie, presented in Box 14.3.

BOX 14.3

SUPERVISORY IMPLICATIONS OF A SUPERVISEE'S ETHICAL DECISION-MAKING STYLE

Jessie is a 28-year-old graduate student in a master's program in counseling. At the beginning of her internship, her supervisor encouraged her to articulate her ethical decision-making style by completing an ethical genogram. In the course of doing this exercise, Jessie learned quite a bit about herself and the origins of her ethical decision-making style.

She noted that her father's style of making tough decisions was to take a great deal of time in order to think through the decision and its ramifications. This process often was overwhelming, and as a result, he avoided making most decisions. On the other hand, her mother's style reflected her feeling of being forced to make the hard decisions her husband didn't or wouldn't make, and she vented her anger and vengeance accordingly. When it came to tough moral and ethical decisions, her mother tended to be strict and dogmatic, while her father reacted with hesitation and relinquishment. Jessie summed up her own implicit style by saying that she would consider all the facts and then act, "but never dogmatically." She was surprised to discover that her implicit style of making ethical and moral decisions was an uncomfortable blend of her parent's diametrically different styles. A much fuller description of Jessie's history is presented in Chapter 2.

What do you view as the implications of Jessie's ethical decision-making style with regard to client issues? With regard to discussion of these issues in supervision?

Based on this information, Jessie's supervisor might conclude that, as a counselor, Jessie would be vulnerable to viewing ethical situations as ambiguous, and while knowledgeable of the ACA professional code of ethics, she is likely to question her ability to appropriately apply the codes and standards. For instance, suppose one of her clients, Ben, with whom she has worked in counseling for three weeks while he is on medical leave from his job, now requests a letter attesting to his fitness to return to work. In the initial evaluation, Ben admitted that he has abused prescription medications in the past, and although he would like to stop taking any potentially addicting medications, he suffers from chronic muscle spasms and takes Valium, an anti-anxiety and muscle relaxant medication, as needed. At two recent sessions, Jessie noted that Ben exhibited slightly slurred speech and inattentiveness, common side effects of Valium, but she said nothing. Jessie realizes that this client really wants to return to work, yet she has concerns about his substance use. She hopes that, if he is cleared to return to work, his self-esteem will increase and work will distract him from his pain. Since she doesn't want to impede his job prospects, she writes a favorable letter for Ben without mention of his substance issues. Only after sending the letter did she mention it in supervision.

In this instance, her clinical supervisor would do well to focus their supervisory sessions on Jessie's pattern of siding with those she perceives as "underdogs" and avoiding confrontation, fearing it might negatively impact the therapeutic relationship or harm the client—Ben might not be cleared to return to work and may actually be terminated. As a result, Jessie may delay or not take appropriate action when it is ethically, morally, or legally necessary. In addition, the supervisor might suggest a supervisory group where Jessie can express her concerns and receive feedback in a safe environment, or advise/refer her to psychotherapy to process her unresolved issues related to these countertransferences or "blind spots."

Relational-Multicultural

The relational-multicultural dimension of supervision invokes the need for supervisors to recognize that differences between the supervisor and supervisee always exist and must be taken into account in the development of the supervision relationship. These differences may reflect differences of age, gender, race, ethnicity, sexual orientation, religion and spirituality, and culture, but always include differences in personal experiences of relationships with authority figures. Gender, race, and culture differences in and of themselves suggest experiential differences in relationship to power and authority. Persons who represent minority communities of color, ethnicity, gender, religion, or sexuality have almost always had experiences in which they have felt oppressed or marginalized.

In the supervision relationship, such experiences are going to affect both supervisor and supervisee and are best made available for discussion within the supervision relationship, as appropriate. The development of the supervision agreement, as discussed above, provides the context-setting opportunity for multiculturally sensitive supervisors to meaningfully include supervisees in discussions about what is most important for them to address in the proposed supervision experience and how they would prefer to address issues of difference and culture that may come up during the supervision process. The supervisor who acknowledges the importance of multicultural issues in supervision and who openly invites discussion of such issues in a welcoming and nondefensive way characterizes the Perspective III relational supervisor.

Traditional versus Relational Supervision Perspectives. The codes of ethics of the various professional associations for counseling and psychotherapy are basically sets of prescriptions and proscriptions that counselors are expected to internalize and perform in their clinical practices. They are sets of rules, some affirmative but many negative, to which counselors are expected to conform. For example, the American Counseling Association affirmatively encourages supervisors and counselor educators "to make an effort to infuse material related to human diversity into all courses and/or workshops that are designed to promote the development of professional counselors" (American Counseling Association, 1995, para. F.1.a). In contrast, like all professional counseling and psychotherapy associations, the American Counseling Association (1995) underscores the negative injunction that "counselors do not engage in sexual relationships with students or supervisees and do not subject them to sexual harassment" (F.1.c).

These rules are grounded in broad mission statements emphasizing client welfare and the principle of "do no harm," or nonmaleficence. They are also grounded in an understanding of ethics based on individual rights and duties and highlight the responsibilities of the supervisor to the supervisee. For the most part, the codes of ethics are fairly silent about the responsibilities and duties of the supervisee toward the supervisor. The codes of ethics reflect the justice or rights and duties orientation of contemporary jurisprudence that situates obligations within an individual context.

There is an alternative understanding of ethics that is rooted in an ethic of care and developed in the work of Carol Gilligan (1977, 1982). In this understanding of ethics, which emerged from Gilligan's challenging of Kohlberg's (1981, 1984) justice and obligation model, moral responsibility is directed toward the relationship rather than toward rights and duties. In the ethic of care, moral decision making is focused on how the relationship, rather than the individuals, would be affected by particular actions or inactions.

McNamee and Gergen (1999) have also articulated a relational view of ethics, but from a social constructionist perspective. In their view, relational responsibility requires (a) a recognition that relationships are the primary source of what people value as "good" and should therefore be affirmed and appreciated to the extent that is reasonable, (b) a recognition that individuals themselves represent many people or many voices (for example, the voices of parents, teachers, lovers, friends, supervisors, colleagues, etc.), (c) a willingness to reflect on how the other in a relationship is inviting one to be and to respond in the moment (for example, blameworthy and therefore guilty; lacking in understanding and therefore insensitive), (d) a willingness to actively consider other potential sets of responses than what might be routinized or default responses (for example, thoughtfulness instead of defensiveness), and (e) a community perspective that links individual actions to the larger group or constituency that such actions represent.

In the traditional justice model of ethics, supervision is guided by the first filter; namely, professional ethical codes and relevant law. The second, third, and fourth filters, in descending order, are the client's welfare, the supervisee's welfare, and the supervisor's welfare. The final filter is the program or agency's needs (Association for Counselor Education and Supervision, 1993). This traditional justice model of supervision ethics could be considered a top-down model, moving from application of a general principle down to a particular situation. Conversely, the relational model of supervision could be considered a bottom-up model, moving from the particularities of a situation up to the determination of what principle might apply (see the case example in Box 14.4 on page 414).

Roles and Responsibilities of the Supervisor and Supervisee in Relational Supervision. Relational supervision invites the experience of mutual accountability rather than the experience of fear of negative evaluation through a process of ongoing iterative conversation and reflection. Adherence to legal and professional standards and codes of ethics, promoting client welfare, facilitating the development of the supervisee's clinical skills and performance, and ultimately making evaluation and endorsement decisions are still supervisory responsibilities in relational supervision, but they are done within a context of mindfulness about the socially constructed nature of the supervision relationship and its potential for plasticity.

Emotions in the supervision relationship have probably been underemphasized. A justice-only orientation can lead to a skewing of the supervisee's emotional responses in the direction of fear—fear of not being competent, fear of being negatively evaluated, fear of violating a code of ethics or law, fear of being sued, fear of being disciplined by the licensing bodies, fear of losing one's job. The relational view of supervision encourages the supervisor to take into account the ethic of care model and to pay more explicit attention to the nature of the supervision relationship itself and to the mutual goals being performed in that relationship.

A relatively new idea emerging from findings in neuroscience may have interesting applications in the supervision relationship and add to the importance of attending to the ethic of care model. New understandings of how the brain works and the relationship between emotion and reason suggest that emotion underlies reason and decision making, and that all thought is tagged with emotion (Crossley, 1998; Crossley, 2000; Damasio, 1994). In applying this perspective to ethical decision making in counseling and in supervision, it seems logical that more role and life-enhancing possibilities would be opened through a relational supervision approach, insofar as ethical decision making could be tagged with more positive emotions than would be the case in the justice model. Emotions springing from contexts of mutual collaboration and mutual accountability are more likely to be positive than those springing from contexts in which the evaluation is one-sided and top-down.

The relational supervisor openly discusses how what is taking place in the supervision relationship is linked to the authority and requirements of licensing boards, professional regulation, and cultural understandings of superior–subordinate relationships. In relational

BOX 14.4
CASE EXAMPLE OF RELATIONAL VERSUS TRADITIONAL SUPERVISION

Carla was a doctoral-level supervisee with some experience in school and mental health agency settings. Her current position was as a high school guidance counselor, and she saw clients in her university's mental health clinic as part of her doctoral internship. Regular supervision was a requirement of her internship, and Carla reported to her supervisor that she was not experiencing any particular problems with her clients. When her supervisor asked Carla what her most challenging case was, Carla responded that she didn't really have one and that all her cases were going well.

The supervisor experienced Carla as resentful, uncooperative, and dismissive when he set up two meetings for live supervision in the university clinic. After the live supervision, the supervisor assessed Carla's skill in establishing rapport with her clients as limited and felt that Carla was not communicating to her clients that she had heard their stories and understood them.

In the traditional model of supervision, Carla's supervisor would give her feedback about his observations and suggest some strategies for skill development, recognizing that the clients' welfare was at stake should Carla not improve her skills. If Carla's uncooperativeness and dismissiveness of supervisory feedback were to continue, the supervisor might insist that Carla enter personal counseling before being allowed to continue seeing clients at the university clinic.

From the perspective of relational supervision ethics, the supervisor might ask Carla to describe the meaning of supervision to different audiences: for example, to her clients, to her coworkers, to her nonprofessional friends, and to herself. Through these questions, the relational supervisor is opening up the possibility for Carla to think about the many meanings that supervision might have for different audiences and to perhaps redefine it for herself as less threatening. The relational supervisor might also ask Carla to imagine what influence the process of supervision might have on her clients even though they are already doing well, thereby appreciating and affirming Carla's commitment to them. The relational supervisor might also ask Carla to talk about who she feels she is supposed to be and how she feels she is supposed to act (as a seasoned professional, an expert, a subordinate, a researcher, a curious participant, etc.) in the current supervision relationship, thereby allowing for commentary about the nature of the current relationship and expanding the set of relational possibilities.

supervision, the supervisor has an obligation to explore the effects of these larger cultural narratives on what is happening in the here and now of the particular supervision relationship. The relational supervisor also has the obligation to work with the supervisee to create preferred and appreciative supervision relationships that are inclusive of the voices of the supervisee, the client, the supervisor, and the larger organizational and societal bodies whose interests are all represented in clinical supervision. Ideally, it is a model in which all voices are recognized and none marginalized.

Reciprocally, the supervisee has the obligation to reflect, in self-conversation and in conversation with the supervisor, on the questions posed by the supervisor and to account for the clinical choices and decisions that he or she makes. The supervisee has an obligation in relational supervision to consider how the way he or she is looking at clients and thinking about their presenting problems is linked to larger cultural scripts defining normalcy, responsibility, and accomplishment. The supervisee also has a responsibility in relational supervision to participate in conversations about how one's preexisting understandings about supervision might be influencing the nature of the supervision relationship in the here and now and affecting one's emotional and cognitive responses to the supervision process.

This process of reflecting on the origins and history of ideas that influence clinical and supervision relationships and their real effects on both the supervisor and the supervisee is the template for relational supervision. This template requires ongoing attention to accountability, that is, the willingness to consider how our present actions and choices are connected to larger ideas and theories and how these choices of thought and action might affect the persons involved in clinical and supervisory relationships. Relational accountability requires giving up assumptions and beliefs and a willingness to subject those assumptions and beliefs to a process of mutual inquiry. It also requires a willingness to imagine and perform alternative ways of thinking and acting that might generate more satisfying versions of current relationships, be they supervisory or otherwise. Box 14.5 presents a difficult supervisory situation.

BOX 14.5
REFUSAL TO ENDORSE

Perhaps the most dreaded task of a counseling supervisor is to have to tell a supervisee that his or her knowledge base, skills, and level of functioning do not meet the minimal standards of the profession, and he or she cannot, therefore, be endorsed for continuation in training. The traditional supervision model would have the supervisor outline the ways in which the supervisee's skills and functioning are deficient and not easily remediable, concluding with the discharge decision. This is a devastating experience for both the supervisor and supervisee, often leaving both feeling like failures, and it is likely to induce fear of litigation on the part of the supervisor and anger and hurt on the part of the supervisee.

A relational approach does not make the situation easier, but it does introduce some important differences. In a relational approach, the supervisor would open the conversation by commenting on the difficult nature of the evaluation situation for both of them, focusing on the "we" of the relationship. The supervisor would situate him- or herself immediately by acknowledging how difficult the training situation had become and outlining the steps that they together had taken to work on improving the situation, and then talk about the present unsuccessful outcome.

The supervisor might then take on the voice of the unsuccessful trainee and speak from his or her view of the trainee's position, acknowledging the trainee's pain and hurt. The supervisor might also wonder aloud what this experience of failure might be saying to the trainee about where his or her skills and training might be best suited, giving the trainee plenty of time to respond to these reflections and concern. Failure closes the door to one set of possibilities at a point in time and simultaneously opens the door to other possibilities. The supervisor might ask the supervisee if he or she is ready yet to think about where the new door is opening and whether the door is opening to a break and a rest, or to a change. The supervisor might then ask the trainee to speak from his or her view of the supervisor's position and pose any questions that he or she might have, however difficult he or she might think they would be to answer.

There is no way of languaging away the pain of this supervision situation. The above example illustrates the ethic of care involved in handling the refusal to endorse from a relational supervision perspective, juxtaposed against the way in which the same situation would likely be handled from the ethic of justice supervision perspective.

In Chapter 3, we indicated that productive supervision cannot occur when the relationship between supervisor and supervisee is inadequate or problematic. Thus, fostering a healthy supervisory relationship is the essential task at the outset of supervision. Such a strong supervisory alliance serves as a base from which future issues and dilemmas in supervision can be effectively managed. Similarly, ongoing maintenance of the relationship is the supervisor's responsibility throughout the course of the relationship. Furthermore, because supervision involves an evaluative component, it is essential that a strong supervisory alliance be based on mutually agreed-upon expectations about the evaluative aspect of supervision. Incongruent expectations about the goals and tasks of supervision as well as about the process of evaluation can lead to misunderstandings, criticism, and harmful conflicts.

Research on Supervisory Relationship. One indicator of an inadequate or problematic supervisory relationship is the supervisee's failure to notify or disclose information about clients to supervisors. Since client welfare might be compromised and because superiors can be held liable as a result of nondisclosure, nondisclosure has been a useful research marker of the supervisory relationship. In a number of studies, it has been shown that one of the most frequent reasons for supervisee nondisclosure is poor quality of the supervisory relationship. Another reason for nondisclosure is negative feelings toward the supervisor. Instead of the supervisor, most nondisclosures were discussed with someone else, usually a peer. The more the supervisor was perceived as negative or uncaring, the more likely that supervisees failed to inform the supervisors of issues arising from their work with clients (Ladany, Hill, Corbett, & Nutt, 1996).

Counterproductive events in supervision, defined as experiences that are hindering, unhelpful, or harmful in relation to the supervisee's growth as a therapist, were assessed in an intensive interview study. Analysis showed that supervisees typically attributed their experiences of counterproductive events to their supervisors' dismissing their thoughts and feelings. Interestingly, supervisees reported experiencing a negative interaction with their supervisors following the counteractive event, yet most did not believe their supervisors were aware of the event's counterproductive nature. Nevertheless, supervisees believed that the counterproductive event weakened the supervisory relationship and led to a change in the way they approached their supervisors. Although they believed the counterproductive events negatively affected their work with clients, most did not disclose their counterproductive experience with their supervisors (Gray, Ladany, Walker, & Ancis, 2001).

"Parallel process" refers to the transfer of treatment from the supervisor, through the supervisee, to the client. The assumption is that how supervisors relate to supervisees ultimately affects clients, for better or for worse. While this theory has appeal and face validity, there are relatively few studies that examine directly the relation of therapist performance and client change to supervision. Nevertheless, there is indirect support for the assertion that the adequacy of the supervisory relationship is related to treatment outcomes (Neufeldt, Allstetter, & Holloway, 1995). Finally, these research studies underscore the importance and necessity of developing relational trust and mutually agreed-upon expectations of roles and responsibilities.

Ethically Sensitive Supervision. To foster positive supervisory relationships, it would seem that training sites should take responsibility for ensuring the quality of their training relationships. Some believe that it is unethical for sites to provide clinical supervision without allocating adequate resources for appropriate supervision (Nelson, Gray, Friedlander, Ladany, & Walker, 2001). Furthermore, it seems that site supervisors, as well as university coordinators of clinical education, have an ethical duty to educate site administrators about the extent of resources necessary to provide responsible supervision. Adequate time must be allotted for supervision to occur as a clinical process, and consultative support for supervisors should be available, particularly for situations in which supervisors experience difficulties with supervisees.

Organizational Ethics–Community Values

As noted earlier in this book, context significantly influences the process and outcomes of the counseling as well as the supervision. This section begins by describing the impact of organizational dynamics on the supervisory process. Then it briefly comments on the potential impact that community values can have on supervision.

The Impact of Organizational Dynamics on Supervision. Every school, clinic, hospital, and human service agency has a unique set of organizational dynamics that influence staff as well as clients. As noted in Part I of this book, an organization's core values are reflected in the organization's structure, culture, leadership, and staff behavior. Not surprisingly, these organizational values and dynamics also impact the supervision process. In some schools and clinical settings, there is a sharp discrepancy between actual and stated organizational values, whereas in other settings there is a close correspondence between the two. The greater the discrepancy, the greater the likelihood for confusion, conflict, and dissatisfaction. For example, it is not uncommon for a human service agency to describe its core values in highly vaunted terms such as *clients come first, quality care is the norm,* and *staff are our most important resource.* However, when the actual values of that agency are that profit really comes first, quantity is the norm, and staff that are not loyal and compliant are expendable, supervisees may experience problems.

Presumably, graduate counseling programs adequately vet training sites in terms of the adequacy of supervision, professionalism of staff, and a culture supportive of training, quality care, and ethical practice. Nonetheless, new leadership, staff turnover, and budgetary changes may shift organizational values in such a way that the site is less appropriate and adequate as a training environment (see the case example in Box 14.6).

Community Values and Impact on Supervision. A discussion of the potential impact of community values on the counseling process was introduced in Chapter 4. Just as the organizational dynamics of a school, clinic, or agency can powerfully influence the behavior and decisions of counselors and therapists, community values and pressure can influence the counseling process and can also influence and impact the process of supervision.

BOX 14.6
DISILLUSIONMENT AT A NEW INTERNSHIP SITE

Having completed her practicum in a child and adolescent residential treatment program, Jan Jacobson was seeking an internship site in which she could get supervised experience working with adults in an outpatient setting. She met to discuss site possibilities with Dr. Gregson, the newly appointed director of clinical education and training in the department of counseling. She volunteered to check out some sites that did not as yet have formal site agreements with the university. A few days later, she found what she thought was the perfect site: a private outpatient clinic for adults that offered supervision with PhD-level psychologists and mental health counselors that was also close to her home. Her interview with Mr. Trintino, the clinic administrator, was cordial and encouraging. She was particularly impressed with the clinic's brochure, which described a caring environment, highly skilled staff, and a commitment to quality care. Her supervision would be Emilio Justine, PhD, who was a licensed as a marriage and family therapist. She petitioned the clinical education and training director for approval of this clinic as her internship site, and it was approved. After her third day as an intern at the site, her enthusiasm dampened as she met with her newly assigned clients and learned of their dissatisfaction with clinic policy and staff behavior. A fellow intern from another university graduate program seemed to corroborate those clients' perceptions. Among other things she learned that treatment plans typically seemed to include three or more treatment modalities: individual sessions, group sessions, and couples or family sessions, regardless of whether these were indicated. These services were apparently billed irrespective of whether clients received the services or not. While assigned as to be group cotherapists, she learned that interns were expected to run groups themselves at times when the assigned staff therapist was not there. In her first supervisory meeting she felt uncomfortable when Dr. Justine commented on her legs and suggested that they might go out for a drink sometime. She indicated that she didn't and that it wasn't appropriate. He said he was only trying to be friendly and just wanted to be helpful to her. Jan was not sure she could trust him and wondered if it was a mistake interning there. The next time they met for supervision, he was very critical of her process notes, case formulations, and documentation. He also assigned her six additional extremely difficult clients. Now she had a caseload larger than other interns who had been there two months or longer. She went to talk to the clinic administrator about Dr. Justine. His only comment was that Justine was one of their best supervisors and that she should let him take her under his wing and learn everything she could from him. Although she had developed good working relationships with most of her assigned clients, she felt anxious and confused about her supervisor. This was not the kind of place or supervision that Jan had envisioned. Perhaps, in her enthusiasm to find a site, she was not more discerning. She had come to trust Dr. Gregson and thought he would be able to advise her. Does Dr. Justine's behavior suggest incompetence or impairment? What might she do? What would you do if you were in Jan's situation?

Community influences can be obvious or subtle, and the ethically sensitive supervisor would do well to recognize and understand community values as they relate to the counseling process. The case example in Box 14.7 illustrates the not-so-subtle impact of community values on the counseling process and the challenge for supervisors.

BOX 14.7

THE CASE OF THE MAGIC PEBBLE

Tina is a school counseling intern who has been assigned to you, an elementary school counselor, to supervise her full-time internship. You had mutually agreed that she will have primary responsibility for facilitating two fourth-grade group guidance classes. While your school district has adopted a commercial group guidance program for the middle grades, the program is flexible enough to be tailored to the interests of students as well as counselors. Tina had recently attended a workshop on spirituality and play therapy and was eager to try out some ideas she had learned. This morning you reviewed her plan for working with both classes this week. She indicated that she was going to use the "magic pebble" technique with her classroom group this afternoon in the unit on enhancing self-esteem. Asking for particulars, you learned that all the students would be given a small smooth pebble that would serve as a reminder to them they could do anything that they set their minds to. The instructions were simple: Close your eyes, and while rubbing the pebble, repeat five times that you are a special and worthwhile person and good things will come your way. After opening their eyes, they will know that the magic has begun.

You recall the uproar a few years ago, in an adjoining school district, when an elementary school teacher attempted something similar with her third-grade class. Immediately, a handful of parents complained to the school principal and to the school board that they did not want their children's minds polluted with "New Age" heresies. Soon afterward, a local evangelical church sponsored a series on the "Demonic Influences of New Age Spirituality." Subsequently, that district came out against the use of any "magic ideas" in their schools.

Since you are aware that similar community sentiments existed among a number of parents in your school and among members of your school board, you decided to discuss the implications of Tina's plan for her afternoon classroom group. She indicated that she hadn't really given any thought to the potential impact of her planned activity on the values of the parents of her students, the principal, or the school board in this community. She agreed that she would replace this technique with something else that would be more religiously and spiritually suitable.

This case highlights the potential for conflict and drastic action when a community's values are not recognized and heeded. The counseling intern appeared to be unaware of both the immediate community's values and sensitivities and the recent events in an adjoining community. Fortunately, her supervisor was quite aware of both and quickly intervened and prevented what might have been disastrous consequences for the intern.

CORE ETHICAL ISSUES IN SUPERVISION

If we view supervision as a relationship of multiples that include the supervisor, the supervisee, the client, and the context(s) that inform all of those participants, basic ethical issues already familiar to counselors can be examined from the perspective of the counseling supervisor. Additionally, there are some ethical issues in supervision that emerge from the specific set of responsibilities unique to the role of counseling supervisor. The common ethical issues in supervision already familiar to counselors are as follows:

- Confidentiality, privacy, and privilege
- The duty to protect and mandatory reporting

- Informed consent
- Boundaries and the use of power, including harassment
- Dual relationships, including sexual attraction, and intimate and nonintimate relations

While familiar, these ethical issues must be considered at a different level when applied to the roles and responsibilities of the counseling supervisor. The common ethical issues unique to the role of the counseling supervisor are as follows:

- Supervisee competency and monitoring
- Fair evaluation and due process

Surrounding both of these sets of common ethical issues in supervision is the influence of cultural issues, especially, gender, race, and class. The following discussion of each of the above ethical issues will include these dimensions: (a) role and responsibilities of the counseling supervisor, (b) stakeholders in the supervision process, (c) an affirmative or life-/role-enhancing view of each issue, and (d) a case example.

Confidentiality

Confidentiality in supervision refers to the dual responsibilities of the supervisor to ensure that the supervisee is respecting and protecting the confidentiality of client information and to ensure that any personal information revealed by the supervisee in supervision is respected and kept confidential. Professional ethics requires the maintenance of client and supervisee confidentiality, unless more compelling interests override that requirement. The supervisor is like a juggler, holding a number of responsibilities in play at the same time. Sometimes two or more of these responsibilities are conflicting (see the example in Box 14.8).

Privacy. Privacy, for one, is at play in this situation. The supervisee has a right to the privacy of his or her beliefs borne out of personal or religious commitments. This right is not absolute, and other supervisory responsibilities may override it, as in the example above. In

BOX 14.8
CHALLENGE OF CONFIDENTIALITY IN SUPERVISION

If a supervisee has a strongly held belief that abortion is wrong and is experiencing difficulty in working with a young woman who recently had an elective abortion, the supervisor may determine that client welfare requires that the case be transferred to another counselor. In such a situation, transferring the case may also require that the supervisor share information about the supervisee's personal beliefs about abortion with other clinical staff who would need to be involved in the case transfer. This necessary divulging of personal information about the supervisee to others in the agency in order to protect client welfare may also open the supervisee up to informal and/or formal negative evaluations by others. What ethical dilemmas is the supervisor juggling in this situation?

this case, protecting the welfare of the client may open the supervisee up to negative characterizations by other staff members who hold opposite views about abortion and who believe that counselors in secular agencies who do not support a woman's right to choose abortion are likely to hurt clients.

The supervisor must also ensure that supervisees protect the privacy of client health information. This supervisory obligation is particularly critical now, in the advent of the federal privacy law, the Health Insurance Portability and Accountability Act of 1996 (HIPAA), which applies to providers of mental health care services. As a result of HIPAA, the right to privacy of personal health information that counselors have typically honored through their professional ethics is now enshrined in federal law. The HIPAA privacy law strengthens the rights of clients to have control over access to their private health information and to prevent unauthorized disclosure of that information. It is a supervisory obligation to ensure that supervisees are aware of HIPAA regulations and adhere to the many requirements of the law.

Privilege. Privilege is related to privacy and confidentiality insofar as it involves the protection of client privacy and confidentiality. Privilege, however, is a legal concept recognizing the right of clients to not have their private psychotherapy and medical information publicly revealed in legal proceedings. Through legislation, most states recognize psychotherapy as a form of privileged communication. Additionally, states usually define the credentials of those mental health providers recognized as legitimate parties to privileged communications. Depending upon the state, professional counselors and marriage and family therapists may or may not be identified as recognized parties to privileged communication with psychotherapy clients.

Where privilege is concerned, it is the responsibility of the supervisor to ensure that supervisees have a full understanding of privilege and that supervisees uphold it. A common misunderstanding about privilege is that the right resides with the therapist. It does not. Privilege is held by the clients, and they may choose to waive privilege, requiring counselors to provide requested information to legal or other sources, even if the counselor does not think it is in the client's best interest for the information to be released. While imposing certain obligations on the supervisor and supervisee, the issues of confidentiality, privacy, and privilege are ultimately best understood as concepts that affirm and preserve the dignity of persons and protect them in relationships in which they are inherently vulnerable (see an example in Box 14.9).

The Duty to Protect and Mandatory Reporting. *Duty to protect.* The duty to protect or warn comes from the *Tarasoff* case (*Tarasoff v. Regents of the University of California*, 1976). In this case, which most students know by name but not by detail, a California court found only that a lawsuit could be filed on the grounds of failure to warn a third party of a threat made by a client in the context of therapy (Meyer, Landis & Hays, 1988). In the case, a client in therapy had made a threat against Tatiana Tarasoff, who had previously rejected his advances. Tarasoff was murdered by the client two months after the therapy session during which the threat had been made. The client had not returned to therapy in the interval between the threat and the murder. The therapist's supervisor had advised the therapist not to pursue action further than what he had already done, which was to unsuccessfully

BOX 14.9
PRIVILEGE IN SUPERVISION

The supervisor of a therapist in a drug rehabilitation center was himself a recovering addict and alcoholic. He attended a large meeting of Narcotics Anonymous (NA) while at a professional workshop in a neighboring town. At the NA meeting, he saw one of his most gifted counseling supervisees pick up a white chip indicating she had been sober for 24 hours. He left the meeting early, knowing that his supervisee had not seen him there. The supervisor felt like he was in a terrible bind. Closed meetings of NA, like the one where he saw his supervisee pick up a white chip, are supposed to be anonymous and confidential. He knew he had a right to be at the meeting to work on his own recovery, yet it was in this anonymous setting in a different town that he learned his supervisee, who was also recovering, had relapsed.

The supervisor was shaken by the information, because he knew that the supervisee could not continue in direct contact with drug rehab clients until she had addressed issues relating to her own relapse. Although the implications for the supervisee pained him deeply at the personal level, the supervisor decided he would meet privately with his supervisee in the morning, tell her how he knew about her relapse, and ask her whether she was willing to tell the director herself about the relapse and request a leave or whether she would prefer that he, as her supervisor, disclose the information and make the leave request to the director. The supervisor went to sleep cursing drugs for the millionth time, because he knew that the agency's clients were going to suffer, too, because the supervisee was such an effective therapist. He drifted off to sleep, wondering how his supervisee was going to make ends meet during her leave and feeling generally bad about the whole situation.

attempt to have the client evaluated psychiatrically. The supervisor feared a breach of confidentiality lawsuit.

The obligations for a supervisor, under this precedent, are to ensure that supervisees are aware of an obligation to warn a third party of a threat against the third party made during therapy, even if it means breaching confidentiality to do so. In the case of a clearly defined threat to harm or kill another, the duty to warn is clear-cut. A challenge for counselors can be figuring out what actually represents a verbal threat or clear and imminent danger.

Do threats concealed as jokes or expressions of wishes that someone would be gone from one's life constitute threats to a third party? Are these examples of threats, or are they examples of ways of expressing anger or hostility? These are not simple questions and bring to mind the possibility of a situation in mental health agencies akin to the one prevailing in schools, in which any utterance of words related to threat, in any context, are responded to as if they were real threats.

For counselors and their supervisors, the ethical issues at play are the obligation to protect others from harm, the obligation to confidentiality, the obligation to promote client welfare by providing effective therapy, and the obligation to protect oneself and one's family from lawsuits. Effective therapy would not be provided in an alarmist context in which the counselor responds to any strong verbal expressions of anger toward a third party by breaking confidentiality and informing the third party.

The supervisory obligation is to assist the supervisee to function effectively in a sometimes ambiguous context and to take reasonable, not extraordinary, measures to uphold the ethical obligation to protect. Clear-cut threats with named intended victims require a clear-cut duty to warn. Beyond those, the situation is not as clear. The supervisor is also obligated to assist the supervisee in drawing distinctions between actions that are therapeutic and actions that reflect a social control function. Therapy and social control are different, and should be understood as the very different functions they are.

The duty to protect goes beyond warning third parties of threats made against them in therapy. It also requires that prompt, proactive measures be taken to promote client welfare, especially when clients face risk or threat. The duty to protect obligates supervisors to assist supervisees in handling client emergencies and to plan sets of potential action strategies ahead of time that could be implemented in the event of suicide, abuse, or neglect (see Box 14.10).

BOX 14.10
ILLUSTRATION OF DUTY TO PROTECT

In June 2000, a 15-year-old boy hung himself in Broward County, Florida, in the shelter for runaway and troubled youth that he was court ordered into. He had become aggressive with his mother and choked her after she had grounded him. She called the police, and the police told her that pressing charges and getting her son into the court system was a way to get him some help. Upon arrival at the facility, the boy told the staff that he had tried to hang himself the day before. It is unclear what, if any, crisis help was provided to the boy after his disclosure, but one thing is clear, he was still allowed to wear a belt. About three weeks later, the boy hung himself in his room with his belt after being sent there for bad behavior. The worker, referred to in newspaper accounts as a counselor, did not attempt to take the boy down but instead took photographs of the boy hanging and said that her supervisor told her to summon authorities to handle the situation. The boy was still alive when he was found hanging but died four months later in the hospital. The counselor was put on trial for child neglect for not taking immediate action to help save the boy, was found guilty, and now faces up to five years in prison (Bierman, 2004).

This tragic account of a real-life situation raises pressing ethical questions at many levels. If we assume the worker or counselor's good faith, how did she choose to not respond immediately? What fears got in the way of the worker taking immediate action? What basis did the supervisor have for ordering that no one do anything until the authorities arrived? So far, the supervisor and other employees who also saw the boy hanging and did not act and have not been charged with a crime. How did the judicial system decide to charge only this worker, and what are the implications of that decision? What about the ethics of the larger system that provides help to low socioeconomic families if the child is in the system, but not so easily if the child is not in the system, forcing families to make terrible choices when they have a troubled youth? What can we learn about ethical decision making from this tragedy?

Mandatory abuse reporting. Like the duty to warn, mandatory reporting of the abuse of vulnerable groups is a social control function that counselors are obligated to perform. Mandatory reporting laws have been established to protect vulnerable groups from physical and sexual abuse and from exploitation. In most jurisdictions, the following are considered vulnerable groups: children, elders over sixty who suffer from the infirmities of old age, and dependent or disabled adults (Behnke, Winick, & Perez, 2000). See the mandatory-reporting dilemma presented in Box 14.11.

BOX 14.11
ILLUSTRATION OF MANDATORY ABUSE REPORTING

The supervisee presented a case she was very worried about to her supervisor. The supervisee's client was a middle-aged woman whose husband had suffered a debilitating stroke and who was hospitalized in the city's only public hospital. The client was despondent over her husband's condition and bitter about the poor medical care she felt her husband was receiving. The client told the supervisee that she was afraid that her husband was unsafe in the hospital. Upon exploring her fear in more detail, the client told the supervisee that she had witnessed a hospital orderly punching a man in a wheelchair in the head with a closed fist on two separate occasions. The supervisee had asked her client whether she reported the abuse to any of the hospital staff or to the authorities. The client had said no, she had not, because she was too afraid that her husband might be abused by the same orderly in retaliation, and she had no money to send him to a private hospital. The supervisee had encouraged and supported the woman to consider reporting the abuse, but the woman was adamant that it would make the situation worse for her husband and refused to make a report. In the supervisee's evaluation, the client was clearly telling the truth and was not delusional. The supervisee was bewildered about what her obligations were and fearful about the safety of dependent disabled patients on the unit in the hospital. How should the supervisor respond to this dilemma?

In this dilemma, the supervisor is now looped into a situation in which mandatory reporting of abuse is required, based on the facts from the supervisee's case presentation. The competing ethical obligations of protecting client confidentiality and responsibility for social control functions like mandatory reporting of abuse are at play. While it seems clear that the supervisor has an obligation to ensure that the abuse is reported, the supervisor has a further obligation to assist and support the supervisee in helping the frightened client through what is going to be a difficult experience for her. Additionally, the supervisee may not be comfortable disclosing to the client her actions in reporting the abuse, fearing the client may lose trust in her as a counselor, and the supervisor has an obligation to support the supervisee through this process.

Informed Consent

The societal value underlying informed consent is regard for the individual's right to self-determination and autonomy (Behnke, Winick & Perez, 2000). The intent of informed consent is to provide individuals with enough relevant information about treatment options, including risks and alternative treatments, to make a free and informed decision to select a particular treatment. The language of "treatment" comes from the medical model, as does the idea of informed consent. Woody and associates (1984) stated that informed consent is the best defense a human services provider can have against a malpractice lawsuit.

The supervisor has a number of obligations in the area of informed consent: (a) an obligation to ensure that supervisees obtain sufficiently detailed and current informed consent from all their clients, (b) an obligation to ensure that the client's informed consent document contains a clear description of the supervision process and how the client's private psychotherapy information will be used in supervision, and (c) an obligation to provide a sufficiently detailed informed consent to supervisees, outlining the supervision process and procedures.

Informed Consent for Clients. Informed consent for clients includes a description of the risks/benefits of the counseling services being offered; a summative description of the processes involved in counseling (i.e., questions, reflections, use of a team or one-way mirror, etc.); a statement about the nature and limitations of confidentiality, including mandatory abuse reporting requirements and the duty to warn; and a statement about fees and payment. The section on the limitations of confidentiality should include a statement about how client information will be used in supervision. For couples and family therapy, the section on confidentiality should also state, in accordance with professional ethical guidelines, that information about the couple or family therapy will not be released to third parties without the written consent of all adults party to the therapy.

Informed Consent for Supervisee. Informed consent for supervision should include a clear description of the processes and procedures used by the supervisor in supervision; goals of the supervision; potential risks of the supervision process; performance expectations for the supervisee; methods of evaluation and endorsement; the limitations of confidentiality in the supervision process; and a statement of fees, if appropriate. The processes and procedures part of the supervision informed consent agreement should include the supervisor's organizing theoretical assumptions about supervision and a description of the degree to which the supervisor emphasizes the educational dimension of supervision, the consultative dimension, and a focus on the person of the counselor.

Supervision goals should be clearly stated and should include general goals (e.g., supervision for licensure and/or professional development) and specific goals that the supervisee has identified as important. Potential risks of the supervision process should be clearly indicated and should include some statements about the degree of personal disclosure and reflection expected and the possibility that such reflection may invoke discomfort or anxiety on the part of the supervisee. Risks of supervision may also include the potential for a less than optimal evaluation or, in rare cases, a refusal to endorse.

Performance expectations should include expected frequency of supervision sessions, the supervisors' requirements for handling client emergencies, and supervisor notification procedures in the event of a client emergency. The performance expectations should also articulate whether supervision is expected to be live, audio/videotaped, to include case notes, or some combination of the three. The methods of evaluation should describe the evaluation procedures and criteria, whether the evaluations are formative or summative or both, whether they are oral or written or both, whose input will be included in the evaluation, and who will receive or have access to the evaluations other than the supervisee.

Limitations of confidentiality in supervision should also be clearly described and should outline what kind of information will be disclosed to third parties (i.e., the supervisee's departmental boss or clinical director). The kinds of information most likely to be disclosed to third parties would include evaluations, the supervisee's handling of difficult or contentious cases, ethical breaches, standard of care below minimal clinical competency, and may also include disclosure of cases that the supervisee handled particularly well. A supervision fees statement, if appropriate, and a signature and date section should also be included at the end of the supervision informed consent agreement. Box 14.12 outlines all of these elements of the informed consent supervision agreement.

BOX 14.12
ELEMENTS OF AN INFORMED CONSENT SUPERVISION AGREEMENT

SUPERVISOR'S THEORETICAL STANDPOINT IN SUPERVISION

Description of Supervision and Clinical Models Informing the Supervisor's Practices

Supervision will include an:

Educational dimension

Consultative dimension

Person-of-the-counselor/reflective dimension

SUPERVISION GOALS

General Goals

Licensure

Approved Supervisor status

Professional development

Other

Specific Goals

List 1 to 5 specific goals that the supervisor and supervisee have collaboratively developed in relation to case conceptualization, skill development, self-of-therapist, and/or development of a professional counseling identity.

Goal 1:

Goal 2:

Goal 3:

Goal 4:

Goal 5:

POTENTIAL RISKS OF THE SUPERVISION PROCESS

Supervisee Performance Expectations

Frequency of supervision meetings:

Supervisee is responsible for setting up or providing:

Live supervision

Videotapes of clinical sessions

Audiotapes of clinical sessions

Case notes

PROCEDURES FOR HANDLING CLIENT EMERGENCIES

Notification of authorities in the case of a client who is a threat to him/herself or others

Notification of family member if authorities called

Notification of third party in case of clear and direct threat to said party

Notification of agency supervisor

Notification of clinical supervisor

Critical incident report including summary of therapist's actions to manage case

METHODS OF EVALUATION

Formative evaluations (frequency, written/oral, whose input is included)

Summative evaluations (frequency, written/oral, whose input is included, who has access)

Criteria for evaluation (case conceptualization, skill demonstration, self-of-therapist issues, difficult/crisis case management, adherence to supervision procedures, etc.)

Endorsement/professional recommendation (Is there an expectation of endorsement for licensure or approved supervisor status or professional recommendation? Has the risk of refusal to endorse been included in the risks section of the supervision agreement?)

LIMITS OF CONFIDENTIALITY

Ethical violations

Poor clinical performance

Failure to follow established supervision procedures

Crisis/high-risk cases

Excellent clinical performance

Who will be notified?

FEE STATEMENT

Supervisee Signature and Date

Perhaps most importantly, in order to help a supervisee give truly informed consent for supervision, the supervisor has an obligation to let the supervisee know how much self-of-therapist work might be included in the supervision and the degree to which the supervisor would expect the supervisee to reflect on personal issues in their lives as they relate to cases under supervision. Supervisees, in order to honor their autonomy and freedom to choose, have a right to know the proportion of supervision that would include counseling, educational, and consultative dimensions. Supervisees are likely to feel most vulnerable in situations in which the self-of-therapist's issues are emphasized by the supervisor and they have not really been prepared for that in advance (see Box 14.13).

BOX 14.13
NOT ENOUGH OR TOO MUCH SELF-OF-THERAPIST SUPERVISION?

A new faculty member was hired in a mental health counseling and family therapy doctoral program. In general, students were quite pleased with the added perspective that the new faculty member brought to their program in the area of object relations and family-of-origin therapy. However, in practicum and internship classes, students began to complain that they were uncomfortable with the level of self-disclosure requested, especially about their families of origin. One student, who was a recovering alcoholic and who had a history of child sexual abuse, was so uncomfortable in the class that she went to the department chair and, while crying and agitated, explained that she did not feel she consented for supervision that included such a strong focus on self-of-therapist and family-of-origin issues. Further, the student said that she was not willing to continue in the class and that she did not expect her grade to suffer as a result of a supervision context that she did not agree to in the first place.

In this case, a number of professional values and goals have collided. It is acceptable for a supervising therapist to have a preferred theoretical framework and model of practice. A focus on self-of-therapist issues can also be important in ensuring that therapists or student counselors in training receive personal counseling when needed in order to protect their future clients and enhance their own personal and professional development. What is not acceptable is for a counseling supervisor to neglect to engage in dialogue with supervisees at the beginning of the supervision process about basic elements of the supervision process. These elements include, but are not limited to, the level of self-of-therapist focus, the theoretical orientation of the supervisor, what preferences the supervisees have in terms of supervision style, and how a situation might be handled if the supervisee felt uncomfortable. Supervisees have basic rights to information about the nature and process of supervision in order to make an informed consent. Supervisors have rights to practice from their preferred orientations and responsibilities to act as professional gatekeepers for the purpose of consumer protection and upholding of minimum standards of care.

Conflicts of Interest and Boundaries

Conflicts of Interest. Conflicts of interest in supervision are parallel at the next level up to conflicts of interest in psychotherapy. A conflict of interest in supervision arises when a supervisor is involved in competing roles or has competing interests that could affect the supervisor's ability to faithfully exercise sound professional judgment and skill (see Box 14.14). In supervision, conflicts of interest are most likely to occur when boundaries between the supervisor and supervisee are not clear, when the supervisor is in a position to exercise undue influence over the supervisee, as in the case of a supervisor who is also the co-owner with the supervisee of a psychotherapy practice, and when the supervisor has multiple roles or relationships with the supervisee. As is discussed below, dual or multiple relationships in supervision are not always avoidable and are not unequivocally harmful. The criteria for determining harmfulness are whether the roles or relationships are exploitative and whether the supervisor, because of those roles, is in a position of undue influence or power over the supervisee. The ethical requirement for the relational supervisor is to assume the stance of a continuously reflective supervisor, open to ongoing examination of the power differential and potential for conflicts of interest and abuse of power within the supervision relationship.

BOX 14.14
CONFLICT OF INTERESTS: A SUPERVISOR'S FAILURE TO DISCLOSE DUAL ROLES

An agency director supervised counseling interns in a difficult case involving the Department of Children and Families, who had removed the children from the family for reasons of neglect. The parents were seen at the agency in order to ultimately facilitate changes in their lives and relationships that would increase the likelihood of their children's being returned to their custody. The agency director took a very pro-reunification stance with the parents, DCF, and court system, and directed the interns he was supervising to write letters to the court encouraging serious reconsideration of family reunification. Some of the interns involved in the case had reservations about reunification so soon, as did the guardian *ad litem,* who was also involved in the case.

During the ongoing work with the family, the agency director resigned from his position at the agency, and a new director was hired. The new director was court ordered to bring videotapes and no associated documentation to a court hearing on the case. When she arrived at the hearing, the videotapes were taken from her by the DCF authorities, and the new director was shocked to see the previous director introduced as an expert witness in the case. The case had been under the jurisdiction of the agency, and the previous director, who functioned also as the clinical supervisor, did not notify the agency of his role as an advocate expert witness. The result was that the agency, who had legal responsibility for the case, was effectively shut out of the process of dialogue and recommendations-making because of the previous director's lack of disclosure of his dual roles: He was now assuming the role of a paid expert witness on a case that he had been involved in only through his role as the previous agency director. The key conflict of interest in this case was the supervisor's lack of disclosure, both to the agency having responsibility for the case and to DCF, of his dual roles, leaving open questions about his motivation.

Use of Power. Issues of power immediately invoke the ethics of relationship and the question of what is the moral way to consider the other. In the traditional justice model of ethics, the supervisor in clinical supervision is seen as having greater power over the supervisee than the supervisee has over the supervisor. So, the power relationship is one of unequals, in which the supervisee is more vulnerable. The ethical obligation incumbent on the supervisor in clinical supervision to be mindful of the power differential is designed to protect the more vulnerable party, namely, the supervisee.

Power and privilege are closely connected, so inquiry into who is privileged at a historical point in time will dialectically point one's attention to who is less privileged. In our time and place, racial minorities, women, and those of lower socioeconomic status, by virtue of those attributes, are more likely to be less privileged and therefore less powerful. Perhaps more importantly, even when emerging from conditions of diminished power and privilege, women, racial minorities, and persons of lower socioeconomic status carry with them the cultural imprint of domination, sometimes oppression, and powerlessness that is not reversed in a historical moment. Consequently, issues of gender, class, and race are potentially highly charged in supervision, a relationship in which the supervisor has evaluative power. Because of the real effects of evaluation in terms of endorsement, licensure, promotion, and career trajectories, whether the role of evaluator constitutes actual coercive power is a question that Bernard and Goodyear (1998) suggest has not been researched in regard to clinical supervision.

Suffice it to say, in a relationship that is unequal to begin with, the addition of gender, racial, and/or socioeconomic differentials introduces an additional layer of complexity into the relationship between supervisor and supervisee. The usual and customary way of addressing these power differentials in supervision is to talk about them and to respectfully engage the supervisee in open conversations and reflections about the meaning of the power differential in supervision for the supervisee. Fine and Turner (1997) refer to this process of openly reflecting upon and talking about power differentials as "transparency."

Sensitive supervisors who are inspired by either the traditional or relational models of ethical decision making are mindful of the importance of attending to power differentials in supervision. Those supervisors whose preferred model is relational, however, are more likely to subject the process of supervision itself to systematic inquiry, recognizing that the supervisor, by virtue of role, does not in fact possess superordinate wisdom about what is the best way to manage clinical cases. These relational supervisors, following Foucault (1975), are interested in examining the effects of the construction of the role of "supervisor" on those who participate in the supervision relationship and are generally more willing to pose questions about the imputed ability of the supervisor "to gaze" into the heart of clinical practice and make evaluative decisions that are fundamentally "right."

Boundaries. In structural family therapy, boundaries demarcate the generations and separate the parental from the spousal from the sibling subsystems. In clinical supervision, boundaries are a way of ensuring that the supervisor does not step over the line and take direct action in relationship to a client that, by virtue of role, should be taken by the supervisee. The supervisor interacts directly with the supervisee, who interacts directly with the client. Boundaries also clearly demarcate the relationship between the supervisor and supervisee as a supervision relationship as opposed to a therapeutic relationship or a purely educational or consultative relationship. The supervision relationship is hallmarked by its evaluative nature. See the case example involving boundaries in Box 14.15.

BOX 14.15
TALKING ABOUT BOUNDARIES IN SUPERVISION

The supervisor lays out his understanding of the supervision relationship to his female supervisee and invites questions, the expression of uncertainty and confusion, and reflections on the process of supervision itself: "Supervision is a complex and perhaps paradoxical relationship. It works best when there is openness and trust between the supervisor and supervisee, yet there is no getting around the evaluative aspect of supervision. As the supervisor, I am acutely aware of the constructed nature of supervision and the power inherent in the role of clinical supervisor. I myself have had both good and bad experiences in supervision and wonder what the history of your experience in supervision has been. Could we talk about what it was about those experiences that made them either good or bad? If you had similar supervision experiences today, do you think you would find yourself reacting similarly as you did in the past or differently? What kind of person and counselor did you find yourself invited to be in your past good experiences of supervision? What kind of person and counselor did you find yourself invited to be in your past not-so-good experiences of supervision? What has helped you to feel secure in the supervision relationship as opposed to fearful about the process or the evaluative aspects? Do you bring with you any concerns about my being male and your being female and how gender differences may affect our work together?

"I want to invite you, at any time, to question or comment on the questions I ask you in supervision and the way of looking at things those questions represent. If you do not agree with suggestions I might make, I would ask you to tell me so we can look at our different ways of looking at things together. If I am confused or unclear about your thinking in a clinical case, I will ask you questions about it, and I want you to do the same with me. If you are unclear or confused about what I am saying or wonder about my thinking, I want to encourage you to stop me and ask me any questions you may have. I am concerned in this supervision process that my voice never drowns out yours, and I would ask that you join me in being watchful about that."

Dual Relationships in Supervision. *Boundary violations versus boundary crossings.* A number of authors have provided a useful distinction between boundary violations and boundary crossings (Gutheil & Gabbard, 1993; Lazarus & Zur, 2002; Smith & Fitzpatrick, 1995; Zur, 2004). This distinction between boundary violation and boundary crossing is helpful for both supervisors and counselors in evaluating the ethics of proposed supervision or therapeutic relationships or strategies. In supervision, boundary violations occur as a result of exploitation of supervisees, abuse of power, coercion, deception, or misrepresentation. The classic example in therapy is the counselor who engages in a sexual relationship with a client. This classic example could also be applied at the next level up, to the clinical supervisor who decides it is acceptable to become sexually involved with a supervisee in active supervision and over whom the supervisor has evaluative and professional endorsement obligations. Such a situation in supervision would involve exploitation of the supervisee, a profound power imbalance, and the operation of undue influence, which is, by definition, harmful to the supervisee. Boundary violations that include exploitation of the power imbalance between supervisor and supervisee and an erosion of a sense of clear boundaries between them are not isolated, discrete events within the context of supervision, but rather are culminating events in a process of ethical and boundary erosion that has taken place over time (Peterson, 1992). By analogy, in the field of chemical dependency, clients are taught to think of relapse not as the taking up of the first drink or drug again, but rather as the thinking and acting that preceded the relapse, in other words, as a process of impaired thinking and decision making, not as a single event.

Boundary crossings, on the other hand, are described by Lazarus and Zur (2002) and Zur (2004) as any deviation from emotionally distant, psychoanalytically derived, office-based therapeutic practice and may be tremendously helpful for clients and also, potentially, for supervisees. An excellent example of a boundary crossing in supervision is the use of reflecting teams, in which the supervisor purposefully steps aside from the "expert" role in supervision and actively participates with his or her supervisee as an equal member of a reflecting team in therapy. In this capacity as a reflecting team member, the supervisor may share personal stories and reactions to the client's story to the same or even greater degree than the supervisee, thus revealing his or her own humanity and vulnerability. This moving away from the hierarchy and rigidity of the psychoanalytically dominated rules and regulations organizing both therapy and supervision is excellently exemplified by the reflecting team format for supervision.

Sexual attraction and sexual relationships. The codes of ethics of the major counseling and family therapy professional associations enjoin supervisors to avoid sexual relationships with supervisees. The American Counseling Association's (1995) ethical code states that "counselors do not engage in sexual relationships with students or supervisees and do not subject them to sexual harassment" (F.1.c). The Code of Ethics of the American Association for Marriage and Family Therapy (2001) introduces somewhat more complexity by addressing the particular period of time involved in the evaluative or training relationship with supervisees: "Marriage and family therapists do not engage in sexual intimacy with students or supervisees during the evaluative or training relationship between the therapist and student or supervisee. Should a supervisor engage in sexual activity with a former supervisee, the burden of proof shifts to the supervisor to demonstrate that there has been no exploitation or injury to the supervisee" (para. 4.3).

Most counseling professionals and trainees understand the greater vulnerability of supervisees in the supervision relationship and the significance of the power differential, and therefore endorse the prohibition against sexual relationships between supervisor and supervisee. That being said, it is also important to recognize the context of supervision and the intellectual and emotional intimacy that can be generated through appropriate supervision practices involving the processing of family-of-origin or self-of-therapist issues. The supervisee may become sexually attracted to the supervisor, the supervisor to the supervisee, or both to each other. Bernard and Goodyear (1998) emphasize the importance of the supervisor's not denying the sexual attraction to her or him, suggesting that denying or minimizing the attraction would limit the supervisor's ability to reflect clearly on it and would increase the risk of acting on it.

There are not too many guidelines for deciding whether and how to talk about sexual attraction within supervision. Would talking about the sexual attraction make it more likely that it would be converted into an actual sexual relationship? There may be some basis for thinking so, given that sexual attraction involves so many biological processes, including a flood of sexual hormones and feel-good neurotransmitters that are very powerful, and that confessing the attraction to the supervisee might indeed trigger an increased release of these biochemicals. The flood of hormones and feel-good neurotransmitters in the presence of an unequal power relationship may be too potent to overcome. It is not clear that, in the situation of supervisor attraction to the supervisee, talking about the attraction would advance the interests of the supervision relationship. The ethical obligations for the supervisor experiencing a sexual attraction to a supervisee are to attend to its early signs and to seek a supervision-of-supervision consultation so that outside help for managing the attraction and making supervision decisions can be obtained. If the sexual attraction is predominantly one-sided, flowing from the supervisee to the supervisor, it is probably easier to talk about the sexual attraction in supervision in ways that are helpful for the supervisee, by collaboratively looking at the context of the attraction and the meaning of the supervision relationship to the supervisee.

Non-intimate dual relationships. Non-intimate dual relationships in supervision include business relationships with supervisees, social and friend relationships with supervisees, supervision with relatives, simultaneous therapy and supervision relationships, and simultaneous supervision relationships with those who already hold evaluative power over the supervisee. Dual relationships introduce complexity into the supervision relationship and therefore invite greater attention to the dynamics of the supervision relationship and the ethical decision making of the supervisor. The values underlying the encouragement to avoid dual or multiple relationships in supervision are the nonexploitation of someone in a relationship in which there is unequal power and the obligations to promote client and professional welfare. These obligations could get compromised if the preexisting relationship invited the supervisor to focus less time and attention on the supervision aspect of the multiple relationship or to go easier on the supervisee who is also a friend or business associate.

However, there are times when dual relationships are difficult or undesirable to avoid. Karl Tomm (n.d.) has taken a clear stance opposing the AAMFT's global restriction on dual relationships, citing the possibilities for personal and professional enhancement that such relationships may generate, while also acknowledging the effort and time involved in successfully maintaining them. Tomm (n.d.) states:

> It is my opinion that the AAMFT is doing our field and our communities a major disservice by imposing such pervasive restraints on dual relationships through the *Code of Ethics.* Far more research and exploration into the nature, complexities, and consequences of a wide range of dual relationships is needed before such a broad restriction on duality is allowed to become entrenched in our professional attitudes. Not only is the issue of exploitation being confused, human enrichment possibilities are being restrained, professional hierarchy is being privileged, and social alienation is being enhanced. (p. 6)

Tomm has recognized the frequency of such dual or multiple relationships in the professional world and their possibilities for enrichment as opposed to diminishment and exploitation. The question of the desirability or undesirability of dual relationship is illustrated in Box 14.16.

BOX 14.16
A DUAL RELATIONSHIP IN SUPERVISION

Louis is a counselor in a large mental health agency headed by a family therapist with a national reputation. Although not Louis's direct supervisor, the family therapist has taken on the responsibility of providing clinical supervision for Louis in couples and family therapy. Louis was trained as a mental health counselor, did not have much experience in family work, and wanted to improve his skills in that area. Louis felt very fortunate about having the well-known family therapist as his supervisor and was enjoying immensely his work with him. The family therapist's collaborative style of supervision and his way of helping Louis to think through his clinical questions and interventions had enabled Louis to develop some important family therapy skills and begin to feel much more confident when working with families. Louis admired the family therapist greatly and saw him as a role model whom Louis wanted to emulate.

During the period of Louis's clinical supervision, his youngest sister, who was 13, began to have some serious academic and behavioral problems. She started staying out late and being disrespectful to her Cuban mother and grandmother, who were bewildered and hurt by his sister's new attitudes. There was some suspicion that Louis's sister had also begun to smoke pot and drink on a regular basis. Louis's mother and grandmother asked Louis what they should do, and Louis could think of no better family therapist in the tri-county area than his supervisor. At his clinical supervision session tomorrow, Louis planned to ask the family therapist if he would see his own family in therapy because they were in crisis.

Should the supervisor agree to Louis's request? Is this situation one in which the multiple relationships of supervisee, staff member, and client would put him in a too vulnerable position? Or is this a situation in which Louis's personal and professional life and the life of his family would be enhanced by the willingness of the supervisor to openly manage the two roles of clinical supervisor to Louis and family therapist to Louis's family? Because a counselor may already have a professional relationship with a highly skilled therapist, does that mean that he can't avail of that counselor's services when he needs help for his own life? Must he go to someone he believes has lesser skills for his own family? How would this dilemma be handled from the perspective of a justice model of ethics? How would it be handled from the perspective of an ethic of care model?

Competency

Supervisor Competence. The issue of monitoring supervisee competence brings into play again the idea of power and the power differential between supervisor and supervisee. In supervision, monitoring competence is reflexive in that it requires the monitoring of one's own competence as a supervisor while also monitoring the competence of the supervisee. To decide to assume the professional role of supervisor is itself an ethical act, suggesting that the supervisor is bringing to the table a history of personal clinical competence and a history of dedication to both professional development and ongoing reflection about the meaning and implications of one's supervision practices for supervisees and clients. In terms of supervisory clinical competence, many states now require that supervisors for candidates for licensure have a minimum number of post-licensed years (usually two or more) before they can be identified as eligible supervisors.

Competence as a supervisor is not a steady state that, once arrived at, is automatically maintained. It requires commitment to ongoing professional training, supervision of supervision, and personal therapy as a resource for developing more enhanced ways of being in relationship with oneself and others. Good supervisors participate continuously in self-supervision of supervision, just as good counselors have learned that the ultimate goal of all formal supervision is learning how to do regular self-supervision.

Impairment versus Incompetence. There is currently little consensus on what constitutes impairment and what constitutes incompetence in supervisors. Some believe the two are essentially the same, as when Bernard and Goodyear (2004) define impairment as gross incompetence (p. 21). Others, like Lamb, Presser, Pfost, Baum, Jackson, and Jarvis (1987), contend that impairment is a reversal of previously adequate functioning and that incompetence is an ability to perform required functions. Still others prefer to avoid the terms entirely and would rather use designations like "ineffective supervisor qualities" (Watkins, 1997) or "lousy supervisor behaviors" (Magnuson, Wilcoxin, & Noiren, 2000) instead. Since ethical codes and legal statutes address incompetency and impairment, we will define and distinguish them. Furthermore, because of the power differential between supervisor and supervisee and because the gatekeeping function is an integral part of the supervisory role, we describe the impact of supervisory impairment on supervisees. Competency is also discussed in greater detail in a subsequent section.

Supervisory Incompetence. Supervisory incompetence can be defined as the incapacity to perform the function of the supervisory role due to a training, experience, unwillingness, or inflexibility. As noted in a previous chapter, in its Ethical Guidelines for Clinical Supervisors, the Association for Counseling Education and Supervision (ACES) indicates four supervisory functions: (a) monitoring client welfare; (b) encouraging compliance with relevant legal, ethical, and professional standards for clinical practice; (c) monitoring clinical performance and professional development of supervisees; and (d) evaluating and certifying current performance and potential of supervisees for academic, screening, selection, placement, employment, and credentialing purposes. Generally speaking, incompetence is the result of lack of training and/or experience, while unwillingness and/or inflexibility are less common; however, either may confound the training and experience deficits (see the example in Box 14.17). Usually, involvement in a formal training or one-to-one coaching in the art of supervision are the interventions of choice for lack of knowledge and experience.

BOX 14.17
DIANE AND A SUPERVISORY DILEMMA

Jacob graduated with a PhD, received psychology licensure one year ago, and thereafter joined the staff of a community mental health center. Recently, he has been asked to provide supervision to internship students from a local university graduate program. Five weeks ago, he started his first supervisory relationship with Diane. Diane is pursuing a master's degree in counseling

(*continued*)

BOX 14.17 CONTINUED

in order to achieve licensure so she can practice psychodrama. At the time she began her internship, she had logged over 800 hours of supervised psychodrama experience as an "assistant" in a psychodrama group that was headed by two psychiatrists who were well regarded in the professional community. She understood at the outset that little, if any, of this experience would count for the university program or licensure. Rather, she looked upon it as "additional" training in a specialty area. When she mentioned her interest and experience in psychodrama to Jacob in their first meeting, he nodded and said nothing.

She began seeing a caseload immediately, and in their next meeting, she started to present one of her cases from a psychodrama perspective. Jacob interrupted and indicated that, from henceforth in their supervision, she must only conceptualize cases, plan treatment, and execute interventions from a cognitive behavioral perspective. He added that her clients would be confused by such a "radically different approach" than the cognitive behavioral they were used to receiving. Diane had little knowledge or interest in that approach and told Jacob that she had already developed treatment agreements with her six clients and all were agreeable to her approach. Jacob was not happy to hear this and angrily forbade her to use anything other than the "standard" approach, which was supposedly the "unwritten policy" of the clinic. Diane immediately complained to the clinic director and to her university supervisor, saying she was not valued as a person or for her expertise. She wanted to be reassigned. In discussion with the clinic director, Jacob admitted he knew basically nothing about psychodrama and was not interested in learning anything about it, particularly from a "master's student that was trained by psychiatrists." Unfortunately, no other supervisor was available at the site, so she remained there for the rest of the semester, reluctantly agreeing to practice the "standard" therapy with her clients. Despite reasonably good clinical outcomes and very good client satisfaction ratings, Jacob evaluated her with a "minimal pass" for the semester. Diane was surprised, since she thought things had gone reasonably well in their supervision. Jacob had not provided a midterm evaluation, nor did he discuss the possibility of a poor evaluation or suggest any remediation.

In terms of the four ACES supervisory functions, Jacob may have exhibited "minimal" functioning on evaluating and certifying Diane's clinical performance and professional development. Might this, as well as Jacob's apparent inflexibility regarding theoretical orientation, constitute supervisory incompetence? Explain. Mindful of the power differential that supervisors hold and the "standard" therapy policy of the site, might things have turned out differently had Diane taken another tack? If so, why? If not, why not? If you were in a similar situation, what would you do?

Supervisory Impairment. Supervisory impairment can be defined as the incapacity to perform the function of the supervisory role due to a debilitating medical, substance-related, or psychological condition that results in diminished functioning from a previously higher level of functioning. Manifestations of impairment include clinical depression, substance abuse, sexual harassment, sexual misconduct, and other boundary violations, personality disorders, severe burnout, and medical conditions such as senile dementia or stroke. Psychotherapy or medical treatments are common forms of remediation for impairment; however, sometimes limitation or loss of licensure or imprisonment is imposed, as in the case of sexual misconduct. Unlike the incompetent supervisor, the impaired supervisor is able to sustain some semblance of professional demeanor and supervisory functioning in the supervisory role before exhibiting recognizable incapacity of function characteristic of impairment.

Impact of Supervisor Impairment on Supervisees. In an earlier chapter, the Integrated Developmental Model (Stoltenberg et al., 1998) was discussed. As you will recall, this model articulates three levels of counselor development, and the model suggests how certain styles and patterns of supervision can foster development. Based on these developmental levels, it is possible to extrapolate how supervision can negatively impact supervisee development (Muratori, 2001). In this section, we'll briefly consider the impact of the impaired supervisor on supervisees at each level.

Level 1 supervisees tend to be highly motivated, extremely anxious, and dependent on their supervisors for guidance and structure. For all practical purposes, they could be considered to be in their professional infancy moving toward toddlerhood. They have a strong desire to emulate experienced therapists and supervisors as a means of developing skill and confidence (Stoltenberg et al., 1998). Thus, they can become quite anxious and confused when working with an assigned supervisor who is impaired. Generally speaking, supervisees at this phase of development are at risk of being harmed, to varying degrees, by such supervisors. Even Level 1 supervisees who are confident in their perceptions that their supervisors are acting in an inappropriate and ethically questionable fashion are likely to be adversely affected by such a supervisory relationship. Their disenchantment with their supervisory experience may conceivably be manifested in a variety of ways, including low morale and an increasingly pessimistic view of "counseling"; symptoms of their own distress (e.g., depression, anxiety); or the decision to reevaluate their educational and career plans and leave the helping professions altogether (Muratori, 2001).

Level 2 supervisees can be likened to adolescents who are struggling to establish a personal identity; in their efforts to establish a professional identity, they vacillate between functioning independently and regressing toward the dependency of Level 1 (Stoltenberg et al., 1998). As Level 2 supervisees come to recognize supervisor impairment, they are likely to experience despair, confusion, and a sense of instability. One devastating consequence of working under the guidance of an impaired supervisor at this level can be the suppression of the supervisee's emerging sense of professional independence.

Level 3 supervisees typically have completed graduate training and are involved in professional practice. They make seek supervision to log hours for licensure or to further develop and refine skills. Characteristically, they are able to focus on the client, the process, and their own personal reactions simultaneously (Stoltenberg et al., 1998). Accordingly, of the three levels, these supervisees are the least likely to be negatively impacted by supervisors' impairments.

To more accurately gauge the impact of impairment on a supervisee, it is necessary to specify the nature and severity of the supervisor's impairment in addition to the supervisee's level of development. For example, a severely burned-out supervisor who expresses little regard for client welfare and whose personal and professional disillusionment prompts him or her to lash out at trainees in a sarcastic manner will likely elicit different reactions from supervisees at each level. For instance, Level 1 supervisees with little or no prior supervised experience may personalize a supervisor's sarcastic and critical remarks to mean that they are completely incompetent. This perception, compounded by the high level of anxiety characteristic of this level, can leave them feeling defeated and may cause them to seriously question or even abandon their career plans and dreams of becoming therapists or counselors. In reaction to the severely burned-out supervisor, Level 2 supervisees may regress to a state of dependency characteristic of Level 1 after internalizing the supervisor's sarcastic and critical remarks as an indication that they are performing inadequately, and thus should refrain from taking the kind of risks that would lead them to a higher level of development. Conversely, Level 2 supervisees could disregard all supervisory feedback in an effort to practice more autonomously than their skills and competence warrant. Unfortunately, either reaction would be detrimental to their professional growth and to the welfare of their clients. On the other hand, Level 3 supervisees are more likely to be able to identify the supervisor's behavior as symptoms of burnout and may be sufficiently professionally mature to maintain adequate boundaries and filter out the supervisor's negative influence (Muratori, 2001).

Monitoring Supervisee Competence. In the justice model of ethics, the supervisor's role is vested with authority before the supervisor ever even works with supervisees. In Foucault's (1975) terms, this authority represents the power of professional disciplines to determine acceptability and to separate the competent from the incompetent, according to particular standards that have become discursively privileged. In the ethic of care model, the supervisor's role is a performative one, in which the supervisor is accountable to the supervisee for encouraging the supervisee's development of skills and professional confidence within the framework of care, compassion, and openness. In this model, the supervisee is also accountable to the supervisor to participate in conversations designed to explore the meaning and implications of the supervisee's clinical thinking and to practice with the end in mind of opening up possibilities for expanded ways of thinking and doing therapy.

The justice model directs supervisors to set up predetermined criteria for evaluating competence. The criteria would include general competence having to do with personal maturity and the ability to interact in interpersonally appropriate ways with clients. The criteria would also include specific standards having to do with client assessment, case conceptualization, clinical skills development, crisis management, referral making, ability to communicate effectively with both clients and peers, and ability to work as a team member, to name some of the most important. In the justice model, supervisees would be measured against a normative standard for all of the criteria.

In the ethic of care model, the supervisor and supervisee explore together the influence of those preestablished criteria on their work and on their lives as professionals. For example, in situations in which the supervisee is anxious or fearful, the supervisor and supervisee talk together to identify the larger cultural scripts that may be operating on the supervisee in an oppressive or colonizing way. They would also consider what steps the supervisee might take to minimize or escape the influence of oppressive or colonizing professional scripts on the supervisee's performance as a counselor. The ethic of care model invites ongoing reflection on how professional roles, professional identities, and notions of professional competence are socially constructed. In this model, should a significant difference emerge between the point of view of the supervisor and the supervisee about the nature of an evaluation, one option would be to include a third professional voice in order to expand the possibilities for thinking about the situation, or to interview the multiple voices that each (supervisor and supervisee) represent within the supervision relationship until a negotiated outcome can be found. See the example of potential supervises incompetence illustrate in Box 14.18.

BOX 14.18
MONITORING A SUPERVISEE'S COMPETENCY

Legal liability and risk management are high-priority considerations in a not-for-profit community mental health clinic in an inner-city neighborhood. The clinic's mission is to work with clients in supportive, strength-based, nonpathologizing ways. The executive director and board of the clinic also run a school and a recreation program and are more in touch with those areas of their organization than they are with their clinic. The clinic staff members are hardworking, dedicated counselors who are stretched to their limits working under pressure of inadequate administrative support and resources and who don't have either the time or inclination to do public relations work to get more attention from their executive director and board.

Most of the clinic's clients are economically disadvantaged multiproblem families referred by the courts, the Department of Children and Families, or the Department of Juvenile Justice. These referring sources require routine status reports and evaluations of the clients they refer. The staff, and especially the clinical director, feel that they are caught in a Catch-22 trying to do nonpathologizing work with clients whose referring networks want medical model, evaluative reports. They also feel caught in a bind in relation to their own administration, who want the clinical services provided, but who are also constantly warning the clinical director and staff to do everything they can to avoid getting involved in lawsuits and litigation.

With a small grant, the clinical director had hired a contract clinical supervisor to work with her and two other counselors. During supervision, the clinical supervisor accompanied the clinical director to court to hear the director's testimony about a particularly difficult case. The clinical supervisor was questioned very aggressively by an agency attorney about whether the mother in the case, in the opinion of the clinical director, was competent to care for two of her children during unsupervised visitations. The clinical director had been involved in the case for eighteen months, and her new supervisor was horrified to hear her answer the attorney by saying that the mother would do the best she could. Since the children had been removed from the home because of allegations of neglect, the attorney asked the clinical director whether that would be good enough if the mother had to deal with an emergency involving one of the children. The clinical director repeated only that she thought the mother would do her best. The attorney and agency workers were angry that they did not get any help to make an informed decision about whether to institute unsupervised visitations. The clinical director was bewildered, afraid to take a stand for fear that she and her agency would be scapegoated by the court should something bad happen to the children during an unsupervised visitation that she had recommended. She also had realized during the attorney's questioning how attached she had become to the mother and wasn't really sure whether the mother could protect her children in an emergency.

Is this a case of clinical incompetence? Should the clinical director have made a fuller assessment of the mother's capability to mother and protect her children in an emergency? Does the clinical supervisor have an obligation to notify the executive director of the details of the case and court involvement? What are the broader agency and cultural issues bearing on the case and on the clinical director's decision to respond the way she did? How have these broader cultural issues affected the clinical director's ability to perform effectively? In supervision, how could the clinical director be helped to escape the double binds that she is operating within, short of resigning her position?

SPECIAL CONSIDERATIONS IN SUPERVISION

Fair Evaluation and Due Process in Supervision

Fair evaluation and due process rights are important ideas, within the justice model of ethics particularly. Since the justice model assumes the authority of the supervisor, fair evaluation and due process rights ensure that the supervisor cannot use that authority in arbitrary and capricious ways and without giving a vulnerable supervisee a way to remediate identified problems and skill deficits. Due process also ensures that, in the event of a negative evaluation by a supervisor, there must be a way of disseminating that information to the supervisee, a review of the basis for the negative evaluation with the supervisee, an opportunity for the supervisee to present his or her perspective, a plan for improvement or remediation, and a reasonable time period to bring skills and/or professional behavior up to standard, before disciplinary or punitive action can be initiated against the supervisee (see the case example in Box 14.19).

BOX 14.19
FAIR EVALUATION AND DUE PROCESS IN SUPERVISION

Ariel was completing her internship at a university clinic. On three occasions during the semester, she failed to show up to see her scheduled clients and did not notify the clinic staff that she would be absent. Her faculty supervisor had spoken with her at length after the first two incidents about the importance of professional behavior and accountability and also about the issue of client abandonment. Ariel said she did not think that she was abandoning her clients, because she knew there would be other counselors or the director at the clinic to see them. She had told her supervisor that she was having some personal difficulties and that she understood the importance of professional behavior. After the third incident, the faculty supervisor gave Ariel a failing grade for the course and felt it was pointless talking with her again because the first two times did not seem to make any difference. The supervisor had made supervision notes about her first two conversations with Ariel in regard to her attendance and client abandonment. After the third incident, she simply assigned the "F" without further discussion, feeling that she had already gone over the same ground twice before.

Has Ariel been afforded a fair evaluation and due process in this situation? How did the supervisor's frustration influence her handling of the supervision issue? What accountability obligations did both Ariel and her supervisor have?

In the ethic of care model, due process is not as central, because the authority of the supervisor to make negative evaluations is itself subject to inquiry. Negotiated outcomes between the supervisor and supervisee would be the rule rather than the exception in evaluation disagreements, making due process somewhat moot.

Fair evaluation includes a number of elements and relates to other common ethical issues in supervision already discussed. Fair evaluations are made by caring supervisors dedicated to promoting best practices in the counseling profession and who are free from prejudice, to the extent possible, and aware of the operation of important contextual and multicultural factors in supervision, in particular those of race, class, and gender. Fair evaluations assess agreed-upon criteria (both general and specific) that the supervisee knew in advance and consented to in an informed consent agreement. Fair evaluations provide an opportunity for supervisee as well as supervisor input. Fair evaluations are designed to encourage professional development and to discourage self-doubt and fear of engaging with clients.

Multicultural Issues in Supervision

The supervision relationship, like the therapeutic relationship, is shaped by the multicultural and contextual histories of the participants. It is also shaped by the discourse of the mental health professions and the power of professional authority vested in the supervisor. It is not possible to conceive of the practice of counseling and counseling supervision without paying attention to the centrality of cultural and contextual factors. In 1991, Pederson proposed the notion that all counseling is multicultural. In so doing, he recognized and affirmed the universal influence of cultural factors of race, gender, class, ethnicity, religion, age, and sexual orientation on people and the relationships they participate in. As in counseling, all counseling supervision is multicultural, and these cultural factors are continuously in play, influencing and being influenced by the participants. Supervisors and supervisees bring personal and cultural histories of oppression or privilege, struggling and survival, subjugation or rising above subjugation to their relationship. These personal and cultural histories interact within the supervision relationship and emotionally tag cognitive responses to situations and events. Box 14.20 helps the supervisor to explore some of the aspects of his or her cultural history.

BOX 14.20
CASE EXAMPLE: SUPERVISOR ACCOUNTING PRACTICES

In order to attend to our own practices of power as clinical supervisors, the following questions might suggest some opening-up dialogues with oneself and with supervisees:

What aspects of your own cultural history stand out for you and why?

With what aspects of your own cultural history are you most familiar? Least familiar?

What ideas does your cultural history give you about the exercise of authority?

What ideas do your professional identity and affiliation give you about the exercise of authority?

How does your cultural history inform your thinking about marginalization?

Does the voice of authority speak loudly or softly, and how does it include the other?

How have your experiences in supervision informed your ideas about what good supervision means?

Foucault (1975) directed our attention to the power of professional discourse to shape reality and to classify reality. His work invites us to question our taken-for-granted assumptions about supervision and the authority of the supervisor to classify and legitimate. Professional discourse, in particular the discourse of mental health and illness, can be used to disqualify and delegitimate personal experiences. The supervisor, as a representation of professional mental health discourse, carries this authority to render judgment on the lived experiences of supervisees. As in all relationships of power, the ethical imperative requires that supervisors examine and account for their practices of power.

Religious and Spiritual Issues in Supervision

Just as professional ethical standards require counselors and therapists to be sensitive to cultural issues, counselors and therapists are similarly required to be sensitive to religious and spiritual issues influencing their clients. Chapter 4 detailed the ethical implication of a number of religious and spiritual issues in counseling practice. Not surprisingly, many of this issues surface in supervision. This section briefly notes some of the more common of such issues in supervision.

Perhaps the most important and most common issue involves the imposition of the supervisee's values on the client. In that earlier chapter, we noted that counseling and therapy are not value-free and that values influence every facet of counseling process: assessment, goals of treatment, interventions used, and evaluation of treatment outcomes. We distinguished value exposure from value imposition. Value exposure involves the disclosure of the counselor's values when appropriate and without an agenda, whereas value imposition involves disclosure with an agenda. Most commonly, value imposition involves effort to proselytize or to criticize the client.

We noted that the Association for Spiritual, Ethical, and Religious Values in Counseling (ASERVIC) had proposed list of spiritual and religious competencies for inclusion in CACREP standards (Favier, Ingersoll, O'Brien, & McNally, 2001, pp. 178–180). Among others, these include the capacity to assess a client's religious and spiritual concerns, the capacity to demonstrate empathy involving a client's spiritual and religious beliefs and practices, and the capacity to assess the relevance of a client's spiritual and religious issues with regard to therapeutic goals. Presumably, supervisors are aware of these specific competencies and the level of the supervisee's competencies and will discuss the influence and impact of such client values and beliefs on treatment process when operative.

Supervision may be the first and only time trainees have the opportunity to begin to understand and deal with issues of transference and countertransference. It should not be too surprising that countertransference issues often arise when clients are describing or dealing with spiritual or religious matters. Supervisors would do well to acquaint themselves with specific strategies for managing countertransference involving such religious and spiritual issues. A clinically useful reference in this regard is Spero (1981).

Besides ethical issues involved with assessment of religious and spiritual values, beliefs, and concerns, supervisors should be comfortable and willing to discuss and offer advice on the use of spiritually oriented interventions and methods. There are situations in which such interventions appear to be warranted. There are also situations and circumstances in which there are absolute contraindications as well as relative contraindications for such interventions (Sperry, 2001) (see Box 14.21). One of the most sensitive and complex ethical issues that supervisees face is a client's requesting them to pray with him or her. The advisability of utilizing prayer as a treatment intervention is an important professional and ethical consideration, and fortunately, the matter of indications and contraindications has been addressed (Koenig & Pritchett, 1998). Even though supervisors may not be fully conversant in these matters, it is expected that they have access to such information through references or consultation.

BOX 14.21
ANOTHER LOOK AT THE CASE OF THE MAGIC PEBBLE

Earlier in the case of Tina, a school counseling intern who has been assigned to Evelyn James to supervise her onsite training in an elementary school in a small rural community, Tina had been to a workshop on enhancing self-esteem and had learned a technique called the "magic pebble," designed to be used with elementary students in a classroom group setting. Tina had planned to use the technique with one of her guidance classes that day that is until she reviewed her plan with Ms. James. James was well aware of community values and sentiment against anything that was perceived to be in any remotely connected to "New Age" techniques. It was clear to the supervisor that the magic pebble activity would be negatively received by parents and church leaders in this small rural community. She vividly recalled how an adjoining community had reacted negatively to a teacher who had used a similar exercise in her class. The teacher's action was denounced as "heresy," and soon afterward a local evangelical church sponsored a series on the "Demonic Influences of New Age Spirituality." Subsequently, that district came out against the use of any "magic ideas" in their schools. The supervisor discussed the implications of Tina's plan for her afternoon classroom group. Tina indicated that she hadn't really given any thought to the potential impact of her planned activity on the religious sensibilities of the parents of her students, the principal, or the school board. She agreed that she would replace this technique with something that would be more religiously and spiritually suitable. This case represents the supervisor's care and concern for clients, that is, students, their parents, the principal, the school district, and the community, as well as for her supervisee. It also reflects the importance of the supervisor in helping supervisees to assess and understand community's religious and spiritual values.

Clinical Supervision, Case Consultation, and Peer Consultation

It is important to distinguish roles and responsibilities of those providing supervision from those providing consultation, since many view consultation and supervision as essentially the same. They are actually quite different in terms of roles, purposes, and responsibilities. The role of a clinical supervisor is to provide clinical supervision. This should be distinguished from the role of the consultant, who provides consultation. In counseling and psychotherapy training programs, this distinction of roles can be noted in a graduate program's clinical education: its practicum and internship training. For instance, students involved in internship training typically work with a clinical supervisor at an off-campus clinical site, as well as attend a weekly internship seminar at the university. At the clinical site, their assigned clinical supervisor provides clinical supervision, while their university instructor meets with student interns to consult on their work at off campus sites, a process called case consultation. Unfortunately, this distinction is blurred when university instructors are referred to as university "supervisors" to distinguish them from site supervisors. The reality is that university faculty involved in practicum or internship seminars function as consultants, not supervisors.

Consultation. Consultation has been defined as a "process in which a human services professional assists a consultee with a work-related—or caretaking-related—problem with a client system, with the goal of helping both the consultee and the client system in some specific way" (Douherty, 2000, p. 9).

Clinical Supervision versus Consultation. While there are a few similarities between consultation and supervision, the differences are quite pronounced. One obvious similarity is the number of parties involved. In supervision, there is a supervisor, a supervisee, and a client or client system. In consultation, there are also three parties: a consultant, a consultee (i.e., the person receiving the consultation), and the consultee's client or client system. While there are multiple roles in supervision—teacher, coach, mentor, advisor, evaluator, and gatekeeper for the profession—there is one primary role in consultation: advisor. While there are multiple responsibilities in supervision—responsibility for welfare of the supervisee, responsibility, usually indirectly, for the welfare of the client, and sometimes, responsibility to an agency—there is only one responsibility for the consultant: advising the consultee.

The most important difference between the two involves the nature of the relationship. Supervisors are experts in the supervisory relationship as well as authority figures, in that they have an evaluation function, serving as gatekeepers for the counseling profession. In consultation, consultants may assume an expert-advisory role, but their advice is purely informational and not binding on the supervisee. There is no evaluative function in consultation. Finally, we have made the case that effective supervision usually requires a collaborative relationship based on trust and mutually agreed-upon goals and roles. Such a relationship, while sometimes desirable, is not necessary for effective consultation to occur, particularly if the goal is to seek or receive advice.

Case Consultation. In case consultation, the supervisee has no responsibility for following the consultant's specific directives about a case, whereas in clinical supervision, the supervisee has the responsibility of following the supervisor's specific directives with a given client. Making this distinction reduces liability to some extent.

Peer Consultation. Peer consultation is the process of conferring with a colleague to ascertain how other reasonable, similarly trained counselors would practice in the same set of circumstances. Peer consultation is particularly important in meeting the legal standard of care. "By consulting with others, a counselor can prove later that they indeed met the standard of care by doing what other, presumably reasonable counselors advised or agreed upon' (Remley & Herlihy, 2001, p. 17).

Organizational Consultation. Organizational consultation is a form of consultation that involves working with a client system that may include a work team or group, a division of an organization or corporation, or the entire organization or corporation. Organizational consultation focuses on work-related issues, and the purpose is to increase productivity, morale, employee commitment to the work team or organization, and so on. Counseling skills overlap to some degree with consulting skills. Not surprisingly, mental health professionals have been exploring organizational consultation as an alternative to counseling practice in a managed care environment.

Ethical Issues in Consultation. Many of the same ethical issues that are operative in counseling and in supervision are operative, to varying degrees, in consultation. These include confidentiality, informed consent, competency, and the welfare of clients. Interested readers can find detailed discussion of these and other ethical and legal issues in Chapter 13, "Ethical and Legal Consideration," in Brown, Pryzwansky, and Schulte's *Psychological Consultation,* fifth edition, published in 2001.

LEGAL ISSUES AND CASE LAW AFFECTING SUPERVISION

Perhaps the main legal issues in supervision involve the matter of liability. We began this chapter by noting that the failure to supervise properly is a rather common cause of disciplinary action taken by regulatory boards against mental health professionals (Sacuzzo, 2002). Supervisors can be held liable not only for their own negligent actions but also for the actions of their supervisees. So what is liability? Liability is defined an obligation one has incurred or might incur through a negligent act. Negligence is defined as the dereliction of a duty, such as providing a reasonable standard of care, that directly causes damages. This section describes two types of liability: direct liability and indirect or vicarious liability. It also discusses the matter of risk assessment and provides some strategies for reducing the risk of liability in the context of supervision.

Direct Liability and Vicarious Liability

Direct Liability. In the context of supervision of students and unlicensed clinicians, supervisors can be held directly liable for their actions. Typically, the liability is due to their negligent acts, usually in the form of negligent supervision. Liability is proved when a link can be established between the actions of the supervisor and client injuries. Lack of proper monitoring is perhaps the most common factor in direct liability. Unless the supervisor is impaired or incompetent, direct liability is a relatively rare cause of malpractice. On the other hand, vicarious liability is a more common basis for a malpractice action.

Vicarious Liability. Vicarious liability is also known as indirect liability. Derived from the legal doctrine of *respondeat superior,* a supervisor can be held liable for the actions of those he or she supervises, regardless of any fault on the part of the supervisor (Disney & Stevens, 1994). This liability exists regardless of whether the supervisor breached a duty. Three elements must be shown to prove the supervisor is liable.

First, the existence of an employer–employee relationship must be established—that is, there must be selection and engagement of the supervisee and thus the power to dismiss and control the supervisee's conduct. For example, the "student may be under the general direction and supervision of professor at the university as well as under the license of a hospital or community facility. Under these circumstances, supervisory liability may be determined by the *borrowed servant rule*" (Sacuzzo, 2003, p. 10). In terms of university students securing training off-site, the university or university supervisor is considered the *general employer,* and the site director or supervisor is known as the *special employer.* The essential test or criterion is the existence of the power to control the supervisee at the time of the commission of the negligent act (Sacuzzo, 2003, p. 10). Furthermore, the theory of enterprise liability might be operative. It emphasizes the foreseeability of a supervisee's actions when a supervisor or clinic bills for the client contact hours of supervisees, and thus claims the supervisor should bear the risk of damages to clients. This theory is probably more applicable for privately arranged supervision.

Second, the act that injured the client must be within the supervisee's scope of employment. Courts use five factors to determine this: supervisor's power to control; whether supervisee had duty to perform the act; the time, place, and purpose of the act; the motivation of the supervisee regarding the act; and whether the supervisor could have reasonably expected the supervisee would commit the act. "When a student or unlicensed therapist is treating a patient under the supervision of a licensed practitioner, it is difficult to imagine any conduct that would not be considered within the scope of employment" (Sacuzzo, 2003, p. 9).

Third, the supervisee's client must prove that he or she was injured. In other words, the client has the burden of proving all elements of negligence. Proper monitoring by the supervisor can reduce or even eliminate the probability of vicarious liability.

Proper Monitoring of Supervisees: Some Practical Considerations

Considering the responsibility of monitoring a supervisee's clinical work on a continuum is useful in delineating a standard of care for supervisors. Such a continuum ranges from minimal and passive monitoring or scrutiny to maximum and active monitoring or scrutiny and has been described as follows (modified from Shoener, Milgrom, & Gonsiorek, 1989):

- Self-report (verbal, process notes, transcriptions)
- Examination of treatment records
- Audiotape
- Videotape
- Session-by-session formal clinical outcome data reports from client and supervisee
- Live observation
- Co-therapy

A legal scholar has recently concluded that "It thus appears as though the time has come in which self-report, or self-report in conjunction with record review, will not meet the minimum standard of care in supervision" (Sacuzzo, 2003, p. 10). Thus, it would not be unreasonable to expect that regular, ongoing monitoring at the active/maximum end of the continuum—scrutiny of videotapes, ongoing clinical outcomes data, careful monitoring of progress notes—would be indicated for beginning supervisees such as practicum and internship students. On the other hand, self-report monitoring may be sufficient at the completion of training, such as at the postdegree level, at which the supervisor has fuller recognition of the supervisee's strengths and limitations (Sacuzzo, 2002; Vasquesz, 1992).

Box 14.22 illustrates a case supervisor advice that may involve direct or vicarious liability.

BOX 14.22
UNEXPECTED SUPERVISOR ADVICE

Jeremy is a mental health counseling intern at a county mental health agency and has been at the site for two weeks. In his second session with a prepubescent female, he notes several bruises on her arms and legs that weren't visible during their first session. When the client is asked about the bruises, she looks away and says, "I don't know." After the session. Jeremy immediately seeks out his clinical supervisor, Norma, and reports his observation. He says that he is planning to call the child abuse hotline and asks her how he should document this in the client's chart. Norma acknowledges his concern but indicates that the call is not necessary because the case is already under investigation for a different injury that was reported to the hotline approximately one month ago by Kim, the client's previous counseling intern. At first, Jeremy is taken back by the supervisor's advice, but because he assumes that she must be correct, he does not make the call. This case gives rise to a number of questions: Did Norma meet her ethical responsibility as a supervisor? Her legal responsibility? If a complaint were filed against Jeremy, could he defend himself by saying he was an intern following the recommendation of his clinical supervisor? Is Norma or the clinic subject to direct liability? To vicarious liability? If you were in this situation, what might you do? How would your plan reduce or limit your liability and your supervisor's liability? How is your plan ethically sensitive? If you subsequently learned that this particular agency was known for consistently "underreporting" abuse, what might this suggest about the agency's organizational ethics?

Key Legal Cases Involving Supervision

Tarasoff v. Regents of the University of California (1976). In this case, of a therapist failing to sufficiently warn Tatiana Tarasoff that his client had threatened to kill her, the Supreme Court of California ruled that the therapist's supervisor could be held liable, because he had direct knowledge and control over the client's treatment. As a result of this, the supervisor had assumed a duty of care for Ms. Tarasoff as if he were acting as the primary therapist.

Altamonte v. New York Medical College (1994). In this case, a supervisee who revealed to a faculty member that he was a pedophile sexually assaulted a child he was treating. The court held that the educational institution was a supervisory institution, and so was liable for supervisory negligence because it had a duty to the supervisee's client.

Andrews v. United States (1984). A supervisor heard a complaint about sexual misconduct and confronted the supervisee, who denied the allegation, after which the supervisor dropped the matter. The U.S. Court of Appeals found that the supervisor had been negligent in his duties, because although he had knowledge of allegations of sexual misconduct, he failed to sufficiently investigate the matter.

Simmons v. United States (1986). An administrator expressed concern to a therapist's supervisor about the therapist's sexual impropriety with a client. The supervisor made no effort to take action. The court ruled that the supervisor was liable for negligent supervision for the client's attempted suicide and for the anxiety and depression suffered by the client.

CASE ILLUSTRATION OF ETHICAL-PROFESSIONAL DECISION MAKING IN SUPERVISION

This section applies the ethical-professional decisional strategy to a supervisory dilemma, presented in Box 14.23. An analysis utilizing the seven-step strategy is described.

BOX 14.23
A CASE OF A SUPERVISEE AND HER IMPAIRED SUPERVISOR

Earlier you were introduced to Jan, who had just begun an internship at a large private clinic serving primarily Title 19 clients. It was the first internship a student from Jan's graduate program had taken training there. While her first impressions of site were quite positive, based on meetings with Mr. Tritino, the clinic administrator, and Dr. Justine, her clinical supervisor, she became discouraged after her first week there. Her clients' complaints about staff and billing irregularities were bothersome, as was her first supervisory session with Dr. Justine. She felt some of his comments were inappropriate. When she rebuffed him, he appeared to retaliate by being overly critical and perhaps even vengeful by assigning her several additional clients who were extremely difficult to treat, particularly for a new intern. She felt trapped: There was no other internship site available this semester and apparently no other site supervisor, and she didn't think she could tolerate Dr. Justine's abusiveness; yet she needed to finish her internship this semester. She felt she was in a very difficult place and was uncertain about how to handle this professional dilemma with ethical ramifications. She decided to review her situation using the Ethical and Professional Practice Decisional Strategy.

Step 1: Identify the problem. Jan began by describing in writing the situations and circumstances that led to her belief that her supervisor was impaired. She used the following questions (modified from Muratori, 2001) to clarify her thoughts and feelings: If I suspect that my supervisor is impaired, what are the behavioral indicators that he has a problem? Do these behavioral indicators clearly impairment? How am I affected by my supervisor's impairment? Has my level of development as a counselor been negatively impacted as a result of his impairment? How are my clients affected by it? How are the clinic's policies and procedures influenced by this supervisor's impairment? What needs do I have under these circumstances that may affect my judgment or cloud my thinking? Given my developmental level, how might my need to function autonomously as a counselor affect my perceptions and impressions of my supervisor and his behavior? If I am feeling reluctant to take action, is it because I am fearful of retribution by the supervisor or the staff of the clinic? What repercussions do I anticipate if I take action? How might my clients and I be affected if I choose not to directly take action? She concluded that impairment was clearly the problem.

Step 2: Identify the participants affected by the decision. The participants included herself, her site supervisor Dr. Justine, the clinic administrator, clinic staff, the newly appointed university director of clinical education and training, and her eight clients at the clinic. Her relationship with Dr. Justine had become problematic and uncomfortable, and while he appeared to be friendly and said he wanted to be helpful, Jan was not sure she could trust him or other staff at the clinic. Although the training director was new, Jan felt he could be trusted and believed he had her best interest at heart. She had developed good collaborative relationships with all of her clients and was concerned that they might be negatively impacted by the current situation.

Step 3: Identify potential courses of action, along with possible benefits and risk for the participants. Because identifying a supervisor as impaired is a serious allegation, Jan carefully considered several potential courses of action: (1) informal resolution with the supervisor; (2) approach the clinic director about taking action; (3) approach the supervisor's colleagues at the clinic; and (4) consult with the university's director of clinical education and training. The benefit of option 1 is that, if the confrontation is respectful, sensitive, and well received, a positive resolution might result. The risk of option 1 is failure and retribution. It has been observed that, when a professional is in a one-down power position, directly approaching an impaired professional may have negative outcomes, since the majority of reported attempts at such direct, personal confrontations by those in a one-down power position have failed (Kilburg, Nathan, & Thoreson, 1986). Muratori (2001) recommends direct confrontation only in situations in which the supervisee is confident that retribution would not be a consequence of the confrontation. The benefit of option 2 is that Mr. Trintino, the clinic administrator, would take action, whereas the risk is that he would not, making the situation even more complex and stressful, such that Jan might conclude she has no choice but to leave the clinic and perhaps lose a semester. The benefit of option 3 is that Dr. Justine's clinic colleagues would confront him and report him to the licensure board if he does not seek treatment. The risk is that they might minimize or discount the complaint. The benefit of option 4 is that the university's director of clinical training has a vested interest in having her supervisees matched with effective and cooperative site supervisors. Presumably, the university director would confer with the clinic administrator about a resolution. Irrespective of the course of action she chooses, Jan can increase her credibility by describing her experience with Dr. Justine with specificity and objectivity. It will be important that she report observable behaviors in a dispassionate fashion without attacking the character of her supervisor.

Step 4: Evaluate the benefits and risks for each course of action.

Contextual Domain Considerations

In terms of the personal-developmental dimension, Jan appeared to be at Level 2 of counselor development. She was also aware of her tendency to righteousness and criticalness of authority and wondered if these factors influenced or precipitated her current dilemma. The university director of clinical education discounted this observation, suggesting that some recent information he had just learned from a clinical education at another university suggested prior instances of impaired functioning in Dr. Justine. With regard to the organizational dimension, Jan's inquiries revealed that issues of incompetence and impairment were not new to the clinic, and that staff, leadership, and the very culture of the clinic were basically unresponsive to impairment issues in both its written and unwritten policies. Besides the concern about Dr. Justine's possible sexually harassing statement, there appeared to be no other gender or multicultural considerations operative with regard to the clinic's stance on impairment. Accordingly, courses of action 2 and 3 seemed untenable.

Professional Domain Considerations

Jan reviewed the literature on impairment only to find almost nothing written about supervisor impairment. In conversation with Dr. Gregson, who had been on the impaired professionals' committee of the state licensing board, she learned more about impaired therapists and supervisors and strategies for dealing with them.

Ethical Domain Considerations

The five moral principles of the helping professions were considered: autonomy, beneficence, nonmaleficence, justice, and fidelity. Jan considered the following questions: Does my supervisor seem to embrace all of these principles? If not, which ones seem to be overlooked? How are my clients affected by my supervisor's unwillingness or inability to adhere to the principles? How am I affected? (Muratori, 2001). Autonomy was the only principle that the supervisor seemed to exhibit. Jan also learned that an intern a year ago had unsuccessfully confronted that supervisor about his abusive manner. Accordingly, course of action 1 seemed untenable.

The ACA (2005) Code of Ethics and Standards of Practice addresses ethical guidelines for the supervisory role in Section F and, specifically, the issue of impairment in Section C.2., which essentially states that counselors should refrain from offering professional services when their physical, mental, or emotional problems are likely to harm a client or others. Furthermore, they should recognize the signs of impairment, seek assistance for problems, and if necessary, limit, suspend, or terminate their professional responsibilities. The state's licensure law specified provisions similar to ACA code and required colleagues to report impaired professionals to the licensure board's committee on impairment. Jan learned that the university's director of clinical training and education had completed a term as a member of the state counseling licensure board's impaired professionals' committee. Course of action 4 seemed promising.

Step 5: Consult with peers and experts. Jan sought both peer and expert consultation. Peer consultation included interns in her university internship seminar, who primarily provided emotional support. Expert consultation included the director of an impaired professional clinic at the university medical center, as well as Dr. Gregson, the university's director of clinical education and training, who was experienced in matters of professional impairment.

Step 6: Decide on the most feasible option and document the decision-making process. Jan explored the following questions: How will all parties involved be affected if the impairment is not addressed? How might future supervisees and their clients be affected if Dr. Justine's impairment worsens? She then weighed each option by writing down a list of the best-case scenarios and worst-case scenarios for each course of action. For option 1, if informal resolution effort is unsuccessful, what steps can be taken to protect me from negative repercussions? If no support is available within the clinic (options 2 and 3) or the university (option 4), who might be willing and able to offer the supervisee support and adequate protection? In the unlikely event that Jan cannot identify one trustworthy professional, could she turn to a university ombudsperson for protection? Based on her answer to these questions and on her evaluation in Step 4, it seemed that option 4, consult with the university's director of clinical education and training to resolve the matter and possibly explore an alternative internship site, was the best alternative.

Step 7: Implement, evaluate, and document the enacted decision. Jan applied four ethical "tests" to evaluate the decision: publicity, universality, moral traces, and justice. Because these "tests" were satisfactorily met, Jan felt more confident about her decision. She formally requested the director's assistance in resolving the matter. Unfortunately, his attempt to have the clinic administrator take action with Dr. Justine was unsuccessful. Since it appeared untenable to keep Jan at the clinic and fearing retribution of some kind, he found another placement for her. The downside was that she "lost" about 100 hours, because neither Dr. Justine nor the clinic was willing to certify the hours Jan completed at the clinic site. Finally, because thorough documentation is of paramount importance, Jan planned to keep a record of all incidents involving the incompetent supervisor, including specific incidents, conversations with colleagues, and so on.

KEY POINTS

1. Administrative and clinical supervision differ in the amount of control or authority that the supervisor has over the supervisee.
2. Supervisors need to be sensitive to the due process rights of their supervisees, especially with respect to the obligation to provide ongoing feedback and evaluation of supervisee performance.
3. Informed consent for supervision must be obtained from both the client and the supervisee.
4. Points that should be discussed between a supervisor and supervisee before they enter into a working relationship include (1) the purpose of supervision; (2) the logistics of supervision; (3) information about the supervisor's qualifications and supervisory style; (4) the expectations, roles, and responsibilities of both parties; (5) evaluation; and (6) specifics about ethical and legal practice.
5. A written supervision agreement is recommended that specifies the nature of the supervisory relationship and that captures the key provisions discussed (Cf. #4).
6. The major components of supervisor competence have been described, as well as the ACES standards for counseling supervisors (1993). Supervisors need to possess the competencies described in this document, to be aware of the need for continuing education in supervision, to develop cross-cultural supervision skills, and to self-monitor the boundaries of their competence.
7. The requirements to keep client information confidential in counseling relationships apply equally to supervisory relationships.
8. Boundaries in the supervisory relationship must be managed carefully. Supervisors should not engage in close personal or social relationships with their supervisees, nor should they enter into business relationships with them, nor establish a counseling relationship as a substitute for supervision. Obviously, sexual intimacies between supervisor and supervisee are unethical and illegal.
9. Supervisors have large scope of responsibility and a number of parties to whom they are accountable. Under the legal principle of vicarious

liability and to the extent that supervisors have direct control and authority over their supervisees, supervisors may be held liable for their supervisees' negligence.

10. Both the supervisor and the supervisee have certain rights and responsibilities in the relationship. It is essential that both parties understand these rights and responsibilities in order for supervision to work, that is, facilitate supervisee growth while protecting client welfare.
11. Trainees also utilize case consultation and peer consultation. Because consultants generally do not have direct control and authority over those who receive their services, they typically cannot be held accountable legally for the negligence of the consultee.
12. Consultants must take care to safeguard the informed consent and confidentiality rights of both consultees and clients.
13. The ethical decision-making model is utilized by a supervisee faced with a weighty challenge involving a supervisor.

CONCLUDING NOTE: PERSPECTIVE III AND SUPERVISION

Supervisors operating from Perspective III tend to view supervision as a process of personal and professional growth for both themselves and their supervisees. Typically, they function as Level 4 supervisors; such supervisors possess considerable technical and relational supervisory skills and are adept at integrating theory in practice. Not surprisingly, they can accurately and effectively monitor and evaluate supervisee performance. In our experience, these supervisors are the ones that consistently work well supervising a wide range of trainees. Interestingly, such supervisors seldom seem to be involved in liability issues, probably because they anticipate potential ethical and legal considerations and proactively work with supervisees to maximize counseling outcomes while minimizing risks. Because they are lifelong learners, issues of incompetence are not likely. Since self-care and wellness are valued and considered essential by these supervisors, issues of impairment are seldom noted. It is for these and other reasons that we advocate striving for a Perspective III mindset for all clinical supervisors.

REVIEW QUESTIONS

1. What would you do if you felt that you were not being provided with adequate supervision during your practicum or internship?
2. Under what circumstances would it be appropriate to socialize with your supervisor?
3. What would you do if your supervisor were attracted to you? What would you do if you were attracted to your supervisor?
4. What qualities do you think an ideal supervisor should possess?
5. How would you feel if your supervisor had to assume vicarious liability for your negligent actions?

REFERENCES

Altamonte v. New York Medical College, 851 F. Supp. 34 (D. Conn. 1994).

American Association for Marriage and Family Therapy. (2001). *Code of ethics* (rev. ed.). Alexandria, VA: Author.

American Counseling Association. (2005). *Code of ethics* (rev. ed.). Alexandria, VA: Author.

Andrews v. United States, 732 F. 2d 366 (4th Cir. 1984)

Association for Counselor Education and Supervision. (1993). *Ethical guidelines for counseling supervisors.*

Retrieved February 28, 2004, from Association for Counselor Education and Supervision (ACES) website: http://www.acesonline.net/ethicalguidelines.htm

Behnke, S. H., Winick, B. J., & Perez, A. M. (2000). *The essentials of Florida mental health law: A straightforward guide for clinicians of all disciplines.* New York: Norton.

Bernard, J. M., & Goodyear, R. K. (2004). *Fundamentals of clinical supervision* (3rd ed.). Boston: Allyn and Bacon.

Bernard, J. M., & Goodyear, R. K. (1998). *Fundamentals of clinical supervision* (2nd ed.). Boston: Allyn and Bacon.

Bierman, N. (2004, March 17). Shelter worker left teenage boy hanging. *The Miami Herald,* pp. B1–B2.

Brown, D., Pryzwansky, W., & Schulte, A. (2001). *Psychological consultation* (5th ed.). Boston: Allyn and Bacon.

Crossley, N. (1998). Emotions and communicative action. In G. Bendelow & S. J. Williams (Eds.), *Emotions in social life: Critical themes and contemporary issues.* London: Routledge.

Crossley, N. (2000). Emotion, psychiatry, and social order: A Habermasian approach. In S. Williams, J. Gabe & M. Calnan (Eds.), *Health, medicine, and society: Key theories, future agendas.* London: Routledge.

Damasio, A. R. (1994). *Descartes' error: Emotion, reason, and the human brain.* New York: Putnam.

Disney, M., & Stevens, A. (1994). *Legal issues in clinical supervision.* Alexandria, VA: American Counseling Association.

Dougherty, A. (2000). *Consultation: Practice and perspectives.* Pacific Groves, CA: Brooks/Cole.

Favier, C., Ingersoll, R., O'Brien, E., & McNally, C. (2001). *Explorations in counseling and spirituality: Philosophical, practical, and personal reflections.* Pacific Groves, CA: Brooks/Cole.

Fine, M., & Turner, J. (1997). Collaborative supervision: Minding the power. In T. C. Todd & C. L. Storm (Eds.), *The complete systemic supervisor: Context, philosophy, and pragmatics* (pp. 229–240). Boston: Allyn and Bacon.

Foucault, M. (1975). *The birth of the clinic: An archeology of medical perception.* A. M. Sheridan Smith, Trans. New York: Vintage Books.

Gilligan, C. (1977). In a different voice: Women's conceptions of self and morality. *Harvard Educational Review, 47,* 481–517.

Gilligan, C. (1982). *In a different voice: Psychological theory and women's development.* Cambridge: Harvard University Press.

Gray, L., Ladany, N., Walker, J., & Ancis, J. (2001). Psychotherapy trainees' experience of counterproductive events in supervision. *Journal of Counseling Psychology, 48,* 371–383.

Gutheil, T. G., & Gabbard, G. O. (1993). The concept of boundaries in clinical practice: Theoretical and risk-management dimensions. *American Journal of Psychiatry, 150,* 188–196.

Kilburg, R. R., Nathan, P. E., & Thoreson, R. W. (Eds.). (1986). *Professionals in distress: Issues, syndromes, and solutions in psychology.* Washington, DC: American Psychological Association.

Koenig, H., & Pritchett, J. (1998). Religion and psychotherapy. In H. Koenig (Ed.), *Handbook of religion and mental health* (pp. 323–336). San Diego: Academic Press.

Kohlberg, L. (1981). *Essays in moral development: Vol. 1. The philosophy of moral development.* New York: Harper & Row.

Kohlberg, L. (1984). *Essays in moral development: Vol. II. The psychology of moral development: Moral stages and their nature and validity.* San Francisco: Harper & Row.

Lamb, D., Presser, N., Pfost, K., Baum, M., Jackson, R., & Jarvis, P. (1987). Confronting professional impairment during the internship: Identification, due process, and remediation. *Professional Psychology: Resource and Practice, 18,* 597–603.

Ladany, N., Hill, C., Corbett, M., & Nutt, E. (1996). Nature, extent, and importance of what psychotherapy trainees do not disclose to their supervisors. *Journal of Counseling Psychology, 43,* 10–24.

Lazarus, A., & Zur, O. (2002). *Dual relationships and psychotherapy.* New York: Springer.

Magnuson, S., Wilcoxin, S., & Noiren, J.K. (2000). A profile of lousy supervisors: Experienced counselors' perspectives. *Counselor Education and Supervision, 39,* 189–202.

McNamee, S., & Gergen, K. J. (Eds.). (1999). *Relational responsibility: Resources for sustainable dialogue.* Thousand Oaks, CA: Sage.

Meyer, R. G., Landis, E. R., & Hays, J. R. (1988). *Law for the psychotherapist.* New York: Norton.

Muratori, M. (2001). Examining supervisor impairment from the counselor trainee's perspective. *Counselor Education and Supervision, 41,* 41–57.

Nelson, M., Gray, L., Friedlander, M., Ladany, N., & Walker, J. (2001). Toward relationship-centered supervision: Reply to Veach (2001) and Ellis (2001). *Journal of Counseling Psychology, 48*(4), 407–409.

Neufeldt, E., Allstetter, S., & Holloway, E. (1995). Supervision: Its contributions to treatment efficacy. *Journal of Consulting and Clinical Psychology, 63*(2), 207–213.

Pedersen, P. B. (1991). Multiculturalism as a generic approach to counseling. *Journal of Counseling and Development, 70,* 6–12.

Peluso, P. (2003). The ethical genogram: A tool for helping therapists understand their ethical decision-making styles. *The Family Journal: Counseling and Therapy for Couples and Families, 14*(3), 286–291.

Peterson, M. (1992). *At personal risk: Boundary violation in professional–client relationships.* New York: Norton.

Remley, T., & Herlihy, B. (2001). *Ethical, legal and professional issues in counseling.* Upper Saddle River, NJ: Merrill Prentice-Hall.

Sacuzzo, D. (2002). Liability for failure to supervise adequately: Let the master beware. Part I. *The Psychologist's Legal Update, 13*(1), 1–14.

Sacuzzo, D. (2003). Liability for failure to supervise adequately: Let the master beware. Part II. *The Psychologist's Legal Update, 13*(2), 1–13.

Schoener, G., Milgrom, J., & Gonsiorek, J. (1989). Thereapeutic response to clients who have been sexually abused by psychotherapists. In G. Schoener & J. Milgrom (Eds.), *Psychotherapists' sexual involvement with clients: Intervention and prevention* (pp. 95–112). Minneapolis, MN: Walk-In Counseling Center.

Simmons v. United States, 805 F. 2d 1363 (9th Cir. 1986)

Skovholt, T., & Ronnestad, M. (1995). *The evolving professional self: Stages and themes and therapist and counselor development.* New York: Wiley.

Smith, D., & Fitzpatrick, M. (1995). Patient–therapist boundary issues: An integrative review of theory and research. *Professional Psychology: Research and Practice, 26,* 499–506.

Spero, M. (1981). Countertransference in religious therapists of religious patients. *American Journal of Psychotherapy, 35,* 565–575.

Sperry, L. (2001). *Spirituality in clinical practice: Incorporating the spiritual dimension in psychotherapy and counseling.* New York: Brunner/Routledge.

Stoltenberg, C., McNeill, B., & Delworth, U. (1998). *IDM supervision: An integrated development model for supervising counselors and therapists.* San Francisco: Jossey-Bass.

Tarasoff v. Regents of the University of California, 551 P. 2d 334, 331 (Cal. 1976).

Tomm, K. (n.d.). *The ethics of dual relationships.* Retrieved February 22, 2004, from the University of Calgary, Family Therapy Program website: http://www.familytherapy.org/documents/EthicsDual.pdf

Vasquesz, M. (1992). Psychologist as clinical supervisor: Promoting ethical practice. *Professional Psychology: Research and Practice, 23,* 192–202.

Watkins, C. E. (1997). The ineffective psychotherapy supervisor: Some reflections about bad behaviors, poor process, and offensive outcomes. *The Clinical Supervisor, 16,* 163–180.

Woody, R. H., and Associates (1984). *The law and the practice of human services.* San Francisco: Jossey-Bass.

Zur, O. (2004). To cross or not to cross: Do boundaries in therapy protect or harm? *Psychotherapy Bulletin, 39,* 27–32.

PART IV

ETHICS AND EFFECTIVE COUNSELING AND PSYCHOTHERAPY

Part IV contains only one chapter, Chapter 15, entitled "Striving for Personal and Professional Excellence: Ethics as a Way of Life." This chapter is unlike any of the previous chapters in this book. It does not contain a list of learning objectives, key definitions, new subject matter, nor specific ethical standards or legal statutes. Instead, it provides a glimpse into the daily lives of actual persons who are striving to integrate ethics into their personal and professional lives. Hopefully, it will make the ideas and themes of this book seem more accessible and real.

CHAPTER 15

STRIVING FOR PERSONAL AND PROFESSIONAL EXCELLENCE

Ethics as a Way of Life

LEN SPERRY AND JAMES BITTER

As the introduction to Part IV noted, this chapter differs from all other chapters in this book. Instead of broaching additional ethical considerations in professional practice, this chapter details a typical week in the lives of two counseling professionals who are involved in teaching and supervising students, as well as in providing counseling services.

Bill James and Geri Jackson are pseudonyms, used because both of these professionals wanted to ensure the confidentiality and privacy of the clients and students they mention, as well as that of themselves and their families. Both Bill and Geri are highly regarded and considered to be master counselors or therapists by their peers, which means, presumably, that they operate primarily from Perspective III rather than from Perspective I or II. It also means that they have achieved a sufficient integration of their personal and professional lives, so that they can experience their work with students, colleagues, and clients as enriching, challenging, and satisfying.

We asked both to recount a typical week in their professional and personal lives. A typical week could be a particular week, or it could be a composite of common experiences. They were requested to describe the kind of professional practice situations and issues that arose and reflect on any related ethical considerations involved. Our hope was that they would feel free to include all such considerations, personal and professional, for the whole week, not just their work days. We asked that they provide a tape recording or written report in a diary format. Both submitted recordings in the first person, which were transcribed and appear in the following sections, following our brief background statements that situate their counseling practices.

A WEEK IN THE LIFE OF BILL JAMES

William R. James, PhD, who prefers to be called Bill, is a licensed mental health counselor. Bill has been in practice for fifteen years, following completion of his doctorate in Counseling Psychology and his postdoctoral internship. While he had been a full-time faculty member for about four years, he decided he was better suited to full-time clinical practice, with some part-time involvement in graduate training of therapists, than to full-time academic work. He really enjoys supervision of interns and facilitating a group counseling course, more so than attending department meetings and serving on university committees, the kinds of things expected of full-time faculty. Because he has been an adjunct faculty member in the department for several years, he has accepted the part-time position of Assistant Director of Clinical Education. As such, he is assigned a handful of interns to advise each semester. Dr. James is widely regarded for his technical and interpersonal competence as well as his sensitivity and commitment to professional ethics. While Dr. James does not teach a graduate course in legal and ethical issues in counseling and psychotherapy, he does incorporate ethical thinking, ethical issues, and ethical sensitivity in the counseling theories and methods course and the group counseling course he does teach, as well as in his supervision and advising activities. Here is his report.

Monday

Monday is the first day of our semester. I was driving over to class and smiled as I recalled how much my approach to teaching has changed over the years. Now, when I plan my courses, I ask myself the question, What do I want my students to be thinking and feeling when this course is completed? Because I've come to believe that ethical sensitivity and professional competence are intertwined, I now focus the content of my course on theoretical and research-based aspects of counseling and psychotherapy, including both their ethical and professional dimensions. I try to treat ethical issues like other topics that I introduce into a course, from a practical, clinical perspective rather than a purely theoretical perspective. I look for case material that is both clinically relevant and illustrative of main theoretical points. And, I try to include at least one case example each class meeting that has both professional and ethical aspects.

The purpose of the case material is to give my students the opportunity to think through and wrestle with typical counseling practice issues that arise in daily clinical practice. The case material also challenges them to link theory and practice and increase their recognition that ethical practice issues are not separate from professional practice issues but are two sides of the same coin. I really enjoy encouraging and challenging students to consider various courses of action first from a professional practice perspective, that is, from theory, research, and clinical lore, and then from and ethical and values perspective.

In addition to case material, I've been seriously considering how I might utilize other teaching methods and techniques in my classes. Well, it's been a serious consideration in the past two weeks. I sat in on a three-hour seminar on teaching strategies that was offered to adjunct faculty two weeks before classes began. I was struck by a comment that another faculty member made during the seminar. The seminar leader said the criterion for choosing an educational technique should be which technique leads to the best educational outcome. That faculty, from the school of business, responded that his criterion in choosing a teaching method when both techniques had equally good educational outcomes was which technique would be better at actualizing one of the core ethical values he is holding up for his students. For example, he might consider which technique more respectful of the students. Or, which technique is more just or fair. I was quite taken with those criteria since they were so consistent with my overall course objective of aiding students in thinking about the link between professional practice and ethical practice issues. I believe that using such teaching method criteria would also heighten my own awareness and facilitate my efforts to model ethical sensitivity and commitment to our students.

Tuesday

This afternoon a soon-to-be graduating master student that I've been advising has a meeting with me to talk about job prospects. The student, Marty S., mentions that he's been asked to apply for a position in a rural community mental health center about 50 miles from the university. Marty was raised in a small rural community similar to the one with the job opening. He has fond memories of the close and caring community in which he was raised and recalls that professionals in the community seemed like everyone else. That is what worried him. Specifically, he was concerned with the prospect of boundary problems and the ethical dilemmas associated with small-town practice. He was quite interested in the position but wondered about the matter of dual relationships. I listened attentively and easily identified with Marty's concern, since I too was reared in a small community. We discussed the ethical standards regarding dual relationships and conflict of interest and their applicability in communities where there are only a few counselors and therapists. Based on his reading of that ethical standard, he imagined that professional life would be untenable in such communities. I noted that the underlying principle and basic ethical consideration with dual relationships was not that they should be avoided entirely, but rather the extent to which clients' interests overshadow the professional's interests. As we talked further, Marty seemed to become more comfortable with a more nuanced view of the dual relationship standard.

Wednesday

This morning, I met with a 14-year-old male client, Rocky L., in my private practice. Rocky was referred to me by a school counselor because he had been experiencing depression and underachievement in his academic work. He is the youngest of three children to parents who have alcohol abuse histories. Though the boy's father regularly attended AA meetings, he appeared to have problems managing his anger. Rocky said that his father has lately been berating him for his lack of interest and commitment to school and long-range career plans. While I found no evidence today that either parent or other family members was physically disciplining or otherwise physically abusing this client, there was concern of possible verbal abusiveness. This was only our fourth session, and I was planning on extending treatment to include his parents in the near future. Interestingly, the reporting statute in this state essentially says that any form of abuse that is distressing should be reported. While mindful of the state's statute, I considered the option of reporting such possible verbal abuse and not being able to provide therapeutic help to this adolescent and family since the likelihood is high that the parents will stop treatment. My preference is to continue treatment, involve the parents in the treatment process, and attempt to change or modify stressors and whatever patterns of verbal abusiveness exist in the family. Now, if Rocky had given any indication of physical abuse, or I had observed any indication of physical abuse, I would have immediately reported that abuse. I've thought long and hard about the professional and ethical considerations involved the reporting of possible verbal abuse, and I have learned through experience that achievement-oriented families in his community are often hard on family members who are not meeting the family's expectations for academic, sports, or social achievement. I know there may be only one chance to help such clients and their families change such verbal-abuse-prone patterns. I also know from clinical experiences that overly enthusiastic reporting of such presumed behavior typically results in a child or adolescent being pulled out of counseling prematurely.

Thursday

This afternoon, I met with Jeanette R., a counseling intern that I've supervised weekly for the past eight months. Jeanette will be graduating in a month. In the beginning of the supervision, I monitored and reviewed her cases very carefully. In the last two months, because of her increasing confidence and competence, I allowed her more independence in her practice decisions. Today, after reviewing her case, the conversation shifted to a personal concern of hers. She had already been offered a position in the clinic, and one of her high school friends whom she had not been in contact with for sometime had met her at a social gathering. She learned that Jeanette would soon be graduating and employed at the community clinic and asked Jeanette if she could make an appointment with her for personal counseling. This presented a dilemma for Jeanette: Should she decline to work therapeutically with someone whom she knew as a friend while in high school or agree to see this individual for counseling? Jeanette asked me about the professional and ethical considerations facing her. I distinguished providing professional counseling services to a family member or relative from providing such services to a colleague or friend. Family members and relatives are different from colleagues and friends in many respects, and prohibitions about working with family members are well justified. On the other hand, I believe that in some specific circumstances it might be acceptable to engage in a professional counseling relationship with colleagues and some friends.

On Thursday evening, while I was getting some records and receipts ready for my tax accountant, I recalled the experience of being audited eight years ago. The IRS had found some dubious deductions that I had taken. At first, I was indignant at the accusation of dubious deductions. But I had to admit that I wasn't particularly careful with my record keeping back then. I blamed the tax system instead of taking responsibility for my actions. In time, however, I started to view my tax preparation not simply as a burden and necessity, but rather as an exercise in ethical training. As I look back I see clearly how, over time, I became committed to the idea of doing my taxes with complete honesty and striving to become increasingly aware of the tendency to cut corners or claim questionable business expenses. And, whenever I would find myself becoming impatient in getting my tax materials together, I checked to see what motives and emotions, such as greed or fear, were influencing me. Then I set out to transform my motives and emotions. As a result, tax preparation became a lesson in personal growth rather than as an unfair trial or ordeal. In time, it was possible to view IRS agents as my teachers showing me where I was being careless, unconscious, or unethical. The result is I no longer feel anxious doing my taxes and no longer cringe when I receive mail from the IRS.

Friday

Early Friday evening, I got on a plane to a midwestern city where I would be conducting the second of three weekend workshop on group therapy counseling with adolescents. The workshop is sponsored by a graduate counseling program that offers graduate credit for this group training. Graduate students taking this 45-hour workshop can receive three graduate credits and substitute this training for their required group counseling course. The workshop consists of three parts. The first is didactic training in group dynamics and group process. The second is observation and review of actual group therapy with adolescents. The third component involves an experiential process wherein participants function as a working group. In that graduate program, the required group counseling course has two components: a didactic part lasting about one hour, taught by a full-time faculty member, and an experiential portion that is facilitated by an adjunct faculty member. This arrangement attempts to avoid the potential problem of dual roles. The concern is that a full-time faculty member teaching both the didactic and experiential portions becomes aware of personal information about students that could unduly influence decisions about the student continuing in the program, etc. It's my belief that since I have no evaluative role with regard to students continuing their program, dual role issues are minimized. I think I can objectively evaluate students' performance in this workshop because of the nature of the written assignment required for those seeking credit for the course.

The way I handle this is to require that students not identify themselves in the written assignment other than by their student identification number. Furthermore, I don't share any information about students in a workshop with the graduate program director or any other faculty. In my experience, when the didactic and experiential portions of a group counseling course are separated and led by two individuals, there is an unfortunate disconnect between theory and practice. On the other hand, one instructor can integrate theory and practice by highlighting aspects of the experiential portion and discussing the theoretical aspects of that particular group experience. However, at my own university, the group counseling course is offered in the conventional split mode, a format I haven't been successful in changing.

Commentary

Dr. James is an experienced therapist, teacher, and supervisor. Over the years, he has developed and maintained a reputation of integrity and professional expertise. He seems to be quite committed to and enjoying his professional work and his personal and family life. For him, professional counseling appears to be a calling, a way of professional life in which he can make a difference in the lives of clients and students. He clearly espouses Perspective III and seems to have developed a high level of ethical sensitivity and professional competence. Furthermore, he seems to have integrated his professional philosophy of practice with his personal philosophy of life. While not everyone may agree fully with his views on specific professional and ethical considerations—for example, the way he teaches the group counseling course—he has apparently thought through the ethical considerations attendant to specific professional practice decisions in a responsible manner that is respectful of both of students and clients.

A WEEK IN THE LIFE OF GERI JACKSON

Geraldine S. Jackson, PhD, who prefers to be called Geri, is licensed as a mental health counselor and as a marriage and family therapist. She has been in practice for thirteen years, following completion of her doctoral training in Counseling with a minor in Marriage and

Family Counseling/Therapy. She is a tenured professor in a graduate counseling program that trains master's-level counselors in school, mental health, and marriage and family counseling/therapy. She teaches graduate courses in multicultural counseling, counseling processes, couples therapy, and child counseling. She consults widely on multicultural, cultural, and ethical matters. She incorporates ethical thinking, ethical issues, and ethical sensitivity in all her courses and supervision. Here is her report.

Monday

It is 8:30 A.M., and I have a class that starts at 9:20. I am arriving at my office for posted office hours, and Kathy has been waiting for me for about half an hour. This is the first day of the first week of courses for the fall semester, and Kathy finished the summer session with an F in a core course, but I do not know this yet. She has received nothing but As in the rest of her 18 credits completed in our Counseling Program.

Geri: Have you been waiting long?

Kathy: Not really. I just need to talk with you.

Geri: Okay, let me get the door open. Come on in.

Kathy: I ran into some problems this summer: personal problems.

Geri: Do you want to tell me about them?

Kathy: Well, I had this one problem, and I decided that I couldn't complete the course on trauma and abuse. So I withdrew.

Geri: Okay.

Kathy: Then I had a bigger problem, and I didn't withdraw from my other course, and I got an "F." I talked to the instructor, but he says that there's nothing he can do.

Geri: Can you tell me what the "bigger problem" is?

Kathy: Well . . . (a long, long pause) It's medical, I guess.

It is clear to me that Kathy is hesitant to talk about whatever "problem" she has. I don't want to push her on it, but I know she is in some minor academic difficulty that I might be able to help resolve if I have more details. I start to wonder: Okay, it may be a medical problem. Maybe it's a medical problem that's life threatening or very embarrassing to discuss, especially early on a Monday morning. Maybe it's a medical problem that happened to someone else, perhaps her twin, and perhaps it totally galvanized her attention for the rest of the summer. I could respond to this as simply an academic problem, but she seems more distressed than that. If I open up the possibility of being concerned about her personal life, am I entering into a "counseling" relationship? Is one session a relationship? Is the fact that I have a teacher–student relationship with her the determining factor about how personal I can get? Are these very thoughts already compromising my ability to respond to her as a human being with sympathy and compassion? And what is the line between sympathy for a student and empathy as a counselor? Should there even be a line between the two? The professional requirement to avoid dual relationships and to not be both a counselor and a teacher for the same student is important, but not without impact at a lot of different levels (see ACA Code of Ethics [ACA, 2005], A.5.c and F.10.e).

Geri: I can tell this is hard for you. I am willing to hear whatever you want to tell me, but if it would be easier for you to talk to someone else, we can arrange that.

Kathy: No. I don't want someone else. I just need to take care of this "F."

Geri: Okay, let's start there. Changing the grade may be quite difficult. You have already talked to the instructor, and for whatever reason, he seems unwilling to work with you on this.

Kathy: Yes. That's right.

Geri: Your next level is to appeal the grade to the Chair of the Department, but she is unlikely to override the instructor or facilitate a change of grade without a very, very good reason—and something a little more specific than a medical problem. (pause) On the other hand, you have nothing but "As" in all of your other courses. That has to be taken into account. In fact, you have enough "As" so that you have not even dropped below a 3.0. You are not even on Academic Probation because of this "F." You can, if you choose, simply retake the course. Both grades will remain on your transcript, and you may have to explain that to a potential employer someday, but if your grades are kept up and you pass comprehensive examinations, you graduate with your degree.

Kathy: (with some sadness in her voice) I have to think about this.

Geri: Okay. I'll be free tomorrow between 1 and 3 P.M. if I can help in any way.

Tuesday

I arrive for my office hours to find Kathy waiting for me. She is ready to talk, but she does not want anyone else to know what she is going to say.

Kathy: Will you guarantee me total confidentiality on this one?

Geri: Yes, of course.

Kathy: Well, this is hard for me to say, especially to you, because I know you are pro-choice, and you know that I am a Christian . . . (pause) and I suspect you are not. But I need help, and I don't think you will be upset with me. (another pause) I got pregnant this summer. My parents did not even know I was dating anyone. I didn't want my whole life ruined. I was so selfish. (She is crying now.) I . . . I had . . . an abortion.

I can remember all the other times I have mourned with friends or clients the loss they have sometimes experienced—even when they freely chose to abort in the best interests of their own lives and any future child. I am flooded with emotions. And Kathy is flooded with emotions: hers, more conflicted than mine and more desperately felt. This is not the time to suggest a referral. We will have to work at the edges of this dual relationship together.

Geri: I feel such great sadness with you right now. There is so much loss in the sound of your words. I know that you experienced the fetus as a baby growing inside you, and you must mourn the loss. You are probably mourning the loss, too, of what you believed about yourself, what was important to you. But mostly, you must have felt very much alone.

Kathy: I was so alone on this. I am so . . . alone.

For the next hour, I listen. I do my best to understand and care, because I do care about her and what a significant turning point this marks in her life. I reaffirm her value as a person and suggest that mourning is, in fact, an important part of whatever healing will still come. And I reassure her that healing will come—as will forgiveness both internally and externally. And I hear all of this coming from my mouth, the mouth of a basically caring, but nonreligious person. I, her teacher and future practicum supervisor, am present with her, and I am counseling her: It is a dual relationship that I will never let harm her, but she does not know that at this minute. She merely needs to talk, to sort, to be heard and not judged. I want her to know that her secrets are safe with me: They will never leave my office without her permission. Even this written account has been changed enough, combined with data from multiple other students, to protect her identity. We also talk about her need to re-find herself as a Christian and for emotional support. She allows me to get her in touch with both a Christian feminist therapist and the support group. This does not end the dual relationship I will have with her for the rest of our experience together. I will always know and need to protect her secrets, and she will always know that I know. It does, however, place the dual relationship in a less dangerous position.

Wednesday

Today, I teach a section of the group counseling course. It will be the only course that our students get in this vital area. We need at least two required group courses and a practicum, but there is no room to fit all of that in with other accreditation requirements and the mandate of the university to keep our degree at 48 credits. When the time arrives, I walk into class; it is our first day together. I introduce myself, and I note that this course, as with others in our program, is experiential, and that a good part of the training experience will be participating as a group member and even coleading a group of one's peers at times.

The dual relationship problems here are immense, and it is my job to make sure students understand this and have options (ACA, 2005, A.8, and Standards of Practice (SP) 6, 12, and 41]. I tell the students that it is part of my professional obligation as a counselor educator to evaluate them during their time in the program for "fitness" with regard to the counseling profession (ACA, 2005, F.5 and SP 42). I further note that the faculty has listed in their student handbook the qualities, traits, and values that are essential to good practice. There is due process delineated for this evaluation procedure: No one is simply dismissed from the Counseling Program without several meetings with faculty members, the opportunity to receive guidance and direction in terms of remediation, when necessary, and even the possibility of appealing any interim or final decisions.

What does all of this have to do with group? I tell them that I work very hard not to let what I learn about them in group influence my evaluation of them later on, but I am not perfect, and I am not always clear about all of the things that enter into my evaluative impressions. I will never use what I learn in group sessions when having student evaluation discussions with other faculty members: That I can guarantee.

One option they have to avoid this problem is to take advantage of being a member of a group in another part of the university, such as our Student Counseling Center or in the community at a mental health agency. Those who would choose this option would still have to come to class, but they would be excused from participation in the group process. No one, in more than a quarter century of teaching this course at different institutions, has ever taken advantage of this option, making it doubtful that it is a real option at all in the minds of students. Then, there is the matter of grading the course and making sure that this evaluation process does not impact the group experience or place students in the bind of wondering if something they say will impact their grades (ACA, 2005, F.7.b and SP 42). Here, I am on somewhat easier (safer) ground, thanks to modern technology. Like most other counseling courses, this course is on our department website, where I have placed three multiple-choice tests covering reading materials and classroom lectures. Students can log on and take the test at any time they feel they are ready. If they get the grade they want on the first test, they stop: That will also be their final grade for the course. If they get a low grade or one that is at least lower than they would like, they may take a second test, and I will give them the higher grade of the two. If they require a third test, I ask them to meet with me personally first to see if I can help them with test preparation, and then, when they take the third test, their final grade is the average of the third test with the higher grade of the two previous tests. If a student does not need help, I never know his or her grade until I officially record it at the end of the course. Even with all of these options and possibilities, the grades still tend to distribute evenly within what is typical for graduate courses, and yes, there are students who take all three tests.

Next, I must address the issue of prescreening of group members. I point out to the students present that only in the most general of ways were they prescreened. They did, after all, engage in our daylong individual and group interviews to be considered for admission into the Counseling Program. They were even informed that many, if not most, of our courses would at least contain experiential parts—just as part of the admission interview, itself, was experiential. But nowhere was the process of this group experience described; no student was invited to consider whether the group was appropriate for her or him, what goals she or he might have in joining the group, or what roles and expectations there might be for group membership. There are several reasons for this lack of prescreening: (a) It parallels what will actually happen in community agencies and schools (where people will often be assigned to groups as a matter of process); (b) for training purposes, a group experience is required by our program, and if the person is not fit for the group experience, then that person is probably also not fit for the program or the profession; and (c) prescreening is not acceptable to me as a group leader.

There used to be a phrase in the ACA and ASGW codes of ethics that recommended screening "when consistent with one's theoretical orientation," but the most recent codes deleted this phrase altogether (ACA, 2005; ASGW, 1989). "Counselors screen prospective group counseling/therapy participants" (ACA, 2005, A.8.a). No wiggle room there. I am further required to prescreen group members to eliminate anyone "whose needs and goals are (in)compatible with goals of the group." This mandate presupposes that the leader determines what the goals of the group are rather than the group itself—and has done so before the group has even met. Again, this is a stance that few group leaders theoretically or pragmatically support. I am also asked to accept only group participants "who will not impede the group process." This, too, is to be determined before the group has even met.

On what is this judgment to be made? Knowledge of the client from another setting? The counselor's intuition? An interview of indeterminate length? In my experience, the practical judgment of fitness for group participation comes down to one thing: Does the group leader like the person or not? Because of my theoretical orientation, I reject screening of group members as against the democratic principles that are the foundation of my therapeutic orientation. I am in technical violation of the ACA ethical code regarding screening every time I begin a group—and so, I would guess, are the majority of counselors who run groups in residential treatment centers, most community agencies, and schools.

After I introduce myself, talk about the dual relationship and grading problems that must be addressed, and note why I am against the prescreening group members, it is a wonder that anyone wants to stay with the class at all, but amazingly they do. We start our group by asking each of them take fifteen minutes and go interview another person in the group and let that person interview them. I hope that the students will come back and introduce each other in the larger group session. During the introductions, I listen very carefully to what each person has been willing to share with someone else. It gives me clues about the participants' openness and safety needs. I also set as my goal an ability to say back everyone's name at the end.

Somewhere in the early part of the session, I like to introduce the Johari Window. Although thirty-five years old, it is still one of the best ways I have of talking about stretching the boundaries of what we risk with each other. I want to caution participants about "jumping into the deep end"; research has long shown that group process can be misused, and people have been hurt, but no group proceeds without some risk. My hope is that the group will become a safe enough place for people to risk a little more than they might normally do. The group experience ought to provide participants a safe haven.

Most groups have as one of their first tasks the forming of group agreements. I use the word *agreements,* rather than *rules* or *ground rules,* because a democracy requires agreements and contracts into which social equals enter of their own free will. The entire notion of ground rules dates to our autocratic past and reflects an almost authoritarian positioning when announced by a group leader. Agreements are facilitated; rules are delineated from above.

Almost inevitably, the question of confidentiality—what it means, how it will be implemented between us as members of a group, and what its limitations are—will arise during the period we explore mutual agreements. On the rare occasion that it does not come up naturally, it is the one area I will ask the group members to consider and address. A consideration of confidentiality is required by our ethical codes and standards of practice (ACA, 2005, B.2.a), but it is also essential to building trust and creating the safety zone for personal disclosure.

Thursday

Practicum starts at 1:30 P.M. I have a new student cohort to see. We have not worked together in our Community Counseling Clinic before, but we will be taking over clients first seen by others during the summer, and we will have new clients coming in, seeking our help. I have already met with these students the spring before. We have talked about how I supervise Practicum. We have talked about which theoretical orientations they choose to follow and what skills and interventions they currently favor. But they are new to the profession. We will all have to see what emerges in real practice. All sessions are taped. I can monitor up to five sessions at a time in our clinic, and that is exactly the number of Practicum students assigned to me this fall. One last time, before the first clients arrive, we go over our informed consent process, role-playing it once again, and going through the steps required by law and professional practice in the disclosure of the limits of confidentiality (ACA, 2005, B.1.d). Every student is praying that he or she won't ever have to face a time when he or she is forced to break the foundation of trust that supports our work.

In the late afternoon, Jennifer comes for counseling with her two boys, having been referred to our clinic by the school counselor of the older child. Her children are Michael and Robert, ages 8 and 6, respectively. Jennifer is a single parent who works at a fast-food restaurant—and she is exhausted. The student counselor has gone through informed consent with the client and has the client's signed agreement of understanding.

Jennifer: I have always been single. The boys' father was around for a while. Then he went to jail. Now he is out, but he never sees them. He wants to get back together with me, but he doesn't even ask about the boys. He's not coming around.

Counselor: So you have had to make a go of it alone with your children. Every word you speak here tells me how exhausted you feel—almost like you haven't had a break in eight years.

Jennifer: I don't think I have. I'm always tired.

Counselor: Yes. I can only imagine. (pause) Can you tell me what brought you here today?

Jennifer: Michael's counselor at school, Mr. Bowen. Michael gets in fights. He gets angry. All the time, he gets angry, not with me though—I won't let him—but at school, and he gets in fights, and then the school calls me. They call me at work, but there's nothing I can do about it. I can't leave work.

Counselor: So the school counselor wanted us to see Michael because of his anger and fighting?

Jennifer: Yeah. I guess so.

Counselor: Okay, well, I think we can talk to Michael about that. What about Robert? Is he in school? And how does he do?

Jennifer: Yeah, he's in first grade this year. He doesn't get in fights at school. He and his brother fight all the time. The noise drives me crazy at night. They are at each other all the time. You can't get them to bed: They sleep in the same room, but all they do is fight and hit. I get so mad at them. I whip them both. I do it hard, too, but it doesn't do any good. They just scream and cry, but they don't learn. Sometimes, I have to whip them three or four times a night.

Counselor: So the boys fight, and the noise really gets to you, and you try to stop their fighting by spanking them.

Jennifer: Yeah. I whip them both with a belt, across their butt and legs, but it doesn't do any good.

Counselor: And do you think you hurt them?

Jennifer: Oh, it hurts all right. They have the marks to prove it.

Counselor: Do you mean, like, black-and-blue marks?

Jennifer: Yep.

Counselor: Do either Michael or Robert have those marks on them right now?

Jennifer: I don't think right now. They haven't been in school long enough yet to get it real bad this year, but they're going to tonight, because of this—having to come here and all.

Counselor: Okay, I'm really sorry about this, but I am going to have to take a small break here and consult with my supervisor. Do you remember the man I introduced to you before we started? (Jennifer nods.) Well, I need to talk with him briefly, and then I will be back. Okay?

It is the counselor's first client. What she hears sounds like child abuse to her even though the mother clearly thinks of it as "only spanking." And I have been listening to the conversation, and even though I think all spankings are child abuse, I have to wrestle with what meets the legal definitions in our state for child abuse. And I have to help this counselor in training sort through what to do next.

Supervisee: Dr. Jackson, have you been listening? Is this child abuse?

Geri: I have been listening. What are your thoughts about it?

Supervisee: I think she is talking about child abuse, isn't she? I mean black-and-blue marks: It sounds over the top to me.

Geri: Yes, that's what it sounds like to me too.

Supervisee: So do I have to report it? She says the boys don't even have any marks on them at the moment.

Geri: Just that they're going to have them tonight.

I am wishing with all my heart that this situation were different. I already feel that we will have to report this and the consequences will not serve anyone well. Child protective services will investigate the case in a week or two—maybe as long as a month from now. There are a lot of cases, and there are very few investigators. If there are no bruises or obvious marks on the children, they will file a report in some cabinet, but nothing will happen either for the mother or the boys. If we saw them here at our center, we could do filial therapy with the boys in our play therapy room. We could help Michael understand his anger, what motivates his behaviors at home and school, and consider new possibilities for interacting with his brother and others. We could help Jennifer understand her anger at the boys and find alternative ways to parent, and we might even be able to help her find some relief from her exhaustion—a break once in a while so that she could do some things for her own well-being.

If we report her to child protective services, she almost certainly won't come back. None of what is possible will even have a chance to work. Hope will simply be supplanted by one more legal mandate that is supposed to protect and help, but like most such interventions, winds up being ineffective—doing too little, too late. True ethics would not require me to report this woman. Back when ethics was about virtue, doing the greater good, and building the kind of connections that led to the "good society," I would not have had to break confidentiality at all. I would be able to offer this woman and her children real services that might make a difference in their lives. I am tempted, even today, to ignore the law, since its ineffectiveness is a moral abomination in and of itself. But I have a student, a university, and colleagues within our center to consider too. I am not acting in a vacuum, and I have multiple people to protect here. I am also a teacher who has an obligation to be very careful with the exercise of relative morality in front of new students with little or no experience in the field.

My supervisee and I are watching the two boys in our playroom with another student. It is late summer weather outside, and both of the children are in short shorts. If there are bruises on them, they are not visible to us. Still, the mother's own report certifies the abuse. We have no choice.

Geri: How you present this to Jennifer is very important. I want you to start by reiterating that we understand how hard it has been for her to raise two children alone. Then, she needs to hear what is possible for her here if she chooses to come back. But we also need to tell her that we are bound by state law to report this and to let her know what will most likely happen.

Supervisee: I think I can do that first part where I empathize with her, but I've never done the rest of it. I've never even seen it done.

Geri: Do you want me to come in with you?

Supervisee: Yes.

As we enter the room, Jennifer stands up, and I reintroduce myself to her. I remind her that I am her counselor's supervisor, and I indicate that the counselor has asked me to be present while we talk over what must happen next.

Counselor: I just want you to know that I understand how hard it is for you to have come here today. I can hear how exhausted you feel, and I know that you want the best for your sons even though they can be very hard to raise sometimes. The problem I have relates to that discussion we had at the beginning of the session and the paper you signed. When you tell me that you sometimes spank the boys so hard that it causes black-and-blue marks, that really constitutes abuse, and I am required to report that.

Jennifer: I don't do nothing they don't have comin' to them. There's nothing that needs reporting here.

Counselor: I hear that. (pause)

Geri: Raising two boys alone is very hard. We both understand that. We very much want to help if we can. We have a play therapy room in which your children are both having a good time and are having their behaviors and feelings acknowledged. This is something that both of the children need a lot if they are going to learn to stop fighting so much. We can teach you to do this with them. We have plans to help Michael with his anger and to learn to act on different choices when he is provoked. We might even be able to help you get some relief so you are not so exhausted in your parenting all the time. But first, we have to tell child protective services what you have told us: that sometimes you spank the boys hard enough to cause bruises. The most likely thing that will happen is that someone will come to investigate. If there are no bruises on the children, and you tell them you are here getting some help, they are likely to only file a report in their office and let it go. I really hope that you will come here for a while, and let us see if we can help you with Michael and Robert.

Jennifer: I don't know. I don't want no report happening. I know a friend of mine, and they took her children away. I don't want any report.

For the next twenty minutes, the counselor and I will acknowledge Jennifer's fears, try to differentiate her situation from what was happening in her friend's home, and reiterate our hope that she can come to our center where we will work very hard to make her life better with her boys and for Michael at school. When she is ready to leave, she says she will have to think about it—whether she is coming back or not. She still doesn't want a report to be made, and we let her know that we will have to make one, but it doesn't have to turn out badly. After Jennifer, Michael, and Robert leave, our closing with each other is rather short:

Counselor: She's not coming back, is she?

Geri: Probably not.

Friday

After I help the counselor-in-training make the required report, I meet with the practicum students to discuss how the day went and what we need to do to prepare for our next meeting. We talk about the difference that all too often exists between our mandate to do good (benevolence) and the professional requirements imposed on us by state law. I am asked, "Are there times when we should just break the law, because it is wrong?" In my heart, I know that the answer is, "yes," but I tell them that no profession can exist if the members operate in an idiosyncratic state of civil disobedience and relativism. If we believe, individually or as a profession, that a law is wrong or misapplied, it is our duty to advocate for change. All of this is true, of course, and all of this is easier said than done. Later, I will wonder if I had been seeing Jennifer and her two sons privately, would I have reported them to child protective services? Probably not.

I have one last client to see; she has been held over from a previous semester. The client knows that practicum students will be watching our session. We were watched last semester, too. Like Jennifer, my client Mary is poor. She has had a rough and sometimes brutal life, but she has persevered. She does factory work, but she barely makes enough to keep herself and her two children alive. Still, Mary has courage. She has also gained some confidence in herself during the last year. And integrity and pride are important to her. She does not have money for therapy, and none is required. I have told her numerous times that her payment is allowing graduate students to watch me and learn what I have to teach them. To her, however, this is not enough.

Mary grows flowers. She grows them in her yard from seeds she has harvested the year before, and she even has a plastic tent with a grow light at her house so she can grow the flowers during the winter months. She loves flowers, and she knows that I love them too. Each time she comes, she brings me some flowers, usually in an old ketchup bottle or sometimes in a jar she's found on the road. It is her way of paying for her counseling. It is bartering (ACA, 2005, A.10.c), an exchange of my services for her material goods. In this case, it is not exploitive, because I will never do anything other than accept her flowers happily and gratefully. If Mary were doing something significant to my well-being—laying a driveway for me or cleaning my house, as examples—with the potential for me to be dissatisfied with her work, the possibility of conflict would clearly undermine the safety and value of the counseling relationship. But my acceptance of Mary's flowers actually supports her dignity and brings a sense of equality of value to our working arrangement. While bartering is discouraged by my professional code of ethics, in this case, it seems more appropriate to accept her bartered payment.

As to the other requirements of code A.10.c, I am clearly in violation. Mary has requested the bartered agreement, so I am okay with it on that account, but as with most such arrangements, this agreement has been sealed with a handshake. Requiring her to sign a written contract with me regarding our arrangement would be disrespectful and a needless intrusion. And in any case, I could never demonstrate that bartering is "accepted practice among professionals in the community." Mary lives out in the countryside. I am sure she barters for other services there, but in the city where I live and the university where I work, I am probably the only person to engage, on occasion, in bartered services. The fact that I would offer this service for free to her is significant, but it does not change the fact that Mary and I have this arrangement. I consider and reconsider regularly whether our agreement supports her therapy or distracts from it: After more than a year, I still feel it is a useful part of our work.

The week ends. Next week, there will be additional challenges—more reflections and additional reconsiderations. The absence of harm in counseling and therapy is not the same as the provision of quality help and service. Real ethics is more often a struggle for what is the better of difficult choices than I wish. The challenge is there, and I'm up for the challenge because I'm so passionate about my work of teaching and counseling.

Commentary

Like Dr. James, Dr. Jackson is an experienced counselor, teacher, and supervisor and has achieved an enviable reputation for integrity and professional expertise. For her, professional counseling is clearly a calling rather than simply a job or career. Her professional life reflects Perspective III, and she seems to have well integrated her philosophy of practice with her personal philosophy of life. It is somewhat uncanny that both Bill and Geri seemed to have resolved the professional and ethical dilemmas about group counseling training in similar ways. Clearly, Geri is a master counselor and therapist and serves as an important role model for her students and professional colleagues.

CONCLUDING NOTE

In counseling and other mental health specialties, ethical positions are too often addressed in coursework and workshops as either easily resolvable issues or as strategies for avoiding malpractice or professional censure. In the daily practice of a counseling, however, issues constantly arise for which there are no "right" answers, or for which personal ethics may be at odds with legal statutes, ethical standards, organizational dynamics and community mores, empirical research, and best practices. This chapter has provided the reflections of two counseling professionals on the ethical and professional dimensions in their counseling practice that reveal how they deal with such issues and dilemmas.

REFERENCES

American Counseling Association. (ACA). (2005). *Code of ethics and standards of practice*. Alexandria, VA: Author.

Association of Specialists in Group Work. (ASGW). (1989). *Code of ethics*. Alexandria, VA: American Counseling Association.

APPENDIX A

ETHICAL THEORIES

The actions of counselors and therapists are guided by their ethical perspectives. These ethical perspectives reflect one or more ethical theories. Regardless of whether counselors and therapists recognize and understand their preferred ethical theory, this theory influences their ethical decision making. For most, this theory is implicit, meaning that, while it guides one's actions, it is not consciously recognized or understood. We contend that it is advantageous for practitioners to recognize, understand, and appreciate the theories that guide their thoughts and actions in making decisions in counseling practice. Since increasing self-awareness and self-knowledge are critical factors in developing personal and professional efficacy, the information in this appendix should prove useful in increasing self-knowledge as well as understanding ethical theory, an often overlooked but extremely important criteria and source of support for counseling practice decision making.

Philosophers have recognized and utilized a number of ethical theories. In this appendix, six common ethical theories relevant to the practice of counseling and psychotherapy are presented. Before turning to those specific theories, a brief discussion of ethical theory and types of ethical theories ensues.

ETHICAL THEORY

So what is an ethical theory? An ethical theory is a perspective on ethical situations. It is the way in which an individual's values are acted out in the world. An ethical theory is the way one chooses to live out and interpret one's values. An ethical theory considers one's underlying values and provides a means of determining which values take priority in any given situation. Such a theory is the means by which individuals can interpret and apply their values in the world. In other words, it is the way a professional puts into practice the choices made about what is valuable in his or her profession.

An ethical theory has at least two purposes. The first is to provide an orientation toward ethical situations. Such a theory involves a set of assumptions about how ethical situations ought to be addressed and which component of an ethical situation takes priority. The second purpose is to resolve conflicts among standards and values. When standards come into conflict or when competing values cannot both be acted on, an ethical theory provides a hierarchy of values to evaluate this conflict and provide a rationale and defense for one's decision. In sum, it enables one to resolve ethical dilemmas and defend the solutions reached (Brincat & Wikes, 2000).

In short, an ethical theory is the broad perspective an individual brings to his or her ethical experience, to the living of his or her professional and personal lives against the backdrop of a commitment to values.

TYPES OF ETHICAL THEORIES

Two types of ethical theories can be differentiated: doing theories and being theories. Doing theories develop rules for action, while being theories depend on the moral agent expressing his or her character, relationships, or life. Doing theories include consequentialist ethics, rights ethics, and duty ethics. Being theories include virtue ethics, care ethics, and narrative ethics. Each of these six theories is described in terms of its origin, its assumption about what constitutes right action, its applicability to ethical decision making, and an assessment of its strengths and weaknesses. See Brincat and Wikes (2000) for a fuller discussion of ethical theories. Table A.1 summarizes the key points of this discussion.

Consequentialist Ethics

Consequentialism is an ethical theory that aims at realizing the best consequences. It is future oriented and endeavors to achieve the best possible outcomes. The consequentialist would compare how much good and harm come from doing nothing against the amount of good and harm that comes from an anticipated action. From the consequentialist perspective, an action is considered right only if it tends to produce more good consequences than bad consequences for everyone concerned. In other words, the basic injunction is to perform the action that maximizes good or positive consequences for all concerned. Consequentialism is a broad ethical theory initially formulated by John Stuart Mills and Jeremy Bentham. Advocates of consequentialism differ in how they define the good that consequentialism endeavors to realize. Contemporary versions of this theory vary from egoism (Edwards, 1990; Hinman, 1994) to situational ethics (Fletcher, 1996).

Operating from a consequentialist perspective is relatively straightforward. First, consider the available options. Second, list what particular persons are affected, either positively or negatively, by each option. Third, assess the degree of good or harm that will likely result to each of the persons under each of the options. This can be accomplished by quantifying the worth or even by assigning a numerical figure to the good or harm that comes to each person. For example, using a scaling technique where, for example, 1 is considerable harm and 10 is considerable good, rate each option for each person. Fourth, evaluate the ratings for all individuals and choose the right action that brings about the more good than harm.

While this approach sounds simple, unfortunately there can be complicating factors. For instance, deciding whether a particular option will result in good or bad consequences to a person, and estimating how much good or harm will come to a person from specific an option, can be challenging. While consequential theory utilizes a seemingly objective, calculative process, an element of subjective assessment is involved, and predictions about the future are never easy.

A major strength of consequential theory is its systematic, inclusive, and logical process of decision making. It is process that is designed to be fair, since the interests of all

TABLE A.1 Comparison of Ethical Theories

THEORY	BRIEF DESCRIPTION	STRENGTHS	WEAKNESSES
Consequentialist Ethics	Aim is to realize the best possible consequences. An act is considered right if it produces more good consequences than bad consequences for everyone involved.	Values each individual's good equally and has a comprehensive procedure for calculating what is right.	Cannot determine consequences exactly and sacrifices individual rights for the sake of the larger good of the community.
Rights Ethics	Assumes that individuals are the bearers of rights that are granted them. An act is considered right when it respects rights and wrong when if violates rights.	Respects the values of the individual and is compatible with individualism.	Cannot determine an individual's rights with certainty and sacrifices community good for sake of individuals' rights.
Duty Ethics	Considers the intention of the person choosing, the means, and the nature of the act itself. An act is considered right if it is done for the sake of duty, has a good motive, its means are acceptable, and/or the nature of the act itself is good.	Respects the values of the individual and recognizes the complexity of moral situations, motives, means and ends, and the nature of the act.	Tends to ignore consequences and can sacrifice the larger good of community for the sake of individuals' duties.
Virtue Ethics	Virtues make one a morally good person. Ethics is primarily about one's internal dispositions and character rather than one's external behavior or actions.	Person-centered rather than rule-centered and recognizes experience among individuals and situations.	Doesn't explain how to move from virtue to right action; not universally applicable since virtue is construed differently among persons and cultures.
Care Ethics	Ethical decisions are made by focusing on relationships. An act is considered morally right if it expresses care or is done to maintain a caring relationship.	Person-centered rather than rule-centered and stresses the relational and emotional aspects of individuals' lives.	Doesn't explain how to move from caring to right action; not universally applicable since caring is construed differently among persons and cultures.
Narrative Ethics	Ethical decisions are made by focusing on narrative or story and its context. An act is considered right if it reflects the ongoing story of an individual's life and the culture and tradition within which he or she lives it.	Person-centered rather than rule-centered and stresses the consistency and wholeness of individuals' lives.	Doesn't explain how to move from narrative to right action; is not universally applicable because of the uniqueness of individuals' narratives.

Adapted from Brincat & Wikes (2000).

involved individuals are equally considered, and the good and harm to each of these individuals is considered in weighing and calculating the decision. On the other hand, consequentialism requires that the decision maker predict consequences that are hardly certain. Furthermore, in its quest to be comprehensive and inclusive, the emphasis on achieving the greatest amount of total good for all, irrespective of for whom the good accrues, is itself problematic. Consequentialism works to benefit the group, the community at large, and arguably overlooks or is willing to sacrifice individual goods and rights.

Rights Ethics

In marked contrast to consequentialist theory of ethics, a rights theory of ethics maintains that an action is morally right when it respects the rights of individuals and wrong when it violates those rights. A right is a morally or legally justified claim or prerogative of one individual—the claim holder—to demand something from another individual or from society. Thus, the right to privacy would require that counselors and therapists maintain client confidentiality. A right to equal treatment requires that clinics, schools, and agencies not discriminate against minorities, the homeless, and others. Rights theory holds the view that the rights of the individuals are the most important consideration in ethical considerations. In short, an act is right only if it upholds rights. Prominent ethicists who espouse rights theory are Ronald Dworkin and Robert Nozick (Dworkin, 1977; Nozick, 1974).

How would a rights theorist engage in ethical considerations? First, the rights theorist would consider whose rights are at issue. Then he or she would determine how to preserve and uphold these rights. While it may not be immediately obvious which option is best in terms of upholding rights, the rights theorist would assess which rights are overriding or whose rights take precedence. Finally, the rights theorist reflects on the situation and the individuals involved and arrives at the alternative that does the best job of honoring rights. He or she would have to decide whose integrity or privacy ought to count more and which rights are more fundamental. But this decision is not particularly easy or straightforward, given a number of questions that arise: Is the right to integrity more basic than the right to equal treatment? Which rights must be satisfied first? What rights do individuals really have, since individuals can claim a right to something that they do not actually have? Who decides what rights individuals have? Where do rights come from? These are difficult questions facing rights theorists.

On the positive side, rights ethics recognizes the intrinsic worth of each individual and that individuals are accorded certain rights by virtue of being human. Rights theory contends that ethical decisions about right and wrong grow out of one's understanding of individuals as the bearers of rights that are granted to them by God or by nature or by society, as in the Bill of Rights of the U.S. Constitution, which specifies rights accorded its citizens.

On the negative side, rights ethics face certain problems involving its justification and application. There is little consensus about which rights are basic rights, what rights individuals possess, and where these rights originate. Rights theorists must also contend with the question of whether individuals can lose their rights. A major criticism of this perspective, leveled by many including consequentialists, is that, in focusing exclusively on individual rights, rights theory ignores the good of the whole community. Unlike consequentialist ethics, rights theory defines what is right in terms of individual ethical prerogatives rather than of good consequences for all. In so doing, rights ethics sacrifice the good of the community for the sake of ensuring individual rights.

Duty Ethics

Note that a person using duty theory is not bound to any particular conclusion. A duty theorist may decide to take some action, or to do nothing. We cannot tell what duty theorists would decide, but we do know why they make their decisions. We know that they will reach a decision by considering what to do, especially by considering duties, and not consequences or rights. A person using duty theory may pick the same action as that picked by a consequentialist or a rights theorist, but the duty theorist will reason toward this course of action in a different way. In duty theory, the rightness or wrongness of an action does not depend solely on whether it produces good or bad consequences. A duty theorist wants to do the right thing, regardless of the consequences. Furthermore, a duty theorist believes that certain things like keeping promises and upholding commitments made in the past are right, regardless of whether the consequences of doing so are good or bad.

The duty theory is unique insofar as it looks at the motive or intention of the person choosing, the means by which the act is accomplished, and the nature of the act itself. Hence, duty theory considers many aspects of moral situation—motives, means, the act itself, rights, consequences—and never decides what to do solely on the basis of the consequences or the rights at stake. According to duty theory, an act is right for at least one of the following reasons: It is done for the sake of duty, it has a good motive, its means are acceptable, and/or the nature of the act itself is good. Duty theory extends back to Thomas Aquinas. He focused on the intrinsic nature of the act itself and considers some actions to be inherently good or evil (Finis, 1980). Immanuel Kant contended that the motive, or intention, was the key factor in determining right or wrong, and he insisted that an individual is acting rightly only when acting for the sake of duty (Kant, 1785/1964).

In one sense, the duty-based decision-making process is easier than the consequential, but in another sense it is harder. It is easier because there is no prolonged process of calculating future consequences, assigning values to each consequence, and totaling good and bad consequences. The duty-based process is simpler because it is not a detailed, calculative affair. On the other hand, its process is harder than the consequential, for just this same reason. It has no easy way to compare the various duties at issue and contrast the nature of one act to another. The duty-based process depends more on intuitive or supposedly self-evident claims. For instance, a duty theorist might say that an act that inflicts harm is by nature more wrong than an act that avoids inflicting harm. A duty theorist may find it hard to explain why one duty is more pressing than another.

The duty theorist counts as relevant many aspects of a moral situation, such as the motive, the means, the nature of the act, and even, for some duty theorists, the consequences. It is valuable to look at all of the aspects of a moral situation before deciding which aspect of the situation is overriding. Duty theory also respects the dignity of individuals and the obligations owed to them. It does not endorse permitting the good of all to always supersede the good of a particular individual. For duty theory, a duty or promise to a single person can be more morally compelling than good consequences to a whole community. Our experience backs up the duty approach by acknowledging situations in which the good of a single person is more important than the good of a whole community. Witness, for example, psychiatrists and investigative reporters who refuse to divulge information about clients and sources, even when faced with arguments claiming that the good of the community depends on having that information.

The main problem with duty theory is twofold. First, some versions of it exclude any consideration of consequences. This seems rather extreme. Given its attempt to be attentive to the complexity of moral situations, it seems only reasonable to assess consequences along with the other variables in the situation. We know from our experience that there are times when the consequences are clear, predictable, and certain, and it would be foolish to ignore that sort of information in deciding what to do. Second, duty theory may underemphasize the communal aspect of our lives by allowing individual duties and promises to supersede our concern for the effects of our actions on others. If human experience is necessarily social and shared with others, then, critics fear, duty theory is dangerously isolationist. Duty theory permits persons to use their own reasoning to identify duties, recall promises, and so on, and it does not require that persons assess how their actions will affect others. This is seen as a weakness, particularly by those who believe strongly in the connectedness of persons and the communal nature of our lives.

As we have seen, all moral theories have strengths and weaknesses. We will differ in terms of how serious the weaknesses seem to us. Your evaluation of each moral theory will depend on whether you agree or disagree with the assumptions it makes about the nature of human persons and human actions. We also must hold open the possibility of combining several theories so that the weaknesses of one can be offset by the strengths of another. Let us now leave the "doing" theories, with their emphasis on dictating action, and turn to the "being" theories and their concern for the person acting.

Virtue Ethics

Virtue refers to a positive or good character trait or disposition as a tendency to act in a way that promotes the human good or human flourishing. The opposite of virtue is vice. A vice is a bad or negative character trait or disposition. Accordingly, vice is a tendency to act in a way that fails to promote the human good or human flourishing. For instance, courage is a virtue, as is justice and benevolence. Their opposites—cowardice, injustice, and malevolence—are vices. According to virtue theory, an act is right if it reflects virtue or good character, that is, if it is the sort of act a virtuous individual would do. Ancient versions of virtue ethics originate with Aristotle (1980). Aristotle listed several virtues including justice, friendliness, truthfulness, and courage. A contemporary version is articulated by Alasdair MacIntyre (1984). A best-selling book on virtues by William Bennett (1993) considered faith and work to be basic American virtues.

Virtue theory maintains that good individuals engage in right actions. Thus, knowing what is right requires knowing what a good individual is, from which can be derived what a good individual does. Accordingly, the only requirement is that an individual acting must act virtuously, must act for the sake of virtue, or must act in the way an individual of virtue would act. Not surprisingly, then, the standard for ethical action has nothing to do with consequences, motives, rights, relationships, and so on. Instead, the standard for action is the virtuous person or the virtue itself. The role of the virtue theorist is quite simple: Outline what virtues are at stake in a situation, consider how each option would or would not realize the virtues, and then pick the course of action that expresses either more virtues or the more important virtue.

Unfortunately, the virtue theorist cannot automatically discern whether benevolence and loyalty to one's boss or benevolence and justice to one's colleagues is the better choice. To provide a fuller ethical perspective, virtue ethics needs guidance from other ethical theories. For example, it would seem that a virtue whose expression affects more individuals would be preferable to the expression of a virtue that affects only single individual. Expressing benevolence to many individuals would seem preferable to expressing benevolence to one. Furthermore, it would seem that a choice that expresses many virtues may be preferable to a decision that realizes only a few virtues. In this way, consequentialism provides guidance to virtue theory. Consequentialism informs the virtue theorist that realizing more virtues is better than realizing fewer virtues, and that those virtues that have an effect on more people are more important than those that have an effect on fewer people.

Yet, a virtue theorist need not accept guidance from consequentialism. Instead, a virtue theorist might decide that it is not always better to realize more virtues rather than fewer, contending that fewer virtues are more important than the many. In other words, virtue theory cannot develop ways that are not consequential to decide which virtue to express nor which action best expresses the virtue. Conceivably, a virtue theorist could rank the virtues or decide that in certain relationships the virtues must be expressed first toward some individuals and only later toward others. For instance, virtue theorists can claim that individuals should pay back a loan before giving gifts to their friends, or act in ways that benefit one's parents before acting to benefit oneself or one's friends.

Virtue theory is attractive because it is focused on individuals rather than on rules. It is a holistic and humane perspective because it evaluates the whole individual and not isolated actions. It is also flexible in that it allows for virtue be practiced differently toward family than toward friends. In addition, virtue theory does not require that all individuals be treated identically, nor each situation the same. On the other hand, virtue theory is not particularly practical, since there is no easy or clear way to translate traits of character into concrete actions. Oftentimes, a virtuous and good person may have little idea of what to do in complex situation when all the person has to rely on is his or her good character. Universality of the virtue is another thorny problem with this perspective. Philosophers and ethical theorists have yet to reach, and may never reach, consensus on what the virtues are or which are the most important virtues. Furthermore, virtue is construed differently among various cultures, with no two cultures espousing the same list of the most important virtues. Arguably, virtue theory seems to be little more than a subjective perspective for resolving ethical problems.

Care Ethics

Also referred to a relational ethics, care ethics is an ethical theory that emphasizes the way in which individuals in intimate relationships, friendships, families, and communities mutually support and care for each other. According to care theory, right and wrong do not exist independent of persons, situations, and relationships. Instead, there is only the caring thing to do in a particular situation; the caring action is the right thing to do, while the uncaring action is the wrong thing to do. Acts are right or wrong insofar as they manifest or fail to manifest caring for and about others. In short, an action is right if it expresses care for another or is done to maintain or further a caring relationship. Care theory has largely been articulated by women and some feminists (Manning, 1992; Noddings, 1984). The beginning of care ethics can be traced to Carol Gilligan (1982) in the 1970s. She noted that girls demonstrated different ethical attitudes than boys, in that girls tended to focus more on relationships, while boys tended to focus more on rules.

In particular situations, using a care theory mean finding ways to foster the expression of care and to sustain relationships. It means avoiding embarrassment, neglect, and harm and instead seeking to express care toward the greatest number of people, including individuals that most need or deserve care. While this theory seems straightforwardly altruistic, it raises some interesting questions, such as, Is it better to express more care to a few individuals or to express some care toward more individuals? Are certain individuals more deserving of care than others? Another concern with care theory is that in its early forms it was modeled on the maternal figure, which many regard as the personification of the caring, nurturing person. The matter of the universalizability of care theory is a major concern. To maintain its viability as an ethical theory, it seems that care theory must become more inclusive, since neither mothers nor women are the only ones who care.

Like virtue theory, a theory of care is rooted in persons and relationships to them. Unlike other theories, ethical decisions are made in care ethics by focusing on persons, especially on their relationships, rather than by attending to actions, duties, consequences, or virtue. It is a most humane and personal approach to decision making. The theory views the emotional, spiritual, physical, and rational dimensions of life and insists that the basis of all ethical action is caring relationships with others. One reason care ethics is such a persuasive ethical theory is because of its holistic incorporation of these dimensions. On the negative side, care ethics suffers from the same defects as virtue theory. Up until now, care ethics has yet to specify a clear and detailed account of how to translate care into actual practice, that is, what it means to care concretely.

As noted earlier, universalizability is another major concern. It does not appear that care is or should be the universal standard for women and men across all cultures. Currently, the theory lacks sufficient detail and development to counter criticism of its subjectivity and the relativity inherent in caring. Other questions to be addressed include, Should individuals care only care for those who care for them? Should individuals care for those whom they do not care about? Should individuals care for those they do not know?

Narrative Ethics

In narrative theory, an act is right if it reflects the ongoing story of a person's life and the culture and tradition within which he or she lives. Ethical decisions are based an individual's unique history, goals, culture, and situational context. Ethical decision making is done by particular persons who are at particular points in the stories of their lives. Thus, from this ethical perspective, decisions must be based on what is known about the decision maker's life, how he or she has been mentored, the histories of other individuals involved in a particular situation, the traditions and cultures of these persons, and so on. Narrative theory is a rather recent development and is associated with philosophers like Alasdair MacIntyre (1984) and Paul Ricouer (Ricouer, 1985–1989; Rosentstad, 1997).

Narrative theory insists that ethics is about the unfolding of a life within a culture, and neither about an individual's character nor about specific relationships. This theory is contextual and attentive to individual histories and social traditions. The aim of narrative theory is to empower individuals to make choices within the particular context of who they are, what they care about, and what they have done, rather than requiring them to act for the sake of the virtues or duty. Narrative theorists use the story to make sense of ethical situations and ethical decision making. In applying narrative theory to a particular case, the narrative theorist endeavors to understand the context, the histories, and beliefs of the individuals who find themselves in a particular situation. Important considerations include the individual's childhood history; education and training; family and professional roles; career aspiration; successes and failure; beliefs and core values; previous decisions; and the laws, traditions, and cultural practices of the organization in which the individual is affiliated. Such information about the context of an ethical situation helps understand the life stories of the characters in it. From a narrative perspective, the more information available about individuals' lives and cultural traditions, the more likely the decisions made will best fit the individual's needs and circumstances.

Applying narrative theory can be problematic since it is seldom clear how a narrative can be used to establish an ethical standard. In other words, it is unclear what an understanding person's history and goals suggests about what an individual's actions ought to be in an ethical situation. The matter becomes even more perplexing when there are many individuals, each with one's own history and narrative. Additionally, there is the problem of how the narrative theory can be universalizable. How can it make use of general rules if it claims to take into account unique persons and histories? Arguably, narrative theory is important and necessary but is not sufficient as a complete ethical theory.

To its credit, narrative ethics is person centered. It views actions and decision making as part of the continuum of a life and a culture. It includes the choices an individual makes as part of the ongoing drama of the individual's life and culture. As an ethical theory, it provides a sense of wholeness and continuity both to individuals and to cultures, and for this reason, it provides a corrective to other theories.

As previously noted, application of this theory is a major concern. It is not evident that by viewing their lives as stories, individuals will know what to choose when faced with an ethical dilemma. It may well be that narrative ethics is more of a technique for describing a moral situation than a theory that explains how to respond to it, since narrative theory does not set a moral standard. Individuals set some standard or some goal that is separate from "life as a narrative" in order to have a basis for making choices within that narrative. Furthermore, the universalizability of narrative theory is also a concern. Its emphasis on narrative uniqueness necessarily limits its universality.

CASE ILLUSTRATION: THE ETHICAL THEORIES IN COUNSELING PRACTICE

Many consider ethical theories to be academic and ethereal and not relevant to daily personal or professional life. The reality is that ethical theories influence the thinking and decisions of counseling professional on a daily basis. Professionals are often surprised when this pointed out to them. On further examination, they may also struck by the differences in ethical views espoused by their colleagues. The case in Box A.1 illustrates these points in terms of a rather common ethical dilemma.

BOX A.1
ONE CLIENT AND FIVE DIFFERENT THEORIES

Marisa Garcia is a 20-year-old Mexican American female who was referred for counseling with Sylvia, the mental health counseling intern, by her academic adviser at the university. The advisor noted that Marisa "seemed a little depressed and ambivalent about continuing at the university." In their first session, Marisa was quiet, seemingly withdrawn, and made little eye contact with Sylvia. When Sylvia inquired about her family background, Marisa reported that her family migrated from Mexico when she was 6 years old and that she had two younger brothers, Jaime, who was 18, and José, age 15, as well as a younger sister, Maria, who was 7. During most of their second session, in which Marissa remained very quiet, Sylvia asked, "What can I do to make this counseling more helpful to you?" Marissa thought for a moment and said, "Maybe you could come to my home for a meal and meet my family. This Sunday is my little sister's first communion and there will be a big family celebration. All my relatives will be there. I really would like you to come. Maybe if my father could meet you he wouldn't be so negative about me coming for counseling. He says that your counseling puts bad thoughts in my head."

Sylvia presented this case to the supervision group at the clinic where she was interning. The discussion soon turned to the underlying ethical dilemma: avoiding dual relationships while remaining sensitive for the cultural demands of Marissa's world. As the discussion continued, it became clear that members of the supervision group espoused very different ethical theories.

Jesse, a clinical psychology intern, indicated that Sylvia should do whatever would result in the greatest good for the greatest number of people. He argued that making Marissa's father happy might not be in the best interest of everyone involved, including the other therapists and clients at the clinic. He did not believe that Sylvia should accept the invitation. Jesse's view seems to reflect the utilitarian theory of ethics.

Cassandra, a clinical social work intern, told Sylvia that maintaining the ethical standard of avoiding dual relationships was absolutely essential. "You can't make exceptions whenever you want to because you think a particular client has special needs. That's why we have ethical standards, to keep therapists from behaving inappropriately." It was clear to her that it would be a terrible mistake for Sylvia to accept the invitation. Cassandra's sentiment seemed to reflect a duties, or rule-based, theory of ethics.

Jamal, a mental health counseling intern, said that he thought that Sylvia should accept the invitation as a sign of respect for Marisa and her father. He indicated that his upbringing had taught him that family is really important, and being a good son or daughter meant respecting the family's wishes and being loyal. Jamal said that it seemed to him that Marisa was experiencing a conflict between being loyal and respecting of her father and trying to be true to herself at the same time. Jamal believes that going to dinner would be viewed by Marisa's father as a sign of Sylvia's respect for him and the family. "The father would see that you are a person of good character and would probably give his blessing for Marisa's counseling." Jamal seems to be espousing the virtue ethics theory.

Jackie, a licensed mental health counselor and supervisor, pointed out that attending to the therapeutic relationship was critical, and that meant showing caring and concern. "In this case showing caring and concern means recognizing and dealing with cultural and religious factors that seemed to be impacting the therapeutic relationship." She encouraged Sylvia to begin exploring Marisa's world as a Mexican American woman and what her interactions might be with the European American female therapist who held position of power and prestige. Jackie asked Sylvia, "How much have you considered the differences between your world and Marisa's? What are the implications of these differences for your relationship with her and her family?"

Sylvia said that she believed the cultural differences were significant but not insurmountable. She wondered if going to dinner with Marisa's family in order to build trust and rapport would meet Marisa's needs without jeopardizing her welfare or exploiting her. Jackie said she believed that it was not only possible but necessary. Jackie added that establishing an effective therapeutic relationship with Marisa was largely dependent on first establishing a social relationship with Marisa's family. Jackie's sentiment seems to reflect the ethics of care theory.

CONCLUDING NOTE

Ethical theories provide an ethical mindset for addressing and resolving moral problems. Each theory offers a way of thinking about and deciding about ethical issues and dilemmas. As noted, no ethical theory is complete or perfect. Each has its strengths and weaknesses. In the beginning, we suggested that all counselors and therapists have a preference for a particular ethical theory. It is useful to take to the time to recognize and understand one's favored ethical theory. Or, one can choose another theory or decide to use different theories in different situations when circumstances favor one theory over another, or one can combine theories and, by incorporating different perspectives, build on the strengths of the different theories. Whatever the case, there is some wisdom in using that ethical theory or theories consistently in all ethical decision making.

REVIEW QUESTIONS

1. Which of the six ethical theories makes the most sense to you? Explain your answer.
2. Which of the six ethical theories is problematic for you? Explain your answer.
3. Can you think of someone you know who strongly espouses one of these theories by his or her behavior or decision-making style?
4. Do you think it's possible to use a combination of these theories in counseling practice?
5. Which of the ethical theories do you think is most commonly used by counselors?

REFERENCES

Aristotle. (1980). The *Nicomachean ethics*. Trans. D. Ross. Oxford: Oxford University Press.

Bennett, W. (1993). *The book of virtues*. New York: Simon & Schuster.

Brincat, C., & Wikes, V. (2000). *Morality and the professional life: Values at work*. Upper Saddle River, NJ: Prentice-Hall.

Edwards, P. (1990) . *Utilitarianism and its critics*. New York: Macmillian.

Dworkin, R. (1977). *Taking rights seriously*. Cambridge, MA: Harvard University Press.

Finis, J. (1980). *Natural law and natural rights*. Oxford: Oxford University Press.

Fletcher, J. (1996). *Situational ethics: The new morality*. Philadelphia: Westminister Press.

Gilligan, C. (1982). *In a different voice: Psychological theory and women's development*. Cambridge, MA: Harvard University Press.

Hinman, L. (1994). *Ethics: A pluralistic approach to moral theory*. Forth Worth, TX: Harcourt Brace.

Kant, I. (1785/1964). *Groundwork of the metaphysics of morals*. New York: Harper & Row.

MacIntyre, A. (1984). *After virtue* (2nd ed.) Notre Dame, IN: University of Notre Dame Press.

Manning, R. (1992). *Speaking from the heart: A feminist perspective on ethics*. Lanham, MD: Rowman & Littlefield.

Noddings, N. (1984). *Caring: A feminist approach to ethics and moral education*. Berkeley, CA: University of California Press.

Nozick, R. (1974). *Anarchy, state, and utopia*. New York: Basic Books.

Ricouer, P. (1985–1989). *Time and narrative. Volumes I–III*. Chicago: University of Chicago Press.

Rosentstad, N. (1997). *The moral of the story: An introduction to questions of ethics and human nature*. Mountainview, CA: Mayfield.

APPENDIX B

DICTONARY OF KEY ETHICAL AND LEGAL TERMS

academic development: One of the three areas of competence reflected in the profession's national standards and national model, targeting attitudes, skills, and knowledge contributing to (a) effective learning in school and across the lifespan; (b) academic preparation regarding postsecondary options; and (c) an understanding of the relationship of academics to the world of work and life at home and in the community (ASCA, 2003).

accountability: Within the school counseling context, this term has become associated with showing academic, career, and personal/social student outcomes resulting from participating in school counseling programs.

accreditation: The process whereby an educational program meets high standards for preparation of professionals beyond standards required for offering a degree.

accrediting bodies: Organizations that qualify educational programs as meeting standards beyond those required of colleges or universities to offer degrees. Professional accreditation of graduate counseling degrees occurs through the Council on Accreditation of Counseling and Related Educational Programs (CACREP) of the Council on Rehabilitation Education (CORE). In psychology, the American Psychological Association accredits doctoral programs.

ad hoc fallacy: In logic, *ad hoc* is short for the Latin phrase *ad hoc ergo propter hoc*, which translates into "because one thing follows another once, one thing will always follow another." In terms of the ethical prohibition on dual relationships, the syllogism is "All exploitive relationships are bad. Exploitive relationships are dual in nature. Therefore, all dual relationships are bad." It is often used as the explanation for banning all multiple relationships, in order to avoid the "slippery slope."

American School Counselor Association (ASCA): A professional organization whose members are certified/licensed in school counseling with unique qualifications and skills to address the academic, personal/social, and career development needs of all students (Preamble to ASCA's *Ethical Standards for School Counselors*, 2004).

Americans with Disabilities Act (ADA): The civil rights seminal legislation for persons with disabilities, enacted in 1990.

AMHCA: American Mental Health Counselors Association, one of the primary professional bodies overseeing the practice of professional mental health counseling.

applied ethics: The division of ethics that focuses on cases or situations and uses them to understand or develop standards, rules, and theories. Applied ethics is subdivided into professional ethics, organizational ethics, environmental ethics, and social and political ethics.

aspirational ethics: Standards beyond those mandated by professional ethics that are deemed by a profession to be compatible and consistent with achieving positive and healthy results for clients, counselors, and the mental health profession as a whole.

autonomy: The ethical value and principle of taking responsibility for one's own behavior and self-directedness; freedom to choose without interfering with others' freedom. In a counseling context, it refers to the right of clients to determine their own thoughts, actions, and futures, and to regulate their own behavior.

beneficence: The ethical value and principle that guides actions consistent with contributing to the well-being of others. This value implies doing good to others.

benevolence: The ethical value of being altruistic and caring, sharing, help, and acting generously toward others.

boundary: The frame and limits surrounding a therapeutic relationship that define a set of roles and rules for relating for both client and therapist. Because of a power differential between client and therapist, and because clients are in a vulnerable position, adequate boundaries serve to protect the client's welfare. The concept of boundary is central to understanding conflicts of interests and involves two polar positions: the categorical boundaries view and the dimensional boundaries view, wherein boundary crossings and boundary violations are a major point of contention.

boundary crossings: A benign and typically beneficial departure from traditional expectations about the settings and constraint of clinical practice. They involve any deviation of clinical behavior from the standards of practice associated with traditional or conservative treatment approaches that emphasize emotional distance or reducing clinical risk and liability. Accompanying a phobic client in riding up and down in a small elevator during exposure therapy or greeting a Hispanic client with an embrace—a culturally sensitive practice—are examples. Such crossings are commonly accepted in many humanistic, behavioral, and systemic forms of psychotherapy. There is evidence that boundary crossings may promote both the therapeutic alliance and positive client outcomes.

boundary violations: Exploitive or harmful practices in psychotherapy that occur when therapists cross standards of professional behavior for their own sexual, emotional, or financial gain. Examples include becoming sexually involved with a client, entering into a business partnership with a client, or confiding personal information to a client to satisfy the therapist's own emotional needs.

breach of contract: Failure to provide agreed-on services considered to be contracted services.

breach of duty: The failure by a professional to perform a legal duty imposed by professional ethics, statutes, or case law. One of the bases for filing a malpractice lawsuit.

care ethics: The ethical theory that is rooted in persons and relationships, wherein ethical decisions are made by focusing on relationships rather than on actions, duties, or consequences. An act is considered morally good and right if it expresses care or is done to maintain a caring relationship.

career development: One of the three areas of competence reflected in the profession's national standards and national model targeting attitudes, skills, and knowledge contributing to (a) self-knowledge and informed career decisions; (b) achieving future career goals with success and satisfaction; and (c) an understanding of the relationship of personal qualities, education, and training for the world of work.

case closure: Often referred to as status 26 closure, indicating an individual has been working successfully for at least ninety days.

case consultation: Also called expert consultation; a process of conferring with a knowledgeable, competent professional to obtain a second opinion or advice on an issue or issues concerning a particular case.

categorical boundaries: The categorical approach to boundaries takes the view that boundaries are a part of human interactions and in place to delineate role functions and facilitate the therapeutic process. These are set *a priori,* and are, by and large, immutable and not open for debate.

categorical boundaries view: The view that boundaries are part of human interaction with the purpose of delineating role functions and of facilitating the therapeutic process. In this view, boundaries in professional relationships are considered immutable, not open to debate, and not to be crossed for any reason. Furthermore, such boundary crossings are viewed as a slippery slope that eventually results in serious boundary violations.

classroom guidance curriculum: Structured developmental lessons infused throughout the school's overall curriculum, presented systematically in K-12 classrooms, and designed to assist students in achieving desired competencies related to improved academic, career, and personal/social outcomes.

client assistance program: A state program that advocates for the consumer in situations in which there is a discrepancy between the needs and wants of the consumer and the services provided by the state vocational rehabilitation program.

clinical supervision: An intervention provided by a more senior mental health professional to a more junior one that is evaluative, extends over time, and purports to improve the junior's professional functioning, to monitor the quality of services provided to clients, and to serve as a gatekeeping function for the profession.

collaborative decision making: Includes therapists and counselors and their client and client's family and/or social network, where appropriate, in cooperative conversations to identify problems and develop treatment plans and strategies to address them. Collaborative decision making also includes all key stakeholders in making decisions about the nature of treatment, options to treatment, whether treatment is effective or not, and when to terminate treatment.

community values: Refers to the ideals, beliefs, norms, and ethos that arouse an emotional response for or against them in a given community.

competence (client): The capability of clients to make decisions about their own well-being. It is a precondition to providing informed consent.

competence (counselor): A counselor's or therapist's capability to provide a minimum quality of service within the professional's and his or her profession's scope of practice. For legal purposes, competence is measured by what other reasonably prudent counselors would do under the same circumstances.

confidentiality: The obligation of counselors or therapists to respect the privacy of clients by not revealing to others the information communicated to them by clients during counseling sessions. In couples and family therapy, it is granted primarily to the whole (e.g., family) rather then to the individual, unless otherwise stated.

conflict of interest: Arises when a counselor or therapist has competing interests that would interfere with faithfully exercising his or her professional judgment and skill in working with clients.

consequential ethics: The ethical theory that aims at realizing the best possible consequences. An act is considered good and right only if it tends to produce more good consequences than bad consequences for everyone involved.

consultation: A formal arrangement wherein a counselor or therapist obtains a second opinion, advice, or supervision on an issue or issues of concern from a knowledgeable, competent colleague.

consumer: A term used in place of *client* or *patient* by some rehabilitation professionals in order to show the choice that the person with a disability has in the process.

Council for the Accreditation of Counseling and Related Educational Programs (CACREP): An independent agency recognized by the Council for Higher Education Accreditation to accredit counseling and related educational programs whose aim is promote excellence in professional preparation in a number of fields including school counseling.

creaming: Employment networks select consumers with the best chances to be successful in the job market and discourage or are passive with other consumers.

cultural encapsulation: A tendency for a counselor or therapist to treat clients and others relative to their own cultural perspective, without regard to cultural differences.

cultural sensitivity: The capability to recognize and appreciate differences in cultural values, mores, and practices in individuals and groups of other ethnicities and cultures.

deposition: A form of pretrial discovery that consists of statements taken by a witness under oath in a question-and-answer format as it would be in a court of law, with opportunity given to the adversary to be present for cross-examination.

dimensional boundaries: The dimensional approach to boundaries takes the view that relationships that have power differentials are not inherently abusive or exploitive. Hence, although boundaries are not eliminated, they can be discussed openly and co-created by client and counselor, and become woven into the relationship definition.

dimensional boundaries view: The view that, although professional relationships involve power differentials, relationships are not inherently abusive or exploitive. Even though boundaries are useful and necessary in professional relationships, they can be discussed openly by mental health professional and client, and boundary crossings, when appropriate, can facilitate the therapeutic relationship and treatment outcomes.

diminished capacity: A state of mental functionality that falls below a normal standard.

direct liability: Liability that results when the harm done by a supervisee is a result of the supervision itself.

disability: An identifiable physical or mental condition wherein recognizable functional limitations may be overcome with appropriate accommodations.

dual relationship: In general terms, refers to engaging in more than one role with another individual; thus, a dual relationship involves two roles. In a counseling context, it refers to having both a counseling and another kind of relationship, i.e., personal, social, or business, with a client simultaneously. When a relationship involves more than two roles, it is referred to as a multiple relationship.

duty ethics: The ethical theory that considers the intention of the person choosing, the means, and the nature of the act itself. An act is considered morally good and right if it is done for the sake of duty, has a good motive, its means are acceptable, and/or the nature of the act itself is good.

duty to protect: The obligation of a counselor or therapist to safeguard the intended victims of a dangerous client. This is a broader duty than the duty to warn. Some consider this duty to apply to clients with suicidal intent.

duty to report: The obligation of a counselor or therapist to report abuse or suspected abuse of children, the elderly, and in some states, the disabled, in a timely manner.

duty to warn: The obligation of a counselor or therapist to inform an endangered party or parties when it is believed that a client poses a serious danger of violence.

essential functions: Those duties of a job that make a job unique.

ethic of care: Cf. *care ethics.*

ethical climate: The dimension of organizational culture that reflects the shared perceptions that staff and colleagues hold concerning ethical procedures and practices occurring with an organization.

ethical dilemma: Situation involving an ethical consideration that confuses a professional either because there are competing or conflicting ethical standards that apply, or because there is a conflict between and ethical and moral standards.

ethical principles: Higher level norms or directives within a society that are consistent with its moral principles and that constitute higher standards of moral behavior or attitudes. They build on and give meaning and direction to one or more ethical values.

ethical sensitivity: The capacity to recognize situations and circumstances that have implications for the welfare or well-being of another. Ethical awareness is a prerequisite for ethical sensitivity.

ethical theories: Broad perspectives that provide an orientation to ethical situations and are the way one chooses to live out and interpret one's values. Major ethical theories include consequentialist ethics, rights ethics, duty ethics, virtue ethics, care ethics, and narrative ethics.

ethical values: Beliefs, attitudes, or moral goods that are useful guides in everyday living. They are single words that identify something as being desirable for human beings. Common ethical values in counseling and psychotherapy are beneficence, nonmaleficence, fidelity, autonomy or responsibility, justice, fidelity, compassion, integrity, and respect for persons.

ethical virtues: Ethical values that are routinely practiced and incorporated into one's basic character.

ethics: The philosophical study of moral behavior, of moral decision making, or how one leads a good life.

ethics audit: An audit or investigation in which the implementation of ethical policies as well as ethical incidents in an organizational setting are reviewed and evaluated.

fair evaluation and due process in supervision: Two rights that ensure that a supervisor cannot arbitrarily evaluate a supervisee without providing a way to remediate identified problems and skill deficits, or without some notice of the intent to provide a negative evaluation.

Family Systems Theory: The theoretical underpinnings of most schools of couples and family therapy. Among other things, it allows for multiple contexts and perspectives of the same event or set of circumstances.

fidelity: The ethical virtue and principle that directs individuals to keep commitments or promises.

HIPAA: Health Insurance Portability and Accountability Act of 1996. Designed to, in part, protect clients' privacy related to their medical information. The federal law designed to standardize procedures across the United States for ensuring the privacy and confidentiality of protected health information (includes counseling and psychotherapy information). The law was thought to be necessary in order to increase consumer confidence in the storage and distribution of client health information in an age of instantaneous electronic dissemination of information and mammoth electronic databases.

impairment: The incapacity to perform the function of the counseling role due to a debilitating medical, substance-related, or psychological condition that results in diminished functioning from a previously higher level of functioning.

incompetence: The incapacity to perform the function of the counseling role due to insufficient training or experience, unwillingness, or inflexibility. Three types of incompetence are technical, cognitive, and emotional.

independent living: Movement of the early 1990s to emphasize living needs of persons with disabilities.

informed consent: The client's right to make the decision about whether to participate in counseling or therapy services—which includes assessment and interventions—after such services have been adequately described and explained in a manner that is understandable to the client. Information about the proposed services should include the purpose, risks and benefits, and possible alternative treatments including the option of no treatment, as well an adequate description ofexceptions to confidentiality and, where appropriate, what kind of reporting is required for court-ordered or mandatorily referred clients.

integrity: The ethical value and principle that involves promoting accuracy, honesty, and truthfulness while striving to keep one's promises and to avoid unwise or unclear commitments.

justice: The ethical virtue and principle that fosters fairness and equity and provides equal treatment to all individuals.

layered supervision: The type of supervision in which doctoral students, who are themselves being supervised by faculty, supervise master's students.

liability: An obligation one has incurred or might incur through a negligent act. Negligence is defined as the dereliction of a duty, i.e., providing a reasonable standard of care, that directly causes damages.

long-arm statutes: These statutes allow a state to assert its jurisdiction over an out-of-state resident for the purposes of litigation if he or she conducts commerce in that state (particularly cyber-therapy).

malpractice: A violation of a professional duty or duties expected of a reasonably prudent professional and involves performing below the professional standard of care.

mandatorily referred clients: Clients whose conditions of legal status, probation, visitation or custody of children, mental health status, or other aspects of their lives governed by either the judicial or mental health system require that they participate in counseling or therapy in order to receive some benefit from the judicial or mental health system. Mandatorily referred clients participate in a *quid pro quo* arrangement with the judicial or mental health systems; for example, release from jail for agreeing to participate in DUI psychoeducation, or unsupervised visitation of their children for participating in family therapy and parenting education.

MCO: Managed care organization. Any entity that administrates or oversees the delivery of mental health services by someone other than the clinician and the client for the purpose of quality-care assurance and cost control (generally an insurance company).

multicultural dimension: Understood broadly, it refers factors such as ethnicity, nationality, economic status, gender, age, disability, sexual orientation, and religion and spirituality that impact the counseling process.

narrative ethics: The ethical theory that insists that narrative, or story, and its context are important in ethical decision making. An act is considered morally good and right if it reflects the ongoing story of an individual's life and the culture and tradition within which he or she lives.

National Career Development Association (NCDA): The professional association connected with career counseling.

National Model for School Counseling Programs: Model based on national standards developed for the school counseling profession in 1997. This model is competency based and addresses the academic, career, and personal/social needs of students, while providing direction regarding delivery, management, and accountability for a comprehensive developmental program.

National Standards for School Counseling Programs: Research-based standards developed in 1997 by Campbell and Dahir directing the vision and goals of school counseling. The standards provide the structure for a systematic, collaborative, and comprehensive model for school counselors to use as they integrate developmental goals addressing the academic, personal/social, and career needs of students into the educational curriculum of the school.

natural supports: A term used to emphasize using people and things that are natural in the environment as reasonable accommodations for persons with disabilities.

negligence: Dereliction of a duty, i.e., providing a reasonable standard of care, that directly causes damages.

No Child Left Behind Act of 2001: Also known as Public Law 107-110, this law requires increased accountability for student achievement outcomes. Schools must demonstrate progress toward academic goals for all students as measured by standardized tests. Partly as a result of this act, school counseling programs have sharpened their focus on achievement outcomes through developmental programs targeting academic outcomes and the removal of social barriers to learning.

nonmaleficence: The ethical value and principle requiring that individuals refrain from any action that might cause harm. Also called nonmalfeasance.

online counseling: Counseling or psychotherapy between a licensed, credentialed therapist and a client involving minimal or no face-to-face contact and in which the process and content of therapy sessions is conducted through email or other electronic, Internet-based formats.

organizational ethics: The form of ethics that recognizes the impact of organizational factors and involves the intentional use of values to guide decision making in organizational systems. Unlike business ethics and professional ethics, which characteristically view a given ethical concern from an individual perspective, organizational ethics views the same ethical concerns from a systems perspective.

peer consultation: A process of conferring with a colleague to ascertain how other reasonable, similarly trained counselors would practice in the same set of circumstances.

person with a disability: An individual with a physical or mental impairment (a) that substantially limits one or more of the major life activities of such individual, (b) who has a record of such impairment, or (c) who is regarded has having such impairment.

personal ethics: The form of ethics that reflects an individual's internal sense of how he or she should live and what he or she should strive for, and serves as the basis for moral decisions or judgments and guiding behavior. An individual's "moral compass," or conscience, reflects these ethical beliefs and values.

personal/social development: One of the three areas of competence reflected in the profession's national standards and national model, targeting attitudes, skills, and knowledge contributing to (a) developing self-respect and an understanding of others; (b) setting goals and making decisions regarding the planning and monitoring of action steps to achieve those goals; and (c) an understanding of safety and survival skills.

PHI: Protected health information. Any information related to the client's condition or health status protected by law.

play therapy: A specialization for couples and family therapists for working with children. Therapists use play to observe and decode children's representational worlds and perceptions of their environment, their experience, and their relationships to others.

privacy: In ethics, the right of a person to be free from unwanted surveillance and to have control over their personal information. Counselors have an obligation to protect client privacy.

privileged communication: Generally understood as communication between psychotherapist and client that is protected by statute from forced disclosure to third parties, except as specified by law. Privileged communication is based on a legal acknowledgment that psychotherapy must be private to be effective and that psychotherapy promotes the mental health and well-being of the citizenry.

power: In the counseling domain, the ability for one person (the counselor) to influence the behavior of another (the client). This can be beneficial to the client or, in cases of abuse, harmful.

profession: A collected body of individuals committed to acquiring specialized knowledge and skills in order to serve the needs of others and act in a competent and ethical manner, and that has a self-governing organization that establishes standard of competency, ethics, and practice guidelines for the provision of services.

professional: A member of a profession who applies specialized knowledge and skills based on the profession's standards of excellence for meeting client's needs rather than advancing the professional's personal needs or interests.

professional and ethical practice decisional strategy: A nonlinear, seven-step decisional strategy that emphasizes the integration of contextual, professional, and ethical considerations rather than simply ethical and legal considerations.

professional and ethical decision making: Decision making in professional practice and ethical practice involves a similar strategy and process. They are also interdependent in that sense that professional input and analysis (i.e., research, best practices, theory, or clinical lore) are first considered, and then ethical input (i.e., theory, values, principles, and codes) is considered in order to reinforce, refocus, or fine-tune the decision.

professional boundaries: Can be understood as the limitations, constraints, or framework that structures and defines the nature of the relationship between persons in professional relationships. In counseling, the nature of the relationship is governed by the obligation to act in the best interest of the client (beneficence), to avoid doing harm to a client (nonmaleficence), to promote client autonomy, and to provide competent clinical counseling services as promised (fidelity).

professional competence: The professional's capacity to provide a minimum quality within the professional's and the profession's scope of practice. Such competence can be measured by what other reasonably prudent professionals would do under the same circumstances.

professional counseling: The application of mental health, psychological, and human development principles through cognitive, affective, behavioral, and systemic intervention strategies that address wellness, personal growth, and career development, as well as pathology.

professional ethics: The form of ethics that endeavors to help professionals decide what to do when they are confronted with a case or situation that raises a ethical question or moral problem; it considers the morality of one's professional choices and is informed by a code and standards of ethics specified by one's profession.

reasonable accommodation: Any thing or adaptation that allows the essential functions of a job to be done and may include equipment or adjusted work schedule.

relational dimension: A broad dimension that refers to factors that both reflect and influence the connection between individuals and their capacity to collaborate in the counseling process; the capacity for trust, mutuality, ethical sensitivity, and acceptance of uniqueness. It facilitates both process and outcome.

relational supervision: A process of supervision explicitly recognizing the situatedness of both supervisor and supervisee within larger domains of professional and social discourses and the influence of those discourses on the process and outcome of supervision.

religion: The search for significance through the sacred, within the context of a shared belief system, via doctrines and communal ritual practice, e.g., liturgy or public worship.

respect for persons: The ethical value and principle that involves honoring the dignity, worth, individual differences, and rights of all individuals to privacy, confidentiality, and self-determination.

rights ethics: The ethical theory that assumes that individuals are the bearers of rights that are granted them. An act is considered morally good and right when it respects rights, and wrong when it violates rights.

rights of children: Broad-based understanding of children as an inherently vulnerable special group because of their dependence on others for their freedom and survival, and endorsing the rights of children to be protected from undue harm and to be provided with basic requirements for the growth and development of their physical and emotional health.

scope of practice: The extent and limits of activities considered acceptable professional practice by an individual who is licensed or certified in a profession; a recognized area of proficiency involving specific competence, proficiency, or skills acquired through appropriate education and experience.

self-determination: Refers to the capacity and right of the individual to act as an agent on his or her own behalf and to direct one's own future, including one's own choices, actions, and cognitive/emotional behaviors.

self-supervision: The active, ongoing conversations counselors have with themselves about their clients, their own thinking about their clients, their clinical case conceptualizations, their assessments of their professional effectiveness, and their attention to the political and ethical effects of their own clinical formulations and interventions on their clients.

slippery slope argument: The contention that a certain course of action will lead to increasing erosion of moral restraint. With regard to dual relationships and boundary crossings, it is the belief that small "innocent" boundary crossings will eventually result in gross, exploitive ones, such as sexual contact with clients.

SOAP notation: One of the most widely used formats for clinical notation. SOAP is an acronym that stands for *subjective, objective, assessment,* and *plan,* which corresponds to the type of information contained in each section of the note.

spiritual sensitivity: The capacity to be aware of and to recognize the importance and/or influence of religious or spiritual beliefs, values, and other factors on another's life.

spirituality: That unsatisfiable, deepest desire within everyone, and the ways individuals deal with that desire: how they think, feel, act, and interact in their quest to satisfy this unsatisfiable desire; the transcendent aspect of life that gives a sense of meaning and purpose to our lives.

standard of care: A description of the conduct that is expected of an average member of the profession practicing within his or her specialty, and that is a measure against which a defendant's professional conduct is compared.

supervisor impairment: The incapacity to perform the function of the supervisory role due to a debilitating medical, substance-related, or psychological condition that results in diminished functioning from a previously higher level of functioning.

supervisor incompetence: The incapacity to perform the function of the supervisory role due to a lack of training or experience, unwillingness, or inflexibility.

supported employment: The employment model for individuals who need assistance of a job coach for a short period of time when a job is first being learned.

threats to others: In the counseling context, refers to threats against the physical safety of third parties made by clients to counselors.

undue hardship: The idea that a reasonable accommodation should not present an employer with results that will hurt the overall running of the business, either financially or architecturally.

value: The quality making something useful or desirable.

vicarious liability: Supervisor's liability that results from the negligent acts of supervisees if the acts are performed in the course and scope of the supervisory relationship.

virtue ethics: The ethical theory in which ethics is primarily about internal dispositions and character rather than external behavior or actions. Basic to this theory is the assumption that virtues make one a morally good person.

work orientation: Work orientation refers to a view and attitude toward work as determined by intrinsic values and aspirations and the experience of working, which is reflected in thoughts, feelings, and behavior about work.

AUTHOR INDEX

Adams, J. E., 391
Ahia, C., 14, 25, 132, 151, 159
Alexander, K., 190, 214
Alston, R. J., 362, 367
Anderson, H., 112
Aponte, H., 291, 339, 341
Aristotle, 477
Arredondo, P., 41, 339
Atkins, B., 366
Barrett, R. L., 104
Barstow, S., 232, 233, 234, 235,
Bates, D. W., 94
Baumeister, R., 148
Beauchamp, T., 361, 387
Behnke, S., 6, 120, 121, 159, 160, 424
Bellah, R., 148
Bennett, W., 477
Bernard, J. M., 32, 39, 155, 403, 432, 435
Bernstein, B. E., 249, 250, 252, 257, 299, 300, 306, 307
Berzoff, J., 131
Bevcar, D. S., 339
Bierman, N., 423
Blake, N., 219
Blumenfeld, W. J., 218
Bolton, B., 394
Bottoroff, N., 57, 162
Bowen, S., 58
Boyle, P., 56
Bozarth, J. D., 384
Bradley, L., 39
Brems, C., 158
Brigman, G., 183
Brill, P., 64, 65
Brincat, C., 12, 13, 25, 26, 30, 147, 472, 473, 474
Brooks, D., 270, 271
Brown, D., 445
Brown, S., 261, 264
Brubaker, D. R., 360
Bullis, R., 220
Burns, C. I., 385
Byington, K., 362, 367
Cameron, S., 235
Campbell, C. A., 169, 175, 183, 198
Capuzzi, D., 207
Carter, B., 293
Catalano, S., 132
Caudill Jr., O. B., 266, 331, 337, 338
Chan, F., 391
Chan, T., 367
Clarkson, P., 247, 253, 255
Collins, N., 181
Coale, H. W., 251, 310, 311, 312, 313, 314, 317, 345
Conger, J. A., 393
Conte, H., 24
Corcoran, K. J., 268, 270
Corey, G., 25, 77, 127, 132, 291
Cornille, T. A., 333
Cottone, R. R., 40, 77, 238, 356, 357, 363, 364, 365, 379, 383, 384, 385, 388, 389, 390, 391
Cozolino, L. J., 97
Crossley, N., 413
Dalton, H. L., 380
Damasio, A., 96, 413
Daniels, J.A., 210, 239, 268, 270
Davidson, J., 148
Davis, A., 40, 77
Davis, J. L., 181
Denkowski, K., 390
Dineen, T., 247, 249, 250
Disney, M., 445
Douherty, A., 444
Doyle, K., 127, 141
Dreyfus, H., 151
Duncan, B., 38
Durham, M. L., 100
Dworkin, R., 475
Dye, H. A., 200
Eberlin, L., 31
Edelwich, J., 131
Edwards, P., 473
Ells, C., 56, 175
Emner, W. G., 392
Erickson, S. K., 336
Erk, R., 217
Farber, B., 157
Favier, C., 49, 50, 442
Fawcett, S., 393
Fay, A., 126, 247, 249
Ferrell, O. C., 363
Ferrin, J., 386
Fine, M., 430
Finis, J., 476
Fisher, J., 362
Flaherty, S., 392, 393, 394
Fletcher, J., 473
Flowers, J. G., 378
Folberg, J., 336
Ford, C., 181, 257
Ford, G. G., 251, 252, 256, 257, 259, 298, 299, 300, 304, 305, 306, 307, 313
Foucault, M., 438, 442
Fowler, C., 366
Fraenkel, P., 332, 333
Frain, M., 379
Freeman, A., 241
Garcia, J. G., 44, 45, 237, 238
Gaston, L., 96
Gatens-Robinson, E., 361, 364, 365, 366, 378, 387
Genia, V., 238
Gilligan, C., 29, 38, 94, 412, 479
Glick, I. D., 299, 305, 313, 334
Glosoff, H. L., 214
Goodyear, R. K., 385, 399
Gottlieb, M., 32, 34
Gottman, J. M., 115
Gray, L., 416
Greenwood, R., 363
Guess, D., 387
Guiterrez, L., 393
Gutheil, T. G., 127, 431
Gysbers, N.C., 183
Haber, R., 291
Handlesman, M., 9, 32, 378
Harding, A., 380
Hass, L., 24
Heiman, J., 334
Heinlen, K. T., 278, 279
Henderson, P., 200
Herlihy, B., 199, 200
Herman, M. A., 172
Hermann, M. A., 210
Hill, M. R., 127
Hinman, L., 473
Hoffman, R. M., 253
Hopkins, B., 379
House, R. M., 176
Howard, M. L., 109, 112
Howie, J., 363, 387
Hoyt, M. F., 100
Hubble, M. A., 96
Hubert, R. M., 261, 264
Hummell, D. L., 390
Ibrahim, F. I., 237
Ingersoll, R. E., 175
Isaacs, M. L., 106, 181, 240
Ivey, A., 362
Jacobson, N. S., 330
Jennings, L., 16, 39, 162, 319
Jensen, J., 24
Kant, I., 476
Kermani, E., 380
Keith-Spiegel, P., 155
Kieffer, C., 393
Kilburg, R. R., 449

Kitchener, K., 25, 26, 32, 77, 291, 361, 387
Kitchner, K. S., 252
Knapp, S., 380
Koenig, H., 49, 50, 375, 443
Kohlberg, L., 38, 412
Kolata, G., 365
Koocher, G., 389, 390
Kosciulek, J., 386, 394
Kottler, J., 157
Kottman, T., 335
Kuczewski, M., 116
Kuehn, M. D., 369
Kuther, T., 32
Ladany, N., 416
Lamb, D., 155, 435
Lambert, M. J., 16, 29, 38, 96, 249
Lazarus, A. A., 127, 132, 133, 139, 247, 248, 249, 251, 255, 311, 312, 314, 431, 432
Leape, L. L., 94
Leahy, M. J., 356, 357
Lens, V., 99
Leslie, R. S., 266, 288, 290, 326, 327, 330, 332, 337, 338
Levine, L. S., 382
Linde, L., 187
Littrell, J., 181, 182.
Lonborg, S., 175, 221
MacIntryre, A., 477, 479
Magill, G., 57, 58
Magnuson, S., 435
Manning, R., 479
Margolin, G., 298, 299, 300, 305, 306, 313
Marshall, C., 361, 362
Maton, K. I., 394
McCarthy, B. W., 334
McCurdy, K. G., 114
McFarland, W., 211
McNamee, S., 38, 128, 412
McWhirter, J. J., 207
Melchert, T. P., 380
Meyer, R. G., 421
Middleton, R. A., 362
Minuchin, S., 291
Mitchell, C. W., 105
Moffic, S., 57
Muratori, M., 437, 438, 448, 449, 450
Myers, J. E. B., 105
Myrick, R. D., 170, 176, 183, 184, 187, 194
Nash, L., 56, 59, 60, 63, 64, 65
Nelson, M., 39, 40, 417
Neufeldt, E., 416
Noddings, N., 479
Norcross, J. C., 333
Nozick, R., 475
Odell, M., 340, 341
Olarte, S. W., 132
Olney, M. F., 393
O'Malley, P., 320, 321
Ong, L., 390
Orlinsky, D., 38
Page, B., 200
Pape, D., 361
Parson, F., 352
Patterson, C. H., 382
Patterson, J. B., 360, 378, 380, 382, 383, 386, 387, 388, 390
Peluso, P., 32, 236, 291, 292, 293, 410
Pedersen, P., 41, 42, 441
Peterson, C., 311, 324
Peterson, M., 134, 432
Pines, A., 157
Pinsoff, W. M., 115
Pope, K. S., 24, 244, 247, 249, 250, 251, 252, 253, 255, 257, 298, 299, 300, 304, 305, 306, 307, 311, 314
Prochaska, J., 96, 157
Reamer, F., 66, 67, 69, 127, 132, 133
Reddy, M., 210
Remley, T., 77, 105, 180, 181, 207, 209, 214, 216, 405, 444
Rich, J., 147
Ricouer, P., 479
Robson, M., 291
Rogers, C., 38
Rosentstad, N., 479
Rosoff, A. J., 112
Rounds, J. B., 375
Rubin, S., 251, 253, 371, 387, 391
Sacuzzo, D., 403, 445, 446
Salomone, P., 382
Sanders, J. L., 261, 262
Saunders, J. L., 385, 386
Scheflin, A. W., 251
Schnarch, D., 334
Schore, A. N., 97
Sciarra, D. T., 206
Sears, S. J., 183
Seelman, K., 394
Sermat, V., 194
Shah, S. T., 241
Shelton, C., 56
Shertzer, B., 360
Siegel, D. J., 97
Siegel, M., 240, 241
Simons-Morton, B., 393
Simonson, N., 194
Sims, R., 54
Sink, C., 174, 217
Skovholt, T. M., 9, 12, 27, 39, 91, 151, 152, 158, 162, 237, 319, 407
Smart, J., 362
Smith, D., 127, 431
Smith, T., 32
Sommers-Flanagan, R., 247, 248, 249, 250, 251, 310, 312
Spero, M., 49, 442
Sperry, L., 6, 9, 10, 13, 16, 46, 50, 54, 57, 65, 76, 274, 330, 443
St. Germaine, J., 127
Stanard, R., 379, 380
Stake, J. E., 127
Steere, D., 45
Stevens, P., 257, 259
Stenger, R. L., 214
Stoltenberg, C., 9, 21, 22, 23, 153, 236, 408, 409, 437
Stone, C., 218
Strupp, H., 38
Sue, D. W., 41, 175, 237, 378
Super, D., 375, 382
Szymanski, E. M., 355, 364, 391
Tarver-Behring, S., 217
Tarvydas, V., 44, 77, 361, 363, 385, 386
Taylor, A., 336
Taylor, H., 365
Tomm, K., 132, 133, 314, 317, 433
Van Hoose, W. H., 378
Vash, C. L., 364
Vasquez, M., 247, 251, 310, 312, 447
Verchsoor, C., 58
Verona, T., 381
Walden, S. L., 230, 261
Walter, M. I., 112
Wampold, B., 16, 29, 39
Watkins, C. E., 435
Weber, M., 148
Wedding, D., 233, 234, 235, 266
Weed, L.L., 214, 234, 235, 289
Welfel, E., 42, 77, 361
Wendell, S., 378
Wheaton, J., 366, 367
White, M., 100
Wilkins, M., 32
Williams, C. B., 261, 262
Williams, M. H., 247, 248, 249
Williamson, E. G., 352
Wilson, K. D., 367
Wittmer, J., 183
Wolf, C. T., 238
Wolfensberger, W., 392
Woods, G., 380
Woody, R. H., 127, 298, 313, 323, 425
Worthley, A., 13, 56, 57
Wrenn, C., 43
Wright, B., 361,
Wright, G., 365
Wrzesniewski, A., 148
Yalom, I. D., 273
Zingaro, 181
Zur, O., 127, 132, 133, 139, 140, 247, 248, 249, 251, 253, 254, 255, 312, 313, 431, 432

SUBJECT INDEX

A

Abuse, *See* Mandatory reporting
Accountability, 61, 66, 407
Accreditation, 61, 66, 169, 174
Accrediting bodies, 174
Ad hoc fallacy, 317
AIDS/HIV, duty to warn, 379–381, 395
Altamonte v. New York Medical College, 447
American Association for Marriage and Family Therapy (AAMFT), 104, 297
American Counseling Association (ACA), 6, 104, 123–124, 239–240
American Mental Health Counselors Association (AMHCA), 231–232, 239–240
American Psychological Association (APA), 104
American School Counselor Association (ASCA), 169, 175, 216–217
  Ethical Standards for School Counselors, 176, 180–181
  National Model: a Framework for School Counseling Programs, 175
Americans with Disabilities Act (ADA), 215, 369, 391–392
Andrews v. United States, 447–448
Approved clinical supervisor, 376
Arnold v. Board of Eduction of Escambia County, 212
Applied ethics, 12–13
Aspirational ethics, 25–26
Association for Counselor Education and Supervision (ACES), 236, 435
  Ethical Guidelines for Clinical Supervisors, 435
  Standards for Counseling Supervisors, 451
Association for Specialists in Group Work, 188–189, 271–273
Association for Spiritual, Ethical, and Religious Values in Counseling, 442
Association of Multicultural Counseling and Development, 41
Attachment, 97
Autonomy, 26, 28, 29, 96, 112–114, 116, 259

B

Beneficence, 25, 28, 29, 94, 376
Benevolence, 26, 28
Boundary/ies,
  in career counseling, 375
  in couples/family counseling, 309–319
  generally, 90, 126–130
  in mental health counseling, 245–256
  in school counseling, 192–196
  in supervision, 430–434
Boundary confusion, in couples/family counseling, 310–311
Boundary crossings
  generally, 127, 139–140,
  in mental health counseling, 249–251
  in school counseling, 192–196
  in supervision, 431–432
Boundary issues. *See* Dual relationships
Boundary permeability, 311–312
Boundary rigidity, 312
Boundary violations
  in couples/family counseling, 312–313
  generally, 126–140
  in mental health counseling, 249–256
  in supervision, 431–432
Breach of duty. *See* Malpractice
Buckley Amendment. *See* Family Educational Rights and Privacy Act
Burnout, 156–159, 236–237
Business ethics, 56

C

Care ethics, 31, 94–96, 412
Career counseling, 353–354
  contextual issues in, 357–360
  core ethical issues of, 373–375
  legal issues affecting the practice of, 375–376
  Perspectives I-III, 376–377
  routine practice of, 354–355
  special issues of, 375
Career development, 216–217

Case consultation, 444
Categorical boundaries, 126, 247–248
Categorical boundaries view, 126
Caveat emptor, 337
Center for Credentialing and Education, 376
Certification
  in career counseling, 376
  in couples/family counseling, 332–334
  in divorce mediation, 336–337
  generally, 152
  in play therapy, 335–336
  in rehabilitation counseling, 385
  in school counseling, 199
  in sex therapy, 334–335
  in substance abuse/drug addiction, 270
Child abuse or neglect, reporting. *See* Mandatory reporting
Child custody
  evaluations, 299–300
  legal issues for counselors, 299–300
Classroom Guidance Curriculum, 187
Client welfare, 26
Clients, empowerment of, 386–8, 392
Clinical supervision, 443–444
Clinical supervision agreement, 405–407
Codes of ethics, 31–32
Collaborative decision making, 109, 116
Commission on Rehabilitation Counselor Certification (CRCC), 356
Community values, 69–71, 417–419
Competence
  in career counseling, 373–374
  as a continuum, 150–152
  in couples/family counseling, 287, 319–323
  and credentials, 153–154. *See also* Credentials
  as ethical and legal concept, 149–150
  generally, 90, 145–164
  maintaining, 28, 150, 154–155
  in mental health counseling, 257–262
  in rehabilitation counseling, 377–378
  in school counseling, 196–201
  in supervision, 434–439
  and technologies, 197
  in testing, 287
  training issues, 153, 332–341
Competencies
  cultural, 42–43
  spiritual and religious, 49–50
Competency (client), 374
Compliance audit, 66–67
Complaints against counselors
  for breaching confidentiality, 262–268. *See also* Duty to warn, Duty to protect, Mandatory reporting
  defending against, 265–268
  immunity, 265–268
Computers. See Technology, Web counseling
Confidentiality
  basis of, 93
  and brain sciences, 96–98
  breaches of, 265–266. *See also* Duty to warn, Duty to protect, Mandatory reporting
  in career counseling, 374–375
  in couples/family counseling, 297–304
  defined, 93
  exceptions to, 100–106
  generally, 90–100
  and HIV/AIDS, 379–381
  legal issues affecting, 98–100. *See also* Duty to warn, Duty to protect, Mandatory reporting
  in mental health counseling, 240–243
  and organizational ethics, 62
  in rehabilitation counseling, 378–381
  in school counseling, 179–186, 202–203
  in supervision, 410–424
Conflict of interest
  in career counseling, 375
  in couples/family counseling, 309–319
  generally, 90, 126–142
  in mental health counseling, 245–256,
  in rehabilitation counseling, 383–384
  in school counseling, 192–196
  in supervision, 428–434
Consequential ethics, 31
Consultation
  accountability in, 443–445
  competence, 445
  confidentiality in, 445
  contracts, 444–445
  defined, 444
  ethics issues in, 445
  freedom of choice in, 444
  informed consent in, 445
  organizational, 445
  peer, 444
  relationships, 444

Context, 76
Continuing education, 154–155
  to maintain competence, 154–155
  for supervisors, 409
Council for the Accreditation of Counseling and Related Educational Programs (CACREP), 174
Counseling Alliance, 97
Counseling profession, 147–148
  history, 5–6
Counselor education, 139, 173–174, 361
Couple/family counseling,
  contextual issues in, 291–296
  confidentiality in, 297–304
  core ethical issues of, 297–324
  counselor competence, 319–323
  divorce and child custody issues, 300–302
  legal issues affecting the practice of, 325–332
  privileged communication in, 299–300
  routine practice of, 286–290
  special issues in, 325–341
  and systems theory, 293–294
  training, licensure, and certification, 332–341
Court orders, 243
Creaming, 369
Credentials, of counselors, 199
  misrepresenting, 373–374
Cultural audit, 67
Cultural diversity, generally, 40–41,
Cultural encapsulation, 43
Cultural sensitivity, 41–42
Cyber-therapy. *See* Web counseling

D

Dangerousness of clients, 263–264, 328
Davis v. Monroe County Board of Education, 211
Developmental issues contract, 407
Developmental perspective of counselors, 21–24, 236–237
Developmental perspective of supervisors, 408–410
Dimensional boundaries, 126, 248–249
Diminished capacity, 244–245, 306–307
Direct liability, 445–446
Disability, 377–378356
Discrimination
  and Americans with Disabilities Act, 214, 369, 391–392
  and career counseling, 355
  and justice, 26
  and rehabilitation counseling, 363, 366
  and school counseling, 218
Distance credentialed counselor, 376
Distress, 156–159
Divorce mediation, 336–337
Documentation
  for self-protection, 234–235
  in supervision, 407
Drug addition. *See* Substance abuse.
Dual relationships. *See also* Sexual dual relationships
  and boundaries, *See* Boundary/ies
  between faculty and students, 218
  boundary violations. *See* Boundary violations
  complementary relationship, 132
  conflicting relationship, 132
  ethical decision making model, 141–142
  generally, 90, 132–133
  in career counseling, 375
  in couples/family counseling, 313–319
  in mental health counseling, 246–256
  in supervision, 431–434
  post-termination relationships with clients, 133
Due process, and fair evaluation, 440–441
Duty ethics, 31
Duty of fidelity, 270
Duty to protect
  in career/rehabilitation counseling, 330–331
  in clinical supervision, 421–424
  generally, 100–105
  in mental health counseling 262–265
  in rehabilitation, 379–381
  in school counseling, 207–210, 212
Duty to report. *See* Mandatory reporting
Duty to warn
  in career/rehabilitation counseling, 330–331
  in clinical supervision, 421–424
  generally, 100–105
  in mental health counseling 262–265
  in rehabilitation, 379–381
  in school counseling, 207–210, 212

E

Education for All Handicapped Children Act, 213, 215
Eisel v. Board of Education, 212
Equal Access Act of 1984, 220
Ethic of care. *See* Care ethics
Ethical acculturation, 34
Ethical autobiography, 32
Ethical climate, 54–55
Ethical decision making
  in career and rehabilitation counseling, 394–398
  in couples/family counseling, 341–348,

cultural considerations, 44–45
generally, 6–7, 14–15, 33–34, 44–45, 77–85
in mental health counseling, 275–281
models, 77–85
personal, 15
in school counseling, 221–225,
in supervision, 410–411, 448–451
Ethical dilemma, 14, 57
impact of organizational dynamics on, 61–62
Ethical genogram, 291–293
Ethical principles, 25
Ethical sensitivity, 7, 8, 15, 34
Ethical theories, Ethical Models, 30–31
Ethical values. *See* Values, ethical
Ethical virtues. *See* Virtues, ethical
Ethics
defined, 12
positive, 9
Ethics audit, 66, 374
Ethics compliance audit, 69
Evaluation
competence to evaluate, 440–441
and informed consent, 424–428
objectivity in, 408–409
Ewing v. Goldstein, 264–265, 329

F

Fair evaluation and due process in supervision, 440–441
Family counseling. *See* Couple/family counseling
Family Educational Rights and Privacy Act (FERPA), 213, 215
Family systems theory, 293
Fees
collection of fees in private practice, 287
and informed consent, 113, 116
in supervision, 426–427
Fidelity, 27, 28
Florence County School District v. Carter, 213
Free and appropriate public education (FAPE), 215

G

Gathright v. Lincoln Insurance, Co., 212
Gerber v. Lago Vista Independent School District, 212
Gifts, from clients, 129, 194–195
Global career development facilitator, 376
Group counseling
competence in, 272
confidentiality in, 272–273
and informed consent, 188–190

H

Health Insurance Portability and Accountability Act (HIPAA), 99–100, 116, 232–234, 287–290
Hedlund v. Superior Court of Orange County, 263–264, 328

I

Illegal behavior, 133
Immunity, 325, 327–330
Impairment, 156–159
Impairment vs. burnout, 157–158
Incompetence, 155–156, 374
Incompetent clients. *See* Competency, client
Independent living, 356
Independent practice. *See* Private practice.
Individualized educational plan (IEP), 215
Individuals with Disabilities Education Act (IDEA), 190, 215, 217
Informed consent, 244–245, 304–309, 374, 382
in career counseling, 374
and confidentiality, 114, 186
in couples/family counseling, 304–309
diversity issues in, 116
elements of, 113–116
in evaluation, 115
generally, 90, 109–123
in group counseling, 188–190
in individual counseling, 187–188
and involuntary commitment, 120–122
and minor clients, 118–120, 187–191
in online counseling, 122–123
and organizational ethics, 62
problems in, as basis for lawsuit against counselors, 112–113, 261–262
in rehabilitation counseling, 381–383
in supervision, 424–428
systemic issues, in, 116–118
Integrity, 27, 28
International Association for Marriage and Family Counseling (IAMFC), 297
Internet counseling guidelines (NBCC), 337
Involuntary commitment, 120–122

J

Jaffee v. Redmond, 99, 214, 266–267, 329, 389
Justice, 26–27, 28
Justice model of ethics, 413

K

Krikorian v. Barry, 266–267, 328

L
Lawsuits, 261–262
Least restrictive environment (LRE), 215
Leebaert v. Harrington, 212–213
Liability, 445
Licensure, of counselors
  and career counselors, 376
  and competence to practice
  and scope of practice, 152–153
  state boards, 261
Long-arm statutes, 337

M
Malpractice, 160, 323–324
Managed health care, 64, 268–270
Mandatory reporting, 100–104, 204–206, 325–327, 376
  in supervision, 421–424
Master career counselor, 376
Master career development professional, 376
Master therapist, 27–30, 39, 162–163
Mcdonald v. State, 211
Medical model, 353
Mental health counseling
  contexual issues in, 236–239
  core ethical issues of, 239–262
  legal issues affecting the practice of, 262–268
  routine practice of, 231–235
  special issues in, 268–275
Mental health model, 353
Minor clients
  and confidentiality, 105–106, 179–186, 202–203
  conflicts between law and ethics, 105–106
  legal status of minors, 374
  and parent rights, 105, 202–203
  parental permission, 187–189
  in rehabilitation counseling, 390
Moral principles, 25, 180
Morality, defined, 12
Multicultural counseling. *See* Cultural diversity
Multicultural dimension, 40–45
  in supervision, 441–442

N
Narrative ethics, 31
National Association of Social Workers, 104
National Board for Certified Counselors (NBCC), 376
National Career Development Association (NCDA), 373–347, 373–374, 375
National Council for the Accreditation of Teacher Education, 174
National Standards for School Counseling Programs, 169
Negligence, 159
No Child Left Behind Act of 2001, 176
Nonmaleficence, 26, 28, 29, 94, 376

O
Online counseling, 122–123
Organizational culture, 296
Organizational ethics
  and career counseling, 359–360
  and conflict with personal ethics, 66–67
  and couples/family counseling, 294–296
  defined, 239
  and efficiency and expediency, 64–65
  and financial considerations, 63–64
  generally, 13–14, 55–69
  and rehabilitation counseling, 367–373
  and school counseling, 176–179
  and supervision, 417
Organizational ethics inventory, 67–68
Organizational systems, 54–55
  administrative subsystem, 54–55
  cultural subsystem, 54
  environmental subsystem, 55
  and leadership, 58
  structural subsystem, 54
  staff subsystem, 55
  strategy subsystem, 55
    mission statement, 55
    vision statement, 55

P
Parallel process, 39
Peer consultation, 444
People of the State of Illinois v. Hubert, 381
Personal ethics, 14, 55–57, 238–239, 294
  conflict with organizational ethics, 59–60, 65–66
Perspectives, ethical
  I, 10, 11, 25, 90, 107, 113, 124, 127, 160–161, 260–261
  II, 10–11, 162
  III, 11–12, 25, 90, 93, 100, 104, 107, 110, 113, 124, 127, 141, 143, 161–162, 163, 185, 191, 196, 201, 243, 254, 260, 269, 302–304, 308, 318–319, 322–323, 376–377
Play therapy, 335–336
Power, 130–131, 245–251, 375, 386–388
Power differential, 130–131

Privacy, 96. *See also* Confidentiality, Privileged communication
in supervision, 420–421
Private practice, 231–232, 287, 375
Privileged communication
asserting the privilege, 98
in career counseling, 358
in couples/family counseling, 299–300
defined, 98, 241
exceptions, 98, 267–268
generally, 98–99
in mental health counseling, 241–243, 266–268
origins, 99
rationale for, 98
in rehabilitation counseling, 377, 389–390
in supervision, 421
Profession, 147
Professional, 147
Professional associations, 261–262
Professional boundaries. *See* Boundary/ies
Professional competence. *See* Competence
Professional counseling, 8–9
Professional and ethical decision making, 75–77
and contextual considerations, 76
and ethical considerations, 76–77
and professional considerations, 76
Professional and ethical practice decisional strategy, 17, 78–85, 275–281
Professional ethics, 13, 55–57, 239, 294
impact of organizational ethics on, 62–63
Professional liability insurance,
and school violence, 210
Protected health information (PHI), 232–235, 288–290

Q
Qualified immunity, 330

R
Reasonable accommodation. *See* Americans with Disabilities Act
Records
access to, 213–215, 233–234
clinical case notes, 233
computer storage. *See* HIPAA
confidentiality, 90, 270–271
federal law and, 213, 214–215
laws and legal requirements, 232–235
Referrals
for involuntary commitment. *See* Involuntary commitment
and school counseling, 188–189
and school violence, 210
and web counseling, 337–338
Rehabilitation Act of 1973, 215
Section 504, 215
Section 504 Plan, 216
Rehabilitation counseling, 354
contexual issues in, 360–373
core ethical issues of, 378–388
legal issues affecting the practice of, 377, 389–392
Perspectives I-III, 392–394
routine practice of, 355–357
special issues in, 385–388
Relational connection, 28
Relational dimension, 38–40
Relational supervision, 412–413
Relational supervision agreement, 405–407
Religion, 46
Religious dimension, 45–50
in supervision, 442–443
Respect for persons, 27, 28, 96
Rights of children, 105–106
Rights ethics, 31

S
Sain v. Cedar Rapids Community School District, 211
School counseling
and Individuals with Disabilities Act, 189
contextual issues in, 172–179
core ethical issues of, 179–201
ethical standards for, 176–179
and large group guidance, 189–190
legal issues affecting the practice of, 201–221
routine practice of, 171–172
sexual behavior, 218
students with special needs, 216–217
Scope of practice, 151, 152–153
Searcy v. Auerback, 266–267, 328
Self-care, 135–137, 158–159, 200–201
Self-determination, 112–114
Self-disclosure, counselor, 138, 139–140, 194, 248
Self-supervision, 435
Sex therapy, 334–335
Sexual dual relationships, 131–139, 247, 249, 250, 252
between counselor educators and students, 218
characteristics of offending therapists, 131, 137–139
counseling client victims, 218
former clients, 133

Sexual dual relationships (*cont.*)
harm to clients, 132–133
in supervision, 431–434
Simmons v. United States, 448
Simonsen v. Swenson, 380
Slander, 265–266
Slippery slope argument, 313–314
Smith-Fess Act of 1920, 367
SOAP notation, 215–216, 234–235, 289–290
Spiritual assessment, 49
Spiritual dimension, 45–50
Spiritual sensitivity, 46–47
Spirituality
in career counseling, 375
in couple/family counseling, 338–341
generally, 45–47
in mental health counseling, 274–275
in rehabilitation counseling, 388–389
in school counseling, 174–175, 219–220, 221
in supervision, 442–443
Standard of care, 79, 159, 257
Stecks v. Young, 266–267, 328
Subpoenas
of records, 243
responding to, 243
Substance abuse, 270–271
Suicide, 101–104, 207–210, 212, 332
Supervisees, rights and responsibilities, 413–416
Supervision
agreements, 405–407
and community values, 417–419
clinical, 404–451
confidentiality in, 420–424
contextual issues in, 407–419
core ethical issues in, 419–439
cultural diversity in, 441–442
defined, 443–444
documentation in, 407
dual relationships in, 431–434
due process, 440–441
evaluation in, 440–441
in rehabilitation and career counseling, 385–386
in school counseling, 200
informed consent in, 424–428
legal issues affecting the practice of, 445–449
peer, 444
privileged communication in, 421
recording sessions, 446–447
routine practice of, 405–407
sexual intimacies in, 432–433
special issues in, 440–445
Supervisors
administrative, 443–444
clinical, 443–444
competence, 434–435, 438–439
impairment, 435–438
incompetence, 435–436
roles and responsibilities, 413–416
Supervisory relationship, 416–417
Systems audit, 67

T

Tarasoff v. Regents of University of California, 104–105, 262–265, 328, 379–380
in supervision, 447
Taylor v. Vermont Department of Education, 214
Technology. *See* Web counseling
Threats to others. *See* Duty to warn and Duty to protect
Third party reimbursement, 64, 268–270
Thompson v. County of Alameda, 263–264, 329
Transference and countertransference, 49
"Two-hat" dilemma, 65

U

Unethical behavior, 57–58, 59
United States v. Chase, 267–268, 329

V

Values, ethical, 25–31
Vicarious liability. *See* Indirect liability
Virtues, ethical, 29, 31
Vocational guidance model, 353

W

W. B. v. Matula et al., 213
Wagner v. Fayetteville Public Schools, 211
Web counseling, 337–338
Wilkinson v. Balsaam, 266–267, 328
Wilson v. Valley Mental Health, 263–264, 329
Wojcik v. Aluminum Company of America, 380
Work orientation, 148–149